Nomadic Literature

European Connections

edited by
Peter Collier

Volume 35

PETER LANG

Oxford· Bern · Berlin · Bruxelles · Frankfurt am Main · New York · Wien

Jane Fenoulhet

Nomadic Literature

Cees Nooteboom and his Writing

PETER LANG

Oxford· Bern · Berlin · Bruxelles · Frankfurt am Main · New York· Wien

Bibliographic information published by Die Deutsche Nationalbibliothek.
Die Deutsche Nationalbibliothek lists this publication in the Deutsche
Nationalbibliografie; detailed bibliographic data is available on the
Internet at http://dnb.d-nb.de.

A catalogue record for this book is available from the British Library.

Library of Congress Control Number: 2013942351

Cover image: 'Vivid Seam' © Simon Fenoulhet 2010.

ISSN 1424-3792
ISBN 978-3-0343-0729-1

© Peter Lang AG, International Academic Publishers, Bern 2013
Hochfeldstrasse 32, CH-3012 Bern, Switzerland
info@peterlang.com, www.peterlang.com, www.peterlang.net

Printed in Germany

Contents

Illustrations

Acknowledgements

It would not have been possible to research and write this book without support from UCL in the form of generous research leave. I am particularly grateful to the Faculty of Arts and Humanities and to the School of European Languages, Culture and Society for enabling this leave and for financial support towards my research costs. I would also like to thank the Association for Low Countries Studies for their support through the award of a grant to help with publication costs.

I am particularly grateful to my brother Simon Fenoulhet for providing me with a striking image for the cover. For me, this photograph of one of his light installations reminds me of literary translation, with light as literature and the shift in colour as the language shift. In the case of other images, every effort has been made to trace copyright holders and to obtain their permission for the use of copyright material. The publisher apologizes for any errors or omissions in the list of illustrations, and would be grateful for notification of any corrections that should be incorporated in future reprints or editions of this book.

Finally, I would like to acknowledge the enormous contribution from colleagues, students, friends and family who have given me the encouragement needed to see this project through to completion, who responded to my ideas, and who shared their readings of Cees Nooteboom's writing with me. Special thanks to my husband Jeremy who never questioned my need for time and space in which to write this book.

Jane Fenoulhet
University College London

Introduction

Moving between languages, speaking several but mastering none, living in a constant simultaneous translation, is a possible location for the nomadic sensibility which best expresses itself in creative writing.
— ROSI BRAIDOTTI, *Metamorphoses*

I Introducing Cees Nooteboom and the Dutch Literary Field

This is a book about Cees Nooteboom, a novelist, poet and travel writer who writes in Dutch. It is not a book about Dutch national literature, though part of it is about literature in Dutch. I have chosen Cees Nooteboom as my subject for two reasons: first, because I think he is an interesting and important writer who deserves more attention in English-language criticism and second, because of the transnational nature of his literary presence. As the editors of a recent volume on translating Nooteboom say, 'Nooteboom is well known as the most cosmopolitan and transcultural of authors from the Dutch language area'.[1]

What I want to investigate in this book is the extent to which Cees Nooteboom can be said to embody a mode of existence that offers a possible solution to the problem of how to approach the local, or regional, in a globalized world. His way of life and his writing are not only literally nomadic in that he narrates his own wanderings and those of his characters,

---

[1] 'Nooteboom staat bekend als een van de meest kosmopolitische en transculturele auteurs uit het Nederlandse taalgebied.' S. Evenepoel, G Rooryck and H. Verstraete, eds, *Taal en cultuur in vertaling: De wereld van Cees Nooteboom* (Antwerp and Apeldoorn: Garant, 2004), 10. Unless otherwise stated, all translations from Dutch in this book are mine.

but also nomadic metaphorically and philosophically speaking. Expressed as a cliché, travel broadens the mind; that is, it may well give rise to a fundamentally different way of thinking and being in the world. The opening quotation by Rosi Braidotti takes this idea to its limit when it envisages a state of constant linguistic mobility in which translation becomes the dominant mode of existence. In the case of Nooteboom, it is at the very least debatable whether this point has been reached, and the idea provides a horizon against which to view both the author and his work. The writer himself has in recent years gained recognition in the Dutch-speaking world, and so might be said to be considered a 'master' of that language. But his position is an ambiguous one because of his many cultural experiences and allegiances. Moreover, his use of Dutch challenges many of the established conventions of literary writing in Dutch and, I will argue, bears traces of other languages and literatures. When considering Nooteboom's residencies and appearances in many countries, it becomes clear that for some of the time at least, he does live in the state described by Braidotti above. A related dimension is the writing itself which has been translated into many languages and which taken as a whole – that is all the realizations of all the works in all the languages – can also be said to fit Braidotti's description. In this sense at least, Nooteboom's writing an be considered a location for nomadic sensibility.

This book is intended as an exploration of this nomadic sensibility in the person and the work of Cees Nooteboom. The philosophical aspect of nomadism will be outlined in the second part of this introduction to *Nomadic Literature* and will be discussed more fully in relation to literature in translation in Chapter 2. At this point I want to make clear that it is not my intention to present Nooteboom as some kind of literary exponent of philosophical nomadism, but rather to take these ideas as a guide for exploring Nooteboom's writing and the extent to which it can be viewed through this particular lens.

So where might home be for a writer as nomadic as Nooteboom? In a particular territory, or in the language itself and its artefacts? And is Nooteboom a complete exception in Dutch literature, or indeed in Dutch culture at large? There is a Dutch diaspora, though it is not often described as such. As well as the emigrants discussed below who left the Netherlands in the years after the Second World War, there are Dutch communities around the globe following paths mapped out by Dutch multinational companies such as Royal Dutch Shell, Philips and TomTom. Even if Dutch employees around the world frequently work in English, they still read and speak Dutch, and their children are usually educated at least partly in Dutch to enable a return to the Netherlands. Chapter 3 will return to the theme of the nomadic in Dutch culture.

Despite the fact that Nooteboom's preferred mode of existence involves repeated travelling, he still roots himself firmly in the Dutch language. This raises questions of identity and belonging and the extent to which these are connected with a sense of responsibility and locatedness. The feminist philosopher Rosi Braidotti whose work provided my epigraph and is concerned with subjectivity and personal transformation as part of a project to assert female difference and tradition, highlights multiplicity as crucial to a nomadic mode of being as well as the need for a sense of (partial) belonging. Despite a desire for an identity through transitions 'the nomadic subject ... is not altogether devoid of unity; his/her mode is one of definite, seasonal patterns of movement through rather fixed routes'.[2] She is sceptical about notions of the global or cosmopolitan citizen, emphasizing the need for an engaged local belonging as a necessary part of any global aspiration.

How any of this applies to Nooteboom and his writing will be the subject matter of my book: how does Nooteboom combine being at home in the small world of the Dutch language with his persona as global traveller? How are we to see the many affiliations which can co-exist without the need for any one of them to supersede another, even though they expand and recede depending on circumstances and location. In Nooteboom's case, there is the European citizen, but also the German one, the Spanish one and, legally speaking, the Dutch national, as well as the global traveller. These different kinds of belonging certainly have an impact on the way such a writer is read and on his reception by the critical establishment in his country of origin. Nearly sixty years after his literary debut in the Netherlands,

2   Rosi Braidotti, *Nomadic Subjects: Embodiment and Sexual Difference in Feminist Theory* (New York: Columbia University Press, 1994), 22.

Nooteboom is now being recognized for his literary contribution, even if his reception in the Low Countries did not possess the appropriate words or ideas with which to characterize him fully and to locate his contribution during the early part of his literary career. In Chapters 2 and 3 I look at both old and new belongings, or national identity and how it is affected by mobility and globalization.

There is another dimension to belonging: that of shared experiences. I am thinking here of the experience of growing up during the Second World War in a 'small' European language and culture by comparison with the hegemonic languages of Germany, France and the United Kingdom. Both the experience of war and that of speaking a 'small' language will have had a particular impact. At the time when Nooteboom was writing his first poems and fiction, more than half a million Dutch people were emigrating to the United States, South Africa, Canada, Australia and New Zealand to escape the small overpopulated world of the Netherlands and the narrow confines of Dutch domesticity. Reflecting on smallness offers an interesting perspective for considering the background to Nooteboom and his work since it is a characteristic that can be analysed on a number of levels. Here, I focus on two of them. First, as a feature of the Dutch way of life: the smallness of Dutch minds, for example, was much criticized by Dutch intellectuals in the 1930s and again after the war; also the main unit of social organization was small, being the nuclear family, or *gezin*, as opposed to a more extended *familie*. Second, at the level of European politics: during the 1930s, there was a growing sense of vulnerability in the Dutch body politic because of the country's small size and limited capacity to defend itself. This was reinforced by the Netherlands' speedy capitulation after the German invasion in May 1940. This feeling of political insignificance generated a sense of patriotism rooted in history and culture, and expressed in popular histories, the most famous examples being Jan Romein's *De Lage Landen bij de Zee* (The Low Countries by the sea, 1934) and *Erflaters van onze beschaving* (The fathers[3] of our civilization,

---

3   *Erflaters* are the individuals who are responsible for creating Dutch heritage. The book does include one 'mother'.

1938), a series of portraits of significant Dutch public figures throughout history, written with his wife Annie. The intellectual dilemma was clear: nationalism was considered a force for the bad, but the vulnerability of the Netherlands called for the creation of a 'local' identity. Both historians and historical novelists contributed to the project.[4]

After the war, Dutch literature flourished, even though many of its practitioners have been criticized for the small, restricted world they depicted in prose. This had been the case since the 1930s when the critic Menno ter Braak was scathing about the domestic realism of women writers, and fifty years later the literary historian Ton Anbeek commented on the inward-looking world of Dutch writing.[5] This self-imposed literary confinement could be seen as a response to external threat. Perhaps the knowledge that few outsiders had access to Dutch culture because the language was not widely learned by fellow Europeans, reinforced the sense of safety, creating a linguistic haven or fortress; or, for those who felt alienated in some way, even a linguistic prison. At any rate, the awareness of cultural 'smallness' and insularity might be expected to shape the attitudes of the generation of writers who had their debut in the years after the war – the late 1940s and 1950s – which includes Nooteboom. Eventually this sense of smallness would in certain cases become a powerful stimulus for embracing other cultures, whether motivated by empathy with other 'smaller' cultures, or by an ambition to penetrate hegemonic cultures, or simply by a desire for larger audiences. In the second part of the Introduction and in Chapter 3 I explore whether the cultural attitudes suggested here can be better understood in the light of Gilles Deleuze and Félix Guattari's concept of 'minor literature' as introduced later in this Introduction in the section headed 'Central concepts'. Contradictory as it may sound, Nooteboom's lasting contribution to Dutch literature may be as an exponent of a 'minor

---

4   See Jane Fenoulhet, 'Towards a Critical Patriotism', *Modern Language Review* 99/1 (2004), 112–30.

5   See Jane Fenoulhet, *Making the Political Personal: Dutch Women Writers 1919–1970* (Oxford: Legenda, 2007), 26–7; and Ton Anbeek, 'Aanval en afstandelijkheid: een vergelijking tussen Amerikaanse en Nederlandse romans', *De gids* 144/2&3 (1981), 70–6.

practice of major language' as Deleuze and Guattari put it, opening it up to new subjectivities and new sensibilities. This will be explained in more detail in the second part of this Introduction.

Institutions of the Literary Field in the Netherlands

As well as being a book about Dutch literature and culture, *Nomadic Literature* is about the relation between literary history, comparative literature and translation studies; indeed, it moves across and seeks to remove the boundaries separating these three approaches to understanding literature, with Cees Nooteboom's work as the focal case study. Because he writes in Dutch, his first readership is relatively small, since the pool of Dutch speakers from which they are drawn is around twenty-two million – a much smaller number of native speakers than the languages of the Netherlands' three large neighbours, the United Kingdom, France and Germany.[6] Leaving aside the question of whether Nooteboom himself originally had an ambition to reach wider audiences, he subsequently became one of the most successful Dutch writers in translation. In the same postwar period spanning his authorship, Dutch cultural policy certainly did aspire to reach an audience beyond the borders of the Netherlands. Since the 1950s, national policy has included and valued translation as an important part of being a smaller European culture. It was in 1954 that the Ministry of Education, Arts and Sciences provided the funds to set up a foundation to promote Dutch literature abroad through its translation into

6   It is notoriously difficult to give exact figures for numbers of speakers since it depends on the definition of a 'speaker'. Given that my aim here is to give an impression of relative size of readerships, I will give numbers of native speakers as listed in Wikipedia: English 328–350 million; French around 77 million or 128 million francophones; German around 101 million. <http://en.wikipedia.org/wiki/List_of_languages_by_number_of_native_speakers> accessed 21 July 2010.

other languages.[7] That organization exists today as the Dutch Foundation for Literature (Nederlands Letterenfonds).[8]

In fact, translation plays an even more pivotal role in Dutch literary culture than the unidirectional externally-focussed Foundation might suggest. Certainly, outward movement from Dutch into other languages is much desired and therefore has public money invested in it, but at the same time, research shows that a significant proportion of what is published in Dutch originated in other languages. In an essay on small countries and cultural globalization, Johan Heilbron notes that 'the percentage of translations in the national book production [of the Netherlands] rose from less than 10 per cent at the end of the 1940s to more than 25 per cent after 1990'[9] The Foundation's new policy recognizes this state of affairs and states an intention to shift the balance by taking steps to promote other literatures than the Anglo-Saxon ones, i.e. to ensure that translated literature in Dutch nevertheless represents a diversity of languages and cultures. The aim is to arouse the curiosity of 'Dutch readers, teachers, university lecturers, students, booksellers and publishers for literature from countries whose cultures are less familiar'.[10]

---

7   See Guy Vandeputte, 'De Nederlandse literatuur in vertaling', *Handelingen Tiende Colloquium Neerlandicum* (Woubrugge: Internationale Vereniging voor Neerlandistiek, 1988), 93.

8   Until 1 January 2010 it was known as the Foundation for the Production and Translation of Dutch Literature (Nederlands Literair Productie- en Vertalingenfonds, abbreviated to NLPVF). It has just published a sophisticated policy document for the period 2009–2012: see <http://www.nlpvf.nl/nl/downloads/beleidsplan_20092012.php> accessed 21 July 2010.

9   'het percentage vertalingen in de nationale boekproductie steeg van minder dan 10 procent eind jaren veertig tot meer dan 25 procent sinds 1990.' Johan Heilbron, 'Nederlandse vertalingen wereldwijd: Kleine landen en culturele mondialisering' (Dutch translations worldwide. Small countries and cultural globalization), in Johan Heilbron, Wouter de Nooy and Wilma Tichelaar, eds, *Waarin een klein land: Nederlandse cultuur in internationaal verband* (Amsterdam: Prometheus, 1995), 218.

10 'Nederlandse lezers, leraren, universitair docenten, studenten, boekhandelaren én uitgevers nieuwsgierig maken naar literatuur uit cultureel minder bekende landen': NLPVF, *De Nederlandse literatuur in de wereld: Beleidsplan 2009–2012* (Dutch

In a fascinating piece of research into the Dutch and Flemish literary fields, Marc Verboord and Susanne Janssen looked at the reading behaviour of non-professional book readers and literary mediators such as librarians, booksellers and reviewers. Although the research was comparative, I shall confine my comments to the literary field in the Netherlands and the small section of the findings that deals with the origin of the two books most recently read by these influential informants. More than 50 per cent of these two books was neither Dutch nor Flemish in origin, but rather translated literature. The actual results for the origin of the two books read by Dutch literary mediators, of whom 124 participated in the research, are as follows:

> Book 1 – 37 per cent Netherlands; 6 per cent Flanders; 57 per cent translated
>
> Book 2 – 42 per cent Netherlands; 4 per cent Flanders; 54 per cent translated.[11]

One advantage of this kind of field analysis which involves empirical research is that its methodology is not national(istic), in contrast with traditional Dutch literary studies. This piece of research by Verboord and Janssen, conducted in 2005, shows that literary reality in the Netherlands is nowhere near as Dutch as the national literary histories would seem to suggest.

Once translation is viewed as being integral to literary life in the Netherlands, it follows that the study of the Dutch literary field can no

---

literature in the world: Policy outline 2009–2012), 16: <http://www.nlpvf.nl/nl/downloads/beleidsplan_20092012.php> accessed 21 July 2010.

11   Marc Verboord and Susanne Janssen, 'Informatieuitwisseling in het huidige Nederlandse en Vlaamse literaire veld. Mediagebruik en gelezen boeken door literaire lezers en bemiddelaars' (Exchange of information in the contemporary Dutch and Flemish literary field. Media use and books read by literary readers and mediators) in Ralf Grüttemeier and Jan Oosterholt, eds, *Een of twee Nederlandse literaturen? Contacten tussen de Nederlandse en Vlaamse literatuur sinds 1830* (One or two Dutch literatures? Contact between Dutch and Flemish literature from 1830) (Leuven: Peeters, 2008), 319.

longer focus solely on works originally written in Dutch. It would need
to take into account the Dutch literary diaspora as well as translated literature published in Dutch. However, when such a study is undertaken in
the form of literary history, it necessarily filters out these significant but
non-traditional parts of Dutch literary culture in the interest of creating
a 'pure' national canon. This, too, is part of Dutch cultural policy and as
such serves a particular political purpose. For some time now this purpose
can be seen as part of a response to the global domination of English and
the fear of the national language and culture losing ground whether it
be in the context of European enlargement or of inward migration. This
sense of the need to preserve or strengthen Dutch informs the policy of
the Dutch Language Union (DLU); in the five-year policy document
covering the period 2008–2012 the first stated goal in the policy overview is 'to preserve and strengthen Dutch as a language that can be used
in all domains and in all social situations'.[12] For a period of at least eight
years, the Dutch Language Union invested in the production of a history
of literature in Dutch.[13] In its policy document cited above (see n. 9), the
Dutch Foundation for Literature, formerly NLPVF, also states its intention to create a new 'canon of literature in Dutch' consisting of literary
classics from the Netherlands and Flanders.[14]

The Dutch Language Union is in fact an intergovernmental treaty
organization responsible for matters concerning the Dutch language, and
Dutch-language culture and education. Originally set up to cover the Dutch
language in the Netherlands and Flanders (the Dutch-speaking part of

12   (het Nederlands te behouden en te versterken als taal die gebruikt kan worden in alle
      domeinen en in alle sociale situaties) *Nederlands zonder drempels. Meerjarenbeleidsplan
      2008–2012* (Dutch without obstacles. Four-year plan and policies 2008–2012)
      <http://taalunieversum.org/taalunie/meerjarenbeleidsplan0812.pdf> accessed 24
      February 2009.

13   The annual amounts vary from €237.285K in 2003 to €5.904K in 2005 after an initial
      annual funding of around €180K. See Dutch Language Union annual interim reports
      and the policy document for 1998–2002: Nederlandse Taalunie, *Meerjarenbeleidsplan
      1998–2002*: <http://www.taalunieversum.org/taalunie/publicaties> accessed 24
      February 2009.

14   NLPVF, *De Nederlandse literatuur in de wereld*, 13.

Belgium), the Dutch Language Union now also includes Suriname in its remit. It is also noticeable that current policy acknowledges globalization, promotes Dutch as a global language and seems to be moving away from promoting literature as a national identity-forming entity in the direction of promoting reading using a wide range of materials, both digital and printed.[15] Nevertheless, the literary histories themselves are still appearing. A significant one to mention here is the volume that covers the postwar period, *Altijd weer vogels die nesten beginnen: Geschiedenis van de Nederlandse literatuur 1945–2005* (History of Dutch literature 1945–2005) by Hugo Brems, published in 2006. This open and democratic literary history does not privilege any particular national narrative, and seeks to include as many women writers, migrant writers, colonial and postcolonial writers and genres as possible. Cees Nooteboom features much more fully here than in any other literary history published in Dutch. Significantly, however, he occupies a prominent place in a recent literary history published in German in 2006: *Niederländische Literaturgeschichte*.[16] And this brings me to the other gap in the structure of literary studies: that between national literary fields. When studying literature in translation, it is not possible to pretend that there are two separate literary fields – in the case of this book on Nooteboom, the English (with the American/British problem still to be answered) and the Dutch – and assume that translated texts simply surface in the new culture from time to time. One aim of this book, therefore, is to formulate some ideas about movement between fields; as Ton Naaikens puts it 'the transition between the two cultures, the two worlds, the two languages'[17]

---

15   The English pages of the DLU website contain regularly updated information on policy: <http://www.taalunieversum.org/inhoud/english-general-information> accessed 3 December 2012.

16   Ralf Grüttemeier and Maria-Theresia Leuker, eds, *Niederländische Literaturgeschichte* (Stuttgart: J.B. Metzler, 2006).

17   Ton Naaikens, 'de overgang tussen de twee culturen, de twee werelden, de twee talen' ('Een wereld van verschil. Over taal en cultuur in vertaling' (A world of difference. On language and culture in translation)), in S. Evenepoel, G. Rooryck and H. Verstraete, eds, *Taal en cultuur in vertaling: De wereld van Cees Nooteboom* (Antwerp and Apeldoorn: Garant, 2004), 17.

or, put another way by Mueller-Vollmer and Irmscher, 'a complex practice of cultural transfer.'[18]

II Mobility, Nomadism and New Belongings

On the English-language website <www.ceesnooteboom.com>,[19] produced by the Dutch publishing house De Bezige Bij, the headlines present Cees Nooteboom as 'Novelist –Traveller – Poet – Art Reviewer', and a short video clip shows the writer on a harbour wall watching ships coming and going, speaking in German with English subtitles. Mobility is a mode of existence not only for Nooteboom the individual in his travel writing, but also for his fictional characters. He has frequently been described as a nomad, particularly by commentators on the travel writing. The impact of this mobile life on Nooteboom will be an important question for this book: In what ways has it acted as a force for change for the author personally? How has it affected his subjectivity, and how has it found its way into his work?

Philosophy as a Mode of Literary Inquiry

Mobility brings with it what sociologist John Urry calls new 'sociabilities' involving contacts with strangers, automobility which creates new subjectivities, and 'aeromobility' with its 'global lines of flights.'[20] Urry's use of the phrase 'line of flight' both refers to the form of travel and at the same

---

18　Kurt Mueller-Vollmer and Michael Irmscher, 'Introduction', in Mueller-Vollmer and Irmscher, eds, *Translating Literatures, Translating Cultures: New Vistas and Approaches in Literary Studies* (Stanford: Stanford University Press, 1998), xii.

19　Accessed 17 February 2013.

20　John Urry, *Mobilities* (Cambridge: Polity Press, 2007), 104, 127, 149.

time echoes Gilles Deleuze's 'lines of flight' which connect singularities, or individual points, and which Deleuze describes as a 'fibre strung across borderlines'.[21] Deleuze's philosophy will form an essential part of my approach to Nooteboom's writing and it supplies many more concepts than that of a 'minor literature' mentioned in the first part of this introduction. I first came to Deleuze's philosophy through the work of the vitalistic feminist philosopher Rosi Braidotti whose reading of it foregrounds personal transformation through embracing minority and multiplicity, two concepts which require further explanation as they are distinctive concepts of nomadic philosophy. The absence of linearity and hierarchy in this philosophy is conceptualized through the branching rhizome which consists of lines constituting a map of border and threshold crossings. Such lines of flight[22] become the means by which deterritorialization occurs, the process by which new belongings come into existence. Deleuze has used these concepts to write about literature and film, and I have chosen them because they enable me to work with a matrix of concepts that I envisage will provide the tools for the complexities of literature, and particularly of literature in translation, to be mapped out in subsequent chapters of this book which presents an experiment in viewing literature through philosophical thought.

In what follows, I aim to introduce the relevant philosophical concepts and indicate how they will be used to reflect on the writer Nooteboom, his literary preoccupations and to produce readings of his poetry and prose. The mobilities paradigm as expounded by Urry in his book *Mobilities* with its dynamic, mobile view of human society provides a relevant framework for studying the work of Cees Nooteboom that can take into account not only his travel writing and nomadic themes and characters, but possibly also the mobile nature of his works and their afterlives in translation. At the same time, however, in thinking more broadly about literature in translation and

---

21   Gilles Deleuze and Félix Guattari, *A Thousand Plateaus: Capitalism and Schizophrenia*, trans. Brian Massumi (London: Athlone Press, 1988), 249.

22   An alternative translation of this phrase is 'lines of escape'. See, for example, the translation by Dana Polan of *Kafka: Toward a Minor Literature* (Minneapolis: University of Minnesota Press, 1986).

how it establishes itself in new, other cultures, I want also to reflect more deeply on national literatures, cultural identities, and nomadic subjectivity. To do so, I turn to what is termed 'philosophical nomadism' in order to try out an approach which is quite distinct from the mobilities paradigm. The latter concerns itself with the physical world and human behaviour from a sociological point of view, placing the focus on the importance of movement, and on forms of mobility and their impact on individuals and societies. The adoption of this paradigm requires scholars to take a fresh look at many aspects of their discipline.[23] Philosophical nomadism, on the other hand, is a philosophy of the human subject which rests on a non-unitary vision of the subject. It privileges ideas of movement across boundaries, minority positions, multiplicity and complexity, and the new structures of thought that these engender. It also challenges conventional disciplinary structures.

In order to do justice to the fact of literature in translation, I am nevertheless also concerned with the different modes of textual mobility: physical, cultural and intellectual. In the English-speaking world, it could be said that many texts in translation occupy a minority position to some extent since they are not successful in their attempts to belong to the new English-language culture in which they find themselves, remaining marginal in the host literary field. Nooteboom is one of the few Dutch writers who has moved from the outer margins of the English literary field to a place of recognition, albeit still a relatively marginal one. I will be comparing Nooteboom's place in the English literary field with his very different position in Germany in Chapter 3.

Nomadic Literature will investigate the extent to which philosophical nomadism, and the associated concepts introduced above, can shed light on literary lines of flight. I have explained my decision to bring philosophy to bear on literature rather than taking the sociological 'mobilities' approach. This does not mean, though, that the material world is irrelevant – far

---

23 For instance, this way of thinking is applied to language learning in Jane Fenoulhet and Cristina Ros i Sole, eds, *Mobility and Localisation in Language Learning* (Oxford: Peter Lang, 2010).

from it. Rosi Braidotti, to whom I will turn for an account of nomadism, already brings together the material and spiritual world, the empirical and the symbolic in her insistence on the embodiment of subjects:

> The 'body' in question is the threshold of subjectivity; it is to be thought of as the point of intersection, as the interface between the biological and the social – that is to say between the sociopolitical field of the microphysics of power and the subjective dimension.[24]

I first became familiar with the work of Gilles Deleuze through Braidotti who builds on it as she develops her own philosophy of becoming. She interrogates Deleuze's fundamental idea of 'becoming woman' as the first step in becoming minor, or in moving from the centre to the margin, from a feminist perspective. As a woman working in literature, it is important to me to keep this perspective in mind, which is why Braidotti's work has become so important to me personally. I am equally concerned to draw on Deleuze's own work on literature, which is why I refer frequently to both philosophers. Although the main focus of this book is on literature in translation, more specifically Nooteboom in translation, and on nomadic subjectivity and its representation in literature, the literary representation of gender and sexuality is also a constant concern.

The following section of this Introduction outlines the main concepts I shall be taking from philosophy in order to discuss literature. When I transfer concepts from one discipline to another there is no intention to contribute to the field from which such concepts derive, since I write as a scholar of literature rather than philosophy. My translation of them into the domain of literature aims to preserve their particularity and take them to a point across a boundary between disciplines, and so could itself be said to constitute a Deleuzian line of flight. And according to Braidotti on the subject of transdisciplinarity and the borrowing of ideas, 'Deleuze calls this technique "deterritorialization" or the becoming-nomad of ideas.'[25] I chose a nomadic framework because of its literal and symbolic relevance to my

24   Braidotti, *Nomadic Subjects*, 182.
25   Braidotti, *Nomadic Subjects*, 37.

topic, but it has rapidly become part of my interdisciplinary approach. It represents a distinct and conscious departure from the literary tradition in which a book devoted to a single author would contribute towards that author's national canonical status. Rosi Braidotti writes as a woman who lives and works in the Netherlands, grew up in Australia in an Italian migrant family and studied for her research degree in Paris, clearly maintains multiple cultural allegiances. Recently, she has made her own contribution to the inclusion of new citizens in the Netherlands in what in some respects has become a self-conscious national(istic) culture in the course of the last decade.[26] In her subsequent writings Braidotti tries to envisage what a new vision of non-unitary subjectivity might mean, moving towards a vitalistic and ethical vision of (post)human life.[27]

Central Concepts

There are three sets of theoretical concepts that I will explore in the rest of this introduction: those surrounding the notion of 'mobility'; those connected with nomadism and subjectivity; and those relating to belonging and new belongings.

In the introduction to a collection of essays on the impact of new mobilities on language pedagogy, Cristina Ros i Solé and I summarized the effect of understanding human societies as fundamentally mobile rather than static:

> The 'mobilities turn' involves recognition of deterritorialised, multiple identities and belongings, of overlapping memberships of different groups, and of a new kind of capital – what Urry, following Bourdieu, terms 'network capital'. In a similar way,

26 In particular, her co-edited volume to accompany the Netherlands' pavilion at the 2007 Venice Biennale represents a significant contribution in this area. See Rosi Braidotti, Charles Esche and Maria Hlavajova, eds, *Citizens and Subjects: The Netherlands, For Example: A Critical Reader* (Zurich: JRP/Ringier, 2007).

27 Rosi Braidotti, *Metamorphoses: Towards a Materialist Theory of Becoming* (Cambridge: Polity Press, 2002) and Rosi Braidotti, *Transpositions: On Nomadic Ethics* (Cambridge: Polity Press, 2006).

language learners cannot be conceived any longer as individuals affiliated to a single territory, language and culture.[28]

The simple fact of Nooteboom's extensive travel writing in which he narrates his travels from the 1950s to the present day means that he exemplifies mobility as a fundamental way of life rather than an interruption to a basically static existence. As he puts it himself in the introduction to the collection of travel stories published in English as *Nomad's Hotel*:

> I packed a rucksack, took leave of my mother and caught the train to Breda. An hour later – you know how small the Netherlands is – I was standing at the side of the road on the Belgian border sticking my thumb in the air, and I have never really stopped since.[29]

For a writer from a small European culture and compared to many of his fellow-writers in Dutch, Nooteboom's network capital is unusually high: in addition to all eight elements of network capital, or capacities to be mobile, enumerated by Urry, he has 'the possibility of escape into "sheer inaccessibility"'.[30] Whether this leads to some kind of postnational identity as Urry suggests, will be explored in Chapters 2 and 3. The extent to which Nooteboom's network capital as a writer is due to his personal mobility, or to the transfer of his literary texts into other languages will be assessed as part of the complex interplay of subjectivity and literature that is the subject of this book.

That mobility leads to deterritorialization, multiple identities and new belongings can be understood in a rather obvious commonsensical way as activity that severs the fixed link between location and identity. In *Kafka: Toward a Minor Literature* Deleuze and Guattari describe this as 'real' deterritorialization when they refer to the migration of Kafka's father, a Czech Jew from a rural community speaking a rural Czech to

---

28   Fenoulhet and Ros i Solé, *Mobility and Localisation*, xv.

29   Cees Nooteboom, *Nomad's Hotel: Travels in Time and Space*, trans. Ann Kelland (London: Vintage Books, 2007), 2.

30   For more on network capital, see Urry, *Mobilities*, 197; the short quotation is from page 201.

the German-speaking town. They develop the idea of a minor literature, to express the minority position of Kafka himself, writing in Prague in a dominant but deterritorialized language – German – that is not his 'own'. In this case it is not Kafka himself who is mobile, but the German language which crosses the border because of the power structures that existed at the time in which Kafka was writing. Deleuze and Guattari see this special position as one which produces great intensity and solidarity, 'and if the writer is in the margins or completely outside his or her fragile community, this situation allows the writer all the more possibility to express another possible community and to forge the means for another consciousness and another sensibility'. The concept of 'minor' then allows for 'a minor practice of major language', and the possibility of the margin as a state of mind. 'We might as well say that minor no longer designates specific literatures but the revolutionary conditions for every literature within the heart of what is called great (or established) literature.'[31] Deleuze and Guattari go on to show how Kafka's writing is structured in a rhizomatic way in which elements are connected along lines of flight. Although these elements can continue branching in an unlimited way, the structure remains finite and therefore capable of being grasped by readers. Clearly the linguistic position of Kafka is not directly comparable to Nooteboom's. All the same, Nooteboom does share a rhizomic mode of expression, especially in his travel writing. Deterritorialization is also a feature of Nooteboom's use of Dutch, precisely because the language is the 'home' he takes with him on his travels. And although Dutch is one of the official languages of the European Union, the discussion of Dutch as a small language and culture earlier in this introduction makes it clear that its speakers and politicians have been only too aware of its minority position, which is not to say that they necessarily adopt a minoritarian stance.

Up to this point I have used the terms 'nomadic' and 'nomadism' with deliberate openness both to allow for the dictionary meaning of 'roaming, wandering' and to keep the door open for them as philosophical ideas. However, I do not mean to suggest that being on the move automatically

31 Deleuze and Guattari, *Kafka*, 12, 17, 18.

engenders nomadic sensibility, or nomadism. And it is this which provides the web of ideas for this exploration of Nooteboom and his work. Key concepts will be taken both from Deleuze and from Braidotti, and include rhizomatic structure, multiple subjectivity, and the importance of desire, intensity and 'becoming' as positive movement within a subject who embarks on a process of becoming-minor.

The Structure of this Book

Like its introduction, my book as a whole is organized into two parts, the first of which concentrates on theory and literature, while the second focuses solely on Cees Nooteboom's writing. Chapter 1 will survey and discuss the question of national literatures in a mobile world. Are they irrelevant in a postnational, global culture, or do they provide a much-needed 'local' counterweight to the globalization of culture and a remedy for the fear of loss of a particular language and culture, a fear which may loom larger in the smaller European cultures? Is the whole idea and function of the national changing in response both to globalization and to new or rediscovered nationalisms? And which academic disciplines provide the best framework of ideas for considering these questions? The focus of this chapter will be on the academic disciplines of individual languages and cultures (in this case Dutch Studies), on comparative literature and on translation studies.

Chapter 2 will delve more deeply into concepts of translation that take a positive approach to the transfer of meaning across language boundaries, such as Paul Ricoeur with his notion of 'linguistic hospitality ... where the pleasure of dwelling in the other's language is balanced by the pleasure of receiving the foreign word at home'.[32] The idea of cosmopolitanism and its relationship to both the global and the local will provide a different way of reflecting on highly mobile subjects. These discussions will prepare the

---

32   Paul Ricoeur, 'Translation as Challenge and Source of Happiness' in *On Translation*, trans. Eileen Brennan (London and New York: Routledge, 2006), 10.

ground for my discussion of Cees Nooteboom's own relationship with translation in Part 2: his experience of translation, his interaction with his own translators, and the role of translation in his poetry and prose works.

New ways of elaborating national identity will be explored in Chapter 3 through the nomadic, cosmopolitan or intercultural figure of Cees Nooteboom as an author who has acquired quasi-national status in Germany, is read in many languages and yet understands his own Dutchness in highly specific and important ways. Through his writing, Nooteboom resists any attempt to pigeonhole him as a Dutch writer and makes it almost impossible for readers and critics to view him in an essentialistic way. Since his travel writing consists of highly personal accounts of encounters with other cultures and his novels create avatars who think, feel, and sometimes write about the nature of human existence, I will link the question of subjectivity and its expression in writing to identity in a way that allows for multiple and new belongings.

In Part 1, then, I consider three aspects of the paradigm-shift away from national literary study: the impact of this shift on humanities disciplines; the centrality of translation in the new paradigm; and the impact of this shift on national identity.

In presenting my account of Cees Nooteboom and his work in Part 2 of this book, I am mindful of my own responsibility towards the literature of the Netherlands and towards the writer who provides the material for what will be a substantial case study. My aim is to provide a full and open representation that does justice to the translatability and mobility of the writer and his work. The fact that I write in English and view Dutch literature and culture from outside the Netherlands does provide an opportunity to introduce and discuss the literary oeuvre of an important European writer whose medium is the Dutch language from a distanced perspective. At the same time, however, as a scholar of Dutch literature since the 1970s, I aim to share both my attachment to Dutch literature and my understanding of the cultural background to the writing to which some of my readers may not have access.

Part 2 of this book takes Nooteboom's writing as its focus with a chapter devoted to each of the three main genres in which he publishes: fiction, poetry and travel writing. I will experiment with detaching Nooteboom's texts from the territory of the Netherlands by basing my discussion where possible on the oeuvre in English; that is, on those texts that have been published in English, thus refraining from viewing them as intrinsically or essentially Dutch. It is clear from Nooteboom's autobiographical writing that many texts were not produced on Dutch territory, nor do they show a primary connection with it in the form of their settings. This deterritorialization goes beyond real border crossings to virtual ones both on the part of the author and his translated texts. The transformations or 'becomings' that are engendered by this deterritorialization will be an important theme of *Nomadic Literature*.

I will certainly argue that Nooteboom's nomadic way of life has the effect of altering the link between the Dutch language and the territory where it is the major language and I will assess the impact of such deterritorialization on Nooteboom's reception in the Netherlands with particular emphasis on the fiction and poetry. It is the case that for many years the writing produced by Nooteboom in the Dutch language was not welcomed as part of national literary life, in part because of the literary marginality in the Netherlands of two genres practised by him – journalism and travel writing (to be discussed in Chapter 6). In her book on Italian travel writing, Loredana Pozzi notes that Claudio Magris writes in the deterritorialized Italian of the border city of Trieste, and that furthermore, his well-known book *Danubio* is 'perceived as ambiguous (thus deterritorialized from the canon) and possibly belonging to a marginal, minor genre such as Italian travel writing'.[33] *Danubio*'s success outside Italy, like that of Kafka beyond Czech borders suggests that marginality, whether linguistic or generic, may have the effect of enabling border-crossings. Nooteboom's use of the Dutch language can be seen as a highly accomplished literary practice of a minor European language in genres that have been marginal in the Netherlands suggests that a fruitful line of exploration will be that of his becoming-minoritarian. Whether this is a matter of biography, genre or other feature of his work is something that remains to be discovered. One

33   Loredana Polezzi, *Translating Travel: Contemporary Italian Travel Writing in English Translation* (Aldershot: Ashgate, 2001), 190.

thing that Nooteboom and Magris have in common is that they have both been translated into a language and culture where travel writing is not marginal: English.

My account of Nooteboom's writing begins with the novels, which have almost all been translated into English. In this case, there is an English oeuvre which is rather different from the Dutch one. For example, books do not appear in the same order, or at the same time as their Dutch counterparts. Given that my aim in Part 2 of this book is to give readers an overall sense of Nooteboom's writing based primarily on the English versions, there will not be a systematic parallel treatment of all the texts. Taking the English texts as its starting-point, Chapter 4 will refer to the Dutch versions and their reception where there are interesting points to note. For example, the study of the novels' English reception will provide important insights into the ways in which they have come to belong in their new cultural surroundings, and have bedded into the new landscape. In addition, the discussion will show how the protagonists of the novels enact new forms of belonging and are engaged in processes of becoming, such as becoming-minor and becoming-imperceptible. On the other hand, the chapter which deals with Nooteboom's poetry will of necessity be based to a significant extent on the poems in Dutch, reflecting the dearth of English translations of this genre. It is important that they are included for a full understanding of Nooteboom's writing, since he has published volumes of poetry all through his writing career, and the poetry shares the themes and preoccupations of the novels. At the same time, the chapter features an in-depth discussion of the one anthology of his poetry in English translation, as well as a detailed and comparative reading of the three published translations of a single poem, 'Basho'.

In the final chapter, which is devoted to the travel writing, I discuss the three main English publications *Roads to Santiago*, *Nomad's Hotel* and *Roads to Berlin*. Here, questions of self-fictionalization, cosmopolitanism and nomadism come to the fore, as does translation itself as something multiple, contingent, fluid, which can be both a powerful force for cross-cultural understanding but also one for the commodification of culture. This will depend, I argue, on the nomadic stance of the writer in question.

PART I

Literature and New Belongings

CHAPTER I

Literature on the Move: Finding a Disciplinary Framework

Mobile Literature: The Classics

Literature has always travelled, crossing different kinds of frontiers as it does so. In Europe, the literature of ancient Greece and Rome is still in motion after more than two thousand years. Though a history of the Classics would be out of place here, the literary texts of ancient Greek and Rome provide a particularly fine illustration of the mobile condition of literature. Because of their special place in the development of European culture, they crossed and re-crossed frontiers at many different times throughout history, and in different forms for different audiences. Such textual peregrinations are emblematic of the mobile view of literature I am proclaiming and will serve as the starting-point for my reflections on literary border crossings, cultural capital, translation and the availability of academic disciplines for studying them. This chapter will map the disciplinary terrain with a view to arriving at a framework of ideas, approaches and methods for discussing mobile literature written in Dutch and the work of Cees Nooteboom in particular.

The strictly defined political boundaries that have determined the map of Europe since the creation of nation-states from the eighteenth century onwards are a relatively recent phenomenon when viewed in relation to the cultural legacies of Greece and Rome. In contrast, there have always been physical barriers such as sea, mountains, rivers and marshes which played an important part in checking the development and distribution of languages and the cultures associated with them. When cultural transfer was primarily oral, they would have been all-important, but such geographical barriers continued to have an effect as long as texts travelled in manuscript or book form. This latter form of movement, i.e. 'the physical movement of *objects* to producers, consumers and retailers' is one of the 'five "mobilities" that produce social life organized across distance and which form (and re-form) its contours', according to John Urry.[1] Modern engineering and mechanized travel may have minimized the impact of physical barriers, but electronic means of transmission in the new mobility-system of networked computers have eliminated it. The digital circulation of texts has created a sphere in which political boundaries themselves cannot be policed or maintained and the geographical displacement of a writer or physical transportation of his/her paper text is no longer necessary for the spread of literature. A distinguishing feature of Classical literature is that it travelled widely across European linguistic boundaries in the original language as well as in translation. This was possible because it represented such valuable cultural capital that networks of schools and universities throughout Europe taught ancient Greek and Latin and the literatures written in them for centuries from the Middle Ages to the Renaissance and into the twentieth century, though what remains today is a small group of specialist scholars. Aldo Scaglione ascribes this durability to the existence of a stable canon of texts within uniform curricula in a particular educational system: the liberal arts. He also points out that the curricula and texts circulated 'beyond the Christian West well into the Greek Orthodox East and even the Arab world'.[2] By the sixteenth century this stability was challenged by the new municipal education in which Renaissance humanism used classical culture as the key to social mobility. Or as Pascale Casanova puts it, 'Latin – together with Greek, reintroduced by humanist scholars – had accumulated all of the literary and, more generally, cultural capital then in existence'.[3] She points out that the humanist enterprise was an attempt

---

1   Urry, *Mobilities*, 47.

2   Aldo Scaglione, 'Comparative Literature as Cultural History: The Educational and Social Background of Renaissance Literature' in Clayton Koelb and Susan Noakes, eds, *The Comparative Perspective in Literature: Approaches to Theory and Practice* (Ithaca and London: Cornell University Press, 1988), 149.

3   Pascale Casanova, *The World Republic of Letters*, trans. M.B. DeBevoise (Cambridge, MA: Harvard University Press, 2004), 48.

to reclaim a secular Latin heritage in the face of scholastic tradition thus challenging the monopoly of the church. This was also to be challenged by the Reformation which emphasized the importance of direct access to the bible for the laity, thus undermining the dominance of Latin. An important milestone was the publication of Luther's complete translation of the bible into German in 1534.[4]

The Netherlands saw an explosion of translation activity from the mid-sixteenth century, just like other European countries. In his introduction to a volume of reflections on translation in the Low Countries in this period, *Door eenen engen hals: Nederlandse beschouwingen over vertalen 1550–1670* (Through a narrow channel: Netherlandic reflections on translation 1550–1670), Theo Hermans attributes this to a number of factors besides humanist influence: urbanization, the growth of a patriciat and of a middle class. 'The translations and imitations of the Classics are the most innovative and prestigious from a cultural perspective. Since these activities, together with the practice of new disciplines, present the vernacular languages with new tasks, progressive language-lovers pay them particular attention. Furthermore, in an era of nation-building, the use of the mother tongue also acquires an ideological dimension.'[5] I will return to this last point. The cultural capital of the Classics in humanist education still survived in the twentieth century in a weak form in more traditional branches of education where they were seen as a civilizing influence. In his

4   There had been many translations before this, but Luther's translation was a watershed because it was part of the institutional challenge to the Catholic Church and as such was soon followed by translations into other European languages. See the entry 'Bible' in *The Encyclopedia of Protestantism* (London: Routledge, 2004), vol. 1, 223.

5   'Uit cultureel oogpunt het meest vernieuwend en prestigieus zijn de vertalingen en navolgingen van de Klassieken. Doordat de volkstalen zich hiermee, en met de beoefening van nieuwe disciplines, voor nieuwe taken geplaatst zien, besteden vooruitstrevende taalliefhebbers er speciale aandacht aan. Daarbij komt dat, in een tijdperk van natievorming, het gebruik van de moedertaal vaak ook een ideologische dimensie krijgt.' Theo Hermans, ed., *Door eenen engen hals: Nederlandse beschouwingen over vertalen, 1550–1670* ('s-Gravenhage: Stichting Bibliografica Neerlandica, 1996), 12–13.

book *What is World Literature?*, which proposes a dynamic approach to literature, David Damrosch cites the example of Henry Cabot Lodge who in 1909 opened his ten volume anthology *The Best of the World's Classics* with the statement that readers will be improved by reading Seneca, Cicero and Socrates. By this point Classical education had been in decline since the advent of the philological movement in the late eighteenth century, linked to European nationalisms, the reintroduction of 'self-consciously national languages and, subsequently, the creation of "popular" literatures'.[6]

It is clear from this quick excursion into the mobility of Classical texts in Europe that, as Urry suggests, this mobility of objects does not occur in isolation, but rather in complex intersection with other mobilities and social structures, including translation practices, whether as a pedagogical practice in the process of learning a classical language, or as part of a system of producing printed texts.

Accounts of the history of translation in Europe have drawn attention to the different modes in which the Classics have found their way into vernacular texts, through a range of practices between the poles of 'word-for-word' and 'free' translation. The notion of a word-for-word rendering or 'faithfulness' to the source text has persisted through the ages, perhaps owing to its connection to the translation of sacred texts, as Lawrence Venuti suggests in his introduction to *The Translation Studies Reader*. Maybe because of their special status as what Bourdieu calls 'consecrated' texts as part of a system of symbolic capital, literary texts tend more generally to be translated faithfully. I will return to this aspect in my next chapter when I discuss translation in relation to textual and human mobility in more depth. The nature of intertextual relationships will also be dealt with in Part 2 of this book, where I discuss those works by Cees Nooteboom that have been translated into English. The translational dimension of his writing will be looked at alongside those texts that are the result of interlingual translation.

At the 'free' end of the scale of modes of translation there is the process of rewriting, which covers *imitatio*, paraphrase and adaptation in which a freer treatment coincides with a focus on the new audience for the text.

6   Casanova, *World Republic*, 48.

Beyond these practices which can all be considered as translation, elements of plot, character or thematic content can be reworked and incorporated in new works in a variety of ways so that the connection with the prior text becomes tenuous. Such reworkings have the character of an allusion so that only readers with special knowledge of the prior text will detect the reference. Many of Cees Nooteboom's works are rich in classical allusions, which is one of the means by which he clearly inserts himself into a European, if not a world, literary tradition.

Literary Mobilities and Academic Disciplines

Literary mobility is dependent on the translation of texts into the language of the receiving culture. Consequently, it might be expected that translation studies would be the primary discipline from which to approach textual mobility. Commenting above on the link between consecrated, or canonized, literary texts and the degree of faithfulness in translation, I have implied that the case of Nooteboom's works in English will be a straightforward one in the sense of a close and faithful rendering of a literary source text in a target language. In practice the picture is more complex because literary genre stands in a dynamic relation to the canonization process. For example, the majority of Nooteboom's prose works have been translated into many languages according to prevalent norms that can be located towards the faithful end of the scale. However, closer study reveals that Nooteboom's travel-writing has received a different treatment from translators and editors as it moves across the linguistic and cultural boundaries separating Dutch and English. One of the translated travel works in particular, *Nomad's Hotel*, does in fact exhibit a more flexible, audience-oriented approach that might more accurately be termed adaptation. The explanation for this fact cannot be provided by translation studies alone if it is to be sought in the idea that different genres have differing status, and that the novel is a more privileged genre that commands more respect than travel writing. The question of the relative status of different genres is one that will vary across the various translating cultures, and needs to be tackled using the means of comparative literature as well as those of translation studies.

Having said that, an understanding of translation processes is crucial for an appreciation and adequate account of the literary oeuvre of Cees Nooteboom, given that his work has been translated into thirty-five languages.[7] This oeuvre also lends itself to an exploration of the differential impact of translation into English as opposed to other languages. This would require an approach that takes into account literary institutions and intercultural power relations. Consider the powerful function of Latin as a *lingua franca* that enabled it to persist long after it had ceased to be learned as a first language. This suggests that the function of English as a global *lingua franca* will have some bearing on the spread and reach of translations into English when compared with translations into other languages. How do publishers and translators respond to the challenge of a global market for Nooteboom in English? Nooteboom in English is translated for and marketed to English-speaking countries, but this does not mean that the readership has English as their first language. Although the larger question concerning translations into a *lingua franca* will not be fully addressed in the present study, it is nevertheless a factor to be borne in mind in my discussion of Cees Nooteboom's English oeuvre. One thing is certain: Nooteboom's work in Dutch is highly unlikely to cross political, linguistic, social and cultural boundaries other than in translation. And his work in English has the possibility of travelling very widely, not just in the English-speaking world, but beyond it as well.

The mobility of literature as I describe it here, and its intersection with other mobilities such as digital and translational mobilities, does not fall neatly within the remit of any one academic discipline. The social science mobilities paradigm outlined by John Urry does provide a framework,

---

7   Information taken from the database of the Dutch Foundation for Literature (Nederlands Letterenfonds) <www.nlpvf.nl/vertalingendb/resultaten1.php?q=C ees+Nooteboom&nrows=10&lang=searchtype=simple> accessed 20 July 2010.

if the mobilities just listed are rephrased as the 'physical movement of objects' interacting with 'communicative travel' producing an 'assemblage of humans, objects, technologies and scripts'.[8] Conceptualizing translation as a technology which enables movement and extends the social and cultural networks of a writer and her/his works is useful, but clearly does not capture all that is involved in the process of translation, if the textual dimension is also to be explored. As I indicated in the introduction, nomadic philosophy will provide an intellectual home through its non-linear approach to thinking and writing. At the same time, I want to position myself among the humanities scholars reflecting on the role and future of humanities disciplines; what such scholars have in common is a sense of the continual evolution of the humanities, the indispensability of working across disciplines, and the goal of social relevance.[9] In my view, in order to do justice to the social and cultural complexities of literary mobility, the social science approach to mobility will need to be complemented by the kind of humanities disciplines that will bring in the study of languages and cultural texts. In what follows, I will present a discursive map of the different humanities disciplines that have responded to the changing context of literary production, concluding with the recent debates that attempt to take processes of globalization into account.

A cartographic approach is useful for mapping a complex and pluriform landscape – in this case both a cultural and an institutional one. My inspiration for this approach has been the work of Rosi Braidotti, and I base my description of its key features on her book *Metamorphoses. Towards a Materialist Theory of Becoming* where she explains the nomadic mode of writing as a means of attacking linearity and binary thinking and

---

8   Urry, *Mobiities*, 47–8.
9   This kind of agenda can be seen most clearly through the presence and activities of certain centres and institutes of the humanities, for example: the Centre for the Humanities at the University of Utrecht, under the leadership of Rosi Braidotti: <http://www.uu.nl/faculty/humanities/EN/centreforthehumanities/Pages/default. aspx> accessed 30 December 2012, and the Mahindra Humanities Center at Harvard, directed by Homi Bhabha: <http://mahindrahumanities.fas.harvard.edu/content/ directors-letter> accessed 30 December 2012.

its style as 'multi-faceted and web-like'. Her idea of the relation between writer and reader is of a 'mutual pact of tolerance for complexities'.[10] As Braidotti points out in her previous book *Nomadic Subjects*, a cartography can only be produced from a situated point or points: 'you must be located somewhere in order to make statements of general value. Nomadism, therefore, is not fluidity without borders but rather an acute awareness of the nonfixity of boundaries.'[11]

In mapping the territory of academic disciplines capable of dealing with an author like Cees Nooteboom in a way that takes his literary hypermobility into account I will start from that discipline which lends itself for investigating the entire output of a writer, though whether this includes works that have appeared in translation is a matter for debate. The obvious academic field of study is literary history which places a writer and his or her works in a specific time and culture but which, as practised in Europe with the Netherlands as a prime example, has no mechanism for operating across linguistic boundaries. In the Dutch case it does now cross the political boundary between the Netherlands and Flanders, the Dutch-speaking part of Belgium to present writers born in Flanders, though the effect is one of expansion of the canon, rather than investigation of cultural exchange. The two primary disciplines already mentioned in this chapter are comparative literature which takes many forms including comparison of two or more European literatures/writers; and translation studies which among other things looks at the role of translation in the development of literatures.

A further question is whether it is necessary or helpful or even possible to define the three disciplines, if that is what they are. Either way, my primary aim here is not to attempt the impossible and arrive at a definitive statement of the disciplinary way forward – I aim to give the contours of the terrain including contested areas and shifting boundaries. As Susan Bassnett makes clear in her 1993 survey of the history of comparative literature, too much time has been spent on debating what comparative literature is, and

---

10   Braidotti, *Metamorphoses*, 172.
11   Braidotti, *Nomadic Subjects*, 36.

she demonstrates forcefully that the way disciplines are defined depends on changing factors and is thus itself subject to change.[12] In the following pages I explore what each subject area has to offer, concluding with a section in which I discuss recent ideas on literature and globalization, relating these to nomadic practices taken from philosophy and put into practice in the context of literary studies.

Literary history is the discipline least equipped to deliver an adequate account of translated literature. It came into being as a result of the need of newly emergent European nations to establish a distinct identity. In *The World Republic of Letters*, Pascale Casanova sees this as the second stage in the development of national literary economies after the establishment of the vernacular as the language of education and social mobility in the Renaissance. Language and culture were powerful tools in this process, and the creation of a historical narrative of a given national literature had and still has the power to establish a tradition reaching back into the prenational past, thus lending weight to the claims of national distinctiveness. The notion of comparative literature, according to Susan Bassnett, arose at around the same time in the early nineteenth century. It seems to have had the function of reinforcing national identity through its capacity to establish national characteristics through the simple mechanism of comparison highlighting contrasting features of cultures. In this way it contributed to the development of essentialistic national identity. At the same time, according to Bassnett, it 'was associated with the desire for peace in Europe and for harmony between nations. ... Comparative literature seems to have emerged as an antidote to nationalism, even though its roots went deep into national cultures.'[13] This apparent tension between the nationalistic effects of comparing literatures and the desire for harmony between European nations might be seen as an interesting indicator of the longing for peace as an acknowledgement of complicity in the development of nationalisms. In her Bourdieusian account of literary markets, Casanova

---

12   Susan Bassnett, *Comparative Literature: A Critical Introduction* (Oxford: Blackwell, 1993).
13   Bassnett, *Comparative Literature*, 21.

certainly sees nations and national economies and national literatures as in competition with one another and understands literary history to have played an active role in this.

Looking ahead to the next section of this chapter, where I look at the history of Dutch literature and the role it has played in creating a national identity, I note that with the resurgence of nationalisms in the last decade or so, especially in the smaller European countries, literary history is still implicated in the (re)establishment of national awareness and the creation of national sensibilities. Given its dependence on fixed national boundaries, it would have to reinvent itself quite significantly to maintain its relevance in a mobile world, and I will look for signs that the ground is shifting. For the moment, I will turn to those disciplines or fields of research that are more likely to take transnational, crosscultural movements into account: comparative literature and translation studies. In Bassnett's account of the genesis and history of comparative literature cited above, she demonstrates all too clearly the discipline's lack of a clear identity caused by the lack of agreement as to its object of study. In 1903, for instance, comparative literature was declared not to be a discipline by Benedetto Croce, who favoured literary history as the proper subject for studying literature; and comparative literature was seen as the 'cultural equivalent of the movement towards a United Nations Assembly' by Wellek and Warren after the Second World War. But it also became a restricted and restrictive discipline in Europe and the United States with its insistence on literature in the original language. By 1959, Wellek was describing comparative literature as in crisis, and in Bassnett's view it did not recover, although she acknowledges that it has risen again outside Europe and the US, revitalized by postcolonial approaches. This more political comparative literature once more participates in identity formation, but this time formerly marginal identities are asserting their place in the discipline and the academy. Bassnett ends her 1993 account of the academic field by declaring: 'Comparative literature as a discipline has had its day. Cross-cultural work in women's studies has changed the face of literary studies generally. We should look upon translation studies as the principal discipline from now on, with comparative literature as a valued but subsidiary subject area.'[14]

Ten years later in *Death of a Discipline*, Gayatri Chakravorty Spivak argues that comparative literature as practised in the United States and Europe is not able to deal with literature in today's postcolonial globalized world. In an acknowledgement she notes that comparative literature has responded to globalizing forces by joining them to provide 'the literatures of the world through English translations organized by the United States.'[15] Her book, which was first presented as the 2000 Wellek Lectures in Critical Theory, argues *against* this homogenization of literature based on a notion of translation as unproblematic, and *for* a new kind of comparative literature:

> The new Comparative Literature makes visible the import of the translator's choice. In the translation from *French* to *English*[16] lies the disappeared history of distinctions in another space – made by the French and withdrawn by the English – full of the movement of languages and peoples still in historical sedimentation at the bottom, waiting for the real virtuality of our imagination. If we remain confined to English language US Cultural Studies, we will not be instructed either by the staging of restricted permeability or by the disappeared text of the translation from and into the European national languages that form the basis of what we know as Comparative Literature.[17]

Like Bassnett, she thinks that the future of comparative literature is closely bound up with translation studies, though she argues that the latter discipline will be the force that revitalizes the former.

The disciplinary background sketched in above brings to the fore tensions inherent in the study of European literatures which have been present since the formation of national awareness. From the start, a nationalistic literary history and canon were seen as denying the dynamic interplay

---

14   Bassnett, *Comparative Literature*, 12–30, 4, 161.
15   Gayatri Chakravorty Spivak, *Death of a Discipline* (New York: Columbia University Press, 2003), xii.
16   She is discussing Philcox's translation of Condé's *Heremakhonon* as exemplary.
17   *Death of a Discipline*, 18–19.

between different languages and cultures. The earlier emphasis of comparative literature on linguistic and cultural difference came to be seen as restrictive since scholars and students were limited to study of literature in the languages they knew. Unfortunately, because of the link between globalization and the widespread use of English the solution to this has tended to mean literature in English translation. A related development is that of the conceptualization and practice of world literature, which Spivak and others object to as part of a project promoting United States cultural dominance. Translation studies is the discipline which has the potential to expose cultural tensions to scrutiny, in Spivak's view, whereas the less polemical Casanova reflects on developments affecting the position of literature(s) in the world. Pursuing for a moment some of the implications of the concept of 'world literature', whereas Bassnett saw postcolonial studies as a productive development for comparative literature (though ultimately unable to redeem the discipline), a decade later, Spivak was proposing the next stage in comparative literature's trajectory. Her conclusion was that it is time to find an alternative to a postcolonial comparative literature of dominant versus dominated cultures. However this might proceed, it is clear that comparative literature itself cannot be defined; nor need it be. Relationships of power between literatures are fundamental, and multidimensional and multidirectional.

The passage from Spivak cited above raises important points which need to be taken into consideration if the aim is to discuss literature in a way that reveals differences and the culturally layered nature of texts viewed as part of history. In the concluding section of this chapter I will propose steps towards a practical cartography of the entire and manifold oeuvre of a single writer, including those oeuvres that appear in translation, based on the ideas currently under discussion. My project is to find an appropriate set of concepts for discussing literary works from one of the smaller European cultures which has been powerful, so in a sense belongs with the postcolonial dominant as a former colonial power, but which is relatively powerless in the context of Europe where Dutch culture is marginal and its written culture hardly visible.

World Literature and Literary History

Spivak advocates the notion of 'planetarity' as a necessary alternative to globalization, since the latter is for her an extension of the dominant United States–European culture. She envisages an expanded scope for comparative literature in which 'the proper study of literature may give us entry to the performativity of cultures as instantiated in narrative'.[18] And she argues that teachers should be training students' imaginations as powerful tools in the cross-cultural project. In as much as Spivak argues for the specificity of cultures and the importance of translation studies as the means of ensuring that comparative literature remains alive to difference and nuances of difference, her new idea for literary study is one that I subscribe to. The position of Dutch literature demonstrates that even being part of the dominant United States–Western European culture is a complex matter of differential statuses, just as in Deleuze and Guattari's *Kafka*, where German is the language of a 'minor' literature. In what follows I discuss world literature as a contested space viewed against the background of complex and multilayered cultural belongings.

The need for European nations to assert their sense of identity and nationhood reappears at times of conflict or significant cultural shift when those self-understandings are perceived as under threat. In the introduction I described the state of affairs in the Netherlands in the years before the outbreak of the Second World War when literature participated in such a process of reaffirming Dutchness. They did this most notably by turning to a somewhat neglected genre – the historical novel. This allowed recourse to iconic figures representing a wide variety of Dutch characteristics, as well as dwelling on iconic landscapes and townscapes, the geographical and social factors that were seen as shaping the people.[19] A similar process of heightened national awareness has again been underway in the last decade or so. As a smaller European country, the Netherlands, together

---

18   Spivak, *Death of a Discipline*, 13.
19   Jane Fenoulhet, 'Towards a Critical Patriotism', *Modern Language Review* 99/1 (2004), 112–30.

with the Dutch-speaking part of Belgium – Flanders – has felt its language and culture to be threatened by the recent expansion of English both as a *lingua franca* and as the medium of imported cultural products such as films and TV programmes. The European Union and its enlargement has added to the anxiety about the wellbeing and even the future survival of the Dutch language in competition with many languages in addition to English. Another factor is the arrival of new languages and associated cultures in the Netherlands through migration.

It is still the case that reasserting the nation involves emphasizing attachment both to the language and to cultural expression in that language. In the Netherlands, this is seen most clearly in the 2006 report of the Committee for the Development of a Canon of the Netherlands which again turns to national history to foster national awareness.[20] This new nationalism is by no means supported by all citizens, but it has played a prominent part in political and social life in the Netherlands since the turn of the current century. The cultural policy outlined in the Introduction to provide financial support for the creation of authoritative histories of literature in Dutch can be viewed against this background. However it cannot be seen as a straightforward expression of nationalism. For a start the funding body is an intergovernmental treaty organization, the Dutch Language Union, created to look after matters concerning the Dutch language and culture, the original signatories to the treaty in 1980 being the Netherlands and Belgium, but with a current brief to support the Dutch language wherever it is spoken in the world.

The investment in a new literary history was clearly politically acceptable at a high level, and was part of a policy to strengthen the position of Dutch in Europe. And since, according to the organization's website the project was initiated in 1997, it clearly predates the right-wing nationalistic response to inward migration.[21] Indeed, the history's two senior editors,

20   See, for example, the policy document *Cultural Policy in the Netherlands* (The Hague/ Amsterdam: Ministry of Education, Culture and Science, 2009), especially section 3.2.8 'The Canon of the Netherlands and the National History Museum'.

21   <http://taalunieversum.org/literatuur/literatuurgeschiedenis/> accessed 16 July 2012.

Arie Jan Gelderblom and Anne Marie Musschoot conclude a presentation on the new initiative with a reference to European positioning: 'It is of course not entirely by chance that the new literary history at this time of European union should present the literature of the low countries as a coherent entity, in a historical development, within a larger European framework.'[22] This sketch reveals the complex layered nature of the local and regional contexts: in the matter of literary history, the Netherlands has joined forces with the Dutch-speaking part of Belgium, though the background is nevertheless one of a cultural policy in the Netherlands to strengthen the position of the Dutch language and culture through fostering national awareness. The local and regional allegiances are embedded in the larger one of the European Union. In turn, European cultures have had a life of their own in the world for centuries and are only incidentally connected with the European Union.

One way in which the different languages and cultures are connected is if one sees literary markets as linked to economic markets. Marx and Engels saw the link between a world market and national literatures in 1847 in *The Communist Manifesto* when they pointed out the connection between a world market for goods and a growing cosmopolitan character of production and consumption. In *What is World Literature?*, David Damrosch prefaces his book with the well-known quotation from Marx and Engels that ends with the sentence: 'National one-sidedness and narrow-mindedness become more and more impossible, and from the numerous national and local literatures, there arises a world literature.'[23] The birth of the idea of world literature is generally tracked back to Goethe's use of the

---

22 'Het is natuurlijk niet helemaal toevallig dat de nieuwe literatuurgeschiedenis in deze tijd van Europese eenwording de literatuur van de Lage landen presenteert als een samenhangend geheel, in een historische ontwikkeling, binnen een ruimer Europees kader.' Arie Jan Gelderblom and Anne Marie Musschoot, 'Veranderingen in een bedding van continuïteit: de literatuurgeschiedenis in een nieuw jasje', in G. Elshout et al., eds, *Perspectieven voor de internationale neerlandistiek in de 21e eeuw* (Woubrugge: Internationale Vereniging voor Neerlandistiek, 2001), 8.

23 David Damrosch, *What is World Literature?* (Princeton: Princeton University Press, 2003).

term 'Weltliteratur' in a letter to Eckermann in 1827 to convey his view of literature as literatures in contact with one another in contrast to a closed national literary paradigm. In the light of Goethe's and Marx's and Engels' percipience, it becomes clear just how persistent the nationalist tradition has been in the sense that the dominance of literary history along national lines has been able to obscure the travels of literatures in translation. In Pascale Casanova's account, Goethe's far-sightedness meant that he understood the translator as a central figure in the world market 'not only as an intermediary, but also as a creator of literary value'. She conceptualizes world literary space dualistically between the global and the national: between 'a literary and cosmopolitan pole' and 'a political and national pole'.[24] According to her it is internationally ambitious, cosmopolitan writers themselves who seek out a career beyond national boundaries.

In a collection of essays on Dutch literature outside the Netherlands, Susanne Janssen reflects on the Netherlands as a small country in a global context and sees the cultural elite as being oriented towards the larger influential countries with the result that a small country like the Netherlands imports more cultural products than it exports, with English as the dominant culture since the 1990s.[25] Perhaps the insistence on (trans)national literary history serves as a corrective to this state of affairs. In this way the Dutch literary field behaves like one of Casanova's 'small literatures' which need to assert their own literary norms and identity by means of national literary history at the political pole of global literary space. In the Dutch context, literary history has a particular emphasis on the product rather than the process of literary historiography. It is as though Dutch literature does not exist unless the national canon is defined or constructed in a panoramic work. So a book like this one about a single author, especially one who is still living and writing, is clearly not literary history, though it provides material for the literary historian, and does make a distinct contribution

---

24   Casanova, *World Republic*, 14, 108.
25   Susanne Janssen, 'Grenzeloze literatuur? Een vergelijkend onderzoek naar het internationale gehalte van de literaire berichtgeving in Duitse, Franse, Nederlandse en Amerikaanse kranten in 1955 en 1995', in Petra Broomans et al., eds, *Object: Nederlandse literatuur in het buitenland. Methode: onbekend* (Groningen: Barkhuis, 2006), 169.

to the canonization process. All the same, I choose to view the creation of a narrative about an author and his work, all of which has been published in the past, as a literary historical act. And a single-author history calls for more detailed literary analysis than is found in historical surveys, so provides a welcome complement to those overviews which cannot make the space for discussion of what authors actually write. Whether this kind of literary historical contribution can be linked to the national project will probably depend on the texts under discussion and the language in which they are published. I want to argue that, in a globalized world, the fact that Dutch writers have published in other languages is the living proof, as it were, that Dutch literature has vitality and can bridge the gap between Dutch culture and other cultures, thanks to the work of intermediaries such as translators and publishers.

In keeping with the bird's-eye perspective adopted by literary history, it has frequently been maintained that literary history of the kind that produces a diachronic survey needs distance in time in order to produce a correct judgement of literary value, based on the commonplace that these works must stand the test of time. This widely held notion is used to legitimize the national canon that emerges as a result of literary historical endeavour. The *Lexicon van literaire termen* (Lexicon of literary terms), published in the Netherlands in 1980, defines the canon as referring 'to the group of classic works, to the "immortal" works, of a national literature'.[26] Casanova's analysis of a national canon of foundational texts goes on to explain that the classics, having acquired 'the status of timeless works of art, have defined their literary capital as nonnational and ahistorical'.[27] While this may apply to the larger literatures, and it is certainly borne out by the 'naturalization' of certain writers such as Tolstoy or Flaubert in English, to judge by the Dutch case, the smaller literatures do not have this international aspiration.

26 '[...] naar de groep klassiekers, naar de "onsterfelijken" van een nationale literatuur', H. van Gorp et al., *Lexicon van literaire termen* (Groningen: Wolters-Noordhoff, 1980).
27 *World Literature*, 15.

The idea of longevity, rather than immortality is in evidence in a more recent publication by Mads Rosendahl Thomsen in *Mapping World Literature* who sees the canon as a much more complex and dynamic entity and advocates a 'culture of criticism that is perpetually seeking, reading and criticizing alternatives'.[28] He both adheres to the concept of 'the test of time' and acknowledges the need to include contemporary literary production in the process of critical assessment. Ultimately his interest in national canons is as a source of knowledge about the evolution and composition of the world literary system. This high-level approach seems to take as given the processes of value assignment and like Casanova, he regards the products, i.e. the canonized works, as cultural capital. The advantage of Thomsen's approach for my project is that it integrates the national level as part of the way literature functions in the world; it accords a place to the national which might perhaps now in some contexts be described as the g-local, to follow Braidotti's usage.[29]

The Bourdieusian, sociological, approach seeks to understand the process of value assignment which is based on an individual professional reader's interpretation of individual literary works. It clearly distinguishes between analytical activity and the kind of activity by literary scholars that seeks to participate in the assignment of literary value, suggesting it is possible to write literary history and, rather than exercise the power to make value judgements, to assess instead the place of a writer and his or her writing in culture and society, as the recent history of postwar Dutch and Flemish literature by Hugo Brems amply demonstrates. Brems's approach is informed by and contributes to a literary field analysis, since it discusses the roles of publishers, reviewers, performance, the media and new technologies in disseminating ideas and judgements about literature. In other words, it takes into account the way that society itself produces literary reputations through the changing responses to authors and individual works. Brems does much more than this: he provides a synchronic picture of literary life

---

28   Mads Rosendahl Thomsen, *Mapping World Literature: International Canonization and Transnational Literature* (London: Continuum, 2008), 31.
29   See, for instance, Braidotti, *Metamorphoses*, 14.

in one year for every decade covered. This allows for a full account of all writers in all genres, thus avoiding the exclusion of those writers who do not fit a particular line being taken. This history – *Altijd weer vogels die nesten beginnen: geschiedenis van de Nederlandse literatuur, 1945–2005* – is volume seven of the Dutch Language Union-funded eight-volume literary history discussed in the earlier part of this chapter.

Another strength of Hugo Brems's history of postwar literature in Dutch is the fact that he writes transnational literary history in a small, regional form; his subject-matter covers the literature of the two Dutch-speaking areas of Europe: the Netherlands and Belgian Flanders. The question of whether there are two literatures or one is much discussed inside the Dutch language area, particularly since the intergovernmental treaty organization charged with looking after the Dutch language, the Dutch Language Union, promulgates the principle of one language in use across the two national entities. However, it is certainly possible to isolate two literary fields along national lines with their own institutions such as publishers and news media. In the case of Dutch literature, therefore, an adequate contextual description implies a layered approach: mapping at national level combined with some form of supranational mapping, given the existence of an institution at precisely this supranational level. In *Death of a Discipline*, Spivak speaks of the negotiation of the 'nation-region divide' in comparative literature with the introduction of the concepts of Francophony, Teutonophony, Lusophony, Anglophony and Hispanophony, though it is unlikely that she means to include Dutch under Teutophony.[30] Anyhow, her point is to suggest that these broader categories still reflect a colonial perspective. Since there is no adjective in English for the Dutch-speaking community and no noun for the Dutch-speaking world, I will have to make do with the loan translation 'Dutch language area'. Given that this book is focused on a single writer from the Netherlands, its main transnational dimension will be provided by the writer's oeuvres in translation with a particular focus on English. How relevant the Flemish dimension is for Nooteboom's position as a writer in Dutch will be of minor interest here.

30   Spivak, *Death of a Discipline*, 9.

Conclusion

At this point in my discursive mapping of disciplines which all have something to contribute to literary study, let me take stock of the discussion so
far while proposing the ways in which I will engage with these disciplines.
Although this monograph on Nooteboom will of course be available in
future to Dutch and Flemish literary historians, its primary aims are: i) to
contribute to our understanding of the mobility of literature – what happens to a writer's words when they cross borders and how does this affect
the position of the writer?; ii) the presentation of Cees Nooteboom to an
English readership. And if literary history's primary role is on the national
level, then my transnational aim suggests that another discipline or subject area will provide a more appropriate home than literary history. But
as we have seen in this chapter, the discipline of comparative literature is
contested and shows the strain of adjusting to literature's changed circumstances. Although I have touched on the position of translation studies, it
will be discussed in greater depth in the next chapter. Ultimately, a nomadic
approach should mean that I cease to look for a permanent disciplinary
home, taking up temporary residence where I find concepts that help me
to address different aspects of my study.

Viewing literary history as an academic and cultural practice, this
book will participate incidentally in the process of critical assessment of
a writer and his work which ultimately feeds into literary history and
thereby into a national canon. In the view of Mads Rosendahl Thomsen,
this national canon in turn has the potential to contribute to the world
canon, but I think that this potential is unlikely to be realized in the case
of a small literature. The case of Cees Nooteboom is rather interesting in
this respect, since I consider him to fit Casanova's description of the 'international' writer upholding an autonomous conception of literature in an
international literary field. 'In other words, the writers who seek greater
freedom for their work are those who know the laws of world literary space
and who make use of them in trying to subvert the dominant norms of
their national fields.' It is worth mentioning here that Casanova states that

she does not see these writers as operating according to 'consciously and rationally elaborated strategies.'[31]

The main discussion of Nooteboom and his work requires a collection, or assemblage, of ideas that is appropriate to today's mobile, globalizing world. For me this rules out the old discipline of comparative literature, at least as practised in the past in the West, with its ongoing search for its object of enquiry and its fatal indecision over matters of language and nation, and over Eurocentricity and postcolonialism; and with its use of static categories. According to both Bassnett and Spivak, though with different emphases, this leaves translation studies as the dynamic discipline fit for the purpose of analysing literature as it moves across boundaries. Perhaps as a way out of the comparative literature-translation studies impasse, scholars such as Casanova and Damrosch turned to the concept of world literature to provide the way forward, even though influential figures such as Spivak and Linda Hutcheon still see possibilities for renewal in comparative literature. As we saw earlier, Spivak advocates a planetary perspective which is distinct from a global one, and in so doing intends to emphasize difference as opposed to processes of homogenization; Hutcheon also sees a future comparative literature as addressing cultural specificity and providing a counterweight to recent movements away from Europe as an object of study. For Hutcheon, the project is no less than the 'cultural redefining of Europe' and the vision is to embrace diversity and difference, or even discord within the unity of Europe. The idea underpinning this is that 'in a postmodern world in which individual as well as national identity is "multi-laminated" and complex, difference is both constitutive of identity and something to be constantly negotiated.'[32] Framed in these terms of complexity and dynamism, the project sketched by Hutcheon comes very close to my own, especially since Nooteboom as a representative of

---

31 Casanova, *World Republic*, 109, 178.
32 Linda Hutcheon, 'Comparative Literature: Congenitally Contrarian', in Haun Saussy, ed., *Comparative Literature in an Age of Globalization* (Baltimore: Johns Hopkins University Press, 2006), 227–8.

European literature has participated in a redefining of European literature through his willingness to engage with cultures outside Europe as well.

Europe is part of a globalized world and although European cultures and societies can be precisely located geopolitically, they are intimately connected with all parts of the globe through historical and current migrations and movements as well as their colonial histories. David Damrosch delineates a multiple canon of world literatures that accepts complexity and layeredness, maintaining that it is too simple an idea that the 'Eurocentric canon' has disappeared. According to him, there was a two-tiered world canon of major and minor authors, but this has now been replaced by a three-level system of hypercanon, countercanon and shadow canon.[33] This new layered system creates a cultural space for 'subaltern and "contestatory" voices of writers in languages less commonly taught and in minor literatures within great-power languages' in the countercanon, while preserving the European 'greats' in the hypercanon and accommodating writers who were formerly part of the main canon in the shadow canon. This approach places Nooteboom firmly in the countercanon, which does not preclude the possibility of his entry to the hypercanon, should his translated work stand the test of time. The canons themselves have no regard for political, geographical, linguistic or other boundaries.

Mads Rosendahl Thomsen conceives world literature as much more than a set of canons or an object of study; indeed it 'cannot be perceived as a whole. It can be mapped and navigated in order to address its complexity'. He sees it as a paradigm 'that encompasses both the study of internationally canonized literature and the ambition to investigate and to be interested in all kinds of literature'. While accepting the existence of national canons as part of a layered picture, he also notes that 'there are groups of writers and works which could be said to form subsystems that are transnational. Three very different examples are much in evidence: Holocaust writers, migrant writers and instantly translated authors.' The latter are an interesting case

---

33   David Damrosch, 'World Literature in a Postcanonical, Hypercanonical Age' in Haun Saussy, ed., *Comparative Literature in an Age of Globalization* (Baltimore: Johns Hopkins University Press, 2006), 45.

because according to Thomsen, these writers have become detached from the national literature – detached from the literary culture and criticism – to which they once belonged. He asks, 'Have they not been transformed from being writers belonging to a nation, to writers belonging more to the world, thus transcending the comparative aspect of comparative literature?' This is one of the key questions that I will be exploring throughout this book in relation to Nooteboom and the texts he has written. For as long as they are hosted in new cultures by virtue of being translated, there is a comparative dimension for scholars seeking to understand the differences between the 'same' text in its different new homes. As for method, Thomsen's approach can be summed up in his proposed shift from world literature as object of study to paradigm which 'combines, first and foremost, a primary curiosity with a realistic observation of circulation and critical valuation, that will mix and balance the particulars with the main streams'.[34] It is this primary curiosity that legitimizes the study of any literature regardless of boundaries and categories. The particular cultural embeddedness of a given work of literature will be explored in a manner which places the literary field, literary institutions at the centre of enquiry as well as key individuals such as an author or translator. Thomsen acknowledges that Bourdieu himself discussed literature in a national context, but considers the notion of the field too fruitful a research tool to leave behind since it enables researchers to analyse the fine detail of culture and art. In particular, it can be used to clarify canonization processes, the concept of symbolic capital being particularly important. In fact, Thomsen identifies two more key terms in the investigation of world literature after Bourdieu and the field concept: Ulrich Beck and the concept of cosmopolitanism; and Homi Bhabha and the notion of hybridity as expressing the changes that occur in culture as a result of migration.

My collection of ideas for discussing Cees Nooteboom and his work certainly includes concepts of the literary field and cultural capital, since attention to the producers of books and of literary reputation is crucial to an understanding of how literature works in translation into other cultures

---

34 Thomsen, *Mapping World Literature*, 2, 23, 23, 26.

than the one in which it was first generated. In an afterword to *Literary History: Towards a Global Perspective*, the four volumes which contain the results of a large research project, Stefan Helgesson concedes that the project has demonstrated just how far thinking in terms of global literary study still has to go. He concludes by proposing four paradigms for globalizing literary studies, 'namely, the archival, canonical, formal and circulational approaches'.[35] It is the fourth of these approaches which comes closest to my project since it is focused on 'such (hugely different) works of literature that are transferred to localities, languages and interpretive communities at a remove from their primary site of emergence. Such an approach places a heavy emphasis on reception and translation as well as on the transformations of literary evaluation in different times and places'. He goes on to note – and this is a criticism that can certainly be levelled at my project: 'It can be accused … of being an excessively loose approach in terms of method, but in its directedness towards singular and changeable historical moments it can also supply a wealth of insights, both as regards specific (re)interpretations of texts and historical knowledge of transcultural interactions.'[36] An element of my project not included in Helgesson's list of scholarly activities is that I also engage in the act of reinterpretation in my readings of Nooteboom's work. This places me methodologically in the field of literary criticism, yet one more facet of the interdisciplinary nature of this research project. This is where the concepts of nomadic philosophy allow me to link the mobility of literature to Nooteboom and his writing. In similar vein to Thomsen, I will use the contemporary philosophical notions to gain an understanding of Cees Nooteboom as a mobile, international writer, referring in particular to ideas of cosmopolitanism as well as nomadism.

The final question I want to address in this opening chapter on the way in which different cultural and literary disciplines might be used in

---

35 Stefan Helgesson, 'Going Global: An Afterword' in Stefan Helgesson, ed., *Literary Interactions in the Modern World 2*, vol. 4, *Literary History: Towards a Global Perspective* (Berlin: De Gruyter, 2006), 308.

36 Helgesson, 'Going Global', 315.

my project to approach literature in translation is the role of translation studies itself. Unlike Spivak, I do not choose to see translation studies as a means to renew comparative literature, although I concede that this would indeed be the best way forward for comparative literature simply because of its history of traditional practices associated with bounded literatures that are to be compared. The complexity of literary afterlives in translation and of the processes of moving a text to a new language and culture means that no bounded discipline can adequately support the study of this cultural phenomenon. In the course of this survey across disciplines it has become clear that this project must take cognizance of national literatures and their histories while at the same time operating in a space without national allegiances. For this reason, many of my central ideas and concepts are drawn from philosophy and critical and social theory and are not considered part of literary criticism or history. This creates a scholarly space for the exploration of my aims and the material I have chosen to work with. Whether or not such an approach can be thought of as translation studies is a topic that has attracted some attention. In his study of translation and travel, *Across the Lines: Travel, Language Translation*, Michael Cronin has noted that translation studies has problems of self-definition which he attributes to the nature of the phenomenon it studies:

> [...] one could argue that certain disciplines such as anthropology and translation studies are particularly prone to nomadic restlessness. In other words, it is not just the translating subjects of the discipline that are engaged in a nomadic practice as they translate; rather the discipline itself is nomadic in its disciplinary journeying from subject area to subject area.[37]

This nomadic discipline of translation studies sounds like an attractive and appropriate location for my study, but I wonder whether such a nomadic discipline is actually a discipline at all. Susan Bassnett expresses exasperation with such reflections, stating in a 2011 contribution to 'studies in world writing': 'both translation studies and comparative literature are

---

37   Michael Cronin, *Across the Lines: Travel, Language, Translation* (Cork: Cork University Press, 2009), 104.

not disciplines – both are methods of approaching the study of texts'.[38] In my case, this method would be a complex one which draws on a number of disciplines and study areas.

In the next chapter, I look at the extent to which reflection on translation can provide a framework of ideas for considering Nooteboom as a translated author, and his work, whether written and received in Dutch, or written and received in English. Furthermore, I consider how nomadic philosophy can be used in tandem with thinking about translation as a nomadic practice to consider questions of belonging and identity in contemporary subjectivity.

38   Susan Bassnett, 'From Cultural Turn to Translational Turn: A Translational Journey', in Cecilia Alvstad, Stefan Helgesson and David Watson, eds, *Literature, Geography, Translation: Studies in World Writing* (Newcastle: Cambridge Scholars Publishing, 2011), 72.

CHAPTER 2

New Belongings:
Translation, Travel and Cees Nooteboom

Hospitality in Language

Nomadic practices, whether in the pursuit of a discipline, or undertaken by a traveller and writer, lead inevitably to new belongings which co-exist with older forms of belonging. The possibility of multiple belongings does not, however, dispense with the notion of home. Questions of what is home and how a nomadic individual creates a sense of home become important, and it is no longer necessary to equate home with a fixed geographical or territorial location. In the next chapter, I discuss the way in which Cees Nooteboom provides himself with a sense of home, of dwelling. In this chapter, I shall be asking how textual new belongings differ from human ones, and where a translator fits in as an indispensable operator in the process.

In 'Translation Functions and Interculturality' Lourens de Vries addresses this question, agreeing with the translation theorist Anthony Pym that translators can no longer be seen as part of the target culture. De Vries tentatively positions translators in the intercultural spaces between source and target cultures. At the same time, though, he insists that the 'products of those translators, their translations, are firmly located in target communities.'[1] This is an interesting point: that translators can and do position themselves differently from their texts in relation to the target culture. It confirms that experienced translators can choose to reposition themselves

---

1   Lourens de Vries, 'Translation Functions and Interculturality' in Stella Lin, Maarten Mous and Marianne Vogel, eds, *Translation and Interculturality: Africa and the West* (Frankfurt-am-Main: Peter Lang, 2008), 140.

culturally so that they stand beside the languages and cultures with which they work, rather than inside them. However, just what is entailed by a firm positioning of a translated text in the target culture – to paraphrase De Vries – is not yet clear. I hope to shed more light on this aspect of literary translation through studying the phenomenon of Nooteboom's work in English. What if a translated text fails to sell and therefore remains for the most part unread, for example? Is it still part of the target community simply because it has been translated into that community's language? And how does the appearance of subsequent translated works affect the embeddedness of earlier translations?

At the end of the previous chapter I concluded with Cronin's notion of translation as a nomadic practice. Returning for a moment to the epigraph chosen from Braidotti's *Metamorphoses* to introduce to this book, while it is not difficult to see that her words chime in with my project on literature and translation, it is not yet clear how her ideas can be mapped on to the territories of literature and intercultural interaction. Braidotti sees plurilingualism – 'moving between languages, speaking several but mastering none' – as a nomadic mode of being. It is significant, I think, that she rejects the notion of mastery of a language, since this act involves a refusal by the plurilingual subject to place herself firmly in control of any one language. Braidotti shares the idea of being between languages with De Vries, though her emphasis is on the dynamic traversing of this space. Furthermore, she seems to imply an ethical stance in which each language is treated with respect as a kind of open house which allows individuals the possibility of a creative encounter with a particular language. Mastery, on the other hand, entails a language being learned as building blocks to be utilized according to a closed set of rules, so that the speaker has tamed and can dominate the unruly beast of language. In the epigraph Braidotti goes a step further and suggests that creative writing can be seen as a privileged site where 'the nomadic sensibility ... best expresses itself': the starting-point and crux of my project.

In *Across the Lines*, Michael Cronin speaks both of the 'fundamental nomadism of language'[2] and of language as a home. Closely linked with the idea of language as providing a home, a place in which to dwell beyond geographical space, is the notion of hospitality espoused by Paul Ricoeur in *On Translation*. According to Cronin,

> Translation is conceived of [by Ricoeur] in a nomadic mode as a guest/host relationship. The host opens up his/her house of language to the other but any attempt to diminish the guest's otherness, to impose dominant norms of behaviour or expression on the other, is to violate the laws of hospitality.[3]

This is translation as an ethical project which connects with Braidotti's refusal of mastery over a language, where the speaking subject sought to dominate the 'house of language' itself rather than another person. At the same time, the ethical dimension that I infer from both thinkers involves the guest in a language retaining some of her or his cultural distinctiveness and neither guest nor host engaging in linguistic power play. Perhaps the translator's skill should be seen not as ease of movement from one language into another, but rather as a flexible ability to negotiate the reconciliation between the roles of host and visitor through cultivating generosity. The power dimension of the guest/host relationship may also provide an interesting framework for thinking about the translation of a work from a small European literature into a global, dominant language such as English, for example, by providing the basis for a commentary on asymmetrical relationships in translation, and on the ways in which a target language is opened up to the source text by the choices a translator makes. Perhaps it is her location in the intercultural space which allows her the room to move to and fro between both texts, shifting her own ground in the process. This deep intercultural engagement and mental flexibility can be expected to have an impact on the translator's subjectivity. I wish to argue that in a nomadic approach, not only the text is transformed, so is the translator.

2   Cronin, *Across the Lines*, 36.
3   Cronin, *Across the Lines*, 92.

This aspect will be discussed in more detail below in the section entitled 'The Translator as Transformer'.

In a later book, *Translation and Identity* (2006), Michael Cronin discusses translation as a 'potentially transformative practice' by conceptualizing it as a practice which can simultaneously convey difference and similarity. He views it in the context of the 'mutable mobile', a concept of family resemblance used by Wittgenstein, and relates it to Maria Tymoczko's paradigm of metonymic translation. He goes on to explain an important advantage of this approach: 'The perception of translation as a mutable mobile which operates within a topology of fluidity ... would usefully put paid to the conventional habit of dismissing translation as synonymous with loss, deformation, poor approximation and entropy.'[4]

It may well be that the translator has much in common with the traveller, since both can be conceptualized as located in the spaces between cultures. The figure of the traveller is, however, not the same as the philosophical figuration of the nomad, a point emphasized by Rosi Braidotti. In subsequent sections of this chapter, I return to these two figures, the traveller and the translator, in order to explore them as figurations of nomadic subjects. First, though, I turn to a topic which I have not yet addressed explicitly but which will play an important role in assessing the position of both translators and travellers: cosmopolitanism.

Cosmopolitanism and Translation

Given that I have chosen to discuss translated literature as an intercultural phenomenon and as a nomadic practice, and given that I do not consider my discussion of Nooteboom's writing in Part 2 of this book as a contribution to the narrative of Dutch literature as a national literature, this raises the question of how I view Dutch-language culture in relation to other

4   Michael Cronin, *Translation and Identity* (Abingdon: Routledge, 2006), 28.

cultures. As we saw in the discussion of world literature in the previous chapter, there is clearly a need to find a place for a specific regional, or local, literature and to relate it to the global context and to other literatures. In Chapter 1, I reviewed the ways in which different academic disciplines have approached this challenge. In Chapter 2 I map out an interdisciplinary terrain for my explorations. This need to relate the local and the global also exists at the level of individual writers: since Nooteboom has been translated into thirty-four languages thanks to the work of translators, his writing clearly stands in some kind of relation to all these languages, some of which are global as well as local languages. In addition, the thirty-four languages can be related to a larger number of distinct cultures.

In *Across the Lines*, Michael Cronin sees translation as having a dual function: that is, both a universalizing and a localizing function, explaining that it is possible to see the universal and the local as mutually interdependent, something he describes as 'genuinely liberatory'. He turns to Braidotti's nomadism as a means of understanding this paradox, since she argues for an aesthetic style of writing which is based on '"compassion for the incongruities, the repetitions, the arbitrariness of the languages s/he deals with"'.[5] Writing is where the polyglot relinquishes the 'illusory stability of fixed identities' associated with familiarity with a particular language. In this sense, writing could be said to be an intercultural space.

Cronin proceeds to dismiss what he calls a 'pseudo internationalism' in favour of 'genuine cosmopolitanism'.[6] In philosophy, sociology and political science, cosmopolitanism has been under discussion since the early 1990s. Steven Vertovec and Robin Cohen open their volume of essays taking stock of the development of cosmopolitan thought some ten years later confirming that 'cosmopolitanism is back'.[7] They ascribe this renewed interest to 'globalization, nationalism, migration, multiculturalism and

---

5   Cronin, *Across the Lines*, 97, 104; he is citing Braidotti's book *Nomadic Subjects* (104).
6   Cronin, *Across the Lines*, 136.
7   Steven Vertovec and Robin Cohen, 'Introduction: Conceiving Cosmopolitanism' in Vertovec and Cohen, eds, *Conceiving Cosmopolitanism: Theory, Context, and Practice* (Oxford: Oxford University Press, 2002), 1–22. Here they are quoting social theorist David Harvey.

feminism' and offer an overview of the various strands of cosmopolitan-ism. Among others, they identify a cosmopolitanism that denotes a late twentieth-century cultural condition emphasizing extreme mobility of people and ubiquitous telecommunications, noting that this can be seen as threatening local cultures. And they go on to describe another variant that seeks global democracy or world citizenship leading to cosmopolitan-ism as a project to create transnational institutions. Despite containing elements that overlap with my project, neither of these is of particular relevance for the question of translated literature. However, Vertovec and Cohen also identify cosmopolitanism as a political project embracing the idea of multiple subjects:

> A cosmopolitan politics, in this understanding, emphasizes that people have – and are encouraged to have – multiple affiliations … such a project entails the idea that 'each citizen of a state will have to learn to become a "cosmopolitan citizen" as well: that is, a person capable of mediating between national traditions, communities of fate and alternative forms of life'.[8]

Such a person might well be a translator, whether by profession or, like Nooteboom, by virtue of a deep engagement with different cultures as a travel writer. In addition, Vertovec and Cohen identify a cosmopolitan attitude or outlook which involves an openness to other cultures and a sense of global belonging which they link to certain behaviours and prac-tices. Although this assessment was made ten years ago, it provides a good starting-point for arriving at a definition of cosmopolitanism that is rel-evant for this book with its focus on multiplicity and mobility as applied to culture and literature.

One particular contribution to the volume stands out as coming close to my project: 'Not Universalists, Not Pluralists: The New Cosmopolitans Find Their Own Way' by David A. Hollinger. According to Hollinger, the new cosmopolitanism began in the late 1990s and the movement has since

---

8   Vertovek and Cohen, 'Introduction', 12–13. Here the editors are citing David Held et al., *Global Transformations: Politics, Economics and Culture* (Cambridge: Polity Press, 1999), 449.

gained greater currency.[9] The important feature of this new cosmopolitanism as distinguished by Hollinger is that it offers an alternative both to the humanist universalism of Martha Nussbaum and to the pluralism and emphasis on group rights of Will Kymlicka, and more generally to the old cosmopolitanism which has its roots in Enlightenment thought. Hollinger thinks that new cosmopolitans will be in a better position to 'find and exploit whatever capacities historically situated human beings may have to form sustaining communities, while engaging problems that affect a human population larger than that embraced by those communities.'[10] Put differently, the way forward is to adopt an ethical stance in which this new cosmopolitan accepts the cultural traditions in which people locate themselves and makes positive use of group affiliations which have the ability to create a sense of belonging. At the same time, the stance is outward-facing and looks beyond any one community. Hollinger suggests that there is a responsibility to assist in solving problems that arise in going beyond the base cultural group which raises the important question of primary belonging. He offers no answer here, but it remains a key question even when the notion of unitary or fixed identity has been relinquished. I prefer to adopt the notion of temporary identification put forward by Richard Sennett in his contribution to the volume, 'Cosmopolitanism and the Social Experience of Cities'. Although he does not develop the idea originally posited by the social theorist Louis Wirth, the notion of a temporal limit on identity suggests a kind of provisionality that I believe is embraced by those who make a point of learning languages and engaging at a deep level with cultures other than the one(s) in which they grew up.

In *Translation and Identity*, in which Cronin continues his exploration of translation (a major focus of his work since the 1990s), he takes his ideas on translation as a nomadic practice a stage further. An important theme is the interaction between the local and the global, which leads him to reflect on translation and the new cosmopolitanism. It is worth summarizing the

9   David A. Hollinger, 'The New Cosmopolitanism' in Vertovec and Cohen, *Conceiving Cosmopolitanism*, 227–39.
10   Hollinger, 'The New Cosmopolitanism', 239.

main ideas here since they are of particular relevance for my reflections on nomadic literature. In his introductory comments, Cronin makes it clear that he will propose a solution for the inadequacies of a cosmopolitanism which has tended to ignore linguistic and cultural practices, and that this 'reworked cosmopolitan version of translation theory can contribute to debate, namely, localization practice, curricular reform of national literature courses and the formulation of translation policy for supra-national institutions'.[11] It was already clear from *Across the Lines* that translation studies as practised around the year 2000 was not a discipline equipped to deal with increasing mobility and globalization. Of the three areas cited above to which *Translation and Identity* aims to contribute, the first two are relevant for this book, most particularly for my discussion of Nooteboom as a travel writer, in Chapter 6.

In his review of cosmopolitan thought since ancient Greece, Cronin works his way towards those elements of recent cosmopolitan thinking which take into account globalization and its effects. He notes that 'there is a conception of the cosmopolitan that presents it primarily as a *practice* or *competence*', defining it as 'the ability to make one's way into other cultures and to actively engage with those living in or through different cultures, languages, or milieux'. Like Cronin, I welcome this attitude of mind as a counterweight to a deeply-rooted negative attitude to translation as impossible or always involving loss. Cronin is also wary of the kind of cultural pluralism that assumes a primary identity: 'So the stress in cosmopolitanism is on multiple affiliations and the possibility of individual choice rather than the unwavering cultural determinism of communities of descent.' Another form of cosmopolitanism where Cronin sounds a warning note is that of the 'cosmocrats' – 'a highly mobile, meritocratic elite'.[12] This is the kind of cosmopolitanism that Craig Calhoun, in his contribution to Vertovec and Cohen's volume, refers to as the 'class consciousness of

---

11   Michael Cronin, *Translation and Identity* (Abingdon: Routledge, 2006), 3–4.
12   Cronin, *Translation and Identity*, 10, 10, 11.

frequent travellers'.[13] Given the tendency of some reviewers to refer to Cees Nooteboom as a cosmopolitan writer in this sense, it will be important in the chapter on his travel writing to assess this perception, and to consider it against Nooteboom's actual travel writing.

The crux of Cronin's argument is that translation and translation studies need to adopt the kind of cosmopolitanism that balances the global with the local, or the universal and the specific, and to this end he begins with Held's definition of cultural cosmopolitanism as being '*the ability to stand outside a singular location*', arguing that this is an 'intrinsic part of the translation process'.[14] However, this in itself is not enough: it is necessary, according to Cronin, for translators to appreciate differences associated with singular locations as well. He proposes the notion of micro-cosmopolitanism as a way of avoiding lapsing into nationalism and particularism while nevertheless welcoming differences. It rests on the concept of 'fractal differentialism' which posits that cultural complexity remains constant whatever the size or scale of a cultural entity. It is intended to assist 'thinkers from smaller or less powerful polities to circumvent the terminal paralysis of identity logic not through a programmatic condemnation of élites ruling from above but through a patient undermining of conventional thinking from below'.[15] This can be done by emphasizing the hybridity and multiplicity of all cultural practices whether in cities or in rural areas and by paying attention to solidarities 'whether based on religion, ethnicity, gender or political orientation'. According to Cronin this will also reveal translocal effects, thus enabling mediation between the local and the global. And finally, bearing in mind the title of this chapter, 'in its unwillingness to be wholly subject to any fixed, permanent, all-encompassing notion of

---

13   Craig Calhoun, 'The Class Consciousness of Frequent Travellers: Towards a Critique of Actually Existing Cosmopolitanism' in Vertovec and Cohen, *Conceiving Cosmopolitanism*, 86–109, and cited by Cronin, *Translation and Identity*, 11.

14   Cronin, *Translation and Identity*, 11–12. The first citation is from David Held, 'Culture and Political Community: National, Global and Cosmopolitan' in Vertovec and Cohen, *Conceiving Cosmopolitanism*; Held's italics.

15   Cronin, *Translation and Identity*, 15–16. This includes an explanation of the mathematical thinking behind the idea of fractal differentialism.

belonging or being, cosmopolitanism is by definition anti-essentialist, an important consideration for how we defend translation against its critics.[16]

In this section I have briefly reviewed ideas of cosmopolitanism as proposed by social theorists and applied to translation by Cronin. I consider nomadic subjectivity, which provides a new way of understanding the subject as having no fixed identity, as linked to cosmopolitanism. In particular, new cosmopolitanism as described by David A. Hollinger, complements nomadic philosophy, providing an account of how to balance the global and the local. A new cosmopolitan will have a primary belonging, according to Hollinger, but is outward-facing with a responsibility to help solve the problems that arise when different cultural groups meet. Cronin goes a step further when he expresses his wariness of communities of descent; he also warns against the global traveller who elides difficulties of communication across cultures. Translators certainly belong to a group which is well-positioned to become the kind of new cosmopolitan with a sense of responsibility towards communication and understanding across cultural lines. In what follows, I explore the translator's role in more depth.

Figurations of the Translator

New cosmopolitanism implies high self-awareness and a willingness to work on the self, while an ethical translation practice in a globalized world likewise ought to involve mindfulness and personal transformation. I am using the term 'transformation' to mean 'a thorough or dramatic change in the form, outward appearance, character, etc'[17] of a text as well as of certain subjects, in particular, the translator, the reader of a translation, or more broadly mobile, nomadic individuals. In the process, I consider three figurations of the translator: as transformer, as pilgrim and as bridge.

16   Cronin, *Translation and Identity*, 19, 20.
17   *Concise Oxford Dictionary* (1995).

In 'Literary Hybrids and the Circuits of Translation: The Example of Mia Couto', Stefan Helgesson examines 'how cultural expression travels and is transformed'. He contrasts the mobility of an artefact with that of a text:

> A book, a story, or a set of poems is removed from its original context and received elsewhere. But the creativity of translation goes beyond sheer transferral. The material properties of a physical object may remain the same even as its significance changes, whereas literary translation by definition entails a wholesale transformation.[18]

Helgesson goes on to describe translation as part of a dynamic interaction between languages, places and cultures which produces something new which is necessarily also hybrid. And the hybridity of the new literary text can no longer be attributed to a single creator since it is not possible to separate translator from author or any other actors in the creative process. Helgesson's case study is of the Mozambican writer Mia Couto and as a post-colonial writer, Couto is already producing hybrid texts because of a need to reshape the dominant colonial language to suit his needs.[19] In this view, writing is also a kind of translating. Here too, the importance of emphasizing the dynamism and fluidity of translation is a way of refusing translation as a one-way process or as inevitably inadequate.

In Helgesson's article, the translator is figured as a powerful transformer: a co-creator of a literary text. Michael Cronin suggests something similar, though on different grounds: he figures the translator as an 'agent of metamorphosis' who derives his or her transformative power from the view of language in which words no longer simply refer to objects in the real world but construct or generate reality. In this way, a translator can carry new meanings from one language into another, subtly altering the target language and culture. Cronin also points out that metamorphoses

18   Stefan Helgesson, 'Literary Hybrids and the Circuits of Translation: The Example of Mia Couto', in Helmut Anheier and Yudhishthir Raj Isar, eds, *Cultural Expression, Creativity and Innovation* (London: Sage, 2010), 215.

19   Although I do not give it a prominent place here, the idea of hybridity, also touched on in Chapter 1, is a kind of textual transformation which is particularly relevant for post-colonial literature and which plays a more marginal role in relation to Nooteboom's work.

can involve a violent or brutal change, citing the 'foundational narrative of the nation-state of Rome'.[20] This kind of violent transformation is not likely to apply to translations of Cees Nooteboom, though as he has now been translated into so many languages, some of them very distant from western European languages, it is not possible for me to say so with any certainty. Cronin links metamorphosis to a very specific kind of location – '"spaces that were crossroads, cross-cultural zones, points of interchange on the intricate connective tissue of communications between cultures"'.[21]

Sites of pilgrimage are one such location. In 'The Changeling', a chapter in *Across the Lines*, Michael Cronin explores the translator's commitment to the mother tongue and the tensions caused by the need to leave home in order to enter new languages and cultural worlds. In the process, he briefly suggests a possible figuration of the translator as pilgrim:

> The pilgrims to Rome, Mecca or Jerusalem are the expression of an ancient link between travel and transcendence. Spiritual quest like the metamorphosis of the hero is the pilgrim's progress from the familiar to the promised land of redemption, illumination, rebirth.[22]

Viewed in this way, there is very little difference between the translator and the traveller. But before I explore this idea in more detail, I will first consider Cronin's idea that translators are themselves transformed by their way of life.

One reason for focusing on transformation in this chapter on belonging is its role in nomadic philosophy which concerns itself with the individual subject as being multiple and in flux, a link which Cronin himself makes. Rosi Braidotti explores this topic at length in *Metamorphoses*, where she explains in the prologue that it is more important now to find ways of representing the process of change than it is to establish identity. She warns against images of fixity of any kind:

20   Cronin, *Translation and Identity*, 105, 108.
21   Cronin, *Translation and Identity*, 105, citing Marina Warner's *Fantastic Metamorphoses, Other Worlds*.
22   *Across the Lines*, 63.

The starting-point for my work is a question that I would set at the top of the agenda for the new millennium: the point is not to know who we are, but rather what, at last, we want to become, how to represent mutations, changes and transformations, rather than Being in its classical modes. ... One of the aims of this book is therefore to explore the need and to provide illustrations for new figurations, for alternative representations and local locations for the kind of hybrid mix we are in the process of becoming. Figurations are not figurative ways of thinking, but rather more materialistic mappings of situated, or embedded and embodied, positions.[23]

Thus, representing the translator as pilgrim enables me to express his or her personal and cultural journey from mother tongue to new language, but also the physical displacement involved in gaining the level of linguistic and cultural knowledge of the new language needed for literary engagement. The new culture acquires a special status in the life of the translator which comes close to being sacred since it requires devotion of much time and attention. The site of pilgrimage, the new place to which translators, like many keen language learners, travel is an intercultural space for them, though not necessarily for those resident in the target culture who share this space. The aim of undertaking a pilgrimage is self transformation, though I do not mean to suggest here that the change a translator undergoes is part of a (quasi)religious process. In keeping with Braidotti's usage of the term figuration, I am not using it metaphorically but rather to explore the kind of deep engagement with alterity that is much more personally meaningful than so-called mastery of a language. Such a figuration lends itself to a more detailed mapping – one which I will essay in my discussion of Nooteboom's most recently published book travel writing on Germany in English in Chapter 6. Michael Cronin puts this deep engagement into words as follows: 'The translator must become the Other while remaining the One'.[24] He goes on to describe the 'One' as fragmented, but I would rather see this as multiple subjectivity, leaving behind the notion of a wholeness which is implicitly desirable and which can be fragmented through the contact with other cultures. Cronin points out that translation can involve loss, trauma and a sense of betrayal of the originary culture. Eva Hoffman's *Lost*

23   *Metamorphoses*, 2.
24   Cronin, *Across the Lines*, 100.

in Translation is perhaps the best known account of the traumatic effects of displacement. But like the pilgrim, a translator sets out both with the expectation of being changed by the experience *and* with the intention of returning, which has the effect of adding new and increasingly complex elements of his or her subjectivity.

Since figurations are ways of representing multiplicity, one figuration does not need to replace another. Their purpose is not to capture and fix reality, but in this case to provide a way of thinking about a particular group of subjects. The translator is sometimes figured as a bridge or broker: Cronin astutely points out that translators nevertheless have a vested interest in separation as well as connection, so that the bridge function is complemented by a kind of door function controlling the direction of the connection.[25] This is a highly complex set of flows which is not regulated by the translator alone, but by the organizations, agencies, publishers and so on involved in Mueller-Vollmer and Irmscher's 'complex practice of cultural transfer'.[26] The figuration of the translator as broker certainly endows the translator with agency to bring about active negotiation between two cultures, and perhaps suggests personal gain from the activity on the part of the translators in a way that other figurations do not. The figuration of translators as transformers is itself multiple: it encompasses transposition of texts from one language to another, transformation of the translator's subjectivity, and perhaps also of the readers of those translated texts.

It is this last aspect that I will now briefly consider. An obvious question to ask is whether the impact of a translated literary text on a reader is very different from the impact of any non-translated literary text in the reader's first or primary language. In the case of the latter, readers enter into the imaginary world created by the writer, and since the writer is an other person, these imaginary worlds are inevitably other to the reader, though they will contain many familiar elements since writer and reader share a language and culture. In the case of translated literature, readers

---

25 Cronin, *Translation and Identity*, 121.
26 Kurt Mueller-Vollmer and Michael Irmscher, 'Introduction', *Translating Literatures: Translating Cultures* (Stanford: Stanford University Press, 1998, xii.

have the illusion of sharing a language and culture with the writer, but it will not be long before the illusion is disrupted. But it is of course also possible for a reader to encounter jarring notes even when s/he and the writer nominally share the same culture. In the case of translated literature, there is at least an expectation of strangeness. Allowing that all literature is potentially transformative, the main difference between translated and non-translated literature may simply be that the power of writers is shared with translators as co-creators of a translated literary text.

Travel Writing and Translation

In a fluid, mobile world, it is no longer surprising that translators can be considered as co-creators of a translated literary text. Similarly, it is not necessary to separate the figure of the traveller from that of the translator, since, as we saw above, they are both engaged in a spiritual quest in their commitment to exploring another culture. Travel writers have even more in common with translators, given their role as cultural mediators through textual means. In the first instance, travel writing is both written and read in the home language of the writer and reader and therefore involves a prior act of cultural translation by the author. Like any other literary text, a piece of travel writing can also be translated into another language, making it in effect a double translation, or retranslation.

A feature of travel writing is that its readers do not need to travel themselves. In *The Art of Travel*, English popular philosopher Alain de Botton acknowledges that some people prefer the anticipation of travel to actual travelling. To illustrate this point, he quotes from Huysman's novel *A Rebours* in which a misanthropic hero, the Duc des Esseintes who lives on the outskirts of Paris, displays a preference for travel to his chosen destination through fantasy and imagination rather than actually going there. But the duke's reading matter was Baedeker's guide to London, emphatically not a literary account. Travel writing can also inspire readers to undertake a particular journey: for example, I am acquainted with an English reader of Nooteboom's *Roads to Santiago* who felt inspired by this very literary representation of a personal encounter with Spanish culture to undertake part of the journey Nooteboom recounts, so effective was the author's evocation of this other culture. Whether this is transformation or tourism is something that will be discussed in the chapter on Nooteboom's travel writing, prompted by J.M. Coetzee's review of the same text.

Cronin sees travel as a form of lived translation and notes that the art of travel writing is to make readers undertake the same journey, though he, too, does not mean literally. According to him, this reading-travelling can take two forms, what he terms the 'ocular' and the 'epistemic'. Ocular travelling refers to the capacity of the travel writing to describe sights in such a way that readers can imagine being there. Epistemic travel as defined by Cronin is the transformative aspect: it entails readers 'being persuaded to leave behind the safe berth of received opinion and to explore elements of their own or other cultures that they take for granted'.[27] Although Cronin is here discussing work by, for example, Paul Theroux and Bill Bryson, i.e. English intralingual travel writing, it seems to me that these two concepts also apply to interlingual travel, such as Nooteboom's accounts of Spain. Given that this kind of reading-travelling has the power to disrupt traditional ideas, and generate curiosity towards both one's own and the other culture, this provides a means for transforming subjectivity. I also think that this effect of epistemic travel is likely to apply to translated literature more generally.

The similarities between travel and translation can be summed up as follows: both are located in the spaces between cultures and both entail movement across political, social, cultural and linguistic borders. Travel refers to bodily displacement across some or all of these borders. Even in intralingual travel, as Cronin's discussion of English intralingual travel writing shows, cultural translation is necessary and brings with it linguistic effects. The act of textual translation itself does not entail travel, but it does presuppose previous travel by the translator in order to achieve a

27   Cronin, *Across the Lines*, 37.

certain level of proficiency in another language. The two activities are thus interconnected in complex ways. At the same time there is one crucial difference: translation always involves movement across linguistic and cultural boundaries and therefore also some form of deeper engagement with another culture, whereas travel does not necessarily bring with it insights into and understanding of the new cultures visited by the traveller, at least not those that entail access via language, since not all travellers possess the relevant linguistic knowledge.

While it would simplify matters in this context to distinguish between the traveller and the tourist on the grounds that the former involves some kind of engagement with the destination culture while the latter does not, to my mind, this is too reminiscent of the social distinction attaching to elite forms of travel as opposed to mass tourism which, according to John Urry, developed in the second half of the twentieth century.[28] In their introduction, Urry and his co-author for the third edition of *The Tourist Gaze*, Jonas Larsen, list nine social practices involved in tourism including the tourists' search for the culturally typical or traditional. This is emphatically not the kind of travel that I am discussing here, since it suggests a globalization of place which is dependent on images and views of special or 'sacralized' locations which form tourist destinations. Strangely, nowhere in their introduction do Urry and Larsen mention language.

I share with Cronin the aim of encouraging localization practices, so a crucial question for my enquiry into Nooteboom's travel writing in Chapter 6 will be whether and how it does indeed contribute to processes of localization, or whether it serves to enhance the desirability of certain tourist destinations. A travel writer who can be described as a new cosmopolitan, can be expected to value the specificities of the new cultures s/he visits and to seek novel ways of communicating this cultural specificity for her or his home audience, and I suggest that it is not possible to do this without knowledge of the language or spending a considerable amount of time in the location that is the subject of a travel account.

28　John Urry and Jonas Larsen, *The Tourist Gaze 3.0* (London: Sage, 2011). See Chapter 2, 'Mass Tourism'.

The focus, then, is on how the travel writer approaches life in the 'contact zone', a term first defined by Mary Louise Pratt in her seminal book on travel writing, *Imperial Eyes. Travel Writing and Transculturation.* Although Pratt was primarily concerned with colonial and postcolonial travel writing, she demonstrates the power of such writing to shape outsiders' views of a particular culture. And she shows how the contact zone is characterized by imbalances of power between European travel writer and those s/he surveys. She defines the contact zone as 'social spaces where disparate cultures meet, clash, and grapple with each other, often in highly asymmetrical relations of domination and subordination – like colonialism, slavery or their aftermaths as they are lived out across the globe today'.[29] Such asymmetrical relations are potentially present in Nooteboom's travel writing contained in *Nomad's Hotel* dealing with countries outside Europe.

Intercultural Subjectivity and Nomadic Literature

The extent to which a reader might be changed by encountering literature that originated in another language and culture must depend on many factors that can be brought together in the notion of the individual receptive moment. By focusing on individual subjectivity, I want to move away from the idea of an inbetween, intercultural space between two cultures which is where translation takes place. While this idea was a useful starting-point for thinking about the positioning of translators, it risks seeing cultures as bounded entities rather than sets of practices, ideas and attitudes that are constantly in touch in a number of ways. Ultimately it is within the individual subject where these practices, ideas and attitudes are welcomed in, tried out and combined with pre-existing cultural practices, ideas and attitudes.

29   Mary Louise Pratt, *Imperial Eyes: Travel Writing and Transculturation* (London and New York: Routledge, 1992), 4.

In 'Strangerhood and Intercultural Subjectivity', Simon Coffey is of the view that it is 'the intensification of globalization [that] requires different models of intercultural subjectivity which acknowledge our fears of difference and which encourage these to be confronted in local home spaces'.[30] Drawing on Claire Kramsch's work on multilingual subjectivity, he goes on to note that the idea of a third cultural space between the foreign and the domestic has 'ceded to a theorizing of the individual (language learner, migrant) as a navigator in complex landscapes'. Coffey also proposes that within each subject is an element of strangeness which is activated in some way by an encounter with a new and unfamiliar culture. He uses autobiographical narratives to research 'how individuals make sense of – interpret – the familiar at individual moments'. Given that Nooteboom's travel writing can be seen as a form of autobiographical writing, it will be interesting to apply this idea of the stranger within to him as a writing subject. In *Nomadic Literature*, I will not be investigating readers in general, although I will look at professional readers' responses to Cees Nooteboom's work in the second part of this book when discussing his writing in both Dutch and English. In my readings of Nooteboom's work I will focus on the ways in which Nooteboom himself represents subjectivity, and I will also read his texts in the light of his own personal transformation through travel. At the same time, I will be considering how his translators have participated in the transformation of his writing into texts with a life of their own in a new culture.

In order to conclude Part 1 of *Nomadic Literature*, I return to the core concept of nomadic literature which I use to embrace different aspects of texts, their production and translation, their reception, and also the personal dispositions and sensibilities of writers as well as qualities of their writing. I use the term nomadic in two senses: first, to refer to a particular form of human and cultural mobility which involves an ability to dwell in more than one language and culture, and second, to denote those aspects

---

30   Simon Coffey, 'Strangerhood and Intercultural Subjectivity' in Jane Fenoulhet and Cristina Ros i Solé, eds, *Journal of Language and Intercultural Communication*, 13/3 (forthcoming).

of translation and travel that engender new belongings. These ideas allow me to interrogate the writings of Cees Nooteboom taking into account their extreme mobility as translated works, with a particular focus here on their afterlife in English. Alongside this aspect, I am interested to know the extent to which nomadic concepts of multiple subjectivity and becomings are found in the works themselves. Reading the texts through this nomadic lens is a way of making the link between the texts and their generator by investigating the extent to which certain works contain nomadic elements. But first it is time to present the author himself more fully. I conclude Part 1 of *Nomadic Literature* in the next chapter with an account of the writer as an individual moving to and fro among cultures – How does he manage the new belongings he brings about through travel? Does he have a sense of home and where is it located?

CHAPTER 3

Nomadic Subjectivity and Identity: Or, Cees Nooteboom and Dutchness

Rethinking Identity and Belonging

The aim of this chapter is to return to questions of subjectivity and identity and explore them in more detail as they relate to Cees Nooteboom. I also return once more to Braidotti's *Metamorphoses: Towards a Materialist Theory of Becoming.*

> Philosophical nomadism is a philosophy of transformation or 'becoming' which emphasises affect, intensity and the embodied structure of the subject: nomadic embodied subjects are characterized by their mobility, changeability and transitory nature. Their power of thinking is not the expression of in-depth interiority, or the enactment of transcendental models: it is a tendency, a predisposition which expresses the outward-bound nature of the subject.[1]

Part of Braidotti's aim is to find new ways of speaking about 'the kind of internally contradictory multi-faceted subjects that we have become'. She views subjectivity as a process and uses figurations of the subject to denote the range of alternative subjectivities which according to her have emerged in postmodernity. These should not be seen as types, but rather as 'contested, multi-layered and internally contradictory subject-positions'. This non-unitary vision of the subject stands in contrast to the traditional idea of the coherent, centred self. Where does this new understanding of subjectivity leave the notion of identity, and is it even possible to speak

---

1   *Metamorphoses,* 70.

of an individual's identity? In fact, rather than call identity into question as a way of speaking about belonging, Braidotti seeks to show that in the nomadic world she is describing, identity itself is complex and shifting.

'Becoming' is the process by which new subject-formations come into being. It is an effect of desire, of positive energy which 'push[es] the subject to his or her limit in a constant encounter with external, or different others'.[2] According to Braidotti, 'all becomings are minoritarian' in the sense of moving the subject towards the minor or marginalized 'others' of traditional European culture. Examples of such becomings are: becoming-minoritarian, becoming-woman, becoming-animal, becoming-insect, becoming-machine.[3] In a world of multiplicity, belonging cannot be taken for granted: it is a work in progress. One positive effect of this is that all notions of an essential nature or of fixed characteristics whether of an individual, race or people are rendered useless. In Europe, the idea of citizenship has changed: it is now much more flexible and allows for hybridity. This has the effect of weakening the national, in that individual choice is a decisive factor once certain requirements such as residence have been met. Citizenship, nationality and national identity are not inextricably linked, creating room for new belongings – what Braidotti in a subsequent book calls a 'functionally differentiated network of affiliations and loyalties'.[4] For some commentators, this development opens up the possibility of a post-national Europe in which civil society exists across the borders of the nation-states. Like Braidotti, I see a link here with the growth of new European nationalisms: elections in 2010 saw the anti-Islamic party in the Netherlands, the Freedom Party, increase its number of seats in parliament from fifteen to twenty-four to become the third largest party, while in Flanders in 2010, the Dutch-speaking part of Belgium, the Flemish separatists, the New Flemish Alliance, gained twenty-seven seats in the Belgian parliament, becoming the largest party. Rosi Braidotti acknowl-

---

2   Braidotti, *Metamorphoses*, 6, 13, 119.
3   Here Braidotti is working with Deleuzian concepts. However, I will not develop this point further in this book. For those readers who wish to pursue these ideas, see Braidotti, *Metamorphoses*, in particular Chapter 3.
4   *Transpositions*, 79.

edges that, for an individual, leaving behind fixed identities and exclusive national affiliation will be difficult and painful, and that individuals will experience a sense of loss. But she also posits that the affirmative character of nomadism can provide a counterweight to the loss of an idea of a fixed origin in the 'active production of multiple forms of belonging and complex allegiances'.[5] There is a parallel here with literary translation itself which balances between its sense of the fixed origin of a text and the power of translation to create a new text capable of new cultural belongings.

Taking this multiple view of identity, and reflecting on the complexities surrounding, for example, the production of a history of Dutch literature explained in my first chapter, it is clear that I do not subscribe to a clearly defined and therefore fixed notion of Dutchness; of course there is no such thing as singular Dutchness. I would suggest that there never has been, though there have been times of apparent consensus, or acceptance of a received notion of Dutchness. In recent years national identity is a much contested area in the Netherlands. In her book on the Dutch-Moroccan writer Hafid Bouazza, *Homeless Entertainment*, Henriëtte Louwerse surveys the recent debate which began when Pim Fortuyn, the Dutch politician assassinated in 2002, published his 1997 book *Tegen de islamisering van onze cultuur* (Against the Islamification of our Culture). She notes that around 2000 there had been tentative suggestions that writers from outside Dutch culture who had adopted the language and literature might bring much-needed renewal, but that this cultural optimism was supplanted by calls for a return to a narrowly focused national culture. As well as the voices calling for a national literary canon and a museum of Dutch history was a suggestion that Dutchness is characterized by 'uncertainty about what it means to be Dutch and the fear of losing one's culture and its achievements in an increasingly globalised and multicultural society with this inherent ambiguity'.[6] There have been successive inward migrations to the Netherlands since the Second World War, starting with migrants from

---

5   *Transpositions*, 84.
6   Henriëtte Louwerse, *Homeless Entertainment: On Hafid Bouazza's Literary Writing* (Oxford: Peter Lang, 2007), 31.

Indonesia after independence was declared in 1945, who were followed by migrants from Turkey and north Africa and later from Suriname which gained its independence from the Netherlands in 1975. Furthermore, there had long been a general assumption that outsiders had no access to the Dutch language and culture. This led to a strange kind of insularity marked by a resistance to any incomers who tried to 'infiltrate' the language and culture. This focus on language came sharply into focus over the question of the Dutch Book Week gift in 2001. Every year the Foundation for the Promotion of the Dutch Book commissions a short work which is given away to book buyers during Book Week. In 2001 it was Salman Rushdie who wrote the gift book. In a revealing piece, the literary journalist Elsbeth Etty saw this as a betrayal of the Dutch language and culture. Louwerse notes:

> Here, perhaps unwittingly, Etty confirms the outsider position of the migrant authors by problematising language itself. The use of Dutch as the language for literary expression is, according to Etty, a conscious choice and in extreme cases it may have caused 'pain'. Whether this is true or not is less relevant than the observation that language, in this case, Dutch, is expected to be a different experience for multicultural authors than for monocultural authors. Language is given an additional charge of conscious self-definition and positioning.[7]

Superficially the case of Cees Nooteboom is the obverse of Hafid Bouazza's, since Nooteboom is a (partial) outward migrant from the Netherlands who could have chosen to write in other languages. And yet there is no doubt that for Nooteboom, too, the Dutch language carries this 'additional charge of conscious self-definition and positioning'. The point I want to make is that the impact of Nooteboom's extreme mobility and nomadic way of life has consequences for his writing that are part of the same picture of cultural fluidity drawn by Louwerse in relation to Bouazza: 'His writing is both local and "extraterritorial", both rooted in Dutch literary tradition and reaching far beyond it.'[8]

7   *Homeless Entertainment*, 32.
8   Louwerse, *Homeless Entertainment*, 59.

Nooteboom: A Condensed Life History

Up to this point, whenever the name Cees Nooteboom is mentioned it has denoted Nooteboom the writer. But perhaps the question of Nooteboom's identity it best addressed in the first place by going back to his roots as an individual. There is no book-length biography of him, nor has he produced a full-length autobiography, but there are a number of personal writings which provide insights into the way Cees Nooteboom sees himself. Many of these do not have the considered quality of a more formal autobiography which intends to take stock of a life, and they have to be gleaned from speeches and the pages of what is generally described as travel writing. What becomes clear on tracking these autobiographical moments is that there are certain key narratives that are repeated, and that shift subtly over time. My two main sources of stories of this kind are both recently published collections of sketches and stories with a strong personal dimension, including reflections on a personal biography with many gaps in it. They are: i) *Nooteboom's hotel*, published in English as *Nomad's Hotel*, an intensely personal collection of what one reviewer called 'a contemporary nomad's meditations and mus-ings on the move'[9] which first appeared in 2002; ii) *Rode regen* (Red rain), described on the back cover of the 2007 Dutch edition as 'stories' and as a 'personal collection'. Much of *Rode regen*, which has not yet been translated into English, is told from an intensely personal standpoint, giving a portrait of the author in his contemporary surroundings on the Spanish island of Menorca where he has spent his summers for some forty years. At the same time, it also revisits the familiar, though sparse, narrative of his early years, his schooling, early independence and first journeys beyond the borders of the Netherlands. However, the most touching self-portrait, in my view, is to

---

9   Guy Mannes-Abbott, 'A Contemporary Nomad's Meditations and Musings on the Move', *The Independent* (9 March 2006). It should be borne in mind that this com-ment was made about the English version, which is very different from the Dutch text. The question of adaptation and translation will be discussed in more detail in chapter 6.

be found in the introduction to *Philip and the Others*, the English translation of Nooteboom's first novel, *Philip en de anderen*.

Biographical accounts are largely unhelpful since detail is hard to come by – most sources give the same summary information. The website devoted to Nooteboom and his work is another such source, but with the advantage of a version in English.[10] Unfortunately, the main Dutch literary biographical dictionaries were published in 1985[11] and 1986[12] and in addition to being out of date, the entries on Nooteboom are relatively sketchy, perhaps reflecting his status as a writer at that time. A good source of supplementary information is the catalogue which was produced to accompany an exhibition on Cees Nooteboom at the Literary Museum in The Hague in 1997–8, especially the section giving a timeline, compiled by Dick Welsink.[13] My biographical narrative will interweave elements of these short biographies with Nooteboom's own autobiographical commentary where relevant in order to arrive at an outline of the writer's life. Another strand will be Nooteboom's trajectory as a writer. After this brief life history I will turn to all Nooteboom's writings about himself in order to assess how he presents himself in relation to his Dutch origins. Finally, I will give an account of his reception in the Netherlands in as far as it addresses the question of Nooteboom's identity as a writer. His position in Dutch literary history will also be included in this section.

Cornelis Johannes Jacobus Maria Nooteboom was born in The Hague on 31 July 1933. The author himself has maintained that he had no recollection at all of his early school years, for example in a piece entitled 'Schooltijd'

---

10   <http://www.ceesnooteboom.com/?cat=7&lang=en> accessed 30 July 2012.

11   G.J. van Bork and P.J. Verkruijsse, eds, *De Nederlandse en Vlaamse auteurs van middeleeuwen tot heden met inbegrip van de Friese auteurs* (Weesp: De Haan, 1985), Digitale Bibliotheek voor de Nederlandse Letteren, <http://www.dbnl.org/tekst/borko01nede01/noot003.htm> accessed 25 March 2009.

12   R.F. Lissens et al., eds, *Lexicon van de Nederlandse letterkunde* (Amsterdam and Brussels: Elsevier, 1986).

13   Dick Welsink, 'Cees Nooteboom: een leven in data' in Harry Bekkering, Daan Cartens and Aad Meinderts, eds, *Ik had wel duizend levens en ik nam er maar één! Cees Nooteboom*, Schrijversprentenboek 40 (Amsterdam and Antwerp: Atlas, [1997]).

(Schooldays) in *Nootebooms hotel*. Unfortunately this piece is not available in English as it was not included in the collection of travel writing published under the title of *Nomad's hotel*. In Chapter 6 of this book, which investigates the travel writing in English, I will look into this adaptation more closely. In fact all the sources of information about Nooteboom's life, with one notable exception, are in Dutch and will be presented here as always in my translation.

A researcher putting together the exhibition on Nooteboom in the Literary Museum in The Hague managed to establish that the Nooteboom family moved eight times between Cees's birth and the outbreak of war in 1940.[14] This information seems to provide Nooteboom with a satisfactory explanation for his amnesia:

> And actually, it fits perfectly: precisely because of moving house so much, the memory fails. The file is languishing somewhere in the dungeons of the shattered memory, and unless and until it is retrieved thanks to some Proustian conjuring trick, it will continue to moulder away down there.[15]

Nooteboom goes on to say that he has chosen not to retrieve the past by means of psychoanalysis. To an outsider there are at least two events that are worth mentioning because they must have been traumatic, particularly against the background of instability whether through moving house so frequently or as a result of life in a country under German occupation: Nooteboom's father left the family in 1943 and two years later was killed in a bombardment of The Hague.

The entry on Nooteboom in the dictionary of Dutch literary biography edited by Van Bork and Verkruisse mentions that the author received a grammar school education at Catholic secondary schools in Venray and Eindhoven run by monks. In fact, he attended four different schools in as

---

14   Welsink, 'Cees Nooteboom: een leven in data', 149.
15   'En eigenlijk klopt het ook schitterend: juist door het vele verhuizen geeft de herinnering het op. Het dossier slingert in de kelders van het geschokte geheugen, en zolang het niet door een Proustiaanse tovertruc wordt teruggevonden zal het daar wel verder schimmelen.' Cees Nooteboom, *Nootebooms hotel* (Amsterdam and Antwerp: Atlas, 2002), 288.

many towns, such was the unsettled nature of his family life. It is hardly surprising that he did not complete his secondary education, leaving home and school in 1951. It was before he left school that he made his first journey beyond the borders of the Netherlands, a cycling trip to Belgium and Luxemburg. He did continue his education at evening school while working in a bank during the day, but has no memories of taking his final exam. This was followed in 1952 by a trip to Brussels and Paris, the first stage by train, the second hitch-hiking.[16] In 1953 he made two hitch-hiking trips, one to Italy and one to the South of France via Denmark.[17] His debut novel, *Philip and the Others*, first published in 1955, could be described as a hitch-hiking novel. In the following year, he published his first volume of poetry, *De doden zoeken een huis* and his first piece of journalism, an article for the Amsterdam daily newspaper *Het Parool* on the Hungarian uprising. More travels followed when he signed up as a merchant seaman with the Suriname Shipping Company at the suggestion of his future father-in-law and worked his passage to the Caribbean where he sought permission to marry Fanny Lichtveld. According to Welsink permission was not granted, but in November of 1957 the couple married in New York. In the years that followed, Nooteboom published stories, more poems, a play and in 1963 another novel – *De ridder is gestorven* (published in English as *The Knight has Died*, though not until 1990). The following year he and Fanny divorced – a time of deep crisis according to the author himself.[18]

In the 1960s Cees Nooteboom worked as a roving columnist for the Dutch daily newspaper *De Volkskrant*, and in 1969 won the national journalism prize (prijs voor de dagbladjournalistiek) for *De Parijse beroerte* (The Paris Riots), his account of the May revolution of 1968. He then became travel and poetry editor of the Dutch magazine *Avenue* where he also made his name as a translator. Many of his journalistic travel pieces were also collected and published in book form during this period. Although

16   Cees Nooteboom, *Rode regen* (Amsterdam and Antwerp: Atlas, 2007), 102ff.
17   Nooteboom, *Rode regen*, 110ff.
18   See Jan Brokken, 'De voorbije passages van Cees Nooteboom' (Cees Nooteboom's past journeys) in Daan Cartens, ed., *Over Cees Nooteboom: beschouwingen en interviews* (The Hague: BZZTôH, 1984), 16.

he continued publishing poetry and another play (this time his translation of a Brendan Behan piece), his next novel did not appear until 1980.
A gap of seventeen years preceded the publication of *Rituelen (Rituals,*
c. 1983). This was his first work of fiction to attract attention outside the
Netherlands; in 1982 it was awarded the Mobil Pegasus Prize which had
been set up by the oil company to cover the cost of translation of 'foreign'
fiction into English. By 1985 *Rituelen* had also been translated into French
and German. All Nooteboom's subsequent fiction has appeared in English
within two or three years of its publication in Dutch. Not surprisingly,
according to the *Encyclopedia of Literary Translation*, the award of the
Pegasus prize marks Nooteboom's breakthrough in English. In Germany,
however it is *Die folgende Geschichte (The Following Story)* that signalled
Cees Nooteboom's crosscultural breakthrough;[19] it also won the European
Aristeion Prize which was 'awarded to an author who has made a significant
contribution to contemporary European literature'[20] and was translated
into over thirty languages.[21] Many more prizes and honours were to follow.
Cees Nooteboom is still a prolific writer, and still publishes across the range
of literary genres. Since 2000 a novel, *Paradijs verloren (Lost Paradise)* and
a volume of stories, *'s Nachts komen de vossen (The Foxes Come At Night)*,
have appeared in Dutch, along with the volume of 'columns, memories,
poems', *Rode Regen*, mentioned above. Judging by numbers of publications
since 2000, he has been at his most productive in the travel writing genre
which in his hands has now become a highly fluid genre. The English page
of his website lists these recent publications as:

19   'Cees Nooteboom' in Olive Claasse, ed., *Encyclopedia of Literary Translation* (London:
      Fitzroy Dearborn, 2000), 1007–8; Ralf Grüttemeier and Maria-Theresia Leuker, eds,
      Niederländische Literaturgeschichte (Stuttgart: J.B. Metzler, 2006), 236.
20   From an EC press release issued by the prize panel in 1994. See <http://presseuropa.
      com/press-releases/meeting-of-the-jury-of-the-aristeion-prize-1994> accessed 1
      August 2012.
21   The total currently stands at 31. See <http://www.nlpvf.nl/vertalingendb/search-
      results1.php?lang=&searchtype=&q=&naam=&genre=&taal=&vertaler=&uitg
      ever=&otitel=2583&allejaren=1&alletitels=1&jaarvan=&jaartot=&limit=40&n
      rows=10> accessed 1 August 2012.

Nootebooms Hotel. Travel stories, essays. Atlas, Amsterdam 2002; *Het geluid van Zijn naam. Reizen door de Islamitische wereld (The sound of His name. Travels through the Islamic world).* Travel stories, poetry; *Tumbas. Graven van dichters en denkers.* Essays and portraits; *Berlijn 1989/2009* Essays; *Raadsel van het licht,* Essays on art; and *Journal de bord. Verre reizen. Travel stories.*[22]

There is also a collection of old and new poetry, *Bitterzoet* (2000), and a new collection *Licht overal* (2012). Translations of Nooteboom's work are appearing all the time: since 2000, work has been translated into all the major European Languages as well as seven non-European languages.[23]

Nooteboom on Nooteboom

National identity is generally one of the most clear cut elements of an individual's identity, even if the individual is Western European and highly mobile. Cees Nooteboom is a Dutch national who was born into a Dutch family on Dutch territory, grew up speaking Dutch and was educated through the medium of the Dutch language. On receiving an honorary doctorate from the Free University of Berlin in 2008, he himself distinguished between his writerly self and 'myself as a real person – a citizen of the Netherlands ... who stands here before you because he is about to receive an honorary doctorate'.[24]

22   <http://www.ceesnooteboom.com/?cat=10&lang=en> accessed 30 July 2012. For
       a more detailed discussion, see the 'Overview of Nootebooom's Travel Writing in
       Dutch' in Chapter 6.
23   See <http://www.nlpvf.nl/vertalingendb/search-results1.php?naam=353&genre=
       &taal=&vertaler=&uitgever=&otitel=&allejaren=0&jaarvan=2000&jaartot=2
       012&alletitels=1&nrows=10&lang=> accessed 9 December 2012.
24   '[...] mijn reële persoon van Nederlands staatsburger ... die nu voor u staat omdat
       hij een eredoctoraat krijgt' from a Dutch version of the acceptance speech which
       was reproduced in a Dutch weekly newspaper: Cees Nooteboom, 'De bevochten

Figure 1   Cees Nooteboom at the Free University of Berlin in 2008
(photograph by Stephan Töpper, Freie Universität Berlin).

The self he relates here is much more than Nooteboom the Dutchman: his open and disarming account accepts that the narratives in which he constructs his past themselves shift and change and may even contain untruths. The self that emerges is fluid and nomadic. The title of an earlier volume of prose-poetry which appeared in 1993 also seems to suggest a multiple sense of self which can be expressed poetically, but not literally: *Zelfportret van een ander* (*Self-Portrait of an Other*, 2011). In the speech, Nooteboom cites the motto which precedes the prose poems and which seems to sum up his subjectivity: 'Transmigration of the soul does not happen after but during a life.'

lichtheid', *Vrij Nederland* (31 January 2009), cited from the database LiteRom on 1 August 2012.

In search of complexity and depth, I turn to more of the writer's own utterances on the subject of his sense of his own identity and belonging. Much of the material is indirect and subtle, and what follows is a composite narrative of mine rather than the author's. Nooteboom's early life history was lived within the boundaries of the Dutch state. It nevertheless deviates from what might be called the Dutch norm: the sheer instability of the family was unusual, and although Catholics were no longer a minority group, social apartheid was institutionalized in the Netherlands which meant that Catholics had their own separate educational, welfare, sports and other organizations from Protestants and liberals. Against a background of historical discrimination against Catholics in the form of exclusion from public life in the Netherlands between the late sixteenth century and 1795, this must in some way produce a distinctive sense of self as Catholic even when no longer practising the religion as in Nooteboom's case. It was his generation in the Netherlands that saw the weakening of the 'pillarised' system of social and cultural apartheid based on religion and ideology. In the decades after the Second World War the new generation moved away from the religious basis of Dutch society. Nooteboom himself is quite clear that it is his protestant 'reformed' colleagues for whom religion plays a part in their writing; he is not troubled by religious hang-ups. At the same time he notes: 'I am extraordinarily content with my Catholic upbringing. An upbringing full of *rituals*.'[25] This comment hints at the possibility of a distillation of Catholicism, or affinities with and traces of Catholic ideas and practices in Nooteboom's thinking and imagination. And there remains the awareness that this in some way sets him apart from those protestant colleagues. It is possible that this is another factor in the mixed reception of Nooteboom's work at home in the Netherlands. Given the after-effects of the pillarization of society and culture, this is certainly an aspect worth considering.

The only direct source of information about an individual's sense of identity are his or her own pronouncements on the subject of the self; if

---

25   'Ik ben buitengewoon content met mijn katholieke opvoeding. Een opvoeding vol *rituelen*.' Cited in Brokken, 'Voorbije passages', 11.

the individual is a writer, this includes interviews or the different kinds of writing he practises that reveal aspects of his sense of his subjectivity. In addition to Nooteboom's short pieces that contain reflections and musings on his life both past and present, there is also the intriguing *Self-Portrait of an Other* that belongs to an in-between genre which for the moment I will call poetic prose. Its hermetic nature means that its best contribution to this investigation of the way Nooteboom positions himself in relation to Dutch society and culture can only be a matter of interpretation, of my personal reading. Beyond the basic facts already related in the previous section, there is in any case little in Nooteboom's writing to feed a hunger for the straightforward. Far from it, since it undermines the very notion of identity itself, where identity is understood as something unitary and singular. The question of this multiplicity, which has been described as fragmentation, will return in the discussion of Nooteboom's work, in Part 2 of *Nomadic Literature*.

The construction of Nooteboom as subject with a particular focus on his sense of where he belongs brings together many of his self-narratives which develop and vary over time. Theologian Rowan Williams sees the construction of such a story both as prosaic, something everyone does, and as 'an act', with consequences, like other acts, in the world and speech of others'. And for this reason, 'every "telling" of myself is a retelling'.[26] The subtle variation within repeated stories about the self is a kind of rehearsing of a self that it always moving and changing rather than an establishing of an identity. This telling and retelling is the process through which deterritorialization occurs. In *Kafka* Deleuze and Guattari envisage such a process as one in which the writer imagines new possible communities and which allows him 'to forge the means for another consciousness and another sensibility'.[27] For Nooteboom the idea of other possible communities is not prominent, perhaps because his focus is on forging a new consciousness in relation to the past. What is relevant is how the narratives vary through

---

26   Rowan Williams, *Lost Icons: Reflections on Cultural Bereavement* (London: T. & T. Clark, 2000), 144.

27   Deleuze and Guattari, *Kafka*, 17. See also Introduction, 16–17.

time. Nooteboom himself is well aware of this dimension, particularly in his most recent autobiographical writing, *Rode regen*, where he speaks of 'my invented past'.[28] All the same, there is a lasting impression of a kind of *Bildungsroman*, a 'portrait of the artist as a young man', to borrow Joyce's phrase. In conversation with the Dutch journalist Margot Dijkgraaf, the writer himself speaks of 'his own Genesis' as something that everyone makes up for themselves.[29]

The preface to *Philip and the Others* opens with the words:

> A long time ago, an eternity of over thirty years, a young man with whom I share a first name sat down in the municipal library of a provincial town in the Netherlands. He was going to write this book. By the uninterrupted machinations of time I have stopped resembling him; and when they show me a photograph of this thin, romantic stranger, I am aware of the cruel distortion of his youthful features that has become my face.
>
> He, in his day, had already been marked by the chaos of war and a medieval upbringing in an Augustinian monastery school; but somehow he had managed to keep a dream intact that had nothing to do with his, or with Dutch, outward reality.[30]

Nooteboom openly fictionalizes his past self, by making the distance between his narrating and narrated selves visible through the use of the third person to denote the past self, and the first person for the narrator. At the same time, the 'I' narrator makes it quite clear that the author is constructing his own past. Given the impossibility of full recall, perhaps this is the most honest, or truthful approach.

Some twenty years later in *Rode regen* Nooteboom returns to the same theme in the reminiscences collected under the title 'Eerste reizen' (First journeys) where he relates the discovery of old diaries. The first journey of the title is the cycling trip to Belgium undertaken in the summer holiday of 1950, while he was still at the school run by Augustinian monks. In this brief memoir called 'Grenzen' (Borders) he describes himself not only

28   '[...] mijn verzonnen verleden', *Rode regen*, 100.
29   Margot Dijkgraaf, *Nooteboom en de anderen* (Amsterdam: Bezige Bij, 2009), 9.
30   Cees Nooteboom, *Philip and the Others*, trans. Adrienne Dixon (Baton Rouge: Louisiana State University Press, 1988), v.

as a completely other person but also as someone he doesn't really like. 'You don't want to have been that person, easily infatuated, romantic, an emerging person who would take a very long time before he amounted to much.'[31] In the Dutch source for this quotation, Nooteboom uses the striking phrase 'iemand in wording', literally 'someone [who is] becoming', though translated by me as 'an emerging person' because of the ambiguity of 'becoming' used in an adjectival position in English. The Dutch phrase calls to mind the importance of processes of becoming in the philosophies of Gilles Deleuze and Rosi Braidotti who both emphasize the many possibilities available to individuals. It is important to note here that the term becoming cannot be used interchangeably with development which still relates to the idea of *Bildung*, or organic development of an individual in which he gradually moves towards a state of full realization. Becomings, on the other hand, are individual responses to many kinds of threshold-crossing, and Nooteboom's narratives of becoming involve randomness and impulse which generate intensity.

In 'Borders' he again retells the familiar story, but he refers to his use of the third person as deception:

> If I were to put forward something in his defence, it would have to be the wretchedness of war, divorced parents, dead fathers and foster families, but I don't want to, if only because of the deception of the third person by which means I attempt to keep that youthful version of myself at arm's length ... Does the seventy-four-year-old staring with more aversion than affection at his own rounded handwriting from the past ... resemble that earlier lonely romantic?[32]

31   'Je wilt zo iemand niet geweest zijn, een beetje dweperig, romantisch, iemand in wording die er nog heel lang over zou doen voor het wat werd.' Nooteboom, *Rode regen*, 100.

32   'Als ik iets tot zijn verdediging zou willen aanvoeren, kom ik uit bij de miserabilia van oorlog, gescheiden ouders, dode vaders en pleeggezinnen, maar ik heb er geen zin in, al was het maar door het bedrog van de derde persoon waarmee ik die jeugdige verschijning van mezelf op afstand probeer te houden ... Lijkt de vierenzeventigjarige die met meer afkeer dan liefde naar zijn eigen bolle handschrift van toen kijkt ... op die vroegere eenzame dweper?' *Rode regen*, 100–1.

He says that he had to learn 'that you can only invent the past, including your own'.[33] Parts of the narrative of early life and becoming a writer appear in slightly different forms in speeches, in *Nootebooms hotel* and in the exhibition catalogue *Ik had wel duizend levens en ik nam er maar één* (I had a thousand lives and I took only one of them) referred to earlier in this chapter. Part of a series of illustrated lives of writers, this particular volume which is devoted to Nooteboom opens with a series of photographs with accompanying autobiographical texts taken from two collections of travel writing, *Waar je gevallen bent, blijf je* (Where you fall is where you remain), and *Van de lente de dauw* (Spring dew), as well as some which appear to have been specially written by the author. Photographs play a particularly important role in Nooteboom's travel writing because of his friendship with the photographer Eddy Posthuma de Boer who accompanied him on certain trips as did his partner, Simone Sassen, also a photographer.

So far, the picture that emerges is of the writer's separation or even alienation from the young adult self whose main characteristic seems to be his dreaminess. In a more positive earlier account, the young man's dream is identified as having nothing to do with outward, Dutch reality. The second piece contained in the memoir of first journeys, 'Wie was Arthur Edell?' (Who was Arthur Edell?) is based on a diary from 1952. It includes a telling quotation from this diary of a young man who is not yet twenty: 'I shall be a tramp along God's roads, a person without cares ... May I escape from the pull of this endlessly sombre country.'[34] The early 1950s were austere and gloomy during the phase of reconstruction after the occupation of the Netherlands during the Second World War. All the same, Nooteboom's overwhelming urge to experience other places, other cultures, was not typical of his generation. Fellow writers such as W.F. Hermans and Gerard Reve depicted the sense of claustrophobia, or desolation felt by young men who stayed at home in the immediate postwar period.

33 '[...] dat je het verleden, dus ook dat van jezelf, alleen maar kunt verzinnen.' *Rode regen*, 101.

34 '[...] Ik zal een zwerver zijn langs Gods wegen, een mens zonder zorgen ... Mag ik wegtrekken uit de ban van dit oneindig sombere land.' *Rode regen*, 109.

Another part of the familiar self-narrative is the account of Nooteboom's love of reading and unusual choice of books in his youth – what he wryly calls the 'delicious years of untutored lust for reading'.[35] Lacking guidance, he read great writers like Voltaire, Sappho and Cervantes alongside more popular Dutch and Flemish novels. Or, in an alternative version in conversation with Margot Dijkgraaf:

> So was it then all because someone had to earn his living by the age of eighteen and read Faulkner much too soon in a minuscule boarding house room, but also Alain-Fournier's *Le grand Meaulnes*, and Truman Capote's *Other Voices, Other Rooms*, and some time later, after a first big hitchhiking trip through Scandinavia, *Le Mas Théotime* by Henri Bosco ...?[36]

More than four decades later in his acceptance speech on being given an honorary doctorate at the Catholic University of Brussels he talks about his lack of a university education, his love of reading and learning and he admits to being envious of erudition 'in his secret autodidact's heart'.[37] I have spent some time on this fragmentary narrative of becoming because in much of his prose writing, whether fiction or travel, Nooteboom creates an impression of a writer alive in the moment, but with an appreciation of the past in the present. This writing persona that I had imagined to myself over the years of reading Nooteboom's work, is a solitary one with a distinctive take on the world, but also one apparently without a great deal of personal baggage which is why the gradual, though limited, revelation of personal detail from his formative years holds such fascination.

Recently, Nooteboom has written about his 'other' life on the island of Menorca:

35   '[...] opwindende jaren van de ongevormde leeslust', *Nootebooms hotel*, 304.
36   'Kwam het dan toch doordat iemand op zijn achttiende al zijn eigen brood moest verdienen en op een minuscule pensionkamer veel te vroeg Faulkner las, maar ook Alain-Fourniers *Le grand Meaulnes*, en Truman Capotes *Other Voices, Other Rooms*, en nog weer later, na een eerste grote liftreis door Scandinavië, *Le Mas Théotime* van Henri Bosco ...? Dijkgraaf, *Nooteboom en de anderen*, 8.
37   *Nootebooms hotel*, 306.

I have two lives, it seems, one over there where I come from, a life that is growing
shadowy, it doesn't really exist. The other is here, I had only interrupted it. You
can't add them together to equal two whole lives, and yet it does seem as though
life lasts longer. The other life is one of people, events, journeys. In that other life,
times change, they are called arrival, the time of your plane, appointment, here time
is sand, all I have to do is turn it the other way up each day and the same grains mark
the same hours.[38]

It is as though he is allowing the reader into his private life instead of keeping her at arm's length. These are not confessional pages by any means, but
rather a more personal form of registering his immediate environment, of
being in the world, which is similar to the travel writing. The narrating 'I'
sometimes becomes a 'we' to include his partner. The opening sentence of
'Kip' (Chicken) – a story in *Rode regen* – manages to convey both the first
person singular and plural: 'I am a nomadic tribe of two people.' Readerly
persistence pays off in this collection of stories, that is, if one is seeking
proximity to the writer. Eventually the memories come: of the woman
(now dead) with whom he made his first journey to Morocco, of school
and reading Homer, of the diaries and early journeys already mentioned
earlier in this chapter, of special friendships, of life as a sailor on the Gran
Rio, of a drinking session in Ibiza.

The Netherlands never quite disappears, though it fades dramatically.
It seems as though the country of Nooteboom's birth makes few claims
on him for at least some of the time when he is at his house in Menorca,
and when he is travelling. His genesis story suggests that this is a pattern
that became ingrained early on and that is integral to his subjectivity as
a writer. His early curiosity for and encounters with non-Dutch writers
seems to have been translated into curiosity for other places, languages, and

38   '[...] Ik heb twee levens, lijkt het, één daar, waar ik vandaan kom, een leven dat nu
      schimmig wordt, het bestaat niet echt. Het andere is hier, ik had het alleen maar
      onderbroken. Je kunt ze niet bij elkaar optellen als twee hele levens, en toch lijkt
      het of je langer leeft. Het andere leven is er een van mensen, gebeurtenissen, reizen.
      In dat andere leven veranderen de tijden, heten aankomst, vliegtijd, afspraak, hier
      is de tijd van zand, ik hoef hem alleen maar elke dag om te draaien, dan benoemen
      dezelfde korrels dezelfde uren.' *Nooteboooms hotel*, 330.

cultures, as he explains to Dijkgraaf: 'one thing I know for certain: that in that year [1953], roving and reading, I opened the door to my freedom.'³⁹

The Dutch Critics and Commentators on Nooteboom's Position as a Dutch Writer

It has often been said that the quality of Nooteboom's writing went unrecognized by his compatriots in the early part of his career, and this is certainly part of the received view of Nooteboom in the Netherlands. Part 2 of this book will look in detail at the reception of several works by Nooteboom in Dutch and in English across the three genres of novel, poetry and travel writing in order to produce a more nuanced understanding of Nooteboom's reception at different stages of his career. The subtitle of an article on Nooteboom's 2008 tour of Germany by the Dutch literary critic Jeroen Vullings encapsulates the received view by explicitly subtracting the Netherlands from Europe to express how out of touch the Dutch critics are: 'How Europe (minus the Netherlands) glorifies its dreamed-of Nobel prize-winner, how our eastern neighbours cherish him: Cees Nooteboom, self-made world writer.'⁴⁰ Vullings accompanied Nooteboom on a tour of Germany, and a constant theme of his published account of the trip is the contrast between the reception at home and in Germany. Vullings thinks that German audiences respond differently to writers in general and show much more appreciation of writers appearing in person and reading from their work, something the Dutch consider pointless. Vullings also points

---

39   'maar één ding weet ik zeker: dat ik in dat jaar [1953] reizend en lezend de deur naar de vrijheid voor mijzelf heb opengedaan.' Dijkgraaf, *Nooteboom en de anderen*, 12.

40   'Hoe Europa (min Nederland) zijn gedroomde nobelprijswinnaar verheerlijkt, hoe onze oosterburen hem liefdevol koesteren: Cees Nooteboom, selfmade wereld-schrijver.' Jeroen Vullings, 'Als God in Duitsland', *Vrij Nederland* (6 December 2008).

out that Nooteboom does all he can to smooth the path for other Dutch writers wanting to make a name abroad.

The most recent publication about Nooteboom at the time of writing this is Margot Dijkgraaf's account of her extended conversation with the author. In it, Nooteboom imagines that the Italian writer Calvino had written the same works but in Dutch, and suggests that not only would Calvino not have counted among the top Dutch writers, but he would also not have enjoyed quite the same success in translation.[41] This hypothetical case is symptomatic of a lingering doubt about the effect of writing in a less commonly known language and in a culture that has not been considered to be a language of high culture and that is perhaps less at ease with a cosmopolitan figure like Nooteboom. It may also be that there is a time lag somewhere in the reception of Nooteboom at home – views of a particular writer are frequently echoed by other critics, which can prevent them seeing with fresh eyes. This is due in the main to the way literary and social norms influence the judgements of critics. Vullings also sees something systematic in the negative view of Nooteboom, describing him as 'systematically lambasted, sidelined, belittled' and naming the influential daily paper *NRC Handelsblad* as the ringleader.[42] He also believes that there is a gap between the way literary journalism viewed Nooteboom and the Dutch reading public at large, suggesting that the latter may have led the way towards acceptance of Nooteboom by the literary field. Cultural change is multi-speed with some embracing the new and others clinging to tradition, with many positions in between, and the time lag effect may well apply to writers themselves as well as their readerships: a writer who is disappointed with his reception may still feel that way even after opinions have shifted.

Whether it is the Dutch public that led the way, or whether the Dutch press has been responding to cultural changes in the world at large, and

---

41   Dijkgraaf, *Nooteboom en de anderen*, 43–4.
42   '[...] maar in de vaderlandse kritiek stelselmatig gekapitteld, in de hoek gezet, klein gemaakt, vooral in NRC Handelsblad.' Vullings, 'Als God in Duitsland', *Vrij Nederland* (6 December 2008).

in particular to the growth in inward migration in the Netherlands and its impact, there is no doubt that critics are more accepting of a nomadic way of life and of a style of writing that reflects this. The back cover of Dijkgraaf's book contains the following remarks:

> Cees Nooteboom, it appears, is an outsider, an observer, a pilgrim, a writer who is seldom in the Netherlands and is always travelling, an islander who for years has spent his summers on Menorca in order to write. Nooteboom's only real dwelling-place is the Dutch language.[43]

The fact that this comment is published as part of a marketing text indicates that the separation of language from national territory is something that is expected to appeal to the target audience, and so it can be regarded as evidence of a particular strand of the culture of the Netherlands; the unbreakable bond is with the language itself, not with the place. It is this identification with the language that is held out to prospective readers as the solution to Nooteboom's troubling un-Dutch presence in Dutch life and letters.

Cultural Complexity and Nooteboom's Reception

Here I look in more detail at Nooteboom's reception in the Netherlands, and particularly at the question of whether the critics' sense of the writer's Dutchness has any influence on their judgement. My starting-point is the view discussed above and repeated as recently as 2008 by Vullings that Nooteboom has not found full recognition, though it is hard to say at this point why this impression should persist if one reviews the many

---

43   'Cees Nooteboom, zo blijkt, is een buitenstaander, een kijker, een pelgrim, een schrijver die zelden in Nederland is en altijd op reis, een eilander die sinds jaar en dag zijn zomers doorbrengt op Menorca om te schrijven. Echt wonen doet Nooteboom alleen in de Nederlandse taal.' Margot Dijkgraaf, *Nooteboom en de anderen*, back cover.

prizes that he has received for his work since the publication of his first
novel. By way of preparation for a short reception study, a brief survey of
his literary work now follows. Since I am discussing the Dutch works in
order of publication, I will give the titles in Dutch in the text, followed by
their English translation at the first mention. Later on in the book, when
I discuss the English oeuvre, English titles will take precedence.

According to the entry on Nooteboom in Van Bork and Verkruijsse, to
the Poetry International website[44] and to many other sources, Nooteboom
sees himself primarily as a poet. The Dutch academic and literary historian
Jaap Goedegebuure describes Nooteboom as 'an author who has emphasized
in many interviews that of all the genres in which he works, he has always
attached most value to poetry. Above all he wants to make his mark as a
poet.'[45] Unfortunately Goedegebuure does not give his sources and this has
the feel of one of those 'truths' that circulate among critics, possibly ema-
nating from the author. Vullings describes poetry as the 'quintessence of
Nooteboom's oeuvre' and tells us that Nooteboom considers his poetry to
be the best of what he has to offer. It seems to me that Nooteboom himself
expresses his relationship with poetry carefully, for example in his response
to an interviewer's comment that poetry is not incidental to his work but
is central to it, when he replies, 'I have kept it a bit apart from my other
work.'[46] And in his acceptance speech in Berlin he points to the intensely
personal and intimate relationship a poet has with his poems.[47] What is
certain is that this is a firmly established perception in the Low Countries
which has not taken root in the English-speaking world, no doubt because

44   <http://www.poetryinternationalweb.net/pi/site/poet/item/4001/Cees-
     Nooteboom> accessed 8 August 2012.
45   '[...] een auteur die in diverse vraaggesprekken heeft benadrukt dat hij van alle door
     hem beoefende genres aan de poëzie altijd de meeste waarde heeft gehecht. Voor alles
     wil hij als dichter gelden', Jaap Goedegebuure, Over 'Rituelen' van Cees Nooteboom
     (Amsterdam: Arbeiderspers, 1983), 7.
46   'Ik heb het een beetje afgeschermd van het andere werk.' Brokken, 'De voorbije pas-
     sages', 25.
47   Cees Nooteboom, Roads to Berlin, trans. Laura Watkinson (London: MacLehose
     Press, 2012), e.g. 303.

the writer is not perceived as a poet all because of the lack of availability of his poetry in English. Nooteboom's first published volume of poetry was *De doden zoeken een huis* (1956, The Dead are Seeking a House) and he has continued to publish poetry regularly throughout his career. He won the poetry prize of the city of Amsterdam in both 1960 and 1965, and the Jan Campert Prize in 1978 for *Open als een schelp, dicht als een steen* (1978, Open like a Shell, Closed like a Stone). In 1984 his collected poems 1955–83 appeared as *Vuurtijd, ijstijd* (Fire Time, Ice Time).

Whether Nooteboom regards himself first and foremost as a poet or not, the newest Dutch literary history presents him in an emphatically different light. He features here as a significant literary figure because of his prose, both fiction and travel writing; his poetry is mentioned only once in passing.[48] In fact he also made a name for himself with his first novel, *Philip en de anderen* (1955, *Philip and the Others*) which won the Anne Frank Prize. Although his next novel, *De ridder is gestorven* (*The Knight has Died*), was also awarded a prize in 1963, its year of publication, fiction became a problematic genre for Nooteboom whose next novel did not appear until 1980. As I noted above, when *Rituelen* (*Rituals*) did appear it was awarded an international prize, was reprinted many times, and by 1985 had been translated into English, German and French.[49] There now followed his most successful period as a writer of fiction which still continues at the time of writing this book. The novels will be discussed in detail in Chapter 5, but for the sake of completeness, I will list the remaining ones here: *In Nederland* (*In the Dutch Mountains*), *Het volgende verhaal* (*The Following Story*), *Allerzielen* (*All Souls' Day*), and *Paradijs verloren* (*Lost Paradise*).

Generally speaking, the reception of individual works will be discussed in Part 2 of *Nomadic Literature*, while this section considers opinions of Dutch newspaper and academic critics affecting Cees Nooteboom's position within Dutch culture, guided by the following questions: Do the

---

48   Hugo Brems, *Altijd weer vogels die nesten beginnen. Geschiedenis van de Nederlandse literatuur 1945–2005* (Amsterdam: Bert Bakker, 2006).

49   For a list of prizes awarded to Nooteboom, see <http://www.ceesnooteboom. com/?cat=6> accessed 9 December 2012.

Dutch critics make any comments on the author's perceived identity? Are there negative aspects to the reception of his work, and if so, to what are they attributed? Is his work valued differently at different times? Although I have made a point of Nooteboom's lack of recognition in the Netherlands, there is some evidence that the literary world beyond Dutch borders is aware of Nooteboom's unusual position at home, which is perhaps not surprising when Nooteboom's international literary networks are taken into consideration. Interestingly, the *NRC Handelsblad* which Vullings had singled out as being the most persistently negative, reprinted an article by the Argentinian writer Alberto Manguel in Dutch translation in which he goes so far as to suggest a reason for Nooteboom's rejection at home:

> Perhaps the Dutch have rejected Nooteboom as a major writer precisely for the reason that Nooteboom refuses to offer them a uniform narrative of their geographical and historical identity. This is so often the case for a writer who does not want to latch on to local colour and vague sociology, but instead chooses a more generous, all-embracing point of departure. To the Dutch, Nooteboom must seem guilty of sacrilege.[50]

In order to explore the development of this negative reception I have looked at the Dutch reviews of *Rituelen*, the novel which appeared in 1980 after Nooteboom's long silence. Before this the reception of his first novel, *Philip en de anderen*, had been generally positive but with some mixed reviews. There seems to have been little in the way of negative comments, and the short debut novel gained official recognition in the form of the Anne Frank

---

50   'Misschien hebben de Nederlanders juist wel om die reden, omdat Nooteboom weigert een gelijkmatig verhaal van hun geografische en historische identiteit te bieden, hem als hun belangrijkste schrijver afgewezen. Dit geldt zo vaak voor een schrijver die niet wenst in te spelen op couleur locale en milde sociologie, maar in plaats hiervan een royaler, alomvattend uitgangspunt verkiest. Voor de Nederlanders moet Nooteboom schuldig lijken aan heiligschennis.' Alberto Manguel, 'De wereld is het verhaal', *NRC Handelsblad* (25 July 2008); cited from LiteRom, <http://literom.knipselkranten.nl/IndexJs?#dofilter_f_301356885400624_t_Recensent_ts_S_v_zoekstandaard%3DCees%2BNooteboom%2B%26zoekauteur%3D%26seli tems%3D_sep_Titel%253DAlgemeen%2520_sep_Recensent%253DAlberto%2520 Manquel%2520_sep_%26orderby%3D1> accessed 27 March 2009.

Prize, awarded by the Netherlands–America Foundation. The reactions to
the next novel *De ridder is gestorven*, published in 1962, were mixed and
included some appreciative reviews by established commentators such as
Jan Greshoff and Ben Stroman. At this point, no hostility or dismissal
has emerged, even though there are some negative comments. The critics'
views are more polarized by the time *Rituelen* was published. Of course,
Nooteboom was a well-known figure by now, known mainly for his journalism – travel pieces for the Catholic daily newspaper *De Volkskrant* and articles for the glossy magazine *Avenue* – though he was also forging a literary
persona as a poet. However it does appear that it is this journalistic activity
that has influenced some of the critical opinion: one reviewer comments
that Nooteboom deals with trendy topics 'as though a marketing agency is
behind it', and sums up with two short sentences, 'It is still modish twaddle.
Second-life literature.'[51] The reviewer in the quality weekly newspaper *Het
Vaderland* confirms this reason for Nooteboom's position as an outsider
on the Dutch literary scene, though he simultaneously distances himself
from the standard 'Calvinistic' response:

> He made a name for himself purely as a professional traveller, chiefly for Avenue, but
> we are generally too Calvinistic to regard the account of these journeys as a literary
> genre like they do in England, certainly when those texts have already appeared in
> print alongside glossy adverts. I fear that Nooteboom's new book will not do much
> to alter his position as an outsider in the literary world. Rituals is in every respect
> an un-Dutch book; it is written in such an expert and measured way that the style
> comes across as almost international, the subject, put very pointedly: loneliness,
> is not wholly unusual [in Dutch literature], but when it does occur, all distance is
> lacking and the smell of boiled sprouts is overwhelming.[52]

---

51 'Alsof er een marketingbureau achter zit ...', 'Het blijft moedieus gezeur. Second-
life literatuur.' Reinjan Mulder, 'Wintersport, whisky en oorsterse rituelen',
NRC Handelsblad, 12 December 1980, cited from LiteRom, <http://literom.
knipselkranten.nl/artikel/index/25871> accessed 11 May 2009.

52 'Alleen als beroepsreiziger, hoofdzakelijk voor Avenue, verwierf hij zich een naam,
maar we zijn er doorgaans te Calvinistisch voor om het verslag van die tochten ook
werkelijk als een literair genre, zoals in Engeland, te beschouwen, zeker als die tek-
sten ook al eerder naast luxe advertenties hebben gestaan. Ik vrees dat Nootebooms
nieuwe boek niet veel aan zijn positie van outsider in de literaire wereld zal veranderen.

These examples give an idea of some very specific reasons for the Dutch literary field's reluctance to recognize Nooteboom. These are connected with the social and cultural complexities I alluded to earlier in the section 'Nooteboom on Nooteboom' when I described the Netherlands as moving away from pillarization. Whereas before the war, the literary and cultural world had been part of the system of social and cultural separation along confessional and ideological lines, participating in structures which had included separate newspapers and magazines, after the Second World War this rather rigid and closed system rapidly began to break down. But the tradition of approaching literature from a confessional standpoint still persisted in some quarters, and clearly affected Nooteboom's reception. The repercussions of these cultural tensions and complexities are still present, though they are receding all the time. One example is the fact that Nooteboom's collected works have been published in German, in nine volumes, but that his Dutch publisher has not yet taken such a step. In fact, this led to a break with Atlas, the publisher Nooteboom had been with for many years, and to his move to De Bezige Bij, who had promised to bring older work back into print.

And an important literary prize in the Netherlands, the P.C. Hooftprijs (P.C. Hooft Prize), was awarded to Nooteboom's near contemporaries some thirty years before he received this honour in 2004: Gerard Reve in 1968, W.F. Hermans in 1971 and Harry Mulisch in 1977. The most significant prize of all, the Prijs der Nederlandse Letteren (Prize of Dutch Letters) which is normally awarded every three years to a Dutch or Flemish writer, was given to Nooteboom in 2009. By this time, however, enough has changed in the Netherlands for Nooteboom's cosmopolitanism to be valued. In fact,

---

Rituelen is in allerlei opzichten een on-Nederlands boek; het is zo vaardig en beheerst geschreven, dat de stijl haast internationaal aandoet, het onderwerp, heel toegespitst gezegd: eenzaamheid, komt wel vaker voor, maar dan ontbreekt meestal iedere vorm van distantie en is de spruitjeslucht te snijden.' Daan Cartens, 'In het klooster van de tijd', *Het Vaderland*, 3 January 1981, cited from LiteRom, <http://literom. knipselkranten.nl/IndexJs?#dofilter_f_221356886291981_t_Recensent_ts_S_v_zoe kstandaard%3DRituelen%2B%26zoekauteur%3D%26selitems%3D_sep_Recensen t%253DDaan%2520Cartens%2520_sep_%26orderby%3D1> accessed 11 May 2009.

King Albert II of Belgium who presented the prize addressed him as 'the cosmopolitan Cees Nooteboom' and described the prize as a celebration of the fact that Nooteboom gives Dutch literature a place in world literature.[53]
　　When the Dutch politician and journalist Hans van Mierlo presented the P.C. Hooftprijs to Nooteboom he emphasized the writer's important contribution to 'the stumbling progress towards European awareness' through his recognition in other European countries:

> all these prizes and honours that were then awarded to you and will continue to be, are the recognition of what you have meanwhile become in Berlin and Madrid and all of Europe in between: a great European writer. Thanks to the fact that now everything you write or say in Europe is translated into all the important European languages, a recognition effect is created that is inherent to true literature.[54]

So according to Van Mierlo the recognition received in Europe means that the Netherlands must accept that Nooteboom's work is 'real literature', whether they like it or not. Van Mierlo also claims that his European readers see Nooteboom first and foremost as a European, and then as a Dutchman. Dutch readers do not seem to be included in the notion of European readers. Van Mierlo also attempts to describe the crosscultural dimension of Nooteboom's European reach, which he sees as contributing towards European unification:

53　Speech of H.M. Albert II, King of the Belgians on the occasion of the award of the Prijs der Nederlandse Letteren, 18 November 2009: <http://prijsderletteren. org/2009_toespraak/> accessed 9 August 2012.

54　'[...] het strompelende bewustwordingsproces van Europa', and 'al die prijzen en onderscheidingen die je daarna in de hoofdsteden ten deel vielen en zullen blijven vallen, zijn de erkenning van dat wat je in Berlijn en Madrid en al het Europa daartussen bent geworden: een groot Europees schrijver. Dankzij het feit dat nu alles wat je schrijft of vertelt in Europa vertaald wordt in alle belangrijke Europese talen, ontstaat op macroniveau het herkenningseffect dat inherent is aan echte literatuur.' Hans van Mierlo, 'Laudatio bij uitreiking P.C. Hooftprijs 2004', in László Földényi, et al., *In het oog van de storm: De wereld van Cees Nooteboom* (Amsterdam and Antwerp: Atlas, 2006), 217.

If you make cultures known to each other, transport beauty across borders and above all expose that which is recognizable generally in the particular, if you thus stir the emotions in different places simultaneously, then you are unintentionally providing what at this moment is most lacking in the integration process. This is the answer to the question of what Europe actually is.[55]

While the national prize for literature certainly marks a form of acceptance by the cultural establishment, there remains the question of Nooteboom's presence in Dutch literary history. From a passing mention in Van Bork and Laan's 1985 volume *Twee eeuwen literatuurgeschiedenis* (Two Centuries of Literary History), for example, Nooteboom makes slightly more of an impact five years later when Ton Anbeek published his literary history, *Geschiedenis van de Nederlandse literatuur tussen 1885 en 1985* (A History of Dutch Literature between 1885 and 1985). Nooteboom's established contemporaries Harry Mulisch, Gerard Reve and W.F. Hermans had most definitely become part of the national narrative at this point. While Anbeek does include Nooteboom, the treatment of him is minimal compared with these contemporaries; one page out of 270 pages of text is given over to more detailed discussion of his work, and his name his mentioned several times in lists of writers, for example, of those using classical mythology and Christian imagery in their writing.[56] However, when the next history appears in 1993, Nooteboom does not appear as a writer in his own right, though he is mentioned twice in passing as having been discussed by the influential critic J.J. Oversteegen and his novel *Rituelen* is cited as an example of literature translated into film.[57]

55 'Als je zo culturen aan elkaar bekend maakt, schoonheid over de grens tilt en vooral in het bijzondere het algemeen herkenbare zichtbaar maakt, als je zo op verschillende plaatsen tegelijk ontroering tot stand brengt, dan voorzie je ongewild in wat op dit moment het meest ontbreekt in het integratieproces. Dat is het antwoord op de vraag wat Europa eigenlijk is.' Van Mierlo, 'Rede', 217.

56 Ton Anbeek, *Geschiedenis van de Nederlandse literatuur tussen 1885 en 1985* (Amsterdam: Arbeiderspers, 1990), 240.

57 M.A. Schenkeveld-Van der Dussen, ed., *Nederlandse literatuur, een geschiedenis* (Groningen: Nijhoff, 1993), 760, 768.

As noted in the Introduction and Chapter 1, the volume of the newest literary history dealing with the period 1945–2005 was sponsored by the Nederlandse Taalunie which gives it a certain official status. There is no question of Nooteboom being neglected in it: no fewer than ten book titles are mentioned, some of which are discussed individually, including his travel writing. What is most striking about this treatment of Nooteboom is that he is now integrated into the narrative of Dutch literature, from his debut in the 1950s through to the closing section of the book which is headed 'Bestaat de Nederlandse literatuur?' (Does Dutch Literature Exist?) and which deals with literary mobility and open cultural boundaries.

Conclusion

In this chapter I have charted the life, the work and the position of Cees Nooteboom as a writer. I portray him as fundamentally nomadic with a multiple, shifting identity, emphasizing the effect of his extreme mobility on his subjectivity – his sense of himself and his sensibilities. In the section 'Nooteboom on Nooteboom' it becomes clear that Nooteboom frequently positions himself in relation to the past, that is, to his own personal past by means of autobiographical narrative. His sensibility precludes nostalgia for the past and seems to fit with the Braidottian idea of work on the self and thinking not as an inward dwelling on ideas but as an expression of 'the outward-bound nature of the subject'. Nooteboom's approach to the past could be described as matter-of-fact if it weren't the case that central to his engagement with the past is the recognition that it is constructed, so that it is in some sense a fiction.

This relationship to the past is important for Nooteboom's complex interaction with Dutchness, whether personally as told here using his auto-biographical writing or in his literary writing, which will be discussed next. It is certainly not the case that he has rejected his country of birth though he has had an uneasy relationship with some aspects of Dutch society and culture. This contrasts with his appearances in Germany where audiences and literary figures as described by Jeroen Vullings are warm and respectful towards the writer and his work. Nooteboom's travels took him around Europe as a young man, then to the Caribbean, and his travel journalism funded trips to America, Africa, Japan, Australia and the Arab world. This extreme mobility raises questions which will be discussed in Chapter 6 on the travel writing: is this travel which borders on tourism? To what extent does Nooteboom engage with the many new cultures he encounters, and does this engagement vary depending on factors such as length of stay, knowledge of the language, or the stage in Nooteboom's career? While this career is completely international it has not left behind the world of national, or local, culture. The postnational paradigm does not seem to be an appropriate one for discussing Nooteboom's sense of culture or his personal sense of belonging. Also, his literary works are transnational in ways that Nooteboom himself can never be, since they present themselves to new audiences in their own languages – many more than the author speaks. And they reach audiences in far greater numbers than the author on tour can ever reach.

A nomadic subject can encompass the tourist, the traveller, the pilgrim, the poet, the novelist, the boundary-crosser, the Dutchman. Of course Cees Nooteboom is a Dutch writer. That is why his relationship with Dutch audiences and literary figures is complex and involves tensions. There is a definite sense, according to him in his Berlin acceptance speech that the Netherlands is still home. On the subject of his next novel, he says:

> The new novel which is still only in my head, will, I suspect, feature Italy, and in a very particular way the Netherlands. Because I cannot and will not escape the Netherlands. My feeling is that my real home is in the Netherlands, even though Simone and I spend the summers in Menorca. My books, my paintings, my drawings are in Amsterdam and so is my archive. And I have never wanted to give up my status as a resident even though that would have been financially advantageous. Put simply, the Netherlands is there, and I cannot be without my language.[58]

58   'De nieuwe roman die alleen nog in mijn hoofd zit, zal met Italië te maken hebben en op een heel bijzondere manier met Nederland, vermoed ik. Want onder Nederland kan en wil ik niet uit. Voor mijn gevoel staat mijn echte huis in Nederland, ook al

He has insists on the importance of the Dutch language for him – 'the love of my life' – and 'the reason why the centre of my being is here [in the Netherlands] and not anywhere else.'⁵⁹ Nevertheless, he has found full recognition in translation in other European countries, most notably Germany, but also Spain, Italy and France. This recognition not only preceded his acceptance into the Dutch literary establishment, it also paved the way for it. King Albert explicitly mentions Nooteboom's recognition by the Free University of Berlin as a factor that changes Nooteboom's status as a writer, and it was his treatment by his German publisher that provoked Nooteboom to switch from his old Dutch publisher to a new one who would manage his back list better. And of course, articles like the one by Vullings cited in this chapter also have the function of raising awareness not only of Nooteboom's elevated position outside the Netherlands but also of making the Dutch literary establishment look a little behind the pace.

What this chapter shows most eloquently is that from the beginning of a long career of travel and writing, Nooteboom's literary sensibilities were anticipating what would become the most significant cultural development of the late twentieth century and early twenty-first century. His nomadic exploration of self was most certainly a rejection of the well-documented postwar frustration with what the younger generation saw as the small-mindedness of the Dutch. That this multiple selfhood found widespread approval outside the Netherlands before it became generally acceptable within that society and culture, is both understandable and fortunate for Nooteboom's career. But perhaps the writer's most important contribution in an age of globalization is his acknowledgement of his local belonging and attachment to the Dutch language, without a trace of nationalistic pride: a firmly cosmopolitan position.

---

leven Simone en ik 's zomers op Menorca. In Amsterdam staan mijn boeken, mijn schilderijen, mijn tekeningen, daar is mijn archief. Ik heb mij ook nooit willen laten uitschrijven, al zou dat financieel voordelig zijn geweest. Nederland is er gewoon, dom gezegd, en buiten mijn taal kan ik niet.' Vullings, 'Als God in Duitsland'.

59   '[...] de liefde van mijn leven' and 'de reden waarom ... het centrum van mijn bestaan zich hier bevindt en niet ergens anders', Cees Nooteboom, 'Dankrede bij uitreiking P.C. Hooftprijs 2004', in Földényi et al., *In het oog van de storm*, 224.

PART 2

Cees Nooteboom: The Writing

The Novels: Fictions of Becoming

Nooteboom's English Afterlives

The English Nooteboom is first and foremost a novelist: nine novels and a collection of stories have been published in English since his debut in 1983 with *Rituals*, whereas only a small collection of poems and three travel volumes have appeared in book form. There are also a number of translated poems and stories in periodicals. This chapter aims to give a sense of Nooteboom as a novelist in his English afterlife: the mode and mood of his writing, his distinctive voice and his preoccupations. This reading of Nooteboom's fiction is constructed in dialogue with other critics and commentators, mainly those who write in English and Dutch. Given that Nooteboom is well-established as a writer of fiction in the English-speaking world and that so many of his novels have appeared in English, in this chapter I base my discussion on the English works alone without comparing them with their Dutch counterparts. I do not assume that translation is transparent and that the English versions are identical with the Dutch ones – rather, I set out to read Nooteboom as he is read by the vast majority of his English readers, that is, without reference to the Dutch texts. On the other hand, I am concerned with the contrasting ways in which the texts have been read by others in both languages, and for this reason, I will compare the writer's reception both in the Netherlands and in England and the United States. This experiment in reading translated fiction was hard to sustain, and I suspect that my reading is at the very least coloured by my foreknowledge of Nooteboom as a Dutch writer.

The term 'postmodernism' is acknowledged to mean many things and has been applied to Nooteboom's fiction. *A Song of Truth and Semblance* (1984), *In the Dutch Mountains* (1987) and *The Knight has Died* (1990) are metafictional texts in which writer-characters struggle to create fictional worlds. And in all the novels to be discussed here, intertextuality is a mode of writing; narratives are multiple, discontinuous or circular; characters are multiple or partial. In an account of postmodernism in Dutch and Flemish novels, *Het postmodernisme in de Nederlandse en Vlaamse roman* (Postmodernism in the Dutch and Flemish Novel), Flemish critic and academic Bart Vervaeck notes that Nooteboom and his novels were not located at the heart of his research domain because 'there is still a search for logical coherence, symbolized by the Proustian "madeleine" which is the final piece that finishes off the whole puzzle.'[1] In my readings of the fiction in the main part of this chapter, I see a more rhizomatic kind of structure which provides a different kind of coherence; one that is not logical in any traditional sense. Ideas and preoccupations remain connected while branching out in different directions, and my readings offer nothing to support the idea that Nooteboom's fiction presents a world in which any puzzle can be finished or solved. While Vervaeck refers to modernist features in Nooteboom's work, Ernestine Kossmann – writing some ten years earlier – calls it 'postmodern avant-la-lettre'.[2] It is certainly not my wish to provide a definitive characterization of Nooteboom's fiction in any way, my interest is in works of literature that place themselves on a threshold, on a cultural cusp with the tensions and uncertainties that this generates. In this way, I am not constrained by a dualistic modernist/postmodernist frame of reference. It is certainly the case that I look for the postmodern elements because I feel a personal affinity with the openness and fluidity that I associate with postmodernism – or poststructuralism –

1   Bart Vervaeck, *Het postmodernisme in de Nederlandse en Vlaamse roman* (Brussels and Nijmegen: VUB Press & Vantilt, 2000), 12 (my translation). Vervaeck's comment is made with reference to Nooteboom's novel *Rituals* which will be the first novel to be discussed in detail in this chapter.

2   Ernestine Kossmann, 'Postmodern avant-la-lettre: Over *De ridder is gestorven*', in *Bzzletin* 168/19 (September 1989), 41–4.

in philosophy and literature, including the nomadic philosophy I outlined in my introduction. The resulting readings in this chapter highlight the philosophically nomadic qualities of Nooteboom's fiction.

Does a postmodern interpretative stance mean that what I shall for the moment term the great themes of European literature are no longer possible given that postmodernism eschews grand historical narratives? They are certainly less likely to be present as recognizable themes, and more likely to be found in traces as allusions, as momentary acts or thoughts of a character. For this reason, I prefer to speak of preoccupations through which a writer places himself or herself in a European tradition of writing, rather than of themes. Nooteboom's novels are permeated by the following preoccupations: death; human relationships whether familial, sexual, or friendships; fear and ways of dealing with it; time and memory; and perhaps the most challenging theme of all – life and how to make it meaningful. Seemingly, these preoccupations concern the fundamental elements of human existence. At the same time, love, beauty and truth, as absolute concepts and interrelated values, are absent from the fiction. For a postmodern writer like Nooteboom, these traditional ideals are no longer part of his mode of writing and have been replaced by an intertextual web of creative thinking and a lightness of tone. It is for this reason that I have opted for a Deleuzian, Braidottian nomadic approach in order to do justice both to Nooteboom's development as a writer and as a practical philosopher struggling with the meaning of death as an answer to the problem of how to live. It also opens up the reading to the many threshold-crossings and becomings in the subjectivity of Nooteboom's main characters in particular.

The major part of this chapter will be a chronological account of the English fiction, with attention to its reception. The chapter will conclude with a brief look at one novel in Dutch, English and German – *Philip and the Others* – since its reception history is particularly illuminating.

Nooteboom's Trajectory as a Writer of Fiction

Nooteboom's English debut *Rituals* can be read as the story of Inni Wintrop, told in leaps of ten years – 1963, 1953, 1973 – that are not chronologically ordered in the novel. The sequencing of the chapters is what highlights this novel as a narrative of crisis, of temporary madness, its background and aftermath. In these chapters Inni is first a young man whose marriage has just come to an end; then a youth on the threshold of adulthood; and finally a forty-year-old who is learning how to live. Inni's getting of wisdom occurs through crucial encounters with others, most particularly Arnold Taads in 1953, and his son Philip in the 1970s. Inni's sexual encounters offer readers a way of charting his progress from lost boy seeking close physical contact in Chapter II to married man for whom sex has become an impersonal addiction in Chapter I to a more self-contained less needy kind of lover in Chapter III.

> This is what pleased him most about his strange life – that when he had gotten up that morning, he had not known that he would now be cycling here with a girl at his back, but that such a possibility was always there. It gave him, he thought, something invincible. He looked at the faces of men in the oncoming cars, and he knew that his life, in its absurdity, was right. Emptiness, loneliness, anxiety – these were the drawbacks – but there were also compensations, and this was one of them.[3]

Inni has learned to embrace life, accept fear and anxiety and to love the 'anarchic freedom' of his city Amsterdam.

Back in 1953 the figure of Arnold Taads who leads a withdrawn, eccentric existence dependent on routine, shows Inni the sterility of a life which refuses engagement with the world outside. Inni himself had found it difficult to fit in at school, preferring to remain aloof and might seem at first to have this in common with Taads.

---

3   Cees Nooteboom, *Rituals*, trans. Adrienne Dixon (Baton Rouge: Louisiana State University Press, 1983), 85.

If it meant that he [Inni] was alone in the world, it was correct. That was what he himself felt, too, and it suited him splendidly. Other people, like the man [Taads] facing him now, had to be kept at a distance. And they should not talk too much about him either. As long as they talked about themselves, or about his relations, none of whom he knew anyway, it was fine.[4]

Philip Taads, the abandoned son of Arnold also leads a withdrawn existence, but he has elevated absence to a personal religion, a self-invented practice aimed at denying the body; what the narrator aptly and sarcastically calls 'meditating himself to death.' The character himself represents a kind of meditation on *thanatos*, the urge to death. Philip's desire for physical absence, the minimalist aesthetic of Japanese culture, his monk's cell of a room and the lack of human contact are in some way not enough in the end, and the suicide does not come as a surprise to either the reader or to Inni.

Both Taadses resist and refuse any form of becoming, choosing to be frozen and fixed in their disengaged lives – the very opposite of the way Rosi Braidotti proposes life should be lived in *Metamorphoses*. Surprisingly, perhaps, Philip Taads speaks of himself in terms of multiplicity – 'Sleeping is senseless. A peculiar form of absence that has no meaning. One of all the people you are is resting, the others remain awake.'[5] And he quotes the Taoist Tzu Chuang on the subject of metamorphosis:

All things are in a constant state of self-transformation, each in its own way. In this everlasting change, they appear and disappear. What we call 'time' plays no role whatsoever. All things are equal.[6]

This is at odds with Braidotti's view of time: according to her, to be *in* time is to accept an embodied subjectivity. What Philip Taads is after is a kind of cosmic time in which the individual life becomes insignificant:

4   *Rituals*, 49.
5   *Rituals*, 126.
6   *Rituals*, 127.

What the East has given me is the thought that this I of mine is not so unique. Nothing much will be lost when it disappears. It isn't important. I am a hindrance to the world and the world is a hindrance to me. There will only be harmony if I get rid of both at once.[7]

The Taadses remain in the world through their use of ritual. Paradoxically Arnold's ritual of doing everything by the clock abolishes time passing and turns it into a static framework for the day. Philip's meditation and tea ceremony seem calculated to create an eternal now, since nothing changes and develops. The Taadses are Inni's example of how not to live.

By Chapter III Inni accepts the ageing process, and the narrator emphasizes the passing of time in Inni's world: 'There were days when [...]'; 'It was not 1973, and Inni had turned forty [...]'; 'About an hour later [...]'; 'Suddenly [...]'; 'Half an hour later [...]'; 'Now that he had reached the age of forty [...]'; 'How long ago was it [...]'; 'From time to time [...]'; 'Five years after his first encounter with Philip Taads [...]' and so on. Inni's acceptance of the physical, thus temporal, body separates him from the Taadses, and his sexual encounters can be seen as part of this, and even become life-affirming in the latter part of the novel. Earlier on the narrator describes what could be called Inni's sex addiction as giving him the feeling that 'he existed after all' – a step in the direction of affirming life in the here and now.

Stepping back from the narrative, the main character of *Rituals* is a postmodern literary creation embodying what Bart Vervaeck, citing Thomas Docherty, calls the 'temporal process of metamorphosis':[8] there is no true self that the narrative has brought to light. Inni is also someone who wanders aimlessly, leaving himself open to strange encounters like the three successive doves on the day he first meets Philip Taads. All Nooteboom's main characters are *flaneurs* and meanderers, as we will see.

Beyond the characters, it is Nooteboom's narrator that gives *Rituals* its distinctive voice – the lightness of tone, the edge of cruelty to the ironies, the sharp insights:

7   *Rituals*, 129.
8   Vervaeck, *Het postmodernisme in de Nederlandse en Vlaamse roman*, 70.

It was Amsterdam before the Provos, before the 'dwarfs,' before the long, hot summers. But at many places in that magic semicircle, unrest was sharpening. It seemed an age ago since the Indies had slipped away into one of the last pages of the Dutch history book that later would have to be rewritten so drastically. Korea had been divided by a ruler, by what some called the ineluctable course of history, and there were already people who knew that the seed of Vietnam had been sown. Fishes were beginning to die of things that fishes had not died of in the past, and the faces in the ever lengthening traffic jams along the canals displayed at times that mixture of frustration and aggression that was to make the seventies so unique.[9]

Sometimes the narrative merges with Inni's thoughts, giving a fluidity of expression. Here, the young Inni is listening to a discussion between the atheist Arnold Taads and Roman Catholic priest who is chamberlain to the Pope:

Arnold Taads stared at him and said at last: 'Let us try to avoid an argument. What I have to say on the subject would sound most discourteous to your ears.'
'My ears are but human ears. It is God's ears you might offend.'
Taads said nothing but Inni tried to imagine it. God's ears. Who knows, God might be nothing but ear, a gigantic marble ear floating through space. But God did not exist. The Pope did, that was sure, and this strangely birdlike man was his private chamberlain.[10]

When it first appeared, *Rituals* was interpreted in radically differing ways. The references to Sartre seem to have led some commentators to emphasize aspects that can be associated with existentialism, such as the Guardian reviewer's reference to the 'compost of despair',[11] and the Philadelphia Inquirer's emphasis on 'nausea and boredom'.[12] In the same issue of the Dutch journal *Bzzletin* in which Michael Boll's reception study was published, which is devoted entirely to Nooteboom and his work, Gaby Lefeber's analysis of the Dutch text – *Rituelen* – in terms of existentialism

---

9   *Rituals*, 5.
10   *Rituals*, 62.
11   From a review by Christopher Wordsworth cited by Michel Boll in 'Het oeuvre op reis: De buitenlandse reacties op het werk van Cees Nooteboom' in *Bzzletin*, 168/19 (September 1989), 88.
12   Boll, 'Het oeuvre op reis', 87. Boll is paraphrasing the review by Arthur Sabatini.

reduces the characters to aspects of the philosophy. In so doing, it misses the ironic treatment of Sartre both through Arnold Taads's use of Sartre as a reference point and the young Inni's rather vague notion of Sartrean ideas:

> A meaningless world into which you were thrown, an existence that signified nothing except by virtue of what you made it signify. It still smacked of church. It had a suspect, musty odor of martyrdom. Most of all, thought Inni, it found its expression in the taste and the smell of those Gauloises ...[13]

Nor does Lefeber seem to recognize the fundamental difference between Inni and the Taadses. On the other hand, the perceptive review by Linda Barrett Osborne in the Washington Post, again cited by Boll, sees the novel as a portrait of the modern world, of a society that is too complex to understand, where Inni Wintrop is the survivor because he adapts to his surroundings.

A Song of Truth and Semblance was Nooteboom's second work of fiction to be published in English.[14] It appeared the year after *Rituals* in 1984 and like the later work *The Knight has Died* (1990),[15] it is about the daunting challenge of writing fiction. Both metafictional works feature two writers who are friends. Because of this similarity I shall discuss them together in this section of the chapter. This pair of novels will also serve to make the point that the structure of Nooteboom's English oeuvre does not make it possible to track the author's trajectory as a writer without recourse to the dates of first publication in Dutch. These are of course not difficult to come by, but there are no references to such facts in the English reception of Nooteboom, which serves to reinforce the impression that readers of English translations give little or no thought to source texts or to a translated author's literary trajectory. There is a kind of randomness to the order of works which is dictated by the exigencies of publishing schedules, marketing requirements, or translators' availability and prefer-

---

13   *Rituals*, 43.

14   Cees Nooteboom, *A Song of Truth and Semblance*, trans. Adrienne Dixon (Baton Rouge: Louisiana State University Press, 1984).

15   Cees Nooteboom, *The Knight has Died*, trans. Adrienne Dixon (Baton Rouge: Louisiana State University Press, 1990).

ences. Although I have decided here to be guided by the shared feature of writer-characters who are friends, this consideration is no doubt reinforced by my overall understanding of Cees Nooteboom as a novelist acquired through knowledge of the Dutch works. The effect of discussing *The Knight has Died* and *A Song of Truth and Semblance* at this point, thus deviating from the texts' order of appearance in English, is to restore the original sequence in Dutch.

First published in Dutch in 1963, *The Knight has Died* occupies a particularly significant place in Nooteboom's primary career as a Dutch novelist. It was the long-awaited follow-up to the highly successful 1955 debut novel *Philip and the Others*. When the short novel appeared in Dutch it received mixed reviews: several reviewers praised Nooteboom's virtuosity and skill but objected to what they saw as the literariness of his writing style – not an attribute that was valued by the Dutch literary establishment at this stage. In fact one of them described the book as 'kitschy posing'.[16] None of the reviews I consulted, all in the major daily or weekly papers and magazines, considered the book to be a success, variously describing it as remarkable, problematic, or even a low point.[17] It is certainly the case that the charming novel of Nooteboom's youth could not have prepared them for this next stage in his development, which must explain some of the bewilderment when *De ridder is gestorven* – to give it its Dutch title – appeared. Ernestine Kossmann ascribes this reception – correctly, I think – to the fact that in 1963 there was no concept of a postmodern novel, and reviewers were approaching *The Knight has Died* with a modernist frame of reference.[18]

16　'[...] kitschige aanstellerij'. Ab Visser, 'Nooteboom en Heeresma vernieuwen het proza', in *De Telegraaf* (28 March 1963). Cited from LiteRom: <http://www.knipselkranten. nl/literom/> accessed 3 May 2011.

17　All these attributes are combined in the review by Jan Greshoff, 'De ridder is gestorven: Geconstrueerde chaos en oogverblindend vuurwerk'. In *Het Vaderland* (14 September 1963). Cited from LiteRom: <http://www.knipselkranten.nl/literom/> accessed 3 May 2011.

18　Ernestine Kossmann, 'Postmodern avant-la-lettre: Over De ridder is gestorven', 41–4.

This excursion into the novel's Dutch reception clearly shows that it was a challenging read in 1963, whereas by 1990 when the English version appeared postmodernism was well understood by reviewers. Having said this, it has not been possible to find any English reviews, and I suspect that the translation, which was published in the United States, did not circulate widely. It probably resides mainly in university libraries, as I have not found any evidence of it ever being released in paperback.

In my view *The Knight has Died* constitutes a key moment in the chronological narrative of Nooteboom's fiction in Dutch and merits particular attention, so I will give a fairly full reading of it. The two main characters are writers; one is dead and unsuccessful as a writer, the other is narrating the novel, having been set the task of completing the dead man's unfinished work. The story opens with an image that has become iconic of the postmodern novel's structure: eternal recession or return, frequently expressed in terms of Russian dolls or onion skins. Nooteboom treats his readers to a peculiarly Dutch version:

> I do not need to invent a plot; he has already done that. His book was to have been a book about a writer who died. Another writer finishes the dead man's book. A simple idea, like the nurse on the Droste cocoa cans: in her hand she holds a can on which is depicted a nurse holding ... And so I sit here with eternally receding writers, mine and his, who die with other writers at their heels who then complete their works, but who die, etcetera.[19]

This is a particularly sinister version of the postmodern plot structure because it suggests that our storyteller must also die. On the face of it *The Knight has Died* could be said to have a rather traditional structure: the first and last short chapters provide the framing narrative which encloses the unnamed narrator's literary memorial to the dead André Steenkamp. It presents a figuration of a writer who never actually delivers the goods, but who has the vision, or sensibility of a writer: 'He died before he became a writer, or because he had to become a writer but could not.' The narrator constructs his memorial to enable his friend to 'vanish forever to the realm

---

19   *The Knight has Died*, 1.

of the heroes'.[20] The idea of repetition hangs in the air until the final framing chapter when the narrative returns to the current narrator's time of writing.

> this book was his idea; my lesser nerves, my smaller capacity for the extreme, for what he called suffering, complete it. Exactly in the way he foresaw and intended it. For while I was writing the last chapter, I began to wonder more and more often whether he had not deliberately shunted me onto this track: he starts on a book about a writer who writes about a writer who dies before he has completed the book about the dead writer. André Steenkamp did not manage to finish his book, but with my help he brings it off after all, for he knew exactly to whom to leave his papers. Of course, it is rather a drastic way of writing books, but with the help of someone like me he succeeded.[21]

But at the very last minute the narrator struggles free: 'I free myself from your deadly embrace and put you away. It has not happened. I am the one who flees.'[22]

The eternal return is better conceived of as a narrative of becoming: Steenkamp becomes the unnamed narrator's writer-character, an ultra-manipulative and insane individual whose extreme way of life leads to an ambiguous death-cum-suicide. In this way, he can be laid to rest in the new narrative created by Nooteboom's nameless avatar. The dead writer struggled to translate his artistic impulse into literature; the living writer harbours no illusions: he knows that his André Steenkamp is a construction and – not without irony – he highlights the very different temperament required to produce fiction, which he himself possesses: 'my (so much healthier!) powers of observation'; acting 'out of the crudest opportunism'; 'thanks to the temporary German thoroughness that I have adopted for his sake'. Not much agony and ecstasy here. In fact the narrator describes himself as enjoying the present, referring to his 'irrepressible happiness'.[23] And there is a moment in the book when he emphasizes the ironic distance from his friend in one of his frequent asides on the character he is constructing: '[This

---

20   *The Knight has Died*, 2.
21   *The Knight has Died*, 100.
22   *The Knight has Died*, 102.
23   *The Knight has Died*, 2; 12.

exclamation mark is not included within the quotation marks employed by me. There is no question of irony in these notes of his. Poor A.S.].'[24]

Not only does André Steenkamp become a writer in our narrator's fictional world, our narrator also embarks on a process of becoming: from servant of the manipulative Steenkamp to resistant writer who refuses the misguided and sentimental task of making a hero of André and who allows his own prose to take flight. This short novel has also been interpreted as a transformation on the part of the author, a laying to rest of the romantic, sentimental self that was the young Nooteboom. In an assessment of Nooteboom as a writer, the Dutch academic Harry Bekkering cites the author on this subject:

> I had to rid myself of him, the Nooteboom of *Philip and the Others.* I started out with more talent than sense and with more sentiment than concept, an accidental beginning really. The boy who wrote that was a sentimental, soft character. ... From this has emerged someone who I know better, at any rate.[25]

But according to Bekkering in the same article, the literary diagnosis of Steenkamp's malaise is that he had not determined his writerly stance, had not worked out where he stood on the relation between fiction and reality. The title of Nooteboom's next metafictional work suggests that this is still a preoccupation: *A Song of Truth and Semblance.*

This short novel – a novella really – is interspersed with conversations between two writers: 'the writer' and 'the other writer', whose names we never learn. It is clear from the start that it is 'the writer' who is the protagonist, and he is the one who is uncertain about his role and his technique. He 'invents' two characters on the spot simply in order to carry on a conversation with the other writer, who is ironized from the very first page as a proponent of the dominant concept of writing as a craft or the writer as godlike creator in control of his creation. This immediately calls to mind

24 *The Knight has Died,* 67. The square brackets are the author's.
25 Harry Bekkering, '"In mijn boeken is, behalve het verzinsel, niets verzonnen"' in Harry Bekkering, Daan Cartens and Aad Meinderts, eds, *Ik had wel duizend levens en ik nam er maar één!* (Amsterdam and Antwerp: Atlas, n.d.), 15.

Nooteboom's fellow-writer Harry Mulisch, and I take it as a comment on the literary scene in Amsterdam in the early 1980s. 'The writer'-character's rather superficial approach is a key postmodern feature that Bart Vervaeck links to the novella's very title:

> The nietzschean idea which sees depth on the surface can be found in most postmodern novels. The question of the transition from superficial appearance to real depth is central to *A Song of Truth and Semblance*. The writer sees reality as the semblance of truth and literature as truthful semblance.[26]

The narrative of *A Song of Truth and Semblance* adopts a slightly weary, knowing tone and if it is subtly mocking of 'the other writer' its treatment of 'the writer' is also gently ironic.

> There is something indescribably sad about writers alone in their studies. Sooner or later the moment arrives when they start to have doubts about what they are doing. It would perhaps be strange if it were not so. As a person gets older, reality becomes more obtrusive and at the same time less interesting because there is so much of it. Is it really necessary to add anything? Must the invented be piled on top of the existing merely because someone, in his youth when he had little experience of what is called reality, invented some pseudo-reality and was consequently called a writer?[27]

There is an element of autobiographical 'truth' here, to judge by the echoes of remarks that Nooteboom has made about himself.[28]

The two characters in search of a novel (the colonel and the doctor) gradually take shape before the reader's and the writer's eyes, as does the novella, since the writing process is also represented in the text. At last, in Chapter 4, readers are allowed to enter the inner story, finding themselves in a deeper layer of fiction so that they can read in the familiar traditional manner, believing that the colonel and the doctor are real men, until the end of Chapter 7 when the narrative stops abruptly, marking the spot where the writer had been interrupted by '[t]elephone, someone at the door, a bout of flu, then a lecture somewhere, a two-month trip to Spain'.

26 Vervaeck, *Het postmodernisme in de Nederlandse en Vlaamse roman*, 115.
27 *A Song of Truth and Semblance*, 3.
28 See, for example, Chapter 2 of this book, the section 'Nooteboom on Nooteboom'.

Wilfully banal, with no attempt to cover up the interruption or smooth it over, the writing process emerges as the main focus of the novella. Whether it is authentic or not, the reader will never know, as the narrator himself points out, but the demystifying effect remains the same.

> The reader (the reader!) would never know about those intervening months, would never know that the random word he would now write in order to continue the story was not the word (was probably not the word) he had intended to write four months earlier.[29]

This passage also reveals the large gap between 'the writer' at this point in the story and the narrator of Nooteboom's published text, because the readers do now know – the artifice is exposed. Another stage has been reached in the representation of the writer-character's journey of becoming: from potential (André Steenkamp) to achievement (the narrator) in *The Knight has Died* and from purveyor of illusion (the other writer) to ironic commentator and revealer of the novelist's hidden arts (the writer) in *A Song of Truth and Semblance*.

The writer-character's unassuming stance enables him to undergo a nomadic transformation. He is now in Rome to finish his story about the colonel and the doctor and is so receptive to the impressions of that city that he is forced to rethink his notion of time:

> Even the traces among which he was walking now, which put these wandering thoughts into his mind, were no older than a few thousand years, and they would wear away and disappear like the earth itself. Only time would continue to exist. Or would that vanish as well? But then nothing would have ever existed. Slowly he walked down the steps of the Campodoglio, to regain the Forum by a roundabout route.
>
> It was this notion, more than any other thought or figment of the imagination, that made him and the whole world fictitious, because everything was being undermined by future nonexistence.[30]

The boundaries between fact and fiction had already been fuzzy, but now they are erased and 'the writer' has attained a kind of nomadic

---

29   *A Song of Truth and Semblance*, 21.
30   *A Song of Truth and Semblance*, 65.

sensibility which separates him both from his earlier self – the one that set out to create a historical fiction about the colonel and the doctor – and from 'the other writer'. So his destruction of the work in progress comes across as the next step in his nomadic transformation. The closing chapter achieves a mood of lightness that will characterize Nooteboom's two subsequent novels: *In the Dutch Mountains* (1987) and *The Following Story* (1993). This final chapter of *The Song of Truth and Semblance* celebrates the writer's escape from the clutches of the Dutch literary establishment, and at the same time reminds the reader of the important insight that time is real, though not linear and continuous. It does this by means of intertextual reference not to philosophy or literature: a limerick does the trick:

There was a young lady named Bright
Who traveled much faster than light
She left home one day
In a relative way,
And came home the previous night.

Without being able to explain it, he knew that something like this had happened to him. But to whom could he have explained it if he did not understand it himself?[31]

In the Dutch Mountains is a playful short novel of transformations. It continues the nomadic becomings with a writer-protagonist for whom writing is a holiday, a form of retreat from the character's more prosaic day job of roads inspector. This is also a highly intercultural novel which foregrounds translation and travel. For the first time, the writer and narrator character is not a Dutchman: he is a Spaniard who has lived in the Netherlands, and the novel he is writing is a transformative portrait of the Netherlands that is both critical and affectionate. He creates his work of fiction by means of another transformation, this time of the fairytale 'The Snow Queen'. The main characters, Kai and Lucia, are Dutch cabaret artists whose act has become rather unfashionably dated. In a way, they are doubly distorted representations – of a Dutch man and woman, and of the familiar fairytale characters. They also represent the perfect couple. Through this couple, the

31   *A Song of Truth and Semblance*, 81.

novel shows perfection to be stultifying, and thanks to Kai's abduction by the snow queen both he and Lucia undergo transformative experiences. So although *In the Dutch Mountains* still continues with the writer-character, this novel is altogether different, creating as it does a nomadic world of becomings, not only for the fictional characters, but also for texts which are happily reused to form a new set of meanings.

For the first time, the writer-character is also the narrator of the tale. Alfonso Tiburon de Mendoza, has succeeded in avoiding the angst displayed by earlier writer-characters by seeing writing as an act rather than an identity or calling: 'I like writing but I don't want to live as a writer.'[32] To emphasize the performative aspect of his approach to writing, the narrative shows him composing his story during the school holidays when he is given access to a primary school where he sits at an undersized desk and 'plays' at writing. Far from tearing up his manuscript like the writer in *A Song of Truth and Semblance*, he celebrates the completion of his story with a solitary game of hopscotch in the school playground.

> I felt a ridiculous, uncontrollable urge to play hopscotch. I resisted briefly, but it was three o' clock in the morning and no one could see me in the school playground. I went outside, looked at the squares and realized that I did not know how to play, but I didn't care.
>
> Suddenly I jumped, the way you jump into the sea for the first time in the summer, into the first square, on one foot, and moved with a little skip to the next square. I didn't know what I was doing, but I was happy.[33]

The climax of the novel is the becoming-child of a middle-aged roads inspector, brought about by the completion of the story he has been writing throughout the novel. The man discovers a new dimension of his subjectivity: the ability to engage in the activity of hopping and skipping, and to experience joy. This new or rediscovered element of himself entails both physical and mental lightness. What process has engendered

---

32   Cees Nooteboom, *In the Dutch Mountains*, trans. Adrienne Dixon (Harmondsworth: Viking Penguin, 1987), 73–4.

33   *In the Dutch Mountains*, 127.

this becoming-child? What aspect of story-writing? He has succeeded in turning both the world of the fairy story and the representation of reality upside-down.

Here again, Nooteboom has used a framing narrative – that of Tiburon – and in the inner narrative – the story Tiburon is writing – he dismantles the fairy tale of the snow queen. In his commentary, Tiburon makes his dislike of the genre clear when he compares fairy tales and myths:

> Fairy tales are written by people – that is what is wrong with them. Myths are washed up, written by no one, and only later written down. ... Perhaps in some mysterious way myths were invented by all of us together. But why should someone write fairy tales? Because reality is unbearable? Myths were not written by anyone – it must have something to do with that. The writing of fairy tales is a false longing for the writing of myths, and therefore a longing to be no one, or to be a whole people ...[34]

The whole of the short Chapter 20 is a critique of fairy tales, the main points being:

> Fairy tales are one-dimensional stories. ... Fairy tales are closed systems, that is what makes them so terrifying. ... Everything always tallies; a writer has nothing to seek there. The outcome is fixed, the characters have only one dimension, no lies can be told except in such a way that everyone notices it.[35]

Tiburon rewrites 'The Snow Queen' keeping the same main characters: boy, girl and wicked queen. In the fairy tale the boy is stolen by the queen and rendered a total prisoner until the girl through her devotion and determination tracks him down and dislodges the glass splinter that had kept him in thrall to the queen. Boy and girl are reunited and return home. Their lives can now be resumed and go on as before. Tiburon's girl loses track of time and abandons the search for the boy while enjoying herself with another man – so when she and Kai are eventually reunited, it is no reward for virtue. Meanwhile, Kai has been the Snow Queen's sex slave with never a thought for Lucia. Eventually, when the splinter leaves

---

34 *In the Dutch Mountains*, 94–5.
35 *In the Dutch Mountains*, 100.

Kai's eye thanks to a blow on the head, he experiences double pain since he can now also feel the loss of Lucia. One of the gangsters who have been holding Kai releases him when the game is up (they are surrounded by police), and a fairy godmother figure leads Lucia to Kai. The final showdown is a gruesome one resulting in three dead bodies, including that of the fairy godmother. Kai and Lucia escape, but the story pointedly does not say that they lived happily ever after. During the course of the tale, the perfect couple who were perfectly happy have witnessed traumatizing violence and been unfaithful to one another. Nooteboom, in the guise of Tiburon, has turned the fairy tale on its head and has the last laugh: 'And I sat there happily ever after.' (*In the Dutch Mountains*, 128)

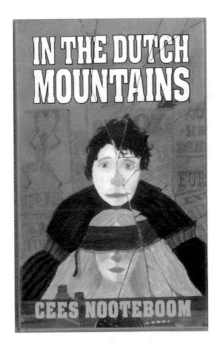

Figures 2a and 2b Contrasting covers: *In the Dutch Mountains* and its Dutch counterpart *In de Bergen van Nederland* (reproduced by kind permission of Arbeiderspers publishing house).

In an essay on contemporary versions of 'old tales', A.S. Byatt writes about *In the Dutch Mountains* together with *The Following Story* which came out in English in 1993. But before I go on to discuss Byatt's reading, the structure of Nooteboom's English oeuvre merits a comment: in the intervening years between the publication of *In the Dutch Mountains* in 1987 and *The Following Story* in 1993, two other short works of fiction by Nooteboom appeared in English: the translation of his first novel *Philip and the Others*, and *The Knight has Died*, which has just been discussed above. This causes problems for the study of the connection between a literary work and its creator. The link to a writer's life emphasizes the embodied nature of subjectivity which therefore exists in and through time. In seeking to describe Nooteboom's trajectory as a writer, I therefore take the structure of the Dutch oeuvre because of its direct link with the author, while at the same time basing my readings of the texts on the English versions.

The Following Story also has a writer as I-narrator, but this time emphatically not a literary character: Herman Mussert writes travel guides. In 'Old Tales, New Forms' Byatt sees *The Following Story* as 'a collection of stories about and against death.'[36] In her introduction in which she bases herself on Calvino's *Six Memos for the Next Millennium*, she identifies certain formal qualities of tales that she thinks are characteristic of the contemporary works she will discuss and that connect them to the old tales. 'He [Calvino] likes the economy, the rhythm and the hard logic of the tales, he says, the stories within stories that show the relativity of time, what he calls the "laconic" tone of them.'[37] At the same time, this description can be used to highlight the shift that has taken place in Nooteboom's writing: the anguish or the frustration and destruction of *A Song of Truth and Semblance* and *The Knight has Died* have made way for the laconic tone of the two short novels currently under discussion. Death and destruction are still present in *In the Dutch Mountains*, but they are contained, made safe, by the framing tale of Tiburon. In Nooteboom's case the laconic element

36   A.S. Byatt, *On Histories and Stories* (Cambridge, MA: Harvard University Press, 2001). See Chapter 4, 'Old Tales, New Forms', 136.
37   Byatt, *On Histories and Stories*, 129–30.

seems to operate beyond the tone, almost becoming a structuring principle. The novel's lightness and quickness come from the way it captures a significant event in the life of a character, like Lucia's sexual encounter with another man, in few words that hint at richness of experience:

> Sometimes a ray of light fell vertically. Then she looked up to see how his head was lit by that ray, and he saw it and smiled from his suddenly more radiant face and pretended to grasp the ray. He whispered 'God' to the light and 'God' as he touched her shoulder or her breasts and 'God' while lifting up a leaf...
> God. That was something she had never concerned herself with, but he said it so often and always with that hum in his voice, so that now, when she looked at water or at a bird, she, too, softly and cautiously, without moving her lips, muttered that odd, short word with which he sealed things. How long had this been so?[38]

And the way Lucia experiences time is relative – at this point it ceases to matter altogether.

The Following Story again combines brevity with richness, particularly of texture, since the text is full of allusions. Take the opening page which in one paragraph places the text in a web of other texts, here Kafka's *Metamorphosis* and Proust's *In Search of Lost Time*. Again, it is laconically done, avoiding grandiosity.

> I had woken up with the ridiculous feeling that I might be dead, but whether I was actually dead, or had been dead, or vice versa, I could not ascertain.

And a little further on in the same paragraph:

> And evidently I was still somewhere: pretty soon it would also become apparent that I could walk, look around, eat (the sweetish mother's-milk-and-honey taste of those little buns the Portuguese have for breakfast lingered in my mouth for hours).[39]

Although everything in this narrative is connected with death, there is a paradoxical quickness and lightness, which I see as connected to a nomadic sensibility. Death, in nomadic thinking, is a becoming-imperceptible. At the

---

38   *In the Dutch Mountains*, 101–2.
39   *The Following Story*, 5.

same time, it is possible to describe *The Following Story* as a cliché in novel form, the cliché that your life flashes before you at the point of death. Byatt cites Walter Benjamin on this point, who 'in his essay on "The Storyteller" points out that a man's life becomes a story at the point of death' going on to say that *The Following Story* uses 'the frame of the journey as a shared space for storytelling.'[40]

During the course of the novel the dying Herman Mussert in bed in Amsterdam becomes himself as he was twenty years before; a classics teacher, also known as Socrates. When asked by the biology teacher who was to become his lover to tell her what he thinks 'we' humans are, he replies: 'A cluster of composite, endlessly altering circumstances and functions which we address as "I". What else can I say? We act as if it is fixed and unchangeable, but it changes all the time until it is discarded.'[41]

The man born Herman Mussert does not reveal a fixed identity, but rather a multiple, nomadic subjectivity signalled up to a point by his aliases: Socrates the schoolteacher, and Dr Strabo the travel guide writer. Lisbon is the location for the period of greatest intensity in this loner's life – his unlikely love affair with the biology teacher. In the end, a fight in the playground between Socrates and the biology teacher's husband (another teacher) loses Mussert his job, and results in the death of a pupil and injury to the husband in a car crash after the fight. It was after this that Dr Strabo's wanderings began.

The novel enacts a becoming; it narrates death as a process of becoming: in this case, becoming-imperceptible. In Lisbon, Mussert embarks on a boat (another cliché, and storytelling device) where during the crossing the passengers each tell their own story of dying, all the time becoming imperceptible:

> Our bodies seemed undecided as to whether they wanted to be there; I had seldom seen a group of people with so much missing, every now and again entire knees, shoulders, feet disappeared from view, but our eyes were not in the least disconcerted,

---

40 Byatt, *On Histories and Stories*, 132, 137.
41 *The Following Story*, 44.

they filled in whatever was missing whenever things got too bad, sought out the eyes of the others, as if thereby to exorcise the threat of wholesale disappearance.[42]

In this fictional world, death is a positive process in which the physical body is left behind for a dreamt or remembered body. Helped by the novel's title, its ending:

> And then I told her, then I told you
> the following story

creates the impression that this is the story that has just been read. So the novel offers the possibility of eternity through the return to the beginning of the narrative. Nooteboom represents death as the discarding of the physical body which goes its own way becoming molecules and atoms. Death is also the end of the narrating self as an embodied subject. What remains is the text, this slim novel representing what Braidotti, speaking of the mind, calls a 'synthesis between reason, the memory and the imagination.' Put more simply, again quoting Braidotti, 'It makes the subject into something that "will continue to have been"'[43] in stories and memories.

Writing about writing has become writing about the creative or artistic impulse in *All Souls' Day* (2001), where the central character is a filmmaker, Arthur Daane. Distance from the familiar writer-character is also emphasized through the use of third person narration. Daane and the young woman he has a relationship with are both Dutch, but the novel is set in Berlin and Spain.[44] The tone of this novel is elegiac and the laconic form has been replaced by lengthy musings on the part of the main character, and lengthy intellectual discussions between Daane and his friends in Berlin. The dead, past acts of destruction, and the traces of history are all accepted as part of the present in the same way that the Catholic feast of All Souls is a celebration of past lives by the living. This stance in which the pain of loss and destruction is embraced as part of the present, is what

---

42 *The Following Story*, 85.
43 Braidotti, *Transpositions*, 240 (both citations).
44 For a discussion of Nooteboom's knowledge and experience of Berlin and Spain, see Chapter 6 on the travel writing.

enables a nomadic becoming. Rather than live in the shadow of the past, which in the case of Daane means longing for his dead wife and son, lost in a plane crash, bringing the past into a dynamic confrontation with the present is part of a process of renewal.

Daane makes documentaries and TV programmes to earn a living, and has his own nomadic project which is to film the in-between: twilight, the grey zone between night and day, day and night.

> Whenever anyone asked him what he did with all that footage, he found it hard to come up with an honest answer, or at any rate one he was willing to articulate. No, it wasn't the tag end of something else. No, it wasn't part of a project, unless you wanted to call his whole life a project. ... Half an hour later he emerged from the U-Bahn at Potsdamer Platz: the place Victor had brought him to after their first meeting, the place where he'd had his first lesson on Berlin. No one who had seen this city when it was divided could ever forget what it had been like. Could not forget, would not be able to describe it, not be able to tell the real story. Here he was now, alone, out on the hunt, but for what? For something he'd seen then and would never see again? Or perhaps for what had been there before, familiar to him only from photographs?[45]

He shares his footage with a philosopher friend who points out that Arthur has put himself in the film in the form of a shadow, but with the camera invisible.

> 'An invisible signature. But that's a paradox.'
> 'You noticed it, didn't you?'
> 'Is it because you want to go on living after you're dead?'
> No it seemed logical, but that wasn't it.
> When nobody knew or noticed his presence, that's when he would no longer be there, would become part of all that had vanished. But you could hardly say you wanted to disappear along with the rest when you were putting together a collection to save them all, could you?[46]

Here Nooteboom imagines becoming-imperceptible as an art form.

45 *All Souls' Day*, 52–3.
46 *All Souls' Day*, 65.

The nomad, as Braidotti expresses it, 'stands for the relinquishing and deconstruction of any fixed identity and resists settling into socially coded modes of thought and behaviour. It is the subversion of a set of conventions that defines the nomadic state, not the literal act of travelling.'[47] Arthur Daane may travel a great deal, but his nomadic state in the philosophical sense described by Braidotti is beyond doubt. Not only has he left the conventional Dutch way of life behind, as a film-maker he also resists the conventions for making a meaningful film. And though his sexual encounter with and emotional attachment to the research student Elik Oranje may be normatively heterosexual, their pairing resists any traces of a patriarchal pattern of behaviour.

The travel that comes with Arthur's work brings more complexity to his life and to his subjectivity. During the novel he films in Estonia and Japan. The removal to another culture is described as stepping into another life, becoming another person who is at the same time still Arthur. The climax of the novel happens when Arthur goes to Spain in search of Elik Oranje and is the victim of a violent street attack which leaves him in hospital with head injuries. It also marks the culmination of a process of becoming, this time a kind of becoming-woman. Actually, Arthur's actions and interactions in the novel reveal no overtly masculinist tendencies at all – he has all but 'become-woman'. During the healing process he abandons the last vestige of traditional manly behaviour: he frequently cries openly in the hospital; and when his friends come to visit, he weeps, he sheds tears.

There is an extraordinary epilogue to the novel in which Arthur, having recovered, is on his way back from Spain. The mood is quiet, almost expectant. We have reached the point where Arthur Daane's personal film project, his temporary relationship with Elik Oranje, and his recovery from physical trauma take his nomadic subjectivity beyond becoming-woman to the point of becoming-animal. Here is the penultimate paragraph of *All Soul's Day*:

47   Rosi Braidotti, 'Difference, Diversity and Nomadic Subjectivity', 2002: <http://women.ped.kun.nl/cbt/rosilecture.html> accessed 1 October 2010.

Evening had set in. It wasn't quite dark yet. The man came out of the inn and walked down to the river. He began filming something, though it was hard to see what it might be, unless it was the dancing light as the sun's last rays bounced off the water, silvery glints that slowly dissolved in the approaching twilight. After that he went back inside. In the night he was awakened by a desperate wail, a hoarse cry that answered itself and was so unmistakably mournful that our language even has a separate verb for it, so that the man in the inn wanted to throw his arms around the donkey's neck and comfort him.[48]

In *All Souls' Day* there is no framing narrative, but since narrative complexity is one of the main characteristics of Nooteboom's fiction, it is important to investigate how it is achieved in this novel. Several of the works already discussed have a woven structure where the act of writing is interwoven with the writer-character's creation, whether it be transformed fairy tale, another writer's life or two characters searching for a story. The main narrative of *All Souls' Day* is interrupted from time to time; what is new is that the interruption is unconnected with the main figure and his creativity. It is an angelic voice apparently from the angels who watch over human beings. The angelic perspective is all-seeing but the opposite of omnipotent since the angels are powerless to intervene. Like Benjamin's 'angel of history', they are not subject to linear time, and can see all of Berlin's turbulent and violent history whereas the characters in the narrated present can only see the traces of the past. Though powerless to intervene, the angels do take an interest in Arthur and Elik, almost too close an interest. Though at first glance they may seem like a literary translation of Wim Wenders' film 'Wings of Desire' there is no suggestion that these textual angels could, like their counterparts in the film, choose to join the humans and forsake their angelic perspective.

Nooteboom's most recent work of fiction in English, *Lost Paradise* (2007), is prefaced by a quotation from Benjamin's 'On the Concept of History' in which he takes the Paul Klee painting *Angelus Novus* as inspiration for the angel of history:

---

48   *All Souls' Day*, 337–8.

His face is turned toward the past. Where we perceive a chain of events, he sees one single catastrophe which keeps piling wreckage and hurls it in front of his feet. The angel would like to stay, awaken the dead, and make whole what has been smashed. But a storm is blowing in from Paradise; it has got caught in his wings with such violence that the angel can no longer close them. The storm irresistibly propels him into the future to which his back is turned, while the pile of debris before him grows skyward. The storm is what we call progress.[49]

And instead of a film, the work of art which is presented in *Lost Paradise* is Deborah Warner's 'The Angel Project', an innovative theatre event first put on in Perth, Australia in 2000, in which actors play angels located all over the city. The audience members must seek them out.

Lost Paradise is perhaps the most narratologically nomadic of Nooteboom's fictional works, enacting Deleuze's first step to becoming minor: becoming woman. It all happens in the first few pages of the novel. After the quotation from Benjamin, the author himself, or a fictional avatar, is the first person narrator, an older writer with voyeuristic tendencies on a plane watching a young woman with a copy of a book: 'It's *this* book, a book out of which she is about to disappear, along with me.' This prologue is followed by Part 1 of the main narration which opens as follows: 'Someone left her house in Jardins one hot summer evening while the smell of jacarandas and magnolias filled the heavy humid air'[50] and continues in this anonymous female third person narration of a gang rape before switching to a first person woman narrator. The transitions are handled elegantly:

> what they were really saying was that it had all been her fault, when in fact the thing she did actually blame herself for was that humiliating lie about the cloud, because clouds don't rip your clothes off, men do. It is men who force their way into your body and into your life, leaving behind a puzzle that you will never be able to solve. Or rather that *I* will never be able to solve, since that someone was me.[51]

---

49   Cees Nooteboom, *Lost Paradise*, trans. Susan Massotty (London: Harvill Secker, 2007).
50   *Lost Paradise*, 6, 11.
51   *Lost Paradise*, 13.

Not only does the third person narrator shift to first, via the second person; but his gender changes from male to female in this part of the novel.

While it is not unknown for male writers to create a female protagonist, or even to give her her own voice through a first person narration, in the context of Nooteboom's work as a whole, I suggest that this is more than a narrative device; it is a philosophical practice – what I have chosen to call a nomadic becoming. By saying this, I am also suggesting that Nooteboom's actual writing amounts to this kind of technology of the self which is how Braidotti, following Michel Foucault, describes the process of learning to open oneself to multiplicity. In *Lost Paradise* Nooteboom has taken up a position that is no mere performance, but one that is convincingly situated in a female world of experience. By depicting male violence against women, he shows himself in tune with 'woman' who, in Deleuzian terms, is marginal in a patriarchal society. Moreover, when this character, Alma, reappears at the end of the novel, it is clear that she has not allowed herself to be intimidated by this sexual violence. She has developed her own subjectivity through a sexual encounter of her choosing in which she and a young aboriginal artist agree to stay together for one week, thus avoiding all the temptations to shape the other person. This is a free, light, encounter which is portrayed here as on perfectly equal terms; a coming together without expectations. This is apparently achieved because Alma chooses a man of Australian aboriginal background, and their complete otherness releases them from cultural pressures.

Alma, acting the part of an angel, encounters the Dutch literary critic Erik Zondag who responds immediately to the sight of the angel: he is struck dumb, rooted to the spot, and that night he cannot sleep. He returns the next day which is also the last of the performance, and waits until she is no longer performing the part before he speaks to her. She takes him along to the cast party, a rather banal, debauched beach party which is raided by the police. Erik experiences it all on a different, romantic, plane in which the bright lights expel him from the paradise of a kiss with the 'angel'. When the two of them meet again by chance in Austria, Alma is firm that the encounter will not resume. Their short discussion is very revealing:

> She made a gesture, a flick of the wrist, as if she might be tossing away a theo-
> retical man.
>   'Where I am has never really mattered to me.'
>   'So you told me back then: "The world is my home." You know, that really turned
> me on.' He stood up and grabbed his bathrobe. He wanted to say something, but
> wasn't sure what. 'I fell madly in love with you.'
>   'I know, you were pathetically eager.'
>   'So you were laughing at me?'
>   'No, Just the opposite: I was terrified.'[52]

The portrayal of the generation gap between the middle-aged writer and
the young woman suggests that she has gained some wisdom; her cosmopolitan stance clearly appeals to the man, but she comes across as the more
mature of the two. For Erik she is as unreachable as if she had been an angel.

Lost Paradise was reviewed in the major American and English literary pages, a sign that Nooteboom is fully accepted as an important writer,
though not necessarily one who is widely known. Indeed, the reviewer
in The Washington Post (4 November 2007) refers to him in relation to
the Nobel Prize, while The New Statesman (12 July 2007), referring to the
title's obvious reference to Dante, describes him as having 'the reputation and the chutzpah to lay down a few gauntlets of this sort.' The most
substantial review is by J.M. Coetzee in The New York Review of Books (6
March 2008).[53] He states that he finds 'Nooteboom's tale of Alma and
her two lovers ... somewhat of a puzzle to interpret.' While attentive to
the philosophical dimension of the book, his problem seems to lie with
what he calls the 'thinness of the stories of Erik and Alma' which will
not support a complex interpretation. I disagree with Coetzee when
he describes Alma as Nooteboom's 'romantically inclined heroine': it
is the hero of the second part, Erik Zondag who in my account is the
romantic, and it is precisely his romanticism that comes between him
and Alma. When Coetzee complains that 'It is also hard to make sense of

52   Lost Paradise, 131.
53   J.M. Coetzee, 'Look Homeward, Angel' in The New York Review of Books, 6 March
     2008. Accessed 4 July 2011, www.mybooks.com/articles/archives/2008/mar/06/
     look-homeward.

her grounds for excluding the troubled Dutchman from the paradise he seeks in her arms, namely that angels cannot consort with human beings', he perhaps pays too little attention to the trauma in the character's past and the effect this has had on her approach to herself. To Nooteboom's credit, he created this young woman character-narrator, and the middle-aged writer-character who is shown in a less favourable light, so that it is possible to say that through giving the narrative voice to Alma, he has become woman.

Nooteboom's fiction is generally in novel form; some of the texts are very short and I have sometimes used the term novella, particularly in relation to *A Song of Truth and Semblance*, because it comes across as shorter, with a less well-developed main character, although the definition of 'novella' is somewhat hazy in English. Fitting in with genre conventions is not what postmodern writers are about; what is interesting is to see the many ways in which they subtly disregard or ignore such conventions. Nooteboom's fiction frequently hovers in the border territory dividing novel from novella, and his most recently published fictional work in English, *The Foxes Come at Night*, moves in the direction of an even shorter form: it is his first collection of short stories in English. In an interview on his English publisher's website, Nooteboom wryly comments that 'for once the blurb is right ... the stories are interconnected and could be read like a novel.'[54] There are eight stories of varying length; the longer ones, 'Heinz' and 'Paula' are divided in to numbered sections, or mini-chapters. They are all linked by the theme of death and loss, by their elegiac atmosphere, but not by their narrator. Told in the third person, 'Late September' and 'Last Afternoon' are complex portraits of bereaved older women who find ways of living with their loss: complex, because the man they have lost was both significant for them, but also part of a web of relationships with the tensions and conflicts that these engender. Suzy in 'Late September' takes some kind of comfort in the secret nocturnal visits of the waiter from a local bar who, at sixty-three, is younger than her. He provides sex, she gives

54   Interview with Cees Nooteboom: <http://maclehosepress.com/tag/the-foxes-come-at-night> accessed 7 July 2011.

him presents. In Nooteboom's hands, this story is not seedy; it radiates honesty, empathy and humanity, even if the characters themselves are not particularly admirable or likeable.

The remaining stories are all told by an I-narrator. With the exception of 'The Furthermost Point', this narrator is gendered male. He remembers friends, and in one case a stranger, who died prematurely. The title of 'The Furthermost Point' both describes the female narrator-character's unusual compulsion and the position of the story in the volume, and, for the time being, in Nooteboom's fictional oeuvre so far. At intervals the character treks to a remote headland on a Spanish island to dance and roar with the gale-force wind, the *tramontano*. And whereas in *Lost Paradise* we witness the narrative transformation from male to female narrator, in this story Nooteboom has become woman completely through and in his fiction. Several of the online reviews single out 'Heinz' as the story which made the greatest impression on them.[55] It is a harrowing tale of a Dutch honorary consul in Italy slowly drinking himself to death, characterized by the narrator's humane, if brutally honest account of this friend's decline. As I write, the stories are receiving their English reception. The collection was published in the United Kingdom in June 2011, and by the time of writing (end of July) it has received reviews in most of the significant publications: *The Times Literary Supplement*, *The Independent*, *The Guardian*, *The Financial Times*, *The Herald Scotland* and in Ireland *The Irish Times*. This coverage already suggests that Nooteboom is now well established in the English-speaking world, and the substance of the reviews confirms this. They are overwhelmingly positive, and start from a point of acceptance of Nooteboom simply as part of the literary scene. Alberto Manguel's title 'A meditation on the end of things from one of our most remarkable

---

55   For example: Louise Laurie on The Bookbag, a reviews website: <http://www.thebookbag.co.uk/reviews/index.php?title=The_Foxes_Come_At_Night_And_Other_Stories_by_Cees_Nooteboom_and_Ina_Rilke_%28Translator%29> accessed 25 July 2011; Ed Lake on The National Conversation, a news website for the United Arab Emirates and the Middle East: <http://www.thenational.ae/arts-culture/books/the-foxes-come-at-night-revel-in-the-poetry-of-pain> accessed 25 July 2011.

writers'[56] marks an important shift; through the use of the pronoun 'our' Nooteboom is explicitly counted among English-language writers. Manguel is most likely using what we might call the global 'we/our', thus including Nooteboom among world writers, with English functioning here as the language of global accessibility.

Galen O'Hanlon in the *Times Literary Supplement* notes 'resistance … to the demands of the short story. There is little reliance on drama, compression or intensification.'[57] This is, I think, what makes it possible for the stories in *The Foxes Come at Night* to be read as a meditation on death, loss and remembering. And I agree with the reviewers who find the book a positive, even 'oddly comforting' read.[58] However, this is where the affinity with nomadic philosophy as explained by Braidotti ends, since hers is very much a vitalistic philosophy, whereas Nooteboom's fiction taken as a whole balances between joy and lightness on the one hand and a sense of sadness and loss on the other. But the balance never tips in favour of nostalgia for the past: the novels end with a forward momentum and sense of renewal and continuation. If this is vitalism, though, it is vitalism in muted form.

56   Alberto Manguel, 'A meditation on the end of things from one of our most remarkable writers' on guardian.co.uk (22 July 2011): <http://www.guardian.co.uk/books/2011/jul/22/foxes-come-at-night-review> accessed 26 July 2011.

57   Galen O'Hanlon, 'Memories of Life', *Times Literary Supplement* (22 July 2011).

58   For example, Jonathan Gibbs, review of *The Foxes Come at Night* on independent. co.uk (8 July 2011): <http://www.independent.co.uk/arts-entertainment/books/reviews/the-foxes-come-at-night-by-cees-nooteboom-trans-ina-rilke-2308548. html> accessed 26 July 2011; Eileen Battersby, review of *The Foxes Come at Night* in *The Irish Times* (23 July 2011): <http://www.irishtimes.com/newspaper/weekend/2011/0723/1224301153694.html> accessed 26 July 2011; Colin Waters, review of *The Foxes Come at Night* in *Herald Scotland* (25 July 2011): <http://www.heraldscotland.com/arts-ents/fiction-reviews/cees-nootenboom-the-foxes-come-at-night-maclehose-1.1108492> accessed 26 July 2011.

Postscript: *Philip and the Others*

There is one significant novel that I have omitted from this account of Nooteboom's fiction in English: his very first novel *Philip en de anderen*. One reason for doing so is its lack of nomadic sensibility, even though Dutch critic Wam de Moor points to its intensity and vitalism.[59] The main character, Philip, travels through Europe in search of a particular young woman though finding her does not mean the end of his quest. It has been suggested that the novel contains the main themes of all the subsequent works of fiction, summarized as border crossings: between life and death, future and past, imagination and reality.[60] The novel's reception in the Netherlands was extremely positive, and it attracted attention by winning the Anne Frank Prize. Hugo Brems provides an explanation for the consensus among all the established critics who welcomed the novel's emphasis on following a dream, contrasting it with what they saw as the negative, unhealthy writing of Nooteboom's contemporaries.[61] In short, Nooteboom appealed to the older generation because of a lack of gritty realism in *Philip en de anderen*. Not that this promising beginning meant that Nooteboom was assured of a smooth path as a fiction writer in the Netherlands – far from it, in fact: as we saw, the subsequent reception of his novels was somewhat coloured by prejudice against his work as a travel journalist, but was probably also prompted by the uncomfortable, experimental subject-matter and mode of writing. That *Philip en de anderen* did not appear in English translation was no doubt due to the general lack of enthusiasm in the Netherlands for Nooteboom's work. But once *Rituelen* had won the Pegasus Prize which funded its translation into English and had done well, Louisiana State University Press published both *A Song of*

---

59   Wam de Moor, 'Gedichten over het nooit meer strelen en slapen', in Daan Cartens, ed., *Over Cees Nooteboom. Beschouwingen en interviews* ('s-Gravenhage: BZZTôH, 1984), 35.
60   See Grüttemeier and Leuker, eds, *Niederländische Literaturgeschichte*, 286.
61   Brems, *Altijd weer vogels die nesten beginnen*, 156.

Truth and Semblance and *In the Dutch Mountains*, followed by *Philip and the Others*. The decision to translate the debut novel was prompted by its reissue in the Netherlands to celebrate its 25th anniversary, according to the cover flap. The work is presented as 'profound', 'poetic' and having a 'fairy tale quality', and like the Dutch critics of the 1950s, the cover emphasizes the main character's idealism: his 'quest to attain perfection, to transcend the limitations of his existence'.[62]

In German, the picture is very different: there are two translations of the novel – *Das Paradies ist Nebenan* (1958) and *Philip und die Anderen* (2003). The first version came out early enough to share in the momentum of its Dutch original. At any rate, it was certainly discussed on German radio in 1958, because Hermann Lenz refers to this radio review in a subsequent review of the 1992 paperback version in *Die Zeit*.[63] One of the book's most prominent readers is the philosopher and writer Rüdiger Safranski who was captivated by it as a young man, and who has contributed significantly to Nooteboom's status as an important writer in Germany.[64] In fact, according to the chapter on the postwar period in the recent German history of Dutch literature edited by Ralf Grüttemeier and Maria Leuker, Nooteboom's striking emergence in German literature was due to another influential German critic, Marcel Reich-Ranicki, praising Nooteboom highly on German television. What is more, Grüttemeier and Leuker highlight this moment as the turning point, not only for Nooteboom, but also for Dutch literature in Germany.[65]

What this short account of Nooteboom's first novel in translation in English and German shows, is how different and separate these afterlives of works in translation are. The fact that there are two German translations at all – *Das Paradies ist Nebenan/Philip und die Anderen* – is remarkable and a measure of the huge success of that book in Germany. How differently

---

62 Cees Nooteboom, *Philip and the Others*, trans. Adrienne Dixon (Baton Rouge: Louisiana State University Press, 1988), cover flap, back and front.

63 Hermann Lenz, review of *Das Paradies ist Nebenan* in *Die Zeit* (24 July 1992). <http:// www.zeit.de/1992/31/jugendtage> accessed 12 December 2012.

64 See Grüttemeier and Leuker, eds, *Niederländische Literaturgeschichte*, 288.

65 See Grüttemeier and Leuker, eds, *Niederländische Literaturgeschichte*, 236.

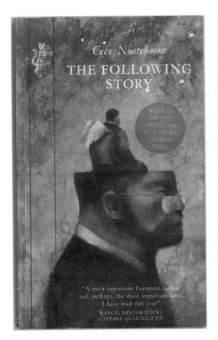

Figures 3a and 3b Contrasting covers: *The Following Story* complete with recommendation from Reich-Ranicki, published by The Harvill Press (reproduced by kind permission of The Random House Group Ltd) and its counterpart in Dutch, *Het volgende verhaal* (reproduced by kind permission of Arbeiderspers publishing house).

Philip and the Others has fared in English, scarcely attracting critical attention. J.M. Coetzee does not mention it in his essay 'Cees Nooteboom: Novelist and Traveller', preferring to concentrate here on *In the Dutch Mountains*. And Nooteboom's other champion in English, A.S. Byatt, discusses this same novel, together with *The Following Story*.

In nomadic philosophy the process of becoming is never completed, which leaves me wondering where Nooteboom's next work of fiction might take its readers. In my view, these readings of Nooteboom's fictional metamorphoses show that nomadism with its becomings and technology of self can be a useful framework for approaching certain literary works and oeuvres. In the next chapter I move on to look at Nooteboom's poetry in relation to the same nomadic ideas I have used to approach the fiction here. And whereas I have based most of my discussion in this chapter on translated work, the situation is reversed in what follows because so little of the poetry has been published in English. As I proceed through Part 2 of this book, questions of translation will gradually come to the fore. I conclude Chapter 5 with a comparison of three published versions of one poem by Nooteboom, and translation is the main focus of Chapter 6 which is devoted to the travel writing.

The Poetry:
'Like a Foreigner in One's Own Language'[1]

Cees Nooteboom is frequently described as seeing himself primarily as a poet. The website devoted to him and his work by his Dutch publisher De Bezige Bij presents him in this light: 'Cees Nooteboom is known mainly for his novels and his travel books. For the writer himself, however, poetry takes first place.'[2] In a short video clip on the same website Nooteboom puts this in his own words:

> Like so many I began with poems. I regard poetry as something so essential that, compared with prose or travel writing, it is simply something for oneself. To me, my life is unthinkable without poetry.[3]

Since Nooteboom has published much less of his poetry in English than his prose, this chapter will be structured differently from the previous one which took the English oeuvre as the basis for discussion. It takes the form of an intercultural experiment in which I first discuss the complete works in Dutch, together with their reception in the Dutch language area,

---

1   Gilles Deleuze.
2   'Cees Nooteboom geniet vooral bekendheid vanwege zijn romans en zijn reisboeken. Voor hem zelf echter komt de poëzie op de eerste plaats.' Unless otherwise stated, all translations from the Dutch in this chapter are mine. <http://www.ceesnooteboom. com/?page_id=224> accessed 12 August 2011.
3   'Ich hab' so wie viele mit Gedichte angefangen. Ich betrachte Poesie als etwas so essentiels daß sie neben Proza oder neben Reisliteratur ist einfach etwas für sich. Ohne Poesie ist mein Leben für mich undenkbar.' It can be argued that Nooteboom's primary audience is the German one, so his use of German is not particularly surprising. My transcription and translation. Source and date of access as above.

offering a reading of the poetry on the basis of the Dutch poems. Then I discuss the small body of work available in English, comparing the poet as he emerges from the English translations with the Dutch poet. I conclude with a different kind of comparison between three published English versions of one Dutch poem.

I will begin by placing Nooteboom the poet in the context of the Low Countries to show how his poetics have been at odds with the poetic tastes prevalent there. In the interaction with the Dutch-speaking literary world, Nooteboom's inner deterritorialization is evident: indeed this is one of the ways in which Nooteboom can be seen as a foreigner in his own language. It is this Deleuzian idea of deterritorialization which connects the poet to my nomadic project. Being out of tune with some literary critics in the Netherlands raises the question of whether Nooteboom's poetic practice is marginal to the dominant modes of poetic diction and so whether Nooteboom's poetry is in this sense a minor practice of a major language. As with my discussion of Nooteboom's fiction, I will again turn to nomadism for a philosophical approach which can open up the poetry to display many features of its poetic landscape, whether imaginative, affective or philosophical. However, in this chapter, I base my readings on the ideas of Deleuze himself rather than Braidotti.

On a practical note, although the poetry in Dutch forms the material for my discussion, I will provide bilingual examples, using published English versions if these are available and otherwise my own versions. In this case, translation functions as an adjunct to the Dutch text since my translations are made with the aim of reflecting the Dutch text. This is intended to solve the problem of readings and interpretations made on the basis of work in one language proving difficult to justify using the translated version. I know from personal experience that literary work in English translation does not always support a reading made using the Dutch text. As it happens, few of the Dutch poems selected for discussion here are available in a published English version so that the majority of the translations are already informed by my interpretations.

Nooteboom the poet is represented by one collection in English, *The Captain of the Butterflies* (1997), as well as translated poems which appear individually or in small groups in poetry magazines and anthologies. In the section on the poetry in English, I will characterize the poet as he comes across in English in the knowledge that this very reduced body of work is all that is accessible to his English audience. Nooteboom himself had some involvement in the project to create an English-language anthology, so this very partial and selective account of him as a poet is at least sanctioned by him. Finally I discuss two works which have attracted the attention of more than one translator. The poem 'Basho' has appeared in no fewer than three translations, while the book of prose poems called *Zelfportret van een ander. Dromen van het eiland en de stad van vroeger* (1993) has appeared in two different English versions. *Self Portrait of an Other* is the most recent of Nooteboom's poems to be translated, appearing in book form in early 2012 in a translation by David Colmer, having previously appeared in a literary journal in the US translated by Duncan Dobbelmann. These short prose pieces described as 'dreams' in the book's subtitle, are clearly designated prose poems on the book's cover.

The Reception of Nooteboom in the Low Countries

Although Nooteboom has not written about poetics, he has made statements about his feelings for and understanding of the purpose of poetry in conversations and interviews with critics. In a revealing interview with Frank van Dijl, for example, he makes it clear that he is not keen to 'theorize about poetry'.[4] He then responds openly to questions and suggestions, declaring himself to be against 'fear of the unreadable':[5] he does not think that readers should want to make immediate rational sense of what is written. Rather than rational analysis, he advocates reading as opening up not

---

4 'Ik heb vroeger ... nooit over poëzie willen theoretiseren', Frank van Dijl, '"Reizen is mijn manier van denken"', in Cartens, ed., *Over Cees Nooteboom: beschouwingen en interviews* ('s-Gravenhage: BZZTôH, 1984), 50.

5 '[...] angst voor het onleesbare', Van Dijl, '"Reizen is mijn manier van denken"', 52.

only to the poem, but also to the poet. And he wants an affective response. He rejects the description of his poems as 'hermetic': as long as a reader feels an emotion on reading a poem, it does not matter if he or she reads it differently from the way the poet had thought of it. He gives examples of uncooperative readings by a Dutch critic who fails to appreciate some of the meanings supplied from outside the words, in this case, by a knowledge of German romanticism. And he makes a connection between this rather restricted approach and the return of Dutch culture in the 1980s to a narrow-minded bourgeois respectability. He is wary of rhyme which is associated with this culture, and which he considers to consist of 'frequently highly dangerous forms, because the fact that they are superannuated can engender a kind of superannuated thought'.[6] Nooteboom's criticism of Dutch poetry as lacking in urgency and intensity reveals an important poetic value. Finally, he suggests life is a train of thought with poetry as a tangible outcome, and at the same time 'a meditation, a form of thinking'.[7]

There has often been an assumption outside the Netherlands that Nooteboom has found recognition as a poet among his Dutch colleagues, and from critics and commentators in the Low Countries.[8] For example, the first edition of the yearbook *The Low Countries* includes an overview of Nooteboom and his work, noting that 'Although Nooteboom regards himself as first and foremost a poet, *and has been acknowledged as such*, it was as a writer of prose that he first achieved really wide public recognition' (my italics).[9] On further examination this acknowledgement masks a mixed reception, but the domain of literary prizes delivers a clear and

6   '[...] vaak levensgevaarlijke vormen, omdat ze door hun ouderdom een soort ouderdom aan gedachten met zich mee kunnen brengen', Van Dijl, '"Reizen is mijn manier van denken"', 53.

7   '[...] een meditatie, een vorm van denken', Van Dijl, '"Reizen is mijn manier van denken"', 57.

8   Whereas in the previous chapter I was particularly concerned with the reception of Nooteboom's novels by his colleagues in the Netherlands, in this chapter, especially when discussing literary histories, I include histories written by Flemish critics and academics, hence the transnational term 'Low Countries'.

9   Frans de Rover, 'Cees Nooteboom', in *The Low Countries: Arts and Society in Flanders and the Netherlands 1993–1994* (Rekkem: Stichting Ons Erfdeel, 1993), 151.

positive message: Nooteboom has won the poetry prize of the City of
Amsterdam three times, in 1960, 1965 and 1970; and the Jan Campert Prize
in 1978. Given the complex reception Nooteboom has received at home
more generally, it is worth exploring how the poetry fares in more considered academic writing. I therefore undertook a short survey of the status
of his poetry in Dutch literary historiography, bearing in mind that those
behind these works are engaged in the construction of the national literary
canon. I first looked at the treatment of the poetry in a number of general
literary histories published since 1989.[10] Only Jaap Goedegebuure mentions Nooteboom's poetry with a few lines on the motif of disappearance.[11]
All the histories discuss poetry as a fundamental part of Dutch literature,
but Nooteboom is not generally reckoned to be one of the poets whose
work merits discussion. There are also a number of books devoted to the
genre of poetry in the period during which Nooteboom has been active as
a poet. Of the three on Dutch poetry by Hugo Brems, for example, only
one mentions Nooteboom, and then only as a writer of song lyrics.[12] And
Nooteboom is nowhere to be found in Redbad Fokkema's history of Dutch
poetry since 1945.[13] However, Nooteboom is mentioned accidentally, as it
were, in Yves T'Sjoen's collection of encounters with contemporary Dutch
poets, *Stem en tegenstem* (Voice and Countervoice). And then it is not his
poetry that is discussed, but the title of a volume of poetry, *Het gezicht van*

---

10 They are: Jaap Goedegebuure, *Nederlandse literatuur 1960–1988* (Amsterdam: De
Arbeiderspers, 1989); Ton Anbeek, *Geschiedenis van de Nederlandse literatuur 1885–
1985* (Amsterdam: De Arbeiderspers, 1990); Erica van Boven and Mary Kemperink,
*Literatuur van de moderne tijd : Nederlandse en Vlaamse letterkunde in de negentiende
en twintigste eeuw* (Bussum: Coutinho, 2006); Hugo Brems, *Altijd weer vogels die
nesten beginnen : geschiedenis van de Nederlandse literatuur, 1945–2005* (Amsterdam:
Bert Bakker, 2006); Theo Hermans, ed., *A literary history of the Low Countries*
(Rochester, NY: Camden House, 2009).

11 Goedegebuure, *Nederlandse literatuur 1960–1988*, 221.

12 Hugo Brems, *Al wie omziet: opstellen over Nederlandse poëzie 1960–1980* (Antwerp:
Elsevier Manteau, 1981); *De rentmeester van het paradijs: over poëzie* (Antwerp:
Manteau, 1986); *De dichter is een koe: over poëzie* (Amsterdam: Arbeiderspers, 1991).

13 Redbad Fokkema, *Aan de mond van al die rivieren: een geschiedenis van de Nederlandse
poëzie sinds 1945* (Amsterdam: Arbeiderspers, 1999).

het oog (Eyesight/The Face of the Eye) that finds its way into a poem by
another poet – Anton Korteweg. What is more, this title is considered by
Korteweg to be an example of one that undermines the desire to read the
poem itself.[14]

This brief survey creates a strong impression that Nooteboom is not
taken seriously as a poet in the Low Countries.[15] Fortunately the poet and
essayist Wiel Kusters is something of an exception, revealing himself to
be more open-minded than his colleagues with a talent for making connections across the work of many poets. For example in *De geheimen van
wikke en dille* (The Secrets of Vetch and Dill)[16] he discusses the theme of
presence and absence in relation to several Dutch-language poets notably Hugo Claus and Cees Nooteboom. There are also a small number of
edited volumes devoted to Nooteboom and his work including the poetry,
which I refer to throughout this book. To my knowledge, there is only one
monograph on the poetry in Dutch: *De tijd and het labyrinth: De poëzie
van Cees Nooteboom 1956–1982* (Time and the Labyrinth: The Poetry of
Cees Nooteboom 1956–1982) by Roger Rennenberg, published in 1982.
It offers a detailed interpretation of the poetic oeuvre at the time of writing, focusing on the major themes of death and time and emphasizing the
pessimistic nature of the poetry. There is much talk of Nooteboom's death
wish, of decay, futility, an absence of redemptive love, and the theme of
time is coupled with death. At the same time, Rennenberg's pronouncements tend to be absolute. For example: 'The poet senses the rhythm of
nature as alien. His basic thought is the following: the cycles will recur but
I will no longer participate in them.'[17] Perhaps as a result of his existential
approach Rennenberg is not open to the changing moods of the poet, or to

---

14   Yves T'Sjoen, *Stem en tegenstem: over poëzie en poëtica: dubbelessays over hedendaagse
     Nederlandstalige poëzie* (Amsterdam: Atlas, 2004), 223.
15   T'Sjoen and Brems are Flemish academics.
16   Wiel Kusters, *De geheimen van wikken en dille* (Amsterdam: Querido, 1988).
17   'De dichter voelt het ritme van de natuur als wezensvreemd aan. Zijn grondgedachte
     is de volgende: de cycli zullen zich wel herhalen maar ik zal er geen deel meer aan
     hebben.' Roger Rennenberg, *De tijd en het labyrint. De poëzie van Cees Nooteboom*
     ('s-Gravenhage: BZZTôH, 1982), 22.

the shape of a cycle of poems which subtly and constantly shifts the poet's and consequently readers' attitudes to the dominant themes.

In response to the opening lines 'ik besta in de wereld/en ik ben er niet' (I exist in the world/and I am not here) of a poem from *Het zwarte gedicht* (The Black Poem, 1960), Rennenberg introduces the interesting idea of the poet as a 'complete stranger, the literary version of the "displaced person"'.[18] But where I will relate this concept to Nooteboom's nomadism and investigate the extent to which his poetry displays Deleuzian lines of flight, Rennenberg accuses Nooteboom of a lack of solidarity with his fellows and a withdrawal into no-man's land. And when Rennenberg says that 'the logical unity of his self has been dissolved',[19] my response is that we are finally arriving at the key idea of multiple, nomadic subjectivity, whereas for Rennenberg we are on psychiatric territory. Of course a term like 'schizophrenic' is used and indeed revalorized by Deleuze, to embrace multiplicity, rather than fall back into the pathology of the split personality. Nooteboom often writes of himself as other, but as I shall argue, this can be seen as a (re)doubling; and there are a number of these other selves, or rather, elements of selfhood. I hope to show how the poetry shifts and changes the nature of these poetic selves and Nooteboom's own selfhood.

In the last chapter, I read the central male characters as fictional constructs. Even when I pointed out similarities with the author's own life, the characters were respected as complex literary creations with elements that relate to the author, though I would not go as far as Coetzee who views them as Nooteboom's avatars. In this chapter, I see the poetic personae, whether expressed as an 'I' or a 'he' as multiple and capable of referring to the poet's self (that is, the poet at the time of writing as the creator of the poem) as well as to others (which can include past selves and future becomings as well as other people).

18   Rennenberg, *De tijd en het labyrint*, 57. Rennenberg is here quoting Hans Meyerhoff's *Time in Literature* (Berkeley: University of California Press, 1960).

19   '[...] de logische eenheid van zijn ik is opgeheven', Rennenberg, *De tijd en het labyrint*, 88.

Nooteboom's Poetry in Dutch

I will begin this account of Nooteboom's poetic themes, preoccupations and trajectory with a largely chronological account of his career as a poet in Dutch. He has regularly published poems since 1956: eight collections of new poems, two volumes of collected poems and an anthology. The development of the poetic oeuvre has some interesting features. In the first eight years Nooteboom published four collections, *De doden zoeken een huis* (The Dead are Seeking a House, 1956), *Koude gedichten* (Cold Poems, 1959), *Het zwarte gedicht* and *Gesloten gedichten* (Closed Poems, 1964). In 1970, a volume entitled *Gemaakte gedichten* (Made Poems) appeared. It contains some new poems together with many old ones. Nooteboom apparently felt the need to explain the existence of *Gemaakte gedichten* in an afterword, emphasizing the practical nature of the undertaking:

> All the previous collections were out of print. That is the reason for this edition, and not any desire for a 'collected poems' or to take stock of my career.

This humble stance is tinged with a reluctance to acknowledge the earliest poetry:

> I hesitated about whether to include the poems from 'The dead are seeking a house'. And I did in the end, except for a few. The collection starts with the new poems 'Present, absent' and then continues backwards in time.[20]

This wariness also seems to explain the unusual decision to publish the poems in reverse chronological order of publication; the first collection

---

20 'Alle vroegere bundels waren niet meer verkrijgbaar. Dat, en niet het verlangen naar een verzameling of "afrekening" op zich, is de reden voor deze uitgave. Ik heb geaarzeld of ik sommige gedichten uit de "Doden (sic) zoeken een huis" nog op zou nemen. En heb dat tenslotte, op een paar na, toch gedaan. De bundel begint met de nieuwe gedichten "Aanwezig, afwezig" en gaat dan verder terug in de tijd.' Cees Nooteboom, 'Verantwoording', *Gemaakte gedichten* (Amsterdam: De Bezige Bij, 1970), 195.

is tucked away at the end of the book and reduced in size. Both these aspects are not only suggestive of distance – they create it. We know from Nooteboom's English foreword to his youthful work *Philip and the Others* that it seems so distant that it is as if it had been written by someone different.[21] This reverse order is also used in subsequent collected works.[22]

The period after *Gemaakte gedichten* was equally productive with three new collections of poetry: *Open als een schelp, dicht als een steen* (Open as a Shell, Closed as Stone, 1978), *Aas* (Bait, 1982) and *Paesaggi narrati* (Narrated Landscape, 1982), a collaboration with the graphic artist Jan Montijn. Soon afterwards yet another volume of collected works appeared – *Vuurtijd, ijstijd* (Fire Time, Ice Time, 1984) – this time with no previously unpublished poems. The volume contains all the poems published to date with the exception of those already omitted from the 1970 volume. The period following *Vuurtijd, ijstijd* sees two collections of poetry appear: *Het gezicht van het oog* (Eyesight/The Face of the Eye, 1989) and *Zo kon het zijn* (It Could Have Been Like This, 1999) as well as the book of prose poems *Zelfportret van een ander. Dromen van het eiland en de stad van vroeger* (*Self-Portrait of an Other*, 1993 in Dutch, 2012 in English). This time the new work is rounded off by an anthology of poems, *Bitterzoet: Honderd gedichten van vroeger en zeventien nieuwe* (Bittersweet: A Hundred Old Poems and Seventeen New Ones, 2000). Nooteboom's poetic oeuvre has one more distinctive feature: the large number of bibliophile editions of poetry, some fourteen according to one website,[23] none of which is listed on the author's website, and none of which is included in the Dutch collected works or the anthology.

Why spend so long listing and detailing the structure of Cees Nooteboom's body of published poems? Not only does this give a dynamic picture of the interaction between creation and reflection, a similar pattern can be seen in relation to the travel writing in the next chapter. When I speak of an oeuvre in this context, rather than something monolithic I mean a

---

21　See 'Preface' to *Philip and the Others*, v–vi.
22　Also pointed out by T'Sjoen, *Stem en tegenstem*, 227.
23　<http://www.schrijversinfo.nl/nooteboomcees.html> accessed 16 August 2011.

totality characterized by its multiplicity – with or without the bibliophile editions, with or without the poems Nooteboom translated, for example, and also a body of work that is constantly changing its mood and diction. And the poetry also has as many other lives as there are languages into which it is translated. For example, what to do about the fact that volume one of the collected works in German does not include *De doden zoeken een huis* and claims to include poems not available in Dutch?[24]

In what follows I will discuss Nooteboom's poetry in chronological order of publication in Dutch. As in the previous chapter, I use the chronology as a basic life framework in which to highlight changes, shifts, continuities and re-envisionings of the self rather than to adopt a linear approach. Again these re-envisionings are more than the poet's own journey as expressed in his poetry: readers encounter different versions of Nooteboom in different languages as the discussion of the English anthology will show. The shape of the poetic oeuvre given by the Suhrkamp collected works is different, and so is the poet who emerges from it: perhaps one with less of the youthful obsession with eros and thanatos thanks to the omission of *De doden zoeken een huis*. The version of the poet I present aims to be a panoptic one: I try to bring all the ages and stages of the poet into the present. And there is no doubt that the very early poems offer a distinctive poetic voice when compared with the voices of other Dutch poets of the 1950s, speaking as it does of a life of intensity at the extremes of existence expressed through the shared vocabulary of European culture. Sadly the English version of the poet is a much reduced one, which is why the main part of this chapter is formed by my readings of Nooteboom's poetry in Dutch which are arrived at in dialogue with some of the Dutch critics.

The poet and critic Adriaan Morriën identifies something unhealthy and feverish about the first two collections, *De doden zoeken een huis* and *Koude gedichten*, and speaks of the poet's lack of resistance to death:

---

24   Cees Nooteboom, *Gesammelte Werke*, Band 1: Gedichte (Berlin: Suhrkamp, 2003): <http://www.suhrkamp.de/buecher/gesammelte_werke_in_neun_baenden-cees_nooteboom_41561.html> accessed 16 August 2011.

Nooteboom's poetry is ravaged by a permanent concealed raised temperature, a feverishness that is responsible for the feeling of cold that turns his world to stone. Despite its basis of resistance, this defencelessness is so extreme that Nooteboom binds himself to, becomes one with death in his poetry.[25]

Morriën concludes that this stance forces Nooteboom to withdraw from the world of human beings. He also sees the motif of rain as symbolic of a position between life and death, something which he takes to be a negative position of 'impotent postponement and self-deception' – a harsh judgement on such a young poet. In keeping with my reading of *The Following Story* in the previous chapter as a fictional representation of death as becoming imperceptible, as a threshold to be crossed in the opening out of the self, I propose later on in this chapter to take a positive view of the poet's relationship to and with death.

Another Dutch critic Wam de Moor opens his assessment of the poetry collected in *Gemaakte gedichten* (1970) with a look back at *Philip and the Others*. He makes a crucial observation that sets the tone for a new reading of the poetry:

> At that time Nooteboom gave an almost ethereal account of an intensely experienced hitchhiking journey through Europe, simultaneously the romanticized story of a youth which was not fed by the usual pessimism, but by an almost awed vitalism.[26]

25   'De poëzie van Nooteboom wordt ... door een permanente verborgen temperatuurs-verhoging geteisterd, een koortsachtigheid die verantwoordelijk is voor het gevoel van koude dat zijn wereld doet verstenen. Ondanks het er aan ten grondslag liggende verzet gaat deze weerloosheid zo ver, dat Nooteboom zich in zijn poëzie met de dood verbindt en vereenzelvigt.' Adriaan Morriën, 'Poëzie geteisterd door temperatuurs-verhoging', originally published in 1959, reproduced in Daan Cartens, ed., *Over Cees Nooteboom: Beschouwingen en interviews* ('s-Gravenhage: BZZTôH, 1984), 27.

26   'Toen gaf Nooteboom het bijna etherisch verslag van een intens beleefde lifttocht door Europa, tegelijk het geromantiseerde relaas van een jeugd, dat niet door het gebruikelijke pessimisme, maar door een bijna beschroomd vitalisme werd gevoed.' Wam de Moor, 'Gedichten over het nooit meer strelen en slapen', first published in 1971, reproduced in Cartens, *Over Cees Nooteboom*, 35.

De Moor also emphasizes a positive aspect of the poet's isolation as being something from which he derives strength. And he makes an important comment on the last stanza of 'F.', a poem about a relationship that has ended from the cycle 'Aanwezig, afwezig' (1970). I will give the poem in its entirety, first in Nooteboom's Dutch, then in my translation:

F.

Zoals een gezicht verdwijnt
heb jij je laten verdwijnen
met je gezicht in de tijd.

En door de tijd heen zie ik het
als ik het zie,
met tijd besmet en bestreken.

En ik die hier stil blijf staan
als een lege doos voor een deur,
in dezelfde tijd zal ik vallen
tot het krankzinnige leven me opheeft
en het niet meer kussen begint

tot de niemand die niet van ons houdt
zijn gezicht van ons afwendt
en het nooit meer strelen en slapen
ons ieder afzonderlijk insluit.[27]

F.

The way a face disappears
is the way you disappeared
face first into time.

---

27   Cees Nooteboom, 'F.' from 'Aanwezig, afwezig' in *Vuurtijd, ijstijd. Gedichten 1955–1983* (Amsterdam: De Arbeiderspers, 1984), 134.

And looking through time it is
as I see it,
smeared and streaked with time.

And I who stand here stock-still
like an empty box by a door,
I shall fall into this selfsame time
till crazy life has consumed me
and the time of no more kisses begins

till the nobody who does not love
turns his face away from us
and the time of no more caresses or sleep
enfolds each of us, apart.

De Moor notes that this last stanza is not about physical death, but about the loss of actions that express the self, that is, a person's mental disposition or mood.[28] Indeed affect, or the expression of mood and feelings, is important both for reader and poet. When the poet seems to be absent from the very early poems it is because he has transformed personal suffering and intensity into poetic vision, one that frequently reminds me of the dark, mysterious romanticism of Caspar David Friedrich, perhaps with a small figure alone in a dramatic moonlit landscape, which is not to say that such a poem attempts to recreate a painting but rather to employ its vocabulary. That Nooteboom draws on the huge web of European culture for his means of expression is one aspect common to both his poetry and prose.

Romantische herfst

schimmig vanavond jaagt die mist de velden
de maan sluipt terug in dodelijke bomen
nu is de grote rafelaar gekomen
een herfst een doodgaan een gekwelde smeekstem

---

28   See De Moor, 'Gedichten over het nooit meer strelen en slapen', 37–8.

hoor ... ademend beweegt de aarde van heimwee
om mensen te bezetten met een adem van verdriet
om koeien zwaar en zwijgend in zich vast te zetten
als schepen, vastgegroeid aan het lichaam van de zee
of de dood, levend aan het gezicht van de mensen,
meeademend, meesprekend.[29]

mist chases over fields this ghostly evening
the moon creeps and hides in deathly trees
now the great unraveller is here
autumn dying a tortured pleading voice

listen ... the breathing earth swells with longing
to fill human beings with a breath of sadness
to anchor cows in itself heavy and silent
like ships, melded with the body of the sea
or death, alive in the faces of the people,
breathing, speaking alongside them.

This early poem with its evocation of landscape and responsiveness to
visual arts is only the beginning of what was to become an important preoccupation and ultimately in Nooteboom's case, a poetic mode. While
'Romantische herfst' evokes a certain German romantic painter for me,
others may have other associations or detect other allusions; a feature that
Nooteboom's poetry shares with his prose. One reason for the effectiveness
of 'Romantische herfst' is the complete absence of a poetic persona, creating
the visionary mode. In other poems, such as 'Ich saz ûf einem steine',[30] for
example, there is an explicit I-figure, in this case one who remembers the
medieval love poet Walther von der Vogelweide. De Moor emphatically
does not agree with Morriën that the lack of an explicit poetic persona
means that the poet has somehow absented himself: '[...] it is also precisely

29   Cees Nooteboom, 'Romantische herfst' from 'De doden zoeken een huis' in *Vuurtijd,*
      ijstijd, 295.
30   From the cycle 'Vervreemde gedichten', *Het zwarte gedicht* (Amsterdam: Querido,
      1960). Also in the collections *Gemaakte gedichten* (1970), *Vuurtijd, ijstijd* (1984) and
      Bitterzoet (2000).

the case with the poetry that in all instances, the poet is present, whether as poetic persona, the main figure in the poem, or as silent observer.'[31]

Wiel Kusters devotes a short essay, 'Een logboek van schuim' (A Logbook of Foam), to Nooteboom's poem 'Gran Rio' from *Paesaggi narrati*.[32] He discusses the time structure of the poem and the way that the poet feels a kind of fear on behalf of his younger self which Kusters considers less than convincingly conveyed in the second half of the poem. According to him, it is this part of the poem that is devoted to the experience of the fear. Kusters draws our attention to an early poem 'Pathetisch scheepsgedicht, boven Trinidad' (Emotive maritime poem, above Trinidad) from *Koude gedichten* which contains disturbing visions of figures jumping overboard. He then raises the very interesting question of the authenticity of the emotion expressed in the poem, suggesting that the very title indicates Nooteboom's own doubt about the authenticity of his fear. The following explanation is worth citing in its entirety:

> Nooteboom's poetry is to an important extent rhetorical poetry. Or rather: the poet experiences many of his poems as rhetorical. There is constant doubt about the authenticity of the emotions rendered in poetry, the poet therefore feels as it were estranged from his own poems. What he can do is to ground the uncomprehended feelings that arise in him in a poem. 'Fear' and 'sadness' – key terms in Nooteboom's work – must be made explicable as emotions *caused* by the language of the poem, so that, being 'artificial emotions', they lose their real threat.[33]

---

31   '[…] maar het geldt nu juist ook voor de poëzie dat de dichter in alle gevallen, hetzij als persona poëtica, hoofdfiguur in het gedicht, hetzij als stille waarnemer aanwezig is.' De Moor, 'Gedichten over het nooit meer strelen en slapen', 38.

32   Wiel Kusters, 'Een logboek van schuim', *De geheimen van wikke en dille*, 145–9.

33   'Nootebooms poëzie is voor een belangrijk deel retorische poëzie. Beter gezegd: de dichter ervaart veel van zijn eigen gedichten als retorisch. Aan de echtheid van de in poëzie gegeven emoties wordt steeds weer getwijfeld, de schrijver voelt zich daardoor als het ware vreemd aan zijn eigen gedichten. Wat hij kan doen is de zich aan hem opdringende onbegrepen gevoelens in een gedicht funderen. "Angst" en "verdriet" – sleutelwoorden bij Nooteboom – moeten verklaarbaar worden als door de taal van het gedicht *veroorzaakte* emoties, opdat ze als "*kunstemoties*" hun reële dreiging verliezen.' Kusters, 'Een logboek van schuim', 148–9.

Kusters certainly flags up a significant feature of Nooteboom's poetry which he seems to see as a kind of therapy for dealing with negative emotions. And I can imagine that other poets, especially Nooteboom's contemporaries for whom authenticity is a key poetic value, will have mistrusted his poetry if they also consider it rhetorical in nature – that is exhibiting some kind of gap between what the poet is feeling and what the poem conveys.

With these comments in mind, here is the poem in question:

Gran Rio   *voor F.D.L.*
1957

Veertien mannen, veertien dagen,
Een schip op de oceaan.
In het grote web van de zomer
Verschuift het schip als de spin.
Een logboek van zeeschuim blijft achter
Dat niemand zal lezen.
Op die plek in de tijd
Heb ik wacht onder de sterren
Die zichzelf niet benoemen.
Angst die ik toen niet had voel ik
Nu.
Ik stond alleen aan de reling
In mijn vroegere, andere lichaam,
Geen gedachte, geen schepen in zicht.
De vracht van de melkweg
Verlichtte de zwalkende vlakte
Totdat die de kleur kreeg van modder,
Het schip anders rolde, en de stuurman zei
Zand uit de Orinoco.
Toen zag ik het land in het water
De mond voor de ogen,
En later de stad van jouw huis.

Fourteen men, fourteen days,
A ship on the ocean.
In the great web of summer
The ship moves like a spider.

A logbook of sea foam remains
That no-one will read.
On that spot in time
I take the watch beneath the stars
That do not name themselves.
Fear I did not feel then I do
Now.
I stood alone by the rail
In my earlier, other body,
No thoughts, no ships in sight.
The vast milky way cast light
On the endless surface
Till it took on the colour of mud,
The ship changed its roll, and the steersman said
Sand from the Orinoco.
Then I saw the land in the sea
The mouth before the eyes
And later the city with your house.

Where I agree with Kusters is in the feeling of estrangement that radiates from 'Gran Rio'; the poet in the writing present is estranged from his youthful self, so either he cannot remember what he was feeling or he perhaps remembers his innocence. What is certain is that the poet knows what lay ahead of the young man, much of it painful: it is this knowledge that causes the poet's sensation of fear: he has temporarily become that young man. I disagree with Kusters when he says that the fear in the second part of the poem is somehow inauthentic or rhetorical: I see the poet as moving from imagining being himself as a young sailor to a kind of active remembering in which the poet's emotions are now in play. However I do agree that there is a gap between feelings and words in the sense that the poetry frequently resists the explicit expression of feelings, preferring instead to use imagery, allusion, mood to convey something that is too complex to fix in words.

To sum up these examples of the Dutch reception of the poet Nooteboom: they tend to stay close to individual poems, to see the poet as death-obsessed or the emotions he expresses as somehow inauthentic. Roger Rennenberg's first chapter on death in Nooteboom's poetry may

unintentionally provide part of an explanation for the poet's treatment
when he places Nooteboom in a Dutch tradition of poets dealing with
the problem of death: Victor E. van Vriesland, M. Nijhoff, J.J. Slauerhoff,
Anthonie Donker, Adriaan Morriën, H.A. Gomperts, Gerrit Achterberg,
Leo Vroman and Ed. Hoornik. They are all poets who made their debut
before the Second World War and who the new generation of the 1950s
wanted to sweep away. And Nooteboom's debut as a poet came in 1956. To
see Nooteboom as a poet dealing with death emphasizes continuity with
the past – and the same is true of the reception of his first novel which
was compared to the early work of Arthur van Schendel (1874–1946).
Much of the criticism I have surveyed dates from the early years, the point
being that its impact reverberates for decades. From my perspective located
outside the Low Countries, there are many other features of Nooteboom's
poetry that I consider to be of more relevance and interest to these times,
particularly his mobility and this preoccupation with human subjectivity.

A Deleuzian Reading of Nooteboom's Poetry in Dutch

To continue my reading of Nooteboom's writing as nomadic I now turn
to other Deleuzian concepts, which lend themselves to a discussion of the
poetry in particular. They are not traditional literary concepts, though
Deleuze has frequently written about literature, resolutely using his own
concepts, some of which I adopt here. My reading of Nooteboom's poetry
will focus on the lines of flight created through the poetry, and on the preoccupation with multiplicity and the process of working towards a nomadic
subjectivity. I do not mean to suggest that Nooteboom has consciously
set out to enact or embed a Deleuzian philosophy in the poetry: rather, I
see an affinity between the philosopher and the writer which leads me to
undertake this confrontation of certain Deleuzian ideas with Nooteboom's
poetry. The process that is central to Deleuze's philosophy involves some
kind of dismantling of the self, in contrast to the 'fragmentation' identified

by Rennenberg, taking a negative view of the process in which the subject loses its 'logical unity'.[34] Deleuze himself puts it rather differently:

> It's a strange business, speaking for yourself, in your own name, because it doesn't at all come with seeing yourself as an ego or a person or a subject. Individuals find a real name for themselves, rather, only through the harshest exercise in depersonalization, by opening themselves up to multiplicities everywhere within them, to the intensities running through them.[35]

In what follows I investigate the ways in which Nooteboom's poetry gives expression to these elements.

Deleuze and Guattari address this process of work on the self in *A Thousand Plateaus*: 'if in dismantling the organism there are times one courts death, in slipping away from significance and subjection, one courts falsehood, illusion and hallucination and psychic death'.[36] Reading the poems in the light of these elements will enable me to break away from the kind of interpretive trap I explored in the previous section. The need to court death in order to participate in this process of becoming immediately places Nooteboom's poetic preoccupation with death in a new light, as something necessary and purposeful. If, as Deleuze and Guattari suggest, in the process of dismantling the self the individual may also court illusion and even hallucination, this will provide a new way of approaching what are recognizable elements of the poems. Finally, dismantling the self is part of a process in which a multiple self 'enters into relations with other multiplicities and changes nature, transforms itself, follows a *line of flight*'.[37] According to Deleuze in 'Literature and Life', writing 'is inseparable from

---

34   Rennenberg, *De tijd en het labyrint*, 88.
35   Gilles Deleuze, *Negotiations 1972–1990*, trans. Martin Joghin (New York: Columbia University Press, 1995), 6.
36   Gilles Deleuze and Félix Guattari, *A Thousand Plateaus: Capitalism and Schizophrenia*, trans. Brian Massumi (London: Athlone Press, 1988), 160.
37   Daniel W. Smith, 'Introduction. "A Life of Pure Immanence": Deleuze's "Critique et Clinique" Project' in Gilles Deleuze, *Essays Critical and Clinical*, trans. Daniel W. Smith and Michael A. Greco (Minneapolis: University of Minnesota Press, 1997), xxx.

becoming: in writing one becomes-woman, becomes-animal or vegetable, becomes-molecule to the point of becoming-imperceptible.'[38] As the discussion of Nooteboom's fiction already showed, Nooteboom's writing can be seen as bearing out or enacting this philosophy. I want to argue here that this process, described by Deleuze as a 'passage of life that traverses both the liveable and the lived' is particularly evident in Nooteboom's poetry as it enters on multiple lines of flight. The intensities which are part of the process can be felt unmistakably in Nooteboom's poetry, and in more traditional readings have frequently been interpreted by commentators as romanticism.

Courting Death

In the early poetry, the speaker seeks intimacy with or envisions intimate knowledge of death. Thoughts of death pervade the first cycle and the poet sees death everywhere and meditates on his own relationship to death, as in the following extract from 'Ik ben de herfst niet':

> Ik ben de herfst niet ik ben anders doodgaan
> moe zingen ben ik niet ik ben net niet meer zingen
> hardnekkig vormt mijn dood zich in mijn hand
> genadig kan ik hem niet meer verdringen
>
> hij heeft hartslag in de kleinste dingen.[39]

> I am not autumn I am a different dying
> I am not tired of singing I have gone beyond singing
> stubbornly my death takes shape in my hand
> no longer can I suppress it with mercy
>
> it finds a heartbeat in the smallest things.

38   Deleuze, *Essays Critical and Clinical*, 1.
39   Cited from the collected works *Vuurtijd, ijstijd*, 291.

The lyrical subject expresses a state beyond tiredness – a kind of exhaustion in which the poet is alive to the paradoxical vitality of death. In a Deleuzian reading, such proximity to death is part of the process of working towards an expansion of the self which necessarily involves the kind of pain and suffering that these poems attest to. In the poem 'Pathetisch scheepsgedicht, boven Trinidad' discussed above in relation to 'Gran Rio', the poet endures a terrible hallucinatory and apocalyptic vision of a shipwreck. While forty of those on board leave the ship for safety, another forty are preserved clinging to the 'tongue of truth, searing and burning'. In the following extract, only the poem's central figure is trapped:

> waarom kan *hij* niet springen?
> wordt hij bewaard of gestorven?
> om zijn middel kwelt een patrijspoort,
> een insect is hij, gewrongen in twee lijven,
> gezwollen, gespannen van twijfel
> en monsterlijk bewegend,
> maar welke beweging?

> why can *he* not jump?
> will he be preserved or die?
> round his waist an agonizing porthole,
> he is an insect, squeezed into two bodies,
> swollen, stretched taut with doubt,
> moving in monstrous ways,
> but which movement?

Poised between life and death, a state in which he asks 'welke kracht kan hem tillen?' (what force can lift him?), the poem ends with the lines 'schuimdieren springen hem naar de keel/openbaring boek vijftig, generlei, generlei' (beasts of foam leap at his throat/revelation book fifty, nonesuch, nonesuch).[40]

---

40 'Pathetisch scheepsgedicht, boven Trinidad', *Vuurtijd, ijstijd*, 255–6.

A number of poems like 'Pathetisch scheepsgedicht, boven Trinidad' create visions of death, destruction and decomposition. The lines 'in deze droom sterf ik duizend keer/altijd bedorvener' (in this dream I die a thousand times/ever more decayed) from 'Wankelend hapert het slaapvuur' not only suggest the process of decomposition but also what the poem calls 'dat tergend liefdeleven' (that tormenting life of love).[41] The poet can experience death in a small way through orgasm, a recurring theme throughout the early works.

Destabilizing the Self

Destabilization of the self in Nooteboom's poetry takes different forms involving multiplicity, from the cryptic 'sterf rustig mijn dichters vanavond' (die peacefully tonight my poets) of the first collection,[42] to the 'dwazen die ik in mijzelf ontmoet' (crazy ones who I meet in myself) whom the poetic persona seeks to kill in the poem 'het moet scherper te zeggen zijn' (it can be put more starkly)[43] to the many doublings of focal figures as in 'Jager en offer' (Hunter and victim).[44]

In 'het moet scherper te zeggen zijn' (it can be put more starkly), the poetic 'I' is troubled by this multiplicity. The poem's first stanza expresses his desire to kill these manifold selves, which he finds unbearable. At the same time, his description of them in the second and last stanza as 'my own butterflies' and his condemnation of the idea of betraying these butterflies might suggest that he is already sensing that there is no going back, or even that the notion of a once simple and cohesive self is an illusion. Although he does not reject these selves, realizing that they are a sign of vitality, this poem does not relate a conscious Deleuzian or Braidottian process of dismantling the self.

41   'Wankelend hapert het slaapvuur', *Vuurtijd, ijstijd*, 232.
42   'Opdracht aan een regen', *Vuurtijd, ijstijd*, 296.
43   'het moet scherper te zeggen zijn', *Vuurtijd, ijstijd*, 277.
44   'Jager en offer', *Vuurtijd, ijstijd*, 160.

het moet scherper te zeggen zijn:
de dwazen die ik in mijzelf ontmoet
vleiers, heldenvereerders,
praatgrage haters,
ofwel, vergelijkenderwijs
maanaanbidders, rozenplukkers,
mieren te paard
ik moet ze verbranden in koude ovens.

het is onverdragelijk om zoveel mensen te zijn
en ze verraden is schaamteloos
maar mijn eigen vlinders staan me naar het leven

it can be put more starkly:
the fools I meet in myself
flatterers, hero-worshippers,
loquacious haters,
or, comparatively seen
moon lovers, rosebud gatherers,
ants on horseback
I must burn them in cold ovens.

it is unbearable to be so many people
and to betray them is shameless
yet my own butterflies are out to get me

'Niemand anders 1' from *Gesloten gedichten*, first published in 1969, presents an unwanted transformation: a butterfly in a glass case which has become a stone. It is the 'nobody else' of the title who uniquely possesses transformative power. In the second and final stanza, the nobody can, in an echo of Christ, distribute his blood so that it takes on shapes or forms. Not only can he multiply this physical essence, he can also perform the same act on his essential being, thus undermining the traditional notion of an indivisible individual essence.

Niemand anders 1
Niemand anders kan het,
een steen zijn die met zijn vleugels werkt,
twee zijden spansels die een steen vervoeren en zijn,
de naalden van het onmogelijke door het lichaam in de vitrine.

Hij verdeelt zijn bloed in gedaantes,
zijn wezen in water: het is onzichtbaar.
Niemand kreeg van de goden ooit meer dan een haarlok.[45]

    Nobody else 1
Nobody else can do it,
be a stone flapping its wings,
two silken sails that transport and are a stone,
the nails of impossibility through the body in the glass case.

He divides his blood into shapes,
his essence into water: invisible.
Nobody ever received more than a lock of hair from the gods.

In 'Nobody else 2', the companion poem to 'Nobody else 1', the poet directly addresses a self left behind after the departure of 'the servant', seemingly a more subservient self.

    Niemand anders 2
Nu, de onderdaan vlucht.
Alleen, het vuur zelf of bij het vuur, blijf je achter.
Jij bent het. Uit de gelijkende koker reikt de nieuwe stank.
Jij bent het, vermomder, het nieuwe.

En dat is de dood, een vergelijking.
In de trappen daarvan ben je gewend, meer dan de anderen.
Terwijl je lichaam in lichaam verandert
Verbleekt en vergaat de gedachte aan je bestaan.

Jou zal niets geweldigers overkomen
Dan het onuitroeibare zelfde.[46]

    Nobody else 2
Now the servant flees.
Alone, you remain, by the fire or the fire itself.
It is you. From the semblance of a cocoon the new smell rises.
It is you, disguised, new.

45   'Niemand anders 1', *Vuurtijd, ijstijd*, 161.
46   'Niemand anders 2', *Vuurtijd, ijstijd*, 162.

And that is death, the comparative.
You are practised in its forms, more than the others.
While your body transforms into body
The idea of your existence fades and decays.

Nothing more dramatic will happen to you
Than ineradicable sameness.

The poem addresses this new creature, the image of a 'cocoon' suggesting a new self emerging from a chrysalis: 'It is you, disguised, new.' The second stanza seems to say that comparison between the new and old selves is deadly, and asserts the reality of the new self by emphasizing its physicality, its bodily solidity. Transformation: new and the same. The butterflies – symbol of multiplicity – reappear later in the collection along with the ambiguous figure of the 'captain of the butterflies' – 'Hij is de afwezige/ die er is' (He is the absentee/who is there).[47] The butterflies have not been destroyed and the captain seems to have found a way of co-existing with them: 'Achter hem volgen zijn vlinders' (Behind him his butterflies follow).[48]

The process of destabilization is portrayed as a kind of radical engagement with the self that is powerful, transformative, but not one that the poet necessarily has under control. Rather he studies its effects, and transforms these into poetry.

Emptiness and Courting Illusion

I have already read the poet's accounts of hallucinatory visions of the drowned and the saved as courting death. The intensity of the process can

47 Cees Nooteboom, 'The Captain of the Butterflies' trans. Leonard Nathan and Herlinde Spahr, *The Captain of the Butterflies* (Los Angeles: Sun & Moon Press, 1997), 33.
48 My translation. Nathan and Spahr: 'His courtiers follow.' I will return to the published English translation in the following section of this chapter on Nooteboom's poetry in English.

lead to exhaustion – a motif particularly in *Gesloten gedichten*. Another part of the process of dismantling the self, according to Deleuze and Guattari in *A Thousand Plateaus*, may involve courting falsehood and illusion. My previous chapter looked in great detail at the way Nooteboom not only practises but also thematizes illusion, for example in *In the Dutch Mountains*. And the concentrated action of poetry also creates visions – textual transformations of affect or lived emotions. Falsehood is an important preoccupation, for example in the first poem of the cycle *Gesloten gedichten* in the lover's lies, or in the 'opgebruikte mythe' (exhausted myth) of the poem 'Een doorregende landstreek'. Perhaps the most captivating fiction of the cycle is the 'captain of the butterflies' himself.

The set of poems 'Liturgie' (Liturgy)[49] opens with a figure on the verge of madness 'schreeuwend om liefde' (screaming for love). A memory of past innocence and the effect of the lack of love bring the poet back: 'komt de dichter/uit het gat van zijn onzin/en bekijkt zijn mens' (the poet emerges from the hole of his non-sense/and regards his humanity). This line is strongly reminiscent of what Deleuze has described as 'hiatuses, hole, or tears that we would never notice, or would attribute to mere tiredness, if they did not suddenly widen in such a way as to receive something from the outside or from elsewhere.'[50] The final short poem of the 'Liturgy', opens with the phrase carried over from the previous poem 'en hij denkt' (and he thinks), which creates a linguistic opening for the poem to slip into the first person: 'ik ben het' (it is I); the poet's subjectivity is reborn.

A subsequent poem in the cycle *Gesloten gedichten*, 'De wetten van de winter' (The Laws of Winter) depicts a state of suspension and emptiness. In his essay 'The Exhausted', Deleuze compares the merely tired with the exhausted person. Whereas the former can no longer realize the possible, the latter goes beyond all possibility. According to Deleuze this has implications for language which needs another dimension or metalanguage – 'no longer a language of names but of voices, a language that no longer operates

---

49   Cited from *Vuurtijd, ijstijd*, 163–9.
50   Deleuze, 'The Exhausted', *Essays Critical and Clinical*, 158.

with combinable atoms but with bendable flows.'[51] One form of flow in 'Liturgy' derives from the very structure of the poem, since it is impossible to say whether it consists of seven short poems, each on a separate page, or whether it flows across the pages in one piece that is at the same time not a single poem. And with its absence of rhyme and traditional metre which emphasize the atoms of poetry, syllables, Nooteboom's poetic diction can be more generally felt as an ebbing and flowing of language.

The courting of falsehood and illusion also requires another language. The first three stanzas of 'Golden Fiction' tell of an 'I' figure whose friends are all dead and buried, sadly waiting for his ship to depart. Without a linking element, the following stanza switches to a 'he' whose main characteristics are that he tells lies and writes things down. He is clearly a writer-figure, perhaps of fiction, given the poem's title (which is also a reference to a brand of Dutch cigarettes). Here are the two final stanzas:

> De bedrieger zit in zijn kamer en schrijft het op.
> Uit welke levens schrijft hij? Uit welke tijd?
> Zal ooit het werkelijke leven bij hem komen,
> hem meenemen?
>
> Nee, het zal hem nooit meenemen.
> De bedrieger zit in zijn kamer en schrijft
> wat de stemmen hem zeggen.

> The traitor sits in his room and writes it down.
> Out of which lives does he write? Which time?
> Will the real life ever come to him
> and take him with it?
>
> No it will never take him with it.
> The traitor sits in his room and writes
> what the voices tell him.[52]

51   Deleuze, *Essays Critical and Clinical*, 156.
52   'Golden Fiction', *Captain of the Butterflies*, 85.

This deceiver – on one level the poet himself – accepts that there is no 'real life' from which to write, only lives, and voices which produce his writing. As Deleuze said, 'no longer a language of names, but of voices'.

Lines of Flight

Lines of flight are an important concept for Deleuze and Guattari, introduced in *A Thousand Plateaus* and denoting trajectories of becoming. They are less obviously discernible in Nooteboom's poetry, but worth exploring nevertheless. In this section I look at the extent to which these lines of flight are part of Nooteboom's poetic world.

Deleuze favours rhizomatic structures, branchings which he uses to envisage a new structure of thought that is not linear and logical. Nomadic becomings can be visualized in a similar way as branchings from a centre which do involve some kind of self-estrangement while retaining a sense of self. 'Being like a foreigner in one's own language. Constructing a line of flight' is how Deleuze describes it.[53] Nooteboom expresses a similar estrangement in the poem 'Nachtuur' ('Nighthour'): 'Ik schrijf/[...]/in een gedicht dat vertaald lijkt/uit het spaans/' (I write/[...]/in a poem that seems translated/from the Spanish). My method here is simply to bring writer and philosopher into contact with each other, to see what resonances there are. For example, the poem 'Getijde 1' (Season 1) can be read as an image of extreme multiple subjectivity:

> Er is geen volgorde aan mijn gedachten.
> Als ik de kathedraal af heb maak ik de symfonie.
> Daarna leer ik en martel,
> ik stuur de regimenten en ontwerp de brug.
>
> Chinees schrijf ik ook, en ik demp het moeras.
> Dan dans ik de tango, ik verzamel de vloot,
> ik schilder de appel op de duizend manieren,

53   Gilles Deleuze and Claire Parnet, *Dialogues*, trans. Hugh Tomlinson and Barbara Habberjam (London: Athlone Press, 1987), 4.

maar hoe vaak ik ook met je slaap
de tijd blijft onzichtbaar.

Hij is er en hij is er niet.[54]

There is no order to my thoughts.
After the cathedral I make the symphony.
Next I will study and torture,
I send the regiments and design the bridge.

I write Chinese too, and reclaim the swamp.
Then I dance the tango, I assemble the fleet,
I paint the apple in the thousand ways,
But however often I sleep with you
Time remains invisible.

It is both there and not there.[55]

These imagined selves seem to be so many lines of flight without a return
to the centre that they leave the poet unchanged and so cannot be seen as
becomings. They are more imagined possibilities or references to historical
others. Another point of contact in this and the other poems in the cycle
Getijde is the sense of being outside the kind of time that can be measured
by a clock – that is of embracing Aeon, or timeless time, as opposed to
Chronos, or clock time, expressed in Deleuzian terms.[56]

Taken as a whole, the cycle 'Open als een schelp, dicht als een steen'
(Open as a shell, closed as a stone) shows an awareness of the dimension of
time within which transformations occur. In the poem 'Koffer' (Suitcase)
the lyrical subject experiences a vision of his own disappearance, disintegra-
tion, and of entering a new state of being – of growing older, which makes

---

54 'Nachtuur', in 'Open als een schelp, dicht als een steen', cited from *Vuurtijd, ijstijd*,
    83.
55 'Nighthour', *Captain of the Butterflies*, 87.
56 For an explanation see, for example, Daniel W. Smith, 'Introduction' to Deleuze,
    Essays Critical and Clinical, xxxv–xxxvi.

nostalgia possible. The poem offers a new kind of becoming – becoming-object – which seems to be the opposite of a Deleuzian vitalistic becoming. I cite the second half of the poem:

wilt U
mijn verdwijning betalen
met het geld voor een foto

totdat

niet het glas maar de scherven
niet de stof maar de rafels
niet het onheelbaar hele
maar de ontbrekende hand van het standbeeld,

totdat

ik de koffer mag worden
die weer omvalt als dingen.[57]

will you
pay for my disappearance
with money for a photo

until

not the glass but the shards
not the fabric but the threads
not the impossible whole
but the missing hand of the statue,

until

I can become the suitcase
that topples over as things do.

57 'Koffer' in 'Open als een schelp, dicht als een steen', cited from *Vuurtijd, ijstijd*, 91–2.

The 'I' figure wants to disappear, and calls on the help of an unknown person who is asked to fill these words (the poem) with sand, put the dream in a box, feed empty plates with films in the form of life and pay for the poet's disappearance so that a photograph can be a substitute for him. What the 'I' wants this to achieve is his becoming-thing (in this instance, a suitcase). What might at first seem like an instance of nostalgia for a lost unified solid self is anything but, because he enumerates a process of fragmentation: glass becoming shards, cloth becoming unravelled, and the hand detached from the statue. The suitcase's crucial characteristic is that as an object, it can fall over, presumably to lie there until someone picks it up. All the same, it seems to me that this becoming-object is hard to reconcile with Deleuzian vitalism. What is more, the title of the collection *Open als een schelp, dicht als een steen* suggests that the poet is still working with traditional dualism. Indeed, there is a tension in the collection between the fragmentation of the self, the idea of openness and the closed dualist system. The final poem, 'Slot' seems to proclaim an overcoming of dualism. After the first stanza in which the poet figure places a seal on the lock/castle, the poem asks 'Is hij binnen of buiten?' ('Is he inside or out?').[58] By virtue of his double self as private and public man, he is both inside and outside the locked space.

An important question for me is whether this doubled self is a form of multiplicity which then undermines dualism, or whether it is itself is a dualist construct. Perhaps the cycle 'Chagrin public' from the 1982 collection *Aas* (Bait) can shed some light on this question since it features a poetic 'I' who recognizably shares characteristics with the author.[59] There is nothing in the poems, though, to identify the poet character with Nooteboom in any direct way. They are poems of loss, sadness, and memories, with the poet as lone traveller. While travelling is a form of literal flight, presumably from the poet's everyday life, memory means that the losses and sadnesses cannot so easily be left behind. Instead they are openly displayed in the poems. Although these poems do not thematize exhaustion like those in 'Gesloten gedichten', they do convey to me a sense of exhaustedness with the exploration of self.

58   'Lock', *Captain of the Butterflies*, 37.
59   See Chapter 2 of this book.

New life comes from engaging with visual art. The collection 'Tituli' from *Aas* contains the cycle 'Poemas del Hierro'; poems to accompany photographs by Nooteboom's friend and sometime travelling companion Eddy Posthuma de Boer. In three of them, 'Wijnstruik' (Vine), 'Rotsplant' (Rockplant) and 'Boom' (Tree) the speaker has become-vegetable; the poetic 'I' is a plant, speaks as a plant. This is an example of the way in which writing itself is the location of crossing a threshold, of experiencing a new becoming. The tree exhorts the reader of the poem to become-vegetable: 'Wees mij, word mij' ('Be me, become me').[60] In 1989, Nooteboom published the volume of poetry entitled *Het gezicht van het oog* (Eyesight/The Face of the Eye) in which the poet becomes-artist, creating a landscape of words: 'De dichter is een gemaal door hem wordt het landschap van woorden' ('The poet is a mill that turns the landscape to words').[61] Many of these poems put into words the deterritorialization that occurs when one nomadic subject becomes-other. The zone of becoming is neither that of the other nor of the subject in question. In 'Wat er te zien was 3' (What there was to see 3) writing is seeing: 'Wij komen uit een ander oog. Dat heeft ons geschreven als een veld in augustus, geschroeid, verbrand.' (We come from another eye./It has written us as a field in august, scorched, seared.)[62] Sometimes the language of the poem is unconnected, or to use Deleuze's term: stuttering.

> Of een vrouw, ooit gezien bij een bruiloft,
> tegen de muur van een kerk. Wij weten niets
> van die vrouw. Water in een kreek, onyx, dat wat jij
> zwart noemt. Het raakt ons niet.

> Or a woman, once seen at a wedding,
> against the wall of a church. We know nothing
> of that woman. Water in a creek, onyx, what you
> call black. It leaves us cold.

---

60   'Tree', *Captain of the Butterflies*, 113.
61   'Basho IV', in *Bitterzoet: Honderd gedichten van vroeger en zeventien nieuwe* (Amsterdam: Arbeiderspers, 2000), 64; and *Captain of the Butterflies*, 79.
62   'Wat er te zien was 3', *Het gezicht van het oog* (Amsterdam: Arbeiderspers, 1989), 71.

Here it is not clear who the woman is, who saw her, who 'we' are and who the poet addresses as 'you'. There are only unconnected elements of a scene. All through the oeuvre, many of Nooteboom's poems create landscapes which are not viewed from the outside, but created from within the poet's inner eye. Like Deleuze, Nooteboom connects this kind of evocation with a distinct way of understanding time. 'Silesius droomt' ('Silesius dreams'), also from *Het gezicht van het oog*, expresses this distinction between clock time and indefinite time, between 'Chronos' and 'Aeon':[63]

> De ziel heeft twee ogen, dat droomt hij.
> Het ene kijkt naar de uren, het andere
> ziet er doorheen,
> tot waar de duur nooit meer ophoudt,
> het kijken vergaat in het zien.

> The soul has two eyes, so he dreams.
> The one looks at the hours, the other
> sees right through them,
> to where duration never stops,
> looking is consumed into seeing.[64]

The poem links clock time with looking, i.e. seeing as registering, and flat time with seeing.

This discussion of lines of flight in Nooteboom's poetry shows that he envisages and imagines multiplicity; he creates a poetic persona with a strong sense of other lives recalled in the famous line 'ik had wel duizend levens en nam er maar één!' (I had a thousand lives and only took one!).[65] At the same time there is an expression of a doubling of self at the expense of the unified monolithic self as well as a desire to become object, or to become vegetable which could be seen as a kind of nostalgia for simplicity. In the poetry Nooteboom and his poetic personae are on Deleuzian territory,

---

63   See Smith, 'Introduction' to Deleuze, *Essays Critical and Clinical*, xxxv–vi.
64   Excerpt from 'Silesius droomt', *Het gezicht van het oog*, 62; 'Silesius dreams' in *The Captain of the Butterflies*, 98.
65   From 'In dit getij leer ik mijzelf kennen', *Vuurtijd, ijstijd*, 86.

struggling with their multiplicity and imagining a solid, simple existence which the poet has long since left behind. As Braidotti says, 'changes hurt and transformations are painful.'[66] Nevertheless, the poetry itself can be seen as creating a space of becoming where the process may both be imagined and enacted. The clearest line of flight in the later poetry is Nooteboom's engagement with visual arts and with the resulting deterritorialization of writing itself, in which it is translated into the visual.

Nooteboom's Poetry in English

Although not many of Nooteboom's poems have been translated into English, his poetry has attracted significant critical attention, most notably from J.M. Coetzee who includes him as one of only six poets from the Low Countries in his anthology *Landscape with Rowers: Poetry from the Netherlands*. In this section I will survey the English oeuvre and its reception, and compare it with my account of the poetry in Dutch, closing with the substantial collection of prose poems *Self Portrait of an Other* which is published in its entirety in English.

The Captain of the Butterflies is a perfect example of how to present an unknown Dutch poet to an English audience. The two translators, Leonard Nathan who was himself a poet, and Herlinde Spahr, whose PhD thesis discussed Nooteboom's work, collaborated on the translations, according to Spahr in her introduction, while Nooteboom himself was a visitor to the University of California-Berkeley. Their complementary strengths have served Nooteboom well. Spahr's introduction is brief, but it also captures the main elements of the poetry which she relates to Nooteboom's novels, since seven of these had been published in English at the time. She points out that themes that are painful in the poems take on a more lighthearted

---

66   Braidotti, *Metamorphoses*, 43.

form in the novels. Her short characterization of the poetry is worth quoting here in full:

> The fissured, fragmented self, the dissolution of reality, the shrewd blurring of truth and semblance, these topoi of the postmodern idiom appear first in his poems as personal, existential insights that almost overwhelm the poetic voice itself. If the color red seems to be made up of paint in his novels, it carries traces of blood in his poems, memories of pain. That softly ironic tone which turns his narrators into such worldly, witty observers, is peeled away in his poems to reveal a poet who is completely alone, oblivious of the reader, focused on a world in which poetic meaning has taken refuge in the form of bleached, disintegrating skeletons, in the slower presence of a crumbling rock wall.[67]

The 'topoi of the postmodern idiom' identified by Spahr are also important aspects of my Deleuzian reading which takes postmodern philosophy as its basis. Spahr's introduction sheds light on Nooteboom's involvement in the selection of poems for the anthology, and on other relevant factors. Not only did the poet provide explanations and comments to the translators, he also determined the final grouping of the poems along thematic lines. The translators themselves aimed for a representative selection covering as many periods and styles as possible. They are open about discarding some translations that they felt were less successful.

The poems are grouped quite loosely under four headings: 'Self and Others', 'Travels and Visions', 'Poems and Fictions', 'Thoughts and Theses'. In his author's note Nooteboom confirms that the selected poems come from all periods of his writing. He helpfully and tantalizingly points out that he used less punctuation when young, suggesting that this will help readers to identify the earlier poetry since none of the poems is dated. Reading the anthology itself, it is striking how the poet and his collaborators have decided to start with a clean slate, thus taking into account the audience's complete unawareness of him and his work. However, the general organizational principle seems to be the one employed in the Dutch anthologies discussed earlier in this chapter: that the most recent poems are placed first. This produces a very different effect for new readers; in fact, I would go

---

67   Herlinde Spahr, 'Introduction' to *The Captain of the Butterflies*, 10.

so far as to say this constructs a different poet from the one who made his debut in 1957 with *De doden zoeken een huis*. Any reader approaching the English poems in the order in which they are printed will encounter in the first poem a tone that is closer to that of the novels. 'Meditation' opens in an upbeat mood with a trumpet blast – it is morning in the city – and on a whimsical note – 'the cat on her way to the office'. The poet figure seems to have conquered his demons: 'I'm ready for anything!' However the familiar elements are still there: death, time, emptiness and even butterfly wings.

In my discussion of this new Nooteboom, I will use the same Deleuzian framework to interpret the translated poems as I did for the Dutch works. The two sets of readings will be compared to gain some insight into the way in which the construction of an oeuvre in a new language also constructs a new poet.

Courting Death

'The poem of death' is the third poem in the volume. Judging by its lack of punctuation it is an early poem.[68] There is a sense of the world as an empty, unresponsive expanse, lit by cold moonlight; the poet is absent: this is the poem of death 'which begs and tumbles/in the long drawn arches of the evening,/nobody hears it'. In the fourth stanza there is some colour and energy in the painted birds and the trumpeting angels, but it is inhuman and unearthly. The 'whisperings of dead souls' which had seemed unthreatening in the opening poem 'Meditation' are more threatening here:

those in masks whisper

a house is no house
a thing is no thing
life does not exist.[69]

---

68   It appeared in 1960 in the Dutch literary magazine *De Gids* and also in the cycle 'Waarom zou Tamenund blijven?' in *Het zwarte gedicht*.
69   *Captain of the Butterflies*, 22.

Again, the poem conveys a kind of exhaustion, something that empties out the everyday as well as intimate knowledge of death. In the poem 'Lock', for example, a figure well acquainted with the dead seems to hover on the brink:

> The dead accompany him
> though he knew no-one.
> He seals the wounds
> and memory.
> He seals the lock.
>
> Is he inside or out?[70]

The figure is so intimate with death, that he is no longer sure which side of the divide he finds himself. As 'Melancholia' shows, not all the poems in which death plays a part depict it as a force of annihilation. In 'The Page on the Lily', the poem even satirizes the romantic poet and his intimacy with death:

> The page lies on the lily,
> and on the leaves of the lily.
> The poem is all mirrors.
>
> And he,
> he sits there posturing on the edge of his grave
> and listens to the gulping of time
> in the poem across from him,
> the never-to-be-grasped.[71]

Destabilizing the Self

There is one poem in the collection in which the lyrical subject proclaims satisfaction with his life against a background of 'So many forms of existence': 'Give me some other life and I won't take it./Shells and crickets, my

---

70 *Captain of the Butterflies*, 37.
71 *Captain of the Butterflies*, 84.

cup is full of eternal noon.'[72] But there are several other poems that testify to a fragmentation of the self into two, three or more parts. In the poem 'The Fighters' this becomes an active dismantling of the self, expressed through the motif of the fight. The alienation from the self is performed through the use of both I and he in the following extract:

> He always approaches him, bared,
> to discard me.
> He recognizes him, flinches,
> then yields.
>
> He tears my photo
> and starts bleeding.[73]

Although tearing the photo might at first seem to be only a symbolic dismantling, apparently of the lyrical subject's self by this other figure, it is the other who is physically damaged, suggesting that the two are somehow one. In the final two stanzas they are separate and at the same time mirror images.

Mirrors create the possibility of endless multiplications of selves which Nooteboom perhaps sees as part of a poetic disposition. 'The page on the Lily' closes with the one-line stanza, 'I am in all mirrors.' The poem 'Reflection, Reflector' is addressed to a poet whose self is 'scattered'. The poem suggests that this is a conscious multiplication with the poet not only in control but making a virtue of it in his verse. If the poet in question were Ovid, for instance, then these splinters of self take the form of many transformations or metamorphoses. Since the poem speaks of 'your hexameters' which is the metre used by Ovid in *Metamorphoses* this reading is not altogether fanciful. In 'Tree', Nooteboom's poem enacts a becoming: the lyrical subject speaks as a tree which in its turn exhorts the reader to 'Be me, become me/for once in your turbulent life.'[74]

The Captain of the Butterflies constructs a poet who comes across as less overwhelmed by the pain of the struggle with the self and more

---

72 'Harbalorifa', *Captain of the Butterflies*, 29.
73 *Captain of the Butterflies*, 41.
74 *Captain of the Butterflies*, 113.

accepting because the relentless darkness of the early volumes of poetry is simply not present. 'Midday' evokes this most strikingly: it has exchanged the cold moonlight for 'midday of glittering hours', and though the opening stanza refers to 'himself cut up by himself' this figure is described as in control even though he is

> Someone, somebody scattered,
> the uncollected persona
> in converse with himself, dreaming and thinking
> present, invisible.[75]

While the emphasis is different, the poetry is still preoccupied with destabilization of the self, which involves intense struggle, but the resulting multiplicity of the subject is no longer to be feared once the subject is able to take control.

Emptiness and Courting Illusion

In my discussion of 'The poem of death' I pointed to the sense of emptying out with which the poem concludes. Although the theme of exhaustion which I described in relation to the Dutch poetry is not a prominent one in the English anthology, it appears in the shape of an exhausted Classical culture; the gods have been sleeping for two thousand years surrounded by the remains of their greatness, empty saddles and empty chariots. 'The square of the world is empty, empty the space.'[76] The illusions provided by the old myths are gone, though in a sense a poem like 'Sleeping Gods' also reinvents the myth. This new illusion strips the gods of their power over human lives creating a new space in which the future is shaped by other forces than destiny. The last poem in the volume, 'Order', imagines a para-

---

75 *Captain of the Butterflies*, 44.
76 'Sleeping Gods', *Captain of the Butterflies*, 31. This poem has also been translated by Peter Nijmeijer. See James S. Holmes and William Jay Smith, eds, *Dutch Interior: Postwar Poetry of the Netherlands and Flanders* (New York: Columbia University Press, 1984).

doxical world in which the gods are both mortal and at the same time not able to die; they have lost control of the elements which leaves room for chance. And in Nooteboom's new myth it is chance that gives rise to vision:

> There water turns to fire, sea
> floats through the air, there elements
> lick the sight from one another's
> eyes, there the law of chance breeds
>
> a law without logic, the accident
> that leads to vision[77]

Many of Nooteboom's poems in the anthology can be read as visions of another world which is not subject to clock time and is far removed from the quotidian. This world is frequently elemental, outside of history; it features a rockscape, the sea, a fire, the sun, moon, 'the grit of the stars'. 'Finis Terrae' is a vision of the earth, herself female, 'stripped of all the voices of women':

> she chose the deeper mourning of emptiness,
> left her ceaseless course and wandered
> through the opened mouth of the cosmic seas,
> a leaf on the great river.[78]

This is courting illusion on a cosmic scale which can offer the comfort of 'the time without time of death.'

Lines of Flight

If, as I suggested in my title to this chapter, Nooteboom is already a foreigner in his own language, what is the effect of reading his poems in another language? Is the foreignness of the translation somehow cancelled out, or

---

77   *Captain of the Butterflies*, 116.
78   *Captain of the Butterflies*, 112.

is it doubled? Because the poems are either set in a non-specific world, or, when places are named, they can be anywhere in the world, there is no correlation between setting and language. Nooteboom's foreignness is thus an expression of his cosmopolitanism which comes across equally well in his English-language poetry. In the second stanza of 'Churchill's Black Dog or Mr. Nuszbaum Complains' the lyrical subject's fundamental relation to language is one of translation:

> I who am quite aware
> that a word is only a translation,
> a poor code
> among secretive services,
> I myself have inherited at least
> ten thousand words
> from the large brothel
> toward which the world empties.[79]

The cynical tone of this poem is perhaps not in keeping with contemporary ideas of ethical cosmopolitanism but I will save this discussion for the next and last chapter of this book.

The poem 'The Sea' – like 'Tree' which has been discussed twice already in this chapter – enacts a becoming since it is the sea who speaks; the 'I' is not the poet's voice, but the imagined voice of the sea, addressing 'you', a writer. Put differently, the lyrical subject, who I read at one level as congruent with the poet, has in this poem become liquid. The sea has attained a state of being which is sure of itself, strong and vital: 'I am the music./You are only the strings.' The sea urges the writer-figure to become like itself: 'sway with me in this light/.../and sit down and write.'[80]

Despite the fact that very few of the poems I referred to above in my Deleuzian reading of the Dutch oeuvre are to be found in *The Captain of the Butterflies*, the English anthology does support a very similar reading. New poems come to the fore, and new aspects are highlighted. The exercise serves to underline the fluidity both of Nooteboom's poems and

79   *Captain of the Butterflies*, 46.
80   *Captain of the Butterflies*, 71.

of this kind of nomadic reading which does not aspire to fix meaning. So while the first impression of Nooteboom in English stands in contrast to his Dutch poetic persona read chronologically, this effect is tempered on reading the English volume as a whole.

The Three Versions of 'Basho'

'Basho I–IV' is a sequence of four short poems by Nooteboom inspired by the seventeenth-century Japanese poet of the same name. They appeared in the 1989 collection of poems *Het gezicht van het oog*. In fact they open the volume and have as their theme the poet's eye, or the way Basho and poets more generally transform what they have seen into words. The three realizations of 'Basho I–IV' are by J.M. Coetzee, Leonard Nathan and Herlinde Spahr, and Michael O'Loughlin. In what follows, I will compare the three versions of each poem with the aim of exploring the poet's voice as it emerges from each version. Are there significant differences? How similar is the tone of voice across the three translated poems? Are the poetic diction and mood the same? How do they deal with the intertextuality relating to Basho and other poets? What light does the existence of three versions of the same poem throw on the nature of poetry translation as an intercultural process?

I will start with Coetzee's translation which appeared in the anthology in which he presents six Dutch poets to the English-speaking world, *Landscape with Rowers*. His version of 'Basho I' has a distinctive poetic diction which creates a slightly mysterious atmosphere. The poem has a flowing style achieved through minimal punctuation and complete absence of commas. The order of words in a sentence is frequently unusual, for example 'Here passed by the poet on his journey to the North.' This gives it a poetic feel reminiscent of an older tradition of poetry in English which preserves older forms of syntax that have died out in spoken language, but which are still available to contemporary speakers of the Dutch language. It is possible that Coetzee's Afrikaans heritage plays a part here, which gives the translation a flavour of the Dutch of the original.

In Coetzee's version, the rhythm of the poem is not prominent; in the flow of words, there does not seem to be a strong pattern of syllables or stresses. However there are other structuring elements such as the constant repetition of 'he' and 'his' in the opening lines:

> Old man among the reeds mistrust of the poet.
> He is on his way to the North he is making a book with his eyes.
> He is writing himself upon the water he has lost his master.

and the repetition of the half-line in the final two lines:

> Here passed by the poet on his journey to the North.
> Here passed by the poet finally forever.[81]

Another striking feature of Coetzee's version is its elusiveness or ambiguity, as in the first line quoted above, where it is simply unclear what the connection is between the old man and the poet. This contributes to the poem's seeming mystery which will never yield a closed interpretation. Read alongside Basho's biography, it is clear that the poem offers a representation of the poet at the end of his life, but it suggests much more besides.

Turning now to the translation of the poem by Leonard Nathan and Herlinde Spahr, their realization of 'Basho I' feels rather different. The diction is energetic and the poem moves forward with some pace, while the rhythm is quite bold and more definite than Coetzee's. Even though this version also omits all punctuation except for full stops, it does not flow as smoothly. In fact, this translation of the poem produces a regular anapaestic or reversed dactylic rhythm in places such as line 2:

> (He) goes his way to the North he composes a book with his eyes.

---

81 Cees Nooteboom, 'Basho I', trans. J.M. Coetzee, *Landscape with Rowers: Poetry from The Netherlands* (Princeton: Princeton University Press, 2004), 61.

Coetzee also uses the anapaest in this same line and in this respect both translations reflect the fact that in the Dutch the poem also has a repeated rhythm, though its structure is very different: it has a rhythmic phrase that is repeated in the second half of the line. Nevertheless there is for me a subtle difference between the two translations with Coetzee's rhythm being the gentler of the two. An important line in relation to sound structure is the one referring to the seventeen syllables of the haiku:

> Seventeen the sacred number in which coming-forth is ordained. (Coetzee version)
> Seventeen the holy number in which the apparition is sealed. (Nathan and Spahr version)

Nooteboom's Dutch poem itself has seventeen syllables, as does Nathan and Spahr's translated line, but Coetzee seems to have chosen not to reproduce this effect. At this point I wonder whether there is some resistance to the Dutch poem on Coetzee's part; translation against the grain.

The version of the poem by the Irish poet Michael O'Loughlin is not a direct translation: it was made by him on the basis of a literal version by Peter van Kamp.[82] This is translation in stages, and since the poet responsible for the final version does not know Dutch, some interesting effects might be expected. The resulting poem has a striking rhythmic structure which makes it pleasantly easy to read since it acquires its own momentum in the expectation of a regular beat. Each line has a noticeable pause creating two distinct halves. While this is a feature of the Dutch up to a point and is reflected in the other two translations to a certain extent, in this version it almost becomes a structuring principle. This contributes to the stronger rhythm of O'Loughlin's version. Compare all three versions of line 3:

> He is writing himself upon the water he has lost his master. (Coetzee)
> He writes himself on the water he has lost his master. (Nathan and Spahr)
> He writes himself on water he has lost his master. (O'Loughlin)

---

82   See 'Editor's Preamble', Peter van de Kamp, ed., *Turning Tides: Modern Dutch and Flemish Verse in English Versions by Irish Poets* (Brownsville, OR: Story Line Press, 1994).

The second 'Basho' poem is a less impersonal poem than the first. It opens with 'We' and addresses the poet figure as 'you' as well as 'old master'. It continues the theme of poetry as a translation into words of what the poet has seen. This way, what has disappeared from the physical world is still perceptible as poetry, as is the fact of its vanishing. Coetzee's translation of this poem is less smooth than his version of the first 'Basho' poem. For example, in line 2 he uses commas that are not present in the Dutch. Here are the opening two lines:

> We know poetic poetry the common dangers
> Of moonstruckness, bel canto. Embalsamed air, that is all.[83]

Line 2 particularly stands out for its choice of words: moonstruckness is an unusual word which is not listed in the *Oxford English Dictionary*, although its meaning is transparent. However its sound is rather awkward, perhaps in contrast to 'bel canto' which stands out for a different reason, namely that though naturalized in English, it nevertheless retains its foreign form. And 'embalsamed' is both unusual (again not listed in the *OED*) and awkward with its three syllables and 'em/am' repetition. It also sets off associations with the more morbid 'embalmed'. As with Coetzee's translation of 'Basho I', it seems as though he has chosen a Dutch-sounding word which closely mimics the Dutch word it translates, 'gebalsemde' which means scented. In Nooteboom's poem the scented air denotes the flowery kind of poetry that is the opposite of Basho's concentrated haikus and the Dutch phrase is more accessible than Coetzee's choice. The overall strategy for this poem seems to be one of faithfulness, though words are transposed, preserving something of their foreignness.

The approach taken by Nathan and Spahr is more colourful and explicit than Coetzee's, rendering the expression rather than the language. Compare the two versions of line 1:

> We know poetic poetry the common dangers (Coetzee)
> We know the cheap perils of poetic poetry (Nathan and Spahr)

83   *Landscape with Rowers*, 63.

In the Nathan and Spahr version the poet's voice is more forceful and more everyday, partly because of the normalized word order and partly due to a more direct diction. Coetzee's Nooteboom says 'You, old master, polish the pebbles' to 'bring down a thrush' whereas Nathan and Spahr have 'kill a thrush' in line 5.

O'Loughlin's version reads more like a composed poem than a translated one. There is a distinct rhythmic shape which takes precedence over faithfulness. Take lines 4 and 5, for example:

> You, old master, hewed the stones
> With which you fell a thrush.

This shifts the metaphor used in all the other versions where stones or pebbles represent the words that poetry is made of to something more solid, perhaps the poem itself is like a block of stone. However, the reference in the following line to the poet carving an image works well with the hewn stone.

'Basho 3' is a highly intertextual poem which takes further the idea of vanishing – becoming imperceptible – expressed in the last line of the previous poem: 'so that what vanished is still there as something that vanished' (Coetzee). The poet Basho is present in the third poem through his own words which Nooteboom uses in lines 1 and 5.[84] What is more, 'Basho 3' contains an adapted line from another vanished poet, the Dutch poet and nomad J.J. Slauerhoff: 'Only in my poems can I dwell' in Coetzee's version. Nathan and Spahr again prefer a more straightforward diction which removes some of the ambiguity and in so doing some of the reader's uncertainty, creating quite a different reading experience. Here are the first three lines of 'Basho 3' in their version:

> On his hat of cypress he wrote: *Nowhere in this universe*
> *have I found a settled home.* Death took his hat off.
> As he should. But the line stayed with us.[85]

---

84   In the 'Notes' to *The Captain of the Butterflies* Nooteboom explains that the 'lines in italics refer to lines of Basho himself' (117).

85   *Captain of the Butterflies*, 78.

The opening half line and the use of the colon give the poem a definite feel and the italic line which refers to Basho's work (now doubly translated) is split across two lines. All other renderings of such lines are just that – they are arranged as full lines, just as they were in Nooteboom's poem. There is still some ambiguity in Nathan and Spahr's version: for example, in the second half of line 2 it is not clear whether death took off the poet's hat or his own, perhaps out of respect. The second half of line 3 is again more explicit if it is compared to the Dutch which uses the ambiguous word 'zin' which is both 'sentence' (the grammatical unit) and 'meaning'. Coetzee, in keeping with his airier, more mysterious approach opts for the less concrete 'The sense has remained.'

The third poem enacts a kind of rebirth of the poet Basho through his poetry. The poem opens with his death, and with the surviving line of poetry written on the cypress hat; what in 'Basho 2' had been a motif representing Basho is transferred to his work with the hat's removal by death. The last three lines directly address the hat:

> A little while, cypress hat, and you too will see them,
> The snow of Yoshino, the ice cap of Sado,
> The island that embarks for Soren over gravestone waves.[86]

Through the hat, that is, through Basho's poetry which survives, the poet himself sees again. The poetic conjuring trick is achieved by simple means: the residual ambiguity that resides in 'you'. The magic which works so well in Nathan and Spahr's version is spelled out in Coetzee's version: 'A while longer the cypress hat and you too will see them'.

Michael O'Loughlin also addresses the hat directly: 'A little longer, cypress hat, and you too will see them' so that through the hat's personification the poet Basho is briefly brought to life. When the following line states that 'you' will see 'The snow of Yoshina, the icehelm of Sado' the seeing subject is the originator of the poetic vision as well as its expression. The tone of this version is intimate and almost affectionate. In this version of 'Basho 3', O'Loughlin maintains the clarity of diction of his versions

---

86   *Captain of the Butterflies*, 78.

of the first two poems in the group. In this respect he is closer to Nathan and Spahr than Coetzee, though he does manage to keep the italic first line intact: 'Nowhere in this world have I a home/He wrote on his hat of cypress. Death removed his hat,/as is fitting. The sentence remained.'[87]

In 'Basho 4', the play with the identity of the poet figure takes a new turn: until this point the poem has addressed Basho and his emblematic hat as 'you' and by extension, perhaps, other poets. Now the poet figure seems to be separate from the addressee:

> The poet is a mill that turns the landscape to words.
> Yet he thinks like you and his eyes see the same. (Nathan and Spahr)

Is it now the reader to whom the last poem in the cycle is addressed? And in the last line a lyrical subject speaks for the first time. These are the last three lines in Coetzee's version:

> If he is where he never again will be you read his poems:
> he peeled cucumbers and mad-apples he paints his life
> *I too was tempted by the wind that blows the clouds.*

The 'I' who speaks here is a multiple subject: the lyrical subject; Basho, since this line originates in his work; and Nooteboom. The three versions of the final line use three different tenses of the first verb. Here are the remaining two translations:

> *I too am tempted by the wind that allows the clouds to drift.* (Nathan and Spahr)
> *I too have been lured by the wind which drives the clouds.* (O'Loughlin)

These create subtle shifts in the lyrical subject's self-positioning. O'Loughlin's is the most faithful rendering and seems to place the speaker beyond the experience looking back at his surrender to the wind, or the urge to wander, whereas Nathan and Spahr end the cycle with the poet actively experiencing this urge. And although Coetzee places the experience in the past, we do not know whether the subject succumbed to

---

87   Van de Kamp, ed., *Turning Tides*, 333.

'temptation'. In my view this creates two slightly different interpretations: in one (Coetzee, Nathan and Spahr) the subject is feeling or has felt the urge to wander, while the other (O'Loughlin) makes clear that the multiple subject has acted on the urge.

Reading Coetzee's translation of 'Basho 4' I am struck by the way in which a characteristically faithful rendering and thus a version that preserves some of the linguistic feel of the original poem can produce an English poem that has a more distinctive voice than the other two versions. Despite his strategy of closeness to the original Dutch, Coetzee is not afraid to add to Nooteboom's text, that is, to be more specific. In the penultimate line which refers to the preface to Basho's travelogue *Narrow Road to the Deep North*, Nooteboom simply refers to 'appels' or apples. Nathan and Spahr and O'Loughlin follow him in this. Only Coetzee uses 'mad-apple', a term for aubergine which appears in the English translations of Basho's work. The two other English versions of 'Basho 4' come across as more familiar, more normal, more accessible. They both favour a recognizable rhythm, and Nathan and Spahr are prepared to move away from the Dutch text in the interests of the pleasure of reading the English version. The fact that theirs are the only translations which are not accompanied by Nooteboom's poems in Dutch somehow reinforces their approach. O'Loughlin's versions might be better without the source text in my view. There are unfortunate inaccuracies in presentation which undermine the faith of a reader who knows Dutch: not only is Nooteboom spelt wrongly in the header to the pages, the Dutch poems have not been carefully transcribed so that each line begins with a capital letter when the original poems only do this at the start of a sentence; the capitalization does change their visual character making them more traditional-looking.

Nooteboom's Prose Poem: *Self-Portrait of an Other* or Translation as Rewriting

As the analyses of 'Basho' above demonstrate, each new hybrid version of the Dutch poem is subtly different and in this sense it recasts the author as the originator of the text along slightly different lines. In this section, I discuss *Self Portrait of an Other* as an independent, free-standing English collection of prose poems with no reference to the Dutch version, making Nooteboom a poet in a foreign language as well as a foreigner in his own language. The absence of reference to the source text again raises the interesting question of hybridity and authorship: the words I read are those of David Colmer, the translator, but the poetic diction and imaginative world are recognizably those of Nooteboom. This new book of prose poems is a beautifully executed volume of drawings and facing short prose pieces. It is a collaboration between Cees Nooteboom and the German artist Max Neumann, who are both given on the front cover as the book's authors, with the translator's name, David Colmer, also present towards the lower right-hand corner.[88]

In the opening section of this chapter, I noted that Nooteboom has collaborated with several artists on bibliophile editions of poetry, which have limited distribution. The widely distributed *Self-Portrait of an Other* now gives his English readership access to this aspect of his work. His fascination with the visual is perhaps the most important characteristic of his later poetry, although it has always been present. For example, the visual is the theme of the 1998 volume of poetry *Het gezicht van het oog* which translates literally as both 'The Sight of the Eye' and 'The Face of the Eye'. In his note to *Captain of the Butterflies* Nooteboom refers to the title as 'untranslatable'.[89] And the 'Basho' sequence discussed above pays homage to the Japanese poet's ability to convey the visual with words

---

88   Cees Nooteboom, *Self-Portrait of an Other*, trans. David Colmer, drawings Max Neumann (London: Seagull Books, 2011).
89   *Captain of the Butterflies*, 13.

Figure 4 Front cover, *Self-Portrait of an Other*.

in the concentrated medium of the haiku. At the same time, the poems' double articulation suggests that Basho's achievement is the achievement of poetry more widely.

Self-Portrait of an Other is the most recent of Nooteboom's poetry to be published in English in book form. The original poem was first published in Dutch in 1993. In the Netherlands it appeared in a small text edition with one of Neumann's drawings on the front cover. In the same year, it also appeared in German in a bilingual edition together with the drawings by Neumann that are reproduced in the newly published monolingual English edition. The fact that the English-speaking world had to wait eighteen years for the English version while the German version appeared more or less simultaneously with the Dutch one is more than a reflection of the collaboration with a German artist: it is also indicative of Nooteboom's standing in Germany.

Translation of the visual into the verbal is a major theme of the Basho cycle and is central to the creative interactions in *Self-Portrait of an Other*. Are the images a translation of what is written or vice versa; and what dynamic operates between image and verse? At the end of the *Self-Portrait*, after the thirty-third and last poem, there is an autobiographical note by Nooteboom dated 1992–3. In it, he explains the genesis of the poems, his working method and the relationship of the poems to the drawings. Actually, Nooteboom begins with the relationship between the two men which started with his being fascinated by the sight of Neumann at a party. Later, he felt a particular affinity with Neumann's art which led to a collaboration in which the two artists are equal, as neither is trying to depict or represent the other's work in the other medium. There is no attempt here to translate the visual into the written, although the note does disclose that Neumann's drawing existed prior to Nooteboom's words. Nooteboom describes the procedure as follows:

> instead of trying to describe his work, I would draw on its atmosphere and my own arsenal of memories, dreams, fantasies, landscapes, stories and nightmares to write a series of textual images as an echo, but unlinked, a mirror, but independent of the pictures he had given me.[90]

The title of the volume is less cryptic in the light of this explanation.

In *Self-Portrait of an Other*, Nooteboom and Neumann ask us readers to enter into an unreal world which is populated by creatures which question or even resist the traditional notion of what it is to be human.

90   *Self-Portrait*, poem XXXIII verso.

Neumann's images are of creatures with recognizably human elements, but also non-human parts that resemble everyday objects such as steps or a table. This immediately recalls certain poems by Nooteboom in which the lyrical subject becomes-object as in 'Koffer' (Suitcase) or 'Rockface'.[91] Death, present in the drawings in the recurring form either of a death's head or of absence, and fear, represented perhaps by a horrible dog, are also important features of the drawings. Sexuality is present less insistently, as well as evacuation of bodily fluids and solids. All images are set against a vibrant red background which I find surprisingly reassuring to look at and which helps contemplation of the absurd and unsettling drawings. In what follows, I shall focus mainly on the thirty-three texts which are each shorter than a page, and which each face one of Neumann's drawings.

The flap text prepares English readers for the unconventional nature of the book, describing it as a 'set of prose poems' that are 'full of striking scenes and disturbing images'. The book's subtitle 'Dreams of the Island and the Old City' seems to present the 'dream' as an alternative to 'poem' or 'prose poem'. This has the advantage of releasing readers from any expectation of a link between the poems and reality, or of poetry as a representation of the external world. Instead it is the outward form of an inward poetic disposition. All thirty-three dreams are linked by the presence of a nameless man, 'he', and are therefore told in the third person rather than the first person. Is he another of Nooteboom's avatars, fictional creations bearing similarities to the author found in the novels, and as we shall see also in the travel writing? The hybrid genre of the prose poem creates a space for multiplicity and uncertainty in which a reader may detect resemblances to and echoes of Nooteboom in his many guises, given expression in English by David Colmer:

> He thought of the first word, and then of the last, and imagined that somewhere, sometime, a voice would speak that last word just as that same voice, or a different one, had once spoken the first. (XXXIII)

---

91   *Vuurtijd, ijstijd*, 91–2; *Captain of the Butterflies*, 58.

The first poem in the volume recalls the poem 'Sleeping Gods' in its vision of an exhausted and old Hermes sitting on a rock. The nameless 'he' has apparently woken from a sleep on the beach and watches from a distance. That this is the unreality of dream is suggested by the nameless man's discovery of the old man's sandal prints in the sand: 'Alongside each one, the strange smudge of feathers' (I). The 'dreams' feature shadowy figures – on one occasion his father (XVII) and on another his mother (XXIV) and a dying friend (XIX); but mainly the figures are unknown, whether in anonymous crowds, a threatening mob or as women available for sex. Dogs and ants eat carrion while in other poems the man hunts 'the prey that is himself' (VIII), a theme that was found in the 1969 collection 'Gesloten gedichten', for example. A memory of a wartime train journey from his childhood through which he had passed many times later in life exposes the multiplicity within one human existence: 'There must still be photos with him in them, photos in which he didn't want to see himself. The number of lives in an old body is unbearable.' (VII)

In the poems, the man is not presented as an integrated whole of body and mind: there are the past selves which exist in the present, there is the body which is sometimes separate from the perceiving self. Moreover, there are no clear boundaries separating the humans who populate the dreams from the poet:

> It is spring and he has seen himself at least a hundred times in all his former incarnations: drunk, riven by fear, happy, in the snow on a pavement, at a graveside, in a hospital, a brothel, a monastery, visiting friends and women who are already dead. The city has changed and never changed, he has changed and changed again. (XXI)

The multiplicity is recalled by the image of his shadow, also described in the same poem as 'his dog-headed double' and 'a man walking hand in hand with himself'. In this world of transformations, fluidity becomes an important mode of being for the man and also an important medium. Hence the importance of the sea and river: he swims, and imagines disappearing in the sea. Flying – a different kind of free movement – also offers an escape, quite literally a line of flight. In poem XXII, the unnamed poetic figure hears music coming from a house. This leads to a reflection on silence as music and the sea as rhythm:

> The thought that the silence between the notes is calculated as time moves him. It turns the absence of sound into music, as invisible and inaudible as time itself. Audible, inaudible. In that silence he carries on until the greater silence has absorbed everything, sound and the opposite of sound. Only then has he reached the sea. Rhythm, the number of waves, sequence. (XXII)

As *Self-Portrait of Another* nears its conclusion, there is a stronger sense of silence, of absence that recalls the ending of *The Following Story*. The elements of man reaching his end, of ship and sea are all present, but this time, the ship itself is also disintegrating: 'It was a question of who would hold out the longest, him or the wreck. He leans on the missing rail and sees himself disappearing amid that which must remain, amid all the things that were already there' (XXVII). The following poem XXVIII describes a 'first lesson in absence' as a scene, a visual memory of a woman crossing a square in his direction without seeing him: 'Nothing happened except that he remembered it.' There is a sense of leaving the world of events and sensations behind. Blind and deaf, he can now commune with the bare earth, stripped of associations and human activity: 'He hears the rocks like a rock hearing its own sound, time's unbreakable now' (XXX). In the following poem, he ceases to look like himself and at the same time, in a reversal of Deleuze's becoming-animal, two dogs become human: 'He remembered their faces buried in the intestines: during their meal they had taken on human appearance. It would not have surprised him if they had spoken to each other. ... Still chewing, they had looked at each other briefly, then shrugged their shoulders like people who have been disturbed during dinner' (XXXI). The image this conjures up in words, rather like several of Neumann's visual images, contains an element of a wry humour that adds to the complexity of the emotions the text provokes. Nightmarish and unreal, poem XXXII sees the figure locked in the dark space of self with other faces in the emptiness around him that may or may not also be him. This seems to be a vision of the end of time, life, and the civilized world; he feels constantly under threat with no prospect of closure in the poem which ends with the lines 'The one who constantly threatened him knew what he was doing./That was the third face' (XXXII). The final poem ends with the prospect of silence which is outside of time, which must therefore be always already there: 'All things undone and robbed of their names, words erased until the first word too had never been said. Only then would it be silent again. Only then did it fall silent again' (XXXIII).

There are many echoes of Nooteboom's poetry and prose in these poems. The air of fear and the references to former selves who have lived on the edge of what might be called normal life recall the novella *Een lied van schijn en wezen* – with its setting on a Mediterranean island and its desperate main character. Island settings are also found in many of Nooteboom's poems and the more recent collection of stories *Rode regen*. But there are other prose poems that hint at many cities and landscapes in different parts of the world, such as XXXI in which he is driving 'along a coastal road in the tropics'. Perhaps Nooteboom's travel writing can also shed light on these prose poems, as it can on his other work. Many of his more conventional poems form a kind of record of places around the world he has visited and his experiences in them. In the next chapter I turn to that other genre practised by Nooteboom: his travel writing and to translation itself as a nomadic practice.

CHAPTER 6

The Travel Writing: Translation as a Nomadic Mode

Travel and mobility is central to Cees Nooteboom's existence and is part and parcel of his writing. As we saw in Chapter 4, 'Fictions of Becoming', his fictional worlds show a fascination with many kinds of linguistic and cultural difference, including differences brought about through the passage of time. Even when the setting is Nooteboom's home city of Amsterdam, as in *Rituals*, the narrative deals with the otherness of Japanese culture – the tea ritual as practised in Amsterdam by a Dutchman. And the chapter of this book devoted to Nooteboom's poetry was rounded off with a discussion of Nooteboom's homage to the Japanese poet Basho. These are two small examples of the way Nooteboom embraces strangeness and difference, welcoming it into his writing.

In this chapter, I turn to the writing in which Nooteboom narrates journeys he has undertaken, and in which I start out from the assumption that writer and narrator are one and the same person, that is Nooteboom speaking as himself, though in reality it is not quite this straightforward. Although I refer to this body of work as travel writing, it is a complex entity encompassing journalism, reportage, meditations, historical narratives, appreciation of art and architecture, road stories, fables and minimal autobiography which amount to a personal memoir of a writer's life. My aim in this chapter is to explore in depth the three books of travel writing published in English: *Roads to Santiago* (1997), *Nomad's Hotel* (2006) and *Roads to Berlin* (2012) and to discuss what kind of a travel writer Nooteboom is in English, bearing in mind the enormous differences between his English and Dutch travel oeuvres.

In my exploration, I am guided by the following questions: How does Nooteboom represent subjectivity, and to what extent do his characters and literary personae show nomadic traits? What is the effect of reading

Nooteboom's work as a representation of his own subjectivity – for example what role is played by the 'stranger within'? To what extent can Nooteboom be seen in his writings as a translator of other cultures? What kind of a translator/traveller is he? The first two are the core questions underlying the entire discussion of his work. In addition, I return to the ideas set out in Chapter 2 in which travel writing is seen as a form of cultural translation, with the result that I shall also consider the ways in which translators have dealt with the complexities of travel writing, particularly the question of double, or layered, translation. This will entail comparison with the source texts at relevant points in this chapter, but other than this, the Dutch works will not form part of the discussion beyond the short overview of the travel writing in Dutch that now follows.

Overview of Nooteboom's Travel Writing in Dutch

Not only is there a great deal of Nooteboom's travel writing in Dutch, but also the oeuvre is complex in two different ways: first, many of the books are compilations of short pieces around a theme which may have appeared earlier in newspapers, magazines or indeed other collections; second, the style and mode of travel writing practised by Nooteboom is itself complex and variable. One way of viewing these short pieces can be as a pool that can be dipped into from time to time to produce new combinations for publication, but as I hope this study makes clear, this fluid collection of travel pieces which is a result of decades spent travelling, and of revisiting certain places, yields a fascinating account of the writing and travelling subject that is Cees Nooteboom.

The most immediate way of giving an overview of the Dutch travel oeuvre is to reproduce below the list of his travel works from the website devoted to Nooteboom and his writing:

Een middag in Bruay. Columns, travel stories. De Bezige Bij, Amsterdam 1963.
Een nacht in Tunesië. Columns, travel stories. De Bezige Bij, Amsterdam 1965.
De Parijse beroerte. Essay. De Bezige Bij, Amsterdam 1968.

Een ochtend in Bahia. Columns, travel stories. De Bezige Bij, Amsterdam 1968.
Bitter Bolivia, Maanland Mali. Travel stories. De Bezige Bij, Amsterdam 1971.
Een avond in Isfahan. Travel stories. De Arbeiderspers, Amsterdam 1978.
Voorbije passages. Travel stories, essays. De Arbeiderspers, Amsterdam 1981.
Waar je gevallen bent, blijf je. Columns, travel stories, essays. De Arbeiderspers, Amsterdam 1983.
De zucht naar het Westen. Travel stories. De Arbeiderspers, Amsterdam 1985.
Het Spaanse van Spanje. Travel story. De Bijenkorf, Amsterdam 1986.
De wereld een reiziger. Travel stories, essays. De Arbeiderspers, Amsterdam 1989.
Berlijnse notities. Reportage, essays. De Arbeiderspers, Amsterdam 1990.
Vreemd water. Travel stories, essays. De Arbeiderspers, Amsterdam 1991.
De omweg naar Santiago. Travel stories, essays. Atlas, Amsterdam 1992.
De koning van Suriname. Verhalen. Muntinga, Amsterdam 1993.
De atlas van Cees Nooteboom. Travel stories with photographs by Eddy Posthuma de Boer. Atlas, Amsterdam 1993.
Van de lente de dauw. Oosterse reizen. Travel stories, essays. De Arbeiderspers, Amsterdam 1995.
De filosoof zonder ogen. Europese reizen. Travel stories, essays. De Arbeiderspers, Amsterdam 1997.
Nootebooms Hotel. Travel stories, essays. Atlas, Amsterdam 2002.
Het geluid van Zijn naam. Reizen door de Islamitische wereld. Travel stories, poetry. Atlas, Amsterdam 2005.
Tumbas. Graven van dichters en denkers. Essay, portraits. With photographs by Simone Sassen. Atlas, Amsterdam 2007.
Verleden als eigenschap. Kronieken 1961/1968. Edited by Arjan Peters. Atlas, Amsterdam 2008.
Berlijn 1989/2009. Reportage, essays. De Bezige Bij, Amsterdam 2009.
Journal de bord. Verre reizen. Travel stories. De Bezige Bij, Amsterdam 2009.[1]

Of the twenty-four texts listed here, the following can be regarded as the main source texts for the English versions: *De omweg naar Santiago* for *Roads to Santiago*, *Nootebooms Hotel* for *Nomad's Hotel*, and, for the newly published *Roads to Berlin*, *Berlijn 1989/2009* as well as *Berlijnse notities* (Berlin Notes) and *De filosoof zonder ogen* (The Eyeless Philosopher). My aim here is to give a short impression of the range of Nooteboom's travel works in Dutch, taking as my starting-point the way the stories are assigned

1   <http://www.ceesnooteboom.com/?page_id=84&lang=en> accessed 24 October 2012.

to particular text types. The designations are perhaps best thought of as indicative of the fluid nature of Nooteboom's travel writing.

The list given above contains indications after the titles of the types of travel writing in each book. In the 1960s and 1970s, these were mainly 'columns and travel stories', collections of journalistic short pieces that had previously appeared singly in the news press. *De Parijse beroerte* (The Paris Riots) is described here as an essay, though it is in fact a collection of twelve newspaper pieces written by Nooteboom for the Catholic newspaper *De Volkskrant* during two visits to France, first as a special correspondent in Paris during the unrest and then revisiting Paris for the elections as well as travelling in Brittany and the Auvergne. Here Nooteboom confines himself to describing events from the perspective of a sympathetic, semi-participant and their aftermath in the subsequent election defeat of the left. Perhaps this largely factual account is what gives rise to the description of essay.

In an article about Nooteboom's publications during the long gap between the novels *The Knight Has Died* and *Rituals*, Dutch academic Ton Anbeek charts the development of Nooteboom's distinctive style of travel writing.[2] Anbeek points out that Nooteboom seldom relates conversations with others, preferring to enter into conversation with time itself – and he also notes that in this period of Nooteboom's writing, the idea of travelling and memory comes into play. According to the list above, 1981 sees the first appearance of the combination of travel stories with essays, which is also how *De omweg naar Santiago* and *Nootebooms hotel* are both character-ized. This combination also recurs in two other collections published in the 1990s, though *Berlijnse notities*, published in 1990, is the first piece of travel writing to describe itself as reportage, and this designation is used again in *Berlijn 1989/2009*. Ton Anbeek highlights an increase in what he calls 'homework' – factual information – in the later travel writing, noting that *De omweg naar Santiago* turned into a cultural history of Spain.

---

2   Ton Anbeek, 'Reiziger in ruimte en tijd. Het werk van Cees Nooteboom tussen 1963 en 1980' in *De Gids*, 157, 1994, 565–74: <http://www.dbnl.org/tekst/_gid001199401_01/_gid001199401_01_0098.php> accessed 1 November 2012.

The collection titled *De koning van Suriname* is described as simply 'verhalen', or stories, and according to the Netherlands library service which categorizes it as travel stories, it contains the earliest travel pieces which were written for the Dutch magazine *Elseviers Weekblad* between 1957 and 1960.[3] There are also collaborations with photographers: Eddy Posthuma de Boer, who accompanied Nooteboom to Paris in 1968, and whose photographs form the main body of *De atlas van Nooteboom*, published to celebrate the writer's seventieth birthday; and Simone Sassen with whom he produced the book of graves of writers and philosophers – *Tumbas: Graven van dichters en denkers* which appeared in 2007. Although most of the travel writing speaks with the voice of a lone traveller, these photographers occasionally receive a mention, so that it is clear that the lone voice is a writerly stance, rather than a factual condition. In *Roads to Santiago*, for example, passing mention reveals that Posthuma de Boer is present for some of the journeys.

There is a pleasing lack of fixity in the travel oeuvre which, because of the regroupings, revisiting and repetitions, makes it clear that even the printed word can be a temporary phenomenon – here yesterday as newspaper articles, here today between two book covers, and not completely gone tomorrow, but, rather, reforming under new titles. A remark in *De Parijse beroerte* made on a different topic is almost prophetic in this respect: 'the incessant *becoming* [Nooteboom's emphasis] as opposed to the unchangeable which is always the same as itself ... I notice that it has stayed in my mind, and rightly so'.[4] Although J.M. Coetzee writes in English about Nooteboom, his knowledge of Dutch gives him access to all of Nooteboom's writing. In an essay 'Cees Nooteboom, Novelist and Traveller' he assesses Nooteboom's development as a travel writer as

---

3   From the NBD/Biblion review, accessed via bol.com: <http://www.bol.com/nl/p/de-koning-van-suriname/666802347/> accessed 20 November 20, 2012.

4   'het onophoudelijk *worden* tegenover het onveranderlijke altijd aan zichzelf gelijke ... ik registreer dat het in mijn hoofd is blijven hangen, en niet ten onrechte.' Cees Nooteboom, *De Parijse beroerte* (Amsterdam: De Bezige Bij, 1968), 34.

gradually shifting away from the journalistic travelogue as a genre in which to pass comment, at a necessarily superficial level, on the society and politics of another country, toward travel writing as a matrix within which to reflect on the deeper currents of life of a foreign culture.[5]

All of Nooteboom's travel work that has been translated into English can be seen as forming such a matrix, at least, this is the overall effect even when there are some components that come closer to travelogue. The notion of travel writing as a matrix suggests a form, a structure and a function that go beyond what is possible under the guise of travel writing as it is traditionally understood in English. Another way of looking at it is to say that Nooteboom transforms the genre – this aspect will form another focus of my investigations where I emphasize the rhizomatic structure of individual texts.

Introduction to Nooteboom's Travel Writing in English

Cees Nooteboom has published three books of travel writing in English: *Roads to Santiago*, translated by Ina Rilke (1997), *Nomad's Hotel*, translated by Ann Kelland (2006) and *Roads to Berlin*, translated by Laura Watkinson (2012). While the two 'Roads' books have a clear geographical focus, Spain and Germany respectively, *Nomad's Hotel* ranges far and wide geographically, culturally, and in its form and content. Nooteboom's English travel oeuvre has a very different shape from the Dutch one, and does not participate in the shape-shifting described above, since its origins are so different. Whereas the Dutch travel books are generated from Nooteboom's journalism which consists of individual articles published separately, forming a pool of short prose pieces from which any number of collections can be drawn and redrawn, the English travel books have

---

5   J.M. Coetzee, *Stranger Shores: Essays 1986–1999* (London: Vintage Books, 2002), 65.

their genesis in comparable books in Dutch. This leaves English readers unaware of the journalistic origins of individual components and removes the baggage that had adversely affected Dutch critical opinion in the 1970s and 1980s. Here, I want to argue that the mutability of the Dutch oeuvre, which feels like a resistance to permanence, is successfully translated into a rhizomatic structure and the content in the three English texts, i.e. that it is possible to translate a reforming, regrouping approach to short journalistic pieces into a new literary form by using a rambling, episodic mode, rhizomically structured. Detailed discussion of the texts will uncover aspects of this form, which is not unlike Coetzee's notion of the matrix structure.

How does Nooteboom's travel writing fit in with travel writing in English, where there is an acknowledged literary tradition? In Peter Hulme's survey 'Travelling to Write (1940–2000)', he identifies a new post-war generation that includes Norman Lewis and Patrick Leigh Fermor and whose writing 'rediscovers its connections with journalism and cultural history'.[6] While both journalism and cultural history might seem to be elements in common with Nooteboom, the style and texture of the writing is less complex than Nooteboom's who shares more features with what according to Hulme is an 'emergent genre: allusive and literary meditations, with elements of autobiography and travel writing'.[7] Here he is discussing the work of V.S. Naipaul who produced fiction as well as travel writing, and the above comment was actually made in relation to later fiction of Naipaul's that appeared in the late 1980s and early 1990s. This mobility across genre boundaries not only applies equally to Nooteboom; he constantly explores the border zone between fact and fiction. And when I look in more detail at the travel works, the question of fictionalization will again arise. When discussing his autobiographical writing in Chapter 3, I also looked at the way he fictionalizes himself, for example. As I hope to show, self-fictionalization is also a significant characteristic of the travel writing which adds something

6　Peter Hulme, 'Travelling to Write (1940–2000)', in Peter Hulme and Tim Youngs, eds, *The Cambridge Companion to Travel Writing* (Cambridge: Cambridge University Press, 2002), 88.

7　Hulme, 'Travelling to Write', 89.

new to the genre. *Roads to Santiago* appeared in 1997, and is still in print at the time of writing this: a distinct sign of success in the English book market. One possible reason for this success could be the timeliness of its appearance in English given that, according to Hulme, a mode of writing combining autobiography and travel was becoming popular.

At the same time, however, Nooteboom's travel writing has much in common with the next generation identified by Hulme. Here is Hulme's description of a book by Peter Mathiessen: '*The Snow Leopard* reintroduced spirituality and earnestness to travel writing, with Mathiessen producing a pilgrimage into the unknown where the physical travel doubles as, and intensifies, an inner journey.'[8] Again there are elements that are reminiscent of *Roads to Santiago*, though Nooteboom's pilgrimage is very different and his narrative far less cohesive. The writer whose tone perhaps comes closest to Nooteboom's is Bruce Chatwin in Hulme's account, where his quest is 'constantly ironised, frequently forgotten, and only finally fulfilled in a distinctly unheroic and almost surreal fashion' and his tone is described as 'offhand.'[9] Indeed, in his review of *Nomad's Hotel*, Paul O'Brien links the two writers through their nomadism: 'Nooteboom, like Chatwin's nomads, is at ease with his lifetime of wandering; he is *at home* in it.'[10]

The reception of Nooteboom's travel writing in English has been generally positive. He has been positioned by his publisher alongside Patrick Leigh Fermor, Norman Lewis, Jan Morris and Claudio Magris: the review in which he is admitted to this canon of travel writers is cited on the covers of *Roads to Santiago* and again on the cover of *Roads to Berlin*.[11] And O'Brien predicts in the review cited above that 'he will be in the august company of Magris, Brenan, Fermor and Morris'.

8   Hulme, 'Travelling to Write', 90.
9   Hulme, 'Travelling to Write', 91.
10   Paul O'Brien, 'To Aran or Isfahan', *Dublin Review of Books*, no. 3 (Autumn 2007): <http://www.drb.ie/more_details/08-09-28/To_Aran_or_Isfahan.aspx> accessed 30 October 2012.
11   The review in question is by Euan Cameron in *The Daily Telegraph* (1 February 1997).

Roads to Santiago: Detours and Riddles in the Lands and History of Spain

The long title of this book gives readers a good sense of the kind of text they are dealing with: travel which is not narrated in linear way and ideas which are not presented in a straightforward manner. Before looking at the text in the light of my questions, I will attempt to give an impression, a flavour of the book which can perhaps best be summed up as a declaration of love for Spain. The text is a bit like a riddle itself: it is hard to pin down. When do the narrated events all take place? Who is this narrator with his obsessions with the past, with silence, with ancient places of worship, with Spain? Is this a pilgrimage? And is this really Spain? The book consists of twenty-five chapters, each of which relates the narrator-traveller's arrival at a new place with attendant digressions on history, architecture, painting and musings inspired by his own reading. Sometimes the present in the shape of his contemporary surroundings intrudes when he is describing local meals and people, and reading newspapers.

Although the chapters are not dated, I do detect shifts in the narrator's attitudes to Spain, and to the business of travel writing. Comparison with the source text shows that in the Dutch book each chapter is dated which reveals some interesting jumps in time and makes the book's genesis much clearer. I think an English reader would have appreciated this information since the text itself contains so many references to past visits that the reader is only too aware of the sedimentation effect, but without the means to reflect on it. But first, the question of the narrator's identity is worth a moment's consideration. Since this is travel writing, the convention is that the narrating 'I' is indeed Nooteboom, and I would certainly not want to dispute this. But I would like to point out a couple of instances of self-fictionalization: the passage in the first chapter narrated in the third person, and the matter of Nooteboom as a lone traveller. The narrative of Nooteboom's journey to Spain by boat opens in the dominant mode: 'It is impossible to prove and yet I believe it: there are some places in the world where one is mysteriously magnified on arrival or departure by the emotions of all who have arrived and departed before' (3).[12] This writing mode combines the personal narration of the traveller's consciousness with pronouncements that are framed as general truths either giving Nooteboom's beliefs and ideas, or introduced by a phrase such as 'Legend has it that ...'. However, by page 6, the narration is subtly changing: the 'I' narrator is making way for general description of the boat heading for Barcelona. The narrator becomes part of the crowd – there is one mention of 'we' – and the narrator assumes the more general tone of reportage: 'Guitars and clapping on the afterdeck, people are singing, drinking, the deck passengers are settling down for a long night in their steamer chairs ...'. Then the narrative zooms in on what seems to be the main character of this section: 'The lone traveller' who 'goes to his cabin and lies down ...'[13] Although this passage is no longer than a page, its positioning near the beginning of the first chapter lends it significance: in effect it introduces the conceit of Nooteboom as a lone traveller, which is the dominant type of narrative in *Roads to Santiago*.

In a Dutch article on Nooteboom and Spain, Wim Hottentot has also pointed out the fiction in Nooteboom's travel writing that the author is all alone.[14] We know both from passing references to a travelling companion and from sources outside *Roads to Santiago* that the writer was frequently accompanied by his friend the photographer Eddy Posthuma de Boer and later by his partner Simone Sassen, also a photographer. The travelling relationship between Nooteboom and Posthuma de Boer is explored in some detail by Margot Dijkgraaf in her introduction to *De atlas van Nooteboom*.[15] I want to suggest that in the passage on pages 7–8 of *Roads to Santiago* where the narrative switches to 'he', Nooteboom is fictionalizing himself and that the fictional 'lone traveller' is also incorporated

---

12   *Roads to Santiago*, 3.
13   *Roads to Santiago*, 6–8.
14   Wim Hottentot, 'Aanwezig afwezig', in Harry Bekkering, Daan Cartens and Aad Meinderts, eds, *Ik had wel duizend levens en ik nam er maar één! Cees Nooteboom* (Amsterdam and Antwerp: Atlas, 1997), 123.
15   Margot Dijkgraaf, 'De atlas van Nooteboom', in Eddy Posthuma de Boer and Margot Dijkgraaf, *De atlas van Nooteboom* (Amsterdam and Antwerp: Atlas, 2003), 7–16.

in the 'I' narrator. In other words, there can be no perfect and complete coincidence of 'I'-narrator and Nooteboom because of the shifting nature of multiple subjectivity. Temporality also plays a role in the fictionalization process, since the book is composed at a distance in time and place from the travelling, rather than being an immediate record of experience. Again, Nooteboom makes no secret of this and makes reference to his notebooks which he uses later on when writing up a journey. For example, 'The courtyard is high and empty, there are some purple flowers I cannot identify. Later, I will come across a dried specimen in my notebook and will find it impossible to imagine just how vividly they stood out against these blind walls.'[16]

This seemingly innocent passage deserves closer scrutiny. It is narrated in the present tense as if registering the scene like camera. However, we know that Nooteboom's method of working was to record his experiences in notebooks – what he has called his 'external memory' and only write up his narratives once he had completed the journey.[17] So the narrative looks ahead to the future when Nooteboom will be writing up this moment and at the same time – with the benefit of hindsight, since the scene has of course already been written – he knows what the act of remembering will be like. This temporal complexity serves to highlight the layered or multiple nature of the 'I' narrator.

This discussion goes some way towards answering one of the questions I posed at the outset: what is the effect of reading Nooteboom's work as a representation of his own subjectivity – for example what role is played by the 'stranger within' (as discussed in Chapter 2)? The 'I' narrator can be seen as a representation of a nomadic or multiple subject, and the element of the third person contained within the 'I' can be seen as a representation of the stranger within. The multiplicity is already in evidence from the perspective of temporality: the writing subject looking back on the

---

16   *Roads to Santiago*, 275.
17   See, for example, Dijkgraaf's account of the stolen notebook in 'De atlas van Nooteboom', 11.

travelling subject, and given that the book is a about revisiting key places, there are past selves who are never quite identical.

The interesting question of how the travelling subject deals with strangeness within and without leads me to consider where strangeness is found in *Roads to Santiago*. First of all, Nooteboom characterizes himself as a stranger in the closing sentence of the first chapter: 'a stranger driving a car through the land of Aragón'. And having described the absurdity and chaos of Spain in Chapter III, he identifies these same characteristics in himself – the strange or foreign within – and ascribes his love of Spain to this fact.[18] In the closing chapter he still describes himself as a stranger, though he adds a puzzling comment:

> I was a stranger and would always remain so, but I had also become a stranger who had come to recognize what he already knew, and that was another story.[19]

Here is my own translation of the same passage:

> I was a stranger and would always remain one, which was a good thing, but I had become a stranger who came in order to recognize what he already knew, and that was a different story.

In my version, the traveller embraces his foreignness while at the same time acknowledging a becoming-pilgrim, i.e. that the journey was undertaken with the aim of self-knowledge and that in his case, this knowledge takes the form of finding what was already there.

It is significant for assessing Nooteboom's relationship with Spain that at the end of the journey he reasserts his status as a stranger in the country. Wim Hottentot draws attention to a similar pronouncement of Nooteboom's in *De filosoof zonder ogen* (The Eyeless Philosopher), which appeared in 1997 after the Dutch version of *Roads to Santiago* and in which Nooteboom responds to an encounter with a shepherd with '*I* am the one who does not belong here' as the shepherd becomes one with the

18   *Roads to Santiago*, 33.
19   *Roads to Santiago*, 394–5.

landscape.[20] Hottentot also sums up what he sees as the core of Nooteboom's relationship with Spain: something monastic in the Spanish character. According to Hottentot, this explains the duality of Nooteboom's response to Spain, 'the paradoxical combination of quiet, stillness, wholeness, hierarchy … and chaos, dreaming and anarchy'.[21]

There are two distinct aspects of Nooteboom's travel writing in this book: i) the narrative of his physical and emotional engagement with the country and ii) his self-positioning in relation to its society, culture and history and thus as a traveller-translator. His protestations of foreignness, or of not belonging can be considered against the evident depth of his connection with particular aspects of Spain. This can be viewed as another of the riddles posed by *Roads to Santiago*. Many critics have noticed Nooteboom's near obsession with religious places and spaces, which as he himself frequently points out, is hardly contemporary Spain. He is drawn to the fact of their survival from ancient times and is seeking those moments of intensity when he connects with the distant past, even in a small way. In the following example he is looking at a painting in a church depicting Christ being whipped:

> I look at all those eyes avoiding me, only the Moorish king, a black man wearing black velvet slippers and yellow-and-black striped stockings, returns my stare, as if he and I are the only ones to have any business here; the rest, wise men, soldiers, kings, martyrs, are locked in a silent world of their own, as if they have always known that the drama they are enacting would be invalidated by time and that they would one day be seen by people who no longer understood what they represented, as if to resist their transformation from article of faith into work of art …[22]

This fascination with the past in art and architecture is not nostalgic, there is no longing to return to a bygone age. Far from it: Nooteboom does not lament the loss of Christianity as the foundation of European culture, he sees that his gaze changes the painting's function from a religious to an aesthetic one.

20   '*ik* ben degene die hier niet thuishoort', cited by Hottentot, 'Aanwezig afwezig', 128.
21   Hottentot, 'Aanwezig afwezig', 127.
22   *Roads to Santiago*, 163.

During a visit to the Escorial, a large painting of a battle fails to produce the moment of intensity – 'I walk past as if I am inspecting a military
parade' – instead it is in the throne room of Philip II that the time gap is
erased: 'It is light in this room, light and deserted, as if that little chair with
the red cushion was left just a moment ago by someone who will presently
return.'[23] These places of intensity also give rise to meditations and reflections on history and art history which themselves involve an engagement
with historical and literary texts. Such moments of intensity generate their
own pleasure, a reason, perhaps for their repetition. In an essay on indi-
viduation and subjectivation in Deleuzian thought, Marc Rölli discusses
the role of intensity as underlying processes of becoming. He relates this
to spatio-temporal perception as follows:

> One could say that in the (binocular) 'seeing of depth' the perceiving subjectivity
> is made complicit, namely in the passive syntheses of disparate monocular images.
> From here it is but a short step for Deleuze to associate the original relation of
> perception to its background, its own depth, with the coexistence of the pure past
> within the present.[24]

Although I cannot do justice here either to the intricacies of Rölli's article
or to the complexities of Deleuze's thought, I am nevertheless inspired by
this linking of intensity with the idea of the past in a deep perception of
the present. And since I have presented Nooteboom throughout the book
as a writer who engages deeply with his own subjectivity, without ever
turning it into a coherent, smooth narrative I think that it is this aspect of
the travel writing that links it to Nooteboom's other writing. This is how
Nooteboom explains the effect of travel on himself: 'I am extended by everything I see, consume, amass. It is not a question of higher knowledge, it

23   *Roads to Santiago*, 123.
24   Marc Rölli, 'Deleuze on Intensity Differentials and the Being of the Sensible', *Deleuze
     Studies*, Vol. 3 (June 2009), 42–3: <http://www.euppublishing.com.libproxy.ucl.
     ac.uk/doi/abs/10.3366/E1750224109000476> accessed 1 November 2012. I am
     aware that my reference scarcely does justice to this article – but to go fully into
     the philosophy here would take me too far from my subject of Nooteboom's travel
     writing.

is more like sedimentation. An accretion of images, texts, of all the lasting impressions that come my way from the street, from television, conversations, newspapers.'[25] The English text also describes him as 'bloated' and 'thickened' – is this travel as a kind of pregnancy which results in a travel book?

One of the puzzles of *Roads to Santiago* is the complex question of Nooteboom and Spain. He clearly is no ordinary tourist by virtue of the fact that part of his relationship with the country involves repeated visits and even revisiting certain places. There is no doubting the depth of his engagement partly because of the layering effects of time, whether as history or recorded experience, and this provides the texture of *Roads to Santiago*. Because the moments of intensity occur during visits to ancient buildings and provide prominent reference points in the landscape of the text, it is easy to overlook Nooteboom's engagement with contemporary Spain: for example, he plays down his knowledge of the language. Yet is clear from conversations and what he learns from Spanish media that in this respect, the relationship is a close one. When it comes to the activities of ETA for instance, he is passionate in his support of Spanish democracy and clear that terrorism is not the way forward. His respect for Spanish democracy is born of his historical understanding that as a political system it is still too new to disrupt.

In the early part of the book he seems to refuse the role of cultural translator in the sense that he does not display his mastery of the language or attempt to interpret Spanish culture to the reader. Returning to the conception of translation and travel which I put forward in Chapter 2, I would say that he does not seek to assert himself or dominate Spanish culture. He is a guest in the language and culture who observes and registers what he sees, and responds to it. The visit to the elderly couple in the remote village of Lebeña is emblematic of this position. They invite him into their house for a glass of *orujo*, a strong spirit distilled from grape skins – 'I sip the *orujo*, which cuts through me like a knife'.[26] His respect-

---

25 *Roads to Santiago*, 207.
26 *Roads to Santiago*, 188.

ful, humane attitude allows the old couple the space to tell their stories of participation in war: the old man was wounded in the Spanish Civil War 'on the right side', whereas his brother fought for the Germans in Russia in the Second World War. In the text, Nooteboom reciprocates their hospitality by welcoming their language, Spanish, into his text. Although most of the encounter is narrated in English and is therefore a (double) translation, he relates a comment by the old lady in Spanish as if to remind us that we readers are also guests in a Spanish home.

On the same page as the Spanish sentence, we also find snippets of French, and elsewhere Dutch, medieval Spanish, Latin, but the German and English in the source text have become invisible in English, the former through translation, the latter through lack of contrast with the language of the narrative. The text's multilingual stance suggests that rather than being the kind of global traveller who moves easily across cultural boundaries by ignoring them, Nooteboom's cosmopolitanism is akin to what in Chapter 2 I termed 'new cosmopolitanism' following in the footsteps of David Hollinger and Michael Cronin. The point about this kind of cosmopolitanism is that it is accepting of local cultural traditions while being outward-facing, and in Cronin's view the new cosmopolitan should have moved on from a primary cultural identity to multiple affiliations. On the evidence of *Roads to Santiago*, Nooteboom can be reckoned among the new cosmopolitans. I use this concept here as a way of summarizing Nooteboom's attitude to Spain in this text. In the next section, I look at *Nomad's Hotel* to see if this description still holds good.

Nomad's Hotel: Travels in Time and Space

Unlike *Roads to Santiago* this collection of travel pieces is not focussed on one country, but on many. And whereas the writing on Spain revealed the complexity and multiplicity of Spain through its meanderings and musings on that country's history, art, culture in all its layers, *Nomad's Hotel* provides readers with quirky, humorous yet serious stories of travel in Europe and to Africa, Australia and Iran. While they make pleasurable reading, the volume acquires its depth through the reflective pieces on travel: 'In the Eye of the Storm', 'Nooteboom's Hotel I and II' which alert the reader to other reflective comments made in passing. I want to argue here that it is the self-reflexive element of this book that produces a work of nomadic literature. In what follows I look briefly at the reception of *Nomad's Hotel* before I discuss the narrative methods and representation of the traveller's subjectivity, what kind of traveller-writer emerges from these stories, and the ways in which translation permeates the text.

The text's reception in English has been surprisingly positive for a work that according to one reviewer does not fit in with the genre in English: 'The relatively short works here are not ... pieces that slip easily into the conventional Anglo-American travel-writing genre. (That's part of what renders them rather mesmerizing.)'[27] The use of the term mesmerizing to describe the intense experience of reading finds echoes in other reviews where it often applies to the intensity of experience conveyed by the text: for example, 'Nooteboom's electrifying view of the world' and 'fresh with childlike wonder for the world'.[28] Reviewers also appreciate the meditative qualities of the book – Paul O'Brien in the *Dublin Review of Books* is emphatic about this: 'The exquisite, meditative chapters of *Nomad's Hotel* serve as a fitting testament to Nooteboom's nomadic life and, in the wake of the publication in English of *Roads to Santiago*, it was important that they be translated and anthologised.'[29] Guy Mannes-Abbott sees travel as Nooteboom's ultimate subject, something he describes as 'a meditative movement through unknown places and the bottomless past'; movement

27 Review by Tim Rutten, *Los Angeles Times* (8 April 2009): <http://articles.latimes.com/2009/apr/08/entertainment/et-rutten8> accessed 9 November 2012.

28 Rory MacLean, 'A 30-year Odyssey', *The Guardian* (8 February 2007): <http://www.guardian.co.uk/travel/2007/feb/08/travelbooks.rorymaclean.bookreviews/> accessed 9 November 2012.

29 Paul O'Brien, 'To Aran or Isfahan', *Dublin Review of Books*, no. 3 (Autumn 2007): <http://www.drb.ie/more_details/08-09-28/To_Aran_or_Isfahan...> accessed 30 October 2012.

'not towards God, but "mystery"'. He concludes his review with the interesting remark that 'the meditations on place and time in Nomad's Hotel
achieve a potent state of non-completion', leaving it to his readers to draw
their own conclusion as to the nature of this state.[30] I will return to this
idea when I discuss how Nooteboom represents his subjectivity and the
effects of travel on him.

The reviewers are full of praise for Nooteboom's personal approach to
travel as expressed in these stories which comes across to them as sincere,
kind and inspired by his empathy for his fellow creatures. Guy Mannes-
Abbott's remark that 'He communes with long-departed slaves and a cockroach as big as a child's thumb.' draws attention to Nooteboom's feeling for
those on the margins, something which is there in both his fiction and his
poetry, as we saw in Chapters 4 and 5 of this book. When Sandy Balfour in
The Spectator notes that Nooteboom's method of travelling involves being
there 'as witness not protagonist' I think that this relates to Nootboom's
reluctance to impose himself on his surroundings, as was discussed above
in relation to *Roads to Santiago*. In the quote from Balfour which follows,
the values which Nooteboom the traveller represents for him are clear:

> And there he [Nooteboom] waits, patiently, humanely, intelligently, watching a
> human comedy – or perhaps the human comedy – unfold. He remembers to ask the
> question many would forget: 'At which desk would you have to apply in Holland,
> in order to speak to the Queen?'[31]

What this last question signifies is the humility and reciprocity of
Nooteboom's approach in an act of translation – of his own position into
that of the others who are the object of his gaze.

In *Nomad's Hotel*, we encounter the same process of self-fictionalization
as in *Roads to Santiago*. The first occurrence is in 'Forever Venice' where

---

30   Guy Mannes-Abbott, 'A contemporary nomad's meditations and musings on the
      move', *The Independent* (9 March 2006): <http://www.independent.co.uk/arts-
      entertainment/books/reviews/nomads-hotel-by-cees-nooteboom-trans-by-ann-
      kelland-469219.html> accessed 22 November 2012.
31   Sandy Balfour, 'Watching the human comedy unfold', *The Spectator*, 4 March 2006.

there is a transition from an 'I' narrator to the figure of 'the traveller' via the second-person pronoun 'you' which functions as a bridge.

> It is bound to happen. You have been wandering in the Accademia all day, you have seen a solid mile of painted canvas, it is the fourth, the sixth, or the eighth day and you feel as though you are swimming against a powerful current ...[32]

Next the narration shifts to a general description in the third person plural – 'they' referring to the people, real and mythical, represented in paint and stone:

> So there they stand, a nation of Stone Guests, waving from the facades of churches, leaning out of the *trompe l'oeuils* of the *palazzi* ... The traveller draws back from all the tumult, for the moment he wants no more, just to sit on a stone seat ...[33]

The story 'Musings in Munich' stands out as the only one in the collection that is told entirely from the traveller figure's perspective with no use of 'I' at all. The story deals with two significant features of Nooteboom's writing: minimal reference to the Second World War together with close involvement with the past. In this story the connection between the two becomes a little clearer. Brief references to the main character's childhood memories of German soldiers marching into the Netherlands are never dwelt on and it is this fact that conveys a sense of traumatic memory – 'The past as profession, a form of sickness, surely?'[34] The sight of an old man in anachronistic clothing sparks memories of father figures, and the protagonist-traveller recalls an evening in the United States when an old man who had been a Jewish refugee from Nazi Germany had asked him to read Rilke to him in German. The narrated memory of that evening succeeds in conveying the trauma of loss without actually speaking of the events that gave rise to that loss. In its narrative economy and silences, it performs trauma.

32   *Nomad's Hotel*, 12.
33   *Nomad's Hotel*, 13.
34   *Nomad's Hotel*, 54.

He had read more that late afternoon, but during the final lines of this poem he had seen how the lips of his host were moving in time to his own, and he had been touched, a feeling which now came over him again, as though no gap could possibly exist between that *then* and his *now*. The old man was dead, as was his friend's father, plus a few more of those men who seemed constantly to cross his path, as though a rare form of predestination was involved. ... Survival had wrapped itself about them like a second soul, not the surviving itself, for all five of them were now dead, but rather that which they had survived, and about which not one of them had ever spoken to him.[35]

The mention of what seems to him like predestination suggests that he is somehow on the lookout for a father figure: somewhere beyond the moment being narrated lies another loss which is completely absent from the narrative – that of Nooteboom's own father in a bombing raid in The Hague.[36] At the same time, it is Nooteboom himself who is the survivor. In my interpretation of this passage, which I experience as something intensely personal to the author, I found myself turning to the author's biography and reading the 'he' as if it were an 'I'. Through this self-fictionalization, the narration represents the writer's subjectivity: his confrontation with the traumatic past which is both his own, as someone who experienced a major European conflict, and that of many of the people and places he encounters on his travels.

The stories about the Gambia and Mali are interesting in this respect since they represent a different aspect of Europe's past, its colonial legacy, thus adding another dimension. For one who spends much time reflecting on the past, it is important to note that there is absolutely no trace of colonial nostalgia. These pieces are well-observed accounts of the 'contact zone', as Mary Louise Pratt has called it, in which Nooteboom's mildly amused tone is directed at both the present-day culture and at the English colonizers. However, the decision to represent the Africans' English accent in a crude way may provide some local colour, but is perhaps too reminiscent of racist music hall humour to be a comfortable read for the English

35   *Nomad's Hotel*, 60.
36   This death is narrated later in the book in the episode 'That Earlier War: the Memorial in Canberra', *Nomad's Hotel*, 113.

audience. This is not necessarily a criticism of the writer, since the translator is the one to have created this accented speech and can be seen as having an ethical role to play in deciding how to represent these postcolonial subjects. On the other hand, the 'motley bunch' of passengers on the boat up the Gambia river are also described with a dispassionate eye. Nor does Nooteboom escape the ironic treatment himself:

> I really feel I am in Africa. There are so many stars that even the lights on the fishing boats seem to be included; stars floating on the water. I experience a moment of cosmic pride, undergo a metaphysical relationship with the overwhelming firmament, tempered by clichéd notions like 'only this morning I was in Amsterdam and now I'm in ... et cetera,' and fall asleep, a twentieth-century supermarket-Stanley in a hut with a shower.[37]

Nooteboom emerges from *Nomad's Hotel* as a rather different kind of traveller from the Nooteboom we see in Spain, because we encounter him in such a range of contact zones, some of which are outside Europe and have this postcolonial dimension. The issue of globalization and its relation to the local is much more in evidence here. Although the book itself appeared in 2006, many of the pieces were written decades earlier: 'Moonscape Mali' is the earliest. Dated 1971, this piece follows in the footsteps of many European men who had gone before, whether as explorers, travellers, or as anthropologists, and Nooteboom ironically positions himself in relation to this tradition in the reference to Stanley quoted above. He is aware of his predecessors in 'Moonscape Mali', though his reference to Lévi-Strauss is rather earnest and conveys an appreciation of cultural difference and implied criticism of the European sense of superiority. Nooteboom displays here a determination to look beyond European stereotypes of Africa:

> I lie on the bed and think about my journey, about the man in Paris who, before I left, said to me: 'Africa? It's never been viable, it's not viable now and it never will be either. I used to be enthusiastic too, but I've been going there for twenty years and it's hopeless. Their entire history consists of bloodshed and murder, and that's how

37 *Nomad's Hotel*, 183.

it'll remain.' I do not recognise his despair, or his bitterness. Whenever aircraft are twenty-four hours late, all hell breaks loose among European and American passengers. In spoiled isolation, having become asocial through self-indulgence, the white man travels through Africa and sees zilch.[38]

Nooteboom's pieces in this book testify, bear witness (to use terms from his English reception) to the Africa he encounters. His method is to attempt to register what he sees, and though the resulting text lacks the detail to be ethnographic, I think that it is written in this spirit. The effect of this is to value the local and the specific. For the duration of a visit he operates on local terms without imposing European and American norms and standards – of comfort, for example: he tolerates the cockroach and the giant spider and suppresses any urge to kill which is the standard white man's response to African wildlife. From *Nomad's Hotel*, I think it is possible to say that Nooteboom's cosmopolitanism, even thirty or forty years ago, was one that values the local while at the same time being in the forefront of the early expansion of global travel.

What kind of cultural translation does Nooteboom's approach to the other cultures in *Nomad's Hotel* involve? He records in the Dutch language his experiences in a range of different places with their people, cultures, languages and local practices. He makes references to local languages, even when he does not know the language concerned and gives occasional examples. The translation process involves taking notes primarily in Dutch which are used to produce a discursive kind of translation in the form of the travel writing in Dutch. This is then itself translated into English – and many other languages – so that the resulting translation is triple-layered. The travel pieces attest to a conscious enjoyment of being a foreigner which entails awareness of the local perspective. This is clearly expressed in 'At the Edge of the Sahara'.

> The same old sense of excitement. Seeing things you do not understand, a language you cannot fathom, a religion you do not have any real conception of, a landscape which rebuffs you, lives you could not share. ... If you are unable to join in there is a lot

38   *Nomad's Hotel*, 215.

you can dispense with. Your masks do not count. As far as a Berber from Goulimine is concerned you could easily be from Ohio, so that many of the nuances one has taken pains to cultivate no longer apply.[39]

Nooteboom goes on to describe this kind of travel as 'a pleasant sort of void, a state of zero-gravity in which, although the self does not lose all significance, a good deal does get written off'. The state of mind that this induces stands in contrast to the intense and deep engagement with Spain in *Roads to Santiago*.

There is no source text for *Nomad's Hotel*, i.e. there is no equivalent identical volume of travel pieces in Dutch. There is a volume in Dutch with a similar title, *Nooteboom's hotel*, but even a cursory comparison of the tables of contents reveals that although there are some pieces in common (the opening essay 'In the Eye of the Storm' and 'Nootebooms hotel' as well as the narratives of journeys to Venice, Aran and Zurich), there are many more in the Dutch version, and the remainder in the English version first appeared in other Dutch collections. According to Nooteboom in a round-table discussion, this has nothing to do with translation as such, and everything to do with circumstance.[40] He explains that the first version of the book was actually the German one which came about in response to the demand for his travel writing in Germany and which appeared in 2000. After volumes devoted to European travel and travel in Asia and America, there were still enough pieces left for a more random collection. The conceit of the imaginary hotel that is compiled of bits of many of the hotels in the world where Nooteboom has stayed, was what Nooteboom calls 'the prime idea of the German "ur-text" of *Nootebooms Hotel*'.[41] The Dutch version was prepared on the basis of the German one, and was next to appear in 2002. The subsequent Spanish, French and English versions

---

39 *Nomad's Hotel*, 93–4.
40 Désirée Schijns, ed., '"Maar waar is mijn sprinkhaan?" Cees Nooteboom in gesprek met zijn vertalers', in S. Evenepoel, G. Rooryck and H. Verstraete, eds, *Taal en cultuur in vertaling: De wereld van Cees Nooteboom* (Antwerp and Apeldoorn: Garant, 2004), 106–7.
41 '[...] het grondidee van de Duitse "oerversie" van *Nootebooms Hotel*', Schijns, '"Maar waar is mijn sprinkhaan?"', 106.

are each different according to what publishers in consultation with readers and translators decided to include.

This family of related travel texts provides powerful support for a
theory in which the institution of literature is seen as inherently mobile
and translation therefore as part and parcel of this institution. For a start,
there is no original work in the writer's native language which then needs
to be transposed into foreign languages. In effect, the author provided a
pool of writing from which each receiving culture could select the pieces
which would be published, so what I had originally considered as a feature of only the travel work in Dutch, can now be extended to include the
works in translation. The French version (2003) was constructed on the
basis of the German edition, according to its editor-translator Philippe
Noble.[42] Since there is no 'home' version, I think it is possible to see this
group of texts as nomadic in the sense that each represents a new belonging which remains connected rhizomically to all the others, but which
must provide its own dwelling in each of the languages. With its lack of
a dominant language, it has become-nomad in the philosophical sense.
I see this nomadic textual tribe as the perfect expression of the mobile,
nomadic world that is Cees Nooteboom's writing which confirms that this
particular writer can no longer be adequately discussed solely in relation
to Dutch national culture.

Roads to Berlin: Detours and Riddles in the Lands and History of Germany

This collection of travel pieces and essays is unambiguously presented in
English to connect with the first book of travel writing discussed here:
Roads to Santiago.

---

42   Schijns, "'Maar waar is mijn sprinkhaan?'", 108.

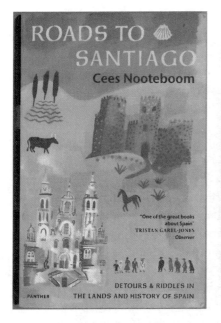 

Figures 5a and 5b The front covers of *Roads to Santiago*, published by
The Harvill Press (reproduced by kind permission of The Random House Group Ltd)
and *Roads to Berlin* (reproduced by kind permission of Querus Editions Ltd).

The title and subtitle of the Berlin book mirror those of the book
on Spain, cleverly creating a feel of coherence to the travel writing part of
Nooteboom's English oeuvre. There are indeed similarities: both books
focus on a single European country, language and culture and do so through
many excursions or detours which take in different aspects of cultural
and political history, and some of these accounts are humorous or ironic,
presenting the culture that is their object of study as complex, puzzling,
intriguing or simply inexplicable. An interesting difference between the
two texts is that *Roads to Berlin* precisely dates all the pieces it contains,
with the exception of the two fictionalized Intermezzi in Part I. This dating
is a significant feature because it highlights the time structure and the
role of reflection and memory as well as the nature of history and history
writing. This will be one of the main areas for discussion in what follows.

Nooteboom's Complex Narrative

Before entering into discussion with and about this book, I will first describe
the complexities of Nooteboom's narrative, focusing on structure, text
type, and the question of fictionalization. The narrative, though broadly
chronological, is emphatically not linear, although at the same time, it is
not a collection of fragments; rather, the structure is rhizomic in that it is
clearly moving along with the flow of time and events and this provides
the central backbone which links the many detours and meditations. The
title makes it clear that Berlin has a central part in this account, but there
are many pathways that can be taken in and out of Berlin, and Nooteboom
certainly follows a large number of them in a kind of quest for the different
Germanies that co-exist alongside one another.

The book opens with a kind of travel journal narrating a visit in 1963
to communist East Germany. These short passages form a kind of preamble and are very similar to Nooteboom's reportage of the Paris uprising in
1968. Part I proper consists of fifteen short chapters, each dated at the end,
starting on 15 March 1989 and taking the reader through the build-up to
the fall of the Berlin wall, the fall itself, and its aftermath. Part I chronicles
the author's residence in Berlin, ending on 30 June 1990 when he takes his
leave, clearly expecting to return: 'when I return everything will be different,
yet still the same, and changed forever'. Much shorter than Part I, Part II
picks up this idea, noting drily that 'It was in itself not a difficult prediction
to make', and going on to explain on his return after a year how difficult
it was to assess what had changed.[43] Part II consists of four sections titled
'Berlin Suite', 'Dead Aeroplanes and Eagles Everywhere', 'Village within
the Wall' and 'Return to Berlin' which contain sketches and 'detours' and
which cover the periods May–June 1991, February 1993 and December
1997. And there is an Intermezzo detailing a visit to Schloss Rheinsberg
in 1997. A similar length to Part II, Part III consists of fragments giving a
picture of Berlin now (2008) from a more distanced perspective, including a boat trip where he assumes the identity of a tourist, that is someone

43   *Roads to Berlin*, 211, 215.

visiting Berlin for the first time; comparison of Berlin now and twenty years earlier; the text of a speech he gave in Amsterdam at an exhibition of work by artists of the Leipziger Schule; a reflection on an American translator and member of the German resistance in the Second World War; reflection on great art, sparked by his presence at the award of a prize to Anselm Kiefer; another speech – this time on receiving an honorary doctorate from the Free University of Berlin; and memories. Part IV is a brief meditation on Europe and is followed by the Epilogue which asks 'Where has Europe gone?'.

Roads to Berlin is an ambitious and deeply personal account of Germany in the second half of the twentieth century. The narrative is complex and shifting. Because of its time structure, the first person narrator's voice itself changes, since the different parts are based on experiences recorded at different times and written up in retrospect and compiled with no attempt at smoothing and levelling the narrative. The semi-fictional traveller figure we encountered in both *Roads to Santiago* and *Nomad's Hotel* reappears here in two of the intermezzi, which are thus clearly signalled as separate from the main body of the personal narrative. And the 'I' narrator of that personal account seems to speak with the author's voice, learning and maturing and gradually making sense of Germany and his own relation to it. This personal voice can be laconic and ironic, but occasionally reveals strong feelings, and political desires. The wry tone of voice, which is also a feature of the fictionalized parts of the book, is similar to the tone of the narrative of *All Souls' Day*, the novel set in Berlin and discussed earlier in Chapter 4. Given the common setting of Berlin, this is perhaps not so strange, and it provides a further opportunity for reflection on the process of fictionalization. In all there are three different Berlin narratives viewed across the two texts: i) the personal travel account where the I-narrator is presumed to be congruent with the writer; ii) the traveller-narratives which tell parts of the journeys and in which an all-seeing narrator follows the traveller-figure and is privy to his feelings about and responses to what he sees; iii) the narrative of *All Souls' Day* with its perspective which is internal to Arthur Daane, the main character, a Dutch film-maker living in Berlin.

There are a number of familiar locations, but Nooteboom's fascination with the village of Lübars on the outskirts of Berlin is one that readers

get to know well. In *All Souls' Day*, Arthur Daane takes his new lover Elik
Oranje there:

> He had often come to Lübars to escape the claustrophobia of Berlin. 'There used to
> be a *Biergarten* there,' he said, pointing. 'You could sit under that lime tree and look
> out over the pasture. And there, where it ends, is where the Wall used to be.' As usual
> he couldn't say why he found it so moving.[44]

He then takes her to the river to the spot where the sign used to be marking
the end of the Western zone. In *Roads to Berlin* Nooteboom was a frequent
visitor to Lübars when the border with the DDR was still policed, and the
river with its midstream sign declaring the presence of the border while 'the
land on the other bank looked the same as the land on our side'.[45] In 'Village
within the Wall', he revisits Lübars in 1993, prompting this meditation:

> After the war, the Dutch poet J.C. Bloem wrote, '*En niet één van de ongeborenen
> zal de vrijheid ooit zo beseffen*' (and not one of the unborn will ever comprehend
> freedom in this way). Standing here, I feel the impact of his words. My path has
> become a field and the forbidden road is now my path. I walk across a space where
> men would once have had to shoot me and I feel a shiver that soon no-one will feel.
> History erases its traces and that is how it becomes history.[46]

In Part III, Nooteboom gives a remarkable account of what he thinks history is in his speech at the Free University of Berlin:

> that special form of memory that we call the past, or better still history, history that
> for me is not an abstraction, but a form of existence, a story written by the world
> and written by each of us at the same time, which often means that we are inventing
> our own history in the midst of the inevitable events that are presented to us by the
> world. I had not made up the war; my memories of it, and the way in which I tell
> them, repeat them, formulate them, invent them, or maybe even lie, belong to me, a
> story that, as you grow from one age to the next, constantly requires new words.[47]

44   *All Souls' Day*, 175.
45   *Roads to Berlin*, 237.
46   *Roads to Berlin*, 238–9.
47   *Roads to Berlin*, 300.

This notion of history both offers an important reflection on the nature and structure of historical writing, and gives an insight into Nooteboom's travel writing as well. This is because in Nooteboom's view, the personal is inseparable from history. Looked at in this way, there are as many histories as there are people, very few of which are ever written down. In *Roads to Berlin*, Nooteboom provides a prime example of one such account of memory and history which is both a study in the division of Germany, reunification and its aftermath and a study in the reverberations of the Second World War that demand reflection and understanding.

This kind of history is highly dynamic and needs a structure that can follow the branchings of the writer's mind which moves from personal experience to cultural or political history, to geographical or aesthetic reflections, and can change with the writer who necessarily visits and revisits places that are significant for the telling of his history. Braidotti points out that the rhizomatic mode 'brings to the fore the affective foundations of the thinking process' and so doing, offers a way of 'putting thought at the service of creation' – an insight that applies to all Nooteboom's writing, and a fortiori to the travel writing.[48]

The Traveller-Writer as Subject

There are three aspects I want to discuss here – Nooteboom's deep engagement with German life and culture, his relationship to language, and the question of autobiography in history.

Roads to Berlin is testament to Nooteboom's enduring connection with Germany – its people, its food, its landscape, its art, its history, its politics and its present. In a list of figurations of language learners as travellers, Cristina Ros i Solé and I distinguish the tourists, the cosmopolitans, and the pilgrims.[49] In the book Nooteboom chooses briefly to act the tourist,

48 Braidotti, *Metamorphoses*, 73–4.
49 See Jane Fenoulhet and Cristina Ros i Solé, eds, *Mobility and Language Learning* (Oxford: Peter Lang, 2011), 18–24.

and displays aspects of the cosmopolitan in the sense that he is highly self-aware and against nationalism, and of the pilgrim in the way he is committed to becoming to some extent part of German culture. Zygmunt Bauman, on the other hand, contrasts the pilgrims who have clearly defined trajectories with the tourists or nomads with their horror of fixity.[50] Clearly neither of Bauman's categories applies to Nooteboom, whose position is much less clear cut. However, such representations of travellers do bring me back to the interesting question of movement and its direction. At the start of *Roads to Berlin*, Nooteboom is a particular kind of tourist – a roving reporter. The nature of the fascination he develops with Germany – a quest to understand its violent entry into his life and that of Europe – seems to demand both movement through place and time and a degree of self-positioning as resident of Berlin.

On the day Nooteboom moves to Berlin, the narrative makes it clear that this is no tourist passing through: 'I am home'. As he says a little later, 'Living somewhere else is different from travelling – I can tell by the way I look at things'. The acculturation process involves the body as well as the mind, since Nooteboom's first reaction to his new apartment involves his senses of smell and sight. Then a phase of mapping and walking the city and adjusting to a German newspaper: 'I read the *Frankfurter Allgemeine* now, a serious business. This country does not treat itself frivolously. There is none of the casual irrelevance I am used to at home. A stern front page, usually without a picture; I probably even look different when I am reading it.'[51] This passage conveys the subtle ways in which a person is changed by a deeper engagement with another culture – to the extent that there is even a possibility that one's bearing or expression becomes different when engaging in a familiar tasks in the new cultural environment. Getting to know Berlin in March 1989 before the fall of the wall is a double task because the two Berlins are so utterly different, and making sense of this inevitably

50   As discussed in Fenoulhet and Ros i Solé, *Mobility and Language Learning*, 22–3. See also, Z. Bauman, 'From Pilgrim to Tourist – or a Short History of Identity', in S. Hall and P. du Gay, eds, *Questions of Cultural Identity* (London: Sage, 1996), 18–36.

51   *Roads to Berlin*, 24, 35, 25.

involves reflection on the past. Simply walking the city is enough to prompt this, since the urban environments bear no relation to one another: stark grey buildings and austerity in the East and on the other side what he calls the 'extravagant West'.

The process of mapping applies not only to the topography of Berlin, but also to concepts in the German language. Nooteboom discusses the telling concept of 'house' in German and contrasts it with Dutch, pointing out that words that appear the same, allowing for linguistic shifts between the two languages, denote subtly different things. 'When someone from the Netherlands asked me what sort of house I was living in, I realised that the Dutch concept of *huis* did not cover it, because my house here was inside another house, and that is that other house, the big one, that they call a *Haus* here in Germany. *Haus* is the name for these huge residential blocks with various layers of homes stacked up around square courtyards.'[52]

The early chapters of Part I of *Roads to Berlin* give readers an unparalleled insight into the travel writer's subjectivity. Not only are we shown the mappings and comparison with Nooteboom's first language, we are also given insights into the uncertainties generated by the whole process of creating a home in a new culture in what might be called passages of intercultural autobiography. Since the whole point of my argument in *Nomadic Literature* has been that individual subjectivity is what is at stake in nomadism, through processes of becoming, I consider such passages as illuminatory and maybe even exemplary of nomadic consciousness. For this reason, the following quote will be given in full, even though it is rather lengthy. For those readers coming to Nooteboom for the first time, it will give a good taste of the way the travel writer exposes his subjectivity without exhibitionism.

> I live in Berlin. It is not only different from the Netherlands; it is different from anywhere else. But I cannot quite express that difference, that *otherness*, in words yet. It has something to do with the people: they are much more my other people than Americans or Spaniards. I am still not sure how to act around them, and I cannot speak their language with confidence. I prefer just to walk in between them; after all

52   *Roads to Berlin*, 35.

you do not need to say very much. I sit on the U-Bahn and observe them. They are often Greeks, Turks, Yugoslavians, Colombians, Moroccans. I am more at ease with them, because they are not as powerful. Or maybe they simply feel closer.

At times it feels claustrophobic. I never felt that way when I was just a visitor. The Wall, the border – you know you can just go over, get out. So it can't be that. Yet even so. I notice it on Sundays. That is when I want to get out.[53]

Strong feelings of uncertainty, powerlessness and claustrophobia are notable, as is the inability to put into words the nature of the cultural differences he senses. The question is: what becomes of these stresses which the subject undergoes, and how are they resolved, if indeed they are?

The essay 'Return to Berlin' in Part II, dating from 1997, provides an example of a location of intensity, a concept already used in relation to *Roads to Santiago*. In 'Return to Berlin' it is the layered nature of the temporal distance as well as geographical distance that enable deep penetration to the heart of the writing subject. Although Nooteboom is far away in Los Angeles, he remembers his first visit to Berlin in 1963, prompted by the unveiling of a piece of the Berlin wall that had been acquired by Loyola Marymount University. Feelings of anguish accompany this trivialization of something that he had known in its all-powerful, fearful state. Back in Berlin, a memory of a particular café displaying a menu bearing the date 1940 allows the bringing together of the personal and the historical:

> And yet, even now, the date on that menu, the unfortunate year of 1940, is forcing me back to my own past. I do not want to linger on this for too long, but even though my life began seven years before that date, I am unable to explain myself to myself without thinking of 1940, if only because that start of the war – which will be over and done with only when everyone who remembers something about it is dead – seems to have erased the first seven years of my life ...[54]

In Chapter 3 of this book, I describe how research for an exhibition on Nooteboom in The Hague brought to light the fact that the family had moved house seven times in those early years, something which led

53   *Roads to Berlin*, 36–7.
54   *Roads to Berlin*, 256.

Nooteboom to revise his idea of himself since he had ascribed this absence of memory to the impact of the invasion of the Netherlands at the outbreak of the Second World War. As he says in an important passage, part of which is quoted in the next paragraph, 'something had been wiped out radically and permanently, by a destructive external force, leaving me with nothing'.

Far from wallowing in this damage, Nooteboom states that he has no need of sympathy as a result of a process of becoming: becoming-writer, which he equates here with life. And on the evidence of *Roads to Berlin*, this is a permanent and dynamic state of becoming-other. According to Nooteboom, it was this loss of memory that

> gave me the opportunity to invent a life for myself by travelling and thinking. More than that, it left me with a fascination with the past, with disappearance, with transience, with memories and ruins, with antiquity, with everything that can be summarised under the heading of 'history'. And I have related this history – because even those personal stories that make up only a very small part of history are still entitled to be called history – in order to explain, not so much to you as to myself, why this city has fascinated me inordinately for such a long time.[55]

He goes on in the same passage to reflect on the roots of this fascination, both linguistic and real: 'All of those gaps, those lacunae, those absences wanted to speak to me about nothingness, about destruction, which in both German (*Vernichtung*) and Dutch (*vernietiging*) is founded on the notion of turning something into nothing'.

Roads to Berlin reveals Nooteboom as a nomadic subject in greater depth and with greater intensity than the other two travel books. Becoming a writer and becoming a traveller are connected in their refusal of a static way of life, but not in the sense that Nooteboom is one of Bauman's rootless vagabonds or wanderers. In *Roads to Berlin* we witness him making a new home in Berlin which is both temporary and permanent: temporary because his physical presence is of limited duration, permanent because of the way in which it weaves itself into his subjectivity. Significantly, he believes that the individual's relationship with her or his language is both

---

55 *Roads to Berlin*, 258.

of limited duration and lasting: 'how peculiar it is that we are born into a language, as though, for the arbitrary span of our lives, we are immersed in a river. But the river never remains the same, and you play a part in changing that river yourself.'[56]

Nooteboom and the Idea of Europe

Whereas Parts I–III of *Roads to Berlin* have previously appeared in Dutch and other languages, Part IV was written specially for the English edition. It deals with the controversial subject of Europe which has been present all along in the sense that German history is European history, and in the years after the end of the Second World War, the idea of Europe was seen as the route to a new compact which would have the potential to remove the old tensions and conflicts. Part IV asks the question of what the new Germany means for the different countries of Europe against the background of the current financial and economic crisis. From his extensive European travels he concludes that the countries of Europe still do not know one another, pointing a finger at a press that repeats stereotypes – 'you only have to read what the British popular press has to say about both the French and the Germans: ancient prejudices, traditional insults so eager to be repeated, deliberate or feigned ignorance, and a fundamental aversion to Europe that extends into the highest spheres', and he adds a rare dig that this is 'based partly on the transparent an imaginary special relationship with an America that is increasingly looking over the Pacific'. Another cause of the failure of European countries to connect with one another is the lack of language skills, according to Nooteboom who makes an exception for the 'minority that travels, reads newspapers and speaks different languages'.[57]

The book concludes with an Epilogue containing three short fables first published in 1993 and dealing with European unification and the distribution of power across different currencies and countries, and the 'miserable

---

56   *Roads to Berlin*, 173.
57   *Roads to Berlin*, 323.

cacophony' of thirty-one national anthems. The heartfelt lament of loss 'Where has Europe gone? Where has it disappeared to? Who has stolen it away?' is at the same time suggestive of a way forward. To an English audience which had not participated in European idealism for decades, this idea that Europe at least provides somewhere to go beyond ever-present and in some cases growing nationalisms is rather surprising and something of a shock. And the author's concluding two paragraphs unambiguously express a desire for a return of the idea of Europe: 'if it still exists somewhere, we would like to have it back, not the Europe of the market and the walls, but the Europe that belongs to the countries of Europe, to *all* of the European countries'.[58]

A well-respected writer making such a plea may only be read by a chosen few, but this is nevertheless a clear position in which Nooteboom reveals a feeling of belonging to the wider Europe and a desire to find a way forward in a Europe that revels in its multiplicity. To make the point through fables and the demand that Europe 'really must be returned to us', the Europeans in all their linguistic and cultural diversity, is a fitting conclusion to what is currently Nooteboom's last book of travel writing to appear in English.

Conclusions

This experiment in subjecting Cees Nooteboom and his writing to a non-national treatment is now ended, and in a sense needs no grand conclusion, since the readings of Nooteboom's novels, poems and travel writing are the practical outcome of the theoretical considerations set out in the first part of the book. I proposed a complex way of approaching a writer and his work which does not see literary texts as intrinsically connected with the country of the writer's birth, while in the second part I put it into

58   *Roads to Berlin*, 326–30.

practice. The approach takes elements from the study of literary institutions and the literary field broadened to take into account transnational mobility and the new set of institutions that welcome a translated work into the culture which will be its new home. These elements are combined with insights gained from viewing translation as a nomadic practice which values cultural hospitality, respect for linguistic variety, and translators as deterritorialized, intercultural figures. In turn these insights inform an understanding of the potential of travel writing as a cosmopolitan, translational, and nomadic practice. Such nomadic practices have a far-reaching effect on both the translator's and the writer's subjectivity, so that deep encounters with new cultures and new texts potentially have a transformative effect on their readers. Because of the embodied nature of subjectivity, travel and the translations that go with it do foster nomadic sensibility in those travellers and translators who strive for de- and reterritorialization. At the same physical mobility is not necessary for the kind of work on the self that engenders new becomings: in Nooteboom's case elements of early deterritorialization and becoming-minor are connected with his Catholicism and lack of a stable home, and later with his position as a speaker of a smaller European language. As well as his travel works, his poetry and fiction can be seen to display nomadic traits.

From my study of the Dutch reception of Nooteboom, it is possible to conclude that, taken as a group, the commentators approach his work from a very particular standpoint which seems to have very little in common with his personal preoccupations and mode of expression. Despite the success of the first novel, subsequent novels received a much more mixed press, perhaps because of their metafictional mode or their playful tone. The poems seem to have been largely ignored, especially by the national literary histories. And the travel writing must have sold, judging by all the collections published in Dutch, but it did not earn Nooteboom respect.

Cees Nooteboom's writing has won acclaim outside the Netherlands, especially in Germany and there can be no doubt about his standing as a world writer. It is likely that his standing outside the Netherlands has contributed to recognition in his country of origin. The aim of my contribution to knowledge and understanding of his work has been to follow its own liberation from its national confines, welcoming it into English culture and academic commentary. Basing as much of my account of Nooteboom's writing as was feasible on the English oeuvre, I have used nomadic philosophy with its emphasis on transformation and on the importance of writing as a means of becoming to discuss the novels, poetry and travel writing. I have found this philosophical framework productive in opening up the works for readings which disregard the local preoccupations of the Dutch literary field, shedding light, I hope, on what it is about Nooteboom's writing that speaks to readers in so many different languages and cultures. Whilst a sincere intercultural disposition fosters nomadic sensibilities, mobility alone without this deeper engagement will never produce nomadic literature.

Bibliography

Works by Cees Nooteboom

All Souls' Day, trans. Susan Massotty (London: Picador, 2001).
Allerzielen (Amsterdam: Atlas, 1998).
Berlijn 1989–2009 (Amsterdam: De Bezige Bij, 2009).
Berlijnse notities (Amsterdam: De Arbeiderspers, 1990).
'De bevochten lichtheid', *Vrij Nederland* (31 January 2009) [LiteRom online database] <http://www.knipselkranten.nl/literom> accessed 1 August 2012.
Bitterzoet: Honderd gedichten van vroeger en zeventien nieuwe (Amsterdam: Arbeiderspers, 2000).
The Captain of the Butterflies, trans. Leonard Nathan and Herlinde Spahr (Los Angeles: Sun & Moon Press, 1997).
'Dankrede bij uitreiking P.C. Hooftprijs 2004', in Földényi, László, et al., *In het oog van de storm* (Amsterdam and Antwerp: Atlas, 2006).
De doden zoeken een huis (Amsterdam: Querido, 1956).
De filosoof zonder ogen: Europese reizen (Amsterdam: De Arbeiderspers, 1997).
Die folgende Geschichte (Berlin: Suhrkamp, 1995).
The Following Story, trans. Ina Rilke (London: Harvill, 1993).
Het geluid van Zijn naam: Reizen door de Islamitische wereld (Amsterdam: Atlas, 2005).
Gemaakte gedichten (Amsterdam: De Bezige Bij, 1970).
Gesammelte Werke, Band 1: Gedichte (Berlin: Suhrkamp, 2003).
Gesloten gedichten (Amsterdam: De Bezige Bij, 1964).
Het gezicht van het oog (Amsterdam: Arbeiderspers, 1989).
In Nederland (Amsterdam: Arbeiderspers, 1984).
In de bergen van Nederland (Amsterdam: Arbeiderspers, 1997).
In the Dutch Mountains, trans. Adrienne Dixon (Harmondsworth: Viking Penguin, 1987).
The Knight has Died, trans. Adrienne Dixon (Baton Rouge: Louisiana State University Press, 1990).
De koning van Suriname (Amsterdam: Muntinga, 1993).
Licht overal (Amsterdam: De Bezige Bij, 2012).

Lost Paradise, trans. Susan Massotty (London: Harvill Secker, 2008).
Nomad's Hotel: Travels in Time and Space, trans. Ann Kelland (London: Vintage, 2007).
Nootebooms Hotel (Amsterdam: Atlas, 2002).
De omweg naar Santiago (Amsterdam: Atlas, 1992).
Open als een schelp, dicht als een steen (Amsterdam: Arbeiderspers, 1978).
Paradijs verloren (Amsterdam: Atlas, 2004).
De Parijse beroerte (Amsterdam: De Bezige Bij, 1968).
Philip and the Others, trans. Adrienne Dixon (Baton Rouge: Louisiana State University Press, 1988).
Philip en de anderen (Amsterdam: Querido, 1987).
Het raadsel van het licht (Amsterdam: Bezige Bij, 2009).
De ridder is gestorven (Amsterdam: Querido, 1963).
Rituals, trans. Adrienne Dixon (Baton Rouge: Louisiana State University Press, 1983).
Rituelen (Amsterdam: Arbeiderspers, 1980).
Roads to Berlin. Detours and Riddles in the Lands and History of Germany, trans. Laura Watkinson (London: MacLehose Press, 2012).
Roads to Santiago. Detours and Riddles in the Lands and History of Spain, trans. Ina Rilke (London: Harvill, 1997).
Rode regen (Amsterdam/Antwerp: Atlas, 2007).
Scheepsjournaal (Amsterdam: Bezige Bij, 2010).
Self-Portrait of an Other, trans. David Colmer, drawings Max Neumann (London: Seagull Books, 2011).
A Song of Truth and Semblance, trans. Adrienne Dixon (Baton Rouge: Louisiana State University Press, 1984).
Tumbas: Graven van dichters en denkers (Amsterdam: Atlas, 2007).
Van de lente de dauw (Amsterdam: Bezige Bij, 1995).
Verleden als eigenschap (Amsterdam: Atlas, 2008).
Het volgende verhaal (Amsterdam: CPNB, 1991).
Vuurtijd, ijstijd. Gedichten 1955–1983 (Amsterdam: De Arbeiderspers, 1984).
Waar je gevallen bent, blijf je (Amsterdam: Bezige Bij, 1989).
Zelfportret van een ander (Amsterdam: Atlas, 1993).
Het zwarte gedicht (Amsterdam: Querido, 1960).

Secondary Literature

Anbeek, Ton, 'Aanval en afstandelijkheid: een vergelijking tussen Amerikaanse en Nederlandse romans', *De Gids* 144/2&3 (1981), 70–6.

——, *Geschiedenis van de Nederlandse literatuur tussen 1885 en 1985* (Amsterdam: Arbeiderspers, 1990).

——, 'Reiziger in ruimte en tijd: Het werk van Cees Nooteboom tussen 1963 en 1980', *De Gids*, 157 (1994), 565–74.

Balfour, Sandy, 'Watching the human comedy unfold', *The Spectator* (4 March 2006).

Bassnett, Susan, *Comparative Literature: A Critical Introduction* (Oxford: Blackwell, 1993).

——, 'From Cultural Turn to Translational Turn: A Translational Journey', in Cecilia Alvstad, Stefan Helgesson and David Watson, eds, *Literature, Geography, Translation: Studies in World Writing* (Newcastle: Cambridge Scholars Publishing, 2011), 67–80.

Bauman, Zygmunt, 'From Pilgrim to Tourist – or a Short History of Identity', in S. Hall and P. du Gay, eds, *Questions of Cultural Identity* (London: Sage, 1996) 18–36.

Bekkering, Harry, Daan Cartens and Aad Meinderts, eds, *Ik had wel duizend levens en ik nam er maar één! Cees Nooteboom*, Schrijversprentenboek 40 (Amsterdam and Antwerp: Atlas, [1997]).

Bork, G.J. van and N. Laan, eds, *Twee eeuwen literatuurgeschiedenis: Poëticale opvattingen in de Nederlandse literatuur* (Groningen: Wolters-Noordhoff, 1986).

Bork, G.J. van and P.J. Verkruijsse, eds, *De Nederlandse en Vlaamse auteurs van middeleeuwen tot heden met inbegrip van de Friese auteurs* (Weesp: De Haan, 1985), Digitale Bibliotheek voor de Nederlandse Letteren, <http://www.dbnl.org/tekst/bork001nede01/noot003.htm> accessed 25 March 2009.

Botton, Alain de, *The Art of Travel* (London: Penguin, 2003).

Boven, Erica van and Mary Kemperink, *Literatuur van de moderne tijd : Nederlandse en Vlaamse letterkunde in de negentiende en twintigste eeuw* (Bussum: Coutinho, 2006).

Braidotti, Rosi, *Nomadic Subjects: Embodiment and Sexual Difference in Feminist Theory* (New York: Columbia University Press, 1994).

——, *Metamorphoses: Towards a Materialist Theory of Becoming* (Cambridge: Polity Press, 2002).

——, *Transpositions. On Nomadic Ethics* (Cambridge: Polity Press, 2006).

——, Charles Esche and Maria Hlavajova, eds, *Citizens and Subjects: The Netherlands, For Example: A Critical Reader* (Zurich: JRP/Ringier, 2007).

Brems, Hugo, *Al wie omziet: opstellen over Nederlandse poëzie 1960–1980* (Antwerp: Elsevier Manteau, 1981).

——, *De rentmeester van het paradijs: over poëzie* (Antwerp: Manteau, 1986).

——, *De dichter is een koe: over poëzie* (Amsterdam: Arbeiderspers, 1991).

——, *Altijd weer vogels die nesten beginnen: Geschiedenis van de Nederlandse literatuur 1945–2005* (Amsterdam: Bert Bakker, 2006).

Brokken, Jan, 'De voorbije passages van Cees Nooteboom', in Daan Cartens, ed., *Over Cees Nooteboom: beschouwingen en interviews* (The Hague: BZZTôH, 1984).

Byatt, A.S., *On Histories and Stories* (Cambridge, MA: Harvard University Press, 2000).

Calhoun, Craig, 'The Class Consciousness of Frequent Travellers: Towards a Critique of Actually Existing Cosmopolitanism' in Steven Vertovec and Robin Cohen, eds, *Conceiving Cosmopolitanism: Theory, Context, and Practice* (Oxford: Oxford University Press, 2002), 86–109.

Cartens, Daan, ed., *Over Cees Nooteboom: beschouwingen en interviews* ('s-Gravenhage: BZZTôH, 1984).

——, 'In het kloster van de tijd', *Het Vaderland* (3 January 1981) [LiteRom online database] <http://www.knipselkranten.nl/literom> accessed 11 May 2009.

Casanova, Pascale, *The World Republic of Letters*, trans. M.B. DeBevoise (Cambridge, MA: Harvard University Press, 2004).

'Cees Nooteboom' [author website], <http://www.ceesnooteboom.com/?cat=10& lang=en> accessed 30 July 2012.

Coetzee, J.M., *Stranger Shores: Essays 1986–1999* (London: Vintage Books, 2002).

—— (trans. and introduction), *Landscape with Rowers: Poetry from the Netherlands* (Princeton: Princeton University Press, 2004).

Coffey, Simon, 'Strangerhood and Intercultural Subjectivity' in Jane Fenoulhet and Cristina Ros i Solé, eds, *Language and Intercultural Communication*, 13/3, special issue 'Romanticising Language Learning' (forthcoming).

Cronin, Michael, *Across the Lines: Travel, Language, Translation* (Cork: Cork University Press, 2000).

——, *Translation and Identity* (Abingdon: Routledge, 2006).

Damrosch, David, *What Is World Literature?* (Princeton: Princeton University Press, 2003).

——, 'World Literature in a Postcanonical, Hypercanonical Age' in Haun Saussy, ed., *Comparative Literature in an Age of Globalization* (Baltimore: Johns Hopkins University Press, 2006), 43–53.

Deleuze, Gilles, *Negotiations 1972–1990*, trans. Martin Joghin (New York: Columbia University Press, 1995).

—— *Essays Critical and Clinical*, trans. Daniel W. Smith and Michael A. Greco (Minneapolis: University of Minnesota Press, 1997).

—— and Félix Guattari, *Kafka: Toward a Minor Literature*, trans. Dana Polan (Minneapolis: University of Minnesota Press, 1986).

—— and Félix Guattari, *A Thousand Plateaus: Capitalism and Schizophrenia*, trans. Brian Massumi (London: Athlone Press, 1988).

—— and Claire Parnet, *Dialogues*, trans. Hugh Tomlinson and Barbara Habberjam (London: Athlone Press, 1987).

Dijkgraaf, Margot, 'De atlas van Nooteboom', in Eddy Posthuma de Boer and Margot Dijkgraaf, *De atlas van Nooteboom* (Amsterdam and Antwerp: Atlas, 2003), 7–16.

——, *Nooteboom en de anderen* (Amsterdam: De Bezige Bij, 2009).

Dijl, Frank van, '"Reizen is mijn manier van denken"', in Daan Cartens, ed., *Over Cees Nooteboom: beschouwingen en interviews* ('s-Gravenhage: BZZTôH, 1984), 48–57.

Dorleijn, Gillis, and Kees van Rees, eds, *De productie van literatuur. Het literaire veld in Nederland 1800–2000* (Nijmegen: Vantilt, 2006).

'EC Press release. Meeting of the Jury of the Aristeion Prize 1994' [online archive Presseuropa], <http://presseuropa.com/press-releases/meeting-of-the-jury-of-the-aristeion-prize-1994> accessed 1 August 2012.

Eco, Umberto, *Mouse or Rat? Translation as Negotiation* (London: Weidenfeld and Nicholson, 2003).

Evenepoel, S., G. Rooryck and H. Verstraete, eds, *Taal en cultuur in vertaling. De wereld van Cees Nooteboom* (Antwerp and Apeldoorn: Garant, 2004).

Fenoulhet, Jane, 'Towards a Critical Patriotism: The Challenge to Traditional Notions of Dutchness from the Historical Novel in the 1930s', *Modern Language Review* 99/1 (2004), 112–30.

—— and Cristina Ros i Solé, eds, *Mobility and Localisation in Language Learning: A View from Languages of the Wider World* (Oxford: Peter Lang, 2010).

Fokkema, Redbad, *Aan de mond van al die rivieren: een geschiedenis van de Nederlandse poëzie sinds 1945* (Amsterdam: Arbeiderspers, 1999).

Földényi, László, et al., *In het oog van de storm. De wereld van Cees Nooteboom. Essays over zijn Oeuvre* (Amsterdam and Antwerp: Atlas, 2006).

Gelderblom, Arie Jan and Anne Marie Musschoot, 'Veranderingen in een bedding van continuïteit: de literatuurgeschiedenis in een nieuw jasje', in G. Elshout et al., eds, *Perspectieven voor de internationale neerlandistiek in de 21e eeuw* (Woubrugge: Internationale Vereniging voor Neerlandistiek, 2001), 151–68.

Goedegebuure, Jaap, *Over 'Rituelen' van Cees Nooteboom* (Amsterdam: Arbeiderspers, 1983).

——, *Nederlandse literatuur 1960–1988* (Amsterdam: De Arbeiderspers, 1989).

Gorp, H. van, et al., *Lexicon van literaire termen* (Groningen: Wolters-Noordhoff, 1986).

Heilbron, Johan, 'Nederlandse vertalingen wereldwijd. Kleine landen en culturele mondialisering' in Johan Heilbron, Wouter de Nooy and Wilma Tichelaar, eds, *Waarin een klein land. Nederlandse cultuur in internationaal verband* (Amsterdam: Prometheus, 1995), 206–52.

Helgesson, Stefan, 'Going Global: An Afterword', in Stefan Helgesson, ed., *Literary Interactions in the Modern World 2*, vol. 4, *Literary History: Towards a Global Perspective* (Berlin: De Gruyter, 2006), 303–21.

—— 'Literary Hybrids and the Circuits of Translation: The Example of Mia Couto', in Helmut Anheier and Yudhishthir Raj Isar, eds, *Cultural Expression, Creativity and Innovation* (London: Sage, 2010), 215–24.

Hermans, Theo, ed., *Door eenen engen hals. Nederlandse beschouwingen over vertalen, 1550–1670* ('s-Gravenhage: Stichting Bibliografica Neerlandica, 1996).

—— ed., *A Literary History of the Low Countries* (Rochester, NY: Camden House, 2009).

Hollinger, David A., 'The New Cosmopolitanism', in Steven Vertovec and Robin Cohen, eds, *Conceiving Cosmopolitanism: Theory, Context, and Practice* (Oxford: Oxford University Press, 2002).

Holmes, James S., and William Jay Smith, eds, *Dutch Interior: Postwar Poetry of the Netherlands and Flanders* (New York: Columbia University Press, 1984).

Hottentot, Wim, 'Aanwezig afwezig', in Harry Bekkering, Daan Cartens and Aad Meinderts, eds, *Ik had wel duizend levens en ik nam er maar één! Cees Nooteboom* (Amsterdam: Atlas, 1997), 121–8.

Hulme, Peter, 'Travelling to Write (1940–2000)', in Peter Hulme and Tim Youngs, eds, *The Cambridge Companion to Travel Writing* (Cambridge: Cambridge University Press, 2002), 87–101.

Hutcheon, Linda, 'Comparative Literature: Congenitally Contrarian', in Haun Saussy, ed., *Comparative Literature in an Age of Globalization* (Baltimore: Johns Hopkins University Press, 2006), 224–9.

Janssen, Susanne, 'Grenzeloze literatuur? Een vergelijkend onderzoek naar het internationale gehalte van de literaire berichtgeving in Duitse, Franse, Nederlandse en Amerikaanse kranten in 1955 en 1995', in Petra Broomans et al., eds, *Object: Nederlandse literatuur in het buitenland. Methode: onbekend* (Groningen: Barkhuis, 2006), 170–93.

Kamp, Peter van de, ed., *Turning Tides: Modern Dutch and Flemish Verse in English Versions by Irish Poets* (Brownsville, OR: Story Line Press, 1994).

Kusters, Wiel, *De geheimen van wikken en dille* (Amsterdam: Querido, 1988).

Lissens, R.F. et al., eds, *Lexicon van de Nederlandse letterkunde* (Amsterdam and Brussels: Elsevier, 1986).

Louwerse, Henriëtte, *Home Entertainment: On Hafid Bouazza's Literary Writing* (Oxford: Peter Lang, 2007).

MacLean, Rory 'A 30-year Odyssey', *The Guardian* (8 February 2007).

Manguel, Alberto, 'De wereld is het verhaal', *NRC Handelsblad* (25 July 2008) [LiteRom online database] <http://www.knipselkranten.nl/literom> accessed 27 March 2009.

Mannes-Abbott, Guy, 'A Contemporary Nomad's Meditations and Musings on the Move', *The Independent* (9 March 2006).

Mierlo, Hans van, 'Laudatio bij uitreiking P.C. Hooftprijs 2004 aan Cees Nooteboom', in László Földényi, ed., *In het oog van de storm: De wereld van Cees Nooteboom: Essays over zijn oeuvre* (Amsterdam and Antwerp: Atlas, 2006), 212–20.

Moor, Wam de, 'Gedichten over het nooit meer strelen en slapen' in Daan Cartens, ed., *Over Cees Nooteboom: beschouwingen en interviews* ('s-Gravenhage: BZZTôH, 1984), 35–40.

Morriën, Adriaan 'Poëzie geteisterd door temperatuursverhoging' in Daan Cartens, ed., *Over Cees Nooteboom: beschouwingen en interviews* ('s-Gravenhage: BZZTôH, 1984), 26–8.

Mueller-Vollmer, Kurt, and Michael Irmscher, eds, *Translating Literatures Translating Cultures: New Vistas and Approaches in Literary Studies* (Stanford: Stanford University Press, 1998).

Mulder, Reinjan, 'Wintersport, whisky en oorsterse rituelen', *NRC Handelsblad* (12 December 1980) [LiteRom online database] <http://www.knipselkranten.nl/literom> accessed 11 May 2009.

Nederlands Letterenfonds [online database of translations of Dutch literature], <http://www.nlpvf.nl/vertalingendb/search-results1.php?lang=&searchtype=&q=&naam=&genre=&taal=&vertaler=&uitgever=&otitel=2583&alleja ren=1&alletitels=1&jaarvan=&jaartot=&limit=40&nrows=10> accessed 1 August 2012.

Nederlands Literair Productie- en Vertalingenfonds, *De Nederlandse literatuur in de wereld. Beleidsplan 2009–2012*, <http://www.nlpvf.nl/nl/downloads/beleidsplan_20092012.php> accessed 21 July 2010.

Nederlandse Taalunie, *Meerjarenbeleidsplan 1998–2002*, <http://www.talunieversum.org/taalunie/publicaties/meerjarenbeleidsplan-1998-2002> accessed 24 February 2009.

Nederlandse Taalunie, *Nederlands zonder drempels. Meerjarenbeleidsplan 2008–2012*, <http://www.talunieversum.org/taalunie/meerjarenbeleidsplano812.pdf> accessed 24 February 2009.

Netherlands Ministry of Education, Culture and Science, *Cultural Policy in the Netherlands* (The Hague/Amsterdam, 2009).

O'Brien, Paul, 'To Aran or Isfahan', *Dublin Review of Books*, 3 (2007).

Polezzi, Loredana, *Translating Travel: Contemporary Italian Travel Writing in English Translation* (Aldershot: Ashgate, 2001).

Pratt, Mary Louise, *Imperial Eyes: Travel Writing and Transculturation* (London and New York: Routledge, 1992).

Rennenberg, Roger, *De tijd en het labyrint. De poëzie van Cees Nooteboom* ('s-Gravenhage: BZZTôH, 1982).

Ricoeur, Paul, *On Translation*, trans. Eileen Brennan (London and New York: Routledge, 2006).

Rölli, Marc, 'Deleuze on Intensity Differentials and the Being of the Sensible', *Deleuze Studies*, 3 (2009), 26–53.

Romein, Jan et al., *De lage landen bij de zee: geïllustreerde geschiedenis van het Nederlandsche volk van Duinkerken tot Delfzijl* (Utrecht: W. de Haan, 1934).

Romein, Jan and Annie Romein-Verschoor, *Erflaters van onze beschaving. Nederlandse gestalten uit zes eeuwen* (Amsterdam: Querido, 1938).

Rover, Frans de, 'Cees Nooteboom', in *The Low Countries. Arts and Society in Flanders and the Netherlands 1993–1994* (Rekkem: Stichting Ons Erfdeel, 1993), 150–2.

Rutten, Tim, review of *Nomad's Hotel*, *Los Angeles Times* (8 April 2009).

Scaglione, Aldo, 'Comparative Literature as Cultural History: The Educational and Social Background of Renaissance Literature' in Clayton Koelb and Susan Noakes, eds, *The Comparative Perspective in Literature: Approaches to Theory and Practice* (Ithaca, NY: Cornell University Press, 1988) 147–61.

Schäffner, Christina and Helen Kelly-Holmes, eds, *Cultural Functions of Translation* (Clevedon: Multilingual Matters, c. 1995).

Schenkeveld-Van der Dussen, M.A., ed., *Nederlandse literatuur, een geschiedenis* (Groningen: Nijhoff, 1993).

Schijns, Désirée, ed., '"Maar waar is mijn sprinkhaan?" Cees Nooteboom in gesprek met zijn vertalers', in S. Evenepoel, G. Rooryck and H. Verstraete, eds, *Taal en cultuur in vertaling. De wereld van Cees Nooteboom* (Antwerp and Apeldoorn: Garant, 2004), 87–116.

Shuttleworth, Mark, 'Polysystem Theory', in Mona Baker, ed., *Routledge Encyclopedia of Translation Studies* (London and New York: Routledge, 1998), 176–9.

Simeoni, Daniel, 'Norms and the State. The Geopolitics of Translation Theory', in Anthony Pym, Miriam Schlesinger and Daniel Simeoni, eds, *Beyond Descriptive Translation Studies* (Amsterdam and Philadelphia: John Benjamins, 2008), 329–42.

Spivak, Gayatri Chakravorty, *Death of a Discipline* (New York: Columbia University Press, 2003).

'Toespraak van Z.M. Albert II, Koning der Belgen, ter gelegenheid van de uitreiking van de Prijs der Nederlandse Letteren aan de heer Cees Nooteboom', <http:// prijsderletteren.org/2009_toespraak/> accessed 9 August 2012.

Thomsen, Mads Rosendahl, *Mapping World Literature. International Canonization and Transnational Literature* (London: Continuum, 2008).

T'Sjoen, Yves, *Stem en tegenstem: over poëzie en poëtica: dubbelessays over hedendaagse Nederlandstalige poëzie* (Amsterdam: Atlas, 2004).

Urry, John, *Mobilities* (Cambridge: Polity Press, 2007).

—— and Jonas Larsen, *The Tourist Gaze 3.0* (London: Sage, 2011³).

Vandeputte, Guy, 'De Nederlandse literatuur in vertaling', in F. Balk-Smit Duyzentkunst, T. Hermans and P. De Kleijn, eds, *Handelingen Tiende Colloquium Neerlandicum* (Woubrugge: Internationale Vereniging voor Neerlandistiek, 1988), 92–100.

Venuti, Lawrence, ed., *The Translation Studies Reader* (New York and London: Routledge, 2004²).

Verboord, Marc and Susanne Janssen, 'Informatieuitwisseling in het huidige Nederlandse en Vlaamse literaire veld. Mediagebruik en gelezen boeken door literaire lezers en bemiddelaars', in Ralf Grüttemeier and Jan Oosterholt, eds, *Een of twee Nederlandse literaturen? Contacten tussen de Nederlandse en Vlaamse literatuur sinds 1830* (Leuven: Peeters, 2008), 307–21.

Vertovec, Steven and Robin Cohen, eds, *Conceiving Cosmopolitanism: Theory, Context, and Practice* (Oxford: Oxford University Press, 2002).

Vries, Lourens de, 'Translation Functions and Interculturality', in Stella Linn, Maarten Mous and Marianne Vogel eds, *Translation and Interculturality: Africa and the West* (Frankfurt-am-Main: Peter Lang, 2008), 123–42.

Vullings, Jeroen, 'Als God in Duitsland', *Vrij Nederland* (6 December 2008) [LiteRom online database] <http://www.knipselkranten.nl/literom> accessed 1 August 2012.

Welsink, Dick, 'Cees Nooteboom: een leven in data', in Harry Bekkering, Daan Cartens, Aad Meinderts, eds, *Ik had wel duizend levens en ik nam er maar één! Cees Nooteboom*, Schrijversprentenboek 40 (Amsterdam and Antwerp: Atlas, [1997]).

Williams, Rowan, *Lost Icons: Reflections on Cultural Bereavement* (London: T. & T. Clark, 2000).

Index

European Connections

edited by Peter Collier

'European Connections' is a series which aims to publish studies in Comparative Literature. Most scholars would agree that no literary work or genre can fruitfully be studied in isolation from its context (whether formal or cultural). Nearly all literary works and genres arise in response to or at least in awareness of previous and contemporary writing, and are often illuminated by confrontation with neighbouring or contrasting works. The literature of Europe, in particular, is extraordinarily rich in this kind of cross-cultural fertilisation (one thinks of medieval drama, Romantic poetry, or the Realist novel, for instance). On a wider stage, the major currents of European philosophy and art have affected the different national literatures in varying and fascinating ways. Many European and North American university courses in literature nowadays teach and research literature in faculties of Comparative and General Literature. The series intends to tap the rich vein of such research.

Offers of contribution are invited, whether studies of specific writers and relationships, or wider theoretical investigations. Proposals from established scholars, as well as more recent doctoral students, are welcome.

The series editor, Peter Collier, is Emeritus Fellow in French at Sidney Sussex College, University of Cambridge. He has translated Emile Zola (*Germinal*, Oxford World's Classics, 1993), and Marcel Proust (*The Fugitive*, Penguin, 2002), has edited several collections of essays on European literature and culture, including *Critical Theory Today*, with Helga Geyer-Ryan (Polity Press & Cornell University Press, 1990) and *Artistic Relations*, with Robert Lethbridge (Yale University Press, 1994), and has written on Proust and art in *Mosaici proustiani* (Il Mulino, 1986) and *Proust and Venice* (Cambridge University Press, 2005). He is a Fellow of the Chartered Institute of Linguists.

Volume 1   S. S. Prawer: W.M. Thackeray's European Sketch Books.
A Study of Literary and Graphic Portraiture. 459 pages. 2000.
ISBN 3-906758-68-0 / US-ISBN 0-8204-5081-2

Volume 2   Patricia Zecevic: The Speaking Divine Woman. López de
Úbeda's La Pícara Justina and Goethe's Wilhelm Meister.
294 pages. 2001.
ISBN 3-906766-91-8 / US-ISBN 0-8204-5607-1

Volume 3   Mary Besemeres: Translating One's Self. Language and
Selfhood in Cross-Cultural Autobiography. 297 pages. 2002.
ISBN 3-906766-98-5 / US-ISBN 0-8204-5614-4

Volume 4   Michela Canepari-Labib: Word-Worlds. Language, Identity and
Reality in the Work of Christine Brooke-Rose. 303 pages. 2002.
ISBN 3-906758-64-8 / US-ISBN 0-8204-5080-4

Volume 5   Hugo Azérad: L'Univers constellé de Proust, Joyce et Faulkner.
Le Concept d'épiphanie dans l'esthétique du modernisme.
474 pages. 2002.
ISBN 3-906769-61-5 / US-ISBN 0-8204-5873-2

Volume 6   Berry Palmer Chevasco: Mysterymania. The Reception of
Eugène Sue in Britain 1838–1860. 284 pages. 2003.
ISBN 3-906769-78-X / US-ISBN 0-8204-5915-1

Volume 7   Sabine Schmid: 'Keeping the Sources Pure'. The Making of
George Mackay Brown. 310 pages. 2003.
ISBN 3-03910-012-2 / US-ISBN 0-8204-6281-0

Volume 8   Walter Redfern: Writing on the Move. Albert Londres and
Investigative Journalism. 266 pages. 2004.
ISBN 3-03910-157-9 / US-ISBN 0-8204-6967-X

Volume 9   Johanna Marie Buisson: Lingua Barbara or The Mystery of the
Other. Otherness and Exteriority in Modern European Poetry.
364 pages. 2012.
ISBN 978-3-03910-057-6

Volume 10   Karl Leydecker and Nicholas White (eds): After Intimacy.
The Culture of Divorce in the West since 1789.
295 pages. 2007.
ISBN 978-3-03910-143-6

Volume 11   Patrick Crowley and Paul Hegarty: Formless. Ways In and Out
of Form. 258 pages. 2005.
ISBN 3-03910-056-4 / US-ISBN 0-8204-6297-7

Volume 34 Bandy Lee and Lorna Collins (eds): Making Sense. Merging
Theory and Practice. 280 pages. 2013.
ISBN 978-3-0343-0763-5

Volume 35 Jane Fenoulhet: Nomadic Literature. Cees Nooteboom and his
Writing. 257 pages. 2013.
ISBN 978-3-0343-0729-1

CBC Canadian

EMERGENT

Literary Awards

VOICES

Stories 1979–1999

Edited by

ROBERT WEAVER

GOOSE LANE

Edited by Laurel Boone.
Cover photograph by Dale McBride.
Cover and book design by Julie Scriver.
Printed in Canada by AGMV Marquis.
10 9 8 7 6 5 4 3 2 1

Canadian Cataloguing in Publication Data

Emergent voices

ISBN 0-86492-267-1

1. Short stories, Canadian (English).*
2. Canadian Fiction (English) — 20th century.*
I. Weaver, Robert, 1921-

PS8329.E63 1999   C813'.0108054   C99-950176-3
PR9197.32.E63 1999

Published with the financial support of the Canada Council for the Arts, the Government of Canada through the Book Publishing Industry Development Program, and the New Brunswick Department of Economic Development, Tourism and Culture.
Canadä

Goose Lane Editions
469 King Street
Fredericton, New Brunswick
CANADA E3B 1E5

CONTENTS

INTRODUCTION

A little more than twenty years ago, when I first began to explore the possibility of organizing a literary competition for CBC Radio, I found out as much as I could — not a great deal, as it happened — about existing competitions in Canada. The largest was the annual short story contest sponsored by the *Toronto Star*, which began in 1976-1977 and still continues. And there were smaller competitions for fiction or poetry or essays in various literary magazines across the country. I guessed that we might receive 1200 to 1500 entries in our first year. In fact, we had about 3000 submissions, and in the years since we have at times had even more. But we have never quite matched the atmosphere of that first year, with the mail bags arriving stuffed with manuscripts and the line-ups of writers with last minute hand-deliveries.

We had prepared a brochure that first year in which we asked for submissions to the competition in three categories: short story, poetry, and what we described as personal essays (meaning memoirs and travel pieces). For half a dozen years in the 1980s the personal essays were replaced with radio plays. But this year, as we celebrate the twentieth anniversary of the Canadian Literary Awards, the three original categories are in place, and by the time this anthology of prize-winning stories is published, the deadline for submissions in 1999 will be upon us.

There have been some changes in the sponsorship of the Canadian Literary Awards during the past twenty years. *Saturday Night* magazine joined CBC Radio to present the awards, and this meant that the prize-winning entries were not only broadcast but also published in the magazine. For two years the awards were co-sponsored by Tilden Rent-A-Car. And in the past two years the CBC and *Saturday Night* have had a welcome third partner in the Canada Council for the Arts.

Each year, a week before the deadline for submissions, a first reading of all the manuscripts begins. There are six readers (I'm one of them), all with experience in writing and editing, book publishing, or broadcasting, and by now with experience working on the Canadian Literary Awards. There is a feeling of anticipation as our work begins. We all like and admire Canadian writers and look forward to discovering new work — all the submissions to the competition must consist of "original, unpublished manuscripts" — by poets, essayists, or short story writers whose earlier work we may already know. We are always hopeful that we will come upon manuscripts by promising new talents.

By the end of the reading period short lists of poems, personal essays and stories have been selected for submission to three judging panels. There are three judges in each panel, and they may be writers, book publishers, editors, teachers, broadcasters. . . . In the past twenty years judges have met in cities across the country from Victoria, British Columbia, to St. John's, Newfoundland. Their task has often not been an easy one.

The brochure describing the Canadian Literary Awards that we distribute every year says that the "competition is open to all residents of Canada regardless of nationality, and to Canadian citizens living abroad." The biographies of the writers whose stories are published in this anthology gives some idea of what this openness has meant. Three of the writers in this book — Caroline Adderson, Janice Kulyk Keefer and Frances Itani — were twice honoured for winning entries by different judging panels, and Ernst Havemann won no less than four awards in the mid-1980s.

I am grateful to Barry Morgan, Radio Arts, CBC Toronto, my associate in organizing the Canadian Literary Awards, and to Laurel Boone and her colleagues at Goose Lane Editions. We all extend our thanks to the thousands of writers who have submitted their stories, essays and poems to the Canadian Literary Awards in the past twenty years.

ROBERT WEAVER

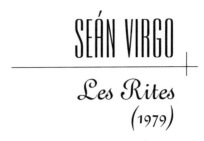

SEÁN VIRGO

Les Rites

(1979)

1

The apple-wood peg hammered into the bank above their mudslide had reeked of beaver-cast seductively on the wind. The big dog-otter had nosed it, breaking water at the head of his family. He galloped up the bank towards the scent, undulating his sleek length over the moss while five cubs trod water, watching. At the last moment his mate whistled from the opposite bank and he swerved, distracted, to romp down the slide. So the trap, instead of breaking his back, closed on the hind legs and the great rudder, flinging a spray of wet fur a yard away. The otter rolled, thrashing and yickering, down to the water, uprooting the peg, and the cubs dived to join the game.

A coneybeare trap is no great weight, but the otter could only hold its own for so long, straining with his front paws. After twenty minutes the mate and her cubs left off nosing the tethered shape which swung with the current in the sombre gut of the pool. The last red bubble of breath had gone winking off down Kumdis Creek.

With the next freshet, body and trap had washed free of the pool, bumping and tumbling downstream with the sticks and moss-rafts through the coffee-dark water. It travelled a mile in the next three days, passing below the Tlell road bridge and on into the darker forest. Two pools down, the trap lodged in the roots of a fallen hemlock, and the stiff otter shape stretched with the flow in the deeper water. A week later the body rotted free, and the head itself snagged on a sunken branch, wrenched off and drifted to the floor of the pool. Leeches seethed in its brain, the fur scummed off and followed the lost limbs downstream, and in the next rains the skull tumbled against a gravel bar and was left there, facing upstream, when the water subsided.

Kumdis Bottom is the most ruinous tangle of forest on the islands. Dark and saturated, it is a senseless grid of fallen trees smothered with mosses, and the ground a succession of trapped black pools, seeping into each other beneath a blotched and treacherous mask of liverworts. Most of the dead trees are young, stretched unnaturally in their search for light and finally starved out, leaning against each other and rotting swiftly in the humid air. There are entire husks of trees, in lichen and bark, thirty feet tall and crumbling into nothing about your face if you should lean on them.

Only the most ancient cedars and hemlocks, whose skins themselves are fire-scarred and marsh-textured, have stability; and as the ground lifts sharply to the south the original unfettered forest permits walking through the giantsleep silence. But down by the creek they stand half drowned or on islands of their roots' own making, blocking out all the light. When they fall they choke the water, which flows, in places for many yards, invisible under the overlapping and half-sunken trunks. There is never any wind here, except when a raven, floating down through the cedar crests, breaks the air with its creaking pinions. That sound is like bats in a cave, and when the ravens call their belling cries hang echoing for minutes in the heavy silence. The texture is almost submarine.

Yet there is life. Underwater it is all one, and the dwarf cutthroat trout arrow across the pools at any stir, while autumn brings a few lost dog salmon blundering up the shallows to spawn in the rare clean gravel. The beavers are young to the islands, but they work half-heartedly along the creek; and the deer (who are immigrants, too) find pathways somehow — their slots are printed everywhere among the liverworts and on the mudbanks, and bright piles of their droppings lie like berries among the sodden litter of hemlock cones.

Moss takes the animals as it does the trees. You will find the shoulder blades of deer, bleached white with the first green lacing of the forest across their palms. Or the skull, in furry green, of a young buck with lattices on its eyes and bristling plumes on its antler hefts. Bone seems a finality, a certain resolution with the elements, but the mosscloak devours swiftly. Everything leaches back into Kumdis Creek through the filter of moss and rain.

But the otter's skull on the gravel escapes the moss, takes on the colour and feel of its stony bed, and stares back up the covered stream while a deer slips past on the bank with lowered head; and a little later, stumbling over the windfalls, a young man follows with a clamouring heart and a gun.

This pedigree of otter and riverbank must stand, because only an earthquake, trundling the Queen Charlotte Islands back into the dark sea bed, will prevent Kumdis Creek, which flows into and out of my story, from pursuing its slow and rack-choked way to the slough when our race, and perhaps the otter's, is quite forgotten.

2

The hotel coffee shop in New Masset faces the volunteer fire hall and the RCMP station. On the wall, above the vinyl seats and the formica table tops, is a picture of the Creation. It is in felt appliqué, white and black and red, a quaint and clumsy rendering twelve feet long of the Raven, hatching first man and first woman from the clamshell out on North Beach. The picture is by two ladies from Old Masset, and their scene is bracketed by the two great clan figures of their people — Raven and Eagle, stiff and uneasy above the heads of the tourists, the loggers, the servicemen, the hippies, the natives.

The hotel bears the name of a great hereditary chief, and in the beer parlour that makes up the other half of the ground floor, there is a list a hundred strong of native people who are banned from the premises.

Behind the hotel is the sprawling reserve of the naval station. The crescents and circles of the married quarters, inturned and inspired as a turkey farm; the three-sided plaza of swimming pool, instruction rooms, and administrative offices; and all dependent on a little blockhouse five miles away on the same North Beach where Raven uttered his fiat. That building is ringed by a towering woodhedge of cedar poles and contributes doubtless to the vigilant security of the great white Lie.

The servicemen do not get involved in fights with loggers or Indians; they are mostly overweight improbable warriors, lounging in the coffee shop or driving through the town. Their wives seem to huddle in their Ottawa-plan homes — eating, dreaming, shopping through the catalogues or at the Capex built tactlessly on the high street. At weekends they may drive with their husbands and children out along North Beach in their dune buggies. It is their only contact with the environment, and in their suburban hearts they whine at the isolation, the rain, the mud, the monotony, the schools, the natives.

Often in the coffee shop you will see a table filled with young men in green clothing, passing the time over coffee and soft drinks, communicating in their closed circle with a foreign tongue. They are so young, so clean-cut and gauche, that their potential as fighting men seems if anything more unlikely than their chubby superiors'. They pass the time, they pass the time, they do not get into fights, they do not explore the wilderness, and they are French.

It is a pedigree of younger sons from families in St. Urbain or Chicoutimi or the townships of Belchasse. Economic blankness, claustrophobia, perhaps an echo of *vingt-deux* legends bring them into the forces. They group, they school, they take courses perhaps in radio technology; they are posted to the Pacific, to the furthest west point of Canada, where, if they ever hiked up the beach to Rose Spit, they could see Alaska on a clear day. They pass the time.

One of them is Raoul Forrestier. He has been sitting here for an hour and a half, discussing cars, Guy Lafleur, the prime minister's wife, watching the other customers coming and going over his companions' shoulders. He drifts away from the group, his mind rewaking a dream from the night before as he hears two truck-loggers talk:

"I tell you — the rack on him. Seven points, no kidding. Biggest I ever seen!"

"Branch Seven is the place . . ."

"No, I'm telling you, this feller stays put. Got to be the one I seen there last spring. Even in velvets he was built like an elk. Next fall for sure I'll get him."

"Get him in the morning . . ."

"Fuckin' rights: camp out all night on the ridge. I'll get him."

And Raoul Forrestier has been dreaming of the deer, too. Of endless dun herds, hooves clicking, passing before him over the muskeg. He has lingered in the Capex at the gun-rack, lovingly taken to himself a 30.30, seen himself tugging down the martini lever to reload, firing into the wave-like herd. It is the old glamour of childhood crazes at work. He is a boy still.

And he withdraws further, pale and certain in his vision, while his eyes take in abstractedly a table full of young natives. Normally he would watch them only in glances, covertly. The full mouth and body of one young girl, with her laughing black eyes, her carelessness of the destiny which leads her — they all know — down her mother's path. And the beautiful young men with naked gums, ten years away from beer bellies and broken complexions.

But his mind is with the gun, with the two days, duty-free, ahead of him. The young Indians sit, laughing, in their separate boredom, and he sees that he has money for the gun and the time to use it. He will rent a car — a pickup — he will go out and hunt deer on the muskeg. Most importantly, though he does not realize it, he will do this alone for his dream. He will brag to no one of his plans, and he will go alone.

3

The dark blade settled between the rear sight's shoulders and travelled a little to the right. It dipped across the pale brow and steadied on the dark left eye. He eased it away slightly, aiming exactly between the staring eyes. One part of him remembered in time that that rifle was shooting four inches wide; another part noted how everything but the gun and the motionless face across the stream had lost focus, even the running water sound. In that instant the strain broke in — he realized he'd been holding his breath the whole time — and the rifle began to leap slightly with each heartbeat. He lowered it and breathed deeply. The sound of the water rushed in. And a raven called, circling above the high forest roof.

The face before him merged back into its place on the bright gravel. He stepped out gingerly over the dark water on a rafting cedar bough and along the crumbling bank. The shot would have been wasted anyway. Would have warned the deer.

He squats on the gravel spit, laying the rifle with care, and picks up the skull. Small enough to hold on the flat of his hand, it is still built massively in its own scale. It is the colour of its gravel perch — dry from within though wet to touch from the lapping flicks of the stream. A flat head, snaky, the lower jaw hinged firmly into the skull, clacking in a dead bite when he releases it. The great overbite of the canines is a cold emblem of savagery — like a saurian fossil or a shark's jaw trophy — and he frowns at its mystery, his eyes going slightly out of focus as if he might clothe it again that way with flesh and fur and learn its name. The word comes suddenly — *loutre*; *l'outre* — as a blaze of dark, fearless eyes. Otter. It was a good omen not to have smashed it with an idle bullet. He eases it into his side pocket and picks up the rifle.

It has not felt right in these woods. His feet have betrayed him at every turn. Not just that he is a stranger under the trees, but that he has failed to condense himself into one simple being. He is out of balance. He had dreamed and foreseen how it would be, but now the clutter of his realities is a trammelling maze where he would walk straight.

And he had felt so straight, so clear this morning as he drove beside the calm inlet, with the truck and the gun and the sun strobing along the spruce ridge to his left. Till he had stopped by Blue Jackets Creek to give a ride to the young couple squatting by their rucksacks. They settled into the cab, and within a minute their cool glances, their patchouli odour, their ease with themselves upturned his patronage. He lost his grip on the helm, jarring the clutch clumsily as he climbed away from the inlet.

He lost himself, and his thoughts oscillated wildly between contempt, affection, communion, envy, confusion. He despised them as he would have on the base; then he was a generous, tolerant Worldly Wiseman; then they held the answer to everything; secretly he was their brother: they were free spirits, he was a novice.

The 30.30 rested against the hippie's knee. "Going hunting?"

Raoul nodded, defensively. He did not like someone else to touch his gun. Or his dream.

"Bad time for it," the hippie said, easily. "Not much meat on them, and you might get a doe."

"Sure, I'll be careful," he said, "just look around."

"We got all ours canned back in November," the girl said. "It's really good with rowanberries."

The hippie's hand rested on the gun barrel. Raoul winced. The hand was twice as big as his. The young man was huge and calm and knowledgeable. It seemed wrong and unfair.

He was rolling a cigarette now with a careful precision that belied the heavy fingers. "Remember the buck holds his head high" — he ran his tongue delicately along the paper — "though even then you can't be sure."

Raoul said, "Sure, I know." He didn't know; he absorbed the lore. The girl looked out the window, laughing at the great parliament of Ravens out on the gravel pits by the garbage dump.

"New gun?" the hippie gestured.

"Yes, I bought him this morning."

The girl moved to laugh at the "him" but smiled and turned instead. "You're from Quebec?"

Raoul nodded.

"Quebec City?"

"Not too far. Across the river, you know. Then Montreal for a while."

"Quebec is beautiful," she nodded gravely. "Really beautiful. Next to here."

Her friend murmured agreement, smiling as he inhaled from his smoke, ducking his chin. The rank Drum tobacco filled the cab. It seemed as exotic and dangerous as dope.

"You sighted the Winchester in yet?"

"No." Raoul was in doubt.

"Should do, man — they get really shagged up in the crates sometimes. You want to stop along here someplace and I'll mark for you?"

He could not be unfriendly. He wanted these people to accept him. But his day was spoiled. He pulled over just past Watun Bridge, feeling as though he were following orders.

The other man picked two beer cans out of the ditch and walked up the road about fifty yards. Across the ditch was a big log pile, a mouldering mass of wasted timber from when the road went through. He set the cans up in front of a log's butt end and stepped back onto the highway. "Okay," he waved.

Raoul was shooting diagonally across the road. He was nervous of the girl beside him at the truck window and of the hippie down the road not quite safely out of the way. He eased six shells into the gun, trying not to fumble, and yanked at the martini lever. That felt better. He was, after all, good with an FN on the ranges. What would the hippie make of that? Control was coming back.

He aimed the light gun, breathing carefully, sighting low on the can because of the short range. He fired and missed. The sound of the shot came crackling back from some echo point on the muskeg. He aimed higher this time and missed again. He flushed and lowered the rifle to inspect the sights. The girl grinned vaguely, unconcerned. He flicked the lever again, but when he aimed the trigger wouldn't pull. He couldn't close the lever, pulled it down again, and the shell in the breech jerked upright, clamped in by its flange. He could not release it, shame overcoming his tenuous poise. "The son of a bitch jammed hup," he muttered to the girl.

The hippie sloped easily, bored, back down the pavement, buttoning his collar. He took the gun. "Yeh, they do that," he nodded. "You've really gotta slam the lever up." He took a Russell knife from his belt. Raoul fell at once in love with its leaf-shaped blade. This young man was so easy with his world, knowing the mysteries. The knife point twisted and the shell fell out onto the road. The hippie slammed the lever home twice and replaced his knife. "You're shooting wide," he said. "I saw your second bullet hit the wood."

He turned casually and aimed back across the road. His left hand did not even close on the stock. He fired, and the lower can leaped, spouting ditch-water. Again, and the other flew out onto the verge. He handed the rifle back. "About four inches to the right," he said, his calm grey eyes resting for the first time straight on Raoul's. "Aim to the left, and you can fix it when you get home. See — the fore sight slides in that groove if you take the guard off." He smiled down at the soldier: "I'll set you up some more cans."

But it was not Raoul's weapon anymore. He ejected the last shell. "No, it's okay," he said, "I'll do it later." And rushed on: "Where you guys heading?"

"Down to Port," said the girl. "Are you going that far?"

"Oh, sure," he shrugged, "I'll take you. I've got nothing to do."

He dropped them outside Port Clements and drove on south towards Tlell. He'd go for ten minutes, and when they were out of the way he'd come back. He didn't know what to do with his day.

And down the hill, by Kumdis Bridge, a deer crossed the road. It was big and unhurried, did not look up. It must be a buck.

The hunting spell re-awoke; he pulled the truck in by the bridge, loaded the gun in the cab, and slithered fast down the bank into the trees. Inside there was frost on the moss still and a smothering silence. There was no sign of the deer.

He carried the gun at port across his body like a movie soldier; knelt to touch a bright pile of droppings like a movie Indian. The hard black pellets were cold. He followed what might have been a trail once and floundered, breathing heavily, over logs and oozing pools, along the river bank and so to the resting place of the skull.

Now, he must take control of his day. He looks around. There is a trail, or clear ground anyway, across the stream again where a solitary crabapple tree lies beaver-felled on the moss. He jumps from the gravel with a bootful of water and looks down at the litter of adze-shavings the beavers have left. The tree's stump points nakedly upwards, chipped round symmetrically as if by axe strokes. He would like to see a wild beaver.

He follows the untidy line of the river bank. There is more sky ahead, more light. For the swamp is not interminable. Someone, sixty years ago, cleared half an acre of the bottom, cut dikes and put stone drains down, and then left his forlorn dream of a homestead and family to die in a different ditch on Passchendaele. And Raoul is approaching a clearing of sorts — a space of matted couch grass, hedged in by the grey embrangling of the wild apple trees. The ditches are vestigial now — the roots of the coarse grass lie in water — but the clearing is firm. Frost has eaten into the mud, and the grass mat will preserve it till nearly midsummer. The crabapples braid into one another — they are cruel, thorny trees, and Raoul's toque is snatched by one branch, his left eye gouged and streaming from its neighbour.

He crouches almost to his knees to win the clearing. When he rises the deer is watching him, thirty feet away across the grass patch. A phenomenal, alert stillness awaits him in the grey head and huge black eyes. The animal is poised for panic, but its nature wills stillness upon it. Raoul's mind is a bloody, racing confusion, but his nature, which he reaches for within, teaches him not to extend that to the deer. His heart knocks, but he fixes his eyes steadily on the animal's and keeps them from the gun which now — unprepared — he must load. He eases down the lever, imperceptibly, then with a prayer slams the breech closed. He winces at the sound, the movement, but his eyes hold steady. A muscle jumps on the deer's shoulder. The hind legs almost gather, but not quite.

He brings the gun round, touches the butt to his shoulder while the muzzle still points away across his body. His left arm swings slowly upwards. The deer holds still, staring. Raoul's left eye streams from its twig-lashing. He brings the sights to rest above the deep alert eyes. Then his finger jerks. Echoes rifle the clearing. The deer's ear is fanned by the bullet. Incredibly, the animal does not move.

Raoul has reworked the lever without thinking, straight after firing. The gun is still up, and he is allowed another chance. *Four inches wide* he curses himself. The sights settle by the deer's right eye. He fires. The deer's whole neck and head flail backwards as though to a great hammerblow, and the body crumples down. The rifle breech is open, oozing cordite, and he has killed his deer. He steps towards the body.

But then, horribly, the deer is up again, or its hind quarters are up. Panic seeds the little grass plot. The animal forces its broken head, its paralyzed front limbs forward with a frenzied rabbit-like working of its back legs. It ploughs itself forwards, colliding with a young spruce tree, through the crabapples and into another open space beyond. It rams itself into a choked ditch and on again.

Raoul is dancing behind it in an agony of remorse and fear and the deer panic charging his own blood. He would like to run away. He rushes upon the creature, the pathetic upturned tail, and does not know what he should do. But the seconds pass — from a mere foot away he fires the heavy bullet into the back of the deer's skull. The head is nailed to the grass, the body leaps once, electrically, and is still. It is over.

He lays the rifle in the grass and walks round and round the body, beside himself. He is waiting for his heart to still, for the possibility of balance to return. He knows that his crime is not to have done the thing but to have done it wrong. And when the next part comes, the cleaning of the carcass, he must be at peace with himself and calm among the witness trees.

He has not done this before but he knows how to. He kneels with his sheath knife and slices at the side of the deer's throat. The eyes are glazed into an impossible deep blue of their own — there is none in the sky. He watches his own face and hands, foreshortened in the blue mirror as in a teapot's side. Not very much blood rolls from the jugular; so much has been wasted already through the shattered skull and the pumping, running legs.

The stomach next. He tugs the deer onto its side, and the legs swing against him, following gravity as if they were scarcely joined to the body. He wills himself into calm, rightness. He cuts from the breastbone down through the long hammock of the belly. Already he knows that it is a doe (that had glared back at him as he chased the poor cripple down the clearing), but he notes the mild genital now, seeing human anatomy as he has all along.

He plunges his hands around the slick heat of the bowels. The smell comes up at him of rabbit guts, his only reference. Do people smell so? The bundle of intestines comes out heavy but easily. There is no blood in the body. Only when he pulls the vivid liver free of its roots. He wipes his hands, front and back, along the grass. A pink, flecked membrane covers the breast-cave, taut. He pierces it with his knife, and with a long sigh the warm, moss-scented breath comes back at him. The human heart is there, and after the lungs, with two more knife strokes the body is clean. He has done this right. He is redeeming himself.

But a shape has fallen free with the last knife stroke. Shrouded in its caul, the still eye and the smiling, lipless rabbit mouth of the fetus discovers him. He stabs the knife again and again into the frosty grass roots — to clean it, to clean himself. He is almost numb. Under one of the apple trees he slices out turf with his knife and chilled fingers and reburies the fawn in limbo. He would pray for its rest and his atonement if there were words.

Carrying the carcass out is clumsy, too, but the woods do not entrap him. He guesses at a drier route, circling round on the higher ground through the big trees; and soon he hears a truck thundering over the road bridge ahead and knows that he has chosen well. His load lightens. And as if in token of that, another deer trots through the shadows at his right, slips round an old cedar and stops to stare back at him. He is seduced, outside himself, considering the feat of the hunter who, with one deer yoked across his shoulders, brings down another.

The deer is facing him directly, and something in the forest air decrees that it shall not move. Raoul lets the body slip off his shoulders — it falls fast, top-heavy, and heaps against his leg. He has the hammer on half-cock this time. He pulls it back as he raises the gun, aims wide, and fires. The deer falls and then, like a shadow, is gone.

He comes back to himself — that the stricken animal may escape to die in pain is like a knife stroke. He lurches down the slope, jolting over tree roots, his breath coming in gasps in a dowse of his victim's state. There is fur scattered everywhere — down the fibrous cedar bark and over the moss — and then, a few feet off, the first great scarlet star of blood upon the ground. And despite himself his brain begins to reason that the creature cannot get far, thus hurt; despite himself the thrill of tracking by a blood-spoor whispers to him out of his childhood reading. His breath comes easily. He is detached and keen.

The track is easy to follow. The blood is brilliant against the moss, the dead wood, the huckleberry stems. But when, across a log, he sees the deer, it is no longer a voyageur's quarry. It is so small and mute, furled gently on the ground, like a faun breathing. He kills it. A doe again, and very small, scarcely a yearling. He cleans it efficiently, his hands working across a cold distance, and drags it back up the hillside. Overhead and back the way he comes, two ravens invoke the forest's echoes. He is observed.

He leaves the smaller carcass and carries the first deer the last two hundred yards to the road. He lays it on the grass verge and tugs down the tailgate. A car is cresting Kumdis hill, and his impulse is to leap like a thief to cover, but there isn't time. The driver sounds his horn three times, cheerily, as he swoops past; a passenger waves. Raoul slides the corpse along the truck bed.

Back in the forest he loses his way. It seems an hour of casting around on the slopes, looking for a landmark. As the afternoon wanes the shadows seem to spill out and eddy across the roots and brushwood. His eyes remember nothing. He is almost ready to work down to the river and retrace his whole journey when a marker leaps at him. Draped on a low stump is a long, gritty shred of lung-flesh. And a few feet further on, the gun and the deer at last.

Yet both piles of guts were far from this place. Something (the ravens?) had dropped this in his path. There is no sound from them now. The offal gleams obscenely against the moss as he trudges back to the road.

4

He'll drive up past Port Clements with his window rolled down, steering with one hand. He'll stop at the other bridge over Kumdis on the Masset road to wash the stink off his hands. And some Haida kids will be waiting across the bridge for a ride, and he'll wave them over. There'll be three in the cab with him and one behind with the deer.

For a while they won't talk much, the two girls embarrassed, murmuring and giggling to each other, the boy remote, staring out with his cheek against the window glass. Raoul will be intensely aware of the girl next to him, her thigh pressed to his, her mocking eyes (however shy) when he glances her way. And the two of them off again in uncontrolled giggling.

Then there'll be a hand slamming on the roof of the cab and, jittery, he'll tread hard on the brakes and throw them all forward. Behind him the rear window will be running wet and red, and through that film the boy in the back, grinning sardonically with teeth gaping and brandishing a jug of Kelowna Red.

The boy in the cab will roll down the window and reach out and back for the wine. As they speed up he'll offer it across the girls. Raoul will hesitate and then take it, tilting it awkwardly, squeezed between the girl Mary and the steering wheel. The wine will go back and forth, and the boy behind will hammer for his share, and they'll all begin to talk and laugh, while Raoul's speech slurs and the dusk grows happy.

The furthest girl, Teresa, will say, "Hey, come on down to the village, blue eyes." And he'll say, "Sure, I always meant to go there." And all four of them in the cab will be laughing wildly while the girls chant, "Beautiful blue, beautiful blue!"

"Hey, good-looking," Teresa will say, "you gonna come to a party?" The boy will laugh nakedly in the darkening cab and say, "Yeah, we'll stop at the bakery first," and they'll be laughing again because the bakery's next door to the liquor store.

It'll be dark almost at the top of Garbage Dump Hill, and a deer's eyes will glow out on the road. Raoul will swerve madly, and the truck's wheels will wrench and skid on the gravel shoulder and almost lose control. But they'll laugh, laugh helplessly with the jug almost empty and the boy in the back beating on the cab roof and yelling, "Goin' down fast, goin' down faast," as they plunge down towards the inlet where New Masset is fairy lights on the dark running tide.

Mary will lay her head on his shoulder and the boy, Adam, will put his arm round her sister and the postilion Henry will scream, "Yee-aiii," as they tear along the inlet. "He's my cousin," Mary will say. "He's reeal crazy." Laughter will take them into the town to Collision Avenue: "Collision Corner, Collision Corner," the girls will chant, and Adam will roll the window down and fire the dead bottle onto the church lawn.

At the liquor store the postilion will jump down, and Raoul will fumble a ten-dollar bill from his pocket — "Put that in the kitty" — and hold it out. And Adam will smirk, "Yeah, put it in your pussy," and Teresa will slap him hard on the brow, and he'll laugh.

Then they'll run the dark and alien mile down to the village and on a ways, up the hill over the church, till the girls shout, "Stop." The truck will come to a jolting halt, and Raoul will know he's had too much already, and his dream of Mary beside him will start to fade even as she grabs his arm by the house door.

They'll troop into the neat warm room where an old woman looks up from the stove. And she'll mutter *Tchi-ay* in disapproval at their state, yet grim in welcome, too. She'll nod and nod her head at Raoul and ask his name, and when he says it Mary will cry, "No, he's Beautiful Blue Eyes," and Teresa will say, "A reeal French lover," and the old lady will cluck and chuckle and tell him to sit down, they've got no manners, they're *lumba* drunk.

In that small room, with its mirrors and gleaming stove and a photograph on the mantel of an old Haida man with a Hawk frontlet, the old one will take him over and say he must call her *Nonnie*, Grandmother, like the girls; and she will chuckle a lot but disapprove of the bottles going around. And Henry, the postilion, will stand apart by the door, sneering.

To Raoul the words will come harder as the girls chatter on and the wine keeps ending up in his hand. But he'll cling to the immense affection that wells out of him to the old lady. To be able to sense the mother in this stranger from a hostile race, to feel what home and belonging mean after this year of prison life on the bases; after the rivalries, the bravado, the pinups on the walls.

He'll make of her the respectable Gaspé matriarch she resembles and blush for her protectively when the youngsters make lewd jests and say they've brought down "a French stud for Nonnie." But she will laugh and laugh at that with them and poke his arm and pinch his chin and say he's "too skinny for me — I need something I can get a good hold on." Raoul will love her the more for breaking his illusion of age and restraint.

He'll know he's letting go of something. That tomorrow he'll be starting in an empty square. Or he'll believe this anyway, and a wave of vertigo will wash around the walls upon him, as though he were poised to jump from a cliff and take his chances with the tides.

Another grandson, Jimmy, maybe thirteen years old, will bang into the house and grow shy instantly at the company. He'll ask about the deer in the truck, and Raoul will say, "Do you want them? Can you use them? Sure — they're yours. They'd only waste I mean." Nonnie will say she'd really like some fresh meat. "Henry never hunts for me no more." She'll glare at the door: "Lazy dog!"

The two boys will go out with Jimmy and carry the carcasses round to the back porch, kicking the dogs away. Raoul will offer to help and half rise, only to sink back to the couch as they laugh at him.

He will feel so fond of these people, yet struggle to keep his eyes from rolling upwards out of weariness and liquor.

Then Henry of the glittering eyes and impatient frame will be back at the door. "Hey, Row, I got to get down to Delkatla and pick up some shakes. Can I take the truck? I won't be half an hour."

He'll see he could never like Henry, but he's included. "Oh, sure," he'll wave and fumble anxiously for the keys, but they're still in the dash.

Teresa will say, "No, don't you let him take it — he'll smash it up for sure. He's always pulling mad stunts like that — he's crazy."

"No, it's okay," he'll say.

And Mary: "Henry, you know you got no licence now. You stay here." But Henry will have gone.

Raoul will slip down to the floor, his back against the chesterfield, and try to catch all their eyes. Maybe a minute later, it seems, he'll half-clamber up again, jolting out of sleep, and realize he had been talking steadily but won't be able to remember what or for how long. He'll see some echoes in the others' eyes of the lanes and fields of his uncle's farm. And he'll realize that he has not been pretending to anyone and that they accept this and that it has all slipped by. He drifts again.

Then the girls will be by the door suddenly, saying, "See you, Nonnie" and, "Goodnight." Mary of the full mouth and limbs will catch his gaze for a moment, and his eyes will reach up feverishly to salvage from the drunken shuttle a moment's touch for the darkness of her eyes.

There'll be no one in the room but himself and Nonnie, and he'll mumble that he must leave her.

"You ain't going to do your Nonnie no harm," she'll say. "You stay now. You're not going *any*where." And she'll squeeze his shoulder, laughing softly, as she limps by.

He'll hear her moving in the other room, and he'll struggle out of his jacket from the stove's heat before he lapses into sleep. Maybe tomorrow, on the street, they won't even know him. Maybe they don't trust the things he has been learning. Never mind the truck and the gun — bad thoughts — never mind tomorrow.

His pocket will knock hollowly against the chesterfield's arm, and he'll fish out the forgotten skull of the otter. The glow from the stove's grille will play over its deep eyes as he struggles to focus on them and bring back into his grasp the day's contrarities.

And Nonnie will be back at her door saying, "What *is* that you got. Geee you're a funny feller, eh?" And he'll relinquish the otter's mask to the trembling hearthrug and slip away from everything while the old woman's voice is still speaking.

The tenses dissolve on that tableau in the hushed living room. Thirty miles down the inlet, over the muskeg, a raven shifts on its roost, dreaming under the cedar canopy high above Kumdis Creek. The water below checks and swirls blindly around the sunken branches. The stars of Orion hang, angled in the sharp January sky. The islands linger on the Pacific.

W.D. VALGARDSON

A Matter of Balance
(1980)

He was sitting on a cedar log, resting, absentmindedly plucking pieces from its thick layer of moss, when he first saw them. They were standing on the narrow bridge above the waterfall. When they realized he had noticed them, they laughed, looked at each other, then turned their backs. In a moment, the short, dark-haired one turned around to stare at him again. His companion flicked a cigarette into the creek.

Bikers, he thought with a mixture of contempt and fear. He had seen others like them, often a dozen at a time, muscling their way along the road. These two had their hair chopped off just above the shoulders, and from where he sat, it looked greasy and hung in tangled strands. They both had strips of red cloth tied around their heads. The dark-haired boy, he thought, then corrected himself, man, not boy, for he had to be in his middle twenties, was so short and stocky that he might have been formed from an old-fashioned beer keg. They both wore black leather vests, jeans and heavy boots.

He was sorry that they were there, but he considered their presence only a momentary annoyance. They had probably parked their bikes at the pull-off below the waterfall, walked up for God knows what reason — he could not imagine them being interested in the scenery — and would shortly leave again. He would be happy to see them go. He was still only able to work part-time and had carefully arranged his schedule so that his Wednesdays were free. He didn't want anything to interfere with the one day he had completely to himself.

The tall blond man turned, leaned against the railing and stared up at Harold. He jabbed his companion with his elbow and laughed. Then he raised his right hand, pointed two fingers like he would a pistol and pretended to shoot.

The action, childish as it was, unsettled Harold, and he felt his stomach knot with anxiety. He wished that he were on the other side of the bridge and could simply pick up his pack and walk back to his station wagon. The only way across the river, however, was the bridge, and he had no desire to try to force his way past them. They reminded him of kids from his public school days who used to block the sidewalk, daring anyone to try to get by. He had been in grade two at the time and had not yet learned about fear. When he had attempted to ignore them and go around, they had shifted with him to the boulevard, then to the road and, finally, to the back lane. As his mother was washing off his scrapes and bruises and trying to get blood off his shirt, he had kept asking her why, why did they do it? Beyond saying that they were bad boys and that she would speak to the principal, she had had no answers. Only later, when he was much older, had he understood that their anger was not personal and so could not be reasoned with.

Every Wednesday for the last six months, he had hiked to the end of this trail and then used his rope to lower himself to the riverbank. Before the winter rains began and flooded the gorge, he wanted to do as much sniping as possible. The previous week, he had discovered a crack in the bedrock that looked promising, but before he had a chance to get out all the gravel, the day had started to fade and he had been forced to leave. The gorge was no place to spend the night. Even at noon, the light was filtered to a pale grey. He dressed warmly, wearing a cotton shirt, then a wool shirt and, finally, a wool jack-shirt; yet within a few hours, he was always shaking with cold. As strenuous as the panning was, it could not keep him warm. The air was so damp that when he took a handful of rotting cedar and squeezed it, red water ran like blood between his fingers. On the tree trunks, hundreds of mushrooms grew. At first, because of their small size and dark grey colour, he thought they were slugs, but then he pried one loose with his fingernail and discovered its bright yellow gills.

Although he had been nowhere near the bottom of the crack, he had found a few flakes of gold, which he meticulously picked out of his pan with tweezers. Panning in the provincial parks was illegal, so he always went right to the end of the path, then worked his way along the river for another hundred yards. Once, he had taken a quarter-ounce of dust and small nuggets out of the river, and he wondered if someone had found out, but he immediately dismissed the idea. Only his psychiatrist knew. When they met each Thursday, he always showed Conklin his latest find. As far as his friends and colleagues were aware, he spent his days off hiking, getting himself back into shape after having been ill for over a year.

As he studied the two men below, he told himself he was letting his imagination run away with him again and to get it under control. There was no good in borrowing trouble. He stood up, swung his pack onto his shoulders and, being careful not to look like he was running away, resumed his hike.

From this point on, the trail was a series of switchbacks. If the two on the bridge were planning on following him and stealing his equipment or wallet, they would probably give up after a short distance and wait for easier prey. Unless they were in good condition, the steep climb would leave them gasping for breath.

Large cedars pressed close to the path, blocking out the light. Old man's beard hung from the branches. The ground was a tangle of sword fern, salal and Oregon grape. In a bit of open space, an arbutus twisted towards the sun. Its bark, deep earth-red, hung in shreds. Here and there, the new pale green bark was visible. That was the way he felt, like a snake or an arbutus, shedding his old skin for a new, better one. The previous year,when nothing else had seemed to work, he had taken his pack and hiked from sunrise to sunset, exhausting himself so completely that he could not stay awake. The sniping, looking for gold in cracks, under rocks, among the roots of trees, had come when he had started to feel better.

At the next bend, he stopped and hid behind a rotting stump. In a couple of minutes his pursuers — he told himself not to be foolish, not to be paranoid — appeared. They were walking surprisingly fast. If the trail had been even slightly less steep, they would have been running.

He wished there was a cutoff that would allow him to circle back. He could, he realized, use his equipment, if necessary, to lower himself to the river, but to do so he would need to gain enough of a lead to have time to untie and uncoil the rope, to set it around a tree, to climb down and then to pull his rope down after him so that it could not be taken away or cut. He then would be faced with the problem of finding a route up. He had to be back by seven. It was the agreed-upon time. Since their mother had been killed, the children became upset if he was even a few minutes late.

He looked at his watch. It was ten o'clock. It was a two-hour hike to the end of the trail, but he could hike out in an hour and a half. That did not leave him much time. First, he wanted to clean out the crack and, if possible, begin undercutting a large rock that sat in the centre of the river. Undercutting was dangerous. It would require that he move rocks and logs to divert the shallow water to either side of where he was going to work. Then he would need more logs to prop up the rock. He didn't want to get the work partly done and have half a ton of stone roll onto him. The nuggets that might be clustered around the base were worth some risk, but there was no sense in taking more chances than necessary.

Ahead, through a gap in the trees, he saw the railway trestle. The two behind him would, he told himself, stop there. Hardly anyone went farther. The trestle was an inexplicable focal point. Every weekend, dozens of people hiked to it, then dared each other to cross over the gorge. Many, terrified of heights, balked after the first few steps and stood, rigid, unable to force themselves to go farther.

That, he reassured himself, was what those two were coming for. They would cross the trestle and scare each other by roughhousing like a couple of adolescents.

He had hoped, unreasonably, that there would be hikers or a railway crew on the tracks. Normally, it was a relief when there was no one there. Hikers were inclined to talk about their experiences, and in the past, he had been afraid that if he was frequently seen on the same trail, his weekly visits might come to the attention of the park warden. To avoid that, he had deliberately arranged to come when the park was empty.

He did not stop but crossed over the tracks and entered the forest on the far side. The path dwindled to a narrow line of crushed ferns. The trees were shagged with windblown moss, and deadfall was everywhere. It was old forest, and in all the time he had come, he had never seen a bird or animal. As a child he had dreamed of living in the forest. In his dreams, his hunting had always been rewarded with game. The discrepancy between what he had hoped for and reality still astounded him.

While he was able to see the railway tracks, he stopped and waited. His legs had begun to tire and cramp. He stretched them, then kneaded his right calf with his thumb and forefinger. Always before, he had valued the silence and isolation. Now, however, as he watched the two bikers look up and down the roadbed, then cross the path, Harold felt the forest close around him like a trap.

He hurried away. Even as he fled, he reassured himself that they had done nothing. Anyone was free to hike wherever he wanted. If he just stopped, they would catch up and pass him by without paying any attention to him.

He kept his eyes on the path. He had no intention of tripping over a vine or slipping on a log. His fear, he chided himself, was not rational. If a Mountie suddenly appeared and asked him what was the matter, what could he say? That he didn't like the way they had looked at him earlier? That they had threatened him? And how was that, sir? He could hear the question. And the answer? The blond one pointed his finger at me. Any Mountie would think him mad.

The moss was so thick that his feet made no sound. There was only the creak of his pack, the harsh sound of his breathing. He would, he decided, abandon his plans, and when he got to the end of the granite ridge that ran along on his left, he would double back through the narrow pass on its far side. People don't assault other people without good reason, he told himself, but it did no good. His panic fluttered like dry leaves in a rising wind.

He wished that he had brought a hunting knife. It would have made him feel better to have a weapon. His mind scurried over the contents of the pack as he tried to determine what he could use in a fight. The only possibility was his rack of chock nuts. It wasn't much. A dozen aluminum wedges, even clipped together on a nylon sling, would not be very effective.

As he came to the end of the ridge, he turned abruptly to the left. The pass was nearly level and, unlike the area around it, contained only a few scattered trees. There were, he remembered, circles of stones where people had made campfires. One day he had poked about and discovered used condoms, some plastic sandwich bags and four or five beer bottles. A broken beer bottle, he thought, would serve as a weapon. He was just beginning to search for one when he saw a movement at the far end of the pass.

He became absolutely still. He felt so weak that he thought he was going to fall down. He craned his neck for a better look. If there were two of them, he could circle back the other way. In a moment, he realized that there was only one. That meant the other was on the path he had just left. He spun on his heel and ran back to the fork. No more than a quarter of a mile away the path ended. At that point, there was nothing to do but return the way he had come or descend to the river. In either case, he was trapped. His mouth, he realized, was so dry he could not spit.

Behind him, he heard someone ask a question that sounded like "Where did he go?" and a muffled reply, but he could not be sure of the words. The ground was nearly level. He was running when he burst out onto an area where the rock fell from the side of the trail like a frozen set of rapids. There were few places here for trees to root. Leaves and pine needles were swept from the pale green lichen by the winter rains. Rather than continue to what he knew was a dead end, he clambered down the slope. He had not explored this area. In the back of his mind was the hope that the rough rock continued all the way to the river. By the time they found out he was no longer on the path, he could have climbed the other cliff. All at once, he stopped. The rough black rock turned into sixty feet of smooth slab.

There was no time to go back. He glanced over his shoulder, then at the slab. It was, he realized, deceptive. It angled down toward the river, then stopped at a ragged edge. No steeper than a roof at the outset, it curved just enough that every few feet the angle increased. Patches of lichen and the smooth texture of the stone guaranteed that anyone who ventured out on it would be engaged in a test of balance.

There was a chance, because of his friction boots, that he could work his way onto the steepest part of the slope. If the two behind him were not pursuing him, they would pass by and he would never see them again. If they were, for whatever reason, meaning him some harm, they would have great difficulty reaching him.

Quickly, he unzipped the right-hand pocket of his pack and pulled out a section of three-millimetre rope. He tied a figure-eight knot in both ends, wrapped the rope around his left hand, then crept down to a small evergreen. Ten feet to the right, in a completely exposed area, there was a gnarled bush. Here and there, stunted trees, their trunks nearly as hard as the rock itself, protruded from cracks.

There was little room for error. If he began to slide, it would be difficult to stop before he went over the edge. At this part of the river, the fall would not be great, but height would not make any difference. Even a twenty-foot fall onto the scattered boulders of the riverbed would certainly be fatal. He leaned out, brushed away some dust that had collected on the rock, then took his first step.

Above him, someone whistled sharply. It startled him, but he kept his eyes fixed on the surface of the rock. He fitted the toe of his boot onto a small nubbin, then his other toe onto a seam of cracked quartz. The greatest danger was that, for even a split second, he would allow himself to be distracted. For his next move, he chose a pebbled area no bigger than a silver dollar. From there, he moved to a depression that was only noticeable because of its slight shadow. He had crossed more difficult areas than this but always with the security of a harness and rope and a belayer he could trust. A fall in those circumstances meant no more than some scraped skin and injured pride.

When he was within two feet of the bush, he felt a nearly over-whelming urge to lunge forward. He forced himself to stay where he was. On the rock there could be no impetuous moves. Patience, above all else, was to be valued. There seemed to be no place for him to put his foot. He scanned the surface. Just below him there was a hairline crack. If he pressed down hard on it, it would hold him long enough for him to step to the side and up and catch hold of the bush.

Slowly, he pirouetted on his left foot, then brought his right foot behind it. He took a deep breath, forced the air out of his lungs, then in one fluid movement, stepped down, up and across. Even as his hand grasped the wooden stem, he felt his feet begin to slide.

When he unwrapped the three-millimetre rope from his arm, he sat with his legs on either side of the stem. He fitted a loop of rope around an exposed root, then slipped the second loop around his wrist. Unless the root gave way, the farthest he was going to fall was a couple of feet.

Only then did he allow himself to look back. There was still no sign of anyone. The area of tumbled rock ran on for a fair distance and, he realized, would take a while to search. He cursed himself for not taking a chance and running back the way he had come.

He hooked his pack to the bush, took out the sling with the hardware on it, then eased himself out onto the steepest section of slab he could reach. Here he crouched, with his back to the trail, his hands splayed against the rock.

There was a sharp whistle above him. It was immediately answered from some distance back toward the trestle. With that, he realized that they had split up. One had blocked the trail while the other had done the searching.

He looked back again. Thirty feet behind him was the dark-haired biker. His blond companion was swinging down from the left. Both of them, Harold could see, were tired. He had, he thought, with a distant kind of pleasure, given them a good run for their money. If they had been carrying packs, he would have outdistanced them.

They both stopped at the rough edge, some ten feet apart, looked at each other and smirked.

"Did you want something?" he asked. He had meant to make it a casual question, even offhand, as though he had no idea they had followed him, but panic sharpened his voice.

They both laughed as if at a joke.

"What do you want?" He was no longer sure that what he had planned would work.

The blond man had a small leather purse attached to his belt. He unsnapped it and took out a bone-handled clasp knife. He pried out the wide blade.

"Are you crazy?" Harold cried. "What's the matter with you? I don't even know you."

They both grinned foolishly and studied their boots. They looked, he thought wildly, like two little boys caught in the middle of a practical joke.

Panic made him feel like he was going to throw up. "Are you nuts?" he shouted. "Are you crazy or something?"

Their answer was to start down the slab, one on each side of him. Their first steps were confident, easy. The surface of the rock was granular and bare at the edge and provided plenty of friction. He could see that neither was experienced. They both came down sideways, leaning into the rock, one hand pressed to the surface. He gripped the nylon sling in his right hand and concentrated on keeping his balance.

The dark-haired one was closest. He was coming down between the tree and the shrub, taking little steps, moving his left foot down, then his right foot, then his left, dangerously pressing all his weight onto the edge of his boot and, even more dangerously, leaning backward, throwing off his centre of balance. Suddenly, a piece of lichen peeled away and his left foot slid out from under him. Instead of responding by bending out from the rock and pressing down with his toes, he panicked. He was sliding faster and faster. His body was rigid, his face contorted with fear, his eyes, instead of searching for a place he could stop his slide, were desperately fixed on the safe area he had just left behind. He made no sound. When he was finally even with Harold, he reached out his hand as though expecting it to be taken. There was, Harold saw, on the back of the hand, a tattoo of a heart pierced by a knife. A red and blue snake wound up the arm and disappeared beneath the sleeve. It was only by luck that his one foot struck a piece of root and he stopped. He was no more than a foot from the edge.

The blond man had come at an angle, picking his way along by fitting his knife blade into a crack. Just before his companion lost control, the blond man had started to work his way across an area where there were no cracks. He seemed frozen into place.

"Why?" Harold shouted at him.

The sound seemed to wake the blond man from a stupor. He turned his head slowly to look at Harold. He squinted and formed his mouth into a small circle, then drew his chin down and ran his tongue along his lower lip. For a moment, Harold thought the biker was going to turn and leave.

"Get me out of here," his companion cried. Fear made his voice seem as young as a child's.

The blond man shook his head, then half-snarled, stood up and tried to walk across the intervening space. It was as though momentum and will held him upright; then Harold swung the nylon sling over his head, lunged forward and struck his opponent on the upper arm. The blow was not powerful, and normally it would have been swept aside. But here, as they both teetered on the steep surface, it was enough to knock them both off balance.

As the blond man skidded down the rock, he jabbed at it with his knife, trying to find an opening. Six feet from the edge, he managed to drive the blade into a crack. The knife held. He jammed his fingers into the crack.

Harold had slipped, fallen, then been caught by the rope around his wrist. He pulled himself back to the shrub and knelt with his knee against the stem.

"Help us up," the dark-haired man begged. He looked like he was on the verge of weeping.

Harold loosened the rope, then untied it. Carefully, giving his entire attention to the task, he retraced his original route. Once at the evergreen, he knew he was safe. His sides were soaked with sweat and he could smell his own fear, bitter as stale tobacco. The two men never stopped watching him.

When Harold reached the top of the slab, the blond man called, in a plaintive voice, "For God's sake, don't leave us here."

Fear had softened their eyes and mouths, but he knew it was only temporary. If he drew them to safety, they would return to what they had been.

"Pull us up," the dark-haired man whined. His red headband had come off and was tangled in his hair.

Around them, the forest was silent. Not a bird called, not an animal moved. The moss that covered the rock and soil, the moss that clung thickly to the tree trunks, the moss that hung in long strands from the branches, deadened everything, muted it, until there were no sharp lines, no certainties. The silence pressed upon them. Harold had, for a moment, a mad image of all three of them staying exactly as they were, growing slowly covered in moss and small ferns until they were indistinguishable from the logs and rocks except for their glittering eyes.

"Tell somebody about us," the dark-haired man asked.

The words tugged at him like little black hooks. He looked down. Their faces were bleached white with fear. He could tell someone, a park warden, perhaps, but then what would happen? If he could be certain they would be sent to prison, he might dare tell somebody, but he knew that would not happen. If charges were laid, he would have to testify. They would discover his name and address. And from then on, he would live in fear. Afraid to leave his house. Afraid to go to sleep at night. Afraid for his children. And what if they denied everything, turned it all around? He had had the necessary equipment to rescue them and had refused. What if one of them had fallen by the time someone came? He could be charged with manslaughter, and the children would be left without mother or father. No matter how he tried to keep his psychiatrist out of it, Conklin would become involved. Harold knew how people thought. His short stay in hospital for depression, his weekly visits to a psychiatrist to siphon off pain and, automatically, he was crazy.

"You bastard," the blond man screamed. "You bastard. Get us out of here." He kept shifting his feet, trying to find a purchase where there was none. "If you don't, our friends will come. They'll get us out. Then we'll start looking for you. There's thousands of us. We'll find you."

The screaming startled him for a moment, but then he thought about how soon the little warmth from the sun would disappear, of how the fog would drift down with the darkness, of how the cold would creep into everything, of how few people came this way.

He wondered if his wife had screamed like that. Six of her fingernails had been broken. *Unto the third generation*, Conklin had said. His children, and his grandchildren should he have any, would feel the effects. Alone in a dark parking lot, desperately fighting for her life, and he had been sitting in his study, reading. "Help never comes when it's most needed."

Then, with real regret for the way things are, he hefted his pack so that it settled firmly between his shoulders and returned the way he had come.

AUDREY THOMAS

Natural History
(1980)

Something had run over her hand. Now she was wide awake and sitting up, the sleeping bag flung off, her heart pounding. What? The rat? No, don't be foolish — a mouse maybe, a vole, perhaps just the cat's tail swishing, as she came back to see if they were still persisting in this out-of-doors foolishness when there were all those comfortable beds and cushions inside. Clytie tried to get the cat to lie down at their feet, but it walked away.

"She probably thinks we're nuts," the mother said.

"Maybe she'll jump in the bathroom window and wait for us to come whining and begging to be let in."

"And she'll say, 'Well, my dears, now you know what if feels like when *I* want in.'"

The cat was old but very independent, except for wanting to sleep inside at night. They often spoke for her, having endowed her with the personality of a querulous but rather imperious old woman.

"Maybe she'll do us the favour of catching that rat," she added.

"You *know* that she won't," the child said. "She's afraid."

"She's not afraid; she's lazy."

But something would have to be done. No mouse could have gnawed a hole like that, right through the outside of the cottage and into the cupboard, under the sink, where the compost bucket was kept. A hole the size of a man's fist. They never saw the rat, but they heard it when they were lying in bed in the other room; and last night, it was on the roof, or rather, *in* the roof, directly over their heads. A determined *chewing* sound. They both woke up.

"I hope that it electrocutes itself on a wire."

"Do they really eat people?"

"No. Some of those old tales from Europe were probably based on fact. Maybe in times of famine — or when it was very cold. Maybe then. But these rats come off the fishboats; they're not starving. Rats are just big mice; there's no real biological difference." So she spoke to reassure her daughter, but nevertheless they lay awake in the big double bed, holding hands, not liking the idea of a long, narrow, whiskered face suddenly appearing through the ceiling. Something would have to be done. She thought of rabies; she even thought of the plague. This morning, she had gone down to the store to see if they carried rat poison.

"Not any more," the storekeeper said. "We used to, but they won't let us anymore. . . . Because we sell food," he added. "In case something spilled, I guess."

So they'd have to take a trip to town and find a drugstore. Would they look at her strangely? She though of Emma Bovary asking for arsenic. She said that she wanted to kill some rats that were keeping her awake. Cramming it into her mouth. Ugh. She would see if it were possible to get enough for only one rat. She came back up the path discouraged. She didn't want to go anywhere. She just wanted to stay here with her child and complete her recovery. Nice word that, re-cover. To cover yourself over again, something essential having been ripped away, like a deep rip in the upholstery. Then there had been the visitors to think about.

They were not sleeping outside because of the rat but in spite of it. They were sleeping outside because of the full moon. They had talked about the moon for days. If it were fine ("And when wasn't it fine, over here in July?" they asked each other), they would sleep out and watch the moon rise. And so, after supper, they carried out pillows and sleeping bags, a thermos of coffee and some cookies in case they woke up early in the morning; and they made themselves a nest under the apple trees. The apples were still small and green, hardly distinguishable from the leaves. They were winter apples. There was a woven hammock that had been slung between two of the trees. She had rigged up a rope, thrown it over a stout branch and tied it, at the other end of the hammock, to a discarded wooden toy, so that one could lie in the hammock and reach up and gently rock oneself.

"The ultimate in laziness," she said. They took turns lying in the hammock, reading, the other one stretched out on an old blanket nearby.

But the moon had taken so long, so long that first the little girl had given a great sigh and turned over, backed up into the warmth of her mother, with her face away from the moon's rising, and slept; and then the mother, too, slept.

But the mother was now wide awake, with the moon high and white and the moonlight falling over on the far side, hitting a white shed that lay beyond the house. Was it moving away from them or towards them? she wondered. Old wives' tales came back to her, about not letting the moonlight strike your face — and the memory of the blind girl that they had met that day, with her round, vacant, staring eyes. Ugh. Too many morbid thoughts.

She got up quietly and walked away a little bit to pee, squatting in the long grass. She had borrowed a scythe from a neighbour up the road, a real old-fashioned scythe, with a long wooden handle and a curved, vicious blade, and had found that, once she got the hang of it, she liked the rhythm of the thing, walking forward, moving her hips just so or the blade wouldn't cut clean, it simply hacked or flattened out the grass; but when they went to pick up the grass, they found that it was still fastened to the earth. She hadn't come around to this side yet with the scythe — perhaps tomorrow. The night was utterly still; even the owl, which they heard so often but had never seen, was silent. And there was no breeze except that, every so often, a ripple would pass through the firs, the alders, the pear tree and the apple trees which almost surrounded the house. It was as though the night itself were an animal, a huge dark cat which twitched and quivered from time to time in its sleep.

"I should sell this place by moonlight," she thought. "Then no one would notice the peeling paint or the cracked windowpanes or the impossible angle of the chimney."

"Describe this house," the blind girl had said, eagerly. "What does it look like?"

"It looks like a witch's house," Clytie said, without hesitation, "like something that a witch might live in." She was showing off — they had been reading Grimm's fairytales — but still, her mother was hurt.

"It's very beautiful," the blind girl's companion said. "The wall that you are leaning against is a lovely mustard yellow, and the couch that we are sitting on is purple."

"What sort of purple?"

"Very nearly the purple of that shawl you bought in Guadalajara."

So she hadn't been blind long. Not long ago, she had seen and bought a purple shawl in a Mexican market. The girl — a young woman, really — was terribly overweight, and that, too, seemed recent. There was something about the way that she moved her body, or moved *in* her body, like a child all bundled up. Diabetes. Lifting the teapot, the mother's hand turned cold. The blindness, as well as the fatness, were merely signs that things inside had got out of control. What was the word? She had heard it often enough. "Stabilize." They hadn't yet been able to "stabilize" the disease. A Seeing Eye dog, a magnificent golden Labrador, lay at the blind girl's feet. A plate of cookies was offered. They had been mixed and baked deliberately for their variety of texture: oatmeal cookies, chocolate chip, hermits. "If I'd only known," she thought. But it was interesting. Once again, the blind girl asked for visual description before she made her choice; indeed, she hardly touched the cookies at all.

Clytie watched every move, fascinated. The girl told them that she was writing poems. "Trying to get some of my anger out," she said with a little laugh. Perhaps she wanted to be asked to recite.

"We're sleeping outside tonight," Clytie said, "under the moon." The girl laughed again, the laugh too small for her large, awkward body. "Be careful not to look at a reflection of the moon in water," she said. "It's very dangerous to do that."

"Why?"

"I think that you're supposed to go mad."

Another old wives' tale.

And there was the moon now — silent, indifferent, unaware of all the myths and tales and proverbs which she had inspired! Words, too, like lunatic, moony. The other day, she said to her daughter, "Stop mooning around and *do* something." As though the moon were aimless or haphazard when, in reality, she was so predictable, so orderly, that her passages could be predicted with extreme accuracy. "July 19th: Perigee moon occurs only six hours before full moon." Growing, brightening, reaching fullness; waning, dimming, beginning the whole thing over again. The old triple moon goddess, corresponding to the three phases of woman. Her little girl, Clytie, named not for the moon but after the sunflower, was very orderly. She had drawn up a schedule at the beginning of the summer and taped it to the refrigerator door. They were going to have to work hard in the garden, yes. They were also going to have periods when each would wish to be alone, agreed; when one or the other would go out to the old shed and work on some private thing. They were going to start a study of intertidal creatures; they were going to paint the kitchen; they were going to learn the names of the constellations. There it all was, on the refrigerator door, all worked out — a calendar of orderly and edifying progression through the long summer, decorated in the corners with orange suns and purple starfish.

And there it remained, because things hadn't quite worked out like that. For one thing, it had been very hot; for another, they both seemed to have been overtaken with a kind of lethargy: the child probably because she was growing so fast, the mother perhaps because she was unwilling to really "come to" and think about the future.

They had worked hard during the winter, getting up at six a.m. and lighting fires, leaving time for a good breakfast before the yellow school bus came. And they went to bed early as well. If someone rang after nine p.m., one or the other had to crawl out of bed in the dark to answer the phone.

She was writing a book, and she worked all day while her daughter was away at school. She sat next to the wood stove, the cat asleep on a chair beside her. The simple life: it was what she craved and what she needed. On weekends, they did the wash in an old wringer washer, shoving the clothes through the wringer with a wooden spoon; they baked bread and cookies, stacked wood, read books and listened to the radio.

"It seems so peaceful here!" the blind girl cried, as they sat in the front room, sipping tea and nibbling cookies. "It must be paradise to be here all year round."

Paradise: "a walled garden, an enclosure." Disaster: "a turning away from the stars."

The blind girl was from Los Angeles. Her companion, older, rather stern-faced until she smiled, was the niece of one of the earliest families on the island. "She wants so much to meet you," the woman said on the phone. "I have been reading your poems to her. It would mean a great deal to her."

She did not want to meet anyone, especially anyone who had suffered, who was perhaps suffering still, but she could think of no graceful way to get out of it. It hadn't been too bad, really. She wondered and worried about her daughter's reaction, but the child seemed more interested than alarmed.

"Nine a.m.: exercises, bike-riding," the schedule announced, as they sat at the kitchen table in their nightgowns, eating scones and strawberry jam. "Two hours a day, intertidal life," it called down to them from where they dozed on the rocks, the green notebook — they were still on seaweed — neglected at the bottom of the towel. They painted each other's toe- and fingernails impossible colours and waved their hands and feet in the air to dry. They timed each other to see who could stay the longest in the icy water. The yellow paint for the kitchen remained in the shed while they lay on the hammock and the blanket and read *The Wind in the Willows* out loud.

"You can't help liking Toad," Clytie said. "I know that I shouldn't like him, but I do."

Strange little creatures done up in leggings and waistcoats, thinking our kinds of thoughts and feeling our emotions. "The English were particularly good at that," she thought. "And look at me, pretending the cat will pass moral judgment on our sleeping arrangements and feeling that, any second now, I'll see her up in a tree, grinning."

But the rat was real. The rat would have to be dealt with. "The cat takes the rat," she thought, "but maybe only in the rhyme."

Sometimes, they drove down to the other end of the island to a sandy beach where the water was warmer, and they spent the afternoon and early evening there. Last week, there had been several young women sitting on the beach with their babies and watching their older children swim. She got into a discussion with a woman that she knew slightly, whom she hadn't seen in months. The woman was very beautiful, with curly dark hair and long dancer's legs. It turned out that her husband had left her and the children to go and live with a younger woman. "I'm better now," she said, "but I spent a month thinking up ways to kill him — to kill them both. Really."

"I believe you," she said. "Last winter, I chopped kindling every day. It wasn't kindling, of course, it was hands and fingers and lips; ears, eyes, private parts. Everything chopped up small and thrown into the stove. We were as warm as toast."

"I'm glad to hear somebody else admit to such feelings," the other woman said, laughing.

"What are all those operas about, those myths, those 'crimes of passion?' We just aren't open about it in these northern climates."

"He says that he can do so much for her," the other woman said.

(And the moon up there, female, shining always by reflected light, dependent on the sun, yet so much brighter, seemingly, against the darkness of the sky; so much more mysterious, changing her shape, controlling the waters, gathering it all in her net.)

It was dark when they drove back up the island, and the eyes of the deer glowed yellow-gold in the headlights. Once or twice, they saw a raccoon with eyes like emeralds.

"Why don't our eyes do that at night?"

"I don't understand it completely," she said. "It's because those animals go out at night. They have something like a mirror, maybe like your bike reflector, at the back of the eye. This gives them a second chance to use whatever light there is. It hits the mirror and bounces back again. Then, what's left over shines out. 'Wasted light,' I think it's called. Your grandfather taught me all that stuff. He knew all about it, but he wasn't very good at explaining it, or at least not to me. Maybe he was just tired or maybe I wasn't very good at listening. I can still remember him trying to explain about the sun and moon, one Saturday morning, when I was about your age. I don't think I *asked* him; I think that he just wanted to explain it! He had an orange, a grapefruit, a flashlight and a pencil. He stuck a pencil through the grapefruit for the earth on its axis, but I got terribly lost. I stood on one foot and then the other, and finally I asked if I could go out and play. I think that he was terribly hurt."

The blind girl told stories about her dog. She made everything gay and light and witty. Once, she and another blind friend had taken their dogs into a posh Los Angeles restaurant. "It's against the law to keep us out," she explained. It was the friend's birthday, so they saved up their money to go out together and celebrate. The waiter was very helpful, and they ordered a fancy meal. Their dogs lay quiet and well-behaved beneath the table. Everybody felt good.

"Then, Samson sort of sat up — I could feel him. He gave a sigh and did a huge shit, right by my chair. It was *so* awful. We could hear the people who were nearest to us saying, 'Well, *really*,' and similar things. The smell was very powerful, and we got hysterical. We were laughing our heads off at the whole idea. We could sort of feel the maître d' hovering nearby, uncertain whether or not to kick these gross blind people out and maybe face some sort of lawsuit, or lose all his patrons, or just try to ignore the whole thing, pick up the poop and carry on."

"What happened?" At the mention of his name, the dog sat up, wagging his tail, as though he, too, were enjoying the story.

"Well, I carefully lowered my big, beautiful, starched dinner napkin over where I thought the pile was — I didn't actually want to get my fingers in it — and then I called out, '*Waiter, waiter.* I'm afraid my dog has had a little accident.'"

"But we never went back there," she added when they stopped laughing. "Never."

"I would not have offered cookies," she thought, "if I had known. I would not have *tempted* her, especially with homemade cookies offered by the young girl who had home-made them." The man who tried to teach her about the motions of the sun and moon and earth on its axis had been a diabetic, too, or had become one, only much later in life than their visitor. He could not give up all the sweet, rich foods that he loved. He was dead now; he did not even know that she had a child. "Just this once," he used to say, as he put sugar on his grapefruit or ordered a dish of chocolate ice cream. And her mother, joining in, would say, "Oh, it won't hurt him, just this once." He had been quite short-sighted, and the thing that made her realize how dead he was, was, after the funeral, finding his bifocals in a drawer. How many cookies had the blind girl eaten? She couldn't remember.

"I don't really feel lonely any more," she said to her friend on the beach. "I used to. I used to think that I'd die from loneliness, as if it were a disease. I suppose that I'll want to be with someone again, but right now I'm content. Only some days — when the fucking clothesline breaks or I'm down to the wet wood, things like that — I wish that there was someone around. But then, I ask myself, 'Is it a husband that I want or a hired hand?'"

"A hired hand might be useful for other things as well."

"Or a hired finger." They giggled.

(He would have dealt with this rat, for instance. He would have got rid of it quick.)

One night, the cat caught a mouse and started munching it in the darkness of the room where she and Clytie were sleeping.

"*Really,*" she said, waking up and recognizing what was going on.

And Clytie, laughing, got up in her long white nightdress and threw the cat outside.

She wasn't the least afraid of that. But she was terrified to be alone in the dark, as her mother had been terrified when she was a child, as perhaps all children were terrified of the dark. Which is why she sat there, now, wide awake and thoughtful, her half of the sleeping bag over her knees, rather than inside the house, sipping a cup of tea and reading until she became sleepy again.

They had done away with mousetraps because they couldn't stand that awful, final "click."

"Ugh," the child said, crawling back in bed, "that crunching sound was really *disgusting*." And they both began to laugh.

"Shall we make her a mouse pie the next time she does that?"

"Would you? Would you really?"

"Why not?"

"It might smell terrible."

"Would you really make a mouse pie with a crust, like in *The Pie and the Pattypan*?"

"Oh, God, I don't know. . . . Probably not."

They caught a rock cod near the government wharf, and when they cleaned it and removed the stomach, there were three small crabs inside.

"I suppose that they have some sort of acid in their stomachs which dissolves the shell," she said.

"I guess everything just goes around eating everything else," her child said.

"Sometimes it seems that way."

The blind girl turned her head towards whomever was speaking; she turned towards the sound. The sunflower, Clytie, following her beloved Apollo as he crossed the sky. The moon, shining always with reflected light.

"Where are all the strong men," the woman on the beach said, "now that there are all these strong women?"

("I'm getting awfully symbolic out here, wide awake beneath the moon." The absolute trust of her sleeping child moved her almost to tears. She would sit here all night, if necessary; it didn't matter.)

"I can't stay on this island forever," she thought. "I will end up like an old witch in a witch's cottage. I've got to give my life some serious attention. It's all very well to sit around reading fairytales and making a game of everything." She glanced at her daughter's long hair which was spread out on the pillow beside her. "*She'll* change; maybe she'll change first. She'll want more than this." Her namesake, turned into a sunflower, gazing blindly towards the sun. The moon (female), shining always by his light.

("Let her be strong," she thought. "Let her be strong and yet still loving." A few years ago, in the city, she had come home from school and announced at dinner that a policeman had come to the school and given a talk about "strangers." Her mother and father glanced quickly at one another. A little girl, her lunchbox beside her, had been found dead in a ditch.

"And what are strangers?" asked her father gently, curious as to what she had been told, yet wanting to keep the story light.

The child's reply was very serious.

"Strangers are usually men.")

"Dis-aster," they read in the dictionary: "a falling away from the stars." "Paradise," from the Persian: "a walled garden." "*Lunaticus*" f. L., "affected by the moon." And who had first made *that* connection? Galileo. He built his "optik glasse" and discovered that the moon (female, shining always with reflected light) was not the "luminous orb" of the poets, but rather full of "vast protuberances, deep chasms and sinuosities."

Later, in England, men looked at a flea through a microscope and saw "the devil shut up in a glasse." Mankind was always wanting more, wanting to make far things nearer, small things larger; to know and understand it all. When the Americans stepped on the moon, one of her friends had written a long mock-heroic poem called "The Rape of Cynthia."

The trick, of course, to try and get the right distance on everything, to stand in just the right relationship to it all. But how? Would her daughter be any better at it than she was? Another image came to mind out of her childhood, a stereopticon belonging to her grandfather. She would sit with it, on a Sunday afternoon, sliding the crossbar up and down, until suddenly, "click," the two photographs taken at slightly different angles (St. Mark's, the Tower of London, Notre Dame) would become one picture, which would take on depth and a wonderful illusion of solidity. *That* was the trick. To slide it all — moon, blind girl, rat, the apple tree, her father's fingers tilting the pencil, her own solitude, the cat, the eyes of the deer, her daughter, this still moment, back/forth, back/forth, back/forth,

until "click,"

until "click,"

until "click" —

there it was: wholeness, harmony, radiance, all of it making a wonderful kind of sense, as she sat there under the apple tree, beneath the moon.

And then, suddenly, because she *did* see, if only for an instant, she bent down and she shielded the child's body as the moonlight, finally, reached them.

"What amazes me," Clytie said, just before she turned over and went to sleep, "is that we're just part of a system. We're all just floating around."

BUDGE WILSON

The Leaving
(1981)

She took me with her the day she left. "Where y' goin', Ma?" I asked. She was standing beside my bed with her coat on.

"Away," said Ma. "And yer comin', too."

I didn't want to go anywhere. It was three o'clock in the morning, and I was warm in my bed.

"Why me?" I complained.

I was too sleepy to think of any more complicated questions. In any case, there were no choices and very few questions back then when we were kids. You went to school, and you came home on the school bus. If your father wanted you to shovel snow or fetch eggs, he told you, and you did it. He didn't ask. He told. Same with Ma. I did the dishes and brought in the firewood when it was required. She just pointed to the sink or to the woodbox, and I would leave whatever I was doing and start work. But at three a.m., the situation seemed unusual enough to permit a question. Therefore I asked again, "Why me?"

"Because yer the smartest," she said. "And because yer a woman."

I was twelve years old that spring.

Ma was a tall, rangy woman. She had a strong, handsome face, with high cheekbones and a good firm chin line. Her lips were full. Her teeth were her own, although she smiled so rarely that you seldom saw them; her mouth tended to be held in a set straight line. She did not exactly frown; it was more as though she were loosely clenching her teeth. Her eyes were veiled, as if she had shut herself off from her surroundings and was thinking either private thoughts or nothing at all. Oh, she was kind enough and gentle enough when we needed it, though perhaps we needed it more often than she knew. But when we had cut knees or tonsillectomies, or when friends broke our hearts, she would hold us and hug us. Her mouth would lose its hard tight shape, and her eyes would come alive with concern and love.

Her lovely crisp auburn hair was short and unshaped, making her face look uncompromising and austere. She wore baggy slacks over her excellent legs, and she owned two shabby grey sweaters and two faded graceless blouses. I did not ask myself why my mother looked this way, or why she had retreated behind her frozen face. One accepts one's parents for a long time without theory or question. Speculation comes later, with adolescence and all the uncertainty and confusion it brings.

But when she woke me that chilly May morning, I was still a child. I rose and dressed quickly, packing my school bag with my pajamas and toothbrush, the book I was reading, a package of gum, the string of Woolworth pearls that my grandmother had given me on my tenth birthday, and some paper to write and draw on. I wore jeans, my favourite blue sweater, my winter jacket and rubber boots. I forgot my hat.

My mother had told me to be quiet, so I slithered down the stairs without a single board creaking. She was waiting at the door, holding a black cardboard suitcase with a strap around it. A shopping bag held sandwiches and some of last fall's bruised apples. She wore a brown car coat over her black slacks, and her hair was hidden under a grey wool kerchief. Her mouth had its tense fixed look, but her eyes were alive. Even at my age and at that hour, I could see that.

We stopped briefly before walking out into the cold night air. The stove in the kitchen was making chugging noises, and from different parts of the small house could be heard a variety of snores and heavy breathing. My four brothers and my father were not going to notice our departure.

For a moment, my mother seemed to hesitate. Her mouth softened, and a line deepened between her eyebrows. Then she straightened her shoulders and opened the door. "Move!" she whispered.

We stepped into the night and started walking down the mountain in the direction of town, six miles away. I did not quarrel with the need for this strange nocturnal journey, but I did question the reason.

"Ma," I said.

She turned and looked at me.

"Ma. Why are we leavin'?"

She didn't answer right away. It crossed my mind that she might not be sure of the reason herself. This was a frightening thought. But apparently she knew.

"I plans t' do some thinkin'," she said.

We walked quickly through the night. North and South Mountains closed off the sky behind us and far ahead, but a full moon made it easy to see our way on the frosty road. The hill country was full of scrub growth, stubby spruce and sprawling alders, unlike the tidy fields and orchards of the Valley. But the frost lent a silver magic to the bushes and the rough ground, and the moonlight gave a still dignity to the shabby houses. It was cold, and I shivered. "Fergot yer hat," said Ma. "Here." She took the warm wool kerchief from her head and gave it to me. I took it. Parents were invincible and presumably would not feel the cold. My mother was not a complainer. She was an endurer. It was 1969, and she was forty-five years old.

When we reached Annapolis, we stopped at a small house on the edge of town, and Ma put down her suitcase and dug around in her purse. She took out a key and opened the door. Even my silent mother seemed to think that an explanation was required. "Lida Johnson's in Glace Bay, visitin' her daughter. Said I could use the house while she's gone. Normie's at a 4-H meetin' in Bridgetown. Joseph's truckin'. We'll wait here till th' train goes."

"Ma," I asked, "how long we gonna be gone?"

She bent her head down from its rigid position and looked at the floorboards of the front hall. She touched her mouth briefly with her fist. She closed her eyes for a second and took a deep breath.

"Dunno," she replied. "Till it's time."

We slept in the parlour until we left for the station.

I guess that six-mile walk had shunted me straight from childhood into adolescence, because I did an awful lot of thinking between Annapolis and Halifax. But at first I was too busy to think. I was on a train, and I had never been inside one before. There were things to investigate — the tiny washroom with its little sink and the funny way to flush the toilet. In the main part of the Dayliner, the seats slid up and down so that people could sleep if they wanted to. I watched the world speed by the windows — men working on the roads; kids playing in schoolyards; cows standing dumbly outside barns in the chilly air, all facing in the same direction; places and towns I had never seen till then. My ma looked over at me and placed a comic book and a bag of peanuts on my lap. "Fer th' trip," she said, and smiled, patting my knee in an unfamiliar gesture. "Mind missin' school?" she added.

"No," I said. But I did. I had a part in the class play, and there was a practice that afternoon. I was the chief fairy, and I had twenty-five lines, all of which I knew by heart already. But this trip was also a pretty special, if alarming, adventure. It had a beginning but no definite end, and we were still speeding toward the middle. What would Halifax be like? We never had enough money to have more than one ride on the Exhibition ferris wheel at Lawrencetown, but here we were buying train tickets and reading comics and eating peanuts and travelling to heaven knows what expensive thrills.

"Ma," I asked, "where'd the money come from?"

She looked at me, troubled.

"Don't ask," she said. "I'll tell you when you're eighteen."

Eighteen! I might as well relax and enjoy myself. But I wondered.

Before long, she fell asleep, and I felt free to think. Until then, it was almost as though I were afraid she would read my thoughts.

Why had we left? How long would we be gone? How would Pa and my brothers cook their dinner? How would they make their beds? Who would they complain to after a hard day? Who would fetch the eggs, the mail, the water, the wood, the groceries? Who would wash their overalls, mend their socks, put bandages on their cuts? It was inconceivable to me that they could survive for long without us.

When we reached Halifax, we went to what I now realize was a cheap and shabby hotel in the South End of the city. But to me it seemed the height of luxury. The bed was made of some kind of shiny yellow wood. The bedspread was an intense pink, with raised nubbles all over it. A stained spittoon sat in the corner. There was actually a sink in the room, with taps that offered both cold and hot water. A toilet that flushed was down the hall. I checked under the bed; there was no chamber pot. But who needed it? There were two pictures on the walls — one of a curly-headed blonde displaying a lot of bare flesh and another of three dead ducks hanging upside down from a nail. I spent a lot of time inspecting both of these pictures.

Halifax was a shock to me. How could the buildings be so huge and the stores so grand? Here I was in the province's capital city before I really understood what a capital city could be. I admired the old stone buildings with their carvings around the doors and windows. I stretched my neck to see the tops of the modern apartments, with their glass and concrete reaching up into the clouds. The buses and cars alarmed me as they rushed up and down the long streets, but they excited me, too. The weather changed; it was warm and comforting, and the wind was gentle and caressing. We went down the hill to the harbour and saw the bridge; rooted in the ground and in the sea bottom, it lifted its enormous metal wings into the sky. I marvelled that a thing so strong could be so graceful, so beautiful. What a lovely way, I thought, to get from one place to another. We walked across the bridge to Dartmouth and watched the ships, far below, headed for Europe, for Africa, for the distant North. My mother, who had started to talk, told me about all these things. It was as though she were trying to tell me something important but didn't want to say things right out. "They're goin' somewheres," she said. Later on, she took me out to Dalhousie University, and we walked among the granite buildings and beside the playing fields. "If yer as smart as the teacher claims," she said, "maybe you'll come here some day t' learn." I thought this highly unlikely. If we couldn't afford running water, how could we afford such a thing as that? I said so.

"They's ways," she said.

We walked up and down Spring Garden Road and gazed in the big windows. I looked at a candy store with at least five million kinds of candy, shops with dresses so fancy that I could scarcely believe it, shelves full of diamonds and gold and sparkling crystal. "Is there ways for all this, too?" I asked my mother. She hesitated.

"Don't need all that stuff," she concluded.

The weather was dazzling — a sunny Nova Scotia May day. We walked through the huge iron gates into the Public Gardens and ate our sandwiches and apples beside the duck pond. I kicked off my rubber boots and wiggled my toes in the sun as I watched the swans and the yellow ducklings. The gardens were immense, full of massive and intricate flowerbeds, winding paths and strange exotic trees. There were statues, a splashing fountain, an elaborate round bandstand and a little river with a curved bridge over it. Lovers strolled arm in arm, and children shrieked with laughter as they chased the pigeons. I asked Ma why everyone seemed so happy. "Dunno," she said. "Weather does things t' people." She looked around. "And maybe some of them's free," she added.

On the second day, we watched women racing to work in the morning, mini-skirts flipping, heels clicking, faces eager, faces tense. We looked on as shopping women pulled twenty-dollar bills out of their purses as though they were nickels. We saw the drunks sleeping on the pavement outside the mission. We visited the courthouse and looked at the pictures of the stern-faced judges as they watched us from the walls. "They fixes things what aren't right," said Ma. I wondered how. "But not always," she added.

We spent an hour in the public library, looking at the shelves and shelves of books, smelling their wonderful book smells, idly turning the pages. On a book dolly, she picked up a copy of *The Feminine Mystique*. She, who had not to my knowledge read a single book since I was born, said shyly, "I read this book." I was astonished.

"You!" I exclaimed. "How come? When?"

"I kin read!" she retorted, miffed. "Even if y' leaves school in grade five, y' kin read. Y' reads slow, but y' knows how."

"But where'd you get it?" I demanded, amazed.

"Y' remember that day the Salvation Army lady brought us that big box o' clothes?" she asked. "Yer pa was mad and said we didn't need no charity. But I hid the box, and after a time he forgot about it. Well, there was other things in there, too — an egg beater, some toys what I gave to Lizzie's kids, even a string o' yellow beads and a bracelet that I bin savin' fer you. And some books. There was comic books and that big colourin' book y' got fer Christmas, and them *Popular Mechanics* magazines the boys read, and a coupla others. And this." She placed the palm of her hand on the book. "Seemed like it was for me, special. So I read it. She was real tough goin', but I read every word. Took me near a year. Finished it last Thursday."

I could hardly believe it. My ma didn't even read recipes. She kept them all in her head. I asked, "Was it good?"

She thought for a moment before answering. "She was a real troublin' book. But she was good."

I couldn't understand that. "If it was so troublin', why was it so good?"

She answered that one without hesitation. "Found I weren't alone," she said. She stroked its cover tenderly before putting it back on the dolly. I liked the library, with all the silent people bent over their books and the librarians moving soundlessly too and fro. I wasn't used to quiet places.

In the afternoon, we climbed the Citadel and went into its museum, walking up and down among the sea things, old things, rich things. Later on, we went to what I thought was a very fancy restaurant. There were bright, shiny chrome tables with place mats of paper lace and green glass ashtrays. I ordered a hot dog and chips, because that was my favourite meal. My mother, her mouth now soft and cheerful, ordered something with a strange name.

"Ain't gonna come all this way and spend all th' hen money just t' eat what I kin eat at home," she said.

The egg money! So that was it. I let on I didn't notice. But a thrill of fear ran through me. I wondered what Pa would do.

In the evening we returned early to the hotel, and I slept deeply but with strange and troubled dreams.

On the third day, Ma said, "It's time. T'day we go home." I asked why.

"Because," she said.

"Because why?" I insisted.

She was silent for a moment and then said again, "It's time." I was pleased. It had been an interesting trip, but it frightened me a little because there were no explanations, no answers to my unspoken questions. Besides, I was afraid that someone else would get to be chief fairy in the school play. "Have you done yer thinkin'?" I asked. She looked at me strangely. There was hope in her look and an odd fierce dignity.

"I has," she said.

We took the bus home instead of the train, and it was late afternoon when we arrived in Annapolis to start the six-mile climb to our farm. The day was damp and cold, and I wore my mother's wool kerchief again. We were very quiet, and I knew she was nervous. Her mouth was back in its taut line, and her eyes were troubled. But even in the wind, her shoulders were straight and firm, and I could feel a difference in her. Fearful though her eyes were, she was fully alert, and you could sense a new dogged strength in the set of her face.

There was no such strength in me except such as I derived from her. Home is home when you are twelve, and I did not want to live a tourist's life in Halifax forever. But I worried every step of the six long miles.

As we turned the bend at Harrison's Corner, we could see the farm in the distance. It was as though I were seeing it for the first time. The house had been white once, but it had needed paint for almost nineteen years. Around the yard was a confusion of junk of all kinds: two discarded cars — lopsided and without wheels — an unpiled jumble of firewood, buckets, a broken hoe, rusty tools, an old oil drum for burning garbage. To the left were the few acres of untidy fields, dotted with spruce trees and the grey skeletons of trees long dead of Dutch elm disease. To the right, close to the henhouse, was the barn — small and unpainted, grey and shabby in the dim afternoon light. We could hear the two cows complaining, waiting for milking time.

When we opened the kitchen door, they were all there. My four big brothers were playing cards at the table, and my father was sitting by the kitchen stove, smoking a cigarette and drinking from a bottle of beer. I had forgotten how darkly handsome he was. But because it was not Sunday, he was unshaven, and his eyes glared out at us from beneath heavy black eyebrows.

Pa rose from his chair and faced us. He was very tall, and his head almost reached the low ceiling. He seemed to fill the entire room. He crushed out his cigarette on the top of the stove.

His voice was low and threatening. "Where you bin, woman?" he said.

She spoke, and I was amazed that she had the courage. Then I realized with a jolt that his words were little different in tone and substance from hundreds I had heard before: "How come my supper's not ready, woman?" "Move smart, woman! I'm pressed fer time!" "Shut up them damn kids, woman!" "Move them buckets, woman! They're in my way!" "This food ain't fit t' eat. woman. Take it away!"

She spoke quietly and with dignity. "You is right to be angry, Lester," she said. "I left a note fer y', but I shoulda tole y' before I left."

"Shut yer mouth, woman, and git my supper!" he shouted, slamming the beer bottle down on the table.

She moved to the centre of the room and faced him. "My name," she began, and faltered. She cleared her throat and ran her tongue over her lower lip. "My name," she repeated, this time more steadily, "is Elizabeth."

He was dumbfounded. My brothers raised their heads from their card game and waited, cards poised in midair.

Pa looked at her. He looked at me. Then he looked at Jem and Daniel and Ira and Bernard, sitting there silent and still like four statues, waiting for his reaction.

Suddenly my father threw back his head and laughed. His ugly laughter filled the little kitchen, and we all listened, frozen, wishing for it to stop.

"'My name is Elizabeth!'" he mocked, between choking guffaws, slapping his thighs and holding his stomach, and then he repeated himself and her, mincingly, "'My . . . name . . . is . . . Elizabeth!'" Then his face changed, and there was silence. "Git over here 'n' make my supper, woman! I'm gonna milk them cows. But my belly is right empty, and y' better be ready when I gits back from th' chores!"

I watched my mother. During the laughter, I could see her retreat for a minute behind her eyes, expressionless, lifeless, beaten. Then she took a deep breath and looked at him directly, squarely, with no fear in her face. Pain, yes, but no fear. My brothers looked down and continued their card game.

"Act smart there, Sylvie," she said to me, as soon as he had left. "I need yer help bad. You clean up, 'n' I'll fix supper." She was already moving swiftly about the kitchen, fetching food, chopping onions, peeling potatoes.

In the sink was a mountainous pile of dirty dishes. Open cans, crusted with stale food, cluttered the counter. I surveyed the scene with distaste.

"Ma," I asked, complaining like the true adolescent that I had now become, "how come they couldna washed the dishes themselves? They goes huntin' and fishin' and has lotsa little vacations in th' winter. We always do their work for them when they're gone. How come we gotta clean up their mess?"

"Listen," she said, cutting the potatoes and dropping them into the hot fat, "the way I sees it is y' kin ask fer kindness or politeness from time t' time. But y' can't expect no miracles. It's my own fault fer raisin' four boys like they was little men. I shoulda put them in front of a dishpan fifteen years ago. Now it's too late. Yer pa's ma did the same thing. She aimed t' raise a boy who was strong and brave, with no soft edges." She wiped her forehead with the back of her hand. "All along I bin blamin' men fer bein' men. But now I see that oftentimes it's the women that makes them that way." It was a long, long speech for my ma. But she went on. "The boys is seventeen, eighteen, nineteen and twenty years old. Y' can't start makin' 'em over now. They's set." Then she smiled wryly, with a rare show of humour. She bowed formally in the direction of the card game. "I apologizes," she said, "to your future wives."

Then she stopped, and looked from one son's face to the next, and so on, around the table. "I loves you all, regardless," she said softly, "and it's worth a try. Jem" — she spoke to the youngest — "I'd be right grateful if you'd fetch some water for Sylvie. She's real tired after the long walk."

Jem looked at his brothers, and then he looked at her. Water carrying was woman's work, and she knew she was asking a lot of him. He rose silently, took the bucket from her, and went outside to the well.

"And you," she said, addressing Daniel and Ira and Bernard, "One snigger out of you, and yer in bad trouble." I'm sure she knew she was taking an awful chance. You can say a thing like that to little boys, but these were grown men. But no one moved or so much as smiled when Jem returned. "I thank you right kindly," said Ma, thereby delivering a speech as unusual as her other one.

You could say, I suppose, that our leaving made no large difference in my mother's life. She still worked without pay or praise and was often spoken to as though she were without worth or attraction. Her days were long and thankless. She emptied chamber pots and spittoons, scrubbed overalls and sheets on her own mother's scrub board, and peeled the frozen clothes from the line in winter with aching fingers. But not all things remained the same. She now stood up to my father. Her old paralytic fear was gone, and she was able to speak with remarkable force and dignity. She did not nag. Nagging is like a constant blow with a small blunt instrument. It annoys, but it seldom makes more than a small dent. When she chose to object to Pa's cruel or unfair behaviour, her instrument was a shining steel knife with a polished cutting edge. A weapon like that seemed to make my father realize that if he went too far — if he beat her, or if he scolded too often or too unjustly — she would leave. After all, she had done it once before. And this time, she might not return.

So there were changes. One day, for no apparent reason, he started to call her Elizabeth. She did not let on that this was remarkable, but the tight line of her mouth relaxed, and she made him a lemon pie for supper. She fixed up the attic storeroom as a workroom for herself. The boys lugged up her treadle sewing machine, and she brought in an old wicker chair and a table from the barn. It was a hot room in summer and cold in winter, but it was her own place — her escape. She made curtains from material bought at Frenchy's and hooked a little rug for the floor. No one was allowed to go there except her. She always emerged from this room softer, gentler, more still.

I never did hear a single word about the missing egg money. Maybe Pa didn't notice, or perhaps Ma attacked the subject with her sharp-edged knife. Possibly it was the egg money that sent me to Dalhousie — that and my scholarship and my summer jobs. I never asked. I didn't really want to know.

When I was home last February during the term break, I stole a look into Ma's attic room. There were library books on the table, material on the sewing machine, paper piled on the floor for her letters to me and to the boys. I respected her privacy and did not go in. But the room, even in that chilly winter attic, looked like an inviting place.

My ma is now fifty-five and has a lot of life still to live. My pa is fifty-eight. He still shaves once a week, and he has not yet cleared up the yard. But he often speaks to my mother as though she were more of a person and less of a thing. Sometimes he says thank you. He still has a raging temper, but he is an old dog and new tricks come hard. He loves my mother and she him, with a kind of love that is difficult for my generation to understand or define. In another time and in another place, the changes could have been more marked. But my mother is a tough and patient woman, and these differences seem to be enough for her. Her hair is worn less severely. Her mouth is not set so straight and cold and firm. She talks more. She has made a pretty yellow blouse to wear with her baggy slacks. She smiles often, and she is teaching her two grandsons how to wash dishes and make cookies.

I often wonder about these things, but when my mind approaches the reasons for all that has happened, my thinking slides away and my vision blurs. Certainly the book and the leaving do not explain everything. Maybe my mother was ready to move into and out of herself anyway, and no one can know exactly what went on in her thoughts before and after she left. Perhaps she was as surprised as I was by the amount of light and warmth she let in when she opened the door to step into the dark and frosty morning. But of that strange three-day departure, I can say, as Ma did of her book, "She was a real troublin' trip. But she was good."

KENT THOMPSON

A Local Hanging
(1981)

There was no question of Wallace Burton's guilt. I want to put that down for history because you know his ghost is going to rise. He was buried in a barnyard without benefit of clergy, and you know how tales will grow. Everyone will be telling them in a week, I will hear this one and that one until I forget which one is true. All of a sudden someone has seen Wallace on the road to the ferry or in the moonlight behind my store skulking among the barrels. There will be confusion and fear. Wallace Burton's ghost will frighten children at night. Grown men will arm themselves against a ghost and shoot at shadows and deny they have done any such thing. Fenceposts in the moonlight will look like Wallace Burton running for his life. The story is more terrible than that.

Wallace Burton was the son of Nell Burton, who was Noble Burton's daughter out on the Foss Mill Road. Noble Burton worked at Foss Mill till Foss closed it, then he tried to get by on his little piece of land out there with some trapping and logging for other fellows. His wife died. He kept Nell at home with him to look after him he said, instead of sending her off some place in service. The winter was cold. The snow came early and stayed late. In the spring he went into the woods and was never seen again. Nell came into my store at the ferry crossing, and you could see the tragedy in her eyes. You did not have to look further. But she bit down and made do. She was young and pretty and strong. There were men who might have married her. All lost. When her time came she had Wallace by herself like an animal. It was the wonder of the community. Talk in the store was that it would have been better if she and her child had died but that it doesn't matter with animals. You can see how the thinking was going. It was a savage beginning for the poor boy. But she did her best. We gave her what we could, and she would not beg. Her clothes were mostly rags and the boy's, too. He was alone with her out there. After Foss Mill closed nobody had any reason to go out that road. We saw them only in the summer until about three years ago, when Wallace asked J. Watkins for work at Watkins Stable. Watkins said he was agreeable to that because he needed the help, and everyone felt sorry for Nell. She was now looking like a witch and was called a witch by the children who played in front of my store at the ferry landing. People will tell tales and make up tales to amuse themselves. They made up tales to hide the truth from the children. She was now bringing blueberries to me to sell on the riverboats. One of the things I did was sell bread, cheese and berries and such like on the riverboats when they docked at Ferry Crossing. You could get off the riverboat here and go by horse coach to Milton. But the children were harsh on Nell. They did not know anything about her of course except that she was strange. They mocked her. They followed her and mocked her walk. They looked dazed and reached for weeds like they were flowers and called out from behind the fence and the barrels and moaned at her, and they ran dancing behind my shed making strange noises. One of these children was Mary Jenkins, so we do not know if he killed her for his own reasons or on behalf of his mother. It was by this time widely believed by all who did not know the true story of Nell Burton that she was a witch. They said her glance would sour milk and her touch give you boils. None of that was true of course. But time had uglied her.

The death of Mary Jenkins was terrible. She was playing with the other children at the crossroads. It was a game which required running and shouting and tagging. They raised a great deal of dust. I had to tell them to go play in the field, not in the road. When Mary Jenkins knew it was time for her to go home, she said goodbye to her friends and went off on the path behind my place to the road where she and her two older brothers and her mother and father lived. They were all good people, all respected in the community. Mary Jenkins was well-loved by everyone who knew her. She was an innocent, beautiful child. Her smile brightened many a dull day. She was caught by Wallace Burton in the dip in the path by the drainage ditch where there are many alders. No more than a few minutes later J. Watkins and F. Stewart came along, so there is no question of Wallace Burton's guilt. This must be recorded. He was still half-naked. He was wearing his boots and shirt but nothing else. His eyes were wild, and he frothed at the mouth. He began to run as soon as he saw Watkins and Stewart, and they of course were startled by what they saw and looked around and found Mary's body no more than twenty feet from the path. He had torn her clothes from her and used her — though whether before he killed her or afterwards we shall never know. It is hoped she died first and so escaped the horror. He had snapped her neck. This was easy enough to do because she was just a thin child. His trousers were beside her body. Stewart immediately took Mary in his arms and covered her poor little body with the remnants of her dress and ran with her back to my store, where we saw that she was dead and recognized the outrage which had been visited upon her. Watkins was meanwhile giving chase to Wallace Burton, his one-time employee, and hallooing out from time to time. He said later that he knew we would be following on and that he wanted Burton to think that a group of men were after him already. He did not relish the thought, he said, of meeting up with Wallace Burton alone because he knew how strong Wallace was, though small. He had seen Wallace hold a team of skittish draft horses, he said, one hand in each bridle. But Wallace looked them in the eye, he said, and they trembled as if in terror. He had a terrifying strength within, said Watkins. He swears this is true and will not be denied.

There were four of us in the store when Stewart came in with Mary's poor little body and news of the terrible occurrence. We immediately set out after Wallace Burton. Those in the group beside myself were: R.B. Butler, A.R. Scott, Walter Merton and James Jenkins, older brother of Mary Jenkins. He was stunned, as if the sight of his poor sister's broken, naked body had broken him as well. He ran as best he could, but he was always last. It was as if he ran in chains. His eyes were tormented with what he had seen. So there were six of us who pursued Wallace Burton and followed the shouting of J. Watkins. We could tell that Wallace Burton was heading for the river. Doubtless he hoped that if he reached the river safely he could find a boat of some kind and follow the current downriver, hiding under the bushes on the riverbank at night until he reached Saint John, and then who knows but what he thought of the sea or thought southward to the States, where all our scoundrels flee.

But he was not so lucky. We caught up to him near the Ellis Bowden place, as he was running down the bank. Watkins was exhausted by this time because he was not so young as the rest of us, and he could only point to the figure of Wallace Burton thrashing through the bush in the distance. Watkins had performed valiantly. We took up the chase. But

Wallace Burton ran with the strength and speed of a demon, and had he not made an error in calculation he might have escaped us forever and therefore justice. He decided to try to steal a boat from Bowden's landing and evidently thought that he could reach the boat more swiftly by swimming along the shoreline than by running. The running was of course difficult because there was no real path, only a dogtrail of sorts. So Wallace Burton plunged into the water, throwing off his shirt and boots as he did so. He swam for the landing and the boat. But we were quicker than he and reached the landing and the boat before him. Seeing us there before him, he changed his tack and sought to swim across the river, hoping we suppose to reach safety on the other side, although he should have known by this time that there was no hope for him. R.B. Butler and myself were in the boat rowing towards him as he swam. He was not a good swimmer, though an active one, and of course when he saw us coming towards him he became panicked and flailed at the water, to his own detriment. But of course he would not come easily, and as we drew near and reached for him he fought us off and pushed the boat away in the currents and tried to tip us over. Butler took an oar and slashed at him, opening a cut at the back of his head and stunning him. There was blood in the water. Butler grabbed hold of his hair then, and I rowed, and we pulled him back to shore that way. The others were waiting on the landing. His filthy clothes were gathered, and he was made to dress himself. We obtained trousers from Ellis Bowden who was willing to donate them when he heard of the terrible crime.

We then held council there on Bowden's landing. Ellis Bowden was now added to the original group. There was discussion as to what should be done. The courts are of course far away at Fredericton and downriver at Saint John. No one has faith in those places and there was some question as to what they might do differently in any case. We did not want the horror of the story to come out in court and drag poor Mary's name through the mud of the newspapers in Fredericton, which are scurrilous, both of them, irrespective of politics. No matter what, some people would think she had led him on. People will think that no matter what. John Jenkins begged us not to force his mother to undergo the hearing of her daughter's name nor the sight of it in print as MURDERED GIRL. It would be hard enough, he said, to tell her that Mary was dead. She would be frantic with worry now, he said, and suspecting the worst. The worst was what was true. We saw further that there had been two witnesses to the crime, and therefore there was no doubt as to the guilt of the accused. We asked Wallace Burton if he had killed Mary Jenkins, and he stared at us wild-eyed but said nothing. His madness was into the bone. We had no jail to hold him in any case. Would you have had us tether him to a stake in the ground like a goat? It fell upon us to make our decision, and we did so. It was agreed that no one should shirk, except that James Jenkins was excused to go break the grievous news to his mother. That was accounted a harder task than that which befell the rest of us. But it was a grim business in any case.

We swore one another to secrecy. Ellis Bowden got straws, cut one short, and the choosing began. We drew separately for each awful task. I was unlucky in two things but accepted that. A man must bear the burdens chance places upon him.

We returned with Wallace Burton to the oak near the landing. The riverboats took their landing sightings from it. It was the obvious tree. I provided the rope from my store; it was afterwards buried in the pit with Burton's body. We all of us went together to the tree and told Burton what was to happen. We asked him if he understood, and he said nothing in reply. We asked him if he wanted to pray, and he said nothing in reply to that, either. Nevertheless we had Butler hold him while the rest of us knelt and prayed for his soul. This seemed to give him comfort, for he gave us no further trouble. He raised up his head to accept heaven. When the rope was affixed to the tree and the noose made we put a barrel under it, and no sooner was it in place than he walked directly to it and would have got up unassisted had he been able. His hands were of course tied, so we had to help him up there, and Walter Merton, who had drawn the straw for this particular task, placed the noose over his head. Again he raised his head to heaven as if to ask for release. He had been a tormented soul since the day of his birth, and now sought, we could see, rest in Abraham's bosom. Then he himself kicked the barrel away. It was to have been my job. We had not given him enough drop so he did not break his neck but choked to death, which was grievous. He danced and writhed and farted in the air. There was a terrible silence on the earth.

The others left except for myself and W. Stewart. I put the ladder up against the tree and climbed up to take his still body down. I cut him loose and he dropped. I put him in the barrow and pushed him over to W. Stewart's barnyard, where Stewart dug the pit. It was when we had tipped him in that his mother came screaming out of the darkness.

She kicked and tore at me and tried to throw herself in the pit. At last I calmed her by holding her, poor woman, and she at last spoke clearly to me. She wanted his boots, she said. She wanted to have something to remember him by. So. W. Stewart got down in the pit where the body was not yet quite covered and removed the boots, exposing the naked white feet. He then commenced to shovel again. She was later seen to be wearing the boots along the road, shuffling and reaching for flowers that were not there. We knew it was to torment us, and it did.

I put this down so that there will be no false tales about this tragedy, in the hopes that Wallace Burton's ghost will not rise.

MICHAEL ONDAATJE

The Passions of Lalla
(1982)

My Grandmother died in the blue arms of a jacaranda tree. She could read thunder.

She claimed to have been born outdoors, abruptly, during a picnic, though there is little evidence for this. Her father — who came from a subdued line of Keyts — had thrown caution to the winds and married a Dickman. The bloodline was considered eccentric (one Dickman had set herself on fire), and rumours about the family often percolated across Colombo in hushed tones. "People who married the Dickmans were afraid."

There is no information about Lalla growing up. Perhaps she was a shy child, for those who are magical break from silent structures after years of chrysalis. By the time she was twenty she was living in Colombo and tentatively engaged to Shelton de Saram — a very good looking and utterly selfish man. He desired the good life, and when Frieda Donhorst arrived from England "with a thin English varnish and the Donhorst checkbook" he promptly married her. Lalla was heartbroken. She went into fits of rage, threw herself on and pounded various beds belonging to her immediate family, and quickly married Willie Gratiaen — a champion cricketer — on the rebound.

Willie was also a broker and, being one of the first Ceylonese to work for the English firm of E. John and Co., brought them most of their local business. The married couple bought a large house called Palm Lodge in the heart of Colombo, and here, in the three acres that came with the house, they began a dairy. The dairy was Willie's second attempt at raising livestock. Fond of eggs, he had decided earlier to import and raise a breed of black chicken from Australia. At great expense the prize Australorp eggs arrived by ship, ready for hatching, but Lalla accidently cooked them all while preparing for a dinner party.

Shortly after Willie began the dairy he fell seriously ill. Lalla, unable to cope, would run into neighbours' homes, pound on their beds, and promise to become a Catholic if Willie recovered. He never did, and Lalla was left to bring up their two children.

She was not yet thirty, and for the next few years her closest friend was her neighbour, Rene de Saram, who also ran a dairy. Rene's husband disliked Lalla and disliked his wife's chickens. Lalla and the chickens would wake him before dawn every morning, especially Lalla with her loud laughter filtering across the garden as she organized the milkers. One morning Rene woke to silence and, stepping into the garden, discovered her husband tying the beaks of all the chickens with little pieces of string, or in some cases with rubber bands. She protested, but he prevailed, and soon they saw their chickens perform a dance of death, dying of exhaustion and hunger, a few managing to escape along Inner Flower Road, some kidnapped by a furious Lalla in the folds of her large brown dress and taken to Palm Lodge where she had them cooked. A year later the husband lapsed into total silence, and the only sounds which could be heard from his quarters were barkings and later on the cluck of hens. It is believed he was the victim of someone's charm. For several weeks he clucked, barked and chirped, tearing his feather pillows into snowstorms, scratching at the expensive parquet floors, leaping from first-storey windows onto the lawn. After he shot himself, Rene was left at the age of thirty-two to bring up their children. So both Rene and Lalla, after years of excessive high living, were to have difficult times — surviving on their wits and character and beauty. Both widows became the focus of the attention of numerous bored husbands. Neither of them was to marry again.

Each had thirty-five cows. Milking began at four-thirty in the morning, and by six their milkmen would be cycling all over town to deliver fresh milk to customers. Lalla and Rene took the law into their own hands whenever necessary. When one of their cows caught Rinderpest fever — a disease which could make government officials close down a dairy for months — Rene took the army pistol which had already killed her husband and personally shot it dead. With Lalla's help she burnt it and buried it in her garden. The milk went out that morning as usual, the tin vessels clanking against the handlebars of several bicycles.

Lalla's head milkman at this time was named Brumphy, and when a Scot named McKay made a pass at a servant girl, Brumphy stabbed him to death. By the time the police arrived Lalla had hidden him in one of her sheds, and when they came back a second time she had taken Brumphy over to a neighbour named Lillian Bevan. For some reason Mrs. Bevan approved of everything Lalla did. She was sick when Lalla stormed in to hide Brumphy under the bed whose counterpane had wide lace edges that came down to the floor. Lalla explained that it was only a minor crime; when the police came to the Bevan household and described the brutal stabbing in graphic detail, Lillian was terrified, as the murderer was just a few feet away from her. But she could never disappoint Lalla and kept quiet. The police watched the house for two days, and Lillian dutifully halved her meals and passed a share under the bed. "I'm proud of you, darling!" said Lalla when she eventually spirited Brumphy away to another location.

However, there was a hearing in court presided over by Judge E.W. Jayawardene — one of Lalla's favourite bridge partners. When she was called to give evidence she kept referring to him as "My Lord My God." E.W. was probably one of the ugliest men in Ceylon at the time. When he asked Lalla if Brumphy was good-looking — trying humorously to suggest some motive for her protecting him — she replied, "Good looking? Who can say, My Lord My God, some people may find *you* good looking." She was thrown out of court while the gallery hooted with laughter and gave her a standing ovation. This dialogue is still in the judicial records in the Buller's Road Court Museum. In any case she continued to play bridge with E.W. Jayawardene, and their sons would remain close friends.

Apart from rare appearances in court (sometimes to watch other friends give evidence), Lalla's day was carefully planned. She would be up at four with the milkers, oversee the dairy, look after the books, and be finished by nine a.m. The rest of the day would be given over to gallivanting — social calls, lunch parties, visits from admirers and bridge. She also brought up her two children. It was in the garden at Palm Lodge that my mother and Dorothy Clementi-Smith would practice their dances, quite often surrounded by cattle.

For years Palm Lodge attracted a constant group — first as children, then teenagers and then young adults. For most of her life children flocked to Lalla, for she was the most casual and irresponsible of chaperons, being far too busy with her own life to oversee them all.

Behind Palm Lodge was a paddy field which separated her house from Royden, where the Daniels lived. When there were complaints that hordes of children ran into Royden with muddy feet, Lalla bought ten pairs of stilts and taught them to walk across the paddy fields on these *borukakuls* or "lying legs." Lalla would say yes to any request if she was busy at bridge, so they knew when to ask her for permission to do the most outrageous things. Every child had to be part of the group. She particularly objected to children being sent for extra tuition on Saturdays and would hire a Wallace Carriage and go searching for children like Peggy Peiris. She swept into the school at noon yelling "PEGGY!!!," fluttering down the halls in her long black clothes loose at the edges like a rooster dragging its tail, and Peggy's friends would lean over the bannisters and say, "Look, look, your mad aunt has arrived."

As these children grew older, they discovered that Lalla had very little money. She would take groups out for meals and be refused service as she hadn't paid her previous bills. Everyone went with her anyway, though they could never be sure of eating. It was the same with adults. During one of her grand dinner parties she asked Lionel Wendt, who was very shy, to carve the meat. A big pot was placed in front of him. As he removed the lid a baby goat jumped out and skittered down the table. Lalla had been so involved with the joke — buying the kid that morning and finding a big enough pot — that she had forgotten about the real dinner, and there was nothing to eat once the shock and laughter had subsided.

In the early years her two children, Noel and Doris, could hardly move without being used as part of Lalla's daily theatre. She was constantly dreaming up costumes for my mother to wear to fancy dress parties, which were the rage at the time. Because of Lalla, my mother won every fancy dress competition for three years while in her late teens. Lalla tended to go in for animals or sea creatures. The crowning achievement was my mother's appearance at the Galle Face Dance as a lobster — the outfit bright red and covered with crustaceans and claws which grew out of her shoulder blades and seemed to move of their own accord. The problem was that she could not sit down for the whole evening but had to walk or waltz stiffly from side to side with her various beaux who, although respecting the imagination behind the outfit, found her beautiful frame almost unapproachable. Who knows, this may have been Lalla's ulterior motive. For years my mother tended to be admired from a distance. On the ballroom floor she stood out in her animal or shell-fish beauty, but claws and caterpillar bulges tended to deflect suitors from thoughts of seduction. When couples paired off to walk along Galle Face Green under the moonlight it would, after all, be embarrassing to be seen escorting a lobster.

When my mother eventually announced her engagement to my father, Lalla turned to friends and said, "What do you *think*, darling, she's going to marry an Ondaatje . . . she's going to marry a *Tamil*!" Years later, when I sent my mother my first book of poems, she met my sister at the door with a shocked face and in exactly the same tone and phrasing said, "What do you *think*, Janet" — her hand holding her cheek to emphasize the tragedy — "Michael has become a *poet*!" Lalla continued to stress the Tamil element in my father's background, which pleased him enormously. For the wedding ceremony she had two marriage chairs decorated in a Hindu style and laughed all through the ceremony. The incident was, however, the beginning of a war with my father.

Eccentrics can be the most irritating people to live with. My mother, for instance, strangely, *never* spoke of Lalla to me. Lalla was loved most by people who saw her arriving from the distance like a storm. She did love children, or at least loved company of any kind — cows, adults, babies, dogs. She always had to be surrounded. But being "grabbed" or "contained" by anyone drove her mad. She would be compassionate to the character of children but tended to avoid holding them on her lap. And she could not abide having grandchildren hold her hands when she took them for walks. She would quickly divert them into the entrance of the frightening maze in the Nuwara Eliya Park and leave them there, lost, while she went off to steal flowers. She was always determined to be physically selfish. Into her sixties she would still complain to how she used to be "pinned down" to breast feed her son before she could leave for dances.

With children grown up and out of the way, Lalla busied herself with her sisters and brothers. Dickie seemed to be marrying constantly; after David Grenier drowned she married a de Vos, a Wombeck, and then an Englishman. Lalla's brother Vere attempted to remain a bachelor all his life. When she was flirting with Catholicism she decided that Vere should marry her priest's sister — a woman who *had* planned on becoming a nun. The sister also had a dowry of thirty thousand rupees, and both Lalla and Vere were short of money at the time, for both enjoyed expensive drinking sessions. Lalla masterminded the marriage, even though the woman wasn't good-looking and Vere liked good-looking women. On the wedding night the bride prayed for half an hour beside the bed and then started singing hymns, so Vere departed, foregoing nuptial bliss, and for the rest of her life the poor woman had a sign above her door which read "Unloved. Unloved. Unloved." Lalla went to mass the following week, having eaten a huge meal. When refused mass she said, "Then I'll resign," and avoided the church for the rest of her life.

A good many of my relatives from this generation seem to have tormented the church sexually. Italian monks who became enamoured of certain aunts would return to Italy to discard their robes and return to find the women already married. Jesuit fathers, too, were falling out of the church and into love with the de Sarams with the regularity of mangos thudding onto dry lawns during a drought. Vere also became the concern of various religious groups that tried to save him. And during the last months of his life he was "held captive" by a group of Roman Catholic nuns in Galle so that no one knew where he was until the announcement of his death.

Vere was known as "a sweet drunk," and he and Lalla always drank together. While Lalla grew loud and cheerful, Vere became excessively courteous. Drink was hazardous for him, however, as he came to believe he escaped the laws of gravity while under the influence. He kept trying to hang his hat on walls where there was no hook and often stepped out of boats to walk home. But drink quietened him except for these few excesses. His close friend, the lawyer Cox Sproule, was a different matter. Cox was charming when sober and brilliant when drunk. He would appear in court stumbling over chairs with a mind clear as a bell, winning cases under a judge who had pleaded with him just that morning not to appear in court in such a condition. He hated the English. Unlike Cox, Vere had no profession to focus whatever talents he had. He did try to become an auctioneer, but being both shy and drunk, he was a failure. The only job that came his way was supervising Italian prisoners during the war. Once a week he would ride to Colombo on his motorcycle, bringing as many bottles of alcohol as he could manage for his friends and his sister. He had encouraged the prisoners to set up a brewery, so that there was a distillery in every hut in the prison camp. He remained drunk with the prisoners for most of the war years. Even Cox Sproule joined him for six months when he was jailed for helping three German spies escape from the country.

What happened to Lalla's other brother, Evan, no one knows. But all through her life, when the children sent her money, Lalla would immediately forward it on to Evan. He was supposedly a thief, and Lalla loved him. "Jesus died to save sinners," she said, "and I will die for Evan." Evan manages to escape family memory, appearing only now and then to offer blocs of votes to any friend running for public office by bringing along all his illegitimate children.

By the mid-thirties both Lalla's and Rene's dairies had been wiped out by Rinderpest. Both were drinking heavily and both were broke.

We now enter the phase when Lalla is best remembered. Her children were married and out of the way. Most of her social life had been based at Palm Lodge, but now she had to sell the house, and she burst loose on the country and her friends like an ancient monarch who had lost all her possessions. She was free to move wherever she wished, to do whatever she wanted. She took thorough advantage of everyone and had bases all over the country. Her schemes for organizing parties and bridge games exaggerated themselves. She was full of the "passions," whether drunk or not. She had always loved flowers but in her last decade couldn't be bothered to grow them. Still, whenever she arrived on a visit she would be carrying an armful of flowers and announce, "Darling, I've just been to church and I've stolen some flowers for you. These are from Mrs. Abeysekare's, the lilies are from Mrs. Ratnayake's, the agapanthus is from Violet Meedeniya, and the rest are from *your* garden." She stole flowers compulsively, even in the owner's presence. As she spoke with someone her straying left hand would pull up a prize rose along with the roots, all so that she could appreciate it for that one moment, gaze into it with complete pleasure, swallow its qualities whole, and then hand the flower, discarding it, to the owner. She ravaged some of the best gardens in Colombo and Nuwara Eliya. For some years she was barred from the Hakgalle Public Gardens.

Property was there to be taken or given away. When she was rich she had given parties for all the poor children in the neighbourhood and handed out gifts. When she was poor she still organized them but now would go out to the Pettah market on the morning of the party and steal toys. All her life she had given away everything she owned to whoever wanted it and so now felt free to take whatever she wanted. She was a lyrical socialist. Having no home in her last years, she breezed into houses for weekends or even weeks, cheated at bridge with her closest friends, calling them "damn thieves," "bloody rogues." She only played cards for money and if faced with a difficult contract would throw down her hand, gather the others up, and proclaim "the rest are mine." Everyone knew she was lying but it didn't matter. Once when my brother and two sisters, who were very young, were playing a game of "beggar-my-neighbour" on the porch, Lalla came to watch. She walked up and down beside them, seemingly very irritated. After ten minutes she could stand it no longer, opened her purse, gave them each two rupees, and said, "Never, *never* play cards for love."

She was in her prime. During the war she opened up a boarding house in Nuwara Eliya with Muriel Potger, a chain smoker who did all the work while Lalla breezed through the rooms saying, "Muriel, for godsake, we can't breathe in this place!" — being more of a pest than a help. If she had to go out she would say, "I'll just freshen up," and disappear into her room for a stiff drink. If there was none she took a quick swig of eau de cologne to snap her awake. Old flames visited her constantly throughout her life. She refused to lose friends; even her first beau, Shelton de Saram, would arrive after breakfast to escort her for walks. His unfortunate wife, Frieda, would always telephone Lalla first and would spend most afternoons riding in her trap through the Cinnamon Gardens or the park searching for them.

Lalla's great claim to fame was that she was the first woman in Ceylon to have a mastectomy. It turned out to be unnecessary, but she always claimed to support modern science, throwing herself into new causes. (Even in death her generosity exceeded the physically possible, for she had donated her body to six hospitals.) The false breast would never be still for long. She was an energetic person. It would crawl over to join its twin on the right-hand side or sometimes appear on her back, "for dancing" she smirked. She called it her Wandering Jew and would yell at the grandchildren in the middle of a formal dinner to fetch her tit as she had forgotten to put it on. She kept losing the contraption to servants, who were mystified by it, as well as to the dog, Chindit, who would be found gnawing at the foam as if it were tender chicken. She went through four breasts in her lifetime. One she left on a branch of a tree in Hakgalle Gardens to dry out after a rainstorm, one flew off when she was riding behind Vere on his motorbike, and the third she was very mysterious about, almost embarrassed though Lalla was never embarrassed. Most believed it had been forgotten after a romantic assignation in Trincomalee with a man who may or may not have been in the Cabinet.

Children tell little more than animals, said Kipling. When Lalla came to Bishop's College Girls School on Parents' Day and pissed behind bushes — or when in Nuwara Eliya she simply stood with her legs apart and urinated — my sisters were so embarrassed and ashamed they did not admit or speak of this to each other for over fifteen years. Lalla's son Noel was most appalled by her. She, however, was immensely proud of his success, and my Aunt Nedra recalls seeing Lalla sitting on a sack of rice in the fish market surrounded by workers and fishermen, with whom she was having one of her long daily chats, pointing to a picture of a bewigged judge in *The Daily News* and saying in Sinhalese that *this* was her *son*. But Lalla could never be just a mother; that seemed to be only one muscle in her chameleon nature, which had too many other things to reflect. And I am not sure what my mother's relationship was to her. Maybe they were too similar to even recognize much of a problem, both having huge compassionate hearts that never even considered revenge or small-mindedness, both howling and wheezing with laughter over the frailest joke, both carrying their own theatre on their backs. Lalla remained the centre of the world she moved through. She had been beautiful when young but most free after her husband died and her children grew up. There was some sense of divine right she felt she and everyone else had, even if she had to beg for it or steal it. This overbearing charmed flower.

In her last years she was searching for the great death. She never found, looking under leaves, the giant snake, the fang which would brush against the ankle like a whisper. A whole generation grew old or died around her. Prime Ministers fell off horses, a jellyfish slid down the throat of a famous swimmer. During the forties she moved with the rest of the country towards Independence and the twentieth century. Her freedom accelerated. Her arms still flagged down strange cars for a lift to the Pettah market where she could trade gossip with her friends and place bets in the "bucket shops." She carried everything she really needed with her, and a friend meeting her once at a train station was appalled to be given as a gift a huge fish that Lalla had carried doubled up in her handbag.

She could be silent as a snake or flower. She loved the thunder; it spoke to her like a king. As if her mild dead husband had been transformed into a cosmic umpire, given the megaphone of nature. Sky noises and the abrupt light told her details of careers, incidental wisdom, allowing her to risk everything because the thunder would warn her along with the snake of lightning. She would stop the car and swim in the Mahaveli, serene among currents, still wearing her hat. Would step out of the river, dry in the sun for five minutes and climb back into the car among the shocked eyeballs of her companions, her huge handbag once more on her lap carrying four packs of cards, possibly a fish.

In August 1947, she received a small inheritance, called her brother Vere, and they drove off to Nuwara Eliya on his motorcycle. She was sixty-eight years old. These were to be her last days. The boarding house she had looked after during the war was empty, and so they bought food and booze and moved in to play Ajoutha — a card game that normally takes at least eight hours. It was a game the Portuguese had taught the Sinhalese in the fifteenth century to keep them quiet and preoccupied while they invaded the country. Lalla opened the bottles of Rocklands Gin (the same brand that was destroying her son-in-law) and Vere prepared the Italian menus, which he had learned from his prisoners of war. In her earlier days in Nuwara Eliya, Lalla would have been up at dawn to walk through the park — inhabited at that hour only by nuns and monkeys — walk round the golf course where gardeners would stagger under the weight of giant python-like hoses as they watered the greens. But now she slept till noon, and in the early evening rode up to Moon Plains, her arms spread out like a crucifix behind Vere.

Moon Plains. Drowned in blue and gold flowers whose names she had never bothered to learn, tugged by the wind, leaning in angles for miles and miles against the hills five thousand feet above sea level. They watched the exit of the sun and the sudden appearance of the moon halfway up the sky. Those lovely accidental moons — a horn a chalice a thumbnail — and then they would climb onto the motorcycle, the sixty-year-old brother and the sixty-eight-year-old sister, who was his best friend forever.

Riding back on August 13, 1947, they heard the wild thunder, and she knew someone was going to die. Death, however, not to be read out there. She gazed and listened but there seemed to be no victim or parabola end beyond her. It rained hard during the last mile to the house, and they went indoors to drink for the rest of the evening. The next day the rains continued, and she refused Vere's offer of a ride knowing there would be death soon. "Cannot wreck this perfect body, Vere. The police will spend hours searching for my breast thinking it was lost in the crash." So they played two-handed Ajoutha and drank. But now she could not sleep at all, and they talked as they never had about husbands, lovers, his various possible marriages. She did not mention her readings of the thunder to Vere, who was now almost comatose on the bluebird print sofa. But she could not keep her eyes closed like him, and at five a.m. on August 15, 1947, she wanted fresh air, needed to walk, a walk to Moon Plains, no motorcycle, no danger, and she stepped out towards the still dark night of almost dawn and straight into the floods.

For two days and nights they had been oblivious to the amount of destruction outside their home. The whole country was mauled by the rains that year. Ratmalana, Bentota, Chilaw, Anuradhapura, were all under water. The forty-foot-high Peredeniya Bridge had been swept away. In Nuwara Eliya, Galways's Land Bird Sanctuary and the Golf Course were ten feet under water. Snakes and fish from the lake swam into the windows of the Golf Club, into the bar, and around the indoor badminton court. Fish were found captured in the badminton nets when the flood receded a week later. Lalla took one step off the front porch and was immediately hauled away by an arm of water, her handbag bursting open, two hundred and eight cards moved ahead of her like a disturbed nest as she was thrown downhill, still comfortable and drunk, snagged for a few moments on the railings of the Good Shepherd Convent and then lifted away towards the town of Nuwara Eliya.

It was her last perfect journey. The new river in the street moved her right across the race course and park towards the bus station. As the light came up slowly she was being swirled fast, "floating" (as ever confident of surviving this, too) alongside branches and leaves, the dawn starting to hit flamboyant trees as she slipped past them like a dark log, shoes lost, false breast lost. She was free as a fish, travelling faster than she had in years, fast as Vere's motorcycle, only now there was this *roar* around her. She overtook Jesus lizards that swam and ran in bursts over the water, she was surrounded by tired half-drowned flycatchers screaming *tack tack tack tack*, frogmouths, nightjars forced to keep awake, brain-fever birds and their irritating ascending scales, snake eagles, scimitar-babblers, they rode the air around Lalla wishing to perch on her, unable to alight on anything except what was moving.

What was moving was rushing flood. In the park she floated over the intricate fir tree hedges of the maze — which would always continue to terrify her grandchildren — its secret spread out naked as a skeleton for her. The symmetrical flower beds also began to receive the day's light, and Lalla gazed down at them with wonder, moving as lazily as that long dark scarf which trailed off her neck brushing the branches and never catching. She would always wear silk, as she showed us, her grandchildren, would pull the scarf like a fluid through the ring removed from her finger, pulled sleepily through, as she moved now, awake to the new angle of her favourite trees, the Syzygium, the Araucaria Pine, over the now-unnecessary iron gates of the park, and through the town of Nuwara Eliya itself and its shops and stalls where she had haggled for guavas, now six feet under water, windows smashed in by the weight of all this collected rain.

Drifting slower she tried to hold onto things. A bicycle hit her across the knees. She saw the dead body of a human. She began to see the drowned dogs of the town. Cattle. She saw men on roofs fighting with each other, looting, almost surprised by the quick dawn in the mountains revealing them, not even watching her magic ride, the alcohol still in her — serene and relaxed.

Below the main street of Nuwara Eliya the land drops suddenly, and Lalla fell into deeper waters, past the houses of Cranleigh and Ferncliff. They were homes she knew well, where she had played and argued over cards. The water here was rougher, and she went under for longer and longer moments, coming up with a gasp and then pulled down like bait, pulled under by something not comfortable any more, and then there was the great blue ahead of her, like a sheaf of blue wheat, like a large eye that peered towards her, and she hit it and was dead.

GWENDOLYN MacEWEN

The Other Country
(1983)

"There is no such country as Kanada," said the lady reporter.

"Yes, there is," he told her. "Right across the lake."

"You know what I mean. I mean no such country as Canada spelled with a *K*, like you just told me. Just Canada with a *C*."

"Well, maybe I'm looking for the other country," he said cryptically, turning away.

"What do you mean?" She was laughing at him now.

"Never mind."

She scribbled something down in her notebook. *Nerves*, she thought. *He's a bundle of nerves, they all are. God, you'd think there were easier ways of killing yourself than this. He wants to find another country; most of the others just want to win this crazy marathon. Well, I guess they all have their reasons for what they're doing.*

In tents set up along the shore of the Niagara River twelve other swimmers were resting, waiting for midnight and the final weather report. There was still time for a few more interviews.

"Good luck!" she called after him. "Hope I see you on the other side!"

At eleven-thirty good weather conditions were confirmed, and the beach began to reek with the smell of sheep as the swimmers were smeared with the lanolin which would cool the friction created when their pores would no longer be able to sweat.

He stood alone on the beach, having sent everyone — including his trainer — away to the dinghy waiting offshore. Ibrahim came up to him with some last minute words of encouragement. "You stink to high heaven," he said, "and although I am an atheist I will pray for you. This is a difficult thing for me to do, but I will manage. Allah listens to me. Even though there is no Allah. You see what I mean."

"Get lost, Syrian jackal."

As he said this he saw the water behind Ibrahim's shoulder turn dark and luminous as a black pearl, and the lake was breathing, breathing.

"No, I mean — do that then. Pray for me, atheist."

The minutes slid towards midnight, and black grease shone all over his body. Chemical lights of a lurid, phosphorescent green were attached to the swimmers' suits to make them visible to the dinghies accompanying them, from their first thrust into the lake until the rendezvous with the pilot boats. Then the lights would neutralize themselves and die out.

Suddenly everyone was gone, including his friend. Everybody was gone, it was five minutes to midnight, and he was standing there on the beach looking like a spaceman or the creature from the black lagoon — absolutely alone. Some of the other swimmers were making nervous jokes and running around in nervous little circles, but they were somewhere else, in some incomprehensible dimension of reality, they weren't where he was.

Everybody was gone; they had gone to another planet and taken his passport so he couldn't go with them. They had stolen his soul and left him beached on this foreign shore. They had run away with his soul. On some planet in a distant galaxy they were wining and dining and laughing at him. Them and his soul. His soul was laughing at him and being wildly entertained. His soul had cuckolded him, his soul was having a ball, his soul had left him in Hell.

A gun went off behind his left ear, and through a green haze the thirteen swimmers charged down the beach and into the waiting water, screams and applause pursuing them, the water a black pearly bosom gathering them in — the heroes, the lemmings, the fools of midnight.

It took a while for him to fully realize that what he had trained for during the past few months was now a reality — he was in the lake and the marathon was on. His trainer shouted to him from the dinghy and pointed his powerlight at the buoy ahead of them which marked their position. He could scarcely remember the first strokes that had swept him down the river and into the lake, and he had only been dimly aware of linking up with the pilot boat. But now full consciousness was his, and it was the consciousness of utter and horrible darkness. He had committed himself to a limbo shared only by a very few. During the long night some of the cruisers would use no lights, because they had a strobe effect on the swimmers as they lifted their heads out of the water to breathe several times a minute hour after hour.

But after a time it seemed to him that the darkness almost became its own kind of light. The lake was a pleasant twenty degrees, and he was doing sixty strokes a minute through flat water. The operator of the pilot boat communicated by radio with the three accompanying boats which carried coast guards, medical experts and supplies, and media people.

"I heard once that the lake is a lady, and she can turn on you when the sun rises," Ibrahim told the captain of the cruiser. "Especially after a really quiet night like this one. One of the swimmers said before they started that they had seen the lake like this before, and they didn't like it."

"They're all a bunch of superstitious children," said the man at the wheel.

"How can he stand it hour after hour," Ibrahim murmured, leaning over the rail and scanning the black water, "not being able to see us most of the time, seeing nothing, going on, going on . . . ?"

"He knows what he's doing," said the captain. "Otherwise, why would he be doing it?"

Ibrahim turned and smiled. "That is a more interesting question than you might think," he said. "He's my friend, but I do not know him. It's all for the folly, perhaps. The folly and the glory. Forever and ever amen," he added grimly.

The night filled up with timid stars and the static of marine radios as the cruiser captains kept in touch with the dinghies and guided them on their proper course. The swimmer propelled himself through a blue-black world of weeds and fish and lamprey eels, through the ink and slime of the night. At intervals he stopped and treaded water and took time to sip Lucosade through a straw or swallow Dextrose tablets or wonder if anyone except himself really cared what he was doing. He floated on his back for two minutes and considered the bland stars. And because they didn't care one way or the other, he turned and pulled forward with extra force, just to spite them.

He must not sleep; he must not sleep and dream — that was the great danger. *Pick up strokes, thrust forward, think of advanced calculus or nuclear fission. Not too fast or you'll go into an oxygen high. Get this thing you call yourself together. Why have you come to this, why are you in this terrible dream? Don't ask this, or you'll fly apart. Thrust forward, thrust forward . . .*

Ibrahim was lakesick for the hundredth time since he had been aboard the cruiser. The captain's voice came from behind him as he puked pitifully over the rail.

"Guess what? Weather report. Thunderstorms coming up. Ain't that grand?"

This is it, Ibrahim thought. *Now everybody's worst dream comes true.*

The Tower and many other places along the lakefront had kept their lights on all night to help guide the boats. Now in the first hour of the dawn they were turned off, and the lake was once more the domain of the sun. The swimmer had been in the water for six hours, and now he couldn't believe it, but he was almost halfway home. During the night someone had jumped into the water and paced him for almost an hour, but his ghostly companion finally got out and left him once again alone. Now he realized that somehow he had passed through the terrible hour of the wolf, the hour before the dawn, and his mind and body were raging against the night's ordeal. As the darkness lifted he was subjected to bouts of cramps and nausea. He vomited several times and kept swimming off in meaningless directions; his trainer had to shout him back on course over and over again. Then he started doing circles in the water, nothing but circles.

Now someone was waving a large square of fluorescent orange material at him. Out of the corner of his eye he could see it fluttering in the wind. The wind from where? All night the lake had been calm, now suddenly there were waves all around him, teasing him, flirting with him. He knew that he would have to get away from that big ugly piece of orange cloth — it meant that they wanted him to come out, to give up. He stroked purposefully away from it. His trainer read his intention and started shouting at him.

"No!" he yelled back over the rising wind. "I'm not coming out, I'm bloody not coming out!"

The silly orange square disappeared. The anger had drawn him away from his endless circles, and now he was back on course. They were letting him stay in — for how long? He lost all track of time, and the morning fell into another dimension of time altogether.

Later the sky began to darken and once again the wind rose — a sickening wet green wind that whipped the waves up to more than three metres high. They were only six kilometres from shore; a short while earlier someone had held up a sign that read: *7.5 km*; this was the signal for him to commence the final sprint that would take him to shore. This was the time to summon up the body's last resources, to bend the will beyond all its limits.

But he did not know who he was; he did not know his name. His name had drowned and had sunk to the bottom of the lake.

In a few minutes and waves rose to four metres and all hell broke loose. The wind shot up to twenty-five knots. Thunder and lightning tore the sky wide open and released a deluge of enormous hailstones.

"Bring him in, bring him in!" screamed Ibrahim. "This is madness, you are all mad!" An hour before, he had joined the others in the dinghy; now as the storm reached its peak the lake sent up sheer walls of water between them and the swimmer.

"Shut up!" the trainer yelled. "I can't even see him to bring him in! He's veered off course a hundred metres, he's lost all sight of us!"

"We're losing him!" Ibrahim cried into the wind. "Jesus Christ, Jesus Christ," he moaned, hanging onto the edge of the dinghy for dear life as a wave caught them broadside. It threw him clear into the water, where he thrashed around blindly and roared at God. Someone managed to pull him back in.

Back in the cruiser the captain was listening to the radio. "One boat's just been swamped," he heard. "Others are way off course, heading for Scarboro Bluffs. One guy's radio is knocked out. Pray we hold together, just pray."

"He's lost," Ibrahim sobbed. "The word is coming to an end in this terrible lake. I should never have come to this crazy country. Oh God, oh God."

The first time he went down he was looking for his name. Somewhere at the bottom of the lake was his lost name, his drowned self. He sank into the awful world of water, only to discover that his body bobbed up again of its own accord. The second time he went down to explore the spaces between life and death, to find what lay there in the self, in that other country.

Take me to the absolute depths, he prayed, *let me give over at last. Let me offer it all up to the black water — the lost loves, the broken dreams.*

I'm dragging it all down with me to the bottom of the lake; the past, the future, everything.

But his lungs betrayed him, forcing him to the surface with repeated bursts of fiendish energy. Could it be so incredibly *difficult* to die? Could it be that death didn't want him, and the lake wasn't interested in his offerings? What then? He was buffeted by mad waves and hailstones. Hailstones, for God's sake. In the middle of summer. What else?

Suddenly he began to laugh because it was all so goddamn funny. What a colossal irony — he couldn't die now when he tried, he who had 'died' so many times in the past. Was it a luxury to even consider death in the midst of life, an unearned luxury? No, it was more than this — it was an error. It was as he had always known. *You couldn't die.* Now he laughed and laughed, his whole being running on pure oxygen. He was higher than the lightning, higher than the Tower which materialized in the jagged light. He knew that he was immortal; he knew it with absolute certainty. He had always been here, and always would be.

It occurred to him that since he was alive he may as well do something about it. And following upon that thought was another — that as long as one was alive, one may as well do it *right*, period. It was a simple as that; it always had been.

He was off course, but it was not difficult to correct himself. The Tower beckoned him, and he would not be lost as long as he could see the Tower. He knew now that he was going to make the last few kilometres. He was filled with a wild certainty that he could do anything in the world and that the world was his. He would not be beached like a dying whale, washed up on the shores of life like all the flotsam and jetsam and dead fish and discarded junk that lined the beaches everywhere. He was painfully, magnificently alive.

"There he is!" screamed Ibrahim during a moment of calm between the waves. "We've got him, we've got him!"

The dinghy was soon alongside of the swimmer. "He's doing eighty strokes a minute," said the trainer. "He's not human."

His only acknowledgement of them was a wave.

"I don't even think he needs us," said Ibrahim sadly.

And it didn't really matter to him what he needed or didn't need; he lived in a moment torn away from time and in a world lit by another sun. As he approached the breakwater and the buildings that looked like Byzantine pavilions and medieval castles along the shore, he was entering the most exciting and mysterious country in the world, with his past behind him and his alternative futures lying in wait ahead.

The sunlight appeared at intervals, bright stripes of time arrested and held within the fluid, changing present. The sky became a naked blue. He remembered something he had once read about that colour. *Blue was darkness made visible.*

He entered the breakwater and began the last short stretch of his journey, along the shore from Ontario Place to the Exhibition grounds. Many people were crowded along the shore, laughing and whistling and clapping; some threw red and yellow flowers into the water, some took photographs, some just stared at him in frightened silence. They knew he had come from another place.

"When you touch the ramp, turn right around and come back to the dinghy," his trainer had warned him. "Don't let anybody near you; don't let anybody touch you. Your body is going to be a raw nerve."

He forgot all about that when his fingers reached out and touched the land. He didn't know where his fingers ended and the land began. He was an explorer who had discovered a new country, and he claimed it in the name of all that was wondrous and real. He stood up out of the water very slowly, and a great roar arose from the crowd and cameras clicked all around him. He stood half naked and wet and shivering, water falling from him like quicksilver.

Ibrahim and the others rushed ashore to isolate him from the more persistent reporters. Ibrahim, who was weeping, put a towel over his shoulders, and he almost shrieked from the touch of it on his skin. It was nine minutes past one in the afternoon; he had made the swim in just over thirteen hours and set a new record. Two hours later the Egyptian would come in, and later on an American and a Mexican would take third and fourth place. The other swimmers had been beaten by the storm.

The police shooed most of the reporters away, and a medical team arrived to determine whether or not he was still alive. He knew that if he stood on his feet much longer he would probably faint. As they started to put him on a stretcher he caught sight of the woman reporter he had spoken to on the other side of the lake.

"Congratulations!" she cried, fighting her way toward him. "You know, I thought you wanted to die out there."

"What country is this?" he asked her as the darkness began to fold in around him.

"This is Canada," she smiled, "Spelled with a C."

"Oh. Kanada," he said. He pronounced it his way.

"What motivated you to attempt such a difficult feat?" she asked, her pen poised in the air. "I mean, my question is really just a simple *why?*"

"It was the only way I knew to come home," he said.

A policeman took hold of her arm and began to draw her away. "Let me finish my story on you," she begged. "Did you find the other country?"

"Yes, I did."

"What was it like? Where is it?"

"Right here," he answered. "There is another country, you know, and it's inside this one."

They moved him away on the stretcher.

"God," he said. "God, the world is beautiful."

He smiled as the darkness claimed him.

Kali was waiting on the beach with the boy. They saw him emerge from the lake, his body covered with shining, watery scales. A week later they all watched as the fireworks at the end of the Exhibition wrote bright signatures across the sky. Then the particles of fire fell back into the lake like rain.

ERNST HAVEMANN

Bloodsong
(1983)

The path of the ancients started somewhere on the tableland, where the clan chief, Insimbi, had his kraal, and it ran through the valley to the east hills, where many of the clansmen lived.

Our farm was part of the white settlement that lay in the valley dividing the clan's land. Natives crossing from one side to the other usually went by government road, but occasionally someone would use the Path of the Ancients. If my father saw him, or her, he would scold, pointing crossly to the sign NO TRESPASSERS. NO RIGHT OF WAY. He had had it translated into Zulu, but since the trespassers could not read, this made little difference, except that the place where the sign stood came to be called the Place of Scolding.

Sometimes a man, though more often an obstinate old woman, would insist on proceeding. My father fumed but did not otherwise interfere. "I suppose they have a right-of-way by immemorial usage," he said, in extenuation of his weakness. The path was not in fact immemorial. All members of the clan knew exactly when it had been established. It had come into use nine generations ago, when Duma of the Battleaxe had led the clan's ancestors down from the mountains to occupy this piece of thornveld. Every man, and almost every boy, could recite his own pedigree step by step back to Duma or one of his band. When you wanted to thank someone or show respect, you called him Duma or Child of Duma.

I knew about the Path and Duma and Insimbi because Ngumbane, the foreman, was my friend. When things had gone wrong with my birth, Ngumbane had run fifteen miles to fetch a doctor. The doctor arrived too late to save my mother, and the desperate run left Ngumbane with a permanent limp. My father gave him a Friesian cow in recompense. The affair also left Ngumbane with a permanent stake in my development. As soon as I could toddle, he began taking me on his rounds with him. He talked to me about animals and insects, the clan's history, farm activities, and the private lives of the farm labourers. For a long time I was more fluent in Zulu than in English, but when I learned to read I would translate bits of the newspapers to him. My father was happy about the relationship. He knew I was in safe and affectionate hands, and that left him free to go away on his hunting trips.

When I was fifteen, my father went off on an extended trip during my school holidays. I stayed on the farm, as usual. One Saturday afternoon, shortly before work stopped, Ngumbane said, "Nkosane, there is something we must talk about." When no other people were present, Ngumbane called me "my little boy" or Child of Duma or perhaps by a fanciful praise-name describing my alleged feats or character traits: Mastiff That Breaks the Dog Chain, Exterminator of Locusts, Shield That Protects Ngumbane from Wrath. His addressing me respectfully as Nkosane signalled something weighty. I sat down, to show I recognized that he wanted a serious discussion.

"Nkosane," he said, "you know that the Paramount Chief, whom we call the Lion, the chief of all our nation, comes next month to visit Insimbi. All the clans around here will meet to give him a royal greeting." I knew, of course; it was a major topic of local news.

Ngumbane went on. "There will be war dances, as in the old days. But the young men do not know all the dances. They have never performed together in regiments, only in little bands. So there will be a gathering tomorrow at Insimbi's place for them to practice together. They do not want to be clumsy when they greet the Lion. Many will come from over there." He pointed to the east hills and paused, as if the implication were clear.

I said, "I am listening, my father."

He resumed, patiently. "Exterminator of Locusts, those people who live over there must cross the valley to get to Insimbi's place. They say that because it is for the honour of the Lion, they will use the Path of the Ancients, as in the old days, before there were white farms here."

I said, "That does not matter. I will give permission to all who ask."

Ngumbane looked at his feet. "They will not ask, Johnny. Some of the older men think they should, but not the young ones. The youngsters say this day will be as in the days of our grandfathers, when the clan could pass freely over their own land. They are full of insolence."

"What do you want me to do?" I asked.

"Why do you not go and visit the white village tonight?" he suggested. "If you are not here, the people will cross over tomorrow morning and return tomorrow night. If you are not here, their offence will not be seen, and there will be no trouble."

I had no intention of going to spend a boring Sunday in the village. "The people will be on the Path," I said. "I shall stay here at the house. They will not see me, and so they will not be uncomfortable, and I will pretend not to know that they are there. After all, one cannot see the Path from the house."

Ngumbane sighed and then nodded reluctantly. "That will be good. Stay well, Johnny." He went off to join the labourers, who had already lined up, ready to leave for the African reserve where they had their homes.

I always enjoyed Sundays alone on the farm. On weekdays the dawn was full of the noises of oxen and mule teams, carts creaking and drivers shouting. On Sundays, in the quiet, one could hear successive waves of chirps and singing from awakening birds and other small creatures. But this Sunday morning the bird sounds were overlaid by something else — a pervasive hum, like that of large, distant beehives. I could see nothing around the house, so I took binoculars and climbed a tall look-out tree that gave a view across the farmlands to the river and the hills.

The Path of the Ancients, hardly noticeable in the normal course of events, was now thronged with an almost unbroken line of people: men carrying oxhide shields and fighting sticks and capped with widow bird and ostrich plumes, and parties of women and girls in beads and ochre, carrying beer pots and food trays on their heads. All the way to the east hills little tributary trails fed more people into the thickening stream on the Path itself.

I had never seen such a sight. It would, of course, be even more spectacular when they and scores of other streams of people met at Insimbi's kraal. Why shouldn't I go there and see?

I quickly saddled a horse. I thought of wearing my riding breeches but decided against it: they would make me look like an official. Better to go in ordinary khaki pants. I stuffed some sandwiches into one saddlebag and a few sticks of tobacco and boxes of matches into the other, for use as gifts. My eye fell on a large grey pebble; I added it, to throw on the cairn that flanked the Path. I set off along the farm road, which ran from the farmhouse over a little ridge. Beyond the ridge it briefly joined the Path.

The Path itself, usually no more than overgrown track obliterated in parts by ploughing, was now sharply defined by the passage of many feet. It meandered to avoid obstacles that no longer existed, curved wide round a marsh long since drained, and twisted between circular patches marking places where trees had once stood.

The marchers resolutely followed the Path's original route, never taking a shortcut, even where the Path ran across a ploughed field or sown pasture.

I waited for a break in the line. Several times people obligingly stopped, saying, "So you're coming with us," but I waved them on, because I knew the horse would be an embarrassment in the middle of a group. Some marchers greeted me, or saluted, or remarked on the horse. Twice a woman called, "Ha, Sea-Eyes!" whereupon her companions all looked at me, saying, "Truly, eyes like the sea." Blue eyes never failed to amaze the Zulus.

The parties of older men marched stolidly, merely muttering a repetitive song phrase to keep time — "The strength of the antbear," "The bees of the mountain," "Kindle fire, my lads, kindle fire." The young men sang more elaborate part-songs or solemnly recited an old war song: "Shame on the man who is burned in his hut. Come out and fight."

Eventually a break in the line allowed me to get onto the Path. I intended to leave it farther on, where it diverged from the straighter farm road, but when I made to turn off, the man ahead of me put out his arm to stop the horse. "That is not the way," he said reprovingly. When we reached the NO TRESPASSERS sign at the Place of Scolding, a number of people turned round and looked at me, smiling, but no one said anything.

The line halted when we reached the stone cairn. It is very bad to pass one of these cairns without adding another stone to it; consequently, all stones for hundreds of yards around had been picked up. Prudent people avoided bad luck by bringing small stones with them if they were to pass this way. Most of the people ahead of me had remembered to bring pebbles and duly threw them onto the pile, sometimes spitting on them first, but some had forgotten and were now having to search the veld. When I reached the stopping place and took my pebble out of my saddlebag, I heard congratulatory shouting and laughter. A girl cried, "Did you bring a stone for me, too?" An old woman reprimanded her for being pert to a white man.

From here onward the Path climbed an escarpment, winding round many bends. I had to dismount and lead the horse. About halfway up, the marchers ahead stopped. When we got moving again, I saw the cause. In a little enclave beside the trail sat a skinny old man, with his leg stretched out and a very twisted ankle. Some young men were comforting him and lashing together sticks to make a crutch. I said, "Can you ride a horse, grandfather?"

The old man grinned through his pain. "I have never ridden a horse, Nkosane. Surely your white man's horse will resent an old black man and throw me off?"

"No," I said reassuringly, "he is tame. He and I both respect old age."

The old man laughed. The youths carefully lifted him to put him on the saddle. Before scrambling over he motioned for them to wait. He took off his leopardskin cape and spread it meticulously over the saddle so that he would not touch the leather with his bare legs. He said quietly, apologetically, "We old folks smell," and then settled on the saddle, gripped the pommel with one hand, and waved with the other. "Look," he declared grandly. "I am a mounted policeman. Salute the servant of the government!" The crowd laughed and cursed happily, enjoying the opportunity to jeer with impunity at a policeman, especially a mounted one.

A boy came forward to take the reins, but I waved him aside. "Never let a stranger touch your reins" was one of my father's rules. I led the horse up the hill, feeling very foolish. No white person was likely to see me, leading a horse like a servant, with a crowing old Zulu in the saddle; but you never know, so I kept my head down.

When we reached the top of the hill, the young men pointed out a kraal close by. We took the old man there. He praised me excessively. "Duma!" he shouted. "Chief of Chiefs! May you grow like a mountain!" I wished him well and headed for Insimbi's place.

Outside the kraal, on the level tableland, I saw hundreds of men. They were forming into companies, most of them with matching shields — black, or black and white, or white, or brown and white. Some companies were in single or double files, stamping to the rhythm of their own chants. Greybeards with long sticks demonstrated songs and steps, shouted orders, and whacked the shins of men who stepped out of line.

I gave the main crowd a wide berth and rode round to the back of the kraal. I halted twenty yards or so from the stockade and waited. A small boy playing there leapt to his feet, shouting, "White man! There is a white man!" Some women peered curiously. Presently a man appeared. He was obviously someone of importance. I dismounted and saluted him. He acknowledged my greeting and then asked, anxiously, "What is the matter, child of a white man? Is there trouble? Why have you come?"

I explained that I wanted to see the dancing. Would the chief please allow me? I presented the twists of tobacco.

He took the tobacco and smelled it approvingly. "You have a great liver," he said, "to come into our country, black people's country, on a day like this. But you know how to show respect. Where did you learn Zulu?"

I told him about Ngumbane. "The limping one," he said. "He used to be a fine dancer. I will tell the chief you are here. Take your horse over there." He pointed to a tree beyond a little ravine. "It will be a safe place, but do not offsaddle."

I dismounted under the tree and gave the horse his nosebag. Presently two little girls appeared, one carrying a small pot of beer, the other a grass mat with a lump of meat. I gave them sandwiches in exchange.

As the day wore on, the drilling on the tableland grew more and more orderly. The smaller companies were amalgamating into regiments, performing manoeuvres in long waves. They advanced slowly; charged, beating their shields; retreated; advanced again; repeating the exercises until their elderly instructors were satisfied or exhausted.

By early afternoon the exercises were breaking up. Women had for some time been carrying out food and beer, and most of the dancers now sat down, slashing and stabbing at an imaginary enemy. A few real fights had also broken out, and some spectators were trying to stop them; others were excitedly urging on the combatants or joining in. The chief and other older men were having to intervene, shouting and laying about them with clubs and whips.

Glancing at the group around Insimbi, I saw several arms pointing to me. Soon afterwards a youth of about my age appeared. He was bleeding from a head wound and had a weal where a whip had got him. He stood provocatively in front of me and said, "Little white man" — he used an insulting diminutive — "little white man, hear the words of the chief. Insimbi says you must go now. He says in the dusk a white man looks like any other wild creature."

I mounted quickly. "I thank the chief," I said. "I send him respects." I added, condescendingly, "Stay well, little lad," and cantered off.

Many of the women and girls had already left, together with older men who were anxious to reach home before dark. They started off in big groups, which shed fragments as family or neighbourhood parties broke off to go their separate ways. No one made way for me. A group of men stood in front of the horse and demanded that I take one of them to ride with me; I had to make a wide detour to get past them. Several times someone said, "What are you doing here, white man?" Once or twice a man deliberately tried to frighten the horse.

I decided not to risk the Path of the Ancients down the escarpment; there were too many little danger points. Instead, I went a long way round on the government road and did not get home until after sunset. A few stragglers were still on the Path, but the main traffic had apparently passed.

I finished supper and was getting ready for bed when my horse became restless. I had tethered him for the night in a little cornfield near the house. The dead cornstalks had been gathered into bundles, which stood like rows of ghostly men in the moonlight. The horse was so disturbed that I feared a predator might be around. Then I heard what had been disturbing him. It was far away but unmistakable: a war song, sung by a great many men. It sounded like a whole regiment.

I had already undone the tether and let the horse canter off before I realized that I now had no means of getting away if I needed to.

The sound came and then went faint. It was an antiphonal song, the leading voices clear and high, the responses muffled but strong. It grew suddenly louder. By visualizing the Path of the Ancients, I could tell how the sound would alter. As the singers went down through the old riverbed, it faded; it grew louder as they emerged and faded again as they went around the hillock at the Place of Scolding. When they reached the ridge opposite the farmhouse, the sound should almost disappear.

After a moment's silence, too soon for them to have reached the ridge, a new song started, a different sound. I could not hear words, and indeed the song had no words: just *Eee yoh haa haa haa*, starting quiet, rising high almost to a scream, and then falling to the deepest guttural that the singers could reach in their throats and chests. High again, then down, down, *haa! haa!* High, then down low, repeated over and over.

I knew the song, because a gang of labourers on the farm had once started singing it. Ngumbane had intervened, very angry, shouting, "We will have no songs like that here!" He told me it was a song that had been sung in the old days when warriors anticipated a great killing. "When you sing it, your blood wants blood," he said. In my mind I called it the Bloodsong.

The sound receded when the singers got to where the Path ran behind the ridge and grew faint as they went down into the old stone quarry. I went indoors with much relief: they were on their way to the hills. Then a great burst of the Bloodsong hit me. A large company of warriors had silently climbed the ridge and was now massing at the head of the clearing that ran down to the house. Obviously the others, on the Path, had gone on singing to provide a cover so that this party could get close to the farmhouse without being detected.

As fast as I could, I shuttered the windows and locked all the doors except the top half of the kitchen door. I put the pressure lamp to shine out through the door, dragged sacks of meal and seeds to form a little barricade, and loaded both barrels of the shotgun. I put in birdshot, because that was what I mostly used, but then I remembered that when the farmers had formed a commando to get the madman who shot his wife and kids, they all loaded up with slugs or buckshot, so I quickly slipped in buckshot instead.

In the moonlight I could see the great shields of the warriors gleam when they turned. They were now singing the battle challenge: "Shame on the man who is burned in his hut. Come out and fight!" As they sang, they shuffled into some kind of formation. I knew what they would do: they would split into three lots to form the bull, the classical Zulu attack formation. The two horns of the bull advance to harass the enemy's flanks while the main body, the bull's chest, awaits the right moment for a frontal charge. My father's friends had not been in the Zulu wars, but they often talked about them; their theory was that if you managed to crumple one of the bull's horns, the whole force was thereby confounded. One had therefore to concentrate on one horn and bring down as many men in it as possible.

Presently two files of men, rather fewer than I had expected, began creeping down the clearing. I tried to gauge the distance — not easy in the moonlight — and desperately wished I could remember what the *Sportsman's Handbook* said about the range, penetration, and scatter pattern of buckshot. As one horn moved diagonally across the clearing, I cocked both hammers and kept my bead on the leader, wondering whether I should aim at his legs or at his chest. If I only wounded him, perhaps the others would not be deterred. But what if I killed him?

I was puzzled, because the two horns were not advancing to surround the house but were moving obliquely towards the cornfield. The singing of the main body suddenly stopped. After a thin scream of command they all charged, shouting and hissing the clan battle cry. I scrambled out of the kitchen into the storeroom, which gave a view of that side of the clearing. I doubted whether I could get set up in there before they had me. I tore open the window shutter and pushed the gun barrels out, ready for the first man who came within range.

No one was there. But in the cornfield the whole company was stabbing and slashing at the upright bundles of stalks, crying, "Die! Die!" or leaping about in shadow combat with unseen enemies. I felt a great warm wetness down my trousers as I shakily put the gun down.

The display in the cornfield lasted only a few minutes. Soon most of the warriors sat down, breathing heavily. I counted only a dozen or fifteen of them. One man walked to the house, deliberately standing in the lamplight. He leaned his shield and sticks against the wall and stood waiting, making a knocking click with his tongue.

I shouted, "What do you want?" immensely relieved that my voice was rough and harsh, not fearful and squeaky. The man saluted in the direction of my voice. I saw that he was a boy, not much older than I was. "Nkosane, we ask for water. We are dying of thirst," he said.

I replied gruffly, "Wait. I am coming," and frantically looked for a pair of trousers to replace my wet ones. I unloaded the shotgun, alarmed to see how shaky my hands were. Then I went out, unlocked the water tank, and gave the youth a tin mug.

He waved to the others. They carefully stacked shields and sticks against the wall and respectfully greeted me. They were all teenagers. Each one drank in turn, taking care not to spill. The last one rinsed the mug and held it over his head, looking at me for permission. I said, "You would not do that if it were beer." They recognized my weak joke as a gesture and laughed uproariously, boasting about their drinking capacities.

I waited for them to go, but they sat down, obviously intending to rest and talk. One youth said, "Nkosane, did you know that old man with the broken ankle?" I recognized the speaker and two of the others as having been among those assisting the old man. I shook my head. He turned to the group and related what had happened. They appeared to know already, for two of them were miming the old man putting down his cape to protect the saddle. Everyone laughed, and someone said, "He smells like a polecat's backside now, but they say he was a great fighter when he was young." Someone else said, "You did a kind thing, Nkosane. Our little band has come to thank you. That old man is greatly honoured in our family. He was a guardian uncle of my father and of this boy's father." He indicated another youth, who seemed to be the leader. The leader said, "Johnny, you took a thorn from the foot of a stranger. So we give you this praise-name: You Pull Out Thorns for Strangers." The rest applauded, drummed on their shields, and cried, "Thorn Puller," "You Pull Out Thorns." We discussed praise-names and the uncomplimentary nicknames of some of the white farmers. My father was called the Dancer, because he stamped his feet when he was angry.

I went into the house and brought out a big tin of rusks and some tobacco. They demolished the food and made rough cigarettes. They asked if I was courting. I fetched a picture of my girlfriend. They stared at it, carefully not touching with their fingers but holding it on open palms, and exclaimed admiringly at her plumpness.

They showed me a big stone axe they had found in a cliff in the hills. They had had it ritually purified in case it had been used to kill a man; the old women said that small yellow cannibals used to live in those cliffs. They asked whether I had not been scared up at Insimbi's, being the only white person there. The boys who had been with the old man said, "We kept an eye on you where you sat under the tree. If any trouble had started, we would have protected you." The leader assented. "With brave men like us you would have been safe. Did you see us attack that enemy in the cornfield? They outnumbered us many times, but we slew them without mercy. We were heroes, were we not?" There was much laughter as various members of the band enacted their own past or future exploits. I fetched the shield Ngumbane had given me. They examined and admired it, and I had a mock stick fight with one of them; several gave me advice or demonstrated cunning blows and feints.

The moon was sinking towards the western tableland before they left. As they went by, each one said, "Stay well, brother," and clasped me by the forearm. Then they all turned round and cried, "Puller of Thorns! You are one of us," and raised their shields in salute. For the next half hour I could hear their voices, clear and soaring *Eee yoh*, then falling low, deep and ominous, *haa haa haa*. The Bloodsong faded, rose, faded, and finally died in the valleys of the east hills.

I often saw members of the band subsequently, loafing around trading stores, working on farms, or trotting down the highway to the music of a mouth organ. They always greeted me with the greatest friendliness, but none of them ever again called me brother or said, "You are one of us."

ERNST HAVEMANN

An Interview
(1984)

The Special Branch official stopped at her gate, looked for a longish time at the nameplate M.P. HOFMEYR, as if it had importance, then came up the steps and knocked. He was a neat, ordinary-looking, freckled man, wearing a Hertzog High School Old Boys' blazer.

He introduced himself as Mr. Peter Gunter, showed his plastic identification card, and suggested that Mrs. Hofmeyr might want to telephone the local police station to check. He waited until she asked him in and stood until she invited him to sit down.

"Well, Mr. Gunter, what can I do for you?" She spoke tartly, to keep the apprehension out of her voice. She thought of herself as nonpolitical, by which she meant that she did not belong to a political party; but she had stood in line with other black-sashed women in the days when such gestures seemed significant, and she was one of the few people to whom Emma Dupreez said goodbye before she fled across the border to Lesotho.

Mr. Gunter took a notebook from his side pocket. It was thin and flat so that it would not spoil the smooth fit of his blue melton blazer. He did not open the notebook but looked briefly at it, as though refreshing his mind on some detail that he could read through the black cover.

It was characteristic of Emma Dupreez that even when she was in flight from the security police her laughter was as frequent and uninhibited as ever. She had described hilariously how Rhoda Cohen had dressed in her, Emma's, clothes. Emma demonstrated how Rhoda had had to pad her hips and bosom and to practice Emma's flaunting walk. Rhoda left through the front door; within thirty seconds they saw the surveillance man move off from the next corner to follow her. A few minutes later Emma slipped through the servant's quarters to the old sanitary lane that ran behind the house — the "shit street," Emma called it, as they had done in their childhood, when it was the route for a cart that collected night soil from backyard outhouses. She strolled down the lane and dodged through an empty yard into the next lane, where she waited for Sammy Govinder to pick her up in his taxi — his conspicuous, broken-down Indian taxi, for God's sake! They were late and Sammy was anxious to leave, but Emma had insisted that she must first say goodbye to Mrs. Hofmeyr.

Mr. Gunter glanced from his notebook to the portrait of Mrs. Hofmeyr's husband. "I remember the late doctor came and made a speech at our prize giving once. They gave me a prize, too. For attendance." He smiled self-deprecatingly. "It was all they could find to praise me for." He had widely spaced teeth, like that comedian who used to say he parted his teeth in the middle. It is supposed to be a sign of good nature. Mrs. Hofmeyr did not want to have a human being-to-human being conversation with Mr. Gunter, but habitual courtesy surfaced before she could control it. "Oh, I'm sure you undervalue yourself, Mr. Gunter," she said.

She had given Emma her gold bracelet. It was inscribed from her husband: *MPH from RH*. It was the only valuable piece of jewellery she still had. The rest was in a deposit box in a London bank; her niece in Scotland had the receipt and the key. Her husband had said, "Just in case. Just in case things blow up here. It will be a way of raising a little unauthorized foreign exchange in an emergency. Diamonds are a refugee's best friend."

Mr. Gunter said, "You are M.P. Hofmeyr, isn't it?"

"You know that, I suppose, Mr. Gunter. Or were you expecting to see someone else?"

He did not change expression. "Mrs. Hofmeyr, there are many facts known to the authorities that we nevertheless still always try to verify with the parties concerned. It is procedure, you understand. Procedure and evidence. Mistaken identity is always unfortunate. It is not nice for an innocent person to have her name on a dossier, like suppose a clerk gets the papers mixed up because he does not understand the information-retrieval system."

He mistook her frown for a question. "It is what we used to call Records and Filing," he explained.

"Please get to your point, Mr. Gunter." She spoke irritably, waiting for him to produce whatever frightening thing he had come to ask or say.

He looked at his notebook, flat in his left hand, opened it, then put it in his pocket. "You and your son, John Hofmeyr, have social relations with Bantu female Edith Xulu" — he struggled with the click and made the name come out as Kulu — "and her son Z.K. Matthews Xulu. Is that correct?"

Relief washed over her. It was only about the Xulus. Two years ago, during the riots, John ran into an African mob. He was knocked down and was being kicked by a lot of feet when someone intervened, standing straddling him. It was Z.K. Matthews Xulu. He came home with John as far as the gate. When they parted John said, "You saved my life. Some time I'll try to do the same for you." Z.K. smiled. "I will appreciate that, man."

She said, "Yes, we are friends of the Xulus." She was irritated to find herself pronouncing the name as badly as Mr. Gunter did. "And what's it got to do with you? It's not a crime to be friendly with a native, much as your precious minister might like to make out that it is."

"I wanted to ask for your help about Edith Xulu."

"My help?" She spoke shrilly now, with courage. "You mean you've come here trying to get something out of me to help you trap those simple, honest people. Well, you've come to the wrong place, Mr. Gunter. Put that in your dossier."

Mr. Gunter remained sitting. He took his notebook from his side pocket, turned a page, and closed it.

"Have you recently lost a gold bracelet?"

"No," she said, hoping her voice was steady.

"A fourteen-carat gold bracelet, inscribed *MPH from RH*, was recently found by the police." He spoke without inflection.

She was silent.

"Is it not your bracelet?"

"It was mine, but I gave it away."

"Could I ask to whom?"

She saw no point in prevarication. "To Emma Dupreez."

"How long have you known Bantu female Xulu?"

She had never had Africans, other than servants, in her house. When John invited Z.K. Matthews Xulu and his mother to dinner, she was so nervous she nearly fell ill, fearing heaven knows what breaches of taste or tact she, or the Xulus, would commit. Mrs. Xulu put her at ease in a matter of minutes, admiring her sewing and making little jokes. She was especially funny about Z.K.'s name. Her husband had much admired an African university lecturer of that name, but neither she nor her son had been able to discover what the initials stood for. When they were depressed they made up hilarious combinations of sounds to fit the letters.

"I've known Mrs. Xulu for about two years," Mrs. Hofmeyr said. "What has that got to do with anything?"

"Mrs. Hofmeyr, people from old important families don't always know what goes on in the communities." He saw her puzzled look. "The non-white communities," he explained. "You know, like I know, some people don't like white people to have black friends. Especially if their black friends visit them in their houses. They say it is bad for property values. Yes, we all know that is so, isn't it? But do we also realize that some blacks don't like blacks to have white friends?"

He paused to let the thought sink in. "When there is trouble, like a riot, or just a bit too much brandy or home brew, then there's usually one or two murders. Do you know, Mrs. Hofmeyr, there are more murders in this one little black township every year than there are white murders in the whole province? But I suppose a person must not be too severe about these things. All nations have their own forms of self-expression, isn't it?"

He waited for Mrs. Hofmeyr to acknowledge what he was saying, and leaned forward. "So now, say, there are a few drunks and they feel angry. There's a lot of anger inside these fellows, you know. What the professors like to call aggression. Sometimes it is not enough for them to stab one another. They look for another kind of target, a political target, perhaps. Like maybe we would if we were in their place."

Against her desire to keep Mr. Gunter at a distance, Mrs. Hofmeyr found herself nodding.

Mr. Gunter went on. "So when a few tsotsis are looking for a target, there is someone like your friend Edith Xulu, what they call an Uncle Tom, a Bantu that likes being friends with white people. She is one of those old-fashioned mission kaffirs, excuse me, Christian Africans. Completely detribalized. They've got no pride in their nation. They want to be like Europeans."

Mrs. Xulu was vehement and amusing about race relations. "Z.K. is mad. They are all mad, these young people who want black power. If you throw out the white people, the whole place will be like the homelands, I tell him. Look how it was before the white people came, I say. No Jesus, no motorcars, no soap, no nylon, no brandy, no wireless; just kaffir beer and assegais and ngoma dancing, and skins to wear. Do you know what they gave my grandmother when she was a bride? They gave her an isidwaba, a skin skirt, to last all her life. All her life, madam, and you can't wash it. That is what it will be like, I tell Z.K."

Mrs. Hofmeyr waited for Mr. Gunter to conclude. He in turn looked at her as if expecting a response. When she remained silent he said, "A person might think they were being kind when they were doing the opposite."

Mrs. Hofmeyr still said nothing.

Mr. Gunter opened his notebook and looked hard at it. Mrs. Hofmeyr could see that the page was blank. He closed the book and said, "We would appreciate your co-operation. Edith Xulu is important to us."

"Important to you? What do you mean?"

How could Edith be important to them? Was he hinting that she was a police informer? No, surely not. She was a lovely, open person. And yet — she did seem to have much more money than one would expect. . . .

Mrs. Hofmeyr stared at Mr. Gunter with horror. He gave a tiny, knowing nod as if to confirm what she was thinking and somehow to suggest that he and Mrs. Hofmeyr were on the same wavelength about Mrs. Xulu. The implication infuriated Mrs. Hofmeyr, but before she could find the words to repudiate it, Mr. Gunter reached into an inner pocket and produced a bracelet. "Is that yours?"

Mrs. Hofmeyr took it and pretended to examine it. It was obviously her bracelet. Mr. Gunter said, "If a piece of found property is not claimed, it is *res derelictae*, nobody's property. It is eventually sold and the money goes into the Police Orphans' Fund. You may as well have it back. I don't think anyone else will claim it."

"Where did you get it?"

"It was thrown from a vehicle that was attempting to evade the police."

It was just like Emma: to bungle the arrangements for secretly crossing the border — the police could probably trace her halfway across town by her laugh and the smoke trail of Sammy Govinder's taxi — and yet to have the presence of mind to throw away the bracelet, hoping that she would thus avoid implicating Mrs. Hofmeyr. Poor dear, where have they got her now?

"Where is Mrs. Dupreez?" she asked. Her voice sounded strangled.

Instead of answering, Mr. Gunter reached again into his inner pocket and held out a half sheet of paper. It was a typed receipt. "If you'll just sign at the bottom," he said, producing a silver pen. The pen was thin and flat, designed to fit snugly into the wearer's pocket without making a bulge. She signed. Mr. Gunter smiled, showing spaced teeth and pink gums, and put the receipt and pen back into his inner breast pocket.

"Where is Mrs. Dupreez?" Mrs. Hofmeyr repeated.

He looked surprised, as if she had revived a subject they had already disposed of. "Where do you expect her to be?"

Did that mean they didn't have her? Or that everyone should know where political detainees were kept? There was that place in Johannesburg. . . . And what about poor Sammy Govinder?

"Can I see her?"

"You will have to make your own arrangements for that, Mrs. Hofmeyr."

Did that mean they did have her?

"Do you happen to have your passport handy?"

"What do you want it for?"

"I think you will find it expires next May. May twentieth, isn't it?"

She went to her desk, took out her passport, and looked at the expiration date. It was May 20. Mr. Gunter half rose and held out his hand politely, as if to receive a cup of tea.

What would he do if she refused to give it to him? Probably insist on his right to inspect an item of government property: there was that statement about the passport's belonging to the government, not to you, wasn't there? Suppose he kept it? Please God, don't let him keep it.

She handed the passport to him. He did not open it but rested it on his knee.

"Did you give anything else to Mrs. Dupreez?"

She shook her head.

"Did she give you anything? Or leave anything with you to keep for her? Any papers?"

One of Emma's parting jokes was a request to the post office to re-address her mail. She gave as her forwarding address the apartment of her cousin, who was now an attaché or secretary of some kind at the embassy in Washington. "I wonder how he'll explain that away," Emma had said exultantly. "He was such a righteous liberal when we were at college. And look at him now. Spineless little crypto-nationalist arse creeper."

"She left a letter for me to post," Mrs. Hofmeyr said.

Mr. Gunter tensed. "Have you got it?"

"No, of course not. I posted it."

"Did you notice who it was for?"

"The postmaster."

Mr. Gunter frowned. "The postmaster? Here?"

"Yes."

He picked up her passport, looked at the photo and then at her, and flipped over two or three pages.

"Yes, it expires May twentieth." He weighed the document in his left hand. "You should not leave it too late. Sometimes applications for renewal take a very long time. Because of all the inquiries involved, you know. It's what people call red tape, but there is always a reason for a procedure, not so?"

He put the passport back on his knee. "Where was Mrs. Dupreez aiming for when you saw her?"

Mrs. Hofmeyr was silent. Mr. Gunter opened the passport again and carefully looked at the stamps on one page. He said "Hmmmm" very quietly, took out his pen, and put it in to mark the place; he seemed to be comparing the stamps with those on another page, and looked inquiringly at her. He said nothing. He looked again at her passport, kept open at that place by his flat silver pen, and back at her.

"She was going to Lesotho."

Surely they must already know. That car evading the police must have been on the road to Lesotho. Emma had not said that the fact that Lesotho was her destination should be kept secret. Perhaps everyone would know that that was where she would head for in the first instance. Botswana would be a better place, because it was not surrounded by South African territory, but it was much farther. But perhaps Emma had assumed she, Mrs. Hofmeyr, would naturally keep it secret. If Emma had got through, perhaps it wouldn't matter whether the police knew. Or perhaps they knew anyway, through their informers: people said they had dozens of agents in all these little countries. If Mr. Gunter took the passport away, what could she do? You couldn't go to court about it. Suppose Emma hadn't got through? If the police had her in custody, they wouldn't be asking about her destination, would they? So she might be in hiding, waiting for another chance to cross the border, and now the police would know which roads to watch. Dear Lord, what had she done to Emma?

"Lesotho. Yes." Mr. Gunter gave a little pleased nod. "If you don't mind my saying so, that desk is not a very secure place for a valuable article like a passport. Why don't you keep it in your bank with your jewellery? I suppose a lady like you must have a lot of diamond rings and things like that."

He dropped his voice, as if giving away important official information to a friend. "We notice ladies don't wear so many valuable items nowadays. Perhaps it's because they have illegally hidden them overseas, eh?"

He once again put his pen back in his breast pocket, and held out the passport to Mrs. Hofmeyr. She took it and held it tight with both her hands on her lap, resisting the temptation to press it to her heart.

Mr. Gunter leaned forward. "In regard to Bantu female Xulu . . ."

CAROL SHIELDS

Flitting Behaviour
(1984)

Some of Meershank's wittiest writing was done during his wife's final illness.

"Mortality," he whispered each morning to give himself comfort, "puts acid in the wine." Other times he said, as he peered into the bathroom mirror, "Mortality puts strychnine in the candy floss. It puts bite in the byte." Then he groaned aloud — but only once — and got straight back to work.

His novel of this period, *Malaprop in Disneyfield*, was said to have been cranked out of the word processor between invalid trays and bedpans. In truth, he wept as he set down his outrageous puns and contretemps. The pages mounted, two hundred, three hundred. The bulk taunted him, and meanwhile his wife, Louise, lingered, her skin growing as transparent as human skin can be without disintegrating. A curious odour, bitter and yellow, stole over the sickroom. Meershank had heard of the odour which proceeded death; now he breathed it daily.

It was for this odour, more than anything else, that he pitied her, she who'd busied herself all her life warding off evil smells with scented candles and aerosol room fresheners. Since a young woman she'd had the habit of sweetening her bureau drawers, and his, too, with sprigs of dried lavender, and carrying always in her handbag and travelling case tiny stitched sachets of herbs. He had sometimes wondered where she found these anachronistic sachets; who in the modern industrial world produced such frivolities? — the Bulgarians maybe, or the Peruvians, frantic for hard currency.

Toward the end of Louise's illness he had a surprise visit from his editor, a vigorous, leggy woman of forty who drove up from Toronto to see how the new manuscript was coming along. She came stepping from her car one Monday afternoon in a white linen jumpsuit. Bending slightly, she kissed Meershank on both cheeks and cried out, "But this is extraordinary! That you can even think of work at a time like this."

Meershank pronounced for her his bite-in-the-byte aperçu, very nearly choking with shame.

He was fond of his editor — her name was Maybelle Spritz — but declined to invite her into his wife's bedroom, though the two women knew and liked each other. "She's not strong enough for visitors," he said, knowing it was the smell of the room he guarded her from, his poor Louise's last corner of pride. "Maybe later."

He and Maybelle sat drinking coffee on the veranda most of the afternoon. The weather all week had been splendid. Birds sang in the branches of Meershank's trees, and sunlight flooded the long triangle of Meershank's side lawn. Maybelle, reading slowly as always, turned over the manuscript pages. Her nails were long and vivid. She held a pencil straight up in her hand, and at least once every three minutes or so she let loose a bright snort of laughter which Meershank welcomed like a man famished. He watched her braided loop of auburn hair and observed how the light burned on the tips of her heavy silver earrings. There was a bony hollow at the base of her neck that deepened, suddenly, each time another snort was gathering. Later, at five o'clock, checking his watch, he offered gin and tonic. For Louise upstairs he carried cream of celery soup, weak tea and an injection for her hip, which the visiting nurse had taught him to administer.

"Are you feeling lonely?" his wife asked him, turning on one side and readying herself for the needle. She imagined, rightly, that he missed her chatter, that her long days spent in drugged sleep were a deprivation. Every day she asked the same question, plunging him directly into blocky silence. Yes, he was lonely. No, he was not lonely. Which would please her more? He kept his hand on her discoloured hip and mumbled the news — testing it — that Maybelle Spritz was thinking of coming for a visit.

She opened her eyes and managed a smile as he rearranged the pillows. He had a system: one pillow under each knee, one at the small of her back and two to support her shoulders. The air in the room was suffocating. He asked again, as he did every day, if he might open a window. No, she said, as she always did; it was too cold. She seemed convinced that spring had not arrived in its usual way, she who'd always been so reasonable.

Downstairs Maybelle stood in the kitchen drinking a second gin and tonic and heating up a noodle pudding she had brought along. She had occasionally been a dinner guest in Meershank's house but had never before penetrated the kitchen. She set a little table on the veranda. There was a breeze, enough to keep the mosquitoes away for a bit. Knives and forks; she discovered them easily in the first drawer she opened. The thick white dinner plates she found stacked on a shelf over the sink. There were paper napkins of a most ordinary sort in a cupboard. As she moved about she marvelled at the domesticity of the famous, how simple things appeared when regarded close up, like picking up an immense orange and finding it all thick hide on a tiny fruit. She wondered if Meershank would ask her to spend the night.

They had only once before shared a bed, and that had been during the awful week after Louise's illness had been diagnosed.

The expression *terminal*, when the doctor first pronounced it, had struck Meershank with a comic bounce, this after a lifetime of pursuing puns for a living. His scavenger self immediately pictured a ghostly airline terminal in which scurrying men and women trotted briskly to and fro in hospital gowns.

The word *terminal* had floated out of the young doctor's wide pink face; it was twice repeated, until Meershank collected himself and responded with a polite nod. Then he put back his head, counted the ceiling tiles — twelve times fourteen — and decided on the spot that his wife must not be told.

The specialist laced clean hands across flannel knees and pressed for honest disclosure; there were new ways of telling people that they were about to die; he himself had attended a recent symposium in Boston and would take personal responsibility . . .

No. Meershank held up his hand. This was nonsense. Why did people insist that honesty was the only way of coping with truth? He knew his wife. After thirty-five years of marriage he knew his wife. She must be brought home from the hospital and encouraged to believe that she would recover. Rest, medication, country air — they would work their healing magic. Louise could always, almost always, be persuaded to follow a reasonable course.

The following day, having signed the release papers and made the arrangements to have his wife moved, Meershank, until then a faithful husband, took his editor, Maybelle Spritz, to a downtown hotel and made plodding love to her, afterward begging pardon for his age, his grief and his fury at the fresh-faced specialist who, concluding their interview, had produced one of Meershank's books, *Walloping Westward*, and begged the favour of an inscription. Meershank coldly took out a pen and signed his name. He reminded himself that the Persians had routinely put to death the bearer of bad news.

Home again, with Louise installed in the big front bedroom, he resumed work. His word processor hummed like a hornet from nine to five, and the pages flew incriminatingly out of the printer. During the day his brain burned like a lightbulb screwed crookedly into a socket. At night he slept deeply. He wondered if he were acquiring a reputation for stoicism, that contemptible trait! Friends stopped by with gifts of food or flowers. The flowers he carried up to Louise's bedroom where they soon drooped and died, and the food he threw in the garbage. Coffee cakes, almond braids, banana loaves — his appetite had vanished.

"Eat," Maybelle commanded, loading his plate.

He loved noodle pudding and wondered how Maybelle knew. "It's in your second novel," she reminded him. "*Snow Soup and Won Ton Drift*. Remember? Wentzel goes into the cafe at Cannes and demands that —"

"I remember, I remember." Meershank held up a hand. (He was always holding up a hand nowadays, resisting information.) He had a second helping, injecting starch and sweetness. This was hardly fitting behaviour for a grieving husband. He felt Maybelle's eyes on him. "I shoulda brought more," she said, sounding for a minute like a girl from Cookston Corners, which she was. "I said to myself, he'll be starving himself."

For dessert she rummaged in the refrigerator and found two peaches. Louise would have peeled them and arranged the slices in a cut glass bowl. Meershank and Maybelle sat eating them out of their hands. He thought to himself: this is like the last day of the world.

"Ripe," Maybelle pronounced. There was a droplet of juice on her chin, which she brushed away with the back of her hand. Meershank observed that her eyes looked tired, but perhaps it was only the eye shadow she wore. What was the purpose of eye shadow, he wondered. He had never known and couldn't begin to imagine.

A character in his first book, *Swallowing Hole*, had asked this question aloud to another character, who happened to be his wife. What was her name? Phyllis? Yes, Phyllis of the phyllo pastry and philandering nights. "Why do you smudge your gorgeous green eyes with gook?" he, the cuckolded husband, had asked. And what had the fair Phyllis replied? Something arch, something unpardonable. Something enclosing a phallic pun. He had forgotten, and for that he blessed the twisted god of age. His early books with their low-altitude gag lines embarrassed him, and he tried hard to forget he had once been the idiot who wrote them.

Maybelle, on the other hand, knew his oeuvre with depressing thoroughness and could quote chapter and verse. Well, that was the function of an editor, he supposed. A reasonable man would be grateful for such attention. She was a good girl. He wished she'd find a husband so he would feel less often that she'd taken the veil on his account. But at least she didn't expect him to converse with wit. Like all the others, she'd bought wholesale the myth of the sad jester.

It was a myth that he himself regarded with profound scepticism. He'd read the requisite scholarly articles, of course, and had even, hypocrite that he was, written one or two himself. Humour is a pocket pulled inside out; humour is an anguished face dumped upside down; humour is the refuge of the grunting cynic, the eros of the deprived lover, the breakfast of the starving clown. Some of these cheap theories he'd actually peddled aloud to the graduating class at Trent a year ago, and his remarks had been applauded lustily. (How much better to lust applaudingly, he'd cackled, sniggered, snorted inside his wicked head.)

He suspected that these theories were leapt upon for their simplicity, their symmetry, their neat-as-a-pin ironic shimmer. They were touted by those so facile they were unable to see how rich with ragged comedy the world really was. But Meershank knew, he knew! Was it not divinely comic that only yesterday he'd received a telephone solicitation from the Jackson Point Cancer Fund? Wasn't it also comic that the spectre of his wife's death should fill him with a wobbly lust for his broad-busted, perfume-wafting, forty-year-old editor? For that matter, wasn't it superbly comic that a man widely known as a professional misogynist had remained happily married to one woman for thirty-five years? (Life throws these kinky curves a little too often, Meershank had observed, and the only thing to do was open your fool mouth and guffaw.)

At nine he checked once again on his wife, who was sleeping quietly. If she woke later, a second injection was permitted. He carried a bottle of brandy out on to the veranda. One for the road, he asked Maybelle with his eyebrows. Why not, she said with a lift of her shoulders. Her upper lip went stiff as a ledge in the moonlight, and he shuddered to think he was about to kiss her. The moon tonight was bloated and white, as fretful as a face. Everywhere there was a smell of mock orange blossoms which had bloomed early this year and in absurd profusion. Crickets ticked in the grass like fools, like drunkards. Meershank lifted his glass. The brandy burned his throat and made him retreat for an instant, but Maybelle became attenuated, lively, sharp of phrase, amusing. He laughed aloud for the first time in a week, wondering if the world would crack down the middle.

It did. Or seemed to. A loud overhead popping noise like the cracking of whips made him jump. Maybelle slammed down her glass and stared. All around them the sky flashed white, then pink, then filled with rat-a-tat-tat fountains and sparks and towering plumes.

"Jesus," Maybelle said. "Victoria Day. I almost forgot."

"I did forget," Meershank said. "I never once thought."

A rocket whined and popped, made ropy arcs across the sky, burst into petals, leaving first one, then a dozen blazing trails. It was suddenly daylight, fierce, then faded, then instantly replaced by a volley of cracking gunpowder and new showers of brilliance.

The explosions, star-shaped, convulsive, leaping one out of the other, made Meershank think of the chains of malignant cells igniting in his wife's body.

He set down his brandy, excused himself, and hurried upstairs.

Meershank, marrying Louise Lovell in 1949, had felt himself rubbing bellies for the first time with the exotic. He, a Chicago Jew, the son of a bond salesman, had fallen in love with a gentile, a Canadian, a fair-haired girl of twenty who had been gently reared in the Ottawa Valley by parents who lived quietly in a limestone house that was a hundred years old. It faced on the river. There was a rose garden crisscrossed by gravel paths and surrounded by a pale-pink brick wall. Oh, how silently those two parents had moved about in their large square rooms, in winter wrapping themselves in shawls, sitting before pots of raspberry-leaf tea and making their good-natured remarks about the weather, the books they were forever in the middle of, the tiny thunder of politics that flickered from their newspaper, always one day old.

The mother of Louise possessed a calm brow of marble. The father had small blue eyes and hard cheeks. He was the author of a history of the Canadian Navy. It was, he told Meershank, the *official* history. Meershank was given a signed copy. And he was given, too, with very little noise or trouble, the hand of Louise in marriage. He had been stunned. Effortlessly, it seemed, he'd won from them their beloved only daughter, a girl of soft hips and blond hair done roundly in a pageboy.

"What exactly do you do?" they only once asked. He worked as a correspondent for a newspaper, he explained. (He did not use the word *journalist*.) And he hoped one day to write a book. ("Ah! A book! Splendid!")

The wedding was in the month of June and was held in the garden. Meershank's relatives did not trouble to travel all the way up from Chicago. The wedding breakfast was served out-of-doors, and the health of the young couple — Meershank at twenty-seven was already starting to bald — was toasted with a non-alcoholic fruit punch. The family was abstemious; the tradition went back several generations; alcohol, tobacco, caffeine — there wasn't a trace of these poisons in the bloodstream of Meershank's virgin bride. He looked at her smooth, pale arms — and eventually, when legally married, at her smooth pale breasts — and felt he'd been singularly, and comically, blessed.

There is a character, Virgie Allgood, in Meershank's book, *Sailing to Saskatchewan*, who might be said to resemble Louise. In the book, Virgie is an eater of whole grains and leafy vegetables. Martyr-like, she eschews French fries, doughnuts and liver dumplings, yet her body is host to disease after disease. Fortified milk fails. Pure air fails. And just when the life is about to go out of her, the final chapter, a new doctor rides into town on a motorbike and saves her by prescribing a diet of martinis and cheesecakes.

There is something of Louise, too, in the mother in Meershank's tour-de-force, *Continuous Purring*. She is a woman who cannot understand the simplest joke. Riddles on cereal boxes have to be laboriously explained. Puns strike her as being untidy scraps to be swept up in a dustpan. She thinks a double entendre is a potent new drink. She is congenitally immune to metaphor (the root of all comedy, Meershank believes), and on the day her husband is appointed to the Peevish Chair of Midbrow Humour, she sends for the upholsterer.

When *Encounter* did its full length profile on Meershank in 1981, it erred by stating that Louise Lovell Meershank had never read her husband's books. The truth is she not only had read them, but before the birth of the word processor she typed them, collated the pages, corrected their virulent misspelling, redistributed semicolons and commas with the aplomb of a goddess, and tactfully weeded out at least half of Meershank's compulsive exclamation points. She corresponded with publishers, arranged for foreign rights, dealt with book clubs and with autograph seekers, and she always — less and less frequently, of course — trimmed her husband's fluffy wreath of hair with a pair of silver-handled scissors.

She read Meershank's manuscripts with a delicious (to Meershank) frown on her wide pale brow — more and more she'd grown to resemble her mother. She turned over the pages with a delicate hand as though they possessed the same scholarly sheen as her father's *Official History of the Canadian Navy*. She read them not once but several times, catching a kind of overflow of observance which leaked like oil and vinegar from the edges of Meershank's copious, verbal, many-leafed salads.

Her responses never marched in time with his. She was slower and could wave aside sentimentality, saying, "Why not? — it's part of the human personality." Occasionally she said the unexpected thing, as when she described her husband's novella, *Fiend at the Water Fountain*, as being, "cool and straight up and down as a tulip."

What she actually told the journalist from *Encounter* was that she never *laughed* when reading her husband's books. For this Meershank has always respected her, valued her, adored her. She was his Canadian rose, his furry imbiber of scented tea, his smiling plum, his bread and jam, his little squirrel, his girlie-girl, his Dear Heart who promised in the garden by the river beside the limestone house in 1949 to stay at his side for ever and ever. What a joke she has played on him in the end.

She has, Meershank said to Maybelle, taken a turn for the worse. He phoned the doctor, who said he would come at once. Then he handed Maybelle a piece of paper on which two telephone numbers were written. "Please," he said. "Phone the children."

Maybelle was unprepared for this. And she had never met the children. "What should I tell them?" she asked.

"Tell them," Meershank said, and paused. "Tell them it could be sooner than we thought."

One of the daughters, Sonya, lived in London, Ontario, where she was the new director of the program for women's studies. (For those who trouble to look, her mirror image can be found in Ira Chauvin, post-doc researcher in male studies, in Meershank's academic farce, *Ten Minutes to Tenure*.) Sonya did not say to Maybelle, "Who is this calling?" or "How long does she have?" She said, "I'll be there in three hours flat."

The other daughter, Angelica, ran a health-food restaurant and delicatessen with her husband, Rusty, in Montreal. They were just closing up for the night when Maybelle phoned. "I can get a plane at midnight," Angelica said in a high, sweet, shaky voice. "Tell her to wait for me."

After that Maybelle sat on a kitchen chair in the dark. She could have switched on the light, but she preferred to sit as she was and puzzle over what level of probability had landed her on the twenty-fourth of May as a visitor in a dying woman's shadowy kitchen. And that was what she was, only a visitor — she was not such a fool as to mistake a single embrace for anything other than a mutation of grief.

The tiles of the kitchen wall, after a moment, took on a greenish glow, and she began to float out of her body, a trick she had perfected during her long years of commuting between Cookston Corners and downtown Toronto. First, she became Sonya flying down an eastbound highway, her hands suddenly younger and supple-jointed on the slippery wheel. She took the long cloverleafs effortlessly, the tires of her tough little car zinging over ramps and bridges, and the sleepy nighttime radio voices holding her steady in the middle lane.

Then, blinking once and shutting out the piny air, she was transformed into Angelica, candid, fearful, sitting tense in an aisle seat at the rear of a plane — she had her mother's smooth cheeks, her father's square chin and her own slow sliding tears. On her lap she clutched a straw bag, and every five minutes she pushed back the sleeve of her blouse and checked her wristwatch, trying to freeze its hands with her will.

Next she was the doctor — springing onto the veranda, tapping at the screen door and taking the stairs two at a time. She drifted then into the amorphous body of Louise, where it was hot and damp and difficult to breathe but where shadows reached out and curved around her head. Her hands lay surprisingly calm on the sheet — until one of them was lifted and held to Meershank's beating heart.

She felt his bewilderment and heard with his ears a long popping chain of firecrackers going off. A window in the bedroom had been opened — at last — and the scent of the mock orange blossoms reached him with a rushing blow. Everything was converging. All the warm fluids of life came sliding behind Maybelle's eyes, and she had to hold on to the sides of the kitchen chair to keep herself from disappearing.

In each of Meershank's fictions there is what the literary tribe calls a "set piece," a jewel, as it were, set in a spun-out text, or a chunk of narrative that is somehow more intense, more cohesive, more self-contained than the rest. Generally theatrical and vivid, it can be read and comprehended, even when severed from the wider story, or it can be "performed" by those writers — Meershank is not one — who like to gad about the country giving "readings."

In Meershank's recently published book, *Malaprop in Disneyfield*, the set piece has four characters sitting at dusk on a veranda discussing the final words of the recently deceased family matriarch. The sky they gaze into is a rainy mauve, and the mood is one of tenderness — but there is also a tone of urgency. Three of the four had been present when the last words were uttered, and some irrational prompting makes them want to share with the fourth what they heard — or what they *thought* they heard. Because each heard something different, and there is a descending order of coherence.

"The locked door of the room," is what one of them, a daughter, heard.

"The wok cringes in the womb," is the enigmatic phrase another swears she heard.

The bereaved husband, a blundering old fool in shirtsleeves, heard, incredibly, "The sock is out of tune."

All three witnesses turn to their listener, as lawyers to a judge. Not one of them is superstitious enough to place great importance on final words. Illness, they know, brings a rainbow of distortion, but they long, nevertheless, for interpretation.

The listening judge is an awkward but compassionate woman who would like nothing better than to bring these three fragments into unity. Inside her head she holds a pencil straight up. Her eyes are fixed on the purpling clouds.

Then it arrives. Through some unsecured back door in her imagination she comes up with "The mock orange is in bloom."

"Of course, of course," they chime, nodding and smiling at each other, and at that moment their grief shifts subtly, the first of many such shiftings they are about to undergo.

JANICE KULYK KEEFER

Mrs. Putnam at the Planetarium
(1985)

Tuesdays Mrs. Putnam locked her flat, walked three city blocks to the subway, passed, with the sombre airiness of a ghost, through grilles and spokes and greedy-mouthed machines, and rode from Jane and Bloor to Museum. Rode in summer, when the cars were full of tourists with cameras clotting their necks and the pale yellow tiles made the station seem a morgue, ice under the hammer heat of asphalt overhead. Rode in winter when the closeness of the cars made Mrs. Putnam, in her Merino wool coat, her black mink toque, clammy, dizzy, ravaged like a book with pages razored out. Did not ride in spring and autumn since those flighty seasons no longer existed for her now. Once there had been day trips to Niagara-on-the-Lake in Tulip Time, or Autumn Splendour in Muskoka with the boarders from St. Radigonde's or, more rarely, much more rarely, outings with Adam to the Island in late May, early September. Long before there'd even been a Planetarium, back when the Museum walls had been the colour of greased soot, and stone lions snarled in the Tomb Garden.

On this Tuesday — mid-November, snowless, skyless — Mrs. Putnam claimed the seat reserved for veterans, pregnant women and old-age pensioners and started for the Planetarium. Across the aisle from her were advertisements for office temps, notices for putting your newborn through university and pamphlets about Careers without College. Mrs. Putnam glued milky brown eyes to them. For the past ten years she had been retired on a pension sufficient for her to maintain her flat, though not to repair the cracks in the plaster or buy poison enough to terminate the roaches. She had neither nieces nor nephews with babies requiring to be sent to Victoria or Trinity College, and since she'd come by her post as English Mistress and later Language Specialist with only a Grade Thirteen Diploma from Harbord Collegiate, Mrs. Putnam had no need to consult pamphlets at all. Yet it was imperative to do so — otherwise she would have had to look upon her fellow travellers, and Mrs. Putnam had no interest in anybody else's story but her own.

Twelve-year-olds with pink or green or orange hair, Jamaicans looking resolutely uncolourful in raincoats, Lebanese waiters mournful as blank television screens, Pakistanis with babies on their laps, babies with perfectly round faces and eyes like black moons in the dank heat or chill of the subway car. Arms sweating, legs jolting, Mrs. Putnam holding tight and tighter to the silver pole in front of doors out which her stop would show, as welcome as the ram to Abraham and in another sort of thicket altogether.

Changing trains she noted men at the newspaper kiosks who reminded her of Adam — no similarity whatsoever in colour of hair or lack of it, no slightest resemblance in build or height, but perhaps the cut of the overcoat, the precise indentation of the fedora. She was not the sort who would have held a lover's hand or gazed into his eyes, but often after he had left her side and was safely showering she would take up his hat from her dresser and press her fingertips along the crease his own had made in the felt. His wife had the vexing habit of presenting him with a new fedora every Christmas. She ordered them by telephone from Creeds; it was one of the few things she could do for him. The little else she could do Althea had told while waiting in Mrs. Putnam's office one rainy Sunday afternoon for Uncle Adam to take her to tea with Aunt Rosamund.

"She's awfully pale, of course, being an invalid, but it's amazing how strong her hands are — she does yards of crochet and knits scarves and vests and things, none of which Uncle Adam can wear, since he's allergic to wool (*though he wore cashmere mufflers and Harris tweeds, as Mrs. Putnam could have told her*), but he does have his office filled with crocheted doilies and coasters everywhere, even under the secretary's typewriter, which shows how devoted they are to one another. Aunt Rosamund's made me all kinds of tablecloths and comforters for my own hope chest — she says I'm like a daughter to her, since she hasn't any children of her own, which is sad, don't you think, Mrs. Putnam? Maybe you feel the same — I mean, having no children, not even a husband even. I mean, of course you did have a husband once, at least you *say* you did, I mean — no offence Mrs. Putnam —"

Mrs. Putnam took none. Pimply, placid Althea, who hadn't the imagination of a pincushion and, thus, any notion of the fact that while Aunt Rosamund was crocheting quiet mounds of doilies, Uncle Adam was taking more than tea with Hilary Putnam. Althea, thick as three planks, who couldn't recite a line of poetry to save her soul (*a soul the colour and consistency of clotted cream, thought Mrs. Putnam*) but who nevertheless passed all of Mrs. Putnam's classes for the six years she was at St. Radigonde's and her uncle at Mrs. Putnam's. Tuesday and Thursday evenings from six to ten and, perhaps half a dozen times a year, an entire Saturday or Sunday when Rosamund could be persuaded there was pressing work to be done at the Trust Company of which her husband was vice-president. Kind Althea, who hadn't meant anything by her remarks, since she hadn't the intelligence to think ill of anyone's peculiarities but who merely parroted schoolgirl gossip about the English Mistress's marriage, which, as Mrs. Putnam knew extremely well, all the girls and over half the staff believed to be a harmless fiction, if not an outright lie.

Southbound to Museum Mrs. Putnam stared at her reflection in the window as the train racketed through a tunnel. The mink toque had been a present from Adam, the last she'd ever had from him. The first had been a ring — one topaz in a (twelve-carat) band. To match her eyes, he'd said — and her hair, which was a watered blond, definitely not twenty-two-carat, but then all her own at least, and hadn't it made the first grey hair scarcely noticeable? Though he'd not been there to notice anything the night that Mrs. Putnam's mirror finally ambushed her. A massive coronary at his desk, or so Althea had announced the day after the funeral to which, of course, his niece's English teacher had not been summoned. Rosamund — Rosamund was still sipping the small beer of invalid life in Rosedale, having, to counterbalance her fringed nerves and amazingly strong heart. Althea had vouched for it — of all her former pupils, Althea was the only one who still sent Christmas cards to Mrs. Putnam, rang her up on shopping trips to town, and never sounded disconcerted by the minute and peculiar questions put to her — not on the subjects of how many children she had and of which sex, but of whether there had been any change in her aunt's condition. There never was.

Mrs. Putnam's was a different case. She had been a carelessly handsome, strong-blooded young woman, and it had been to her the strictest form of punishment to watch as, year by year, the slow blue veins that Adam had once traced along her arms and breasts struggled up to the very surface of her skin like drowning swimmers. Liver spots over her hands, the peevish slouch of skin, cracks in her lips which, in the caustic light over the bathroom mirror, seemed to be fissures or crevasses down which her very soul might slip — these were to Mrs. Putnam stages of a cross made of real and not symbolic wood; they left scars and splinters in her shoulders. Her colleagues at St. Radigonde's would not have noticed — she had no friends among them and no confidantes; they, for their part, regarded her merely as an English Mistress renowned for the strict discipline she kept within her class and for the tedium of the material she set her students. Not even Adam had known that, while she buried his niece under slabs of Pope and all of Milton's *Aereopagitica*, at home, alone, she'd finger a vellum Swinburne, recite from memory the lusher lyrics of Tennyson or read aloud from Keats in a special edition, gilt-edged with plump, fawn-coloured, soft suede covers.

Pigeons were wheeling over the Museum steps or skittering after bits of popcorn that schoolchildren, on their way home from a session with dinosaurs or dusty Indians in the anthropologist's bargain basement, had bought from the Italian vendors. At their yellow-painted carts, crenellated with candy apples, fragrant with the steam from roasting chestnuts, Mrs. Putnam did not so much as glance — nor at the faces of the children, flushed against the chill of this grey air outside, sharp as icicles against their cheeks. Mrs. Putnam liked neither popcorn nor children overmuch — on the one she had lost a quarter of a tooth some twenty years ago; on the other she had wasted forty years. In none of her students had she bred a love of Shelley, Scott or Swift, though she had done a creditable job in teaching them what sentence fragments, comma splices and malapropisms were. For, some fifteen years ago, the Headmistress of St. Radigonde's had decided that English Literature would have to be hatcheted and Contemporary Culture (plus remedial grammar) put in its place if the school were to hold its own against the more prestigious, if less venerable, private girls' schools in Toronto. Mrs. Putnam had lately read that no one taught *Edwin Drood* or *Silas Marner* to schoolchildren these days — it was all Contemporary Song Lyrics and Shakespeare Comic Books. A colleague of hers, retired now from Weatherstone School, had got up a petition against it and asked Mrs. Putnam to sign, but she hadn't. *I do not care, I do not care*, was all that Mrs. Putnam had written in reply.

No one asked Mrs. Putnam for the extravagant sum it cost to get a ticket to the Planetarium: on Tuesdays old-age pensioners were admitted free — into the Museum as well, though Mrs. Putnam refused to set so much as the toe of her ankle boots inside the place, now that they'd changed everything round and destroyed the garden. On Sunday afternoons after Adam's death Mrs. Putnam had walked under the arches and the stone lions, listening to snow or leaves fall as if they'd been the bells that had hung from the roofs of the tombs. Once a man not much older than herself had watched her from the window of the garden door and asked her, after she'd returned, to have tea with him downtown. From his accent she had diagnosed him as Eastern European and refused, not out of loyalty to Adam's memory, but because she'd been raised in the belief that people whose names ended in *off* or *ski* or *vich* might be high school janitors but hardly the social equals of a Stuart or Jones or Putnam — she'd had visions of the man stirring his tea with his index finger. Foreigners had been barred from St. Radigonde's since its founding by an interim Anglican bishop in 1833, though somewhere in the middle of Mrs. Putnam's term at the school *that* had changed as it had everywhere — Mrs. Putnam understood that the country's Prime Minister was married to an emigrant from that country whose flag looked like a checkerboard.

Once inside the Planetarium she walked up and down corridors painted the colour of milk frozen in the bottle, ignoring the displays of information on the walls and joining the small queue in front of the Projection Room. Waiting for the doors to open she looked down at her hands, then lifted them a little cautiously to her face, stroking her cheek with the leather, inhaling its rich, almost meaty scent. Real kid, none of that pigskin business — though she had to eat macaroni and skimp on the cheese four days a week, Mrs. Putnam would have her necessary luxuries, mere tokens of the things she could have had if Adam hadn't betrayed her at his desk that Tuesday morning or, at the very least, if Rosamund's nerves had done her in before he had to die.

Particles of rouge like motes of rosy dust clung to Mrs. Putnam's gloves; all the heating and air-cleaning machines whirring through the foyer made her eyes feel papery, her skin crisp under the powder she had pressed on that morning. Why wouldn't they open the doors, why must they make her wait — seventy years old and with the dignity, the presence of a dowager queen, yet they kept her in line as if she were queuing up for cigarettes at the five and ten. Where on earth was the manager, he would have to be talked to, he would have to — someone in front of her began to whistle; further down the line she heard, distinctly, a belch. Mrs. Putnam drew tighter the collar of her good, her excellent cloth coat, pulled the mink toque down so it covered her ear lobes — shrivelled, hard now like dried apricots — and waited. If Adam had been with her, if ever he could have been with her . . . but then, if there was anything she detested it was whining women, watering their tea with tears over the mistakes they'd made. *She* had made up her mind when she was thirteen — just after her mother had died — that she would marry well or never marry at all, having learned from her parents' case that life as or with a bank clerk was no great addendum to the sum of human happiness.

Adam had been charming to her — it hadn't been his fault that Rosamund had had the tenacity of a wire-haired terrier in her grip on life, on Adam, and on the president of Adam's company: Rosamund's father. And yet if desire, need and hope had anything to do with our lot on earth; if there were justice under the stars. . . . The subjunctive mood, Mrs. Putnam had drilled into her students' heads, is always used for things that one merely wishes or hypothesizes to be true.

But now it was as if the gates of a post-modernist heaven had been opened for the pensioners and straggling students. The inner doors of the Planetarium swung slowly apart and gathered them in like the great skirts of a Mater Misericordia. As quickly as her dignity and arthritic hip would let her, Mrs. Putnam found her customary seat, three rows back from the front and at right angles from a certain twist in the crumpled metal that projected stars on the egg-shaped dome over her head. She drooped into the chair like a bird to its nest on a darkening winter afternoon; back she tilted, closing her eyes until her head had found its cradling place and the low music rising from the projector crept across her like a hand stroking her brow. And then she looked up at the great black bowl, not hard and blank as the subway window but soft, dewy, gelid — like a membrane to which Mrs. Putnam could raise up her hands, poking fingers through to touch the stars.

Lights dimmed, the music faded and a voice fountained from the projector, talking about pole stars and Betelgeuse and Charles's Wain. The names didn't matter to Mrs. Putnam; she was lying in the grass on the Island with Adam — they had rented one of the small canoes and paddled out to the hand's breadth of land that was now a bird sanctuary; they had beached the canoe and were lying on their backs in wild, tall grass, watching the stars. For once he was not wearing his fedora; she had on her finger a ring with one diamond and a band of twenty-four-carat gold. Rosamund was in Mount Pleasant, and even

Althea had been sent back home to Thunder Bay to parents who had at last decided that the advantages of a private education did not outweigh the loving kindness to be found only in the bosom of one's family. Softly Hilary opened lips that time had not so much as crumpled:

> Now sleeps the crimson petal, now the white. . . . Now lies
> the earth all Danae to the stars . . .

and the stars sang back to her. They were not crystal splinters as children imagined them, but round, fragrant as waterlilies you might pick off the mirror of a lake and hold up to your face, breathing in their succulence and fragrance . . .

Across the table from her someone began to snore with all the violence of a chainsaw massacre. It was hot in the darkened room, the leatherette under Mrs. Putnam's hands began to feel like fur, and she was floating somewhere between floor and stars. The voice was talking now about satellites and lasers. Mrs. Putnam remembered hearing on the radio that before long man would be able to orbit messages in space — celestial billboards advertising Pepsi or the other cola, *billets-doux* or messages of condolence that could circle Earth forever, forcing their stories down peoples' very eyes. If it were possible, floating through a darkness cut to ribboned light — what would they say were she to chisel it into the night sky: *Rosamund, detested of Adam who loved Hilary alone,* Hilary who loved Keats and Tennyson and silk against her skin and all the powders and perfumes of Araby she could not wear to St. Radigonde's, but which she would apply each evening upon coming home, whether Adam were coming or not, whether she believed in him or not, coming or going, leaving or loving, Betelgeuse and Charles's Wain, Miss or Mrs. Putnam, Althea and detested Rosamund and petalled stars in the night sky, looking down where she lay, in her story, nobody else's story — head lolling against the squashed leatherette as a voice explained the simulated stars shifting, blooming, exploding on the painted ceiling over the sleeping dark in which Mrs. Putnam lies curled tight, a newborn's fist around some fiction of a finger to grab onto, climbing steep black spaces in between the stars.

JANICE KULYK KEEFER

The Wind
(1986)

Not Gustave Thibault, dying, but the wind woke Father Hartland, invading his ears like some hysterical woman searching out with dagger fingernails those bowels of compassion of which not even Christ Himself could speak without Father Hartland's gorge helplessly rising, a black and bilious balloon . . . Madame Samson pounding the warped panels of the door, giving him the news of old Thibault, making him understand what was wanted of him, again, for of dying and ministering to death there is no end. By the time she'd thudded on down the hall, the old priest had dropped to his knees beside the iron bed and recited his morning prayers, though it was not yet two o'clock and only the wind crowed outside his window. Against the damp plaster wall a twist and droop of metal, rattling. "My God, My King": Father Hartland's small brown eyes downing the crucifix as if it were the shot of brandy given to revive shock victims, survivors of catastrophes. He rose, and forced cold flesh into the serge of his clerical suit. Madame Samson, through skillful, sadistic use of starch and soap, could make the cloth last almost forever, no mean skill in a parish too poor to do more than purchase gold and silver thread to darn the mothy copes and chasubles in the vestry.

In the kitchen the electric light was crackling: a power failure looming, or just the final frying of the flies that had piled there since summer? . . . *Deliver him from going down into the pit* . . . Madame Samson handed him a mug — white institutional china; his fingers trembled with its weight. Black coffee so hot he winced as his lips met the steam. He held the mug close to him, as though his face were a pane of frost-strewn glass to be thawed back to transparency.

Father Schell's scraping walk down the corridor, into the kitchen, to the stiff net curtains over the sink. He pushed them apart, disclosing a small rectangle of night — black, bitter, comfortless as the coffee.

"Cold as hell with that wind, I'll wager." Father Hartland thumped the empty mug on the enamel table. "Cold as hell, I said, man. And what in hell are you looking for out that window — a funeral barge to take us down to Thibault's shack? Drink up your coffee and let's get the thing done with."

Father Hartland was sixty-odd, prone to phlebitis and petty blasphemies. Father Schell had worked with him for the last five years without losing his temper or loosing a single confidence, a continence the older man deplored as spiritual pride. Cultivating mysteries: washing up here on the French Shore from somewhere in Germany via the Sorbonne, or so the Monsignor had let it be known. Appointed as aide to Father Hartland, whom the Monsignor feared was failing; stayed on, despite the old priest's rudeness, his interminable railing at St. Alphonse Bay, where the soil was so poor the very wildflowers were carnivorous, where the sea had become so niggardly they could manage lobster only once a year, for Christmas.

If it hadn't been for the Sorbonne degree, Father Hartland would have dismissed the young priest as a simpleton. For Father Schell seemed to be staying on with him not in some superb act of contrition, nor even in iron obedience to the Monsignor, but in perfect acceptance of a fate as given, unalterable as a multiplication table. Whereas Father Hartland — he had tried to explain to the young priest that first year — how he'd grown up in Manchester, studied art in London after the war, and gone, a frankly lapsed and distanced Catholic, on just one freakish trip to Rome, as much for the women to be found in the Colosseum after dark as for the Treasures of the Vatican. How on a random Sunday morning he'd gone off for an hour to see the mosaics in Santa Maria Maggiore, had stayed on for high Mass and eight years at the seminary across the road. Long enough to know that his faith, God's grace and the Janiculum at sunset were as securely interwoven as the Trinity Itself.

The fall: abrupt, final as from a mountain cable car. From golden stone, blossoming oleander to a spruce-bogged, rockbound coast which didn't even have the sense to look homeward; like a child banished to a corner, it faced the even foggier wastes of New Brunswick. Banishment among a foreign people whose language he could read but barely speak and who resented the Irish-American Monsignor and the strange priests his Roman connections foisted on them. Perpetual exile, for there was nothing else Father Hartland could imagine doing that would not undo his eight years in Rome, nothing, either, that could make him go back as some kind of pious tourist to his soul's birthplace, its only home. All this he'd confessed to Father Schell, who'd merely listened, blank as an unaddressed envelope.

Madame Samson came with their coats. Schell took his silently, the heels of his rubber boots squealing on the pared-down linoleum of the hall. Father Hartland tendered thanks in his arthritic French as she passed him the gloves and scarf that would ward off the wind, gibbering now through the rectory's windows and eaves, making the housekeeper's eyelids shiver. A puffy woman with flesh the weak white of raw potatoes and slow-moving tortoise eyes. Her Christian name was Aurore — an incongruity Father Hartland would hug to himself the way he had, as a child, the small, sharp cars with which he'd pile his bed at night.

Schell wrenched open the door — the wind came lolloping in like a great stupid dog, almost knocking him over. He steadied himself against the metal railing of the concrete steps down which Father Hartland was terrified of falling. He waited for the old man, offering him an arm; together they clumped down and finally touched bottom. Heads bowed, trouser legs whipping and stinging their shanks, they staggered to the rusted-out Ford the village's one rich fisherman had dumped on the rectory, for remission of repair bills if not of sins. Breathing this air was like swallowing sea water. Father Hartland could taste blood, sweat, semen, tears, everything mortal forced down his throat to choke him. He fell, gasping, into the passenger seat, scouring his face with a handkerchief to get rid of the dank salt smell.

The whole world pulled away with them as the car lunged out of the parking lot into wind that rocked the car like a runaway cradle, dashing them against the doors as if to racket their very eyeballs from their sockets. Father Hartland grabbed at the one thing stuck rigid and unwavering in the riotous black: the lightbulbs screwed into the halo of Our Lady, stranded on her concrete pedestal in the dead sea of the church parking lot. She would be lifting eggshell eyes to stars the clouds had shrouded. He could make out only a murky gleam below the blare of her crown.

"*Ave maris stella, Ave* General Electric." He murmured the blasphemy by rote, loosening the scarf from his neck; the rough wool pricked the cuts he'd made shaving too hastily an hour before. His collar would be scrawled with blood — the deceased's wife would complain to the Monsignor again. But Thibault had no wife, he remembered, only a daughter living somewhere down the coast, toward Matou. And he wasn't deceased yet; they were battling down this road, risking demon cold and wind to catch Thibault's soul, as if it were one of the mink that escaped every so often from the little concentration-camp huts in which the farmer penned them. His nostrils dilated — he loathed mink, the sleekness and stink of them. Thibault had no wife, so who would be with him at the shack? No wife and no religion either; why on God's earth had they been called out on a night like this? Even using Christ's arm as a crowbar, who could pry Gustave Thibault from hell's teeth? Not Father Hartland, who heard them grinding even in his sleep . . .

"No religion, that old soak Thibault." Father Hartland said it tentatively, testing his companion. "Damn fool's errand. We might as well have stayed in our beds — not that we were warm, but safe at least. This isn't wind, it's a bloody hurricane, man. Old Aurore's hallucinating. How could there have been a telephone call when there's nothing in Thibault's shack but a mattress and chickens befouling the one chair I saw the time I was idiot enough to visit him. We'll be blown halfway across the bay before we even reach the turnoff."

Schell's words clattered out like ice cubes from a tray. "I could turn round and take you back, Father. I can manage on my own, if that is what you want."

"That's not what I want, and you damn well know it. I want . . ."

The car lurched on. Once the wind, blurting from behind a screen of spruce, clawed and nearly flipped it over; once Father Hartland was on the verge of asking Schell to stop at one of the black ghosts of houses along the highway, to wait in its shelter till the wind died down. The only living thing either saw was what may have been the shadow of a cat, skidding like quicksilver across the path cleared by the headlights. Finally the car slowed, stopped and made the turn onto the gravel path to Weaver's Mills.

Even had there been moon and stars there would have been little enough to see. It was outside their parish; Thibault was the only Acadian among the scattered families, mostly black, all English-speaking. No houses, only a few trailers steadily shedding their aluminum sills and window frames. Laundry lines betraying the impossible number of children squashed inside. They knew it all by heart — the way the gravel guttered suddenly into mud and rocks, the dismal clearings where loggers would pose for a season or two on equal terms with the muck and mosquitoes. *Deck thyself now with majesty and excellency; and array thyself with glory and beauty.* Flogged chesterfields rotting slowly in the ditches; beer bottles, rum bottles, wine bottles, every possible colour and permutation of glass. And always, at some crazed corner, a new, crude raw-box of a Gospel Hall. THE WAGES OF SIN IS DEATH. JESUS LOVES YOU!!! The wages of love are exile on a scratch of soil over sheer rock, under a sky whose clouds are boulders piled against the opening of the tomb. *Credo, credo,* but if only someone could tell him why, after Rome, after morning light on the mosaics, each golden tile dissolving on the soul's sweet tongue . . . I want, I want . . .

"Father Hartland, I am sorry to wake you, but we are here —"

"I wasn't asleep, I was praying."

Diving out of the car, dodging the suck and gust of wind, they soaked their boots in puddled mud and excrement before the door in which the woman waited.

"He lived bad, he's gonna die good."

She didn't need to introduce herself, though she'd never shown her face at mass or confession. Everyone knew the generations of everyone else in and around St. Alphonse Bay. Only Fathers Hartland and Schell were exempt from the genealogical inquisition, the gossip their parishioners spread like jam on toast. This woman, Gustave Thibault's daughter Simone, had never set foot in her father's shack after her thirteenth birthday, when she'd fled to the nuns at Matou and learned to wash, clean her teeth, say prayers. Went to work folding boxes at Comeau's Crates; took night-school courses. Married, quit Comeau's Crates, opened the only florist's shop on the French Shore and now dyed carnations pink and blue for births, for funerals sold blood-black roses. No children. No religion. No one had it any more, even if they did show up for Sunday mass, as sure of Heaven as they were of bingo nights on Wednesday. None who had religion the way you have a birthmark, a stutter, a defective heart, the way Father Hartland had had it all these years since Rome, since his superior and the superior's superiors had decided that John Hartland's spiritual if not aesthetic state demanded he be turned out of doors into a bitter land and bleaker tongue: "notre Sibérie," the first priests in St. Alphonse Bay had called it.

He left Father Schell to talk to the woman and picked his way to the disembowelled mattress where Thibault was choking on his own breath. Father Hartland scratched himself uneasily; lice can smell death miles away, the floor would be crusted with them, staking out a trouser leg, a dangling vestment to mount. The dying man's eyes were half-closed; a viscous liquid had formed at their corners, and there was spittle on his lips. The priest, his own face puffed and pale, bent his head close to Thibault's eyes as if they were some token of a soul caged so long in foulness only Heaven's incalculable grace could have kept one fingertip of it clean. Bent toward Thibault — and drew back as if a fist had ploughed his face, so colossal was the reek of rum. She must have been sloshing it down the old bugger's throat to keep him quiet, to keep him alive until they could get there. Screech and holy oil so he could die good. *His flesh consumed away, that it cannot be seen, and his bones that were not seen stick out* . . . He tried to make a sign to Father Schell, who was standing angular as a coat rack, eyes bruised with tiredness.

Father Schell shrugged, but the woman kept on talking, her voice harsh, whingeing, reminding Father Hartland of the crows, huge as chickens, which nested in the spruce grove by the rectory. She was insisting on something to do with funeral arrangements; she had made small, sharp fists and was holding them up in front of her nobbly breasts. A skimped, stiff woman, hair dyed the colour of fog, a nebulous blond; cheeks and eyelids painted with the precision another woman might put into an embroidery stitch. No children, but a pale pink scarf round her neck, pinned by a gilt brooch in the shape of an S. No religion but salvation of sorts, a climb out of another kind of pit.

Father Hartland, brushing real or imaginary lice from his trouser legs, walked stiffly from the mattress to the door. He asked Schell to make the preparations; he told Thibault's daughter her silence would be an inestimable help and gave her a rosary from his pocket. Then he returned to the dying man on the mattress, emaciated, cruelly twisted as the Christ upon the wall over Father Hartland's own bed. Outside the whirlwind, and the voice from the whirlwind that could wrench golden stones from basilica walls but would not blow down a tarpaper shack. That could command, but never answer, never explain the fault: had he been too glad, too pliantly good, walking to prayers past tubs of oleander, pink and fragrant tongues of bliss, into this sty? *Canst thou draw out Leviathan with a hook?* Some word, some phrase, some small assurance Christ, my King *who laid the foundations of the earth, when*

the morning stars sang together and all the sons of God shouted for joy.
Why this? Why here? And how long, my God, how long and how much
more . . .

The moment of Gustave Thibault's death his daughter sat on a sheet
of plastic she'd draped over the shack's one chair, absently jingling the
rosary like a ring of car keys. Father Hartland closed and weighted the
eyes, and in an involuntary act of compassion put the clean linen cloth
in which the missal had been wrapped over the dead skin and hair and
bone. Father Schell, kneeling beside the mattress, saw something the size
and colour of a woodlouse quit the corpse, scuttle between the floor
boards and burrow down into dirt.

They stopped for coffee on the way back to the rectory, but it was
too early. The truckers' café, like the rectory, should have had a small
enamel plate with "Ring and Enter," a guarantee that all who came to
the door would be received, given their due of meat and drink. Beside
the reflection of his own large, soft face in the café window Father
Hartland could see Schell's, stark as the planks of the Cross. The men
stepped back, returned to the car, and, at Father Hartland's request,
took a small road that branched off from the highway toward the sea.

The wind had died; there was only the barest ruffling of dingy spruce
boughs along this road. Another slow turning and they could make out,
behind a long, low dune of stones, the waters of the bay: flint-coloured,
dishevelled. Gulls were roosting in the trenches of the waves, and the
sun had not risen but merely diffused itself through rags of cloud.
Schell stopped the car beside a weathered clapboard structure that
might have been a changing-hut for swimmers were it not so small and
rickety. The priests walked over the flat grey stones, stopping at a line
of spruce that marked the former shoreline of the bay, the shore to
which the ancestors of Gustave Thibault had stumbled back from exile.
Hulks of spruce, like giant castoff wooden limbs, silvered by a watery
sun. They felt spray on their lips, put out tongues to lick the salt away.
Father Schell crossed himself and began his morning prayers; Father
Hartland turned his back and walked across the stones to the hut.

It was stranded on its own shore of rock and rusted mailboxes,
dissevered antennae and bedsprings through whose coils black mustard
and a few spindly daisies still swivelled up. Five yards from the wooden
steps leading to its door a placard proclaimed "The First Chapel on the

French Shore." Father Hartland pulled from the much-mended depths of his pocket a long iron key, which he fitted to the lock. The priests came, when they remembered, to make sure that nothing inside the hut had been prised from the walls or ruined by rain leaking through the slowly rotting shingles. He genuflected to the plaster figure of the Virgin which he'd ordered from the catalogue some eighteen years ago. But where the Christ should be — marble flesh the voluptuous paleness of whipped cream — he saw only that twist of iron rattling him awake, the mangled bone and skin of the dead man in the shack up the logger's road.

He slammed his eyes shut on little daggers of light. He knew he should say the prayers, make the signs: words without knowledge, sound without voice. *Shall he that contendeth with the Almighty instruct Him? Thine hands have made me and fashioned me together round about; yet thou dost destroy me . . .* Squeezing his eyelids tighter Father Hartland tried to conjure up the images he'd stuck into his flesh like sacred thorns: that Roman morning when the sky's gold rained into his eyes, sweetly blinding as the priest raised the Host, glittering, exultant. But they would not come; no nick against the skin of memory, only the look, the smell, the feel, in that foul shack, of a long-dying animal whose soul was brother to John Hartland's own, crying "I want, I want, I want everything that will not be given me, that I cannot take for myself . . ." Whose nakedness he knew to be that of John Hartland, now and in the hour of his death, before the God who had kept him prisoned in His hand all these years and years hedged in; the God who would not answer, would no longer bless, but who had made him, all the same.

The priest gripped the chapel key in his hand; he could smell iron through the sweat of his palms. Behind him, Father Schell was saying they should be on their way, there would be the funeral mass to arrange. Father Hartland opened his eyes, twisted round to look at the young priest, a presence palpable, impenetrable as the palm of the hand he was holding out to help the old man down. Slowly, Father Hartland turned the key inside the grudging lock. Then, as if he had no longer any fear of falling, he shook his head at the hand stretched out to him. Stiffly, heavily, Father Hartland walked down the chapel stairs to the car. The young priest followed him wordlessly. Their car shifted a few stones as it lurched back to the highway and disappeared into the calm obscurity of day.

JANETTE TURNER HOSPITAL

Queen of Pentacles, Nine of Swords
(1986)

First I noticed her condition, then her startling nose-jewel (a diamond teardrop), and only after that her remarkable face. This was years ago, the first time she came into my ratty apartment on Earl Street. She was eight months pregnant and nineteen years old at the time, and still wearing *salwar-kameez*; but the pantaloons were giving her trouble in the snow, and she had tucked them into boots that a local pig farmer must have given to the Sally Ann. A vinyl stamp on the uppers said *Thurston Farms, Kingston, Ont.* The parka was another cast-off, bilious green, its hood ringed with mangy fake fur. Inside it, she had the eyes of a tiger.

On the sofa that served as my waiting room she sat next to a housewife who edged discreetly away. My customers were uneasy with foreigners. They stared. The girl opened her bag (a drawstring sack, beaded and brocaded with elephants and little mirrors) and began to work: fingers flying, a cream silk streamer of crochet snaking out of her hands, twitching, growing, curling under the sofa like some live nervy creature.

Perhaps it was simply that we didn't know Indian women crocheted. I suppose we thought of it as something our grandmothers once did, as something that went out with lavender pomanders and maiden aunts.

(Months later she was to tell me sardonically that ever since 1851, ever since the Great Exhibition and the Crystal Palace, when all the prizes for crochet went to the corners of the empire, it has been Kenyans, Trinidadians, Tamils — whomever the missionaries taught — who have been keeping the lace-making arts alive.)

But back then we knew nothing of that. We stared.

She ignored us and crocheted as if she were under a curse.

That was seventeen years ago, but it is the first image that comes back to me when Decker calls.

"Metro Toronto Police," he says, "I'm calling in connection with a woman named Sita Ramshankar."

"Oh," I said faintly, bracing myself.

"I know it's a long way, but we'd appreciate it if you could come on into the city, ma'am. Bloor Street station."

"Right now?"

"We'd appreciate it."

In the car, disoriented, I half turn around to see if the boys are safely strapped into the back seat — Sita's son and my son, our little boys who have part-time jobs and are almost through high school now.

I try to remember why the children are not in the car. I stare vaguely at the bunch of keys in my hand and just sit there in my garage.

She is still and always coming into my room with her swollen belly and the diamond blister in her nostril. Something powerful, some strong animal sense, warns me: don't read her cards. But I am cornered, when it's her turn, by the way she holds out the five-dollar bill and by her eyes. Or perhaps it has something to do with the ribbon of crochet that twitches as she loops it up and stuffs it into her bag. She's the last for the day; there are just the two of us.

"I have seen your advertisement," she says, and the English is sterling, crisp as a new pound note, discordant. She smells of poverty in spite of the diamond teardrop, and her eyes unnerve me.

Listen, I want to say, I don't read for True Believers. I put on this gypsy smock and my dangling earrings (the crescent moon on my left ear, the star on my right) and presto: desolate suburban wives are able to unburden themselves. In the cards they see little Markey, who is having trouble at school, and Darlene, who is nubile and recently divorced and always borrowing someone's husband on account of engine trouble, and Mr. Dunlap the electrician who didn't install the baseboard heater properly but won't come back to fix it. I promise a letter from Winnipeg, an unexpected visitor from Montreal. I throw in a bit of solemnity, a little closing of the eyes and deep breathing, a pinch of hope, and they go away happy. The housewife's therapist. I'm cheaper, after all, than a night of bingo or a Sears catalogue binge.

I ignore her five dollars and pour her a cup of tea. "What's your name?"

"Sita." She points to the Tarot pack, implying urgency. Between her palms, the money is rolled back and forth, back and forth; it furls itself tighter, becomes a reefer, a taper, a skewer. She looks at it, puzzled, then places it delicately on my saucer.

There are some people . . . I don't know what it is . . . they give off the same kind of hum as high tension cables. You know from the start that if you get too close you'll be singed. And yet they're the very ones — don't you find this? — who make you understand the moths.

Still, I make an effort to resist.

"I can't take your money," I tell her. "Listen, your husband is a graduate student, right? So is mine. This is how I manage, that's all." I show her the crib in the other room, my baby asleep. "This pays a few bills," I say. "But I can't read your cards, I'm a fraud."

For a moment she stares at me, eyebrows raised, then she laughs — a short, harsh, incredulous sound. "It's the *cards*," she says, as if to the village idiot. "The cards themselves. Don't you understand?" Under her breath she murmurs, "Canadians!" and shakes her head. Without asking, she picks up the deck and begins to shuffle. She shuffles vertically, cards fluttering between her hands, descending, then rising mysteriously like geese in formation. "Read," she says, placing the pack in front of me. And as an afterthought, "Please."

She's intense as a junkie, desperate, but also used to power and accustomed to giving orders. Nothing fits. Stalling, I ask, "How long have you been in Canada?"

Eye to eye over the cards, we breathe each other's breath, I can smell coriander and something else, something musky and irresistible and dangerous.

"I have been here six months. There was the marriage, and then I came. It was arranged." She taps the Tarot impatiently. "You are reading the cards now, isn't it?"

There's a certain peremptory tone I've never cared for. "Read them yourself," I say evenly. "I'm not your servant."

Her knuckles turn white and crack like tiny silver pistols. "Please." The fingers are rigid now — the strain of politeness, of supplication. "The importance is very great."

I don't understand why I do it. I cut three times to the left and draw ten cards.

"Ah," I say flippantly, relieved. "Here, in your current situation, we have the Page of Cups, which means the birth of a child is imminent.

And he's crossed by the Knight of Cups, who is your husband. But who's this in your past, in the Seven of Swords? This trickster making off with stolen goods?"

She is holding her head in her hands like the ravaged woman in the Nine of Swords who dominates the spread. "Again," she says. "Again, again, again." As though she can feel the prick of the nine deadly swords poised above her.

What was the next time?

Quattrochi's, just a week or so later. Quattrochi's, which is such an unlikely store to find in a small Ontario town that I've always half suspected it vanishes when I'm not shopping there to believe in it. Quattrochi's smells of cinnamon and saffron; loops of chili peppers, squash flowers, the mysterious ingredients of *garam masala*, all hang from the walls; there are baskets of mangos, passionfruit, papayas, guavas. I was not surprised, somehow, to see Sita there.

She was stroking the purple bellies of eggplants, prodding their curves with a finger. On the basket, a crayoned sign said: *Spoiled vegetables. Prices reduced.*

"Any day now, I expect," I greeted her politely, leaning across melons and pineapples.

"No," she said, feeling and poking. "It is too late, but they will have to do."

"I meant your baby."

Her eyes widened, then she flashed me that withering look: of scorn? of disbelief? "But I will lose the baby," she said.

I suppose she found me slow or perhaps wilfully obtuse. The need to explain exasperated her. ("*Canadians!*")

"The Nine of Swords." Her fingers drummed on the handle of the shopping cart. "India, England, Canada, it makes no difference."

I blinked. "You're not suggesting . . . ?"

"For me, the predictions are always very bad."

"You're just nervous," I assure her, patting her hand. "I was, too, this close. It's normal."

"You know nothing." She pinched the skin of an eggplant savagely, and amethyst rind came away in her hand. "My father got a second opinion. An astrologer was brought from Madras. It was the same."

"I can't believe . . . I mean, you're educated, you're married to a . . ."

"Oh, yes, I know," she snapped. "I'm *Canadian* now. The cautious people, the safe people."

"There's no need to be —"

"I will show you. You will read for me again."

"I most certainly will not."

And when I did, back in my Earl Street apartment, it was there again: the Nine of Swords. "You cheated," I accused. "It was the way you shuffled."

She ignored me.

Without, I think, being aware of what she was doing, she fiddled in her drawstring bag and pulled out the ivory hook and began to crochet. Faster, faster, the silken thread creamy and skittish. She never took her eyes off the cards. "Look, the Queen of Staves. She's the headmistress at Finchley Academy for Girls."

"Finchley?"

"In England, I hated England. She shipped me straight back to Tanjore after Mr. Timkins . . . he was the history master . . ." She patted her stomach, to indicate the nature of homework for Mr. Timkins, who would have been helpless, I imagine, from the moment she tossed her black mane and fluttered her slow heavy lashes. I remember feeling a spasm of sympathy for him, fellow fly in a web.

"What happened to Mr. Timkins?"

She paused momentarily, puckered her brows, shrugged. "He was fired, I think."

She might have been discussing Mr. Dunlap of unsatisfactory electrical installations, or wanton Darlene. "Anyway, Daddy flew to Bombay to meet me. He didn't want me seen in Tanjore. Poor Daddy. But he couldn't say he wasn't warned." The family astrologer had told them over and over: nothing could be done to offset such an inauspicious time of birth.

The snake of crochet jumped and twitched and lay still.

"So what else could Daddy do? In Canada, Daddy said, they don't even have shame." Add to Canada — Canada! — a student husband, a family with no money: it was what they could salvage, she said. She was married by proxy. Her husband met her in Montreal. She said wistfully, "My sister lives in Paris. She is married to an executive of Burma Shell."

"I imagine Daddy will take care of everything," I said tartly. "Here's the Queen of Pentacles. You're going to be rich and famous."

"Rich." Her lip curled. "My family has great wealth." She made a gesture with her fingers, as of flicking away a dandelion puffball, to show how much great wealth meant. "I'm off Daddy's hands now. I'm Ramshankar's problem. I'll lose the baby," she said.

She did lose the baby, but then there was another, her husband's this time. And then another.

Here's a fresh picture, fallen suddenly into focus:

We are sifting through a table of children's snowsuits at the Salvation Army Thrift Store. Sita is feeling the padding of a powder blue suit, assessing the thin spots. She tugs at the jammed zipper, which comes away in her hands like a tear along a dotted line.

"You can stitch it," I say.

She says: "Ramshankar is leaving me."

"What?"

"He is suing for custody of the children."

"What?"

"On account of my affair."

I stare at her, dumbfounded.

"You know Professor Parkinson?" she asks.

"In the Business School?"

"That one. It's him."

I smooth out the tattered lining of a snowsuit that is covered with blips of mildew and with larger black blotches. Car grease, perhaps. The table stinks of recycled odours. A *lover*, I think. I see bodies gliding and writhing like swans in the quilted tangle of hollow arms and legs. I push my hand down the inside of a sleeve and think hungrily: *another man's skin.* "I had no idea," I mumble. "I've never seen you with —"

"Oh, *seen*! I'm not for being seen with. I'm for hot fucking and sly bragging."

"Well," I say, nervously. "The mother always gets the children."

"Ramshankar knows how to do these things, from Law School. It's interesting, what stirs a man to life." She is racing the broken zipper head up and down its aimless track, up and down. "Ramshankar is so . . . you wouldn't believe how *poor*! I don't mean money; it has nothing to do with money. But he is a *poor* man, a *poor* man." She is spitting the words. "There is no spirit, there is nothing." She pays for the blue snowsuit with her Family Allowance cheque. Her hand is trembling slightly as she signs her name. "Anyway, before I became a little too hot for comfort, Parkie had me write that Admissions thing." She laughs and says sardonically, "Apparently I'm brilliant." She makes a mistake with her address on the back of the cheque and has to initial it. "It will be simpler without the children for a few years, actually. I'm starting a business degree."

In the car, we strap the toddlers into their safety seats. "Anyway," she begins, but suddenly buries her face in the zipperless blue snowsuit and holds it there all the way to the Co-op Nursery School. The boys — my Joey and her Ravi — come running to the car with their play-dough airplanes and fingerprinted pictures of happy families. "Anyway, if I'm destitute, I can always sell crochet. You wouldn't believe what the Yorkville boutiques are beginning to pay for that stuff."

This strikes her as funny. She begins to laugh and can't seem to stop. She scoops up her son and tries to stifle her hilarity by nuzzling the hollow of his neck. She stuffs one of his mismatched mittens into her mouth. Whoops of laughter escape like bubbles under pressure.

Her son looks frightened.

We're in a restaurant in this scene, we're in Toronto in a restaurant off Bay Street. The wine steward is tripping over his own feet with obsequious nervousness in Sita's presence. She orders a bottle of something French, the price of which makes me gulp once or twice, and brushes him away.

"So." She picks at her smoked salmon with a fork, nibbles a flowerlet of parsley. "What do you hear from Joey about Ravi?"

"Well, you know," I say nervously. "Grade twelve and grade ten, they're different countries. It's only during basketball season . . ." I feel ill at ease for being so ordinary: still living in a small town, still married, still on speaking — even on hugging — terms with my children.

"A place like that," she says. "People talk all the time. Everyone knows everyone's business."

"But I never pay attention . . . you know I can't stand that sort of . . ." I have no intention of telling her the rumours. What can you expect, people say, of a kid with a mother who . . . ? It's a town that disapproves of the unusual. (There are people who claim to have seen Sita on lower Yonge Street. Late at night, they say, walking up and down and wearing skin-tight leather pants. People will say anything.)

Ravi, in fact, is often at our house since his father joined a law firm in Calgary. Ravi sort of camps around. But there's too much in the past for me to tell her any of this. There's the business of the kidnapping, for example, and of Ravi and Prem running away again to their father — or perhaps simply back to the known circle of school friends. Anyway, just too much past. "Ravi's okay," I say. "He's an okay kid. He's an *interesting* kid, Sita. Give him time, he'll come to cherish the fact he has an extraordinary mother."

With her fork, she has divided the smoked salmon into multiple thin strips, none of which she has eaten. "Prem writes," she says. "He has to do it secretly. He has to sneak out to the Calgary post office. He wants me to get him away from his father."

With great concentration, I break a dinner roll apart and butter it.

"I had a reading done last month," she says. "Some U of T student wife. Guess what card came up?"

"Queen of Pentacles, I imagine. I can't believe you still go in for that stuff."

"Queen of Pentacles, too, for what that's worth."

"Worth plenty, apparently. Remember I predicted fame and fortune way back? How does it feel to be made a partner?"

"To be the token woman and token black in the company, you mean? I drive them crazy. They can't stand it that I crochet in board meetings."

I try to imagine this. I see a circle of pinstriped men, a flash of smoke and vermilion sparks, a little dervish of crochet twisting and turning on the boardroom table. Sita plays on her snake-charmer's pipes. There is a drowsy smell of incense, and the men with silver hair and combed moustaches begin to sway and rise like cobras with the wisp of crochet. Sita keeps time with her ivory needle, hooking, hooking.

"I'm bored out of my mind in strategy meetings," she says vehemently. "All these people who can only do one thing at a time. I have to listen to their minds crawling along, clunk, clunk, clunk. I'm going to have to move on, find something with more bite to it. Do you ever get the feeling when you wake in the morning that you just want to sink your teeth into the day and suck at it and suck at it? And it never *ever* has enough juice to make it worthwhile?"

"Sita, you can't just . . . can't you see that you're *programming* yourself for . . . I mean, this obsession with the Nine of Swords. And inauspicious birth, for God's sake! You've got terribly self-destructive —"

"Ah," she says cuttingly. "Psychology. The Canadian form of the occult."

"You worry me. You haven't eaten a thing."

"I'm ravenous. *Ravenous!*" she says.

Sergeant Decker is ill at ease. "I can't figure this lady. I just can't figure her. Appreciate your coming all this way." He goes to a file cabinet, rifles through a drawer, pulls out a blue manila folder. "Long drive. How was the 401?"

"Uh . . . so-so." But I cannot remember what the traffic was like. I cannot remember getting here at all.

He is shaking his head. "Third time in as many months. Little twist to this one, though. This time she's not at the receiving end. No smashed-up lip, no bruises." His eyebrows lift. "You didn't know about that?"

For some reason, I notice there is a slat missing in the Venetian blind on the window above his desk. Third from the top.

"She gave you as next-of-kin. She — ah — married to a relative or something? Well, none of my business." He looks through the folder. "Yeah," he says, "Yeah. She has a taste for violent johns."

Then he settles himself into his chair and leans across his desk. "What really blows our minds," he says, and I note the proprietary cast to his voice. He likes to talk about her. His case. "Turns out she's a big wheel on Bay Street. Well, of course you know. I check it our because of the too-fancy car, which I assume is her pimp's and probably stolen. Trail leads to this glitzy building. I step out of the elevator on the sixteenth floor, and she's standing there in this grey suit with a red silk thing around her neck. Looking like the ice princess herself. You could've knocked me over with a feather. Course," he says. "Coloureds. You never know, do you?"

He tosses a sheet of paper in front of me. "Arrest, this time. Shoplifting. Has to appear in court on the fourteenth."

"Now" — he leans forward, resting his chin on his clasped hands — "that lady must make two, three times what I make. Something weird is going on here."

I nod. I feel a little sick. The missing slat in the Venetian blind seems to have ominous importance. I swallow, I mentally rehearse words, I form the question in my mind. But do I want to know? Decker goes on as though I have asked anyway.

"Woolworth's. Fifteen, twenty dollars worth of junk. Yarn. Silk thread. The kind of stuff ladies do embroidery with. Crochet hooks. You willing to take her with you?"

I nod.

When she is brought out, I see the way he gets nervous. Oh, Decker, I think. You too. He rushes her a little with awkward courtesies: returning her labelled possessions, handing her his pen for the signature. A policewoman takes her into the next room for photographs. Decker shakes his head, fondly possessive. "Just can't figure her," he says. "Crazy Paki."

"Sita," I say in the restaurant across from the police station. "I'm taking you home with me."

"Not there," she says with a shudder. "I couldn't ever go back there. That was the worst place, the worst place of all."

"But Sita, they were good years. Those years when the children were little —"

She looks me directly in the eyes, and I feel glib. "You weren't me," she says. She fiddles in her bag and pulls out her ivory hook and a ball of silk. She begins to crochet by instinct, without looking at the work in her hands. "I've got friends who have a cottage north of Barrie," she says. "Tamils. I'll go there for a while. Can you drop me at the Voyageur terminal?"

"No, I'm not going to do that. At least I'll take you home for your car."

"I can't *stand* the car. It's so . . . nothing *happens* in the car. Will you take me to Dundas Street, or do I have to get a cab?"

At the bus terminal, I catch hold of her arm. "Sita, I'm afraid to leave you."

For just the merest second, she permits herself to be held. She butts her forehead against mine. "Don't blame yourself," she says. "No one could have done anything." She clears her throat. "Tell Ravi . . ." Then she shakes off. "Listen," she says. "I don't want you hanging around."

But I do hang around. I stand shivering out on Dundas Street, watching through the grimy glass doors of the waiting room as she sits there crocheting feverishly. I watch right up until a man with a shaved head and a tattoo on his arm saunters over and puts his foot on the chair next to hers. He leans toward her. His boot is close to her thigh. There is something about his swagger that I don't like, I don't like at all. But she smiles up at him and begins to stuff her crochet work into her drawstring bag.

A week later Decker calls.

CAROL WINDLEY

Dreamland
(1987)

In India, Lillian's husband shot and killed a tiger. She did not herself witness this event and found it difficult to imagine her husband, an austere and proper man, intimately involved in that uncompromising moment of blood and passion when the tiger took the shot into its living body. But it was happily conceded by everyone who had been on the hunt: the tiger belonged to Lillian's husband. Its skin was displayed on the polished floor of the house they occupied in Madras State. The tiger's skull was unexpectedly small and innocent; its eyes were gold-coloured glass, blind. Lillian sat with her feet resting on the tiger's back as she read or sewed. Secretly, she asked it to carry her away to the hills, to the far-off mountains.

For nearly twenty years Lillian and her husband lived in India, most of the time in Madras State. They had four children, all boys. At about the time that Lillian could count on the fingers of one hand the years left until her husband's retirement from the Indian Civil Service, he invited her to his office and showed her a map spread out on his desk. The map was of Canada, a country about which Lillian knew absolutely nothing. Her husband pointed to a dot of land on the left-hand side of the map.

"This is where we are going," he said.

Lillian did not understand. She placed her hand on a corner of the desk to steady herself, to keep from falling into the cold, painted waters, to keep from catching her hair and dress on the jagged edge of the ochre land mass. Her husband began to talk about annual rainfall, mean temperatures, a temperate climate, the benign influence of certain ocean currents. He spoke of the mystery, the beauty, of the northern rain forest, of which he had lately read, and in fact heard, from various sources. And the silence, he said. And the distance, the enormous, incontestable distance from India, the India of the British Raj, of which he had had more than enough.

"But we are going home," said Lillian, meaning home to England.

"We are not 'going home,'" her husband said. Then he tapped the map sharply with his finger. "We are going here. This will be our home."

He seemed to gloat; he looked ferocious and triumphant. Lillian thought: the soul of the tiger has entered his soul. She felt afraid of her husband, not, perhaps, for the first time. As soon as she had returned to the house she went straight to a table in the sitting room where she kept writing paper and a pen. She wrote her husband's name quickly on a scrap of paper; then she burned the paper in a brass censer that hung in the sitting room and was meant to be only decorative. But she put it to use. The flames consumed her husband's name, and in this way she removed him from her mind.

That was India in 1919, and now it is one year later, and Lillian and her children actually inhabit the place on the map. It is where they live. They are on the west coast of an island that is itself on the extreme west coast of Canada. They live in a fishing village of perhaps two hundred people or less. Her husband brought his family here and then he returned to India, alone, to finish up the three years until his retirement. He went back to India and left Lillian and the boys here as if this were an entirely reasonable thing to do. "You will be safer here than anywhere," he told Lillian repeatedly. "The boys will be happier here than anywhere else." This new life would make men of them, he said.

While he was with them he had a house built on a piece of land at the edge of the inlet waters, a tall house of wood with a steep roof and two rooms up, two rooms down. He had some furnishings shipped from Victoria by boat: a table and chairs, a sideboard, a bookcase and a wood-burning stove, which he proceeded to install himself. He unpacked a shelf full of his books, including Homer's *Iliad*, Darwin's *Descent of Man*, a volume entitled *Principia Mathematica*. He spoke of the time when he would return and how he would sit in a chair by the window, undisturbed, reading these books. He nailed the tiger skin hastily to the wall, not minding what he damaged.

During the long days of rain that ensued, the tiger glowed like a lamp, like the Indian sun at dawn, only beginning to attain its true brilliance. In Lillian's estimation the tiger's face appeared less blind, less innocent, as if adversity were pushing it toward some new and interesting truth.

Her husband stayed for six months in all. In early December he left on the mail boat in a storm. The mail boat had to go along the open coast, which could be rough and dangerous at any time of year, in any weather. She stood on the dock watching the boat as it plunged into the waves, and at last she called out her husband's name. The name was torn from her, a great cry for help, for assistance of some kind, and she was for a moment appalled at the sound. But the wind was fierce; no one heard her. *He* certainly didn't hear her. The mail boat was swept into the rain and fog, and soon it was obscured.

There is no road out of this village. There is Lillian's house and after that there is nothing much, only a rough trail leading into the bush. At first everything she sees offends her eye: the ugly twisted pines, the straggly cedars, dead snags, blackened stumps where land has been partly cleared and then abandoned — visions of despair, of desperation. Some days she thinks the constant rain and fog will surely destroy her. And then the west wind starts up, chilling her to the bone and making her feel somehow vagrant, dispossessed. Her boys seem to exult in the wind, as they do in everything here. They climb trees, wade in the sea, throw rocks at one another, hide on her when she calls them. They are being made men of, she supposes. She stands listening, watching at the place where the trail leads off into the woods. No one lives there. It is an absence, an absence of life, of all but the most dangerous, elemental forms of life. She can see that it bears no relationship whatsoever to the milder forests of England and certainly none to the light-filled, dry, tumbling vastness of India.

No one Lillian has spoken to in the village can tell her who made this trail or when, to what purpose. It is simply there. As a diversion, almost against her better judgement, she begins to follow the trail into the forest. Underneath the trees she sees a surprising number of plants: sword fern, salal, thimbleberry, water hemlock and a species of frail, wild lily, the name unknown to her. She begins to make a project of naming as many of these plants as she can and to make sketches of those she cannot yet name. All that first spring and summer she does this, drawing pages and pages of wet, inky ferns, the fronds translating themselves wilfully into mouths, eyes, the palms of hands; human features that delight Lillian, although she cannot decipher their meaning or identity.

At night when her boys sleep, Lillian gets up from her bed and travels again down this trail, feeling her way in the dark. She is blind, her eyes full of a wonderful innocence. This is the night and she is in it, like a creature of the forest, a small animal. She feels, she knows, that this is a foolish practice, walking here by herself at night, but she cannot give it up, must not give it up. She feels the danger beating like her heart against her ribs, although more robust and sustaining. Easily she could lose her way, easily fall, tripping over a vine or tree root. And there truly are wild animals out here, dangerous animals. The village is rife with stories of encounters between men and bears and mountain lions. She chooses to discount these stories. Nothing in this forest is in the least interested in her. It even amuses her to imagine her husband's consternation if he were called back from India simply because his wife had lost herself in the forest, in the night, and had been gobbled up by a bear. What does *his* discomfort matter to her, however? What does any of it matter? She is a small forest animal, padding down the trail, snuffling and whistling. Impossible to tell just where Lillian leaves off and the damp night air begins.

As well as the tiger skin there are several other objects brought all the way here from India. There is a collection of brass vessels of different sizes, the largest nearly three feet tall. Lillian likes to fill it with ferns and branches and wild flowers she gathers out in the bush. As a result, the house smells persistently, and not unpleasingly, of damp earth. Upstairs in her bedroom is a plain sandalwood box with a hinged lid in which she keeps her hairpins and combs. These are her own belongings, her possessions. She bought them herself, over the years, at market places in India. She went shopping in a rickshaw pulled by one of the servants. The rickshaw flew over the street, its wheels humming. There was a time when Lillian felt it wrong to be pulled along in this way by another person, by a human being who might, after all, resent being used in this way. Her husband had laughed and said, "Oh, don't be ridiculous, Lillian," and so, after a while, she thought only of the wind on her face, a sense of flight arranged for her pleasure, and now she misses it, she misses all of it. She misses India.

In the marketplace, beggars held out their hands. Her husband warned her, "You will only encourage their indolence." That was the way he looked at it. To her the beggars didn't seem indolent; they seemed rigid with intent and purposefulness. Their hands were lean and dark, sinewy and warm with the stored energy of the omnipresent sun. She gave them money, as much as she could spare. Her husband hated weakness, poverty, sickness. Once he pointed urgently to a dark shape huddled in a gutter and said, "Can you tell, is that a child or a monkey? Can you see which it is?" He had been very agitated.

She said, "Oh, a monkey," but the truth was, from where they were standing, it was impossible to be sure. Her husband was a tax collector; he took money from the Indian people and gave it to the ruling English. That was how it worked. It was an important position her husband held, but he was, at least in this case, a realistic man. He said the taxes were paying for some very fine meals and elegant homes. "Could India survive on her own, however?" He doubted it. "Look at Mohandas K. Gandhi, for one example," he said, "and the trouble he is causing."

An incident occurred in India. Lillian went into her dresser drawer for something, a lace collar to wear with her dress. She pulled her hand out only just in time. Nestled in her folded petticoats and clean handkerchiefs was a scorpion. One of the servants had plainly hidden it in her drawer to hurt her, to kill her possibly. Shaking with anger and fear, she told her husband, and he assembled the servants on the veranda at dusk. The sun was a red disc spinning on the rim of the earth. Her husband went up and down the line of servants, saying, "Above all else, I expect you to be open, honest, above-board. Play fair with me and I will play fair with you." He wore a white suit, a white hat; he was a tall man, dark-complexioned, with dark eyes. Later, he took Lillian aside and said that it was her job as mistress of the household to see that this kind of thing did not happen again. It was obvious to him, he said, that she did not have the respect of the servants. "Less daydreaming, Lillian," he said, "and more attention to the task at hand."

There is one thing from India here in this new house on the inlet, and that is the brass censer in which Lillian burnt her husband's name. She cannot precisely remember packing it in her trunk before leaving India, but here it is, somewhat tarnished it's true, but still beautiful, a lovely object hanging from a hook in the front room. One morning, in a reflective mood, she dips her finger into the bowl of the censer and brings it out coated with a fine white ash. Her husband's name. She puts her finger into her mouth to lick it clean, then stops. In the pantry she scrubs her hands clean with a bar of soap, lathering her arms to the elbows. His ashes, she thinks. How awful, what a thing to do. In her mind, for a moment, it is as if her husband has died and she has desecrated his remains and now he is speaking to her, shouting at her from an omniscient position: do you see where your daydreaming gets you, my girl? Your indolence? You will do anything, won't you?

Toward the end of the second year, she writes to her husband: "I cannot tell what season of the year it is any more. There is one long season, cold and wet, every day the same. You cannot imagine the monotony or how it weighs on the spirit."

Her husband replies: "Last week I was forced to stay in a village stricken with disease. I am now dosing myself with quinine water. In addition, a rather brutal murder has occurred here, a Hindu-Muslim quarrel, I suspect. Every day the same, Lillian? Oh dear, oh dear."

A pod of killer whales swims into the inlet. The whales are in a frenzy, leaping high into the air, sending up great plumes of white spray. The entire village has turned out to watch from the shore, from the wharves. This has never happened before, everyone tells Lillian. The whales careen wildly; the villagers call out, Oh! as if they were at a circus. Wind ripples the furiously churning surface of the water; clouds race past the mountains; everything is happening at once. Lillian drags her sons close, closer to the water's edge. You may never see a sight like this again, she tells them, as excited as any of the others. A rumour spreads that this is an omen, that this strange behaviour on the part of the whales means something, good luck or bad. A man near Lillian says it has nothing to do with luck, it is the whales being whales, it is nature. Yes, Lillian says, yes indeed; nature. Then she thinks, The whales are in love. In love with the sea, the sky. It is too much for them, they cannot contain the energy of their love. She feels sympathy for the whales; they could easily annihilate themselves for this love; they have lost all sense of danger.

She thinks also of the tiger, her tiger, alive and floating through the green and gold air of the mountain slopes, its prey below on the ground, and the tiger's paws flexing, its claws unsheathed, its eyes burning with love, for itself and the object it so desires: the prey.

Lillian walks out into the land at night, where no one else has the courage to go, and she finds it surprisingly peaceful, dark, muted. It is like walking into a pleasant dream. Then she thinks, no, her dreams are not always pleasant; sometimes they frighten her. Sometimes she wakens with a cry and realizes that she is alone, she is alone on what seems the edge of the world; beyond the walls of her house there is only the sea and then nothing. That incomprehensible absence. She can't get back to sleep; how could she sleep, she is too wrought up. She lies awake and listens to the wind, to the rain, to the sea. On the whole she would rather not sleep; she would rather be out there in the forest, playing a sort of game with fate. If I stumble and fall, she thinks. If a mountain lion leaps from a tree, snarling, its teeth bared. Nothing will happen, she tells herself. I am all right, she says. One more step, and then one after that. The ground underfoot is slick, uncertain. And there is the smell of dank vegetation, of death, she thinks. She is brave, unmindful. She walks on.

It occurs to her now that of course it was the children's ayah who put the scorpion in her dresser drawer. The ayah didn't like Lillian; she gave her sidelong glances, full of meaning. She spoiled the children, feeding them candies and hot Indian food, stroking their hair with her plump, scented hands.

The ayah was there on the evening Lillian's husband reprimanded the servants over the issue of the scorpion. The ayah stood slightly apart from the others, as if wishing to disassociate herself from the matter and from her condition of servitude. She was not the same as the other servants, her posture seemed to say. In the warmth of the setting sun her face was rosy, swollen. Lillian's husband went up and down, lecturing. "One of you is responsible," he said, "beyond doubt." The ayah was very pretty standing there, her hands meekly clasped.

Lillian thinks how strange, how very strange that only now, years later, on the opposite side of the world, is she able to clearly recognize in the ayah's combined attitudes of submission and apartness not innocence, but guilt.

Her husband taunted her. Before they left India, he said to her, "There is no society out there, you know. No English society, church teas, fancy dress balls, all that nonsense. You'll be on your own, out there."

"I was never all that much interested," she said, although she had enjoyed the fancy dress balls, the impromptu theatre. In any case, her husband was wrong. In the village there are men and women from England, immigrants like Lillian, anxiously running their hands over the walls of moist air to see if it is real, this prison, this small place they have come to. Wearing gumboots, they wade through mud to play mah jong around kitchen tables; they sing songs together, and dance, and toast one another with glasses of sherry. At the end of all this entertainment, they stand and sing "God Save the King," their mouths alive, biting with great vigour into the words "victorious" and "glorious." The English in diaspora, Lillian thinks. It is the same everywhere. She does not join in the singing but watches the energy of the open mouths with interest. She is amazed that the words still have meaning for these people, not only these words, but any words at all. Any spoken words. For her, words have become as vague and formless as the mist that wreathes the mountainsides. She begins to avoid social occasions; she develops a most unlikely habit of running to hide when people walk down the road to visit her. She hides in her garden behind the trunk of a cedar tree, or she runs into the house and locks the door. Anything she or anyone else might have to say seems suddenly pointless, irrelevant. (Quite, quite irrelevant, she hears her husband's voice saying.) She is a small animal, solitary, making her way down a trail no one else dares to take.

Of course, she isn't an animal. She is Lillian, with her sketchbook and her pen and ink, getting it all down on paper, recording the shapes, the mysterious, scarcely apprehended shapes and forms that green growing plants can take. As she draws, she is fascinated to see human features behind the branches, mixed in with the vining stems and fleshly leaves, appearing magically, independent of her pen. The corner of an eye, the tip of a nose, a full, pouting lower lip.

Even the tiger is there, his black stripes boldly visible against the delicate tracery of a sword fern. The tiger makes her smile. He is arrogant, indifferent, strutting on the paper: did you intend to forget me? he asks.

Lillian ventures farther down the trail than she has ever gone. She plunges on and on through the bush. She scratches her hand on a branch, pauses to pull her skirt free of a thorned vine. Then she arrives at an open place, unlike anywhere else. She has an idea, from studying maps of the area and from hearing people talk, that she has come to the mud-flats, where the sea at last wears itself out and becomes engulfed by the land. The ground is marshy, like a peat bog, and the water is everywhere shallow and blue and motionless. Tall, bearded grasses grow along the shore. A blue heron stands one-legged not far from her. Everything is quiet and seems consecrated to this singular moment. Lillian sits down on a log and places her sketchbook open on her knee. Will she find her way back? she wonders. Will her sons notice that she's been gone for an unusually long time? It is July and surprisingly hot. She is wearing a wide-brimmed hat tied under her chin with a scarf to shade her eyes. It is, in fact, a hat she wore many times in India while engaged in just such an activity as this: sketching the indigenous flora and fauna of the land. She draws a long curved line meant to represent the heron's long neck, which ought to look graceful but is instead strangely clumsy, unmanageable. She turns to a fresh page. Behind her in the bush there is a noise, as if something, an animal, were creeping up on her to have a better look. She doesn't turn around.

Her husband said to her before he went back to India, "I suppose you will forget me once I am gone." He had been at the window looking at the inlet, at the small, dark islands that rise abruptly out of the water. She wanted to tell him that it was too late, she had already forgotten him, she had forgotten his name; she had written it down and let it be consumed by fire. Instead she said, "The children might forget you. Three years is a long time to a child." He replied that it was her responsibility to see that they did not forget him. Then he began unpacking his books, telling her she must encourage the boys to read these books, it was important that they read and exercise their minds. "I will write to them," he said. "A letter for each child, every month."

Of course, even after all this time the boys have not forgotten their father, although they mention him less and less as the weeks and months go by. And even after reducing it to a fine white ash, Lillian remembers her husband's name. She hasn't spoken it aloud since the day he left on the mail boat, but she does remember it. No, the irony is that it is herself she has forgotten. Her self, her physical presence, seems to have become amorphous; parts of her float through the cedar forest; parts of her catch on dead snags. Her husband said, "The great beauty of this place is that you can make anything you want out of it. No one has really discovered it yet. It is a sort of dreamland, waiting. You can make what you want out of it. That's what I want. That's exactly what I want."

He spoke with such enthusiasm; he so badly wanted his dreamland away from the rest of the world, away from India, away from the ancient populated parts of the world. But Lillian knows what her husband does not know, even yet: that the land makes what it wants of you. The land is not clay waiting to be shaped; it is a monster already formed, with claws and a hungry mouth. A shiver runs down her spine. She can sense something behind her, although common sense tells her nothing is there. She is alone, and at any moment she can get up and begin the walk back.

She draws, curving a slender grass stem deliberately across the clean white page. Her hand moves quickly, forming a lattice-work of sea grasses bending as if swept by a fierce wind, only there is no wind. Behind the grasses elusive human features appear, shy, diffident. They lack an identity, although it seems to Lillian they might at any moment assume one. She sees an ear, then the open palm of a hand. The fluttering edge of a scarf, the brim of a sun-hat much like the one she has on her head. And an eye, wide, surprised, knowledgeable.

KATHERINE GOVIER

The Immaculate Conception Photo Gallery
(1988)

Sandro named the little photography shop on St. Clair Avenue West, between Lord's Shoes and Bargain Jimmies, after the parish church in the village where he was born. He had hankered after wider horizons, the rippled brown prairies, the hard-edged mountains. But when he reached Toronto he met necessity in the form of a wife and babies, and, never having seen a western sunset, he settled down in Little Italy. He photographed the brides in their fat lacquered curls and imported lace and their quick babies in christening gowns brought over from home. Blown up to near life size on cardboard cutouts, their pictures filled the windows of his little shop.

Sandro had been there ten years already when he first really saw his sign and the window. He stood still in front of it and looked. A particularly buxom bride with a lace bodice and cap sleeves cut in little scallops shimmered in a haze of concupiscence under the sign reading Immaculate Conception Photography Gallery. Sandro was not like his neighbours any more, he was modern, a Canadian. He no longer went to church. As he stared, one of the street drunks shuffled into place beside him. Sandro knew them all, they came into the shop in winter. (No one ought to have to stay outside in that cold, Sandro believed.) But he especially knew Becker. Becker was a smart man; he used to be a philosopher at a university.

"Immaculate conception," said Sandro to Becker. "What do you think?"

Becker lifted his eyes to the window. He made a squeezing gesture at the breasts. "I never could buy that story," he said.

Sandro laughed, but he didn't change the sign that year or the next, and he got to be forty-five and then fifty and it didn't seem worth it. The Immaculate Conception Photography Gallery had a reputation. Business came in from as far away as Rosedale and North Toronto, because Sandro was a magician with a camera. He also had skill with brushes and lights and paint, he reshot his negatives, he lined them with silver, he had tricks even new graduates of photography school couldn't (or wouldn't) copy.

Sandro was not proud of his tricks. They began in a gradual way, fixing stray hairs and taking wrinkles out of dresses. He did it once, then twice, then people came in asking for it. Perhaps he'd have gone on this way, with small lies, but he met with a situation that was larger than most; it would have started a feud in the old country. During a very large and very expensive wedding party, Tony the bridegroom seduced Alicia the bridesmaid in the basketball storage room under the floor of the parish hall. Six months later Tony confessed, hoping perhaps to be released from his vows. But the parents judged it was too late to dissolve the union: Diora was used, she was no longer a virgin, there was a child coming. Tony was reprimanded, Diora consoled, the mothers became enemies, the newlyweds made up. Only Alicia remained to be dealt with. The offence became hers.

In Italy, community ostracism would have been the punishment of choice. But this was Canada, and if no one acknowledged Alicia on the street, if no one visited her mother, who was heavy on her feet and forced to sit on the sofa protesting her daughter's innocence, if no one invited her father out behind to drink home-made wine, Alicia didn't care. She went off to her job behind the till in a drugstore with her chin thrust out much as before. The in-laws perceived that the young woman could not be subdued by the old methods. This being the case, it was better she did not exist at all.

Which was why Diora's mother turned up at Sandro's counter with the wedding photos. The pain Alicia had caused! she began. Diora's mother's very own miserable wages, saved these eighteen years, had paid for these photographs! She wept. The money was spent, but the joy was spoiled. When she and Diora's father looked at the row of faces flanking bride and groom there she was — Alicia, the whore! She wiped her tears and made her pitch.

"You can solve our problem, Sandro. I will get a new cake, we will all come to the parish hall. You will take the photographs again. Of course," she added, "we can't pay you again."

Sandro smiled, it was so preposterous. "Even if I could afford to do all that work for nothing, I hate to say it, but Diora's out to here."

"Don't argue with me."

"I wouldn't be so bold," said Sandro. "But I will not take the photographs over."

The woman slapped the photographs where they lay on the counter. "You will! I don't care how you do it!" And she left.

Sandro went to the back and put his negatives on the light box. He brought out his magic solution and his razor blades and his brushes. He circled Alicia's head and shoulders in the first row and went to work. He felt a little badly, watching the bright circle of her face fade and swim, darken down to nothing. But how easily she vanished! He filled in the white spot with a bit of velvet curtain trimmed from the side.

"I'm like a plastic surgeon," he told his wife. "Take that patch of skin from the inner thigh and put it over the scar on the face. Then sand the edges. Isn't that what they do? Only it isn't a face I'm fixing, it's a memory."

His wife stood on two flat feet beside the sink. She shook the carrot she was peeling. "I don't care about Alicia," she said, "but Diora's mother is making a mistake. She is starting them off with a lie in their marriage. And why is she doing it? For her pride! I don't like this, Sandro."

"You're missing the point," said Sandro.

The next day he had another look at his work. Alicia's shoulders and the bodice of her dress were still there, in front of the chest of the uncle of the bride. He couldn't remove them; it would leave a hole in Uncle. Sandro had nothing to fill the hole, no spare male torsos in black tie. He considered putting a head on top, but whose head? There was no such thing as a free face. A stranger would be questioned, a friend would have an alibi. Perhaps Diora's mother would not notice the black velvet space, as where a tooth had been knocked out, between the smiling faces.

Indeed she didn't but kissed his hand fervently and thanked him with tears in her eyes. "Twenty-five thousand that wedding cost me. Twenty-five thousand to get this photograph, and you have rescued it."

"Surely you got dinner and a dance, too?" said Sandro.

"The wedding was one day. This is forever," said Diora's mother.

"I won't do that again," said Sandro, putting the cloth over his head and looking into his camera lens to do a passport photo. In the community the doctored photograph had been examined and re-examined. Alicia's detractors enjoyed the headless shoulders as evidence of a violent punishment. "No, I won't do that again at all," said Sandro to himself, turning aside compliments with a shake of his head. But there was another wedding. After the provolone e melone, the veal picata, the many-tiered cake topped with swans, the father of the bride drew Sandro aside and asked for a set of prints with the groom's parents removed.

"My God, why?" said Sandro.

"He's a bastard. A bad man."

"Shouldn't have let her marry his son, then," said Sandro, pulling a cigarette out of the pack in his pocket. These conversations made him nervous.

The father's weathered face was dark, his dinner jacket did not button around his chest. He moaned and ground his lower teeth against his uppers. "You know how they are, these girls in Canada. I am ashamed to say it, but I couldn't stop her."

Sandro said nothing.

"Look, I sat here all night long, said nothing, did nothing. I don't wanna look at him for the next twenty years."

Sandro drew in a long tube of smoke.

"I paid a bundle for this night. I wanna remember it nice-like."

The smoke made Sandro nauseous. He dropped his cigarette and ground it into the floor with his toe, damning his own weakness. "So what am I going to do with the table?"

The father put out a hand like a tool, narrowed his eyes, and began to saw where the other man sat.

"And leave it dangling, no legs?"

"So make new legs."

"I'm a photographer, not a carpenter," said Sandro. "I don't make table legs."

"Where you get legs is your problem," said the father. "I'm doing well here. I've got ten guys working for me. You look like you could use some new equipment."

And what harm was it after all, it was only a photograph, said Sandro to himself. Then, too, there was the technical challenge. Waiting until they all got up to get their bonbonnière, he took a shot of the head table empty. Working neatly with his scalpel, he cut the table from this second negative, removed the in-laws and their chairs from the first one, stuck the empty table-end onto the table in the first picture, blended over the join neatly, and printed it. Presto! Only one set of in-laws.

"I don't mind telling you, it gives me a sick feeling," said Sandro to his wife. "I was there. I saw them. We had a conversation. They smiled for me. Now . . ." He shrugged. "An empty table. Lucky I don't go to church any more."

"Let the man who paid good money to have you do it confess, not you," she said. "A photograph is a photograph."

"That's what I thought, too," said Sandro.

The next morning Sandro went to the Donut House, got himself a take-out coffee and stood on the street beside his window.

"Why do people care about photographs so much?" he asked Becker. Becker had newspaper stuffed in the soles of his shoes. He had on a pair of stained brown pants tied up at the waist with a paisley necktie. His bottle was clutched in a paper bag gathered around the neck.

"You can put them on your mantel," said Becker. "They don't talk back."

"Don't people prefer life?" said Sandro.

"People prefer things," said Becker.

"Don't they want their memories to be true?"

"No," said Becker.

"Another thing. Are we here just to get our photograph taken? Do we have a higher purpose?"

Becker pulled one of the newspapers out of his shoe. There were Brian and Mila Mulroney having a gloaty kiss. They were smeared by muddy water and depressed by the joint in the ball of Becker's foot.

"I mean real people," said Sandro. "Have we no loyalty to the natural?"

"These are existential questions, Sandro," said Becker. "Too many more of them and you'll be out here on the street with the rest of us."

Sandro drained the coffee from his cup, pitched it in the bin painted "Keep Toronto Clean" and went back into his gallery. The existential questions nagged. But he did go out and get the motor drive for the camera. In the next few months he eradicated a pregnancy from a wedding photo, added a daughter-in-law who complained of being left out of the Christmas shots, and made a groom taller. Working in the dark-room, he was hit by vertigo. He was on a slide, beginning a descent. He wanted to know what the bottom felt like.

After a year of such operations a man from the Beaches came in with a tiny black and white photo of a long-lost brother. He wanted it coloured and fitted into a family shot around a picnic table on Centre Island.

"Is this some kind of joke?" said Sandro. It was the only discretion he practised now: he wanted to talk about it before he did it.

"No. I'm going to send it to Mother. She thinks Christopher wrote us all off."

"Did he?" said Sandro.

"Better she should not know."

Sandro neglected to ask if Christopher was fat or thin. He ended up taking a medium-sized pair of shoulders from his own cousin and propping them up behind a bush, with Christopher's head on top. Afterward, Sandro lay sleepless in his bed. Suppose that in the next few months Christopher should turn up dead, say, murdered. Then Mother would produce the photograph stamped Immaculate Conception Photography Gallery, 1816 St. Clair Avenue West. Sandro would be implicated. The police might come.

"I believe adding people is worse than taking them away," he said to his wife.

"You say yes to do it, then you do it. You think it's wrong, you say no."

"Let me try this on you, Becker," said Sandro the next morning. "To take a person out is only half a lie. It proves nothing except that he was not in that shot. To add a person is a whole lie: it proves that he was there, when he was not."

"You haven't proven a thing, you're just fooling around with celluloid. Have you got a buck?" said Becker.

"It is better to be a murderer than a creator. I am playing God, outplaying God at His own game." He was smarter than Becker now. He knew it was the photographs that lasted, not the people. In the end the proof was in the proof. Though he hadn't prayed in thirty years,

Sandro began to pray. It was like riding a bicycle: he got the hang of it again instantly. "Make me strong," he prayed, "strong enough to resist the new equipment that I might buy, strong enough to resist the temptation to expand the gallery, to buy a house in the suburbs. Make me say no to people who want alterations."

But Sandro's prayers were not answered. When people offered him money to dissolve an errant relative, he said yes. He said yes out of curiosity. He said yes out of a desire to test his skills. He said yes out of greed. He said yes out of compassion. "What is the cost of a little happiness?" he said. "Perhaps God doesn't count photographs. After all, they're not one of a kind."

Sandro began to be haunted, in slow moments behind the counter in the Immaculate Conception, by the faces of those whose presence he had tampered with. He kept a file — Alicia the lusty bridesmaid, Antonia and Marco, the undesired in-laws. Their heads, their shoes and their hands, removed from the scene with surgical precision, he saved for the moment when, God willing, a forgiving relative would ask him to replace them. But the day did not come. Sandro was not happy.

"Becker," he said, for he had a habit now of buying Becker a coffee first thing in the morning and standing out if it was warm, or in if it was cold, for a chat. "Becker, let's say it's a good service I'm doing. It makes people happy, even if it tells lies."

"Sandro," said Becker, who enjoyed his coffee, "these photographs, doctored by request of the subjects, reflect back the lives they wish to have. The unpleasant bits were removed, the wishes are added. If you didn't do it, someone else would. Memory would. It's a service."

"It's also money," said Sandro. He found Becker too eager to make excuses now. He liked him better before.

"You're like Tintoretto, painting in his patron, softening his greedy profile, lifting the chin of his fat wife. It pays for the part that's true art."

"Which part is that?" said Sandro, but Becker didn't answer. He was still standing there when Diora came in. She's matured, she'd gained weight, and her twins, now six years old, were handsome and strong. Sandro's heart flew up in his breast. Perhaps she had made friends with Alicia, perhaps Diora had come to have her bridesmaid re-instated.

"The long nightmare is over," said Diora. "I've left him."

The boys were running from shelf to shelf lifting up the photographs with their glass frames and putting them down again. Sandro watched them with one eye. He knew what she was going to say.

"I want you to take him out of those pictures," she said.

"You'd look very foolish as a bride with no groom," he said severely.

"No, no, not those," she said. "I mean the kids' birthday shots."

They had been particularly fine, those shots, taken only two weeks ago, Tony tall and dark, Diora and the children radiant and blond.

"Be reasonable, Diora," he said. "I never liked him myself. But he balances the portrait. Besides, he was there."

"He was not there!" cried Diora. Her sons went on turning all the pictures to face the walls. "He was never there. He was running around, in his heart he was not with me. I was alone with my children."

"I'll take another one," said Sandro. "Of you and the boys. Whenever you like. This one stays like it is."

"We won't pay."

"But Diora," said Sandro, "everyone knows he's their father."

"They have no father," said Diora flatly.

"It's immaculate conception," said Becker gleefully.

But Diora did not hear. "It's our photograph, and we want him out. You do your job. The rest of it's none of your business." She put one hand on the back of the head of each of her twins and marched them out the door.

Sandro leaned on his counter idly flipping the pages of a wedding album. He had a vision of a great decorated room with a cake on the table. Everyone had had his way, the husband had removed the wife, the wife the husband, the bridesmaid her parents, and so forth. There was no one there.

"We make up our lives out of the people around us," he said to Becker. "When they don't live up to standard, we can't just wipe them out."

"Don't ask me," said Becker. "I just lit out for the streets. Couldn't live up to a damn thing." Then he, too, went out the door.

"Lucky bugger," said Sandro.

Alone, he went to his darkroom. He opened his drawer of bits and pieces. His disappeared ones, the inconvenient people. His body parts, his halves of torsos, tips of shiny black shoes. Each face, each item of clothing punctured him a little. He looked at his negatives stored in drawers. They were scarred, pathetic things. I haven't the stomach for it, not any more, thought Sandro.

As he walked home, St. Clair Avenue seemed very fine. The best part was, he thought, there were no relationships. Neither this leaning drunk nor that window-shopper was so connected to any other as to endanger his or her existence. The tolerance of indifference, said Sandro to himself, trying to remember it so that he could tell Becker.

But Sandro felt ill at ease in his own home, by its very definition a dangerous and unreliable setting. His wife was stirring something, with her lips tight together. His children, almost grown up now, bred secrets as they looked at television. He himself only posed in the doorway, looking for hidden seams and the faint hair-lines of an airbrush.

That night he stood exhausted by his bed. His wife lay on her side with one round shoulder above the sheet. Behind her on the wall was the photo he'd taken of their village before he left Italy. He ought to reshoot it, take out that gas station and clean up the square a little. His pillow had an indentation, as if a head had been erased. He slept in a chair.

In the morning he went down to the shop. He got his best camera and set up a tripod on the sidewalk directly across the street. He took several shots in the solid bright morning light. He locked the door and placed the CLOSED sign in the window. In the darkroom he developed the film, floating the negatives in the pungent fluid until the row of shop fronts came through clearly, the flat brick faces, the curving concrete trim, the two balls on the crowns. Deftly he dissolved each brick of his store, the window and the sign. Deftly he reattached each brick of the store on the west side to the bricks of the store to the east.

I have been many things in my life, thought Sandro, a presser of shutters, a confessor, a false prophet. Now I am a bricklayer, and a good one. He taped the negatives together and developed them. He touched up the join and then photographed it again. He developed this second negative and it was perfect. Number 1812, Lord's Shoes, joined directly to 1820, Bargain Jimmies: the Immaculate Conception Photography Gallery at 1816 no longer existed. Working quickly, because he wanted to finish before the day was over, he blew it up to two feet by three feet. He cleared out his window display of brides and babies and stood up this new photograph — one of the finest he'd ever taken, he thought. Then he took a couple of cameras and a bag with the tripod and some lenses. He turned out the light, pulling the door shut behind him, and began to walk west.

CAROLINE ADDERSON

The Hanging Gardens of Babylon
(1988)

"Okay you two, go out now and play," said their father. But because the room was dim, an old dark blanket slung over the curtain rod, he was half hidden in the corner and they had forgotten him. They did not listen now.

There was an unpleasant smell in the room, sour and oppressive; it came from their mother. She lay motionless on the bed, small like a child, her white face passive with discomfort. At her mother's feet Lillian sat watching her brother Rudy, thinking that he didn't know anything. Half on, half off the bed, he was clutching their mother's hand and chatting happily. "Here's a little man, Mommy, going for a walk," he said, smiling. With his two fingers he began to march up her arm, "Dee dee dee, dee dee dee," soft temporary impressions in the white flesh. He crossed her shoulder, turned, and his walking fingers moved gently over her breast. At the base of her stomach, rising under the quilt like a jelly mould, he stopped and in his play-voice squealed, "My, what a big hill!"

"Rudy!" Their father's voice was sharp and tired. "That's enough. Lillian, take him and go get the mail. You can see Mommy again later."

She got up mechanically and tugged Rudy by the arm. "I don't wanna go!" but Lillian easily removed him, forced his small thrashing form through the door, then slipped out herself, looking back for just an instant to see their mother, white-faced, cover her eyes with her hand.

Quietly, sock-footed, Lillian descended the stairs to the kitchen, Rudy trailing. A week ago their mother had taken to bed and it showed, especially in that room. The table was cluttered with cereal boxes and Rudy's toys. Puss-Love's paw prints marked the counters like a pattern in the Arborite. No one had remembered to feed Puss-Love. They themselves had been eating out of cans and boxes. Last night was Easter, the very death and rebirth of their Lord, and in celebration they had had Kraft Dinner and no chocolate eggs. This had made them both cry, Rudy at the table, *Jesus wants for me to have an egg*! and Lillian later, when she was alone. The garbage overflowed in the corner and, curiously, a pair of Rudy's underpants lay on the floor next to the refrigerator. Lillian looked in the bread box. She said, talking into the box, her voice sounding hollow, "There's just crusts. You want one?"

"Yes," said Rudy. "Yes, please."

Earlier Lillian had put the peanut butter in the cookbook drawer so she would not have to keep dragging a chair over to reach the cupboard. But there was no clean cutlery. She eyed the sink full of cold greasy water and most of their everyday dishes. "Go to the china cabinet and get a knife."

"I'm not allowed," said Rudy.

"Go on."

Frowning, he left the kitchen, then came back with a letter-opener. Lillian used it anyway. They put on coats and rubber boots and, taking the mail key from the hook behind the door, went out with their crusts.

"I wanna carry the key," said Rudy.

"You'll lose it."

"You always say that."

"Because I know you will."

They sat on the front steps watching Poke run around on the wet brown lawn. Every few minutes Rudy called out, "Poke! Here, Poke! Poke! Poke! Poke!" spraying sandwich, the dog ignoring him, not even barking, just circling foolishly in his matted sheepdog coat.

"Wanna get a stick and play with Poke?" he asked.

"We have to get the mail."

"What do you wanna do after that?"

"I don't know," said Lillian, dropping the remainder of her crust and standing. She went down the steps and walked the length of the driveway, shuffling and kicking the gravel.

"Hey, wait!" Rudy called, leaping down and racing after her. "Wait for me!"

The way to the mailbox was an old asphalt road patched everywhere with wavering lines of tar. On both sides a dirty crust of melting snow filled the ditches. Aspen scrub, strung with last year's wind-sent debris, screened the black and saturated fields. Pervasive the odour of wet soil, the bright biting green smell of new leaves. Rudy went with his face up and nostrils wide, she behind, hands deep in pockets. They heard the call of one bird to another, dee dee dee, dee dee dee, the answer in variation meaning yes, no, perhaps — meaning, *yes, soon.*

They had walked for several minutes when Rudy slowed and began to talk to himself. He mumbled first, then half-sang, making shapes in the air with his fingers, watching rapt as if it were not he who made them, as if the shapes were independent living creatures. They were contortions of his hands, claw-like animals that flew short distances, tethered to the ends of his arms.

"Hurry up."

But he did not hear her. He growled, laughed, said "No! No!" then stopped in his tracks. He pointed and shouted, voice shrill with excitement. "Lookit! Lookit, Lilly!"

A dead cat in the middle of the road. They approached and, standing over it, stared. Rudy made the sign of the cross.

"Whose cat do you think it is?" he asked solemnly.

It had been run over several times. The head was intact but the body almost completely flattened. It lay gape-mouthed on a star-shaped stain of its own making. Rudy squatted and peered in the mouth. "There's bugs or something living in here. Look, Lillian."

"I don't want to," she said, but kneeled and looked anyway.

Small white worms, like grains of rice, tumbled out of the throat. On the wide crusted-over eye was a pivoting fly. They remained there, in the middle of the road, crouching silently.

"You know what Daddy told me?" Lillian said. "He said that tomorrow they're going to take Mommy and cut her stomach open to get the baby. Cut her open to pull the baby out. What do you think will happen when they do that?"

Rudy did not reply.

"What do you think happens to people when they get cut open like that?"

Rudy still looked at the cat.

"Answer me."

"Poor cat," said Rudy, patting its head gently.

She opened her mouth to tell him again but there came a sudden screaming blare, a car bearing down on them, horn pressed. They froze, still hunkering, not even resigned, not anything. The car swerved. Just beyond, it came to an angry halt. The driver opened the door and, leaning out, shouted at them. "Stupid kids! What the hell are you doing in the middle of the road!"

Lillian hauled Rudy to his feet and dragged him along without looking back at the car, her heart slamming around inside her. Rudy was silent and trembling. A few yards on something dawned on him.

"Lilly! We almost had an accident! We almost had an accident!"

Skipping ahead, swinging his arms like berserk pendulums, leaping, he sang for joy. "Accident! Accident!"

"Did you hear what I told you!"

Rudy turned and smiled. "It's not true."

"It *is* true!"

He faced her fully, taking on the pose of a pugilist, fists clenched and threatening, jaw jutting.

"Oh, cut it out, you," she said, and he deflated.

They walked on.

Rudy came back beside her. He tugged on her sleeve until she withdrew her hand and held his. "Lilly! Tell me about those wonderful things."

"What wonderful things?"

"The seven wonderful things."

"Oh. You mean the seven wonders of the world. I told you yesterday. I told you a hundred times."

"Tell me again."

She sighed. She had read it all in a book, weeks ago. "The statue of Memnon cries for his mother."

"He's a baby. What about the other statue?"

"The Colossus? That's a huge one, I don't remember where. He stands over the water like this." She straddled her legs. "The sea goes under him."

Rudy laughed. "He's peeing in the water."

She pursed her lips and let go of his hand. Rudy reddened. "Sorry," he said ruefully. "Sorry." She took him back, putting both their hands in her pocket.

"And what about the gardens! Those gardens you told me about!"

"The hanging gardens of Babylon."

"Yes!" he shouted. "Go. Talk about them."

She did and smiled a little, for she knew a lot and liked to say what she knew. She told him about the five rising terraces, two hundred and fifty feet high.

Rudy looked straight up at the sky.

The spiral staircase, the queen's look-out, the animals.

"What kind of animals?"

"Cats, dogs, snakes."

"Pigs?"

"Yes, pigs," she said.

"What else?"

"All animals."

"*Which ones*? Tell me," he said, cross.

"Elephants, hawks, chickens, lady bugs, hyenas . . ." She continued until, satisfied, he asked, "Which plants?"

"All plants. That's all I'll say."

"Lilies?" he asked, smiling and squeezing her hand.

"I said all plants."

"Easter lilies," he said.

They were in sight of the mailbox. They had passed a few acreages belonging to neighbour families and now the tree stands were denser and the snow was gone from the ditches, bright green shoots rising on either side like the tips of soft, coloured bayonets. The air was fetid, mildew in the grass, last season's dead newly thawed. Rudy beamed. "I think those gardens are so nice. Where are they?"

"In Babylon."

"Where's Babylon?"

"Far far away. In a desert."

"I'd like to live there. I'd like to live there with you. Let's pretend we're there now."

"You pretend," said Lillian. "I'll watch you."

Rudy began to creep along the road, making exaggerated sweeping gestures with his arms as if he were pushing back foliage. Every few steps he stopped and shaded his eyes with his hands saying, "Hullo, who's hanging in the garden of boobilon?" Then they were at the mailbox, and a boy in a plaid jacket and a tuque that read PUT ON A HAPPY FACE stood there staring at Rudy and Lillian.

"Give me the key," Rudy said.

"You're too little." She opened the compartment.

"Ours was empty, too," said the boy with the tuque. "It's a holiday, remember?" He was staying at his grandparents' for Easter, he told them. His face was dirty, some orange sauce circling his mouth. He tilted back his head and narrowed his eyes. "I got a secret."

"What kind of secret?" asked Rudy.

"Come on," he said.

They followed him back in the direction they had just come from, the boy looking for something in the ditch. "This is it," he said finally.

Together they jumped the ditch and pushed through the aspen scrub into the trees. Then they found themselves standing in a small clearing beside a shallow pond formed by spring run-off. All around and rising up through the trees like cathedral music was the deep, frantic, pulsing sound of frogs. It was hurried and overlapping, repetitive, an urgent chorus like mass in amphibian tongue. A plastic bucket sat next to the pond. The boy went over to it and beckoned.

They came and looked inside. The bucket was half-full of water and teeming with frogs, coupled frogs, one in front that made the motions of swimming, one in back with its ridiculous arms clutching the other's middle. This seemed like such an absurd thing for a frog to be doing, squeezing the breath out of another, not letting go even when the boy put his hand in and stirred.

"Isn't that funny?" said Rudy.

Lillian glanced at the boy and at Rudy, who swayed as if the sound had hands to move him, then back at the frogs. "What are they doing?" she asked.

"Fucking," said the boy.

He waded into the pond and, splashing around, caught up a handful of doubled frogs. Returning to the bucket, he dropped them in.

"What are they doing?" asked Lillian.

"I told you. They're fucking. You know what fucking is, don't you?"

"Of course," said Lillian.

"Isn't it funny?" said Rudy.

She looked again in the bucket at the piggyback frogs swimming in circles, cycling around and around, no beginning or end. The frog song seemed louder now, insistent, listen-listen-listen. She was dizzy, then afraid of the song and the strange boy, this hidden centrifugal clearing revolving with frogs. Clearing, earth, everything, turning, circling.

The boy took Rudy's hand and guided it into the bucket. Rudy drew back quickly and laughed. Listen-listen-listen. The song lulled and agitated. She put her hands on her ears. The way the boy held a pair of frogs, learning their weight, they were something to throw. Listen-listen-listen.

"Funny!" cried Rudy.

"What are you going to do?" she asked.

He shrugged, then wound back his arm. Even airborne the frogs did not uncouple. They sailed straight for a tree, struck it — a terrible jellied splash on the bark.

They ran some of the way, then Rudy was tired and Lillian had to carry him on her back. He was no extra strain for her now, after the things she knew and had seen. She walked thinking of the swerving car, the bulging cat eye, her mother's skin, the bright gelatin stain on the tree. Rudy had his legs twined around her middle and was singing, "Dee dee dee, dee dee dee . . ." When she came to the dead cat, she passed it hurriedly.

"Let me down now," he said. "Please."

She walked slowly so Rudy would not fall behind, but still he dragged along at the end of her arm, yawning. He was rubbing his fist in his eye.

"How much more till we're home?"

"Just a bit."

Then a moment later he announced, "I know what was happening to those frogs."

"Which frogs?" She meant the frogs in the pail or the frogs on the tree.

"All the frogs."

"You don't."

"I do! You think I don't know anything but I know lots! And I know what was happening to those frogs!"

"What then?"

"They were going to the hanging gardens."

And suddenly she was furious. "Don't you know there's no hanging gardens of Babylon? Have you ever heard of that place before? There's no such place as Babylon! It's *made up*!"

She was shaking and he was backing away from her with a fierce angry face.

"There is so!" he cried. "Too bad, Lilly. Too bad you don't know where Babylon is."

"There is no Babylon!"

Rudy ran away up the road.

Through the aspen stand the breeze was filtering. Again she heard that call, dee dee dee, dee dee dee — the bird-call, Rudy-call, then the sound of snow melting in the ditch. Gradually the sound grew louder, becoming the roar of a river or a waterfall, water gushing up out of the open earth, pushing things forward. She saw the tumble of waking insects on the crest, and animals, cats, dogs, snakes, all animals, *which ones? tell me*, all animals and people, sweeping forward, on and on and on to the beginning again. Listen-listen-listen. Listen-listen-listen.

When Rudy finally disappeared, a dark bird flew by. She watched as it dipped and swooped and circled, circled again. Then it vanished, too, in the direction of Babylon. Everything in the direction of Babylon.

PATRICK ROSCOE

Peggy Lee in Africa
(1989)

At night three children float in bed and listen to their father play Peggy Lee records in his room at the other end of the new house. This one is built of cement block and has a tin roof; instead of glass windows, there are wire-mesh screens to let in breeze and keep out snakes. Her cool voice slips out into the hot darkness, *I know a little bit about a lot of things*, silencing crickets, even hushing cicadas. For a moment she is mute; perhaps the father has finally stopped circling his room, ceased sitting on the edge of his bed, large hands curved over knees, head bowed. Maybe he has turned off the light to join the children who now drown in darkness. But then she begins again, over and over incanting the same spell upon a man who is fearful of snakes and who won't ride roller coasters and who feels faint at the sight of his own blood. The tangled jungle pours scent down the Ngondo hills, poisoned perfume wraps around the house.

Sometimes during the day, when only the houseboy is home with him, Richard enters the father's room. On the record covers the woman's face is pale and smooth beneath short waved hair that is more white than blond. Her lips are painted deep red. The last time Richard saw his mother was during a June picnic in the yard behind a relative's house, two years ago in Canada. Cousins and aunts and uncles balance paper plates of cold fried chicken and potato salad, ride coloured blankets that like magic carpets hover just above the grass. Look! someone cries, pointing upward. Behind the fenced yard rises the hill with the hospitals on top. A woman in white stands on a balcony high up there, she waves to the people down below. Richard believes he can see her short blond hair, her deeply red mouth; it will be years before he learns how distance can distort or damage vision, transforming any coiled length of rope into an asp. Someone also wearing white comes from behind the woman and leads her slowly back inside. The people at the picnic begin to play croquet, they send bright balls spinning across the lawn, there is the dull, hollow sound of wood knocking wood.

Soon Lily and MJ are sleeping. Richard can hear them breathing nearby, he still hears Peggy Lee sending messages through the Morogoro night. *I know a little bit about biology,* she confides. She's not here, the father once replied to Richard, running one hand through short black hair, squinting at the sisal fields in the valley below the grey house. Lily squirms in her sleep, something is always trying to get her. The father steps from the kitchen door, flashlight in hand; a weak beam plays upon the darkness, searches for danger undulating nearer on its belly. Tentative, the man takes several more steps forward, retreats back inside. Peggy Lee sings on until dawn.

That old snake in the grass, Lily will write Richard nearly twenty years later from somewhere inside her visions of vipers. Honey, what does Peggy Lee have to do with anything? he once asked me. Apparently, he still thinks MJ will be found, he says he's doing everything in his power to make sure his boy is brought back home, writes Lily from the hospital, poised high above Brale, that Richard pictures having innumerable balconies from which hosts of mothers and sisters wave to people playing summer games below. If you're smart, you won't set foot back upon our native soil, adds Lily in 1985. Don't come back, it's not safe, venom abounds.

During daylight the father is clear-eyed and energetic. After work he changes out of his good trousers, white shirt and thin tie; in a pair of old shorts he throws a basketball at a hoop he has fixed on the side of the house. The children sit in the shaded doorway and watch his skin darken to the colour of an African's. He dribbles and dodges past an invisible opposition, scores two more points. How many does that make? he calls. Inside, the houseboy is fixing dinner. When it is ready, he will set it on the table and go home to the village for the night. One moment after there is bright sunlight, it is nearly dark. Supper cools and hardens on the table, unpacked crates from Canada loom in the dimming rooms. The father goes for one more layup. The children can no longer see him leaping towards the hoop, dropping back to earth. They no longer see him spinning something round between his palms.

While the evening is still early and MJ and Lily still play the Canada game, the father often listens to Frank Sinatra or Ella Fitzgerald. He hums around the house, practises new Swahili words aloud, interrupts the children's games to tell stories of when he was a boy. I was the only boy in town who swam the Columbia River, he brags, everyone else was afraid of the currents, the rocks, the undertow. In detail he describes certain especially perilous swims, while the children's eyes become heavy in their nodding heads. Later, if they waken to Peggy Lee's voice, they will know that in the morning the father will be silent over his coffee, with puffy skin beneath eyes which do not turn even towards children who squabble or bicker or cry.

The father is teaching; Lily and MJ are at school in the ancient nunnery at the top of the college, where the jungle begins and colobus monkeys make the palm fronds sway. Richard becomes weary of following the silent houseboy from room to room; he walks up the hill, among the buildings of the calm college. The father's voice is suddenly near, clear. Through the window Richard sees rows of young men and women with dark skin and white teeth; they gaze raptly at the father, who sits on the edge of a desk and swings his legs back and forth, then springs up to write white on the blackboard. If we know what occurred before, we may understand what happens now, the father explains. His eyes travel around the classroom, across the window; he continues to speak smoothly about an impersonal past, as though he doesn't see Richard at the window, as though Richard were not there. The boy crouches between freshly watered shrubs and digs hands into damp dirt. He paints his face brown with tribal markings, reels at the rich odour of this earth.

One night Lily finds a snake curled in a corner of the children's room. The father's face pales; he grips the machete, and from a distance of several feet stares at the intruder. You can sleep in my bed, he finally tells the children, closing the door of their room tightly, leaving the snake undisturbed, alone, coiled around itself for warmth. The children crowd into the father's big bed; he and the record player have moved into the living room for the night. *I know a little more about psychology*, her voice winds away, charming the snake into lifting its head, extending its length into the air, swaying in sinuous circles. Peggy Lee performs magic until morning, when the houseboy opens the door of the children's room to find the snake not there. The father carefully inspects the window screens, fails to find flaws.

If I could get back to Africa, I'd be okay, Lily writes Richard from the clinic they won't let her leave. There at least the snakes are real, you can close the door against them, Peggy Lee makes them vanish in a puff of smoke. Do you remember the time he suddenly decided we had to learn to swim, packed us into the white Peugeot, drove all morning until we reached the ocean? Anyone can learn to swim in the Indian Ocean, he said, the water's so salty it holds you up even when you don't know how to float. You couldn't drown if you tried. He shouted instructions from shore, he wouldn't even get his toes wet, he already knew how to swim, he said. Float! he called. And we did, didn't we? We floated all afternoon in that water as warm as blood, while on land he turned over rocks in search of shells. I won't always be around to save you from drowning, he said when we were allowed out of the water at last to wobble on legs that had forgotten how to navigate solid ground. I can't always save you from this or from that, he frowned, holding a shell to his ear, listening intently. What faint music did he hear? I no longer hear Peggy Lee in the night. Do you? Does MJ, wherever he is? MJ would get me out of here if he were still alive. I keep thinking he drowned, though that's not what really happened, I know. MJ is still with Peggy Lee in Africa, together they disappeared into the jungle, searching for the source of the river, somewhere at the top of the Ngondo hills, that we could never find. *Missing*, is the official word. Not *dead*. Did you know Mitch has started collecting stamps? Honey, I have to have a hobby to keep me busy now that my babies have abandoned me, he explained in a postcard from Thailand. Apparently he's left Tibet; I take it the wise Buddhists wouldn't have him. Stay away, little brother. Remain in Italy or Greece. The snakes have briefly vanished, which only means they'll soon be back in greater number. Everything would be all right if I could smell the frangipani by the river one more time, writes Lily in another of the letters Richard will not answer, not wanting his messages to her to be read first by the people in white with clean pink skin, with cold Canadian eyes.

MJ says she's in a hospital, Lily insists she's dead. Who? asks Richard. Both MJ and Lily say she didn't really have short waved hair that was more white than blond. She didn't use deep-red lipstick, she didn't sing the same song over and over until you fell asleep. You can't remember, they tell Richard. He remembers riding with her on a roller coaster, Lily and MJ in the car behind, the father watching anxiously from the ground. Climbing slowly, then falling fast, snaking swiftly all the way to the end. The children lurch off the ride, join the father on the ground, watch the mother ride again, without them this time. Her head is thrown back, her short hair whips; they can hear her laughter above other passengers' screams. She rides a dozen more times, laughing like she will laugh when they take her away. (Then Richard stays with an aunt during the day, the old house on Columbia Avenue is quiet at night, the father plays Peggy Lee and prepares to take the children across the world, away from everything.) After finally descending from danger, the mother is silent in her summer dress; her red lips press tightly together as the children and father make cotton candy melt in their months, throw rings at gaudy prizes. Lily wins a big stuffed snake she calls Honey.

At first nothing grows in the dirt around the cement-block house. It is red and cracked from lack of water and too much heat or a field of mud during the rains. It would be a waste of time to start a garden, says the father after one year, since we're only here temporarily. The Peggy Lee records become worn and scratched; a constant hissing beneath her voice threatens to drown her out. Richard grows old enough for school in the nunnery up where the butterflies are brilliant, but even Lily and MJ do not go there now. Sometimes the father gathers his children around the atlas or dictionary for an hour in evening; more often he goes into his bedroom right after supper. When are we going home? MJ asks him once. Why, son, this is our home, the father replies, kneading his left biceps slowly — then says he has work to do, shuts his door behind him, makes Peggy Lee sing once more. Slowly the children's hair blanches beneath the African sun until it is more white than blond. They follow the river that rushes down through the jungle, searching for its source somewhere at the top of the Ngondo hills. They eat green mangos until their stomachs are sore. They file, oldest to youngest, along a narrow path with grass higher than their heads on either side. When they meet the snake, Lily will be the unfortunate one: it will be too startled by MJ, in front, to bite him; it will have already had its fill by the time Richard comes along, at the rear. Unlucky Lily, forever in the middle, sees serpents in the clinic. They are always long and thick, tattooed with intricate designs, patterned by the kind of brilliant colours seen only in jungle or in dreams. Don't bother, Lily replies to the father's last long-distance wish to visit her bare white room. You can't save me from the poisoned fangs, that never was your strong point.

The father cries for help. The children find him at the kitchen sink, a knife fallen at his feet, deep-red blood flowing from his thumb. He leans against MJ, Lily runs for bandages and tape, Richard watches the father's legs tremble. *I'm a little gem in geology*, boasts Peggy Lee, knowing nearly everything. I'm bleeding and it won't stop, Lily tells MJ one day, I don't know what to do. Neither do I, says MJ.

Dear Lily, Richard could write, Peggy Lee is still alive and kicking, though I've heard she no longer resides in Tanzania. The climate, she murmurs, stroking her velvet throat, was not good for my voice. Now the notes are no longer perfectly pitched, now she is old and ill. They prop her on stage in a blond wig and dark glasses, she snaps her fingers through "Fever" for the millionth time. He wrote me you refused his offer to fly across the world to see you, he said it breaks his heart that he can no longer save his children from this thing or the other thing. I always thought everything would be all right as long as Peggy Lee kept singing. She could save us from anything, I believed, Richard might write Lily, who finally coils around herself for warmth: the clinic and Canada are always cold. Sometimes she unwinds her length and flicks her tongue. A slow hiss is her only language now.

Fireflies float through the screen window, drift through the children's bedrooms. The colours blink like lights of an airplane searching for a safe place to return to earth. One day we will fly away from all this, MJ has told Richard. Lately the children have begun picking through the father's things; careful detectives, they leave all the Peggy Lee records exactly as they are. They hunt for photographs of the mother, find only a letter from an aunt in Canada. You must do something with those children, read MJ and Lily — while Richard, who hasn't learned letters, stares at the smooth pale face, remembers Peggy Lee laughing all afternoon behind her locked door in the old house on Columbia Avenue. She wouldn't open it, finally they had to break it down, the wood splintered. Before it's too late, adds the aunt. It's late, fireflies bumble sleepily around the room, Richard hears MJ ask Lily if she's awake. I think so, she says. I don't know, she says a moment later. The father sets the needle back down on the black circle; it will trace a million revolutions before dawn. *But I don't know enough about you,* Peggy Lee finally admits. Her voice is playful, light, certain that tomorrow she will know everything about the ones who pray to her at night.

MARY SWAN

Archaeology
(1989)

Now that we are both old I have gone back to school, and this amuses him greatly. At breakfast we watched through the window while the young girls shuffled through fallen leaves, hair in long braids, plaid skirts and thick red knee socks, and Benjamin looked from them to me, buttering toast, and said, "Do you have your pencils sharpened?" Knowing, of course, that I had spent a day in town, preparing. Buying soft-covered notebooks, with lines and without, and one with graph paper in a delicate green, different sizes and intensities, for who knows — I might want to study geometry one day. Physics. Choosing felt pens, black and red, and three pencils which, yes, I had sharpened. Using a small silver sharpener with a grey smudge in one corner, all that was left of the price tag.

He laughed unfairly, for he too knows the seductive power of these objects; we met, in fact, in a stationery shop. I was very impressed by the way he asked for samples of papers, different weights. Rubbed a corner between thumb and finger, held each one up to the light. He said later that he only wanted to keep me near him, to watch me bend, pulling out various packets, the competence in my fingers. This was during his Pre-Raphaelite phase, as I have heard him say many times.

So he is amused and also annoyed that I am not going at this systematically. It irritates him, the way I take a course here and there, flitting from subject to subject, century to century. "Why on earth don't you work for a degree?" he says. "A thing worth doing is worth doing properly," he says, and I wonder if he hears himself.

There is a pattern, I am dimly beginning to see. Questions answered, needs. I don't expect Benjamin to divine this, don't really want him to, but I am surprised that as a professor of English literature he should think anything random.

It also annoys him, of course, that I am learning things without his assistance, approval. When I come home he is often reading in his study, and he takes off his glasses, says, "There you are. Well, tell me, what did they say? What did they say about *Alastor*?"

And if it happens to be something he agrees with he will say, "Yes, yes, but that's putting it a little crudely, you see. It goes so much deeper than that . . ." Following me out to the kitchen, talking and correcting while I make the tea. He will sometimes admit to this annoyance, flashing a little grin when I least expect it. Benjamin was a poet; he has always been able to acknowledge, disarmingly, most of his faults.

It was not easy at first, armed though I was with my notebooks and pencils, a pile of required and recommended texts. I wrote frantically, trying to take down every word that was said, and in the evenings I transcribed those scribbled notes into another book, neat orderly lines sailing across the page. Benjamin thought it absurd. "You're only auditing the course, for God's sake," he said. "A thing worth doing is worth doing properly," I said, and he glared at me and left the room. Poor Benjamin, he could have understood if I had volunteered with the Red Cross, would have welcomed me home after the bustle of the annual bake sale. At times it seemed like a better idea. But I carried on, scribbling my way through the first term, and slowly began to understand the language, to understand that I *could* understand the language. That, in a course called Marriage and the Family, they really were after the simple answers.

The students took longer to get used to. Some hard, raw edge that I don't remember from my own children with their floating hair and rooms full of incense. In the end I decided that if a boy with green hair and ballet tights found me odd, well, perhaps it was only fair. In the coffee shops and waiting halls I realized that the girls in black with extravagant eyes and twelve earrings were talking about their broken hearts. That the brilliant girl in the Philosophy seminar who brought her baby in a backpack was worried, too, about what to cook for dinner. Now we talk between classes, my fellow students and I, and they often borrow my notes, for my attention to detail has been observed.

This fall I am studying the History of Archaeology, Part I. The course is taught by a young American woman who wears hiking boots and has only been here a year, and this is a great relief. There are too many familiar faces, and more than a few of the professors are former students. It is quite unnerving to walk into a classroom and see, behind the trim beard and half-glasses, the face of a pimply boy who once threw up on our living room carpet.

But this woman, who wants us to call her Gail, has no connection with the more recent past. She lectures well; she has been on digs all over the Middle East and Central America, and she makes us feel that we are getting the inside story. In the first class she talked about the Shanidar cave, the famous Neanderthal burials, and I remembered seeing pictures in a magazine years ago. The uncovering of skeletons: old man, woman, young man, child. According to the article, pollen samples showed that at least one had been buried in a flower-lined grave. Benjamin found me in tears later; I couldn't stop, couldn't explain. He wrote a poem about it, but there he was the one who cried.

This week Gail is telling us about Heinrich Schliemann — the crackpot, she calls him affectionately, the old fart. His life, as Gail tells it, unreels like an old movie. The strange young man surviving shipwrecks, travelling everywhere and mastering the languages of the world, amassing great fortunes along the way. Indulging himself, in middle age, by digging for fabled Troy. On his way to the site in Turkey he decided that it was time to marry, and he wrote to the Archbishop of Athens, asking him to pick out a suitable bride. He was, as Gail says, characteristically precise. The girl should be young and well educated, with black hair. She should be acquainted with Homer and of the Greek type. If not an orphan, she should at least be poor, forced to eke out a meagre living. As a governess, perhaps. The Archbishop selected a number of candidates and sent the information, along with photographs. And Schliemann fell in love with Sophie's picture.

"Was this the face?" Benjamin said when I told him my name. And I didn't know Marlowe then, but I did know poetry when I heard it, and I thought him daft. But I let him walk me back to the boarding house, wheeling his bicycle through the town, stumbling and knocking into me occasionally. He wore his hair rather long, combed straight back from his forehead, and he ran his fingers through it as he talked.

He talked a lot of rubbish, as I recall, trying to impress me. Which was a bit of a waste because I didn't understand half of it, didn't even really know, for example, what a graduate student *was*. I watched him though, the way he tugged at his hair with his fingers, the rusty bicycle clips that rucked up his pant legs. I remembered how, after all the testing and weighing, he had picked out the cheapest paper in the shop, and how he had paid for it with great dignity, as if it was what he really wanted.

When our children were small Benjamin used to tell them stories about where he grew up. The grand house with servants' quarters in the attic. His father's library, his beautiful mother who played the piano all day. He told the children that his parents had opposed our marriage, that out of loyalty to me he severed all ties with his family. But as I remember it they gave us a silver tea service and invited us to dinner, so they can't have minded that much. The house was large but not particularly grand, and I don't remember a piano. They talked about their garden, mostly, and about their other son, Robert, who was a lawyer in Montreal.

We went to the farm a few times, too, in those early years, but the visits were never successful. I don't know what he had expected. Landed gentry, perhaps, fallen on hard times but still with paddocks of fine horses and tea in the afternoon. Or perhaps a quaint little cottage, with chickens scratching delicately in the yard and my mother knitting by the fire. Not the rambling brick house with no front step. Not the makeshift toilet and the clammy sheets in the spare room. He thought that my brothers were savages, not understanding that they were putting it on a bit. Stamping around in their shit-covered boots, calling him Ben and asking if he wanted to come help slaughter a sow. Geld a bull.

He told stories about the farm for years over dinner tables, in the faculty club. "It's incredible," he would say, "another world entirely." Going on to relate a conversation with a cross-eyed neighbour, a trip into town to buy rubber boots. Describing corners named for the great cities of Europe where men mated with their mothers, sisters, sheep. Murder, incest, insanity — to hear him talk you'd think there was a corpse dangling in every barn in south-western Ontario.

But I let him do it, didn't contradict him. I even served up a few bizarre tales myself at those dinner parties. I stepped out of my life for a time, trying so hard to be what Benjamin saw in me. A rough diamond, waiting to be polished by the blaze of his brilliance, his love. The girls in the lecture halls have choices now, and perhaps I did too, but it never occurred to me. Not even when I left once, the first year we were married. After a horrible fight, after a party where I'd sat silent, stupid, trying to follow the darting, swooping conversation. Watching him charm every woman in the room with his talk, his slender hands. We shouted and cried and he struck me on the cheek, not very hard, and I put on my coat and walked out of the house, and he threw a cup or a bottle, it crashed against the doorframe after I had gone through, and he shouted, "Good riddance, who needs you — who needs you?"

I went back to the farm very calmly, deadly, and I cooked and I cleaned and I drove in the cattle and I waited to see what would happen. He came for me a few days later. It was just before dawn, when the sky was grey and still, and he left the car on the road and walked up the lane, and the low leaves of trees brushed his hair and the long wet grass soaked his feet, soaked his pant legs to the knee. He walked around to the back of the house; he hadn't shaved and his eyes were wild, and he stood below my window and tipped his head back, and he shouted "Helen! Hel — en!" until his throat ached.

I was in the barn, collecting eggs. I came up behind him and took his hand.

When he was working on the Helen poems we took the children to Greece for a year, rented a house on a small island. It didn't cost much, but it still used up all our savings, and when we came back I had to work for a while typing essays and reports. "If I could have stayed in Greece," he often used to say, "I would have been a great poet. That wonderful clear light, the inspiration of those ancient skies. Ah — if only I could have stayed, things would have been different."

Well, perhaps, but I don't remember much clear light. The rented house squatted on a rocky hillside, no electricity or running water except for the rain that trickled through all winter. Michael was five and kept wandering away, Jennie trailing after him, and Alison was still in diapers and wouldn't let me out of her sight. Benjamin went for long walks and worked outside beneath a flowering fig tree if the weather was fine.

The Helen cycle was supposed to make his name, and some of it is quite lovely. The book was reviewed kindly, on the whole, and sections are still included in anthologies occasionally. "Helen Weeping" was at one time used in a high school text. Benjamin grew a beard and got tenure and began to work on a second collection. It never appeared, although a few of the poems were printed here and there. There were times when, glass in hand, he would point to me and say, "My Helen. Well, you see . . ." And people in the room would begin to talk loudly about other things. And there were times when he would rage about the house, waving a fistful of bills and shouting that we were destroying him, bleeding him dry. We lived like that for years.

The first heart attack frightened him; he stopped smoking and drinking, began to walk to the campus and home, all about the town. He stood in front of the mirror in the bedroom, patting his flat stomach and saying, "Look at that — I'm in better shape than when I was twenty. I feel better than I have in years."

When they tried to reach me from the hospital I was in bed with Jonas, a quiet man who worked at the post office. We had been meeting on his lunch hour for several months; he had grown noticeably thinner but never complained. I have thought since that at the moment that Benjamin's chest exploded I was probably stabbing my tongue at the base of my lover's spine. Some people would see that as a sign, crime and punishment. Benjamin would, for he is a very moral person; he believes in punishment. But I know that it was just a fluke of timing. I could just as easily have been vacuuming the spare room, pushing a cart through the supermarket. Which is where I said I was, to make things easier.

I've never told him about Jonas, about the others. In the old days, of course, there were his students. All those bright young boys who couldn't impress him any other way. Benjamin was always a good teacher, but he loves a mocking phrase and was often, I am sure, quite cruel, carried away by the sound of the words.

So the young boys came to dinner, came to parties, came to seminar meetings held in our living room with a great deal of wine. And sometimes they would rise to help me, to carry dishes to the kitchen, pour coffee, open a bottle. And sometimes our fingers brushed, reaching for a coffee cup, an ashtray, and sometimes they called me, wrote letters, said there was no one else in the world, and sometimes I thought — but only for a moment. They were just boys, after all; they would have wanted people to know, to guess. The men I have chosen have been different, and they have had nothing to do with Benjamin's world. The carpenter who built our kitchen cupboards, more than twenty years ago. The man who sold us insurance, the high school chemistry teacher. Jonas, who I suppose was the last. All kind, lonely men who wanted simply to give and receive pleasure.

Benjamin has never known; he has never tried to know, although I am sure the signs have been there. For years I wore a silver locket given to me by Phil, the insurance man.

And if he had known where I was when the hospital called, he would have had to make it ridiculous. Geriatric desire — my sagging thighs, the fringe of reddish hair around Jonas's skull. Oh, yes, I can just hear him. For years I tried to make him happy, tried so hard to be what he thought I was. The silent beauty in the stationery shop. "Helen by the sea, with children." I never got it right, and sometime during the years of scotch and rage it ceased to matter. I looked at him across a crowded room, heard him talk, his face flushed and a glass unsteady in his hand, and I knew that it didn't matter what I did, what I was. I saw him then as a child, lost in the scent of pine needles. When all the presents have been unwrapped with laughter and a flurry of crackling paper and it slowly begins to be clear that that one perfect, mysterious, longed-for gift is not there.

Later that evening he read a new poem called "Shanidar." And not long after, we had our kitchen remodelled.

She'd made her bed, they used to say where I come from. And I have been close to saying it myself at times, listening to conversations in restaurants and bus shelters. Or when my daughters call from different parts of the world, talking about leaving a husband or lover. How did you stand it? they say. All those years with Daddy when he was — the way he used to treat you, the way he used to carry on — why did you put up with all that?

I don't know, I tell them. I just did. I do.

And the wires hum with their anger and pain, and then they say, What about the girls though, what about all those girls.

Ah yes, the girls. The girls who came to parties with all those gentle boys, the girls whose eyes sparkled in the light of tall candles. The girls whose names came up frequently at home. A student of mine said . . . wrote . . . quite a clever girl, really . . . Angela. Or Christine, or Sarah. I always knew. I learned that each one would fade away, eventually, but they still caused me a great deal of pain. And maybe that's why I don't tell my daughters the rest of it, the funny part. How now that it doesn't matter I've come to think that he never slept with any of those girls.

Something he said to me in the hospital, where I don't suppose a man would lie. All those grand unconsummated poet's loves.

The second attack enraged him. "I might have known," he said, in a voice thick with significance, "that my heart would betray me after all."

He has not accepted it easily. Retirement and a quiet life, the pacemaker which he blames now for the death of his poetry. He reviews books caustically and is lavishly hospitable to the occasional old student who comes by. He has set up a telescope in the back yard and memorized the known sky, tried to teach me to play chess. He follows his doctor's orders grudgingly, with small flashes of rebellion. A cigar at Christmas, a glass of brandy. I can see him now through the window, rake in his hand beneath a curdled autumn sky. He is not supposed to exert himself, but on a brisk October day, breathing deeply and wearing a navy watch cap to keep the heat in, he stirs the flame-coloured leaves, very slowly.

And now that it no longer matters, there is something I would like to tell him. Something I have learned about archaeology. When Heinrich Schliemann came at last to Hissarlik, he was sure that his lost city must lie in the deepest heart of the mound, and he gouged an enormous trench through the hill. But when he reached the deepest layer, none of it made sense. And he died without ever knowing that he had found his fabled Troy, much closer to the surface. That he had destroyed most of it in his haste to reach the depths.

But then, as I watch through the window, I am suddenly ambushed by memory. A clear spring night in that rented house in Greece. Benjamin out walking, and I had soothed the children to sleep, boiled water on the tiny gas burner, washed the dishes. And he burst through the door, his cheeks flaming and his eyes wide with magic. "Come on, come with me," he said, grabbing my hand.

And I went, surprised, a little grumpily, still holding the dishrag in my other hand. He pulled me into the night, stumbling down the rocky path to the point where the sea became visible. All bathed in silver, the whispering sea and the hillside behind us, the huddled white houses.

"Look at that moon," he said very softly. "Oh, Helen, just look at that moon."

IRENA FRIEDMAN KARAFILLY

Hoodlums
(1990)

It was agreed we would meet by the entrance to the park, where a street vendor stood selling sugar buns with his young, one-eyed daughter. Mother was going to see a doctor, and Basha, who had come from the country to work for us, was off to visit her father in the hospital. This was in 1946, in the Polish city of Lodz, on the first day of Hanukkah. Not that my parents — Father was Jewish and Mother Russian Orthodox — were religiously inclined, but one did not go about flaunting secularity in the vastly diminished Jewish community, especially not if one's wife happened to be a gentile. So Father and his partner, whose name was Kapusta, closed their jewellery store, with Father planning to spend the day doing things he normally had little time for: shopping for clothes and seeing an optician and getting a haircut at the barber's. We were all going to buy winter coats that day, before going to the circus. As Father was only seeing a barber that morning, I was left in his care. He was one of those people said to have little patience for children. In fact, his patience was seldom put to the test, for he saw very little of me. Ever since our arrival from Russia, he had been busy setting up shop and establishing contacts — and trying to trace his family, believed to have perished in the concentration camps.

Father was a tall, dark man with heavy-lidded eyes and a sonorous voice. A Polish citizen, he had escaped to Russia along with other Jews and there, in a city named Orenburg, met and married Mother, thereby taking the last step away from his Orthodox Jewish upbringing. Certainly he made no effort to acquaint me with Jewish traditions. I was six, that first winter in Poland, and possessed only the vaguest notion of what religion meant. I knew nothing whatever about Hanukkah, but being in Father's charge lent the day a somewhat festive air.

It was early winter, November or perhaps December, a few weeks before Christmas. It had rained all night, but the morning was unexpectedly sunny, with the sharp, almost painful brightness which a windy, clear morning brings after a night of rain. That was the morning I saw my first rainbow, arching splendidly across the sky. I had up to then seen one only in picture books.

"Watch out, don't step in a puddle."

The warning was issued rather distractedly. We were walking past the park, circling around rain puddles. Father, dressed in a long dark coat, was holding on to his hat lest the wind blow it. There was, all along the park, a row of yellowing horse chestnut trees and, across the street, several neighbourhood shops: a grocery, a bakery, a shoe repair shop, a pharmacy. The air was fragrant with the damp smell of ripe chestnuts and of freshly baked onion rolls. Father may have been a taciturn man, but this in no way affected my spirits. I was walking down the street with my father, small hand in large one, anticipating the singular privilege of watching him get a haircut. That was enough; it seemed everything that morning.

I had never been to a barber shop before, had never so much as passed one since our arrival in Poland some months before. Recently, however, I had experienced my first dental visit, during which a beguiling dentist extracted a stubborn tooth, having first assured me that all he wanted was to have a look. The dentist had worn a short, impeccably white jacket, with buttons and pockets at the front. What I did not know was that, in those days, every barber and waiter in Lodz wore a similar white jacket. Entering the barber shop with Father, I saw an elderly man seated in a high oak chair, his head thrown back, his scrawny throat drawn taut. He was being shaved but looked, alas, much like a dental patient. The barber, a burly man with a double chin and fair moustache, was not only white-clad, he was holding an unfamiliar, knife-like instrument to the old man's throat.

"Papa." I had stopped on the threshold, panic filling my mouth. "I don't want to stay here, Papa."

Father was hanging his hat on the coat tree. He turned and looked at me from beneath bushy eyebrows. "Pardon?"

"I want to go out, Papa."

"Go *out*?" The dark eyebrows were joined in disapproval. "Didn't you want to see me get a haircut?"

"Yes, but — I don't want to anymore. I want to go out, right now."

These words were uttered with sudden urgency; my eyes were beginning to sting.

"But why?" Father had bent down and was looking straight into my eyes. "What's the matter, Vera?"

"Nothing." I glanced over Father's shoulder at the customer in the barber's chair. "I just don't want to." I had begun to snivel.

Father raked his hand through his dark hair. "But I have to get my hair cut," he said reasonably. "I'm going to Warsaw tomorrow." When this failed to make an impression, Father's mouth stretched wryly; he turned his head sideways and drew a long breath. "What's wrong with you?" he asked with sudden irritation.

I did not, I repeated, want to stay in the shop.

"But why?" insisted Father. "Won't you tell me why?"

I would not say nor let myself be persuaded. I said I would wait outside; it was not too cold, I hastened to point out. Mother, I knew, would never have agreed, but Father, untutored in the ways of children, finally sighed and let me have my way. His decision was abetted by the barber himself who, smiling indulgently, provided a chair for me to sit on, right outside the entrance.

"Sit here and don't budge," Father said sternly, adding, "Wait till I tell your mother." He paused then, vaguely doubtful, casting a quick look up and down the street. There was a kiosk a few feet away selling newspapers and cigarettes and candy. "Wait here." He walked resolutely towards the kiosk, coming back with a red rooster lollipop.

"For me?" I said. It was confusing to be rewarded for my lack of co-operation, but Father often confused me, alternating as he did between indifference and extreme indulgence.

"Yes. Just sit here and eat your lollipop. Call me if anyone bothers you."

"All right, Papa. Thank you," I added as an afterthought. The lolli-pop smelled like strawberries.

I sat in the oak chair, licking the lollipop, watching the passers-by. The shopping street was crowded with harried-looking women, a child or two in tow, and elderly men, heading toward the park. The old men ambled along, chatting companionably, hands knotted behind their backs. Now and then they were forced aside by playful children or brash officers. The army officers were Russian and looked resplendent in their uniforms, their medals glinting in the sun. The old men cast sidelong glances in their direction; they lowered their voices as they stepped aside. I was beginning to enjoy myself. From time to time I would glance into the barber shop to see Father waiting, a newspaper in his hands. Once, our eyes met above the paper. Father smiled through the glass.

It was noisy out on the street. There was the sound of horse hooves and of honking cars and the clanking noise of passing trolleys. A few feet away, a girl my own age was chasing a small, fair-haired boy. They ran about, squealing, stopping beside me to watch a black funeral carriage go by. The carriage moved very slowly, pulled by a brown mare. Three women sat in it, staring vacantly amidst a profusion of flowers. We were still watching, the children and I as well as some passers-by, when the tow-haired boy burst into sudden laughter. He pointed at the road, where the scrawny horse's droppings were falling one by one, dry yellow lumps onto grey cobblestones. Then a woman emerged from a butcher shop, shooing the children on. The rising wind blew the woman's skirt above her knees. It made the girl laugh and pat her mother's skirt into place. She looked at me over her shoulder, walking on.

After a while, I got up and stood staring at my own reflection in the plate-glass window. I was wearing a navy-blue coat with red buttons and a red beret attached to my thin, fair hair with a bobby pin. Father, I noted, was now sitting in the barber chair, getting his hair cut at last. It was reassuring to watch the dark bits of curl fall onto the floor, but the silver scissors, flashing around Father's head, made me feel uneasy. Before I could properly reflect on Father's vulnerability, however, a new noise attracted my attention. It was an odd animal sound, followed by the laughter of children from beyond the kiosk. I glanced over my shoulder, quickly detaching myself from the window.

A bear was making its way up the street, trailed by a small crowd. It was a large bear, brown and shaggy and upright, growling ominously. Despite the laughter, the gay scampering of the children, my heart was pounding madly. I was an intensely fearful child and would have certainly fled had it not been for the fact that, as the bear approached, it proved to be wearing black, shiny shoes, much like my own father's.

"Good morning, Missy," he said, pausing before my chair. He bowed from the waist, surrounded by the children. The bow made me smile and lower my chin toward my coat's top button. I was still holding the sticky lollipop.

"I said good morning," growled the bear. The feigned note of malice sparked up a fresh peal of laughter. I giggled and raised my gaze.

I could see a man's eyes, small and blue, staring out within the fur.

"Good morning," I let out at length.

The bear snorted, scratching at his throat. "And what are you doing here all alone at a barber shop?"

"Waiting for my father." The answer was offered after the briefest hesitation. I was suddenly determined to show myself as brave as any of them.

"And who is your father?" the bear demanded. He peered theatrically into the barber shop.

"Mr. Aaron Stein." I twisted back in my chair. The barber was standing with his back to the window, bending over Father.

"Stein, eh? *Stein.*" The bear paused with a paw held against his brow, as if in recollection. The children, who had laughed hearing my name, laughed some more. "Don't believe we've met," the bear said and gave a shrug. "Oh, well. Time to get back to the circus." He sighed ostentatiously. "Bye, Missy — and don't talk to any strangers."

The last bit of advice elicited a final burst of laughter from the children and nods of agreement from the pursuing mothers. My own mother had issued similar warnings, even in the small town of Orenburg. For although I was fearful, I was also intensely curious and liable to wander off on my own. Having been punished shortly after my fifth birthday, I made a promise, which I had kept for a year, never expecting my resolution to be put to a test by a man in a bear's clothing.

While Father sat, oblivious, getting his hair cut by the barber, I got up and took a few timid steps away from my chair. The children went on laughing as they made their way up the street, prancing about the bear, tugging at his fur. I did not join them but followed gingerly at a distance, sucking on my lollipop. I had passed three or four store windows when a gust of wind came, blowing dust in my face. I stopped, shutting my eyes tight, and rubbed and rubbed, until the tears washed out the blinding dust. When my eyes had cleared, I saw that the distance between me and the frolicking group had widened. I began to run, only to see the bear turn the corner onto the street leading toward the park. I had no intention of following the bear. Having been warned against wandering out of sight, I told myself I would stand on the corner and watch the bear's progress down the tree-lined street. When I reached the corner, however, a new gust of wind blew the beret off my head and onto the sidewalk. There it rested, inanimate red against smooth grey pavement, until the moment when my hand reached out to retrieve it.

All at once, as if under the spell of some impish spirit, it rose again, whirling for a moment, only to land passively further down the street. Once more I reached for my beret; once more it eluded me.

By the time this had been replayed several times, I was almost a block away from the corner which was to have been my boundary. The beret was now resting in the middle of the road, as yet untouched by car wheels or horses' hooves but directly in the path of a quickly approaching carriage. I had never had a beret before and, despite Mother's assertion that blue went better with my sea-green eyes, was passionately attached to red. Watching the carriage approach, I had a sudden vision of the horse indolently defecating on my beret. I began to cry, unconsoled when, at the crucial moment, a merciful gust carried my beret clear across the street toward a large, rectangular building with a multitude of windows. Unaccustomed to crossing alone, I went on crying, wiping my nose against my woollen sleeve, my pale hair blowing in the wind.

Suddenly there were two women standing beside me, two large, thick-necked women with tight blond curls and red mouths pursed in solicitude. They looked strikingly alike, except for the colour of their eyes.

"What's the matter, little girl?" the green-eyed one asked, bending toward me. A little taller than her companion, her eyes were an exceptionally light shade of green, a cat's eyes. Both women were dressed in checkered coats and brown laced-up shoes.

"I — you see, I —" my voice faltered, then broke off altogether; I remembered I was not to speak to strangers. I would have more likely broken this injunction had I found the faces more to my liking. Alas, even in my dire circumstances, there was something about the women from which I instinctively recoiled. I had, on more than one occasion, heard of gypsies kidnapping strangers' children. The two Polish women did not look like gypsies to me, but something about their features — the blinking close-set eyes? the pink gums exposed as they smiled? — suggested foxiness. It was easy to imagine them turned aside, exchanging conspiratorial winks. My tears turned to sobs.

"Oh, don't cry." The second woman's eyes were a pale, washed-out shade of blue. "Don't cry, little girl. Where's your Mama, tell us?"

I would not tell them. I pulled back when one of them reached out to stroke my hair.

"Such a pretty little girl." The women made vaguely soothing sounds between their teeth. "Such a nice girl. So tell us where your Mama is, and we'll take you to her."

I glanced back over my shoulder; then across the street where I had last seen my red beret, lying beside a lamp post. It was no longer there. Suddenly, I remembered the Kapustas' daughter. Father's partner and his wife had once had a child who, I had overheard Father say, was lost in the war. This fact, then and now, made my heart cringe with terror. The word went clattering through my head: *lostlostlostlostlostlost*.

My frantic sobs were beginning to attract a crowd. I was aware of questions and exclamations, of the two matrons acting with the fierce complacence of people in authority.

"We found her right here, crying," one of them stated. "All alone without so much as a hat to cover her ears and —"

"She doesn't know where her mother is," the second one interjected.

There were vague sounds of disapproval from the crowd.

"Imagine leaving a small child unattended," someone said behind me.

"My son would get an ear infection in five minutes, let out in this wind without a hat."

"But where could her mother be?" This was a new, gentler voice. "She must be in one of the shops around here. Perhaps we should go and ask?"

"Oh —" An elderly voice sighed eloquently. "What's Poland coming to, I ask you?"

Alarmed by the growing crowd, I wheeled about, chaotically determined to head back up the street and around the corner to the barber shop. And then I saw Father.

He was coming down the street, coatless as well as hatless, dark eyes flashing with wild anguish. "Vera!" he shouted. "Vera!" His arm was raised, as if to hail a taxi or ward off a blow. He was running toward us. "That's my child!" he cried, "that's my child there!"

I had stopped crying. The crowd too, had all at once fallen silent. We all stood and watched the dark, distraught man dressed in suit and white shirt, his tie flapping in the wind. All of him — body and face and clothing — seemed excessively animated while we, the crowd and I, stood silent and still, appalled. Today, what horrifies me is my own childish inertia, the failure to reach toward Father, to cry out his name. I felt oddly paralyzed, unnerved by the contrast between the aloof, poised man I knew and this frantic, shrill, unpredictable (I could feel the crowd thinking) madman. The word *Papa* was lodged deep in my throat. Watching Father slow down, I began to tremble. I could see the tears shining in his eyes. He was almost within reach when the two Polish matrons deposited themselves directly in front of me, blocking my view of Father. There was, in that gesture, the abrupt, cruel finality of a slamming door.

"That is not a Jewish child," the rheumy-eyed one stated sententiously.

"Not a Jewish child!" cried Father. "She's *my* child. Ask her," he added desperately. "Why don't you ask her? Vera —"

I was about to speak. I was aware of Father's frantic efforts to get around the two women, of the confused mutterings of the swelling crowd. Suddenly, a shrill voice rose above the others.

"Look at her!" It spit out the words. "Look at her and look at him. They look as much like a father and child as a —"

"But she *is* my child!" cried Father, struggling, "she —"

"Oh, go on with you," the shrill voice stated. "We've heard of the likes of you."

"Vera!" Father had elbowed his way to me, only to be shoved aside roughly.

"Go on, you Jewish kidnapper. Go, before the police get here."

The word police, as much as the sight of Father's torn sleeve, at last unblocked my constricted throat. "Papa!" I cried. "Papa!"

But the crowd was restive and heedless by then. They went on arguing with each other; some hurled abuse at Father. I don't know how this would have ended were it not for the fact that, suddenly, a familiar voice cried, "Vera!" Turning, I saw Basha crossing the street amid cars and horses, one hand on her head holding down one of Mother's discarded hats, the other clutching her open coat.

"Basha!" I began to cry again. The crowd, for the second time, fell abruptly silent. They watched, grim-faced, as the young woman hurried determinedly toward us, a fabric bag under her arm.

"Is this your child?" The green-eyed matron addressed Basha, blinking at her impassively, exactly like a cat. Basha was a tall, strongly built woman with splendid amber-colour eyes. She had dark hair, not unlike Father's, but hers was an unmistakably Polish face: wide, ruddy cheeks, a high forehead, a small, upturned nose.

"I'm the maid," she said. She took a step toward me, glancing in Father's direction. Father was struggling with two men.

"You are, are you?" The two matrons were scrutinizing Basha in vague confusion. A country woman, Basha's appearance — perhaps even her speech — no doubt left something to be desired. At the same time, she was clearly a woman who could not easily be trifled with. The crowd seemed torn between scorn and instinctive respect.

"This is not a Jewish child, is it?" the rheumy-eyed woman asked with a frown.

"Well —" Basha hesitated, casting an anxious look toward Father. Someone had blocked our view of him. "She is and she isn't." She looked, at that moment, exceptionally young and flustered, like a child asked for a difficult explanation.

"What does that mean?" an aggressive voice demanded.

"It means — oh, what business is it of yours?" Basha's discomfiture had lasted only a moment. Frowning resolutely, she pushed her way toward me, snapping at the crowd. To my amazement, the crowd stepped back before her will, much as I had seen village children do in Basha's neighbourhood. Muttering amongst themselves — some coughed, others cleared their noses — they broke up their invincible front, shuffling away. They sidestepped Father, who was standing alone now, hands clenched at his sides, his gaze fixed upon the black shoes polished by Basha in the early morning. there was about him an air of melancholy, certainly, but also of obscure shame, of almost palpable defeat.

But these things are clearer in recollection than they were to my child's eyes. At that time, running into Father's arms, what struck me most forcibly was the bloody cut in Father's lower lip, then the odd absence of reproach for my disobedience. And something else, which was that Basha, who had up to then been *the maid*, had suddenly and immeasurably gained in stature. It was, indeed, the beginning of her friendship with Father. Not that there was, as the three of us walked away, anything new in Basha's speech or manner. She looked exactly as she did when the dairyman tried to cheat, measuring out milk in our courtyard, or when coming upon the neighbour's two sons engaged in a fist fight. Her mouth was set tightly; the gold in her eyes a shade or two darker.

"Hoodlums!" she said, struggling with the buttons of her grey cloth coat. "Nothing but hoodlums, Mr. Stein."

JOHN GIVNER

Elizabeth
(1991)

On the day Libby is to take her mother to the hospital for a radical mastectomy, the English tabloids are all agog over an unfortunate incident involving Prince William. Libby scans the story with her daughter, Rifka, peering over her shoulder:

> Defiant Prince William left his school sports day in tears yesterday after a smacking from his mother. Princess Diana lost her temper when he ran away as she was ready to take him home.
>
> She smacked his bottom, ticked him off and drove him back to Kensington Palace.
>
> Full story: Page 3

Her mother, Babu, acquires newspapers randomly, unconcerned that they are several days old. She is part of a complicated network of barter and exchange, whereby neighbours drop off the Sunday supplements, magazines and papers in return for sticks of rhubarb or a cupful of black currants — whatever is in season in the garden. (Recycling has flourished here long before the environmental movement in North America.) It is by this means, on the morning of Babu's departure, that the *Daily Express* arrives like a blessing from heaven. Riveted by the huge headlines — WILLS GETS A WALLOP — Babu suspends her packing.

All week she has been assembling a trousseau, following a list issued by the hospital. She has acquired a dressing gown from one of the charity shops that have sprouted in the little seaside town since the recession. Bringing it home like a trophy, she has modelled it for Libby and Rifka to admire. She has also got a shop-soiled night-gown at a bargain price. It is a pretty baby-blue but of an abrasive nylon fabric, like a hair shirt.

To these Libby has added a plastic denture box from Boots to replace the Tupperware container which Babu has withdrawn temporarily from its normal duty of holding scraps in the fridge. Libby realizes how little her mother understands about the surgical procedure when she asks, "Do they make you take your teeth out?"

Libby is addicted to newsprint, gobbling it up like a greedy caterpillar, and she has passed on her addiction as a genetic trait to Rifka. Each morning they listen to *Round the Papers* on Babu's old wireless set and then decide whether to buy the *Guardian*, the *Independent* or both. Babu is appalled by the extravagance. "Think of all the trees cut down to make paper," she says. Current affairs mean nothing to her because she has lived through two world wars, and she expects to be in a better place before the next one. But royalty is a different matter. Babu believes in the Divine Right of Kings and is an authority on the royal family.

The arrival of the *Daily Express* in pristine condition on its day of publication is due to the confusion of Percy across the street. He has Alzheimer's and should be in a nursing home, but it is government policy to keep people in their own homes as long as possible. Accordingly, he is cared for by visiting nurses, vigilant neighbours and volunteers who provide meals-on-wheels. He comes clamouring at Babu's door several times a morning on various errands or pretexts. She greets him with unfailing courtesy, but she cannot invite him inside because he absentmindedly pockets things. He often asks Babu to tell him what happened to his wife. Tactfully, she says that Clara died of pneumonia. In fact, she, too, had Alzheimer's. Percy, who cared for Clara for ten long years, now says, "The tragedies happen so suddenly."

Pleased that Babu has found a distraction, Libby and Rifka feign interest in the story. Rifka turns to page 3 and reads aloud the captions under the coloured pictures:

Angry Diana grabs Wills.

A cheeky grin from Wills, second from the right, as he plays with sports day friends.

Future king heads home to Kensington Palace in disgrace.

Babu says that Wills has always been a handful. Once he put his father's shoe down the loo and pulled the chain. (Libby assumes that the plumbing arrangements are Babu's own interpolation.)

"Well, I'm sure his dad had an extra pair," says Rifka. "Him and Imelda Marcos."

The exchange follows a familiar pattern. If Babu remarks that the royal family works hard for charity, Rifka says, "The Queen doesn't pay any taxes. She could fund all the charities in Britain if she did."

"If the Queen paid taxes," explains Babu, "she would have to sell Balmoral, and it has been in her family for five generations."

"*Bal*moral," grumbles Rifka. "They should call it *Im*moral."

Normally Babu would take umbrage at such irreverence, but Rifka can do no wrong in her eyes. Years ago, when Libby adopted Rifka, Babu said such terrible things that she and Libby were estranged for years. Now Babu has forgotten that Rifka is adopted, and Libby overheard her saying one day, "You have your mother's feet, Rifka, so you'll always be able to get good shoes on sale."

Babu is even used to her granddaughter's name. She really wishes she were called Elizabeth, but three Elizabeths in the same family was too much for Libby. Babu said, "We could have called her Lisa . . . I never heard the name Rifka before." "It's the Hebrew form of Rebecca," Libby said. Babu recoiled visibly, but she said merely, "Well, Rebecca would have been nicer."

Libby reminds her that its is nearly eleven o'clock and she had better finish packing. Babu has had trouble deciding on a suitable bag for her belongings. She has been packing and unpacking all week like a child preparing for summer camp. Libby offered her good leather case but it was rejected. "Too normal-looking for Babu," says Rifka. "It has to be something crazy, like three string bags." Finally, Babu has settled on the rucksack she used for walks when her husband was still living. He wore it on his back to carry Babu's handbag, which goes with her everywhere like a diplomatic pouch.

When her father fell ill, Libby flew over from Canada to say goodbye, fearing to see him wasting on his deathbed. But he spared her the embarrassment by slipping away before she arrived. Since then, Babu has lost interest in life, partly because his pension died with him and she has difficulty making ends meet. Libby has offered to help, but Babu is fiercely independent and prefers to cut back on what she calls "luxuries." Her world gets narrower and narrower, and Libby suspects that she barely gets enough to eat. This one month when Libby and Rifka come over is the highlight of her year.

Libby dreads the end of the visit when the taxi comes to take them to Gatwick. Babu weeps a little, scrunching up her face as she tries not to. Libby and Rifka, torn between guilt at leaving and happiness to be returning to their normal lives, shout out promises of letters and phone calls. Libby knows that this year it will be harder than ever because they will be leaving Babu in a convalescent home. She would prefer to convalesce in her own little bungalow, but Libby is an only child, and there is simply no one to look after her mother.

Babu says, "Put the dust-bins out on Monday evening and put all the table scraps on the compost heap." "I'll have enough trouble feeding Riffy and me without feeding that compost heap," says Libby. She regrets the comment, for Babu's face is suddenly furrowed with anxiety at the thought of the magnitude and variety of calamities that could befall the bungalow in her absence. Mercifully, Percy arrives at the door again.

Libby reminds him for the fifth time that morning that Elizabeth is going into hospital. He says to let him know if there is anything he can do to help, and his offer brings a smile to Babu's face. Then he starts to tell about his trigeminal nerve. Everyone in the cul-de-sac knows and dreads this story. He claims to have remained conscious during the operation in which the nerve was removed to cure neuralgia, and his memory of the pain is the clearest thing he owns. This morning Libby finds it particularly harrowing.

Percy's life has encompassed more tragedies than any one person deserves — sons killed on the M1 and in Northern Ireland and a granddaughter murdered. Libby wonders if his amnesia is a merciful erasure of his past. Yet, since his wife suffered the same fate, perhaps the cause is environmental. Libby's gaze wanders to the huge pylons in the nearby field where the rabbits play. She has read a sinister article in the *Independent*:

> A two-year study by the US Environmental Protection Agency concludes that there is a significant link between exposure to low-frequency electromagnetic radiation and cancer. . . . It shows that it is inadvisable to live within less than 350 feet of an electricity pylon line . . .

When Babu discovered the lump in her breast, she asked Libby plaintively, "Why is everyone dying of cancer? There was none in our family before. Then your father and now me . . ." Libby privately agrees there is too much cancer in the family. And in the cul-de-sac — two cases of leukemia, including her father's.

The doorbell rings once again, and Babu says, "It'll just be Percy," but Rifka calls out that it's a Boston Strangler, her generic name for uniformed employees of the water and gas companies.

"You want to watch how you talk, Rifka," scolds Babu. "We don't say rude things in this country."

"Oops, sorry, I misspoke myself," says Rifka, whose normal racy speech is toned down considerably out of respect for her grandmother. Once she told Babu that Princess Di had false teeth from eating too much toffee as a school girl. Babu was surprised but totally credulous. She said, "Well, the Queen Mother has her own teeth." "Exactly," said Rifka, putting pictures of the two royal women side by side. "See, the Princess's teeth are too perfect. Admit." Babu admitted, but a month later, when Rifka owned up to the falsehood, she said, "I knew all along you were pulling my leg."

When the taxi arrives, Babu says, "We could have taken the train to Hastings and saved five pounds." As they drive off, Percy is standing by his open garage, where he looks several times a day for the car that was taken away when he started to drive on the wrong side of the road. Rifka in the back seat gives him a royal salute and nudges Babu to do the same. "You owe it to your public to go off in style," she says.

By the time they have had lunch in Debenham's cafeteria and walked up the hill to the hospital, even the spirits of Rifka, the rucksack bearer, begin to flag. The fumes from the traffic exhaust almost choke them. "Why is it so bad?" she asks, and Libby explains that there are no laws governing carbon-monoxide emissions.

When they get to the East Sussex hospital, there are plastic bags of garbage all around the doorway. The place is run down and dilapidated, with peeling paint and scuffed furniture. It reminds Libby of a Dickensian workhouse. The ward to which Babu is admitted has sixteen beds crowded very close together, and an ancient woman, with green tubes in her nose and arms, is dying in one of them. There is a ramshackle curtain rail around each bed to ensure privacy when the patients are undressing. Babu pulls the curtain around her bed and disappears behind it to put on the hair shirt. Rifka, horrified, looks at

Libby and mouths, "We can't leave her here." Babu emerges looking very small and apprehensive. The fresh-faced nurse says, "Don't worry, they soon settle down."

They are both silent as they walk to the station. Libby thinks now that she should have insisted on a private clinic no matter what the expense. The late editions of the tabloids are on the newsstands. Already the royal wallop has sparked a public debate. A member of EPOCH (End Physical Punishment of Children) thinks the princess has set a very bad example. Rifka says, "I just hope they don't start blowing up shops like the animal rights people."

When they get home, Libby feels she needs something stronger than tea. She organizes a foraging expedition under Babu's bed, where she stores whatever has to be concealed from public scrutiny. From behind a chamber pot they unearth bottles of whiskey and brandy intended for medical emergencies. "This *is* an emergency," says Libby. "I'm still in shock from seeing that concentration camp."

On the day of Babu's operation they hang about until it is time to call the hospital from the pay phone at the end of the road. They walk into the town, have a ploughman's lunch at the Duke of Devonshire, and read the papers while they eat. "The good old *Guardian*," says Rifka, "nothing about the Wills and the Wallop. The Queen could leave Philip, Diana could sign on as a Playboy bunny, and they could put up Wills for adoption without the *Guardian* paying the slightest attention. Or it might spare a paragraph in small print on the back page."

Libby, for some reason, has succumbed to *The Times*. She reads that the House of Lords has rejected the bill to bring war criminals to trial. One of the Peers of the Realm says show trials are not the English way. "Leave that to the Hebrews and the Americans."

"What about Oscar Wilde? What about Steven Ward?" asks Rifka.

"They weren't war criminals," says Libby. "They violated codes of sexual propriety and gentlemanly conduct."

Back at the bungalow, Rifka stands at the window of the lounge and says, "Uh-uh, visitors." Libby knows at once that something is wrong when she sees Basil from next door with Winifred on his arm. Winifred rarely goes out because she has trouble walking. She has been waiting two years for a hip operation, and the heavier she gets, the more dangerous it will be. Only a catastrophe of a major order could bring her out, inching painfully on a single crutch and supported by Basil.

Libby is not mistaken. Basil and Winifred offer sympathy and the unlimited use of their telephone. As they watch Winifred make the slow journey back next door, Rifka says, "I'm going to have to take better care of you now that you're an orphan."

Libby can't escape the notion that people choose the moment of their final exit. She is aggrieved that her mother, like her father, has slipped away without warning. Or were there warnings that Libby ignored? The doctor said, "There are always risks, but we wouldn't recommend surgery if we didn't think she had every prospect of a good quality of life for some years. Provided she gets adequate post-operative care, of course."

"Of course," said Libby, knowing that he meant six weeks at two hundred pounds a week in a private nursing home, of which he just happened to be part-owner. She accepted the operation and the post-operative care as a total package. It was all arranged, so what happened? Did Babu slip away to spare Libby the inconvenience of a long decline? Was the idea of the expensive nursing home unacceptable to her independent and frugal spirit? Had she lost heart, alone and frightened, in that mausoleum of a cancer ward? It makes no more sense than one of Rifka's fabricated stories about Princess Diana.

Perhaps it will start to make sense tomorrow when Libby goes to collect Babu's things and disperse them — the hair shirt to Oxfam, the dressing gown back to the charity shop, the eye-glasses to the missionary society and so on. Or perhaps later when they take the remains of Babu herself to the crematorium in Eastbourne. There, someone will say a quick prayer; there will be piped-in organ music ("Praise my soul the king of heaven"), and the coffin will roll away like a cafeteria tray on its little assembly line.

When Libby turns on the wireless for the news the next morning, she hears the national anthem. It is Prince Philip's birthday. The announcer says, "We wish his Royal Highness many happy returns of the day," and then goes on to speak of race riots in Birmingham.

Libby thinks, "Babu was my last link to my native land, and by her death she has dispossessed me. I no longer have an ancestral bungalow, family graves or people of my own. When I come back to England it will be as a tourist, inquiring of the travel agent for suitable bed and breakfast accommodation. My home will be in another country where, as an immigrant, I have no right to criticize the customs. If I should die, Rifka or someone who is no kin to me will scatter my ashes in some corner of a foreign field. It is not my mother I have lost but myself."

The doorbell rings, jingle-jangle. It is Percy. He wants to know if Elizabeth has had her operation. It is very strange about Percy and what he suddenly manages to remember. Libby breaks the news to him. Then, seeing a look of utter desolation cross his face, she improvises a little. "Elizabeth," she says, "passed away in her sleep — very peacefully and without feeling any pain."

She closes the door. She hopes that he will come back soon and often because he is the only person who can answer her present need. She wants to tell him over and over again so that finally she might start to believe it herself — especially the words "very peacefully and without feeling any pain."

CAROLINE ADDERSON

The Chmarnyk
(1991)

In 1906, after scorching the Dakota sky, an asteroid fell to earth and struck and killed a dog. Only a mutt, but Baba said, "Omen." It was her dog. They crossed the border into safety, into Canada. But the next spring was strange in Manitoba, alternating spells of heat and cold. One bright day Mama went to town, stood before a shop window admiring yard goods, swaddled infant in her arms. From the eaves above a long glimmering icicle gave up its hold, dropped like a shining spear. The baby was impaled.

These misfortunes occurred before I was born. I learned them from tongues, in awe, as warnings. My brother Teo said, "Every great change is wrought in the sky."

Grieving, they fled Manitoba, just another cursed place. Open wagon, mattresses baled, copper pots clanking. Around the neck of the wall-eyed horse two things: cardboard picture of the Sacred Heart, cotton strip torn from Baba's knickers. Every morning as she knotted the cloth, she whispered in the twitching ear, "As drawers cover buttocks, cover those evil eyes!" Thus protected, that old horse carried them right across Saskatchewan. In Alberta it fell down dead.

So they had to put voice to what they had feared all along: the land wasn't cursed, they were. More exactly, Papa. A reasonable man most of the time, he had these spells, these ups and downs. Up, he could throw off his clothes and tread a circular path around the house knee-deep through snow. Or he would claim to be speaking English when, in fact, he was speaking in tongues. "English, the language of Angels!" but no one understood him. Down, he lay on the hearth, deathly mute, Baba spoon-feeding him, Teo and Mama saying the rosary. I was just a baby when he died.

But this is a story about Teo, dead so many years. I remember him stocky and energetic, his streaky blond hair. If they had stayed in Galicia, he would have been a *chmarnyk*, a rain-man. In the Bible, Pharaoh had a dream that seven gaunt cows came out of the river to feed on cattails. He dreamed of seven ears of corn on a single stalk, withered and blighted by east wind. But Teo never relied on the auguries of sleep. He could read the sky.

"Rain on Easter Day and the whole summer is wet. If you see stars in the morning from one to three, the price of wheat rises."

He told me this in a field still bound by old snow. He had stood out there the whole night, and I was calling him to Easter Mass, 1929. "What'll it be this year then, smartie?"

"Drought." He pronounced the word like he was already thirsty. "Little sister, listen. The sky is only as high as the horizon is far."

"Well, la-di-da."

Teo was nineteen, I twelve, and the skin of my own dry lips cracked as I echoed: drought. All that spring, smoke rose straight out of chimneys, and every evening the sky flared. "That's dust in the air already. That's dry weather," he said.

Always reading, he got an idea about the cattail. "Ten times more edible tubers per acre than a crop of potatoes."

"Just before a storm," he said, "you can see the farthest."

Since the price of wheat was not going to rise, Teo sold our farm and bought the store in town. There I learned our other names: "bohunk" and "garlic-eater." People didn't like owing us money, but the fact that they did never stopped them writing in the newspaper that we couldn't be loyal subjects of the British Empire. That we would never learn to put saucers under our cups. I refused to wear my embroidered blouses and sometimes even turned to the wall the cardboard picture of the Sacred Heart. It embarrassed me the way Our Saviour bared his sweet breast, as if He didn't care what people thought of Him.

Teo was unperturbed. There was work to be done and I could be his little helper. At Mud Lake, by then half receded, ringed by white alkali scum, he asked me to remove my clothes. Covering my breasts with spread-open hands, I waded in, then clung to a snag slippery with algae while Teo, on shore, named clouds.

"Cumulus. Cumulus. Cumulus."

"Why me?" I shouted.

"Needs a virgin," he called. "A smooth thigh."

I came out festooned with leeches — arms, legs, shoulder even. He chose the halest one and burned the rest off with his cigarette. All the way home I wore that guzzling leech sheltered in a wet handkerchief. Like a doting mother I nursed it. Then we put it in a Mason jar with water and a little stick.

"Leech barometer," Teo said. "Fair weather when the leech stays in the water. Unless the leech is dead."

The next year Mud Lake had disappeared. Rising out of what once was water — a secret charnel-house. Old glowing buffalo bones.

Already farms were being seized. Some families had been paying us in chits since 1929. To one farmer Teo made a gift — an idea expressed to hide the giving. "If he wanted, a man might collect and sell those bones as fertilizer." We saw the farmer working every day. On first sight of the bones his horse had spooked. Now it had to be blindfolded — led like a reluctant bride through the sweltering town, an antimacassar the veil on its head. It strained with the cart, load white and rattling. Vertebrae fell in puffs of dust on the road, provoking feud amongst the forsaken dogs.

I never knew there could be so much death in one place or that the labour of removing it could be so gruelling. Finally, all the bones in a dry heap at the train station, ready to be loaded. Women could go down and have their photograph taken with a huge skull in their lap. Boys swung at each other with the leg bones.

Strangest railway robbery anybody had ever heard of. Overnight it all vanished. Not even a tooth left on the platform. The exhausted farmer lost his remuneration. After that he posted himself in front of the store warning those who entered that Teo was not as stupid as he looked. Declaring revenge was a man's right when he thirsted for justice. He spat so often on our window I made a routine of cleaning it off. The pattern of saliva on the dusty glass was like cloudburst.

It was so dry in the Palliser Triangle, dunes of dust stopped the trains. We tucked rags around doors and window sills, blew black when we blew into our handkerchiefs. In Galicia, Teo would have been a *chmarnyk*, a rain-man. He took me with him, driving where roads were passable, farm to farm. Waiting in the car, I watched him point at the sky. Children circled, staring in at me. They thumbed their noses and wrote "garlic" in the dust on the windscreen. I kept my gaze on Teo as he exhorted skeletal-faced farmers to send their wives and daughters into the fields. Send them into the fields on Sunday morning and have them urinate, for a woman's urine has power to cause rain.

Brandishing brooms, they drove him off their porches. They kicked him in the seat of the pants.

"Why are we doing this?" I cried. His every good deed bred animosity.

Teo said, "They didn't know Our Saviour either." To give me faith, he made a drop of water appear at the end of his nose, glistening like a glass rosary bead. "That's without even trying," he said.

Nobody went into the fields, of course. Just Mama and Baba. And me, squatting, skirts hoisted. I saw my urine pool in the dust, ground too parched to drink. High in a tree a crow was watching me. It shouted down that rain comes at a cost and even then might not come for good.

In the Bible, Pharoah dreamed of seven gaunt cows. By 1932, I must have seen seven hundred so much worse than gaunt. Angular with starvation or dead and bloated, legs straight up in the air.

"Ten times more edible tubers per acre in a crop of cattails than a crop of potatoes!"

"Who told you that?"

"And the fluff! That's good insulation! Mattress stuffing, quilt batting! From the stalks, wallboard and paper! The leaves — baskets, clothing!"

I laughed. Who would wear a cattail? "How come nobody ever thought of this before, smartie?"

"Lots nobody ever thought of! Every great change is wrought in the sky! God made the cattail!" His tongue raced, arms circled in the air.

But the big idea was cheap cattle feed, deliverance from famine. Teo the Deliverer. "Is a cow going to eat a cattail root?" I wanted to know.

"Cows eating pieces off tractors! Cows eating gate latches!" Hardware disease.

And the next morning he drove away from the Palliser Triangle, northward, looking for a cattail slough. I waited. Baba sucked on her bare gums all day, as if that way she could wet her throat. Mama —

always the same stories. "Dakota. 1906. A good doggie." She raised one fist in the air, swept it down with a loud smack into her outstretched palm. Weeping, she mimed the baby in her arms. That lance of ice, it dropped right out of heaven.

Then this, another sorrow: how Papa died. As a child I thought he'd been plucked from the plough and raptured straight on high. Mama used to tell how she had clutched his ankle and dangled in mid-air trying to hold him back. Nothing could be further from the truth. He threw himself on a pitchfork. So much blood, it was like when they killed a pig. This she confessed in the back room of the store as I sat on a lard pail. Suicide triples a curse.

On a red background I appliquéd a cattail. The words: THE EVERY-THING PLANT. For batting I planned to use the brown and gold pollen of the cattail flower. We were going to string it across the back of the car when we, brother and sister, did our tour of the drought towns, made our presentation at the feed stores. We were going to sleep under it at night. I was Teo's little helper.

In the corner of every eye, a plug of dust. I was afraid of crying, of someone licking the water off my face.

I urinated again in a field.

There were no clouds to name.

Now they said we were worse than Jews, almost as bad as Chinamen. I had never seen either. On the counter they scattered handfuls of raisins, railing, "Stones! Stones!" as if they actually paid us. What could we do about fly-infested flour, rancid bacon, the desiccated mouse in the sugar? When the cash register opened, chits flew out like a hundred moths. On all these accusing faces the dirty lines were a map of the roads Teo had gone away on.

Now we wanted Teo to take us away. Baba said she could smell hatred. It smelled like gunpowder.

In Galicia, Mama said, drought is a beautiful woman. She persuades a young peasant to carry her on his back. Wherever he goes crops wither and die, ponds evaporate, birds, songs stuck in their throats, drop out of trees. Horrified, he struggles to loosen the cinch of her legs round his waist, her grappling hands at his neck. In the end, to be rid of his burden, he leaps from a bridge. Drought dries up the river instantly, and, crashing on the rocks below, our young peasant breaks open his head.

Finally a package. Inside, a big tuberous finger, hairy and gnarled. We marvelled it was still wet.

"What is it?" Mama asked.

"A cattail root."

When Baba touched it, she started to cry. What did it mean? Would Teo come for us? Alive, it was holding the rain. That night, to keep it moist, I brought it to bed and put it inside me.

To cure fever, drink whisky with ground garlic. Eat bread wrapped in cobwebs. But I did not think it was fever. Overnight my hair had curled like vetch tendrils and my head throbbed where a horse had kicked me seven years before. Beside my bed, the leech barometer. So many years in the jar, I had thought the leech was dead. Now it shimmied out of the water and halfway up the stick.

Mama said, looking over the town, "Smoke from all these chimneys curling down." When I would not take the bread and whisky, she pulled my hair.

Just before a storm, you can see the farthest. We saw you coming miles away. Dust-maker, you were weaving all over the road, horn pressed. By the time we got Baba down the stairs and into the street, a crowd had gathered round the car. You were standing on the hood, almost naked, wet skirt of cattail leaves pasted to your thighs.

Mama gasped, "Teo has his father's curse."

The sere voice of a crow: *rain costs.*

And I was part to blame. I had given my innocence to a cattail root while you held its power.

From the beating part of your chest, your brow, water had begun to trickle, ribboning downward, the sheen of moisture all across you. Motionless, arms open, fingers spread and dripping — you were sowing rain. We were sweating, too, the day dry and searing, but soon you were dissolving, hair saturated, nostrils and eyes streaming culverts. Then you turned, spun round and spattered the silent crowd. Turned again, kept spinning, faster. Whirling, whirling on the slippery hood, you drenched and astounded us, became a living fountain. And then, amazing! A nimbus, seven-coloured, shimmering all around you.

In Galicia, when thunder sounds, prostrate yourself to save your soul. That day thunder discharged, a firearm, reverberating. Mama and Baba dropped to the ground. A dark curtain was drawn across the Palliser Triangle. Black geyser sky.

You bowed forward and vomited a river.

The crowd fell back. They had never seen a *chmarnyk*.

After Teo made it rain, the whole town was filled with steam, water evaporating off the streets and the wet backs of the men who carried Teo's body away. Dogs staggered out of cover to drink from temporary puddles. And in all the fields, green shoots reared, only to wither later in the reborn drought.

They carried Teo's body away and wouldn't let us see him. "Struck by lightning," they said. How could we argue? I was only fifteen, and neither Mama nor Baba could speak English. The moment he was taken, we had been rolling on the ground. But I remember clearly the presence of that farmer, the one robbed of his charnel-house, his smile like lightning. The English word "shotgun" never had a place on my tongue.

Years later Teo came to Mama in a dream. In the dream he had a hole in his chest big enough to climb into, gory as the Sacred Heart. "I have seen the face of Our Saviour," he told her. "He lets me spit off the clouds."

As for me, two things at least I know. The cattail root holds more than water. Every great change is wrought in the sky.

GAIL ANDERSON-DARGATZ

The Girl with the Bell Necklace
(1992-1993)

When I came in from chores, flocks of birds chirped on our roof. I knew we had guests. Bertha Moses and her daughters and her daughters' daughters were in the kitchen drinking coffee left from breakfast. One of the daughters was dipping hot water from the reservoir on the stove into the coffee pot. I'd polished the stove with butter the day before — those were the days when you couldn't give butter away — and the woodstove shone black as the daughter's hair. I went back out the screen door and yelled across the yard at my mother, "Mrs. Moses and her family are here," and went about the business of being hostess. Bertha Moses and her family were walking from the reservation into town. I knew this because they always stopped at our house on their way to and from town. My mother entered the kitchen, wiping her hands on her skirt. She wore milking clothes identical to my own: a brown skirt, white blouse, gumboots and blue kerchief.

"Bertha," she said. "Good to see you."

Bertha Moses wore a red dress, black stockings and moccasins decorated with porcupine quills and embroidery. She wore several strings of brightly coloured beads. She had no husband and no sons. She would not have a drunk man in her house, so it was a house of women. One of the daughter's daughters was pregnant. Another had webbed fingers. Some of the younger girls had blue or green eyes. Each of the girls' hair was black and oiled with bear grease so it shone, and tied back in all manner of barrettes and ribbons. Someone wore violet-scented talc. One of the daughter's daughters wore boys' jeans and a western shirt that stretched a little at the buttons across her breasts. She was my age. My father never let me wear trousers. The girl wore a necklace of bells strung together. I coveted it. She saw me looking at the bell necklace and jingled it. The room filled with tinkling notes that lit everyone's faces. I watched the girl with the bell necklace. She smiled. The room grew womanly.

My mother told how my father tried to fool the hired men. My father hired older Indian boys, like Dennis and Filthy Billy, who ran away from the residential school in Kamloops. My father said he was doing them a favour because these were the days of Depression when no one else would hire them. They worked for cheap and didn't talk back unless they got drunk. If they got drunk, my father fired them.

"John brought home a porcupine yesterday," Mum said. "He skinned it, cleaned it and said, 'It's chicken.' I said, 'That's not chicken.'

"He said, 'I said it's chicken, so it's chicken.'

"I said, 'Fine, it's chicken.' I cooked it like chicken. Dennis and Filthy Billy come in for dinner and John says, 'Maudie cooked chicken for dinner.'

"Everyone helps themselves and then Dennis whispers, 'Porcie,' and Filthy Billy whispers, 'Porcie.'"

Everyone laughed because they knew my father. The laughter became huge and shook the house. The screen door slammed shut.

"What's this about?" said my father. "What are you laughing at?"

There was a pause, then one of Bertha's daughters said, "Men."

My father pushed me out of his way and stood over Bertha Moses. Bertha became an old woman in my father's shadow; he sucked the air from her cheeks and made her eyes dull.

"You told Dennis not to work," he said.

Bertha stood and her daughters stood behind her. Their combined shadows pushed my father's shadow against the wall.

"I said he deserves more for the work he does."

"You don't know nothing," said my father.

"You hire our boys because they don't know how to ask for what they're worth," she said. "You treat them like slaves. They're not slaves."

"Get our of my house!" said my father.

Bertha Moses's shadow gripped my father's shadow around the throat, forcing blood into his face. He stepped back and pushed open the screen door.

"Get out!" he said, and fled from the house.

"We should be going," said Bertha Moses.

"Yes," said one of the daughters.

The women made the motions of leaving.

"It was good to have you," said my mother.

The daughters and daughters' daughters filed out the door. The girl with the bells jingled her necklace as she went by. She had eyes of two different colours, one blue and one green. She was a half-breed then. Bertha stayed behind and patted my mother's hand.

"Stop in on your way back," said my mother. "Please. He won't remember. He gets angry and it washes away."

I followed the women a little way down the road. Their glittering jewellery attracted birds; purple swallows zoomed around them, crows hovered above them, and songbirds sang from trees as they approached. Bertha Moses and her daughters and her daughters' daughters sang hymns of praise to a white man's god all the way into town.

I spent the morning roaming. I followed the creek up to the benchland overlooking my father's property. Filthy Billy worked down below, stooking alone. My father said Filthy Billy was little more than an idiot. Bertha Moses said Filthy Billy was possessed. It occurred to me that if I ran down that hill, I could fly. I spread my arms and the air carried me.

Filthy Billy was hot and tired and agitated. He was skinny and his hair was greasy. He did not own his voice and this made him agitated. His voice made him say words no one liked, and the best Filthy Billy could do was make the renegade words come out in a whisper. He saw me coming and looked more agitated.

"Hello (fuck)," he said. "Excuse me, hello (fuck)."

"Hello," I said.

"(Shit) your daddy doesn't (fuck) (shit) sorry want me talking to you (shit). Excuse me. Sorry (fuck)."

"Why do you talk like that?" I said.

"I don't know (fucking shit). Sorry. I can't help it (shit). Excuse me."

"What does fuck mean?"

"(Shit) you should go," he said.

"Why?" I said.

Then I saw the spirit around Filthy Billy's neck. It was a skinny, nervous spirit with hands like chicken's feet. The chicken spirit jumped on Filthy Billy, as if his lungs were bellows. Each time the spirit jumped, Filthy Billy spewed a nasty word as if it were a fart.

"(Fuck) sorry," he said. "You should go. (Shit) excuse me. Please. Go."

I ran to the farm. Something followed me in the grass. There was a second path beside mine. I reached the fence, jumped over it, and the sound of swooshing grass behind me stopped. I leaned against the back of the barn out of breath. Two parallel paths stretched out across the field; mine continued through the grass past the fence. The second did not. I saw a pair of hands clutching the boards of the fence, as if someone was leaning on it, but nobody was there.

I kept my back to the barn, my eyes on the fence, backed around the corner and ran smack into someone. I jumped and squeaked. The girl with the bell necklace was standing right there. Bertha and her daughters must have stopped in then, on their way back from town, even after what my father said.

"Hi!" she said.

"Hi!" I said.

She bent forwards and looked at the fenceline. "What you running from?"

"Nothing," I said.

My eyes were drawn to her necklace. She jingled it.

"Like it?" she said. I nodded. "I like your hair," she said, and she did an odd thing. She ran her fingers through my hair for some minutes without speaking. It felt good and calming, like my mother brushing my hair before bed. After a minute I closed my eyes and enjoyed it.

"You're beautiful like an angel," she said, and just then, I felt that way.

I opened my eyes. I became aware of the noisy chattering of birds.

"Where is everyone?" I said.

"In the house," she said. She stopped stroking my hair and sunk both hands into her jeans pockets. I tried to think of something smart to say. I felt silly asking her name because I already sort of knew her, though I'd never talked to her before. She'd been at the house with the rest of Bertha's family so many times, drinking coffee, looking at the walls.

"How was town?" I said.

"Dry," she said. "The streets are all dust, and everybody's kicking it up; all the horses were kicking it up. Town was full of people today, with school starting tomorrow. The dust filled your mouth. I had a soda."

She put her hands behind her and stared up at the red roof against the blue sky.

"I guess you start tomorrow," she said.

"Yeh," I said. I knew she wouldn't, so I didn't ask. She took my hand and held it loosely and we stared at the roof and sky together.

I heard my father yell, from some distance away, in the field. I couldn't hear what he said, but I could see he was angry. We let our hands fall. Finally he came close enough we could hear him.

"You!" he said. "You deaf? Get off my property. Get away from here. Lousy Indian! Get off my property."

He marched at us. I looked at the girl with the bell necklace. Her face had gone stony. She turned and fled, jingling, into the house, followed by my father. The birds on the roof lifted and hovered over the house. Presently the women of Bertha Moses's family filed out the door. They jingled, sang and fluttered, and the birds accompanied them. The girl with the bell necklace looked back at me several times, but neither of us waved.

The next morning my mother woke me with a butterfly kiss. She grazed her eyelashes across my cheek, fluttering them. She entered my dream as a moth carrying my mother's blue eyes on stalks. I shook my head awake, and my mother stood straight and produced a butterfly from behind her back. The butterfly was made from petals of scarlet flax, and my mother's fingers breathed life into it. This was a childish game and I was angry at her for it. I threw back the covers and dressed for school, had breakfast and did my chores. My mother went about the business of her day separately, with sorrow draped around her.

Guilt caught up to me on my way to school. The low clouds oppressed my spirit. At the crossroads something moved in the bush, and I got scared for no reason and ran the rest of the way.

School was a one-room building with a wood heater in the middle and a cloakroom at the back. All the grades were jumbled together; I knew their faces, but I'd never befriended them, my father had seen to that.

During hygiene inspection Mrs. MacKay found a yellow streak of manure on my forearm, from chores. That singled me out for the noon-hour initiations that always took place the first day of school. I'd been their victim before; I'd been forced to steal rhubarb from the Watson property next to the school. The house was haunted and I was terrified. One of the boys jumped at me from the derelict window and I ran home, screaming, sure that Rudy Watson had risen from the dead.

At noon a group of older kids surrounded me as I read on the steps of the school. One of the boys clapped his hand over my mouth, picked me up and carried me over to the Watson property. The other kids giggled and followed him into the house. They had kidnapped Gerald Kennedy as well and were holding him down and undressing him. They stripped me of my underwear and pulled my dress over my head. They pulled off my brassiere and laughed at my nakedness. They held down my legs and arms. Two boys pushed Gerald Kennedy down on top of me.

"Screw her," somebody said.

"Do it, or we'll tell MacKay we found you and Beth together naked."

Gerald humped feebly against my crotch and thighs, pulling against my skin. When the crowd finally had enough of this miserable performance they let Gerald up and I hurriedly put on my clothes. Gerald dressed and ran off. Somebody started a chant.

"Slut! Slut! Slut!"

They stood around me, not letting me get up. Finally, I struggled away, and the chorus chased after me, yelling "Slut!"

I didn't stop at the school. I left my coat and lunch tin and ran down the road, leaving the chorus behind. The clouds finally broke and the downpour began. At the crossroads I saw myself standing in the rain, wet through and sickly, my hands outstretched. I was pleading with myself to stop. I ran past myself and the invisible thing hopped onto the road. I saw its footsteps. I ran harder until I saw Filthy Billy sitting against a stook with his collar up against the rain. He smiled and waved, swore at me and apologized.

"Billy," I said, "something's following me."

"There always is," he said.

The chicken spirit hopped and Filthy Billy swore and apologized profusely. I found no comfort in his company. The thing that followed me took steps closer. I stumbled down our roadway and into the house; the footsteps ended outside, on the front steps. I ran to my room and threw myself on the bed and clutched my pillow. Immediately stones fell from the ceiling. The chair by the window began a slow march towards the bed and my dolls jumped off my vanity and began walking at me. I screamed and screamed and then it seemed if I were to stay very still, then everything would stop. I held myself rigid on the bed. The rocks stopped showering and the furniture in my room went back to its usual place. I felt my mother's footsteps and then her face was over me. She called my name and shook me but I focused on the ceiling behind her head. She called my name louder and slapped my face. She said, "Oh God," and left my room. A little while later she came back with my father. His footsteps shook the bed so I knew he was angry; he looked distorted and huge.

"She saw me, she's awake," he said.

"Whatever could have happened?" said my mother.

"She should be at school."

"She wouldn't have come home unless something happened," said my mother.

She looked into my face.

"Beth dear, what happened?" she said.

Her voice was so tender, so forgiving, I almost answered. But there was a new peace here, in not reacting. Everything seemed in my control. As long as I didn't move, no one could hurt me, nothing could penetrate. She tried for a long time, talking sweetly to me. My father huffed and stomped from the house. My mother cried. Then she left my room and fussed in the kitchen, and I must have slept. When I woke there was no one in the house. I heard the rain on the roof, and my stomach grumbled. I struggled against apathy and shuffled into the kitchen. I drank a cup of milk and ate a piece of unbuttered bread. Then I shuffled back to my room and lay rigid.

I became aware I was being watched. Before I could think I turned my head towards the window. The hands, from the thing that followed, were on the outside window ledge. I threw a blanket over myself and looked again. The hands were gone. I heard footsteps and hurriedly arranged myself as I had been. The window slid open and someone climbed into the room. I heard bells. The girl watched me and jingled the necklace. I sat up.

"You were asleep," she whispered.

"No," I said.

"Your parents aren't here?"

"No," I said.

She sat on the bed beside me with the necklace coiled loosely in her hand. The thing that followed me followed her. It stood behind her with one hand resting kindly on her shoulder.

"Your hair is so golden," she said.

She reached out and gently combed my hair with her fingers. I took the necklace and jingled the bells.

"How was school?" she said.

I shook my head. She nodded as if I'd told her everything.

"Roll on your stomach," she said. I rolled over and lay full length, resting my chin on my hands. The bells smelled tinny. She arranged my hair to one side, and smoothed the material of my blouse as if cleaning a blackboard. She began to draw on my back. It felt smooth and tickly and I relaxed under her hands. After a while I said, "What are you drawing?"

"I'm writing," she said.

"What are you writing?"

"You have to guess," she said.

I followed the circles of her hands on my back.

"I don't know," I said.

"Guess!"

Slowly she formed big looped letters of three words, and repeated them over and over. I understood quickly, but didn't know what to do. I turned over and she continued to write, spelling the words over the sides of my breasts.

"You," she said, mouthing the last word and forming a *U* that cupped my breast. Blood tingled into my cheeks. I sat there for some time, breathless, sitting up on my elbows. She continued to draw a *U* that followed the contours of my breasts, first one and then the other. She grazed her lips over my cheeks and forehead, so lightly it was barely a breath. She lay beside me on the bed and I did my best to imitate her. She ran her fingers up my arms and I ran mine down hers. She pulled me close so our breasts touched. She kissed me. I'd never heard of two people doing anything like this. I began to realize that if I'd never heard anyone talk about this, it must be wrong.

The kitchen door slammed and we jolted apart. The girl grabbed the bell necklace and ran. My father marched into my room, just as the girl was climbing out the window.

"Get out of my house," my father yelled, but of course she was already gone. "I'll skin you," he yelled. "Stupid little squaw."

Then he turned on me. He flipped me over on my stomach and turned up my skirt and slapped my bare bottom with his bare hand. It was an indecent act; I was far too old to be handled in this way by my father. After a few slaps he turned me over again and began yelling.

"You will not have that girl here," he said. "Do you understand? She's a breed. They're filth. They carry lice. Do you understand? It's for your own good. I'm only trying to protect you. Do you understand?"

I nodded. He said this about anyone who ventured to be my friend. I stood up, backed away from my father and fled from the house into the field. My father didn't bother to follow me. The storm had taken on a new fury. Wind blistered the rain and it boiled in all directions. Birds struggled for cover and were carried in the wind like sheets of newspaper. A whirlwind zipped by the hung laundry, flinging my father's underwear and socks up to heaven. I ran back into the house as my father ran to the pasture, with his coat over his head.

I watched from my bedroom window as my father struggled to get the animals into the barn. The cows were excited by the storm and my father's attempts at chasing them looked clumsy and foolish. Seeing my father pitted against the storm in this way, I wondered how I could be frightened of him.

The anger of the storm ended abruptly. An awful calmness smothered the house. I pressed my face against the window and saw a rain begin to fall, so gently the raindrops seemed to float. Then I saw they were not raindrops, they were flowers, violets, fluttering to the ground. In no time at all the rain covered the earth in flowers. I opened my window and crawled out onto the purple carpet. I took my shoes off and paddled around in pools of violets. Their fragrance was intoxicating. The clouds moved on, and still the violets drifted down, from a blue sky.

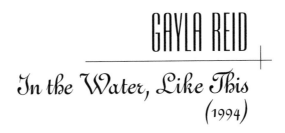

GAYLA REID

In the Water, Like This
(1994)

A small boat on the open ocean in the tropics at night.

The lights from the boat spill out as slivers into the dark of the water. The boat moves, and the lights move, and you are aware of the huge black beyond the lights.

You can feel how soft that blackness is.

Later, there will be a moon.

Paradise, according to popular medieval European belief, still exists on earth — in some distant place. Ninth-century maps locate it in China. The Hereford map, from the thirteenth century, shows it as a round island off the coast of India.

We're out at the edge of the Coral Sea.

She gears up and gets into the water first. Jumps in, hanging on to her mask and regulator. I watch her right herself and see her gloved hand come up. The dive master passes her the housing, with the camera inside.

There's a peppy little current running, so she guides herself on the rope along to the anchor line, to wait for me.

We begin to go down and the water closes over us and I am free.

As far as the normal eye is concerned, we no longer exist.

When we are making our descent she gets tied up in the rope, the one that we use for support against the current when we are entering the water.

Oblivious, she keeps on descending.

And I know her visibility isn't all that good in her mask, and that there isn't much light, but really she should be more careful. I grab her and start unfolding her and I'm right up close to her and I can see her eyes behind that mask, and she's glaring as if I'm interfering, rather than doing her a good turn.

So I give her a pissed-off look right back.

She ignores me as we go down.

We put our flashlights on and they shine green in the water.

People ask me, What was life like before her?

I say it was mainly plainchant, but from time to time Palestrina.

I did okay. Now and then much more than okay.

Their faces ask me this question. They do not use the words.

Sometimes the beginning of tears will come and stand in their eyes. When there is too much about my life that reminds them of their own.

Last week we were diving on a drop-off, going deep for the soft coral. We came around a corner and suddenly the current was tearing at us. It was one of those sneaky, powerful downward currents, and she was directly below me.

Saucers of her air bubbles were floating up past me as I was going down.

As we were swept down in this current I considered, with a detached curiosity, whether she or I would survive.

On balance I gave myself the better chance.

Than just as suddenly the current was gone and we were out of the worst of it.

Tired and elated, hanging on to some coral. Hard, clumpy brain coral, hanging on like crazy.

She didn't know what I'd been thinking.

She gave the small shoulder dance that we use under water to communicate excitement.

Things aren't always so easily resolved. At one time we were diving in the waters off the coast of British Columbia. They call it the emerald sea. You hit a hundred feet and the green deepens into black.

We'd found a great bunch of cloud sponges — the size rhododendron bushes get when they're pampered. They were perched on the side of a quiet cliff, the edge of which fell steeply away into the abyss.

We were taking pictures. Cloud sponges, which grow in these still deep waters, can be a hundred years old. When you come upon them in the gloom, they are a dirty cream. But under a strobe light, they are warm, like parchment. Heavy, living parchment. The quillback rockfish lives in these sponges. It's a small fish of a metallic orange colour. With downturned mouth, it patrols the sponge folds.

The aim is to capture the glassy warm cream of the ancient sponge, in the midst of which that orange pouter is giving you a cranky, domestic look.

We're photographing the cloud sponges and something goes wrong. She loses her mask in the gloom. I can see her eyes saucer big and I know that she is panicking, the fear is upon her.

I can't understand why she's doing this, making a small setback into some massive event.

But she is.

It is an animal fear, the fear of being cornered and trapped in inherently foreign territory.

(The air is full of the wet red soil of the country you are due to leave soon, and now your Jeep, improbably, begins to explode.)

Fear is stored deep in blood and tissue and once unleashed sweeps through the body with bullying, staggering strength.

Each of us has our own mantra for the fear.

I don't know what hers is; she won't tell me.

Down among the cloud sponges, I take her hand, stroke her arm, and lead her upward. She is doing nothing for herself, she has shut her eyes and is keeping her eyes shut, she has forgotten everything she has been told to do.

I look around for the mask and see it, slipping away over the edge of the cliff, down and down.

(She says, later, when we can talk, that the moment I touched her, as soon as she felt the pressure from my gloved hand upon her suit, her body decided to put itself in my trust, utterly. Having done that, she says, her heart stopped its wild thumping. Settled right down.)

At about eighty feet light enters the water, and by fifty feet it is quite bright. She begins to take a bit of interest in her own life again. She opens her eyes and looks around. She fins.

You saved my life, she shouts, when we surface, bobbing about in the chop.

Nah, I say. No way.

Because who wants to be responsible for that, who can bear to acknowledge such a burden?

We rest briefly on the surface, then we keep on going, right up into the sky. We are above the grey-green water and its surface is no longer opaque.

See the white anemones with their seductive, vaginal mouths. See the orange sea pens like quills some monk left behind in mud. Look into the cave where the octopus lives (it stares back with a shy, oblong eye — no visitors, please no). Find the old grey faces of the wolf eels across the way, their mouths opening and shutting like the gummy geriatrics these two are. See the cloud sponges, those rhododendrons, sitting on the edge of the abyss.

See her mask, falling into the abyssal regions, still falling and falling.

My life with her can be like Beethoven's violin concerto, Sir Yehudi playing.

I read her the liner notes.

He wrote it, I tell her, in a state of intense lyric serenity.

He had accepted he was deaf. He had friends.

I told her, I have these two things: water and music.

In love, she assured me, plot is the least of it. Plot, she said, is what comes at the beginning and end. In the middle it is like music, like water, the same themes over and over, corny and classical, revealing themselves: phrases opening up, circling around, rippling away, returning.

Then she said, with church-like solemnity, all big eyes: now you have three.

What was it like? she asks. Nosy.

Why were we on that road, why anyone, why me?

I was there. Period.

So I run up phone bills, sit on committees, make speeches, bla bla yawn.

Because I am unable to forget about the soil (wet, red); the metal; the sky (upside-down); the flesh of my body.

Their complete and terrible candour.

She's got lots of friends. There's not just me.

I know she talks to them about us, although I'd rather she didn't.

She makes herself sound heroic. Knows better but can't resist it. She says, "We have to make special arrangements," and even, "You can't possibly know what it's like."

She's proud of me, I'm one of her accomplishments. Like when I'm in the pool, crashing up and down with my own special butterfly stroke.

It's a competition and I'm winning.

I know she will come to me at the end of the pool, holding out a towel. With a buzz all around her.

She'll lean down and whisper something silly and sweet and lewd.

I'll try to see her clearly, but I won't be able to because I'll still have my swim goggles on. Doesn't matter.

There will be bits and pieces missing.

That's true of anyone, I'd say.

She has her own treasure chests. She teaches art history. She points out to me the spiral, the whorl and the vortex on Minoan vases. She shows me the man in a woman's dress, playing the seven-stringed lyre. Shows me the Minoan octopus, its sensitive arms all around the vase.

Not drowning but waving, she says.

I accuse her of sloppy thinking.

One of our stories:

We are in the waters of the Astrolabe Reef, Fiji.

Above us, somebody has speared a fish, and there is blood in the water. And now there are silkies coming toward us.

Silkies are members of the requiem family of sharks.

There are two silkies, thick, ten-foot sleek creatures, drab khaki on top, pale below. Easy swoosh swoosh of the dorsal fin and they are between us, giving us the once-over.

I look at their mouths.

I glance across at her.

She sends me back a hollowed-out, intense stare.

I understand that there is much I have kept hidden from her, which at this moment I would be rashly willing to share.

Later, she maintains there were three sharks: the two big ones and a baby. The little one, she said, followed in the wake of its mother.

She likes to speak of this baby silky shark, the one that never was. Claims it moved its small dorsal fin elegantly, just like the grown-ups.

Oh, yes, I lie, when she tells this story to strangers. There was the baby, too.

I put my hand out along the couch behind her or touch her leg.

Her mother loved her father. But he came back from the war with head injuries.

Her father: a tall handsome man sitting in his chair on the veranda, in Sydney.

Her father, saying nothing.

Sitting totally still.

She remembers her father lying in his room (her parents had separate rooms). Lying on his bed, with the blinds down, for weeks on end. Shutting out the bright Antipodean light.

Those were the bad times.

We're all on tenterhooks, her mother whispered importantly to the parish priest in the front hall.

She thought that it meant "on tiptoe," because this was how her mother walked during these bouts.

In and out of the hushed room. On tenterhooks.

Her mother, who was English, flew back to England. Just the once. Before she went her mother put into the freezer four months' supply of frozen food. On the fridge door her mother left a diagram of what should be thawed and eaten when.

To look at my father, she says, you would have thought there was nothing wrong with him whatsoever.

A tall, handsome man.

A very simple description.

She saved my life, as once she thinks I saved hers.

An afternoon dive, the third of the day, and I'm down at only sixty feet, looking at a lionfish. The head of the lionfish is excessively decorative. Flaps and flags and spikes hanging off all over. The lionfish has long pectoral fins, about a dozen on each side, poisonous. Its body is dark maroon with cream stripes. The stripes go through its eyes as well.

With all that to notice, I had more than enough to be thinking about.

I ran out of air. It's a stupid thing to have to confess, but I'm not always checking to see how much air I've got left.

It was such a mild, easy afternoon that I forgot.

You can go crazy and die down here, no problem. Rapture of the deep. Tee martoonies, glug glug drown.

Sometimes it seems inviting.

If I leave you, she says, or if you die, I'll get my own place with old oak furniture and lavender in pots. I'll buy antique plates that don't match, with flowers on them.

Give me a break, I say.

I'd like to grab her by the hair, bring her face down into mine, scare her good.

I was a soldier boy, you know. One young dumbfuck. Picked up an attitude, you better believe it.

The trouble is, she says, most of the plates you can find cheap, second-hand, are those dreadful ironstone things from the early sixties, with one crude big daisy or sunflower on them.

Just kidding, I'm a man of peace these days. That's my shtick, you might say. My shtick. My stick.

Anyway I can't reach her hair. I'd need to add half a foot to my arm (ha ha).

There's nothing to stop you, I say, from getting some pots of lavender for our place.

She looks at me as if I have missed the point entirely.

Well, to be frank, I think about leaving her, too.

Most relationships with someone like me break up. They can't take it, the other party. Because a party it ain't.

I've seen that look on her face: she's hanging on and on for dear life, like grim death. She's polishing up her big fat halo. Hanging in with the ole crip.

I can't tell you how it makes me feel, seeing that look.

I think how peaceful my life would be without her, without her discontent. Without her judgements. (And she's very picky; have I told you how picky she is? Muddy wheel tracks on the carpet drive her crazy.)

But when I'm out of air I'm not planning on leaving her.
Or dying.

Not just yet anyway.

I'm looking around for her, and fast.

She's poking about near some tunicates on the edge of a coral outcrop. Tunicates are little living sacs. These particular tunicates are the size and shape of human hearts. Complete with valves and artery-like openings, they pump water as if it were blood. They are blue and white, exactly like the delftware in my mother's china cabinet.

She's over there by the delftware hearts. Open hearts, throbbing away. (In certain lights they are not blue but purple.)

I swim across to her making an out-of-air sign: a slashing motion across the throat.

Her body goes still with this news.

Right away, without any hesitation whatsoever, she takes the regulator out of her own mouth and gives it to me.

I hold on to her.

She's looking pleased with herself because we're doing this right and because she's rescuing me.

Slowly, sedately, we rise to the surface: her breath, my breath. Buddy breathing. Her and me, conspiring in the sunshiny water.

I hear her on the phone one day. He's such a baby, she is saying. She's talking about me.

Now there are times I don't mind being her baby, you understand. But not the whole fucking time. Not on the phone to her friends, who are oh so supportive.

I go into the kitchen and attack the cat-food bowls by running my chair over them. The cat, he's supposed to just have Science Diet but he likes the runny stuff.

I roll my wheels in the runny stuff. Then I roll into the living room, round and round. As I do this I'm thinking about how you used to be able to ruin the phone, when it was attached to the wall. These days the bloody thing would just pop out of its jack.

He yanked the phone right off the wall. Sounds good, doesn't it? Satisfying.

She has to clean up.

Some things are unforgivable, she says, down on her knees, rubbing at the carpet.

They are, I say. They are.

Like me, she gets bored. I've seen her boredom, although she denies it later.

She can be swimming about in a coral garden and everything is moving in the water, everything is alive, sucking, swaying. Or just pretending to be dead, all the better to pounce. Here are the fish you've seen in the aquarium, with their peerless, moving colours.

Consider the harlequin tusk-fish: body of orange-red stripes. Prominent blue teeth.

She can look at those bright blue teeth and shrug.

Beethoven's violin concerto was played for the first time by his good friend Franz Clement, in 1806. Between the concerto's first and second movements, Franz tossed in some pieces of his own, including a sonata which he played on one string with his fiddle turned upside down.

The concerto itself promptly sank into obscurity.

At this moment, on our night dive, she is among the golden sea fans, the gorgonians. I can't see her except when the strobes flash. Then for less than a second I can see the intricate twists of a huge golden sea fan, its irregular, veined beauty. I can see the fan in silhouette, and behind it the density of her body. Her body, hidden now inside her wetsuit. (You should see her peeling off wetsuit and swimsuit; neck shoulders breasts, like cream, like silk, like this.)

Off to my right a turtle goes by me. Precise little flap flaps putting distance between itself and the ugly foreign thing.

The sea fans are golden only under water. If you bring them to the surface, expose them to air, they turn black, they die. I'm hanging here in the tropical water, waiting for her.

Right now I'm having an excellent day.

My minds keeps chugging along — it's stuffy back in our cabin, I don't know how they can bear to swim among these fish and then eat them for dinner, their rates really are a rip-off, maybe I'll have a Deep Springs orange when we get back to the boat — it's a junkyard in there, the usual.

(You want to know how I get down the narrow stairs into that cabin? Well, I'll tell you: I crawl and haul, folks. A forty-eight-year-old crawler-and-hauler, very dextrous.)

But out here, in the water everywhere, above and below and within, there is floating and purring and waving and pulsating.

Then there it is —

The flash of light, the moment of illumination.

She is swimming along in front of me and we are making our way back to the boat. We switch off our flashlights and I can see the phosphorescence coming off her. She moves her legs economically, letting her fins do the working.

I swim behind her.

I imagine that my own legs can move. I pretend they are imitating her legs, keeping in time with her.

Sychronicity.

Like the times she dreams my dreams, or tries (like this) to speak my thoughts.

Minute silver flashes of phosphorescence go right around the edges of her body. I hope she doesn't notice them, because she'll pass me the camera and start doing handstands or waving her arms to swim like a manta ray.

Sometimes she wears me right out.

And all I want is for her to stay like this, moving in the dark waters with me, sparkling.

FRANCES ITANI

Bolero
(1995)

The logs were coming down, the river dark with timber. In a week we'd be back to school. Lyd and I went to bed one night, and when we woke the next morning there was a hush over the river, logs coming and coming in that steady inevitable flow. After breakfast I followed the shore away from the house and up towards higher ground, and I stood on the cliff watching. The river narrowed at the beginning of the rapids, and the mass dipped like a broad dark raft into dark water, whitecaps tossing the logs singly into the air and then catching and concealing them again.

As always, strays drifted to shore in front of the house. Most logs were round and smooth and stamped with the company brand, but some still had bark attached, reminding that these were trees after all. We left the strays to sit in the sun and then went back to peel and crack the bark. We collected insects with latticed wings folded flat the lengths of their backs and used these as bait for bass.

The place we fished bass was below the rapids. Past morning-glory and blunt-petalled wild rose. Past the cliffs and the long meandering ruins of the old hydro wall, a crumbling prop that hemmed the point of land where the river curved at the fiercest part of the rapids. The first day we moved to Quebec, Father took us to see the wall. "Someone had the vision and imagination to harness this energy," he said. "But that was last century, not this. And I'm going to tell you right now. Don't lean on the wall because it's old and cracked, and someday it's going to fall and someone's going to go with it."

Nothing could keep us away. We climbed the wall, straddled it, dug at it, pushed it, and when the water was not too high, walked it. We also feared it.

After the wall, half-mile from the house, the river calmed again and booms were strung out, chained end to end. We were not fooled by the calm. *Down below* was a bottomless place with tough roots twining through mud. Where weeds and bushes snared logs and where bodies drifted after they'd been tossed through the rapids. Our paper boy had drowned in these rapids. In winter, one of the girls who lived in the two rooms behind Le Loup's store had also drowned. Both bodies had been found down below, stuffed under the booms.

It was Lyd who'd first spied the hooks on a rainy day when we were taking turns with our friends climbing the ladder rungs and jumping from the attic platform to the barn floor below. It was years after we'd moved, after Father had bought the house from Duffy. Lyd found the hooks buried in dust behind an old storm door. Bulging pieces of iron with three great curves attached to a braided rope.

"Bodies!" Lyd was the one who dared the rest of us to do what she would not do herself but she commanded our attention because she was the eldest. I had just jumped to the boards and my legbones were wobbling from the impact. I climbed back up and heard her drop into her scaring voice. "Grappling hooks for bodies," she said quickly. "Bodies all stiff and water-bloated. The men drag the bottom to hook a shoulder or a leg. They lower the hooks from rowboats and make a huge splash." Her arms dropped iron through a black surface of river we all knew and imagined. "One man rows, two at the end of the boat drag."

How did she know this? Father hadn't told her because, later, he refused to talk about the hooks when we asked. But he set his mouth grimly and went with the men when they came to the back door after ice break-up the following spring. It turned out that everyone in St. Pierre knew that the village grappling hooks were kept in Duffy's old barn.

After that, one of our games while swimming in the river with our friends became Dead Body. Every summer someone would dip beneath the surface and remember. Would rise with cheeks puffed and shriek, "Dead body below! Dead body!" Our legs ran thickly through water and we scraped knees and feet in the race for shore. Each of us had seen the bloated features of the waterlogged, had felt the hand of the drowned tighten around an ankle; each of us knew that wherever we might place a foot we would step on a body with swollen sealed eyes.

In fact, we never swam down below, by the booms. Our only swimming was in the cove in front of the house, shallow and quiet with its own current but safely above the rapids. It was where we learned to dog-paddle. It was where Mother viewed the river as a danger that could sweep away her children's limp rag bodies into its current. She had never learned to swim and sat on shore on a towel, sunning her legs, crooking a finger at us when we waded out too far. Standing up and hollering when we pretended not to see.

It was the last Saturday in August, and our parents had announced that they were having a corn roast. Not at the usual site on broad shale in front of the house but following the bank up onto the high flat part of the cliffs where there were twelve white pines, grown tall and full with their bundles of soft needles. Quite naturally, we called the place the Pines. It was halfway to the wall. Below the cliffs were the first whitecaps, the place where true fast water began. The river had already begun to rise, and the change of current could be seen from this very spot.

Lyd and I had been helping Father and Duffy and Roy, from the club, collect driftwood and small stray logs along shore. We pretended to find logs that were not branded and dragged them onto the rocks to dry.

The club was not really the men's club; it was the sewing club of their wives — and Rebecque, Duffy's girlfriend. It was the summer the women made sundresses with bolero tops that came halfway down their backs, with close-fitting sleeves ending just above the elbow. *Clever cover-ups with a classic look* was printed on the pattern.

Recently, on a scorching day, Roy's wife, Mona of the little feet, had been shopping in Hull when a policeman approached and advised her that she must put on her jacket. She was carrying her new cotton bolero over her arm. Her shoulders should not be bare, said the policeman, even though he could see that the sundress was held up by a two-inch width of straps. She could be fined fifty dollars or go to jail for one month.

The women of the club were buzzing with this story.

"*Maudit fou*," Rebecque said, of the policeman and of the law, which was suspect. When she spoke this came out sounding like *Moodzee foo.* No one knew if a Quebec ban on bare shoulders really existed. But the enforcement of it came out of the same morality that prevented Lyd and me from wearing our shorts on rue Principale in St. Pierre. Even to run up to Le Loup's for a pound of sliced bologna we had to change into a skirt. We could wear shorts in our yard and in the fields, but if we were seen on the main street of the village the priest would send us home.

Mother's sundress, made from the same pattern used by the other women, was linen not cotton. The colour of deep summer sky embedded with myriad tiny yellow stars. You had to stand close to the material to see the stars, they were so minute. When the last stitches were done, Mother pushed the iron over the new dress, back-forth, back-forth, flattening the straps last. The bolero, not meant to join in front, curved perfectly over her bust. The first time she wore the dress was to buy groceries in Hull. Warned by Mona, she kept the bolero on. Before she left to catch the bus she stood at the long mirror that had once belonged to Duffy's runaway wife. She turned to view all angles of herself and patted her hips. She wanted her dress to be slightly different and had added false pleats at the waist. "Not bad," she said to herself and arched one arm and then the other over her head to check the sleeves.

Rebecque sometimes came over to exercise with Mother in our house after supper. They pushed the kitchen table against the wall and twirled the radio dial till they found music they liked. They sat on the floor, one at each end of the linoleum. Legs outstretched, arms outstretched, palms down, fingertips leading, they crossed the room on their bottoms, shifting forward first one buttock, then the other. When they passed, each collapsed an elbow and pulled an imaginary cord. "Toot-toot!" they shouted, trying to keep the beat of "Ragmop" or "Slow Poke" or "Gonna Get Along Without Ya Now."

Lyd and I refused to watch this display and sat on the steps outside until they were finished. Mother and Rebecque laughed at us. "We are firming our buttocks," they said deliberately. "Just you wait till you're our age, just you wait."

All day Saturday, party food had been arriving. A copper boiler appeared. Duffy carried in a sack filled with corn, and he and Rebecque went down to the river to husk. Duffy laughed like Gildersleeve. He told us he'd driven through field roads the night before and had stolen the corn, and we half-believed him. Lyd and I followed him and

Rebecque to the river and offered to help because *we liked to be near them*. Rebecque was forever teasing about kissing him through his moustache. By now they were living together in Rebecque's house in the village but they were not like our parents or the other couples in the club. *They were not married.*

Father organized a work party to arrange a circle of stones back from the edge of the cliff, and we began to lug wood. We'd been collecting all week, but he wouldn't let us take it to the site until the last minute in case it was stolen. The cliff could not be seen from the house. It was the first time a party would be held there, and I could not see the point of it. Every fork, every stick of wood, every cob of corn and slab of butter had to be carried. It wasn't like ducking in and out of the house when ice was needed or when someone had to use the bathroom.

How would Lyd and I know what was going on?

Would they dance under the twelve pines? How would they get music up there? It wouldn't be pieces like "Coppelia Waltz," played on our record player in the living room while Father and Mother, holding our backs stiff, twirled us, one-two-three, one-two-three. It wouldn't be "Dizzy Fingers" on piano. It would be radio songs: "Secret Love," "Walkin' My Baby Back Home."

It was the music that made Lyd and me decide to sneak to the party after dark. We'd hide in the bushes and watch them dance. We'd go the long way round, skirt the Pines by taking a lower path to the booms, and come back towards the party from down below. We knew every bush that would conceal us and we'd be able to see by the light of the fire. The adults would be drinking, the men beer, the women gin and tonic, and we'd be able to watch them misbehave.

The club women had decided to wear slacks, Mother said, and she pressed her own with a damp cloth during the lull between late afternoon and early evening. Duffy and Rebecque had gone home to change; the fresh corn was piled into three brown shopping bags, ready to be boiled. Father kept changing his mind about the beer. Should he take washtubs and hack at a block of ice to keep the bottles cold? Should he carry up river water and stand the beer in that?

Mother wore a short-sleeved beige sweater to match her plain slacks. She applied lipstick and a spot of rouge on each cheek, rubbed with her finger upward and outward over the bone. "I don't know if I'll be warm enough when the breeze comes up," she said to Lyd and me. "What do you think?"

As if the three of us had planned this together, she went back to the door of her closet and removed her bolero from the sundress on its hanger. She slipped it over top of her sweater. The tiny stars seemed to multiply, to pull inward.

She surveyed herself in the long mirror. "Do you think I look nice? What do you think?"

We watched Father as he turned his head to look at her.

We knew she wasn't really asking.

Lyd and I made cheese and mustard sandwiches and bided our time. We watched the clock and watched the clock and finally set out through the back screen door and got our feet onto a path that was so black it almost disappeared. I thought I knew every root and anthill, but I kept stumbling. What I hadn't allowed for was the roar. Usually I never heard the rapids because they were always there; now they pounded like drums rolling in thunder. It occurred to me that I'd never been deep into the Pines at night. Lyd was starting to change her mind. We took turns hanging on to each other's sleeve.

"Did you know it would be so dark?" she said.

"We're not quitting. We made up our minds."

"Yeah, well, if Father catches us he'll be madder than hops."

"Too bad." I got in front and yanked my arm free. "Whether you go back or not I'm still going."

"Jesus," Lyd muttered. "Jesus cripes." But I could hear her footsteps behind me.

We'd made a wide semicircle and approached the Pines from below as planned. A ridge of old wall leaned out over the rapids in a meandering curve and gave us a landmark to follow. The bushes opened up and the path widened. From here we could see sparks shooting up from the fire, and we heard deep distant laughter.

"Duffy," Lyd said. "I hear the moustache."

She couldn't return now because it was darker behind than in front. We left the path and stuck to a thickness of trees far back from the open cliff. The entire club was there in silhouette, circling a crackling fire. There was Father holding a bottle of beer; Mona, her husband Roy hovering as if he had to be right there to protect her little feet; Rebecque in wonderful tight red party strides, close-dancing with Duffy, who kept kissing her neck.

"It's the perfume," I said. "Where she puts it. Right on the pulse."

"*Ici! Ici!*" Lyd said, jabbing her finger, and we doubled over, loving Rebecque.

We crouched down to settle in. The men were going back and forth to the washtubs for beer, the women dancing with one another's husbands — except for Duffy and Rebecque. A log was kicked into the fire from one side and burst out the other. The laughter was shrill, edged with foolishness.

"They're worse than we are," I told Lyd, but that was okay. We knew who they were, we'd been eavesdropping on them for years. We just wanted to be there to make sure we knew what they were up to and that what they were up to was the same old thing.

Now the radio was playing "Jambalaya." Everyone stopped and pointed glasses and bottles into the air. They planted their feet and became a chorus over the roar of rapids. They could not be said to be in harmony.

"They're half-snapped already," Lyd said.

"Not Mom," I said. "Look."

She did have a drink in her hand and we knew it was gin and tonic, but she wasn't holding it into the air and she wasn't singing, either. She knew every show tune, every line from every musical, every radio song. But she didn't shout them into the sky. Our mother sang privately, to herself and to her children. She'd been doing it since we were born and probably before that, too. In the kitchen, a tea towel wrapped around her waist because she couldn't be bothered tying an apron. Our mother, her dark hair floating over her shoulders, her bolero drenched with stars. Our mother set her drink on boards that had been propped across logs and smiled to herself. She reached down into a paper shopping bag and started dropping corn, one cob at a time, into the boiler.

The members of the chorus, shouting to the treetops, arms around one another's waists, were finding themselves very funny.

"What the hell!" It was Roy. He had his fly open and a dark stream had already arced into the bushes behind us. He turned his back one direction and Lyd and I twisted in the other.

"You little buggers," he said. "Get the hell home before I tell your father." He was fumbling with his pants. We thought he'd shout for Father right there and then.

"How did you get up here?" he hissed at us, his fly finally done up.

"We came the long way," I said. "From down below. Are you going to tell?"

"You bet I'll tell. Now get the hell out of here. Go back the same way you came."

We bolted along the line of bushes into a night as black as the waves, heading for the wall so we could follow its curve to the path. Lyd was in front this time and I was shouting.

"Where the hell did he come from? I thought they were all singing. Goddamn him sneaking up like that. He almost peed all over us."

We reached the wall and leaned against it, and I started shoving as hard as I could.

"Are you crazy?" Lyd said. "The wall's going to fall."

"You're the one who's crazy," I said. "The wall's a foot and a half thick. It'll never fall."

I kicked and shoved some more. But I gave up, and we walked slowly home along the path, hearing the party behind us, never considering the hands groping up out of the black water as we skirted the booms down below.

"Did you see Roy's penis?" I said.

"No, did you?"

We started laughing and ran the rest of the way, climbing in through our bedroom window, even though there was no need to with our parents up in the Pines. We laughed and laughed and laughed and got into our big double bed and didn't draw a line down the middle of the bottom sheet or fight or swear at each other or make threats that would have to be resolved or carried out the next day. We went to sleep thinking of Roy telling or not telling, of almost being peed on, of Rebecque dancing in her tight red pants, of music floating up through the pines. We slept right through the blackest hours of the night and didn't wake until we heard new sounds and crying and shouts in the dark. The barn door banging and the hooks thrown out of the attic to the earth below.

"What," Lyd said. "What." She got out of bed and I could see her long legs in the moonlight as she jumped from one foot to the other. We went through the summer kitchen and stood at the back screen. All the lights had been turned on in the house. Rebecque walked in and pulled us both tightly against her chest.

"What," Lyd kept saying. "What. Tell us what. Please, Rebecque, please tell us."

Because we still didn't know. Because we'd been sound asleep when Mother walked to the edge of the cliff, slept while her left foot tripped and crossed over her right, slept while she lost her balance and slipped silent over the edge, disappearing in full firelight view of her husband and her closest friends. Looking into Rebecque's face we still did not know. And it would be some time before we would be able to imagine the weightlessness, the air rushing past the two spots of rouge on her cheeks, her head bobbing in the white-tipped waves, the breeze resting now, in her hair.

FRANCES ITANI

Poached Egg on Toast
(1996)

December 3, he wrote in pencil on the kitchen calendar: *Robin in front yard*. The robins had migrated before the middle of October and he wondered what this stray would find to eat. It was gone by the end of the day.

December 24, he was shovelling snow from the path that led to the shed, and he looked up to the sky to see Jesus Christ reclining in the clouds. Details were vivid and clear. Christ was wearing a loose robe, and his eyes were kindly as he looked benevolently and sorrowfully towards Earth.

Arthur banged the snow from his boots and went into the warm kitchen. He stood awkwardly, pencil in hand, wondering how to mark this on the calendar, knowing it for the momentous event it was. He decided on the abbreviation *CHR*. If Ada were to ask, he'd say Christmas, one day until. Something like that.

January 31 was the coldest day Arthur had ever lived through, all the years of his life. He walked as far as the clump of trees in the middle of the field and stumbled back to write in his black diary: *I thought the sky above the planet would crack. I understand now what the medievals saw when they described the dome cupped over the flat earth.*

Ada only raised an eyebrow when she came across notations on the calendar. Ada had her three meals to cook every day, which she liked to do, and she had her friend Elizabeth, who lived on the opposite side of the field. Every Thursday night she and Elizabeth went to town to see a movie. Ada did not feel the need to write any of this down.

On April 16, Arthur wrote on the calendar, *The blooming of the lily*, though he hated lilies; they reminded him of death. Ada had brought this one home on the bus from town and carried it in her two hands across the field as she walked from the bus stop.

These were the weeks when Arthur worked furiously in the garden, keeping an eye on grackles that strutted like executioners in their blue hoods. He had to put up with them at his feeders if he wanted to keep the jays.

May 26, he entered in the diary: *Mewling and caterwauling in the trees. The orioles took the string I chopped for them and disappeared.*

That was the same morning he and Ada had the fight over what she'd given him for his breakfast, though he made no entry to mark it.

He'd only mentioned, albeit complainingly, that he was tired of eating poached egg on toast; he'd had it three times in the past ten days.

"I wouldn't be fussy if I were you," said Ada. "There are only so many breakfasts I can think of to make."

That's when Arthur should have kept his mouth shut, but instead he shot back, "Why, I could think of a hundred breakfasts, each one different from the last."

"I'd like to see the day you'd come up with a hundred breakfasts," said Ada, "even in your imagination. Especially when you've never cooked so much as one for yourself."

They sat to a meal together later the same day, but the next morning Ada did not get up.

Arthur posed upright in his chair in the living room and waited and went to the kitchen to put on the water for his tea. He returned to the chair and waited again. Ada did not get up.

He tore a piece of paper from a pad of yellow foolscap.

Corn fritters, he wrote. His stomach contracted in hunger from the writing of it.

Corn flakes, he added. These were pretty harmless.

　　Muffets
　　shredded wheat

He paused and inserted as a heading, *Occasional*, which he underlined.

Ada had to be pretending to be asleep; he knew for a fact that she'd never in her life stayed in bed so long.

　　kipper snacks
　　sardines, plain
　　sardines with tomato sauce

sliced tomato with black pepper, on toast
fish

He changed his mind about fish and turned it into a heading of its own.

Fish
bass
trout
pickerel
salmon (canned)
sole
finnan haddie

He heard Ada stir, and he hid the list inside the dictionary. He got up and put on his jacket and went outside. He walked as far as the trees in the middle of the field. There was a small rise there and he could see all the way around in a broad circle. He placed each foot deliberately, rotating a hundred and eighty degrees. He thought of the word *view* and remembered discovering in the dictionary that one of its meanings was "footprints of the fallow-deer."

When he was a young man and took his rifle to the woods, he was excited by the stillness, the sudden startle of the deer. But there were no footprints this day. There'd been none to notice even before he'd marked on the calendar six weeks earlier, *The last melting of the snow*. It had been twenty-three years since Arthur had hunted. His rifle had been resting in the gun rack all that time.

He stayed outside the rest of the morning and tried to expand the breakfasts in his mind. Without enthusiasm, he could get no further than finnan haddie.

Lunch was ready when he went inside, and he was glad to get some food into him. As soon as Ada turned to the dishes, he sat in the living room and went back to his list:

cottage cheese
apple fritters

Jell-O – orange
      – cherry
      – black currant
      – lime

He included only the flavours he would eat, and he counted each as a separate breakfast. He created another category.

Cold meats
chicken loaf
delicia loaf
mac & cheese
head cheese
bologna, fried

He thought with pleasure of the bubbles that pushed up through the rubbery red circles as they sizzled in the cast-iron pan. The slices had to be exactly the right thickness.

The rest of the day, Arthur turned the earth in his garden and put in seed, and while he worked he considered going to town. He had only vague thoughts about what he might do there and put the trip off to another day. Before he went to bed that night, he lifted the blind and stared out. There was the moon, a slice of lemon, tilted in the sky.

Neither he nor Ada brought up the matter between them. Ada stayed in bed every morning, and Arthur rattled from one room to another, listening for any sound at all. They'd been sleeping on the edges of the bed, careful not to touch. He hated that. He was used to Ada's warmth seeping into him.

Warmed up, he wrote.

giblets
potatoes & cabbage mixed
hamburger boiled, with gravy
meatballs
macaroni
home-made spaghetti with toast
Irish stew

meat pie with crust
turkey and dressing (seasonal)
chicken pot pie

A good run. He had thirty-six but he'd hit a block. He went outside and watched the changing light as the wind cleared the clouds. The first green shoots were lined up unevenly in his garden, and he made a note in his head to mark on the calendar: *Life pushed through earth.*

He felt something like sorrow as he stood there. It was too late in his life to start cooking on his own, pushing pots and pans around the kitchen. He knew Ada would be lying in bed listening. She'd dug in her heels before, and when she was like this there was no telling if she'd give in first, or give in at all. She was still cooking his lunch and his supper, but even though she knew he had to have a good solid meal in the morning, she was behaving as if the idea of breakfast had never been thought of at all.

After lunch, Ada said she was going to visit Elizabeth for the afternoon. Arthur waited until she left, and he took the bus to town. He paced the main street and wished he'd never complained. The tension in the house had clamped over the two of them like the steel trap that hung from a long spike in the shed.

Ada was spending more and more of her time with Elizabeth, and Arthur was no longer privy to the bits of gossip and fun she was used to bringing home.

Arthur watched a man speak rudely to his wife outside the A&P. For a moment he thought that he himself would burst into tears in the street. He went to the next block and walked past the florist twice before he entered the shop. With his head down, he ordered twelve roses for Ada and gave his address to the woman at the counter. She handed him a tiny blank card to fill out, and he stared at it in his large palm. He had not considered this, having to include a message. He gave the card back to the woman and cancelled the roses.

He slipped into the diner by the bus depot and sat in a booth and asked for the breakfast menu, though it was afternoon. He only ordered coffee but wrote on a shred of paper from his wallet:

omelette plain
cheese and mushroom omelette
Hawaiian omelette with pineapple

He did not fancy what the Hawaiians mixed with their eggs in the morning.

pancakes with syrup
pancakes with blueberry sauce

Without ceremony, the waitress appeared beside the booth and took the menu away from him. She lifted it right out of his hands.

Ada was still away when Arthur returned. He started a new column and wrote out the breakfasts he'd borrowed from the diner. After that, he kept on writing.

corn syrup with toast
bacon (not cooked hard)

He'd let Ada know that sometimes she left it too long in the pan.

lasagna (leftovers)
ravioli (leftovers)
cheese chops

He heard Ada coming and stashed the list.

Arthur began to dream about plums served on doilied trays, about grapefruit slit with a delicate silver knife. He woke one morning and thought, *Maybe Ada has forgotten the fight.* And then: *Maybe she's told Elizabeth.*

He imagined the two women laughing over a fight that now seemed to have taken place a long time ago. A fight that was no one's business but his own. His and Ada's, though it was never discussed. Breakfast had simply ceased.

He sat in the chair in the living room while Ada pretended to sleep, and he pressed heavily with a pen into his black diary: *I'm not a useless old fool. I come from a long line of men that were not required to do their own cooking. It's the way things have always been, though once a year at Christmas my father made his four-meat pâté. Rabbit was the fourth meat because it was in the family tradition. I never saw him cook anything else.*

How would he give her the list, even if he did get it done? Somewhere in his mind, he knew he'd attached an unlikely outcome to the hundredth breakfast. Ada would rise early and come to the kitchen in her faded maroon robe and her soft slippers, and she would stir quietly about the room while he sat at the table and waited.

There must have been something else, something besides him complaining about his poached egg on toast. Something deeper, darker, something further back. He couldn't for the life of him think what it might be.

Black pudding, he wrote.

sausage regular
sausage Oktoberfest
bananas, flecked with brown

Fifty.

Thursday morning the following week, Arthur put the kettle on and boiled the water and made a large pot of tea, two bags. He let it sit four minutes and poured the tea into Ada's cup and added a drop of milk. He carried it to their room and stood at the end of the bed.

Ada did not stir; her breathing did not alter. He set the cup on her bedside table, and on his way out of the room he thumped the end of the mattress with his foot.

Before he went outside to work in the garden he put on his cap and tied a bandanna around his neck. As he passed the mirror he glanced back quickly, thinking he'd seen a bandit.

All morning he watered and weeded until his back ached from bending. He scanned the sky, looking for cloud formations, and listened to the birds raise their young. The baby jays were learning to fly. Every once in a while a blue ball of fluff drifted past, slow-landing on the earth.

Everything had its life. He'd read in the paper that trees knew when someone was going to chop them down. Their terrible cries could be measured electronically as the axe hit. Arthur believed this. What was being discovered every day was wondrous.

What he did not like was the way things were reported on radio and TV. Instant this and instant that, everything was instant. War inside your own house the same moment it was happening around the other side of the world. He could do without that. The whole business made him weary.

When he went inside, he could not tell if Ada had drunk the tea he'd made. The cup was washed and dried and back on the kitchen shelf. Ada was nowhere to be seen. Though he was tired, Arthur pulled out the list.

> ham fried
> side pork
> apple sauce (cold)
> Spanish rice (warmed)
> peanut butter on toast
> liver and onions

His favourite. He hadn't eaten liver and onions for a long time. He began to think the list was foolish but he had fifty-six; he was past any point, now, where he could do a back turn.

> toasted cheese sandwich
> hot scones with raisins
> bread pudding, crisped under grill
> cheese biscuits
> waffles with syrup
> bran muffins
> home fries
> fruit salad
> pigs-in-blankets

He went to his room and hauled down the covers, and in the middle of the day, Arthur went back to bed.

When he woke he realized he'd eaten neither breakfast nor lunch. It was Ada's night to go to the movies. Before all this had started he used to mark the films she went to, on the calendar. He never wanted to go himself, but every Thursday when Ada came home, he was used to hearing about the story and the movie stars. He especially liked to hear about the reruns, the old movies done up again, readied for the big screen like old tarts. Bogart and Bacall. Cagney. Rosalind Russell, now there was someone who could act.

He saw that his supper was in the oven. He'd slept a long time. When he looked out across the field he realized it was the first time he'd missed standing at the door on a Thursday evening, watching Ada's back as she crossed the field. She always called on Elizabeth first, before the two of them took the bus to town.

He ate his supper in silence, listening to marauding bands of starlings as they roved from tree to tree across the field. He brought the list to the kitchen.

Salmon patties, he wrote.

dish of prunes

He put down the pencil and picked it up again. He felt his face flush as he wrote and underlined:

Eggs
scrambled
once over
sunny side

He went outside and stood on the step. The sun was being pulled under the hills and there were streaks of charcoal above the horizon. Since last winter he'd checked the sky frequently for signs of Jesus in his robe, but he'd never seen such a vision again. He remembered the date of it, December 24. His mother used to tell him, when he was a small child, that at the stroke of midnight Christmas Eve, all the animals in the barn would speak to one another. Now the seasons seemed to glide past: fall would be here and then winter would cover his roof, his garden, his shed.

He returned to the kitchen table.

boiled egg, 3 minutes sharp
eggs Benedict

These he'd only heard about; Ada had never made them.

Western sandwich
egg-in-the-hole

He went to the gun rack and took down his rifle. As he passed the mirror he saw that he was still wearing the bandanna. He loaded the rifle in the kitchen.

poached egg on toast

He left the house and walked to the clump of trees in the middle of the field.

He sat on the earth, sheltered by trees. He thought he might catch the first star but three blinked together as if they'd been visible all along and he hadn't been alert enough to notice. He closed his eyes and thought about the list. It had been easy enough at first, but he was beginning to run down. He did not know why he'd loaded the rifle, why he'd brought it here, to the rise in the field. He sat holding it, pointing the barrel towards the sky. In an hour or so, Ada would be returning. She and Elizabeth would step down from the bus in the dark and Elizabeth would arrive home first and wait while Ada crossed the field. Ada sometimes called back when she reached the step, to let her friend know she was safe. Not that there was anyone around. They just did that; they were in the habit of calling back and forth through the dark.

He began to feel the coolness of the night as he waited. Birds were settling around him, a soft shudder of wings. Far off, he heard the bus pause to drop its passengers, and it threw out its cones of light as it turned to go back to town. Arthur sat upright, his fingers swollen against the rifle.

A few minutes later, the voices of the two women rose and fell through the dark. There was a murmur as they stopped at Elizabeth's doorstep and then silence when Ada set out alone across the field. She had to pass in front of him; the path was below the clump of trees where he sat stiffly on the ground. It was too late to go back to the house; she would hear him if he moved.

The argument was of no importance, he saw that now. He and Ada had drifted to this place together. They'd been living their lives, and anger had erupted and settled in a still dark pool. He could scarcely imagine why he'd been so stubborn. But she, she was as stubborn a woman as he'd ever known.

She was passing now below the trees. The curve of her shoulder, her silhouette, was as familiar to him as his own unspoken voice. He cocked the rifle and was startled to hear the *snick*. He aimed at the sky and pulled the trigger, and the roar nearly knocked him onto his back. The throb and flutter in the trees fell silent.

Ada's pace did not alter one bit; she did not even look his way. She reached the house and went in, and again he saw the curve of her in the light as she removed her jacket and walked through the living room to close the curtains. He tried to get up but his knees would not hold him. He had to rub his legs and feet to get them to move.

From where he stood in the field he might have been underwater. The lighted house seemed to recede as he waded above the path, his thighs thickening with the chill.

If there was a way of surfacing, he'd never learned it. The list was three-quarters done; Ada would probably never see it. She might not even speak to him when he went inside. He felt foolish holding the rifle, firing it into the air. He did not know how other men and women faced their differences, whether it was all a matter of blunder and chance. He knew only that he'd had to let Ada know he was serious about wanting his breakfast. He only wanted her to understand.

SHAUNA SINGH BALDWIN

Satya
(1997)

Rawalpindi, India, 1937

My heart was black and dense as a stone within me. I told myself I pitied Roop but heard laughter answering me — how difficult it is to deceive yourself when you have known yourself full forty-two years.

I had her summoned to my room in the afternoon when Sardarji had gone to a canal engineers' meeting. When she came before me, I did not speak but took her chunni as though in welcome, so I could study her. I took her chin and raised her face to the afternoon sun, willing it to blind her, but it would do me no such service. I studied her features, her Pothwari skin, smooth as a new apricot beckoning from the limb of a tall tree, her wide and heavily lashed eyes, demurely lowered, innocent.

A man could tell those eyes anything and they would believe him, a man could kiss those red lips for hours and they would look fuller and more luscious for the bruising.

Her hair was long and smelled of amla and of coconut. Unlike mine, it had no need yet for henna. I lifted her plait around her shoulder and examined the tip — too few split ends; it had felt the scissor once at least, if not more. She was a renewed Sikh, then, carrier of the orthodoxy resurging in us all . . . Hindus, Sikhs, Muslims, we are like the three strands of her hair, a strong rope against the Britishers but separate nonetheless.

I unbound her hair. It lay, moonlit-river, in the valley of her spine.

I examined her teeth and found she had all of them still, the back ones still unformed. I hoped when they came they'd bring pain. Her tongue was soft and a healthy pink, and from it a man would hear no truths he could not explain away. I pressed my fingers to her cheek-bones, they were high, like my own. Some remnant of Afridi blood in our past; in other circumstances I might have been her aunt or cousin.

My hands dropped to her neck and encircled it lightly, for I was not trying to frighten her. And I saw that Sardarji had given her a kantha, one of mine. I knew the gold of this one well; I'd ordered it from the sonhar myself. I knew every link in it and the sheen of its red enamel. I wore it last to a party of Europeans, and its brilliance and its weight had comforted me — compensation for my tongue-tied state; the European ladies ignored me once they found I spoke no English.

This I saw now, covering the hollow at her neck, and I wanted to press my thumb in that hollow and wait till her red blood spurted over us both.

I wanted this.

I moved my hands with no sign I recognized the kantha, no hint that she who stood before me was a silent thief.

With such a tremulous placating smile.

I examined her brow. Time was ploughing my own in three horizontal furrows, deepening by the day; but hers was yet smooth. I pulled her hair back over her ears and saw her earrings, the same that Sardarji had given me after my first visit to the first ineffectual Sant. I knew this pair well: three tiers of Burmese rubies surrounded by diamonds — real diamonds, not white sapphires — red-hearted flower-shapes ending in large Basra teardrop pearls.

And Roop was wearing them.

I wanted to tear them from her ears, watch as her tender lobes elongated and parted to give me back what was mine, rightfully mine.

But I moved my hands away.

"Come lie with me in the afternoons. You are alone on your side of the house, I am alone on my side. My pukhawalla is better — he's from my village, our men are strong."

Roop stood, uncertain. If she had been my niece, my daughter, or even a cousin, I would have shouted to her to stay away from me, turn now and run before she could be hurt.

But if I had been her mother, Roop would be my daughter.

And none of this would have been necessary.

"Come," I said again. "It is useless for me to fight Sardarji's will; he is my husband, he has married you. Somehow I must accept that — and you."

Roop's face lit up like a diya at Diwali.

"Oh, Pehenji."

Sister.

I did not feel sisterly at all.

"Oh Pehenji," Roop said. "I'm so glad. I told Sardarji, I will be no trouble, I will be just like a younger sister."

And her silly tears fell upon my hand as I led her to the bed.

I placed myself in the path of the light from the inner courtyard, dismissing the servants. I lowered the reed chics myself till the room, cool and dark, held the sun at bay. A silli of ice covered with a jute sack in the corner of the room wept into a puddle on the floor as it absorbed the heat of the afternoon. The pukhawalla spat a red stream of paan by the door, squatted with the rope over his shoulder, and leaned into his pulling rhythm, setting the huge swath of silk above us creaking back and forth, back and forth. The breeze from his efforts moved from me to Roop and back to me again, doing nothing to cool me. I was white-hot inside — though if I had to speak it out, it would be better to call it hurt or pain.

"Come, lie down," I said, setting aside the roll of the gaudum-takya I reclined on when managing Sardarji's servants. I put a soft pillow beneath Roop's head to cradle my ruby earrings. I heard her juthis plop to the floor behind her as she drew herself into snake-form on my — our — bed. I leaned over her as a mother might have, and I brushed the tears from her lashes with my lips, and I stroked her head and said, "Sleep, little one, we are together now."

And Roop slept, overcome by the afternoon heat.

While I watched her.

So trusting, so very stupid.

Her arm thrown back over her head wore my gold bangles and my rings. Her feet were small and narrow for her height. On her ankles she wore my gold panjebs, on her toes, my toe rings.

I could have torn them from her while she was sleeping, but thievery has never been a trait in my family.

Why was she so trusting? How could she be so confident she would produce a child? How could she not look at me, Satya, and think, "This is what I could become"? How could she not see any danger in blundering deep into the tigress's den to steal the chance of her ever bearing a cub?

Had I been like her once? Had I ever been so witless and still so charming? Young women these days think they are invincible, that they have only to smile and good things will happen to them.

Look at me, I wanted to tell her. Barren but still useful; I manage

Sardarji's whole estate. Do you think that is an easy task? Do you think it is just giving orders? No, little "sister," I wanted to say, the mukhtiar does my bidding because he respects my judgement, he knows he cannot cheat me. I am too watchful and I know the hisab to the anna. Not a pai of Sardarji's money is spent on mere ornamentation or given to the undeserving.

The money I gave to the Sants, however, was a contribution to our future.

Perhaps Sardarji felt I gave them too much — then he had only to say one word. One word in my ear and I would not have spent another pai on intercessors but could have prayed to Vaheguru myself. Only I have never felt Vaheguru listens to women's prayers.

When Sardarji's sister, Toshi — that churail! — when Toshi began her insinuations that Sardarji should marry again, I laughed and said, "Yes, what a good idea."

And I said I would find a good Sikh girl myself, a woman for my husband.

I said this for ten years while my heart sank lower and lower and my body betrayed me every moon-month with its bleeding.

Soon my doom wrote itself into the lines of my hands. The palmists said they saw a daughter or a long-lost sister in my hand; they said this in the "could-be" tone of men who trade the kindness of lies for the wisdom of truth.

They have to make a living.

Still I found no woman ugly enough for Sardarji to marry. In all the Sind-Sagar doab where women are raised like saplings to bend with every wind so long as it speak with a voice of authority, I found no woman pliant enough for my husband. Though I am far from schooled, I found no woman schooled enough to match him. Though I can speak no English, I declared his new mate must know the Git-mit, Git-mit talk and be raised to sit on chairs. And as the times changed and women began to walk in the streets for protest marches, I declared all of them unworthy to come into my presence, let alone his.

When I was forty years old, I read my fate in Toshi's eyes, saw it in the way she and her husband ignored me when they came to visit and no longer asked about me if Sardarji stopped to visit at their home. I went to the Sants and asked them for curses. The told me they were men devoted to God and that I must be self-effacing, humble, grateful for my undiminished status, the magnanimity of my husband, my continued unharmed existence. And I was so angry I began to accuse Sardarji of slighting me when he had done nothing. We would fight so the loving turned sweeter, and I would take care to argue so his long absences inspecting new canals were easier to bear. And Sardarji sent me to Toshi for child-inducing potions and pippal fruit, but such was my state of fear I took none of them in case Toshi was trying to poison me to make way for a new wife.

My mata came to visit with the sowing season and reasoned with me. She said women have been heard of who can have children even till the age of sixty. I said, "I don't have time to wait till then." Mata saw fear had tied my hands and feet, pinned my body to the bed, and she saw how it was draining me like a well that fills by night and exhausts itself by day. She saw how I had almost reverted to the old custom of purdah and laughed at me for wanting the sanctuary of what I once decried. She made sure no one noticed the difference in the daily management of Sardarji's household affairs — many wise men chose her family for their rebirthing.

But how do you talk to a mother about the things that happen between a husband and a wife in the dark? How could I speak of the pain of his touch — so gentle, so forbearing, so kind — when I could not repay it with children? What right had I to share his bed and bring nothing from the coupling? A man is pleasured, Mata said, you can see it afterwards. "But," she said, shelling a Kashmiri pistachio between her strong back teeth, "a woman is merely cracked open for seeding like the earth before the force of the plow. If she is fertile, good for the farmer, if not, bad for her."

Mata came from an honest family.

When Sardarji stopped coming for pleasure, I hid it from Mata. And I asked her questions, like lovers slanting under trapdoors; I prodded her obliquely to name the men in our family who could and would come to my assistance if I should need it. There were a few — my family was not completely powerless — but Sardarji was unarguably the most powerful in our biradari. Any protest from my male relatives would be heard and tolerated, but in the end I would be like a kakar petrified before a tiger; if the tiger were hungry, the kakar must die.

Hai, to die! I cannot bear the remembering.

I knew his body so well, so many years of holding each other in times of tiredness, in times of hope, in times of debt and of loss. How could a young woman know this? How could a young woman know his friends, laugh with them as do those who've learned from living? How could a young woman know he breathes deeply when he thinks too hard, that he wipes his forehead in the cold heart of winter because the tax collector's visit draws near? How would a young woman know how to manage his mills while he is away at shikar, how to give orders that sound as though she were a mere mouth for his words? How would she know his voice is angry with the servants only when he is tired or hungry? How would she know his talk of logic and discipline in the English people's hallways and his writing in the brown paper files about the great boons of irrigation engineering brought by the conquerors are belied by his donations to the Akalis and the Azad Party?

All this was in me as I looked at Roop's sleeping figure, and I remembered the day I could no longer continue my pretence that I was looking for a second wife for my husband. The sorting room was full of apricots brought in big baskets from the orchard and laid out on gunny sacks, their heavy sweet smell mixed with the smell of wet coir. I was supervising the sorting — the damaged ones, even those with small blemishes to be set aside for poor relatives or beggars, the unblemished ones to be kept for serving at Sardarji's table. I felt their skins, I looked for any signs of rot — rotten ones could spoil a whole basket overnight.

I scolded a servant who placed a darkening apricot in a sorting basket of fruit for Sardarji's table, and Mai Mani let out a cackle. "The man was only following what he sees happen in this haveli."

I had lost the one ally every woman should have, if she can afford it: a faithful maidservant.

I did not let Mai Mani see she had hurt me. Instead I took the overripe fruit in my hand and dug my teeth in its softening hide. It was oversweet, pleading to be liked. Its slackening fermenting flesh came away readily, squelching. I told myself it was good; I ate some more. Mai Mani watched, eyes narrowing with amusement. I ate the whole apricot and sucked at its pit. I tasted it, tiny, dry, wrinkled stone in my mouth.

I swallowed it.

Felt no pain as it scraped in my throat, caught like a stopper in my gullet instead of travelling all the way to my womb.

Mai Mani watched me, expressionless, motionless, as I hacked, coughed and spat it out, and said, "Every woman has her kismat." Mai Mani might have come from a family that lost all its land a generation ago, but she retains the talent of the high-born to moralize over the less fortunate.

The next day I sent Mai Mani away to her village, saying she must want to visit her family, and I sent for the munshi. I made him write a letter for me, asking him to sit close to my feet, for I had lost my voice. I dictated to him in a slow tinny rasp, pathetic shadow of my usual haughty one.

When he was finished, I pressed the ball of my thumb to the blue chunk of the ink pad and then to paper, wet ink seeping into the furrows of my thumbprint. No one can make such a swirled oval but I, no second wife can duplicate my mark.

I paid the munshi well — but not too much lest he become suspicious — and I sent the letter to the only woman who owed me anything, my cousin Ruhi.

Ruhi would not deny me, Ruhi would come. In memory of a night of tears twenty years ago by a small bier and in memory of three salwars soaked with blood, she would come. In memory of a birth that was non-birth and a small atma denied a body on this circle of the wheel, in memory of her hands held tightly and screams silenced against my breast, she would come.

I called Ruhi to me now, the letter innocent, gracious, innocuous. "Come and stay a while."

This is how I learned, late but well, that secrets have their uses.

Ruhi came and stayed, and she did not ask why I made her sleep in my room, as though understanding there was no longer any chance Sardarji would visit at night.

Her sons were grown and her position secure by then, but she had dark circles around her eyes and her breath came short and shallow. We spoke little; there was not much to say. And after we heard the news that Sardarji had married a young girl, secretly, surreptitiously, without telling me, Ruhi was there to hold me through the night and wipe my tears as though I had been her own baby, grown now, wounded once again.

Ruhi knew how it would be for me, that I would not be able to face her afterwards, just as she had not found it possible to face me for twenty years after that night by the Indus.

It would be so for me as well.

So in the morning Ruhi was gone and Mata arrived a few days later, clucking like an indignant hen — "Perhaps it is not news but rumours.

You listen to people in the bazaar, this is what I taught you? Go, find a Sant who will sleep with you for money, get a son that way — you have been foolish! Do I have to teach you everything?"

But I was still with longing.

I was remembering our first times, when he would abandon the rough wool of his English suits for the soft white Peshawri kurta-pajama and how he would stand at my back, removing first my jamavar, then my jewellery. . . . And the first years of planning, the way we were partners after his return from England. And I remembered later years, when he was moving up because England-educated Indians were scarce and the British preferred Sikhs, Parsis, and Muslims, whose elevation in the government would be mixed with more gratitude than that of Hindus, recent years when I would tell him to go alone to the gymkhanas, the garden parties, the polo balls and the dinner-dances, times when I asked why would he not bring his office-wallas home and he did, and then they mistook me for a serving woman because I did not speak English.

When Mata was gone, I sat in my private sitting room and cried for myself. Because I had not wanted what he wanted, because I would not change myself just because the British people said we had to, because I wished I did not come from an honest family and that my name was not Satya — Truth — so I could get away from the truth, take refuge in self-pity, take comfort in lies.

And I prayed he had found a woman who was willing to become whatever he wanted her to be.

I looked at Roop's sleeping figure, slender and innocent. She was taller than I so at least she could not wear my clothes. She looked healthy enough; she should be able to give Sardarji sons.

What if she couldn't?

I could not bear it if he was disappointed again. Roop must bear him sons. I would see to it. I would teach her. I would tell her how to be with him.

No.

Never!

Why was she married by her family to a man so much older? Twenty-five years. There must be something wrong with her or her family. Mai Mani said she had no mother — that must be why she was so trusting. A mother would have taught her to beware of other women, especially first wives.

Roop stirred. I rolled over and away. And so we slept, backs to one another.

And I dreamed.

Sardarji lay beside me again, his snoring lending rhythm to the moonlight silvering the courtyard. Roop lay between us, her body pale and hairless, limbs supple and careless. And from between her legs there sprouted apricot buds about to open into flowers.

And Sardarji plucked these, one by one, and gave them to me.

BILL GASTON

Where It Comes From, Where It Goes

(1998)

Not knowing what was afoot in the next room, Mr. Oates told her to stand and take off her blouse. He himself removed the bra straps from her shoulders, carefully so that nothing more fell. It did sometimes make women nervous, this laying their skin bare to him, for they knew he was no official doctor. At the same time they seemed to understand that exposure, that some kind of intimacy, was part of this. To him the clothing didn't matter. It didn't get in the way of his work unless it was distracting, like a fluffy sweater or that scratchy metallic material, like woven Christmas tinsel — lamé? He'd had them all under his hands. Just like he'd had a few women reveal slinky underthings, black or shameless crimson, and these women had an attitude to match, as if seducing him would get them more from him or win some of the Gift for themselves to take home. Well, he would say unto those women, get thee gone.

Standing and facing her, Mr. Oates put his hands on the old shoulders and closed his eyes.

"Okay, den," he whispered, more to himself than to her. "Let's see what ya have dere."

He'd seen from his glance out the round window that it had begun snowing. Soon would begin the season of bad backs from shovelling walks and slippery ice, people he had a mind just to send to the chiropractor in Edmundston. But that was arrogant. All were welcome, like this old woman whose body he could feel wasn't as close to death's door as her eyes had suggested. But she was welcome.

Mr. Oates did his deep breath and long exhalation that tailed, as it should, into the emptiness that grew and turned into a hollowness, a hole into which something must now flow. It was hunger in the shape of his whole body, and yes, into him came tidings of this old woman's pain, first an aching deep mid-back that he could tell never left her. He could also feel the early black whisperings of her eventual death, it felt like distant nuts being cracked, but that was still far off, and anyway it was something that could not be taken, at least not by him. This ache behind her stomach or liver he could probably take. Perhaps he already had, for he could feel it strongly.

Mr. Oates could smell the old woman now, rotten fruit. It was time to finish and move on. She had been in too much pain to bathe, he understood this, but he wanted her to leave. What he did took only seconds to happen or to not happen, but they often had a look of small panic if he took his hands away after what they believed was too short a time. As if one of God's minutes wasn't as good as two, as if miracles had to do with time.

"Mudder, t'anks for comin'."

He had taken to calling all women "mother." He didn't know why, other than at first it had thrilled him and now it just felt good. Even for young girls. Little mothers, something nice in that thought. If it made him more mysterious, there was nothing wrong with mystery.

The old woman — a LeClair from Plaster Rock — put her bra straps up but kept her blouse off, as if she might ask him to have another go. She stood still, staring hard at nothing, looking within. She flexed her shoulders, testing. Then shyly twisted her torso, one way and the other, and though Mr. Oates never cared to know if it had worked or not and looked away as she moved, he was content to have seen her smile rise, lifting the wrinkles in her face.

"Did you sign the form?" he asked, and she nodded yes. "If someone's out waitin' please send 'em in." Carefully not changing his voice in the slightest, he added, as always, "If you would like to show yer t'anks, dere's a shoebox by the door."

He was never certain he had done any good, despite what was said about him. Usually the only sign that he did well came in the amount of money in the shoebox. Sometimes they left little, sometimes they left a lot. It didn't appear to have anything to do with what he did or didn't do. The people around the Restigouche, families he knew, as a rule didn't pay much. They were poor, why should they? And their eggs or ham or offers to plough his drive came in handy. But those who had made a journey generally left the most. Which actually meant they were more bursting with hope. You couldn't blame them. The locals came with headaches and rashes, but the folks from away were often dying. Educated people, who knew medical names for their diseases. They came regularly from Montreal now, and Bangor and Saint John and Halifax of course, and when he tested his memory he could count on his fingers Boston, Toronto, New York City, Baltimore, then the scatter of real foreigners. The two Germans last month, both skinny with AIDS and holding hands — he hadn't changed their condition one bit, he didn't think, but they left a small fortune, in German marks they were called, and which Annette had said the Plaster Rock bank couldn't take and had to send up to Edmundston before they'd change them and put money into his account. But nine hundred dollars. If there were many more like these two, soon he would have his building.

The LeClair woman got her blouse on and went out, the floor creaking with her weight. Mr. Oates sat down. The trailer shuddered when she stepped, closed the door. He could not tell if she had paused long at the shoebox. God bless her.

In twenty years he would be as old as the LeClair woman, and he was already tired. The Gift didn't always tire him, though sometimes as now it felt like a great burden on his body and, if he let it, on his spirit. But in these six years since the Father and His Son and Mary had left him with the Gift he knew how close it was to sin even to let himself feel his fatigue.

But when he was tired, like now, he felt closer to the shabby ground. He could feel in his bones how spring still hadn't come. He could smell mildew in the grey rug, which had to be fifteen years old. The floor of this old mobile creaked almost anywhere you put a foot down, and the room he worked in was damn ridiculous. Annette's bedroom, it was baby-sized. The small round window, which had been someone's idea of a desirable added feature, looked ridiculous, too, even with that crystal dangling in it. The window never got sun and the crystal was wasted there.

So much needed to be better. His own eyeglasses were old-fashioned, and he had heard there was a new kind of lens you could get that made thick ones like his much thinner. There'd be nothing wrong with a decent haircut once in a while. You don't want to look attractive but you don't want to be unattractive, either. You don't want to be a smoothie but nor do you want to be a clown with bottle-bottoms for eye-glasses. Folks thought he was strange already, why add to the picture?

Mr. Oates stood, took a normal deep breath, then touched his toes. He stretched up and touched the ceiling, which he could just barely do. The time had almost come to spend his money. A shrine to the holy Gift he had been given. He would buy a cleared acre on the lee side of a hill closer to Plaster Rock. He would get in a wide, wide lawn like the First Baptist had, buy a small tractor with a mowing tool. Gather the unearthed boulders at the lawn's middle and paint them white.

Maybe it should be nearer Edmundston itself so people could find him easier. No more orange arrows nailed to trees at corners of dirt roads. He would live in enough comfort so he wouldn't be this tired, and so would Annette, in her own bedroom instead of the couch, and she should have a car, one with four-wheel drive. There would be nothing wrong with getting himself a Ski-Doo — though that might signal to the folks that he was willing to do house calls, which he was not. He would keep the same humble shoebox for donations, with its signs on the lid he'd lettered in green marker: GENEROSITY IS THE VIRTUE THAT PRODUCES PEACE. When he'd read these words in a book an early patient had given him, he'd instantly seen them to be true and liked them for his box, even though donations to God's Gift had more to do with thanks than with generosity, as such.

He sighed as he rose to greet the next one. He could hear the heavy footsteps of a man, clunky and self-conscious, probably an embarrassed farmer with cancer or emphysema whose wife had forced him to come. As the door opened to reveal an untidy man in overalls whose bejeesus liver bulged in plain sight of even mortal eyes, Mr. Oates decided to give more thought to the idea he had for the building — it felt Roman or Biblical — of two stone waiting rooms, with that marble panelling, one for women and one for men, with a bath, a Jacuzzi bath, in each, so that they could cleanse themselves before coming in. And they would enter unto him in freshly laundered robes. Not the hospital kind but good bathrobes, either terrycloth or that velour.

The Father, His Son and Mary had given their Gift during a vigil of love at four in the morning with Annette, his daughter and only child, who was in the feverish last stages of what they said was a leukemia, though from the start there were doubts what it was. The look in her eyes that night had made Mr. Oates see her as a young child, eyes so full of fear and hope and trust that her daddy could make life right. It was like she had *become* a baby again, her only chance being to start over, could she please be a baby once more and have another try. Oates could not help but take her up and hold her tight. When his crying lessened and his own fatigue left him emptier than he'd ever been before, he took a slow deep breath, he didn't know why. When he let it out there was a feeling left inside of less than nothing, a cool hunger, a hollowness that invited all. Into him rushed Annette's fever and the horrible wrong in her blood, sour pin pricks by the thousands, it felt like every cell in her body flashed once for him, a sky of prickly fireflies within, then all was dark and warm. Mr. Oates felt close to vomiting up this feeling, this completion, which felt like his daughter's good red flesh, but he didn't.

Perhaps only seconds had passed. He knew something had happened. Perhaps she had died in his arms. He kissed the top of her head and pulled away to look upon her. Annette was breathing steadily. She slept all night, and in the morning she was hungry for the first time in weeks and so beautiful to see that neighbours had to come in and stare at her getting better.

Word was slow to spread. There was only Annette, who couldn't remember her cure. He himself wasn't one to talk. But neighbours could not help wondering at her health. After Mr. Oates's shy descriptions of his loving hug, though no one used the word "miracle," perhaps they made the story colourful when telling it. For an odd young Moncton woman with perhaps twenty earrings visited and asked if he'd seen an angel or if candles had lit by themselves. No, he said, he'd simply hugged her, but a special hug and something had happened.

A month later a desperate woman, Mary Niles, one of the Edmundston Nileses, brought her baby to Mr. Oates and asked him, simply, please try.

After the farmer with the dying liver left he sat tiredly. It was his sleep time, his two-to-three-o'clock break, there was a sign to that effect in the waiting room. But he thought he heard a foot shuffle. He waited for someone to knock, but no one did. He sat for perhaps five minutes, too tired to sleep, watching, through the silly window, a harsh snow falling. He decided he wanted to take a breath of that air, and he stood up quickly and opened his door. There was young Scott Nevers putting the lid back on the shoebox. A handful of bills lay beside it on the table. Mr. Oates stared at Scott and Scott stared back.

"*What?*"

"I —"

"Take 'er!" Mr. Oates yelled.

"Dey —"

"Take 'er 'n' *go!*"

"But dey —"

"GO!"

"But dey said."

Scott Nevers closed his eyes and started blubbering. He was sixteen or so but still had baby fat and there was something wrong with him upstairs. Mr. Oates had seen younger children cuff him with disdain. Scott's word "they" had alerted Mr. Oates and made him not quick to chase the thief.

"Who is 'dey'. What did 'dey' say. Stop cryin', Scott."

"Dey said it was, dey said it was okay."

"Scott, stop cryin'. Who is 'dey'?"

"Dey said if you caught me you'd curse me. Please don't —"

"*Who is 'dey'?*"

"My, my dad. An' Mr. Renous, an' *everyone*. Dey *all* said."

"Why would all of 'em say it's okay dat you steal my money dere, eh, Scott?"

"Dey said you don't care. It's always been like dat."

"You mean you stolen from me before?"

The look Scott Nevers gave him was surprised and then stupidly sly in a way that said much.

"Who ya take the money to dere, Scott?"

"I dunno."

Mr. Oates hit him only the once.

"Who ya take it to? Stop cryin'."

"It's, it's Mr. Renous divvies it out."

"Divvies —?"

"He says it's everybody's and you don't mind."

Mr. Oates touched the lid, reading the little sign, all finger-smudged now, GENEROSITY IS THE VIRTUE THAT PRODUCES PEACE. He lifted it off. Inside there looked to be a like amount of bills as in the little stack on the table.

"What, you take about half, dere, Scott?"

"Best as I can get 'er, Mr. Oates." Fooled by Mr. Oates's tone, he looked ready to smile. "There's cheques to count up, I gotta leave them, so —"

"GET OUT."

Scott looked quickly down at the money, confused about whether he could or couldn't still take it.

"OUT."

"Please don't curse me —"

"OUT!"

Mr. Oates pounded back into the healing room and stood breathing hard. *Damn them.* He looked around quickly, almost panicking at the gritty carpet, the miserly window, the mismatched chairs, the clown-and-balloon wallpaper he'd put up when Annette was born. All looked poorer now. He had only half the money he rightfully should have. His bank account in Plaster Rock, which he pictured as a red thermometer like the United Way used on the City Hall lawn, should be twice as tall. He squinted recalling the Ski-Doo he'd seen Paul Renous riding this winter, he was almost certain it was Renous on that, a model he'd never seen before.

Mr. Oates shook his head in a spasm, as if something obscene had fallen onto the skin of his face and he must fling it off. He found a chair with his hand and sat.

Paul Renous, his facial tics, little jumps of skin in places you wouldn't think were muscles. Could Mr. Oates afford to fight Paul Renous again? It had been years ago. Renous with his cousin dying of cancer, the police, Renous's lawyer from the city acting like *he'd* killed her for christsakes. He'd made no promises, he never made promises. Mr. Oates had had to secure his own lawyer, whom he hadn't liked either, who'd helped only because he was getting richly paid to. The case was eventually thrown out of court, no thanks to the lawyer, whose only usefulness had been to write up the waiver sheet for people to sign, I the undersigned understand that this is not a medical procedure and that Mr. Arden Oates makes no claims to be in any way . . .

This time it would be him going to the police. But it would be impossible. He wouldn't be able to tell them how much had been taken. He could see their eyes as he explained what he did to earn his money.

His door was ajar and someone rapped timidly on it.

Trying to keep his voice steady, he said, "Gi' me two minute, den come in."

He sat straighter to still himself. If the Gift took effort on his part it was in finding the quiet inside. He couldn't be thinking wildly or hard. Putting his hands on his knees, he took a few practice breaths. There had been only one other like Paul Renous. Her eyes dark and accusing, that woman from Cape Breton who had cut out her own tongue, whose husband had brought her, who knows why, how could you restore a tongue? Her mouth was shaped like a complaint. Maybe the desire had been for Mr. Oates to cure her spirit, an evil attitude that had caused her to do that to herself and stare at him with such accusation, smiling cruelly at him as he put his hands on her shoulders and took his good breath.

He stared at the wall and the wall only, casting aside memories of this woman and images of his shoebox, of Scott Nevers creeping up on it every week, or every *day*, how often did they come and rob him? How did Renous "divvy it up," how many people took it, how many people along the Restigouche were robbing him blind and riding *his new cars and snowmobiles and living in his buildings? He would himself appear unto the rabble, he would speak their names and shame them, and they could make restitution according to their shame.*

She was in the room and halfway to him before he saw her, a skinny young woman with glasses thicker even than his. When he looked up at her she stopped and stood.

"Where you from, den, mudder."

"Lachine. Lachine, Quebec. There's so much pollution there, they say that's —"

"Dat's fine. I don' need to know."

She was pale and sickly. Cloudy in the brain or stupid, too. Her eyes went quickly to this and that for no reason and she didn't see any of it. She wore a long-sleeved t-shirt, and he saw no need to touch her skin.

"Stand right dere, mudder, and jus' relax."

He approached and put his hands on her shoulders. He took a few breaths. Then the big one, which he released slowly, till there was nothing.

No hollow feeling arrived. Mr. Oates waited a second. As if a baseball were about to be pitched to him, he shifted his feet and waggled his shoulders. It didn't always happen the first time. He took the deep breath once more and let it out, trying hard to go deeper. Nothing.

"What wrong with you, mudder?" It was a source of pride that he rarely had to ask this.

"The environmental disease. It means I'm allergic to almost everything." She smiled nervously. "First they said it was all in my head, then I almost died."

Copying the knowing voice of a mechanic lifting a hood, Mr. Oates said, "So let's have a look, den."

He breathed deeply, trying again. Then again, and then once more, but he made no connection that he could feel. The woman stood calmly through it. For all she knew this was what he did and maybe now she was cured.

Mr. Oates tried once more before turning from her. He couldn't remember a less fruitful time with anyone.

"Dat's it."

"Well, thank you." She stood where she was, unsure, smiling hopefully. "So that's it? I mean, should I come back? I could stay overnight somewhere and —"

"No, dat's it. I hope you feel better. Maybe come back in six months if you want to. But I don' tink you will."

"Where do I pay?" She was smiling so hard. You could see her dreams rising like bubbles.

"Dere's —"

He stopped himself. In that instant of speaking he thought he felt where it had all come from, and where it had gone.

"If you would like to show yer t'anks, dere's a shoebox outside the door."

NOTES ON THE AUTHORS

CAROLINE ADDERSON was born near Edmonton in 1963 and now lives in Vancouver. She was twice a participant in the May Writing Studios at the Banff Centre, where she was encouraged by, among others, the late Adele Wiseman. Her short stories have been published in *The Malahat Review*, *Saturday Night*, *Quarry*, *Grain*, and other magazines, and reprinted in *Coming Attractions* and *The Journey Prize Anthology*. "The Chmarnyk," a prize winner in the CBC Canadian Literary Awards in 1991, is included in her story collection, *Bad Imaginings* (1993). Her first novel is *A History of Forgetting* (1999).

GAIL ANDERSON-DARGATZ was born in Salmon Arm, British Columbia, in 1963, and she and her husband now live in a rural community on Vancouver Island. Her first book, *The Miss Hereford Stories* (1994), was nominated for a Stephen Leacock Medal for Humour. The author of two novels, *The Cure for Death by Lightning* (1996) and *A Recipe for Bees* (1998), she has won the Ethel Wilson Fiction Prize, the VanCity Book Award, and the Betty Trask Prize (UK), and she was a finalist for the Giller Prize. Her story "The Girl with the Bell Necklace" was a prize winner in the 1993 CBC Canadian Literary Awards.

SHAUNA SINGH BALDWIN was born in Montreal in 1962 and grew up in India. She now lives with her husband in Milwaukee, Wisconsin, where she has an e-commerce consulting practice. She is the co-author of *A Foreign Visitor's Survival Guide to America* (1992) and the author of *English Lessons and Other Stories* (1996) and the novel *What the Body Remembers* (1999). "Satya," the prize-winning story in the 1997 CBC *Saturday Night* Canadian Literary Awards competition, was published in *Saturday Night* in June, 1998

BILL GASTON grew up in Winnipeg, Toronto, and North Vancouver. After spending a dozen years in the Maritimes, he moved to Victoria in 1998 to teach writing at the University of Victoria. He has published a collection of poetry, several plays, three story collections, and three novels, with a fourth, *The Good Body*, due to appear in spring 2000. "Where It Comes From, Where It Goes" won the 1998 CBC/*Saturday Night* Canadian Literary Award for fiction and was published in *Saturday Night* in May, 1999.

JOAN GIVNER was born in Manchester, England, in 1936. After studying at London University and Washington University in St. Louis, Missouri, she began teaching at the University of Regina in 1965; later she edited the *Wascana Review*. She has published biographies of Katherine Anne Porter (1982) and Mazo de la Roche (1989) and two collections of stories, most recently *Scenes from Provincial Life* (1991). "Elizabeth," a prize winner in the 1991 CBC Canadian Literary Awards, was published in a Joan Givner Special Issue of *Room of One's Own* in 1992.

KATHERINE GOVIER was born in Edmonton in 1948, but she has lived in Toronto since the early 1970s. She has taught creative writing at York University and through the Writers in Electronic Residence program. Among her books are the story collection *Fables of Brunswick Avenue* (1985) and the novels *Random Descent* (1979) and *Angel Walk* (1996). Her story "The Immaculate Conception Photography Gallery," a prize winner in the 1988 CBC Canadian Literary Awards, was the title story of a collection published in 1994.

ERNST HAVEMANN was born in 1918 on a farm in what was then Zululand, South Africa; his first language was Zulu. After serving with South African forces in the Middle East during the Second World War, he had a long career as a mining engineer, and he began writing after his retirement when he and his wife lived in Nelson, British Columbia. They now live in New Zealand. "Bloodsong" was a CBC Canadian Literary Awards prize winner in 1983 and "An Interview" in 1984; two other stories won prizes in 1985 and 1988. "Bloodsong" and "An Inter-view" appear in *Bloodsong and Other Stories of South Africa* (1987).

JANETTE TURNER HOSPITAL grew up in Australia, makes her home in Kingston, Ontario, and has lived in the US, England, and India. She is the author of six novels; *The Ivory Swing* (1982) won the Seal First Novel Award. She has also published three collections of stories, a crime thriller, and a French novella. "Queen of Pentacles, Nine of Swords," which was a winner in the 1986 CBC Canadian Literary Awards, was published in *Isobars* (1991), a collection of her short fiction.

FRANCES ITANI was born in Belleville, Ontario, in 1942 and grew up in a Quebec village across the river from Ottawa. She has written short stories, poetry, radio plays, and stories for children. Two collections of short fiction, *Truth or Lies* and *Pack Ice*, were published in 1989. "Bolero," the winner of the 1995 CBC/*Saturday Night* Canadian Literary Awards, is included in *Leaning, Leaning Over Water* (1998), a collection of linked stories. "Poached Egg on Toast," the 1996 winner, was published in *Saturday Night* (June, 1996).

IRENA FRIEDMAN KARAFILLY was born in 1944 in the Ural Mountains; she now lives in Montreal. She has published a story collection, *Night Cries* (1990), and *Ashes and Miracles: A Polish Journey* (1998), a study of Polish society. She is now writing *The Stranger in the Plumed Hat*, an exploration of Alzheimer's disease. "Hoodlum" was a prize winner in the 1990 CBC Canadian Literary Awards and was published in *The Canadian Forum* (August, 1991).

JANICE KULYK KEEFER was born in Toronto in 1952; she now lives in Eden Mills, Ontario, and is a professor of English at the University of Guelph. Her literary criticism includes *Under Eastern Eyes: A Critical Reading of Maritime Fiction* (1987) and *Reading Mavis Gallant* (1989). She has published a book of poetry, a family memoir, three novels, and three collections of stories. "Mrs. Putnam at the Planetarium," a 1985 winner in the CBC Canadian Literary Awards competition, was published in *The Paris-Napoli Express* (1986), and "The Wind," a 1986 winner, appeared *Transfigurations* (1987).

GWENDOLYN MacEWEN was born in Toronto in 1941 and died there in 1987. A writer of great talent and versatility, she wrote novels, travel books, children's books and radio drama, as well as poetry books including *The Shadow-Maker* (1969) and *Afterworlds* (1987), both of which won Governor General's Awards. She published two collections of short stories, *Noman* (1972) and *Noman's Land* (1985), which includes "The Other Country," a prize winner in the 1983 CBC Canadian Literary Awards.

MICHAEL ONDAATJE was born in Ceylon (now Sri Lanka) in 1943. He moved first to England and then, in 1962, to Canada, where he has taught at the University of Western Ontario, London, and Glendon College, Toronto. A poet and novelist, he has had a continuing interest in theatre, film and publishing. His novel *The English Patient* (1992) won the Trillium Award, the Governor General's Award, and the Booker Prize, and it was made into a successful film. "The Passions of Lalla" won the fiction award in the 1982 CBC Canadian Literary Awards and was published in *Running in the Family* (1982).

GAYLA REID was born in Armidale, New South Wales, Australia, in 1945. A Vancouver resident, she works in public legal education. Her story "In the Water, Like This" won the fiction prize in the CBC/*Saturday Night* Canadian Literary Awards in 1994 and was published in *Saturday Night* (May, 1994). Another story, "Sister Doyle's Men," won the 1993 Journey Prize. Both stories are included in her collection *To Be There with You* (1994).

PATRICK ROSCOE was born in 1962 on the Spanish island of Formentera and spent his childhood in Tanzania. Educated in England and Canada, he later he lived in California, Mexico, Spain and North Africa as well as in Canada. Among his books are a book of autobiographical pieces, two story collections, and two novels. "Peggy Lee in Africa," a prize winner in the 1990 CBC Canadian Literary Awards, is an episode in the second of these, *The Lost Oasis* (1995).

CAROL SHIELDS was born in Oak Park, Illinois in 1935, and she and her husband moved to Canada in 1957, eventually settling in Winnipeg. A professor of English at universities in Ottawa, Vancouver and Winnipeg, she has published poetry, short stories and novels and has written plays for radio and the theatre. Among her novels are *The Republic of Love* (1992), *Swann: A Mystery* (1987), *The Stone Diaries* (1993), which won both a Governor General's Award and the Pulitzer Prize, and *Larry's Party* (1997). "Flitting Behaviour," a winner in the 1984 CBC Canadian Literary Awards, is included in her collection *Various Miracles* (1985).

MARY SWAN was born in Wingham, Ontario, in 1953, and she lives and works in Guelph. "Archaeology," a prize winner in the Canadian Literary Awards in 1989, was later published in *The Malahat Review*. Her stories have also appeared in *The Ontario Review*, *The Antigonish Review*, *Best Canadian Stories*, the anthology *Sudden Fiction*, and *Coming Attractions* (1999).

AUDREY THOMAS was born in Binghamton, New York, in 1935, and has lived in Canada since 1959. She divides her time between Galiano Island in the Gulf Islands of British Columbia and Victoria. She has published more than a dozen works of fiction. Her novels include *Mrs. Blood* (1970), *Latakia* (1979), *Intertidal Life* (1984), and *Isobel Gunn* (1999). "Natural History," a prize winner in the 1980 CBC Canadian Literary Awards, was published in her collection *Real Mothers* (1981).

KENT THOMPSON was born in Waukegan, Illinois, in 1936. From 1966 to 1994 he taught English and creative writing at the University of New Brunswick in Fredericton, serving twice as editor of *The Fiddlehead*. He now lives in Annapolis Royal, Nova Scotia. He has edited three anthologies, and he has published two books of poetry, a cycling guidebook, five novels, and two story collections. "A Local Hanging," a winner in the 1981 CBC Canadian Literary Awards, appeared in *A Local Hanging and Other Stories* (1984).

W.D. VALGARDSON was born in Winnipeg in 1939 but spent most of his childhood in Gimli, an Icelandic community on Lake Winnipeg. He is chair of the writing department at the University of Victoria. His novel *Gentle Sinners* (1980) won the *Books in Canada* first novel award, and he has written books for children and young adults and four collections of stories. "A Matter of Balance," a winner in the 1980 CBC Canadian Literary Awards, is included in *What Can't Be Changed Shouldn't Be Mourned* (1990).

SEÁN VIRGO was born in Malta in 1940, immigrated to Canada in 1966, and has lived in the Queen Charlotte Islands, the Gulf Islands, and in recent years in southwest Saskatchewan. He has published five books of poetry, including *Selected Poems* (1990), and seven books of fiction. "Les Rites" won the first CBC Canadian Literary Awards competition in 1979 and is included in *White Lies and Other Fictions* (1980).

BUDGE WILSON was born in Halifax in 1927 and now lives in a fishing village on Nova Scotia's South Shore. A former commercial artist and photographer, she has written more than twenty books, many of them for children and young adults, and has been published in a dozen countries. "The Leaving," a winning entry in the 1981 CBC Canadian Literary Awards, is included in *The Leaving* (1990).

CAROL WINDLEY was born in 1947 in Tofino, British Columbia, and studied at Malaspina College, Nanaimo. Her stories have been published in *Best Canadian Stories* and the *Journey Prize Anthology*. She has published a novel, *Breathing Under Water* (1998), and a collection of stories, *Visible Light* (1993), which includes "Dreamland," a winner in the 1987 CBC Canadian Literary Awards.

ACKNOWLEDGEMENTS

The editor and publisher would like to thank the following for their kind permission to use their stories in this anthology:

"The Chmarnyk" and "The Hanging Gardens of Babylon," by Caroline Adderson, from *Bad Imaginings*, published by The Porcupine's Quill, 1993. "The Girl with the Bell Necklace," © by Gail Anderson-Dargatz. Reprinted by permission of the author. This story was incorporated into the novel *The Cure for Death by Lightning* (Random House of Canada, 1997). "Satya," by Shauna Singh Baldwin, © 1997 Vichar, a division of Shauna Baldwin Associates, Inc. Reprinted by permission of Westwood Creative Artists Ltd. "Where It Comes From, Where It Goes," © Bill Gaston. Published by permission of the author. "Elizabeth," by Joan Givner, is reprinted from *In the Garden of Henry James* by permission of Oberon Press. "The Immaculate Conception Photo Gallery," © Katherine Govier, first appeared in *Saturday Night* and later in *The Immaculate Conception Photo Gallery* (Little, Brown Canada, 1994). Reprinted by permission of the author. "Bloodsong" and "An Interview," from *Bloodsong and Other Stories of South Africa*. Copyright © 1987 by Ernst Havemann. Reprinted by permission of Houghton Mifflin Company. All rights reserved. "Queen of Pentacles, Nine of Swords," from *Isobars*, by Janette Turner Hospital. Used by permission, McClelland & Stewart, Inc. *The Canadian Publishers*. "Bolero," from *Leaning, Leaning Over Water* by Frances Itani. A Phyllis Bruce Book, published by HarperCollins Publishers Ltd. Copyright © 1998 by Frances Itani. "Poached Egg on Toast," originally published in *Saturday Night Magazine*, June 1996. Copyright © Frances Itani. With permission of the author. Winner of the 1996 Tilden/CBC Literary Award. "Hoodlums" © Irena Friedman Karafilly. Originally published in *Canadian Forum*, August 1991. Reprinted by permission of the author. "Mrs. Putnam at the Planetarium," by Janice Kulyk Keefer, is reprinted from *The Paris-Napoli Express* by permission of Oberon Press. "The Wind," © Janice Kulyk Keefer. Reprinted from *Transfigurations* (Ragweed, 1987) by permission of the author. "The Other Country," © Gwendolyn MacEwen, from *Nomans Land* (1985). Permission granted by the author's family. "The Passions of Lalla," from *Running in the Family* by Michael Ondaatje. Used by permission, McClelland & Stewart, Inc. *The Canadian Publishers*. "In the Water, Like This," from *To Be There With You* copyright © by Gayla Reid. Published in Canada by Douglas & McIntyre. Reprinted by permission of the publisher. "Peggy Lee in Africa," from *The Lost Oasis* by Patrick Roscoe. Used by permission, McClelland & Stewart, Inc. *The Canadian Publishers*. "Flitting Behavior," extracted from *Various Miracles* by Carol Shields. Copyright © 1985. Reprinted by permission of Random House of Canada Limited. "Archaeology," © Mary Swan. Previously published in *The Malahat Review*. With permission of the author. "Natural History," © Audrey Thomas. This story first appeared in printed form in *Real Mothers* (Talon Books, 1981). Reprinted by permission of the author and the publisher. "A Local Hanging," from *A Local Hanging and Other Stories* by Kent Thompson. Copyright © 1984. Reprinted by permission of Goose Lane Editions. "A Matter of Balance," from *What Can't Be Changed Shouldn't Be Mourned* copyright © 1984 by W.D. Valgardson. Published in Canada by Douglas & McIntyre. Reprinted by permission of the publisher. "Les Rites," © Exile Editions and Seán Virgo, from *White Lies and Other Fictions*, Toronto, 1980. "The Leaving" by Budge Wilson. Reprinted by permission of Stoddart Publishing, Ltd. 34 Lesmill Rd, Don Mills, Ont. M3B 2T6. "Dreamland," by Carol Windley, is reprinted from *Visible Light* (1993) by permission of the publisher, Oolichan Books.